MONSTERS
OF THE WEEK

THE COMPLETE CRITICAL
COMPANION TO THE

X-FILES

ZACK HANDLEN & TODD VANDERWERFF

FOREWORD BY CREATOR CHRIS CARTER

**ILLUSTRATIONS
BY PATRICK LEGER**

ABRAMS PRESS, NEW YORK

Library of Congress Control Number: 2017956874
ISBN: 978–1–4197–3247–8
eISBN: 978–1–68335–350–8

Printed and bound in the United States
10 9 8 7 6 5 4 3 2 1

Versions of recaps of Seasons Two through Eleven of *The X-Files*, including
crosstalk about *Fight the Future* and *I Want to Believe*, originally appeared
on *The A.V. Club* (www.avclub.com); this material is reprinted and revised
with *The A.V. Club*'s permission.

Abrams books are available at special discounts when purchased in quantity
for premiums and promotions as well as fundraising or educational use.
Special editions can also be created to specification. For details, contact
specialsales@abramsbooks.com or the address below.

Abrams Press® is a registered trademark of Harry N. Abrams, Inc.

ABRAMS The Art of Books
195 Broadway, New York, NY 10007
abramsbooks.com

FOR KEITH PHIPPS,
WHO MADE ALL OF THIS HAPPEN
IN THE FIRST PLACE

CONTENTS

SEASON EIGHT

SEASON NINE

THE X-FILES: I WANT TO BELIEVE

SEASON TEN

SEASON ELEVEN

FOREWORD

We came to Canada for the forests. The alien abduction of Billy Miles in the pilot episode of *The X-Files* was set in the woods, and after a fruitless search in Los Angeles for a pine grove passable as the Pacific Northwest, Charlie Goldstein, the head of production at Fox, suggested Vancouver. As it turned out, the choice to come here was a critical factor in the ultimate success of the TV series. We filmed more than a hundred episodes in Vancouver between 1993 and 1998; David Duchovny liked to say the pilot was two weeks of work that somehow turned into five years.

I'd been to Vancouver before, when my wife was producing a Disney Sunday Movie in 1986. That movie, too, was shot in the forest, and I remember being awed by the size and density of the old-growth trees. That image has brought me back here again and again: for the original run of *The X-Files,* the first and second movies, and the last two event series—a span of twenty-five years. And I'm back now, even as my work on that show is done. I've spent two weeks walking in the woods of Vancouver, under six hundred-year-old cedar trees, to reflect on the show, but also because I love it here. I could grow old here, and I have.

It isn't just the forests of Vancouver, of course; it's really the city itself. Around every corner I come upon an image from the show. Alleys we shot from every angle. The tall statue in Glen Morgan and James Wong's riveting episode from the first season, "Beyond the Sea." Pandora Street, where Bob Goodwin filmed some of the unforgettable images for "The Erlenmeyer Flask." Car chase streets, foot chase streets, neighborhoods we returned to time and again. The Canadian Broadcasting Company, where we created the set for Mulder's original basement office, and where Mulder and Scully met for that fateful first time. Remarkably, from one high vantage, I can scan at least twenty locations where I directed David and Gillian in episodes and a movie. There's an old mental institution called Riverview where we, and so many others, spent hours, days, and long nights. We shot scenes there for the pilot and we were back once again in episodes 209 ("My Struggle III"), 210 ("This"), and 211 (["Plus One"] in which Gillian, in the middle of a take, had to run away from a bear that had stepped out of the woods). We used so many Canadian locations that our original location scouts, Louisa Gradnitzer and Todd Pittson, wrote a book about them—a book from which guided tours were led for fans reliving the show's best moments.

I'm staying in the same hotel as we did in the pilot, full of memories itself. It was here I met Kim Manners in the bar and offered him an episode to direct. That was the first episode of more than eighty he'd go on to direct, and more than 150 of which he produced. Along with Rob Bowman and David Nutter, Kim's brilliance added to the show immeasurably. In Season Two, we got an order for twenty-five episodes, and after the first day of shooting, the unit production manager, J. P. Finn, had a note slipped under my door: "One down, 199 to go." That was back when we'd regularly shoot sixteen-hour days. One morning I woke up in my room here, threw open the curtains and saw a blizzard howling outside: a rarity in Vancouver. It was the first day of shooting "Darkness Falls"—where else?—in the forest. The crew worked through the snowstorm, getting trucks in and out in the slush and ice. They'd all been through these provincial winters and took it in heroic stride.

That's another thing that Vancouver provides: free atmosphere. If you shoot ten months of the year you'll span all four seasons, which include long summer days and short winter nights due to the northern latitude. From September to late spring, you can count on gray days in low light—perfect for a show like *The X-Files*. The local crews here have learned to shoot right through the rain—a badge of pride in a town that loves rather than hates the precipitation that makes the city green and shiny all year. David once made a joke about the rain that was taken not a little unkindly.

But when we came back to do the event series nearly twenty years later, all seemed to have been forgiven. It's a testament to the best reason to be in Canada: its people. The crews here put *The X-Files* on the map. I'd like to think we returned the favor, but Vancouver would've been called Hollywood North over time even without us. Yet I was reminded of just how gracious Canadians can be when I had dinner with Grace Gilroy recently. Grace produced each of the event seasons with a strong, gentle hand that made the work a joy to do. There was simply nothing I could throw at her that she hadn't dealt with before, and she always did it with equanimity and a smile or a laugh. In a business where nerves are often frayed, and where the dramatic arts are practiced behind the camera as much as in the front, she was a delight to work with.

The list goes on and on. Our production designer, Mark Freeborn, made the show not only look great but set a tone for the work. Craig Wrobleski took his sets and locations and lit them with an artist's eye. Our team created an esprit de corps that made it all more than just another showbiz enterprise.

Good work was built on top of the good work that came before it, which is what I'm really here to reflect on as I take my daily walks in the woods. If not for Bob Goodwin, the series' original producer, there would have been no Grace Gilroy. If not for Kim Manners, there would have been no Carol Banker, who directed episode 214 ("Kitten") and was the second woman director ever on the show. If not for Graeme Murray or John Bartley, there would've been no Freeborn or Wrobleski.

They say you can't go home again, and while it's true that this isn't the Vancouver we knew in 1993, it's a place we all think of as home, no matter where our lives have taken us. Gillian, of course, will be forever connected to this place through her daughter, Piper. Like me, David talks about coming back and spending time here apart from the show. It may be because there are some things here that will never change. The natural beauty and the forests are hopefully endless and enduring.

I'm often asked about the legacy of the show, but that's really not for me to answer. I'd like to think it lies in the storytelling, the pushing of limits in production value when TV was a brightly lit, budget-minded pursuit. For certain, many careers began their trajectories on *The X-Files,* though there are but a handful of people who've worked on all 218 episodes of the series. Our composer Mark Snow and his right-hand man Jeff Charbonneau were there every step of the way. But even David and Gillian weren't in every episode—though they were always absent centers. It's hard to imagine the show going on without them.

The mythology of the series has been all-important to the most die-hard fans, and revisiting it through twenty-five years has been painstaking. Following Mulder and Scully's quest to find the truth, both personally and professionally, made it more than a procedural, from Mulder's search for his sister to the birth of William. "Trust No One" has been a drumbeat that has never been timelier than now, when truth itself is threatened in a world of fake news and everyday conspiracies. Through four presidencies, *The X-Files* has charted real history.

That journey, one of the longest in a medium almost eighty years old, is an undeniable part of our legacy, whether you're a fan or not. But if you're reading this, I suppose you must be a fan. And if you are reading it, know that this book, like the show, is for you. Thanks for keeping *The X-Files* alive.

The Truth Is Out There

Chris Carter
Vancouver, B.C., June 2018

INTRODUCTION I

In which Todd makes a case for The X-Files.

The history of television can be told through certain shows, as surely as it can be told through certain personalities or events.

Think of *I Love Lucy*, discovering a way to produce very good TV comedy with speed and exactitude. Or of *The Sopranos*, paving the way for an era of morally complex dramas starring men[1] who rarely worried about doing the right thing. TV as a medium, maybe even more than film or literature, tends to define itself in terms of landmark programs. Shows are seen and assessed in terms of their influences, or in terms of what "era" they roughly fell into.

This is, of course, an oversimplification. No TV series arrives without precedent, and no show so completely defines an era that every other contemporaneous show lives in its shadow. But that oversimplification still helps people who think about television[2] figure out how to classify various artistic movements within a medium that moves quickly and often responsively to events within both the medium itself and the world at large.

But this mode of thinking means that the influence *The X-Files* had on our modern television era has been largely ignored. *The X-Files* aired in an awkward time, between other more obviously notable shows. In an age when most other big TV programs were workplace ensemble dramas that discussed the major issues of the day,[3] *The X-Files* was one part coolly deliberate throwback and one part forward-looking masterpiece. It had bad episodes and good episodes, and its overarching story line about an alien conspiracy to take over the Earth eventually stopped making sense. But it was the rare series that could follow up an episode that barely worked with an episode that made it seem like the best show on television.

If nothing else, week after week, it sent its two central FBI agents out into a scarier, more cinematic America than had ever been seen on the small screen. Mulder and Scully were always in search of some dark secret, some monster that needed stopping. It was a lonely series, as much about an inexorably changing country and world as it was about those terrifying creatures. It was about a moral reckoning with what the United States had done to win the Cold War. And, yes, it

---

1   Yeah, almost always men.
2   People like the authors of this book.
3   See: *ER*, *NYPD Blue*, *Chicago Hope*, *Law & Order*, et cetera.

was about the monsters themselves, ripping flesh from bone, spattering blood, and, in the process, becoming rich metaphors for a nation's evolution.

Let's step back, though, just for a second, from what you might think you know about *The X-Files*—from the flashlights cutting through darkness and the aliens arriving on Earth; from the near romance between Mulder and Scully and the massive commercial and critical success; from the very idea of horror on television. In order to talk about this show as a TV show, rather than a series of images and moments, we have to look at the shows that influenced it, and the ways it influenced television in turn. If you look across the current programming dial, you'll see shows that live in the shadow of *The X-Files* and still other shows that followed its spooky trail into different corners of the woods. *The X-Files* is that rare show that seems to exist both in the time it aired[4] and in the present. It is, beyond all reason, timeless, despite being perhaps *the* ultimate TV show of the 1990s.

If we want to understand how and why *The X-Files* was able to transcend, against all odds, we need to look at both its forebears and the ways the show itself (sometimes subtly) altered television.

There are three core television shows from which *The X-Files* drew inspiration.

The first is *Kolchak: The Night Stalker* (1974–75). *The X-Files* creator Chris Carter has frequently pointed to this one-season series about a monster-hunting newspaper reporter as having a tremendous influence on his show, so it makes sense to start its lineage here. But I would posit that the influence of *Kolchak* extends beyond the fact that its hero tracked down monsters and ghouls haunting the night. Beyond these trappings, *Kolchak* figured out a format through which horror on television could be effective, long before *The X-Files* came along.

Here's the problem with horror on TV: Horror requires the release of tension, often via the catharsis of gore. The monster needs to strike, or the hero needs to vanquish it. The genre needs viewers to believe that the characters are, in some way, in palpable danger. TV, on the other hand, requires a reversion to the status quo. If Fox Mulder and Dana Scully are our main characters, we know they won't die, because if they did, we might stop watching the show. Both *Kolchak* and *The X-Files* put their main characters in danger, but rarely did the audience actually fear for them. That lack of suspense would seem to defeat the purpose of horror.

Yet *Kolchak* saw that horror could exist on the margins of a series. Guest stars could be killed off, and Kolchak could live on, burdened with the existential horror that all was not as it seemed, that the day-to-day thrum of life carried within it something unspeakable and brutal.

When viewed through the eyes of the guest stars, *Kolchak* was, indeed, a horror series, about unfortunate and fatal encounters with unlikely beings. But viewed

---

4 Originally between 1993 and 2002 in its initial run, with one movie arriving in 1998. Another movie arrived in 2008, and two follow-up seasons aired in 2016 and 2018.

through the eyes of Kolchak himself, it became more of a cop drama, with cases of the week and the slow-building weight of a job that sat heavily in his soul.

The X-Files would follow *Kolchak*'s lead and be more of a cop show than a straight horror drama. What's more, *The X-Files* was a '70s cop show, with every episode dropping its protagonists into a new, fascinating milieu somewhere in the middle of nowhere America. Rather than being stationary, our heroes, Mulder and Scully, traveled all over the country, finding new monsters to hunt. Eventually, the horror became existential for them too. They knew the secrets, but nobody would believe them. The darkness was everywhere, but nobody cared.

The second series to prove fruitful for the creation of *The X-Files* was *Moonlighting* (1985–89). This five-season ABC comedy/drama about two bantering detectives, one a guy's guy and the other a girl's girl, might seem to have most influenced the dynamic at the core of *The X-Files*. The romantic tug-of-war between *Moonlighting*'s leads eventually resolved in the two hooking up late in the third season, only for the show to go off the rails soon thereafter.[5] To be sure, the white-hot chemistry between Mulder and Scully (or, perhaps more accurately, actors David Duchovny and Gillian Anderson) and the series' seeming reluctance to consummate that chemistry made it seem as if the show had taken several pages from the *Moonlighting* playbook.

But *The X-Files* borrowed almost as much from *Moonlighting*'s tone as it did from its central pairing. Like the earlier series, *The X-Files* would expand its template to the breaking point. *Moonlighting* offered episode-length riffs on Shakespeare or film noir; *The X-Files* lovingly paid homage to old Universal horror movies and Alfred Hitchcock's real-time filmmaking experiment *Rope*.

Moreover, neither series was entirely comfortable as a "drama." Because *The X-Files* had to have some sort of monster every week, it had less leeway to suddenly burst into sparkling screwball comedy, but it was constantly aware of its own ridiculousness. The longer it ran, the more *The X-Files* took sidelong swerves into absurdism.

The third show that left an indelible mark on *The X-Files* was *Twin Peaks* (1990–91),[6] the show that most immediately preceded it. In the initial spate of reviews for *The X-Files*' pilot and first season, most critics pointed to David Lynch and Mark Frost's remarkable, eerie drama as a clear influence. Especially in the early days, it's easy to see why: *Twin Peaks* sent an FBI agent into the middle of small-town America to discover the horrors at its center; it was filmed in the Pacific Northwest

---

5 The downturn in the show's quality has frequently been *blamed* on the two leads hooking up. I would argue against that interpretation and believe that the hook-up was the right call for that show, but the lesson *Moonlighting*'s ratings drop passed on to other TV shows, nevertheless, was almost always about not shooting your sexual chemistry in the foot by consummating it. I'd argue further, but this isn't a book about *Moonlighting*.

6 There was a follow-up season in 2017, too, but for obvious reasons, that couldn't have influenced *The X-Files*.

and, thus, looked like no other show on the air; and it broadcast some of the scariest sequences ever put on television.[7]

But the element *The X-Files* adopted most from *Twin Peaks* wasn't its shooting location or a sense of horror. It was, instead, a willingness to take its time with the *look* of a series, to come up with visual ways to tell its stories. The scares in *The X-Files* arrive, often, from looking at some everyday location or item in just the right way to ask what darkness could be lurking within it, just as *Twin Peaks* destabilized reality by twisting up the prime-time soap and the small-town drama with nightmare logic.

The X-Files, which calmly and carefully closed a new case every week, couldn't be more structurally different from the open-ended, intentionally obtuse *Twin Peaks*. But the two looked so similar all the same that it wouldn't have seemed all that out of place had the two shows cross-pollinated,[8] and Mulder and Scully turned up in Washington State to solve the death of Laura Palmer.

So: Now that we know from whence *The X-Files* emerged, let's look at the ways it shaped the modern TV landscape. The way I see it, *The X-Files* invented modern television in five major ways.

First, our modern crime dramas are usually just *X-Files* that have jettisoned the supernatural elements. Late in *The X-Files'* run, CBS launched *CSI: Crime Scene Investigation* (2000–15), a science-obsessed, agreeably nerdy show about lab geeks solving crimes by finding DNA evidence and the like.

The success of that series spawned literally hundreds of imitators across the programming grid, many of which are still airing as of this book's publication. What's more, the *CSI*-esque focus on crime-solving and evidence-gathering—as opposed to the personalities behind that process—has proven just as influential when it comes to "case of the season" shows, which focus on investigators trying to close a case over one or multiple seasons.

But go back to the first few seasons of *CSI* and you'll find a show that looks a lot like *The X-Files*, with its focus on flashy imagery, cool blue aesthetics, and fascination with scientific processes. Even if Mulder and Scully proved to be incredibly well-developed characters, they, too, could often be boiled down to "the believer" and "the skeptic"—the kind of simplistic dichotomy that would beautifully suit many crime dramas that followed in its footsteps.

Second, the aesthetics of *The X-Files* expanded the notion of what TV was visually capable of. *The X-Files* took everything *Twin Peaks* had done and proved that other shows could do it too. You didn't need to have a big-name Hollywood director like David Lynch to pull off such sharp cinematic sequences. You just had to budget the time and care to make those sequences matter. As you watch *The X-Files*,

---

7 Especially anything to do with the greasy, long-haired demon BOB, who would turn up in dream sequences just to make everything go south.

8 *The X-Files* even used a number of *Peaks* alumni over the course of its run. Notably, David Duchovny played a minor role in *Twin Peaks'* second season as DEA Agent Denise Bryson.

whether for the first time or the fiftieth, note how many of its scenes, especially its scary ones, are told entirely through visuals with spare dialogue.[9] More and more shows, both its contemporaries and otherwise, have been similarly emboldened.

Third, the serialized storytelling devices used by *The X-Files* have been copied by many genre dramas. The show mostly featured closed-off stories with a "monster of the week."[10] But many weeks, it instead gave itself over to a long-running story about aliens visiting Earth and working with assorted government officials to shady and nefarious ends. Sure, it occasionally made no sense that Mulder and Scully could make huge shattering discoveries about a global conspiracy and then go right back to chasing urban legends down American backroads, but this oscillation between stand-alone tales and serialized adventures has driven many, many other dramas—mostly sci-fi, fantasy, and horror programs but also the occasional non-genre series, like CBS's detective show *The Mentalist.*

Fourth, the series was critical of American foreign policy. While *The X-Files* was not the first series to question whether U.S. efforts to win the Cold War had been worth many of our country's dark deeds during that time, it was by far the most successful show to do so when it aired. Perhaps that is thanks to an accident of timing. *The X-Files* premiered, after all, in the wake of the Cold War's end. Mulder and Scully might have been government functionaries, but their investigations usually uncovered just how horribly the U.S. government had behaved—an undercurrent that has carried forward on everything from *24*[11] to *Homeland.*[12]

Lastly, *The X-Files* mainstreamed modern paranoia. Forget simply modern television, which is full of conspiracy theories and cults and strange hidden secrets perpetrated by the government and shadowy corporations. Forget modern movies, which are full of the same. Instead, think of how much of our current political discourse is driven by a vague, never-proven suspicion that the U.S. government is secretly colluding with [insert suspect entity here] to actively hurt its people. It almost doesn't matter if said paranoid suspicion is driven by actual evidence—as with the growing belief that the Trump campaign worked with Russian agents to influence the 2016 presidential election—or by some random person's certainty that *something* bad must have happened—as with any number of conspiracies lev-

---

9 David Chase, creator of *The Sopranos*, which would similarly break ground for visual storytelling on TV, was considering taking a job at *The X-Files* when HBO picked up *The Sopranos*.

10 Hey, that's the title of the book!

11 Which often suggested the government's bad behavior was, at best, necessary and, at worst, kind of awesome. But that, again, is a different book.

12 Funnily enough, Howard Gordon and Alex Gansa, both early *X-Files* writers, would go on to become writers and executive producers on *24*, with Gordon eventually transitioning to the series showrunner. Gordon and Gansa also cocreated *Homeland,* for which Gansa serves as the showrunner.

eled against essentially every president of the last twenty-five years.[13] *The X-Files* predicted this paranoid reality we all live in so skillfully that when it returned for its follow-up seasons in 2016 and 2018, it occasionally seemed as if the show had been lapped by the real world—impressive, considering this is a show in which a major plot point is the alien invasion of Earth.

But that prescience, above all else, is what makes returning to *The X-Files* twenty-five years after its debut so vital. The show has aged so beautifully (extremely rare for a TV show) because it plays less like an ultracool bit of TV stylishness and more like a mad prophet waving a warning flag to all of us gliding on past it. The world may keep changing. TV may keep changing. Humanity may keep changing. But what's both remarkable and terrifying is how *The X-Files* keeps loping alongside us, never falling far enough behind for us to dismiss its dire predictions for the end of days.

Todd VanDerWerff
June 2018

INTRODUCTION II

In which Zack makes a case for this book.

Let's make this clear: *The X-Files* is important and fun to watch, and it's worth revisiting in a critical context. But why *this* context? Why a book this exhaustive (but hopefully not exhausting) that examines each season episode by episode—a task that goes past heroically Herculean to border on the absurdly Sisyphean? The original nine seasons of *The X-Files* ran for 202 episodes; that run, plus the sixteen episodes of the revival seasons, plus the two big-screen film adaptations, makes for roughly 154 hours of content, all of which have been viewed, dissected, and analyzed here for your enjoyment. Even split between two authors, that's a lot: a lot of monsters, a lot of aliens, a lot of shadowy government figures up to no good. And, let's not forget, a lot of Special Agents Fox Mulder and Dana Scully, bickering, flirting, and leaning on one another in the dark.

It's worth noting how this book came to be at all. The project wasn't originally conceived as a single volume, sit-on-your-coffee-table-to-impress-your-friends affair. In the summer of 2008, *The A.V. Club*, an online site for pop culture commentary, was looking to expand its coverage of classic television. Keith Phipps

---

13 Though if you need an obvious example, consider the certainty that something bad had to have happened during the attacks on the U.S. embassy in Benghazi, despite the fact that every investigation into the event turned up nothing criminal.

decided to start writing on *The X-Files,* with a plan to cover the show weekly with two-episode entries. Midway through the first season, he passed the writing duties on to me;[14] my reviews, which ran up to the midpoint of the second season, ended in September, and the project was put on hiatus. Site commenters asked for more reviews, though, and two years later, Todd and I picked up where I'd left off, with the two of us swapping writing duties till we'd covered the series through *The X-Files: I Want to Believe*—what was then the end.

The original versions of these reviews, then, were written in a very different context; *The A.V. Club*'s approach to episodic reviewing was more informal and conversational than its film, music, and book writing, allowing for the use of the first person and a more laid-back style. The criticism was still expected to be sharp and engaging, but the looser feel was more appropriate to the way these reviews were conceived—not as comprehensive statements about a series but as ongoing works in progress that processed television the way most people processed it: episode by episode. The results were imperfect and often messy, but always curious, engaged, and honest.

What you hold in your hand now is not exactly a compendium of those essays. The originals are still online as of today, and the morbidly curious are welcome to revisit; there's an often lively comments section attached to each, if anyone's nostalgic for the days when *The X-Files* ruled the bulletin boards.[15] The reviews in *this* book have been edited and reworked with an eye toward something more permanent. While (we hope) the vitality and humor of those first drafts remain intact, this new edition has been shaped into something less chatty and more like a critical take of the entire series, from beginning to end. We've also gone back and written reviews for the early season episodes that we missed in our initial run-through online. Ideally, the resulting tome should offer the best of both worlds, capturing the spirit that inspired us during our initial critical engagement with the show but tempered by the knowledge that a book is a little more long term than an Internet post.

This volume, then, is a collection of edited and reworked episodic reviews interspersed with interviews and off-the-cuff observations from much of the show's key staff. The reviews have been collected by season and presented in their original airing order. Anyone coming to *The X-Files* for the first time is encouraged to read along as they go without fear of spoilers; part of the editing process was designed to tailor each essay with an eye toward the new viewer, and that meant saving some

---

14 Keith's reviews are still available online as of this writing and are worth checking out for a different take on those first few episodes.

15 *The X-Files* was arguably the first real phenomenon of the Internet era, its conspiracy narratives and urban legend fixation making it perfect discussion fodder for message boards and chat rooms. In a sense, the reviews for *The A.V. Club* were just a continuation of what those original obsessive fans began. The writing Todd and I did might have been more "official" and less directly interested in plot details, but we were certainly still willing to spill gallons of digital ink on the series.

bigger picture commentary until the end. This book is not intended as a series of plot summaries or deep dives into the mythology, however, and while we discuss story beats throughout, anyone looking for a flowchart detailing the intricacies of the show's long-term narrative would be best served looking elsewhere.[16] As a guide for newcomers, it should work just fine, and for anyone looking to revisit the series, or touch back on high (or low) points, there's plenty of material to keep you occupied.

Speaking of "mythology," there are some terms with which you should be familiar before you start reading in earnest. *Monsters of the Week* isn't intended to be a scholarly analysis, but it does assume you have a basic understanding of how television formats work, especially those from the era in which *The X-Files* originally aired. To that end, here's a brief glossary that will aid you in the pages ahead:

Mythology: The ongoing serialized narrative of the show, first introduced in the pilot episode and built upon for the entire length of the series. As a general rule of thumb, if an episode has aliens, the Cigarette Smoking Man (more on him later), references to Mulder's sister, and/or rumblings of a larger conspiracy, it will most likely fall into this camp. Mythology episodes, which we make sure to identify in each review, are intended to be understood as a part of a larger story, with events in each entry having a lasting impact beyond the scope of their particular hour.

Monster of the Week (or MOTW): The phrase from this book takes its title is also a term used to describe stand-alone, non-mythology episodes of *The X-Files*. While events in these episodes are occasionally referenced in later entries, each MOTW hour functions by itself with little-to-no bearing on the mythology. Each has a beginning, a middle, and an end. Also: There are monsters.

Cold open: The scenes that appear before the opening credits of each episode and that serve as a teaser of things to come. In MOTW episodes, we get a brief glimpse of that entry's monster and usually a death; in mythology episodes, it generally includes a voice-over monologue from Mulder or Scully hinting at the importance of revelations to come.

Structure: A catchall term for how the story of an episode is put together, from the ways it pulls viewers in to the ways it builds suspense, provides exposition, or handles characterization.

As for our own qualifications for the work you're about to read, both Todd and I have been fans of *The X-Files* since its initial run; we'll share a little more of our personal experiences with the series in the pages ahead. Suffice it to say: We've done our homework. Since the majority of these reviews were written individually, we've added our initials to identify who's responsible for each essay. Given the dynamic at the center of this show, it seems only fitting that a partnership should attempt to cover the series as a whole. As to which one of us is the Mulder and which is the Scully, we'll leave that to the reader to decide.

---

16 There are websites for you. So. Many. Websites.

Still, the original question remains: Why *this* sort of book? Well, a large part of the difficulty of writing about television is that there's so *much* of it. A film review covers maybe two hours of experience; a book review, maybe five to ten. But watching a long-running TV show is a time commitment that deserves an equally expansive critical approach. What you are about read represents, to the best of our abilities, an assessment and commentary on the experience of watching *The X-Files;* of falling under the spell of its vision of an America run through with dark forces; of investing in its characters and hoping they will kiss; and of trying to understand just what it is about this show that speaks so clearly to us, and the millions of viewers like us. *Monsters of the Week*, much like the show it discusses, is imperfect, well-meaning, occasionally confusing, and ultimately worth the effort. We may not find the truth by its end but not from lack of trying.

Zack Handlen
June 2018

THINGS THAT GO BUMP

In which Mulder meets Scully.

ZACK: I've seen *The X-Files* "Pilot" half a dozen times or more now, but it didn't occur to me until this latest viewing how little I understand about its actual plot.

There are disappearances; there are strange happenings in the woods; there are these little bumps on people's skin; and at one point, there's a weird, inhuman corpse in a coffin. I know there's a story connecting all these incidents, but every time I watch the episode, I give up keeping track of anything by the fifteen-minute mark. Not because the plot is especially complicated, but because it doesn't seem all that necessary.

While the show's improvisational approach to its mythology would create coherency issues in later seasons, the loose collection of UFO-related apocrypha and horror tropes on display in this episode gel just fine without ever needing to spell out all the details. First episodes often struggle to set a consistent tone, bogged down by exposition and the rules of the show's world. Instead, *The X-Files* nails it right out of the gate.

A large part of that success is due to Chris Carter's deft hand at establishing his leading characters. We first meet Agent Dana Scully (Gillian Anderson) as she is offered a new assignment to the X-Files, a department of the FBI dedicated to investigating unusual or unexplainable phenomena. Her objective is nominally to observe, but her superiors clearly intend for Scully (who we learn over the course of the episode believes unwaveringly in logic and scientific consensus) to discredit the work of her new partner, Agent Fox Mulder (David Duchovny). The two start off as potential enemies—with Scully finding Mulder deep in the FBI basement, hunched over his work like some kind of well-groomed troll—but the chemistry between them is there from the start. Mulder's disarming directness clearly catches Scully off guard, as does his obsession with the paranormal. Their early dynamic mirrors the ideal audience relationship with the show: initial skepticism transforming into attraction and fascination.

The episode works, too, because of that aforementioned alien lore. I love how much the script is a hodgepodge of abduction tropes, best evidenced by the way Mulder and Scully lose a few minutes during a car ride. That scene establishes the universe of *The X-Files:* This is a reality in which nothing is entirely trustworthy, not even the passage of time. The convoluted narrative adds to this sense of instability—and yet, instead of making for a disjointed, confusing hour, the result feels strangely coherent. Its incidents are organized more strongly by theme than by concrete detail, a tactic that would soon become a hallmark of the series.

The other reason this episode works is David Duchovny. Gillian Anderson's Scully would become one of the greatest heroines in television history, and the actress does excellent work in "Pilot," but her role here is largely relegated to audience surrogate. She achieves a crucial balancing act, and helps ground the craziness, but it's Duchovny who makes the biggest initial impression. At times, Mulder seems like the only character on the show with a sense of humor, and his jokes (which are often endearingly lame) and wild enthusiasm for his work make his outlandish ideas that much easier to swallow. His giddiness over every fresh discovery in the first half of the hour is charming, and his story about his sister's abduction (a core piece of the show's mythology) is well delivered.

TODD: I wouldn't call this episode a tremendous example of the TV pilot form, but in its sturdy, functional construction, it transcends many of the issues that should drag it down. When you reflect on how big the show would eventually become, in both popularity and budget, it is a real trip to see such an unassuming first entry, with most of its big special effects sequences achieved by what seems like some giant klieg lights behind trees and leaves blown around with a fan. The hour suggests more than it specifies, which proves key to its success.

I went back, as I often do, to read some contemporaneous reviews of "Pilot" from TV critics, and what struck me was how many of them insisted that UFOs were "played out" as the subject matter for a TV series. Even the positive reviews—and there were many[1]—were worried about *The X-Files* becoming just another UFO series.

This concern, of course, seems like nonsense now. *The X-Files* isn't just another UFO series. It's *the* UFO series,[2] and its treatment of alien conspiracies, government secret-keeping, and what might be lurking in American shadows became so influential that essentially any show airing in its aftermath that tries to play in the realm of "eerie mysteries" has to deal with its legacy. But in September 1993, *The X-Files was* just another show, gasping for air in yet another overcrowded fall season.

So, what exactly did audiences respond to here? The show wasn't a massive hit from the start, but it grabbed a small, loyal viewership that stuck with it through the typical first season stumbles that lay in the weeks ahead. It's not a huge leap to suggest that "Pilot"—with its hints of vast mystery lurking in the woods;

S1 E1

---

1   "If succeeding chapters can keep the pace, the well-produced entry could be this season's UFO highflier," wrote Tony Scott of *Variety*, in a review of "Pilot" that was both very positive and slightly concerned about the show having room to expand in future episodes.

2   Yes, it would deal with all manner of other monsters—just look at the title of this book!—but it was known, first and foremost, as "the show about aliens."

of aliens toying with our very reality; of, yes, even a little sex[3]—put just enough gas in the tank to keep the show quietly running until it was ready to explode into a phenomenon in later years.

Having a rock-solid pilot wasn't *as* important for longevity in the early '90s as it is now because audiences had fewer viewing options back then, but a strong start sure helped. I don't know about you, but when Mulder dances in the rain after experiencing missing time, or when the Cigarette Smoking Man (William B. Davis, playing a mysterious figure with some sort of connection to the alien conspiracy) files away the latest bit of evidence in a government warehouse, or when Scully discovers Billy Miles's muddy feet, I am *in*. The power here is all in suggestion and shadow, and if there's any lesson *The X-Files* learned from its pilot, it was this one.

ZACK: Yes, that dancing-in-the-rain shot is one of my favorites. The scene late in the episode, in which someone torches Mulder's and Scully's hotel rooms and burns all the evidence Mulder's was so excited about, hooks the viewer, and establishes the one-step-forward-one-step-back model that would drive so much of the series mythology. That approach might get tiresome eventually, but it works shockingly well here because there's so little context. Things had been progressing nicely, and then everything hits a wall.

Speaking of when the show debuted, I think one of the other elements that distinguished it immediately from its contemporaries was its commitment to being legitimately scary. "Pilot" is short on monsters, but it has atmosphere in spades, which would keep the season afloat even in its weakest entries.[4] The entire episode is shot through with a perpetual unease, which is fitting for a series so invested in undermining perceived truths. By the time Mulder and Scully are blundering through the woods by themselves, it's not hard to believe that anything could happen.

While it would take a little while for the show's sense of humor and the impressive flexibility of its premise to solidify, the horror was there, right from the beginning, even if it was only atmospheric. "Pilot" instills a terrific sense of dread—which, in combination with a pair of likable heroes, was more than enough to make me a fan for life.

TODD: Dread is really what you want from TV horror anyway. It's hard for TV to effectively execute horror, because it can't truly offer the kind of catharsis that marks the end of a great horror tale. Horror is driven by fear of death or something worse than death, but a television protagonist can't die or suffer too horribly,

---

3 When Scully runs half naked into Mulder's hotel room, it should feel more exploitative than it does, but the moment works, perhaps because the two actors have already built such firm chemistry.

4 Hello, "Space" (S1E9)!

because we need to check in with them again next week. But television shows can spin dread almost effortlessly when they tune in to the right frequencies, and *The X-Files'* earliest hours remind me, yes, of *Twin Peaks*,[5] its most obvious forebearer. These early episodes also make me think of shows that would follow the mold of *The X-Files*, series like *Lost*, which would figure out how to bottle that dread almost as well.

But there's nothing quite like the way this pilot creates an entire world that exists just on the edges of our own. It's clear that the show's creator, Chris Carter, doesn't yet understand how the aliens function, or what they want, or why they're abducting certain people. But he knows they're *here*, and that's almost more important than anything else.

The X-Files' pilot is an extended hand, both to Scully and to the viewer, an invitation to leave behind the highway and step into the woods, where reality becomes patchy and the rules bend and twist like trees in the wind.

---

5   So much of this pilot feels like Chris Carter throwing pebbles at David Lynch's bedroom window to try to get him to come say "hi."

THE FBI'S MOST UNWANTED

And so begins a show that would run on and off for a quarter century. When asked what he remembers about the first days of shooting, showrunner and creator Chris Carter recalls some of the first scenes between the two protagonists of *The X-Files*. "I do remember the first day we were in Mulder's office with Mulder and Scully," Carter says. "It's where I really watched something kind of miraculous happen: I saw the chemistry emerge. We hadn't had the luxury past a table reading of seeing David and Gillian putting a scene up on its feet. So that [day on set] was for me, among the most memorable first days of that shoot."

Staff writer Howard Gordon says that the immediacy of the relationship between Mulder and Scully helped center viewers. "I think the show started with this wonderful self-awareness," says Gordon. "It's a pretty classic construction: 'I'm a believer.' 'I'm a skeptic.' If you start in the broadest contour, that alone gives you an orientation, in terms of when she enters the room and he enters the room, you know who's going to say what or think what. The [clarity] and the specificity and the simplicity of that construction was great. Of course, the key [was] to have this antagonism with an underlying kind of attraction, a shifting attraction."

Gordon also gives credit to the actors for breathing life into these characters who could have otherwise fallen into staid roles: "Mulder's orientation was someone who had been banished to the basement of the FBI and was called 'Spooky Mulder.' There was a cheekiness to it, there was an irony. He wasn't too serious about. I mean, he was entirely serious about his mission, but he recognized that he was considered this mystic. This guy who was disregarded and around whom this whole conspiracy was transpiring. He really had an irony. There was an irony to it and sense of humor that was fun to find. David just played it with deadpan perfection. . . . It's hard sometimes to separate the character from the David and the Gillian of it. It's hard to know what it might have been like without David doing a pitch-perfect deadpan delivery. And Scully's intelligent beauty. She was just so smart. At a certain level, both had a kind of specific and separate charisma."

Another writer, James Wong, also points to the actors as lifting the series off the ground. In the early days, he says, the writers were "discovering ourselves what [Mulder and Scully] were, and how they should interact with each other. I think the fun things that we interjected with David's character are some of the more quirky things. . . . It's those things that we thought were funny, and David and Gillian were very open to doing those things with their characters. It wasn't just this dry procedural. Whatever we thought was fun and funny, we sort of gave them, and when they ran with it, that's when it became really, really fun."

It's no coincidence that Carter, too, is quick to associate the beginning of the show with the strength of Duchovny and Anderson's chemistry, even in the series' very first hour. About his two stars, Carter says, "They're both strong actors. They just understood the roles immediately. It's not like they had to learn to fit into those shoes; they just stepped right into them. There's sexual tension. There's a kind of built-in romantic tension. There's mutual affection, agreements to disagree. It's not like you can just put people together somewhere with a shared goal. These people were always at odds with each other. It provided the argument, and the conflict, and the tension, and the . . . I'll call it the entertainment value that became the show."

Still, even with the attraction evident in the first entry, Carter claims that the executives at Fox wanted the relationship to escalate more quickly. On that scene in which Mulder checks a half-naked Scully for marks, Carter says, "I remember a note that I got was 'Not enough sexual tension.' Meaning, you know, that was supposed to go someplace else. My feeling was, and my argument was: You've got to earn that. You just don't give that to people in the first episode. You'll have nowhere to go. That was a constant battle for me during the beginning of the show, because people didn't quite understand that it's better to ratchet up the tension than to release it with a consummation."

To Carter, "Pilot" (S1E1) makes a better case for Mulder and Scully's emotional relationship, instead of immediately jumping to a physical one. The shift between Mulder and Scully is subtler in the first episode, says Carter: "She comes to believe that Mulder is onto something. That's really how the relationship progressed—that instead of being a spy, she became a scientist and a believer in Mulder rather than a believer in this conspiracy to stop him."

Carter and the writing staff acknowledge that the show and the characters of Mulder and Scully were shaped by the relative freedom the show was privileged to have. According to Wong, "We were a show that wasn't expected to succeed, and so a lot of it was really that Fox didn't pay much attention to us. We were just allowed to do [episodes] that we thought were fun with David and Gillian at the core of it." Gordon concurs, saying, that despite the show having "no real institutional gravity behind it," "The pilot was just really special and really something that felt challenging, but felt like something truly special. [Being] on the Fox Network then was a much more marginal proposition." Carter echoes this claim, saying that the network initially "didn't quite know what they had with *The X-Files*. We got [the Friday night 'death slot'] time slot, which is not the best time slot on television. It's a place where shows oftentimes go to die, because Friday night is where people aren't sitting in front of their television; they're going out and doing things. There isn't a big available audience there. You have to build an audience there, which is what we did slowly but surely."

Viewers were certainly taking notice of this little program, even from the outset. And what drew them to the show? Most claim they were first and foremost interested in the dynamic between the two agents. Vince Gilligan, the future creator of *Breaking Bad*, would come to write for *The X-Files* full-time in its third season. But first, he was an avid fan. When asked what attracted him to the show as a member of the audience, he says, "It was the relationship between Mulder and Scully. . . . It's a man and a woman and they're both young and attractive and of course there's the sexual romantic component that's just simmering under the surface. That stuff always works—it always has, it always will in storytelling. But there was an extra added component beyond that; beyond the boilerplate relationship, there was the fact that they were both really, really smart and they both respected each other's intelligence. They didn't always agree (in fact, they seldom agreed), but they never disrespected one another. You could tell, and in the very earliest episode Scully comes in essentially as a spy for the higher-ups of the FBI, so of course at the very beginning Mulder doesn't trust her and rightly so. But that gets dispensed with fairly quickly, I think even within the first hour. Then that wonderful dynamic goes into full force and these two really respect each other and they really enjoy each other's company. They enjoy working with each other and they always have each other's back. They know that the one can always count on the other and vice versa. I think I just love that.

"And of course, how are you not going to love a show in which there's flying saucers, and aliens, and fat-sucking monsters, and creatures that crawl through sewer lines and eat people's livers. I mean, how are you not going to love that?"

"DEEP THROAT" | SEASON 1 / EPISODE 2
WRITTEN BY CHRIS CARTER
DIRECTED BY DANIEL SACKHEIM

PARANOIA IN AMERICAN TELEVISION
In which a massive conspiracy takes shape.

"Deep Throat" follows that oldest rule in the TV playbook: Make sure Episode Two is largely a retread of the pilot. Sure, it does a few things differently, and its introduction of the titular source nods toward the way the series' ensemble of characters will expand with time. But for the most part, this is another story of anti-government paranoia, strange military experiments, and a little town in the middle of nowhere bedeviled by bright lights in the sky.

The most noteworthy element of the episode—especially in our post-9/11 era—is its laser focus on the American military treating its personnel as expendable, all in the name of perfecting aircraft built with alien technology. This is not to say that the "military treats its soldiers as cannon fodder" theme has completely disappeared from film and TV in recent years, but it's nevertheless surprising to see that this episode directly insinuates that the military is up to no good. Scully might balk at aliens, but she seems to find secret military experiments plausible. And tellingly, so does everyone else Mulder talks to.

This episode distills the fundamental dynamic of the show, wherein Scully believes the government is not above the law and Mulder knows all too well that the opposite is true. The American government, in the world of *The X-Files*, is a monstrous entity that doesn't have the best interests of its people at heart. And yet it employs honorable agents like Mulder and Scully.[6] Expand any organization enough, and it will start to make explicit its own contradictions.

The episode also opens more windows into the alien conspiracy. Even this early in its run, *The X-Files* must suggest a massive, multinational conspiracy on its small budget, which means it must rely on suggestions. When it comes to creating a whole world with a wink and a nudge, Jerry Hardin (who steps into the shoes of Deep Throat) is just the guy. The character appears in only two scenes here, but he doesn't need any more screen time than that to let Mulder know that "they"—including Deep Throat himself—are always watching. *The X-Files* is built out of repurposed 1970s conspiracy-thriller parts,[7] so it's only fitting that Mulder's first major source would be named after perhaps the most famous informant of all time.

It would have been easy for "Deep Throat" to feel perfunctory, like the show going over ground it had already covered just a week before. In some scenes, particularly the one in which Mulder interrogates a couple of local stoners (one of whom is played by a young Seth Green), there's a distinct sense of déjà vu. But this episode also beautifully reintroduces the show in a single, instantly iconic image: Mulder standing beneath a beam of light issuing from a UFO. Just showing a UFO in such detail is more than you might expect the series to indulge in this early on, but the choice pays instant dividends. This is a series about obsession and near-religious fixation. The fact that Mulder spies his quarry (albeit a military-created version of his quarry) this early on, then has the very memory of it ripped away from him, has a mythic potency. Because we see the UFO, it doesn't feel cheap. Because Mulder doesn't remember seeing it, the series drives home its central, essential conflict: Even when he finds a piece of the truth, it will be taken from him.

Beyond that conceit, "Deep Throat" offers a buffet of classic *X-Files* tropes. There's Mulder racing off into the middle of nowhere to chase a UFO and leaving Scully behind to pick up the pieces. There's Scully using whatever advantage she can garner to rescue her missing partner. There's a spirited argument about whether the phenomenon the two observed has a paranormal or scientific explanation, in which you find yourself hoping both could be right. And there's a Scully field report to close it all out.

Really, the only thing that "Deep Throat" has going against it is how obvious it already is that this series can't live and die on UFOs alone. Even here, it's possible to feel how repetitive the series could become, should it simply keep hitting the

S1 E2

---

6   Check out the framing of these two in the bar near the episode's beginning. It feels for all the world like the show wants us to think they could start sleeping together at any moment. Some of that is Duchovny and Anderson's potent chemistry, but just as much is how this scene is shot like a romantic comedy. The show is still figuring out this central dynamic.

7   Note how the "dancing UFOs are replaced by a helicopter" bit at the episode's midpoint is essentially directly lifted from *Close Encounters of the Third Kind*.

"strange lights dancing in the sky" button over and over again. Fortunately for us, there are far stranger mysteries hidden within the X-Files. And fortunately for the show itself, the very next episode would take the series from one that might have attracted a faithful cult audience to one that would, in time, dominate pop culture like few had before it. —TVDW

| "SQUEEZE" | SEASON 1 / EPISODE 3
WRITTEN BY GLEN MORGAN AND JAMES WONG
DIRECTED BY HARRY LONGSTREET |

HERE BE MONSTERS

In which The X-Files *finds a new format.*

Eugene Tooms (Doug Hutchison) is not a likable villain. He's barely even a man. Hutchison gives a sullen, off-putting performance, and during the character's one scene of dialogue (a polygraph test), he's borderline catatonic, muttering each response with the awkward intensity of a creature who can barely form sentences. Yet it's hard not to have a certain fondness for the character, or at least for what he represents. "Squeeze" is an episode of firsts, and among other things, Tooms is the show's first Monster of the Week (or MOTW), representing the start of a venerable tradition that would expand the world of *The X-Files* considerably.

The first two episodes of the first season introduced some of the ideas that would power the mythology through to the end of the show's run. Alien abduction, UFO sightings, government conspiracies, and secrets hidden from plain view made for thrilling, unexpected television. But given that *The X-Files* aired in an era when few series were completely serialized, it needed more diverse subject matter in order to sustain weekly episodes.

The genius of the "X-Files" as a premise lies in its infinite potential. Centering the show around a department of the FBI devoted exclusively to investigating strange or inexplicable cases means *The X-Files* can encompass any number of urban legends, can cross between science fiction, fantasy, and outright horror with ease. This flexibility allowed writers to devote multiple episodes each season to stand-alone stories, making sure that entries focused on the show's ongoing mythology stayed fresh.

"Squeeze" is also Glen Morgan and James Wong's first script for *The X-Files*. The pair would go on to be important voices in the show's earliest years, and their work in this episode helped to establish what would become the format for MOTW entries. While the structure of these stories at times would warp and reflect back on itself, the fundamental core would remain more or less unchanged: There's a monster; Mulder and Scully chase the monster; people die; the monster is caught or killed; and the status quo is restored . . . or is it?

It's a formula that has appeared in genre novels and movies for decades or more. What makes it such a good fit for *The X-Files* is its versatility and the way the idea dovetails with the paranoia and suspicion at the heart of the show's premise. "Squeeze" suggests a world where not even locked doors are proof against horrible death, where malevolent beings with incredible power hide just below the surface of normal life, waiting to pounce. Aliens were bad enough. Tooms has literally been living and killing for over a century before someone finally takes him down.

None of these observations speak directly to the quality of the episode itself, but there's a reason "Squeeze" works so well as an introduction to the MOTW concept. In addition to Tooms, the entry also provides excellent characterization of Scully and Mulder, strengthening their partnership and giving us a clearer sense of just how much Mulder's work has put him at odds with his peers. It's one thing to be told he's been ostracized. It's another to see that alienation acted out, as Mulder's colleagues dismiss his theories out of hand.

Even more important than this portrait of Mulder's work life is Scully's growth as a character. This is her first chance to see what it's like to work on the X-Files full time, and the climax of the episode has Tooms breaking into Scully's house and nearly getting the best of her. Even before then, she's getting lectured by an old friend (a young Donal Logue!) about how sticking with Mulder is more or less career suicide. That Mulder has made himself an outcast is hardly surprising, but watching Scully discover she might be on the same path, and then taking that discovery as an opportunity to stand by her partner, strengthens their relationship.

Then there's the opaque Tooms. With so much of *The X-Files* being about obfuscation and plots-within-plots, there's something gratifying about the straightforwardness of this episode, which smartly gets at some of our basest fears. The show will offer more nuanced (and more sympathetic) threats in the seasons to come, but it's fitting that the format starts with this: a monster we can barely contain, let alone understand. —ZH

S1 E3

THE FIRST MONSTER

When Chris Carter and the writing staff first began developing the series, no one was sure yet what sorts of stories they would tell. James Wong remembers, "When we first started, we asked Chris, 'Does every [episode] have an alien in it? Is this all about aliens?' I think the first day he said, 'Yes,' and then he changed his mind fairly quickly. Because . . . I think all of us suddenly realized that this could be so much more than just aliens. I remember the first pitch, [when] we went to the network. It was me, and Glen, and Howard [Gordon], and Alex [Gansa], and Chris, and we each had our own ideas. [My idea with Glen] was, I think, Tooms. Chris had something else, and, I think, the network didn't know what the show was, and I guess we didn't either."

According to fellow writer Gordon, the character of Tooms from "Squeeze" (S1E3), "opened a door" for the series, "introducing the idea that the show had [a] whole other vocabulary." It was the series' first Monster of the Week episode, the first to forge the stand-alone formula for which the series would become famous. It was groundbreaking, not only for its departure from the more serialized alien narrative, but because its success helped the creative team realize that *The X-Files* could encompass a whole range of genres: alien mythology, weird science, more dramatic stories centered on the personal lives of Mulder and Scully, and horror.

"'Squeeze' showed how scary the show could be," Carter says—even while operating within the confines of network standards and practices. "We can only do things that are so scary because you're limited in the images that you can put on screen and the language that you can use"—not to mention the limitations of time and budget. Carter recalls some key advice he once received from Academy Award–winning production designer Rick Carter for how to tell stories that are not just scary, but "smart-scary": "[Rick] said, 'Do yourself a favor. If you really want to scare people, do it by *not* showing what's scary instead of showing them what's scary. What's scarier is what you don't see, or what you imagine, or what you hear.'" Carter says, "That's something I took to heart."

A FACE IN THE NUMBERS

In which Mulder tries to save someone who is not his sister.

There are two great scenes in "Conduit," both of which happen near the end of the hour. The episode is an opportunity to dive deeper into what drives Mulder, as a new case has him reliving the central trauma of his life: his sister's abduction. Other than that, though, and those two great scenes, the episode fails to make an impression. The biggest problem is a lack of solid story. The pace is somber bordering on somnambulant throughout, and while both Duchovny and Anderson get a chance to do some excellent character work, the episode's narrative is at once too familiar and too thin to work.

The plot is the episode's biggest weakness, as it works largely through hint and innuendo without the necessary connective tissue to build something effectively unsettling: A teenager disappears in a flash of light, her mother saw a UFO as a child, and the abduction occurs at a lake that's well known for unusual sightings. That, plus some mild small-town melodrama, is more or less the whole story. The teenager returns but refuses to tell Mulder anything about her kidnappers, and he and Scully are left more or less where they started.

This subtle, grounded approach has some points to recommend it. As with "Pilot," "Conduit" exploits familiar alien abduction tropes to create an impression of dread without ever providing any explicit connections between events. But where "Pilot" succeeds by piling on multiple twists and setbacks, this episode is considerably sparser, leaning heavily on Mulder's relationship with his sister's case. It suggests more restraint than the series would ultimately embrace, treating arcana like burned trailer roofs and signals from the stars like small cracks in a seemingly normal world, rather than the *Sturm und Drang* they would eventually become.

Although the interesting, if muted, style fails to generate much in the way of excitement, there are, as mentioned, two scenes in which the episode briefly comes fully to life. The first revolves around the abductee's younger brother, whose drawings of ones and zeroes are the closest the script comes to having a hook. Late in the episode, Mulder and Scully find the drawings arranged on a living room floor; when viewed from the stairs above, the binary input (which also contains information from the Voyager space probe) forms an image of the missing girl.[8] In an entry short on visual flair, the reveal here is striking,

---

8   Howard Gordon, who wrote this episode, calls this moment a "big boo" and says that Chris Carter would ask the writers to include "big boos" in every act of their episodes. In Gordon's words, these moments were, "something that made you move forward, or sit up, or jump."

even if, like most every other clue our heroes find, it doesn't actually lead to any further insights.

The second great scene is in the episode's closing sequence, in which audio of Mulder recounting his sister's abduction to a hypnotist is played over a shot of Mulder sitting alone in a church, head in hands. It's a powerful, moving expression of his loss and grief, one that grounds the alien abduction mythos in real, relatable emotion, and it makes the episode slightly more than the sum of its well-intentioned, if too sedate, parts.[9] —ZH

"THE JERSEY DEVIL"	SEASON 1 / EPISODE 5 WRITTEN BY CHRIS CARTER DIRECTED BY JOE NAPOLITANO

PINE BARRENS

In which the show's makeup budget must have been stretched that week.

Through its first four episodes, *The X-Files* has seemed remarkably sure-footed. Yes, some of those episodes are better than others, but they've all been enjoyable genre TV, with a nice blend of science fiction and horror.

Until now.

"The Jersey Devil" is the first genuinely bad episode of the series, and it kicks off a run of the season in which lesser episodes outweigh the classics. Most of this can be chalked up to first-season fumbling, in which the show has to figure out what does and doesn't work.[10] In the case of "The Jersey Devil," it's not hard to sense the specter of network notes lurking behind the worst elements of the episode.

In particular, the focus on Scully's personal life, involving her nascent relationship with a single father she meets at a birthday party for her godson, is the kind of thing that often arises thanks to some network suit wondering if the audience mightn't be interested in hearing about the characters' personal lives. Who is Scully outside of work? Knowing the answer to that question could, theoretically, help us better understand her relationship both to Mulder and to her own professional ambitions. You can certainly see why it would come up as a suggestion.

In practice, however, the story line is a nonstarter. If we're going to worry about what Scully has sacrificed to join Mulder's quest, we need something more than a

---

9 The final exchange is worth quoting here:
   Mulder: "It's telling me that no harm will come to her and that one day she'll return."
   Dr. Weber: "Do you believe the voice?"
   Mulder: "I want to believe."

10 If you're watching a show where this *doesn't* happen in Season One, beware. The crash is coming.

bland would-be boyfriend.[11] This subplot does serve to highlight just how wide the gulf is between the two characters—Scully has an actual life to lose. Mulder (despite looking and sounding like David Duchovny) apparently can't find friends, much less lovers. He's so consumed by his quest to uncover "The Truth" that the thought of him having a serious relationship or friendship is presented as laughable.

There are, of course, some sexist assumptions at play here. Why should Mulder be defined by his work, while Scully ostensibly has to worry about a personal life? "The Jersey Devil" actually tackles this question head-on, as Scully rolls her eyes at the idea that she shouldn't spend so much time at work. Her friend also suggests that maybe she should hook up with Mulder. After all, he's cute, right? (According to Scully herself.)[12]

Scully's romantic travails might thus be more bearable if they weren't wedded to an X-File that squanders a compelling premise. The idea of a Bigfoot-style creature dragging the homeless into the woods to eat them gives the series a chance to play around with one of the most classic paranormal tales of them all: the monster out in the wild, whispered of but barely glimpsed. But *The X-Files* rarely nailed these sorts of tales, too often getting waylaid by how many other takes on the basic material already existed.[13]

Here, after a 1940s-set teaser featuring the monster (who lives just outside Atlantic City) nabbing a family man, the episode turns into a bit of a slog that inadvertently centers on just how little money the series has to depict a legitimate Bigfoot-style creature. Instead, the show decides to split the difference by suggesting that a colony of feral humans lives out in the woods, with the family matriarch sometimes venturing into the city to nab human flesh to feed her children. This leaves much of the episode featuring what appears to be a very normal woman wandering around, naked, with halfheartedly applied makeup meant to suggest she's very dirty. It's all but impossible to take seriously.

"The Jersey Devil," however, has a certain appeal. It's one of those first-season episodes that underlines just how different the series' lush, Vancouver-filmed charms felt when compared with everything else on TV at the time. And a few of the early monster sequences succeed, thanks to suggesting more than showing. But by the time the Devil herself turns up, the episode takes a turn for the worse it never quite recovers from, trying endlessly to justify why it didn't instead put a guy in a schlocky suit and call him an evolutionary missing link. *The X-Files* would

---

11 To its credit, the show almost immediately figures this out. But not in this episode.

12 I'm again struck by how heavily these early episodes play up the prospects of the two of them as romantic partners. This feels like just another network note, but you never know.

13 We'll see this same problem at play in the very next episode, which showcases just how much the show struggled with ghost stories.

make far, far worse episodes than this one, but this is an important bad episode, both because it was the first one, and because the show learned so much about its own limitations from it. —TVDW

| "SHADOWS" | SEASON 1 / EPISODE 6
WRITTEN BY GLEN MORGAN AND JAMES WONG
DIRECTED BY MICHAEL KATLEMAN |

I'LL BE WATCHING YOU

In which you can still be stalked after your stalker is dead.

"Shadows" is meant to be a vaguely comforting tale of a young woman who finds herself protected by a paternal boss, even after his death—though he is admittedly not great at finding ways to look out for her that don't involve terrifying seemingly anybody she meets. It is, then, a fairly classic ghost story. The bonds that formed in life continue beyond the grave, and Mulder and Scully are present for the denouement when the poltergeist has his revenge.

However, the typical *X-Files* final beat employed in "Shadows," wherein the Monster of the Week can never *truly* be banished, is much creepier than I suspect was intended. See, Howard Graves (the aforementioned ghost) sure *seems* like he's still haunting Lauren Kyte (Lisa Waltz) when the episode ends, even though his duplicitous partner has finally been brought to justice.[14] Howard's spirit has followed Lauren to another workplace, in another city, to hurt anyone who dares wrong her—the very figure of an overprotective father who has been given supernatural powers.

Now, if you watched "Shadows" back in 1993, it's not that you wouldn't have caught these undertones, but you might have approached them more in the spirit they were intended: as a solid, spooky scare to close out a humdrum episode. *The X-Files*, like most shows of its era, was written primarily by white men,[15] which means that it sometimes misses the added horrific complications of certain story beats. While Howard's continued existence as a ghost who exclusively haunts Lauren isn't presented as a positive situation, the episode lacks an awareness of the gravity and horror that a viewer watching twenty-five years later might have, in recognizing Howard for what he is: a stalker from beyond the grave. Obviously, the show's writers may very well have arrived at this conclusion and realized how it played even as they wrote it. But considering that the ostensible reasoning for writing this episode was

---

14 The criminal conspiracy here involves an Islamic terrorist cell, which is ripped from the headlines in a very '90s sort of way.

15 And is being reviewed, in this book, by two other white men, so let's be sure to point that out!

to show Mulder and Scully helping someone by ridding Lauren of all of the people tormenting her, it seems unlikely.

It's important not to harp too much on the tiny plot point of the conclusion, even if it helps distract from an episode that spins its wheels a fair amount. It is, ultimately, just a very short moment at hour's end. But focusing on this helps us dig into something that is true of any older TV show: There are episodes of *The X-Files* that don't play well to modern eyes. Some of those episodes involve brief, easily overlooked moments like this coda of "Shadows." Some are full-fledged dives into nonwhite cultures that now come off as insensitive at best. And then there are episodes with hidden messages and themes that weren't as obvious when the episodes originally aired but now are hard to miss.[16]

This is inevitable. TV episodes, more than any other art form, are stuck in the era in which they were made, instantly dated by their fashions, hairstyles, and cinematic conventions. That means their politics and social content wind up stuck there too. "Shadows" first aired in 1993, and it's incredibly difficult to divorce the episode from that era. This ends up saving it, just a little bit, because it's like forgiving a retrograde but essentially harmless attitude from an aging relative. There are plenty of episodes that won't be so lucky.

To make the situation worse, "Shadows" falls into another *X-Files* pitfall: the not-so-scary ghost story. As much fun as it is to see Scully quote *Poltergeist* as a way of gently mocking her partner, the actual mechanics of the ghost plot fall apart the second they become clear, because the ghost story is perhaps the most common and overdone form of horror story. *The X-Files* is better when it takes horror tropes and twists and bends them, but the ghost story has been twisted and bent so many times throughout horror history that there's little for the show to explore or subvert. This is the first time *The X-Files* would fail at telling what amounts to a ghost story, but it's unfortunately far from the last.[17]

That issue leaves the episode flailing a bit, though it ultimately gains a boost from some strong direction, courtesy of Michael Katleman, who would never return to the show. The final sequence, in which Mulder watches as the ghost of Howard Graves unleashes his wrath, is a terrific example of doing a lot with a little. The scene conveys the sheer horror and chaos of being trapped in an *X-Files* episode, using only some swirling paper and a hovering penknife. It's a lesson in minimalism from which many of this season's episodes could learn a thing or two. —TVDW

S1 E6

---

16 Weirdly, this happens in lots of the "comedic" episodes, which we'll discuss later on.
17 Indeed, there are several just around the corner!

	SEASON 1 / EPISODE 7
"GHOST IN THE MACHINE"	WRITTEN BY ALEX GANSA AND HOWARD GORDON
	DIRECTED BY JERROLD FREEDMAN

DAISY, DAISY

In which CTRL-ALT-DEL is a matter of life and death.

It's not particularly surprising that *The X-Files* would do an episode about a malevolent artificial intelligence, given that the concept has been a staple of science fiction since the 1950s, and the '90s saw a rapid development of computer technology. Yet the malevolent operating system that kills anyone who gets in its way is the weakest element of "Ghost in the Machine." Shots of blinking lights and flashing panels have a certain charm, but the threat seems too dated to us now to be memorable beyond its camp value.

The most effective element of this episode is its structure, which starts simply enough before expanding at the midpoint to connect the story back to the season's larger mythology. Once again, we have one of our heroes called in to assist on a case by an old friend, only this time it's Mulder who gets the ring.[18] The reminder that Mulder has a history, and that not all of it is focused on the X-Files, works as good, low-key world-building, and Jerry Lamana (Wayne Duvall) is a well-drawn, seemingly likable guy who's more than willing to exploit his old partner if it will help his career.

Jerry gets just enough character development to give his death weight, and his demise cleverly pushes the plot into a new act. After a slow build, things shift from the immediate danger of a computer-controlled building to the larger threat of evil government forces having that power at their disposal. Deep Throat gets a call, and his intimation that powerful men have interest in developing this technology—a technology that can both research its enemies and kill at a whim—gives the last act some much needed stakes.

The final confrontation, which has Mulder and Scully storming the mad computer building, intent on bringing the thing down from the inside, is both silly and effective. The script finds some inventive, if implausible, ways to keep the operating system a threat (Scully spends several scenes getting blown around in an air vent!). The fact that the tension is not only about our heroes' survival but also about destroying the AI before the government can abscond with it, helps keep the suspense high. It also ensures that the threat, even when technically resolved, still lingers. If someone can do something once, someone else can do it again; you could almost say we're hardwired to try. —ZH

---

18 In "Squeeze" (S1E3), it was Scully who was contacted by a fellow agent to investigate.

WE'RE NOT WHO WE ARE

In which Mulder and Scully try to keep their cool.

Not every monster has a face. "Ice" finds Mulder and Scully trapped at an Alaskan outpost, facing paranoia, alien worms, and alpha male bullshit. Set almost entirely in a single location with a six-person cast, the episode is a claustrophobic nightmare, using its physical limitations to maximum effect. As they established with the Monster of the Week formula in "Squeeze" (S1E3), Glen Morgan and James Wong are more than capable of expanding the horizons of *The X-Files*, this time with a purely biological threat that stretches the definition of "extraterrestrial life."

"Ice" also puts the first serious strain on Scully and Mulder's partnership, forcing them into a situation that breaks down their trust in each other. Though neither of them becomes infected with the worm (which, Scully theorizes, feeds off of impulse control, releasing its victim's most violent tendencies), this detail is almost beside the point. One of the main threads running through the first season is the construction of a relationship that would come to be the heart of the show. It's a bold move to start testing the limits of that bond this early in the series' run, but the gambit works.

This is a testament to both Duchovny and Anderson's strong work in the episode. Both actors are able to build intensity in quick, but plausible, ways, so that Scully's decision to lock Mulder away under suspicion of murder makes sense. More than anything, we see Scully in her element here; she's the sole member of the expedition to keep her head throughout, and even when the tension is high, she makes smart calls, refusing to compromise her judgment for fear. Mulder doesn't come off badly,[19] but he does spend a chunk of time in a storage closet, leaving Scully to deal with the other survivors and serve as the protagonist for much of the episode.

The non-FBI members of the expedition are also well acted and characterized, each one defined by a clear personality type. The two standouts are also the two characters who survive the longest: Xander Berkeley as Dr. Hodge is the sort of prick who makes even a good situation worse, and Felicity Huffman as Dr. Nancy Da Silva makes an impression through her reserve.

The whole cast is great, really, and while we don't get a lot of personal information about any of them, we do get enough to feel a loss when one of them winds up dead. The script is ruthless in its efficiency, establishing the danger in an eerie cold

---

19 His determination to save living samples of the worm, however, is questionable, given the circumstances.

open and then sending Scully, Mulder, and the others into the frozen waste within minutes. Tensions escalate quickly—but not so quick as to seem forced—and the threat plus the setting create a realistic pressure cooker of personalities in which horrors seem all but inevitable.

That efficiency may be due to familiarity. "Ice" takes a large part of its inspiration from John W. Campbell's 1938 novella, *Who Goes There?*, and John Carpenter's 1982 film adaptation of that same story, *The Thing*.[20] As in the *X-Files* episode, both the book and movie follow a group stranded in the frozen tundra who face a deadly alien threat.[21] Unlike in "Ice," however, the monster in those stories is an alien that can perfectly mimic other living entities, but the suspicion and terror of the unknown are similar in each tale.

Yet "Ice" still feels distinct. That's due to the original concept of a worm that induces rage in its host, and to Scully and Mulder's presence, which gives the audience a unique emotional investment in the characters. We're not just seeing new faces turn on one another; we're seeing the two main characters of the show at each other's throats. It's impressive how far the episode seems to go into darkness before pulling back.

While later seasons would expand the show's emotional palette, the first season of *The X-Files* did its best work in horror, peeling back the surface of the world to show the gnashing creatures underneath. "Ice" is one of the highlights—a well-crafted descent into the hell of other people. —ZH

"SPACE"	SEASON 1 / EPISODE 9 WRITTEN BY CHRIS CARTER DIRECTED BY WILLIAM GRAHAM

FAILURE TO LAUNCH

*In which the Face on Mars is indirectly responsible for the
Challenger disaster (maybe?).*

Corner any creator or showrunner of a successful TV series, and you'll inevitably get them to admit at least one episode just didn't work. For *The X-Files* and Chris Carter, that episode is this one, which is admirable, since it issued from Carter's pen.

"Space" is so self-evidently terrible that it's hard not to feel a kind of pity for it. What's fun to see about these early alien-centric episodes is just how all over the

---

20 *Who Goes There?* was first adapted in 1951's *The Thing from Another World*, but since that version forgoes the shape-changing angle of both the novella and Carpenter's film, it's not as relevant here.
21 Another point of similarity: *The Thing* and "Ice" both feature an infected dog.

place they are when compared with the more focused alien conspiracy story lines of later seasons. This is about how the Face on Mars (of supermarket tabloid fame) tormented an astronaut during a space walk, and then it maybe possessed him, and then it quite possibly caused him to create space disasters, including the Challenger explosion. It's a ludicrous premise before you even get to the execution, one that requires you to make five or six separate buy-ins before you can go with it. The best *X-Files* episodes have an elegant simplicity. This has a ghost face.

There was maybe something salvageable here, due to William Graham's mostly capable direction and a couple of nicely executed countdown sequences meant to raise the dramatic stakes. When the agents watch to see if a shuttle they diverted from a disastrous course at the last moment can land safely, there's some genuine tension. Even though he's playing an essentially impossible part—man possessed by the Face on Mars—Ed Lauter as Lt. Col. Marcus Aurelius Belt gives it his all, even when his face is being distorted by strange, ashy darkness meant to represent his inner demons.

You'll perhaps note the episode's main problem lies in that last snarky aside: The series simply doesn't have the budget to do an episode in which our heroes deal with such a wide-ranging conspiracy, at least without collapsing into utter silliness.[22] The effects are awful, the opposite of the perfect minimalism in "Ice" (S1E8). The plotting lurches forward and back. The whole "possessed by the Face on Mars" thing makes less sense the more you know about the show's later alien conspiracy.

Yes, *The X-Files* made worse episodes than this one, or, perhaps I should say, less forgivable episodes than this one. "Space" exists in the first half of Season One, when the show is clearly throwing things at the wall to see what sticks. This episode represents an evolutionary dead end for an experimenting show. The aliens would be back, but not in the form of tabloid fodder, or as beings hoping to infiltrate NASA. Perhaps that's why it's so easy for Carter to throw the episode under the bus in retrospect: He knew this was the first and last attempt at this type of plot. —TVDW

---

22 Yes, the series would often succeed in spite of budgetary limits, but it takes a bigger leap of faith to believe in an unseen entity that is technically just a bunch of rocks than, say, an alien worm beneath someone's skin. All the filmmaking know-how in the world would struggle with an idea this silly.

	SEASON 1 / EPISODE 10
"FALLEN ANGEL"	WRITTEN BY HOWARD GORDON AND ALEX GANSA
	DIRECTED BY LARRY SHAW

THE HUMAN COST

In which we're finally getting somewhere.

"Ice" (S1E8), "Space" (S1E9), and "Fallen Angel" represent a kind of turning point for the show. "Ice" was the best Monster of the Week episode of the first season. "Space" represented a path the show would never again follow. "Fallen Angel" sets the template for dozens of alien conspiracy episodes to come. Whereas earlier conspiracy episodes like "Deep Throat" (S1E2) and even "Pilot " (S1E1) took on questions of abductions and UFOs like a standard crime procedural, "Fallen Angel" begins to suggest that there's a much, much larger picture than we can see, one with a scope even Mulder would struggle to comprehend.

Perhaps more importantly, it introduces Max Fenig. Max, portrayed by Scott Bellis, carries an outsize weight in the series. His memorability is due in part to the performance, sure, but also because he underlines something inherent in the overall story line: The alien conspiracy is ruining people's lives.

To be sure, you can be a Scully—you can believe that Max's problems stem not from frequent alien abductions but from schizophrenia. But the episode avoids this interpretation by siding with the believers, depicting Max hovering in a beam of light with Mulder unable to save him from being returned to his captors. "Fallen Angel" further posits that Max wasn't even aware his visit to a UFO crash site *was* a visit to a UFO crash site. He simply felt compelled, and it's not hard to draw the conclusion that the aliens wanted him back and somehow contacted him. That's where Mulder's logic leads him, and it's a potent early example of the show tapping into the idea of a shadow world, living right alongside our own.

At its most powerful, *The X-Files'* conspiracy plot told a story about forces within the government that operated without any sort of jurisdiction and with shadowy connections to extraterrestrial life. Max is our first real glimpse into a program that involves the aliens abducting and experimenting on a series of hapless humans, all of whom might have lived normal, happy lives but for the fact that they were in the wrong place at the wrong time. Max is a version of Mulder, if it had been Mulder who was taken, instead of his sister Samantha.

One element of the series that has aged poorly in our Internet era is its general sympathy for conspiracy theorist nut jobs.[23] Nowadays, just about any conspiracy theory you can think of will gain enough sympathetic ears to become dangerous. But

---

23 Then again, the series found itself gradually less enamored of conspiracy theorist nut jobs the longer it went along, as we'll see around its midpoint.

in the early '90s, the idea that the U.S. government was hiding information about aliens, and only a few people knew about it, was far enough off the radar to make the show's warm treatment of Max and his Airstream trailer stuffed with conspiracy paraphernalia feel like an embrace of the underdog against the darkness seeking to blot him out.

And, honestly, it's hard to argue with that portrayal of the character. Even if Max were a schizophrenic whose journeys into alien spacecraft happened only in his imagination, he's so far out of the American mainstream as to be all but forgotten. The series embraces this sort of oddball (as long as he doesn't mean harm to anybody else) and the portrayal of Max is in line with the similar portrayal of weirdos who live on the fringes of society in contemporary series *Twin Peaks* and *Northern Exposure*.[24] Max hasn't done anything wrong; he's a victim of circumstance, but said circumstance compels him to keep coming back for more. It's one of the most potent nightmares the show has come up with to this point.

Though he gives the episode its heart, there's plenty more to "Fallen Angel" than just Max. The point-of-view shots that allow the camera to become the invisible alien, searching for a way to escape the government perimeter and find its way back to its ship, are great fun. Mulder's insistence on jeopardizing his own job in the name of finding the truth (and saving Max) beautifully outlines his character. Scully's willingness to follow him ever deeper into hell, all the while saying she's not sure about it, perfectly sets up her voyage through the rest of the season. And the way the episode plays around with the mechanics of an alien cover-up (via a series of ever-shifting government cover stories[25]) suggests something far bigger than Mulder's early investigations turned up. We realize that there's a whole *world* of conspiracy players we have yet to meet, and that they're working very hard to keep the rest of us from knowing what they're up to.

This revelation makes the episode's final moment, in which Deep Throat spares Mulder's life to prevent him from leaking everything he thinks he knows, a sort of trial run for a story point that would recur throughout the series. Honestly, you might wonder, why *doesn't* the conspiracy just kill Mulder already? Yet without Mulder, the conspiracy would apparently be without something vital. It's a question to which *The X-Files* might not offer a terribly convincing answer, but this early stab at it works about as well as any. You almost wish Deep Throat would chuckle wryly and say, "Mulder can't die. Without him, there would be no TV show." —TVDW

---

24 *Twin Peaks* was, as mentioned, a sizable influence on *The X-Files*. *Northern Exposure* is one of the few shows of its era to attain a similar Venn diagram intersection between critical acclaim and audience adoration.

25 One of which—a toxic-waste spill—is another wink toward *Close Encounters of the Third Kind*.

BAD SEEDS

In which the most dangerous monsters are the ones we don't recognize.

Much of the allure of *The X-Files* comes from the way the show capitalizes on the fear of some other, far more horrible reality hiding behind what we think is the real world. It's hard to think of a more unsettling expression of this fear than murderous children. "Eve" is a little too sloppy to be completely successful, but the two little girls and three adult women at the center of the episode are memorable enough to make the script's shortcomings easy to overlook. The result of a government genetics experiment, the young Eves murder anyone who gets in their way—and it's chillingly convincing how close they come to getting away with it.

"Eve" manages some clever misdirection. When a man is found drained of blood in his backyard, Mulder connects the case with cattle mutilations and assumes alien involvement. By now, the show has taught viewers that Mulder's "crazy" theories are nearly always correct, and the episode doesn't immediately tip its hand to the contrary. Teena Simmons (Sabrina Krievins; her twin sister Erika plays the other young Eve) is an almost preternaturally calm child, but she gives Mulder the answers he wants to hear, and it's only when another murder surfaces with the same M.O. that Mulder and Scully start to question their assumptions.

This is a smart, effective way to exploit audience expectations, and it also serves as a structural mimic to the girls' own camouflage. Given their youth and the bizarre awfulness of the crimes, it's easier, and more comforting, to assume the involvement of outside parties, even if those parties are something as implausible as aliens. Even after Deep Throat pops in to provide exposition about the experiment that created the original Eves (and Adams), Mulder doesn't think to suspect the kids, pinning blame on the adult Eves (all played by Harriet Sansom Harris).

That error leads to a suspenseful set piece, with the child Eves trying to poison Scully and Mulder at a roadside restaurant. The audience is already well aware of the girls' murderous intent, having watched them confess their crimes and kill the adult Eve who kidnapped them after their fathers' deaths. Waiting to see if our heroes will catch on to the danger in time makes for nail-biting stuff, and the script and direction do an excellent job of dragging out the tension without overplaying it.

The episode takes a few distracting narrative shortcuts that undercut its effectiveness, relying on the shock of the girls' real intentions to compensate for a variety of issues. The suggestion that the child Eves have some sort of psychic connection is less a legitimate character reveal than it is a method of plastering over plot holes with a modicum of effort. And, while the hour is well paced, the lack of interest in the girls' parents, exploited without their knowledge by one of the adult Eves, leaves the story without an emotional center.

Still, taken solely on the strengths of its monster, "Eve" is a memorable entry in the Monster of the Week pantheon. The Krievins sisters are convincingly sociopathic, their blank stares becoming increasingly threatening as their motive becomes clear, and Harris manages to make each of the adult Eves distinctive. Her work as the kidnapper, convinced she can save the children from themselves, is the closest the story comes to tragedy, and her sincerity makes her death at their hands all the more disturbing. —ZH

SEASON 1 / EPISODE 12
WRITTEN BY CHRIS CARTER
DIRECTED BY LARRY SHAW

"FIRE"

BURNING BRIGHT

In which Mulder faces an old flame.

This episode's best asset is its impressive pyrotechnics, as various stuntpeople and sets are set alight for our enjoyment. The practical effects work makes every expression of Cecil L'Ively's (Mark Sheppard) powers seem legitimately dangerous. By the time an entire house is engulfed by his handiwork, it's almost possible to ignore the hour's shortcomings and just savor the heat.

Unfortunately, "Fire" suffers from a bad case of forced backstory, giving Mulder a new old flame and a terror of combustion that both suffer from obvious contrivance. Phoebe Green (Amanda Pays) is the most basic of stock TV characters, an ex-lover designed to put tension on the hero's current relationship. Scully is reduced to rolling her eyes and looking annoyed, and while Pays and Duchovny do their best to sell the relationship, Green's ridiculous Britishisms[26] make her difficult to take seriously.

The idea that Mulder has been hiding a secret phobia of fire is also a dramatic dead end. It's an all-too-obvious attempt to give Mulder an unnecessary emotional arc, and it fails to connect with anything we already know about the character.

Sheppard is a convincingly menacing creep, but the script gives the actor little else to do. That lack of depth keeps L'Ively from joining the show's canon of great monsters. But hey, it's still a pleasure to burn. —ZH

---

26 Apparently, they had an "indiscretion" on Sir Arthur Conan Doyle's grave.

"BEYOND THE SEA"	SEASON 1 / EPISODE 13 WRITTEN BY GLEN MORGAN AND JAMES WONG DIRECTED BY DAVID NUTTER

SOMEWHERE, WAITING FOR ME

In which Scully is almost a believer.

Twelve episodes into its first season, *The X-Files* had already seen its share of death. But "Beyond the Sea" is the first casualty to hit close to home. The pre-credits scene could almost stand on its own as a short film: Scully, chatting with her parents (Sheila Larkin and Don Davis[27]), and then later, Scully waking up on her couch to find her father sitting across from her, moving his mouth without speaking. At that moment, the phone rings. It's Scully's mother. Her father is dead.

There's something intensely unsettling about this kind of ghost story, a personal and existential crisis that circumvents the series' typical problems with such plots. Our heroes have faced horrifying threats before, but the ghost of Scully's dad presents no immediate danger. He's less a coherent presence than an echo of something, and the effect it elicits is less horrific and more a deep, unnerving sense of loss. In just a few minutes, the episode conveys the shocking awfulness of the unexpected death of a loved one: the disorientation, the pain, and the nagging sensation of some moment misplaced, some vital exchange now lost forever.

Whatever message Scully's father might have wanted to leave for his daughter is a minor thread running through the hour, but the story uses Scully's mourning as a backdrop for a more familiar Monster of the Week. The main case centers around a pair of kidnapped college students and a convicted murderer slated for execution named Luther Lee Boggs (Brad Dourif). Boggs claims to have had psychic visions of the kidnapping and is willing to help authorities in exchange for saving him from the chair. The crux of the episode comes down to whether or not he's telling the truth, and if he is, what that means for Scully and her skepticism.

For once, Mulder is the unbeliever here; his profiling helped put Boggs in the hot seat, and he believes that Boggs is orchestrating the whole crime from the inside as a form of revenge against him. Scully most likely would have taken Mulder's side, were it not for a connection Boggs makes to her father on their first meeting. The vision makes Scully, already vulnerable, more receptive to Boggs's ramblings, putting her in the position of a (however unwilling) believer, trying to convince someone else of the seemingly impossible.

It's a standard complaint that the regular dynamic between the two leads—Mulder's wild theories against Scully's rational doubt—sometimes became

---

27 Davis played Major Garland Briggs on *Twin Peaks*, another indication of that show's influence on this one.

a limitation to an otherwise multidimensional show. Given how often Mulder is right (as we've already seen even this early in the series), Scully's unwillingness to accept the paranormal seems more like a conditioned response than a reasoned scientific approach. But criticism of Scully's attitude isn't entirely fair, considering just how nutty Mulder's theories can be. Her levelheadedness is a key dramatic element, making each case as much about struggling for her belief as it is about tracking down beasties or gathering evidence of alien intelligence. If Mulder can't convince her, how can he hope to convince anyone? By temporarily reversing the two characters' philosophies, "Beyond the Sea" adds more complexity to both Scully and Mulder, showing that their arguments are less a clash of opposing ideals, and more the result of their work to find common ground.

"Beyond the Sea" makes an effort to get a bit more into Scully's head than most episodes have up to this point, first by showing her reaction to the death of her father and his funeral, and then in her interactions with Boggs, as she slowly begins to trust his "visions."[28] Anderson does great work here, and Dourif brings a terrific intensity to the role of Boggs, making the most out of the character's "channeling" sessions. His strongest scene, though, is when he explains to Scully why he's so terrified of being executed. On his first trip to the gas chamber (which ended in a last-minute stay), he had a vision of his victims and felt what they had felt as he killed them; the way that Dourif portrays the horror of that experience makes Boggs more than just a manipulative villain. It doesn't make him sympathetic, exactly, but it does give him just enough depth to make him more than a plot device.

None of this would work if the script[29] didn't have a keen understanding of what drives Dana Scully. The character has never been quite so vulnerable on the show before now, and while it might strain plausibility to have her drop her guard so quickly around a convicted murderer, Anderson and Dourif manage to make their brief connection feel authentic. Scully's clear frustration at needing to communicate and trust someone she knows has every reason to lie to her ensures that the character's rationality is never compromised, and Boggs's directness about his crimes and his gifts make him impossible to dismiss. There's a sense throughout the hour that Scully is on the edge of losing her reserve, that her father's death and her glimpse of his ghost have made her vulnerable to the "extreme possibilities" of which Mulder is so fond.

S1 E13

---

28 An even more obvious influence for this episode is *The Silence of the Lambs*, another story about a female FBI agent who makes contact with a jailed psychopath in order to get his help to track down a killer. Both this episode and that movie derive tension from watching a good person try to negotiate with a monster. According to Chris Carter, the idea that the show would do an episode inspired by *The Silence of the Lambs* "scared the hell" out of the network at the time. Carter had to personally advocate for this episode in order for the network to let it happen, and "it ended up being one of the most memorable episodes of the young series."

29 Another collaboration by Morgan and Wong. The two are responsible for a lot of what works in Season One.

Our sense of Scully's precarious emotional state builds to a powerful conclusion. Earlier in the episode, Boggs offers to give Scully one last message from her dad if she'll be a witness to the killer's execution. She considers the offer, but when the time comes, Boggs goes into the chamber and Scully isn't there to watch it. As Boggs dies, the episode cuts back to Scully by Mulder's bedside at the hospital, where she's already coming up with rational justifications for everything that happened. As she tells Mulder, she's afraid not to.

Scully's fear might not be the most objective motivation to seek a scientific explanation for the episode's events. But this confession makes Scully's consistent refusal to accept Mulder's worldview more than just a writer's trick to create conflict between the characters. The scene acknowledges a truth that Mulder himself seems to have forgotten: Accepting that ghosts and psychic visions are real means accepting that anything else might be. It means giving up the structure of the world as we know it for something that is unmoored from any reasonable notion of reality. It means accepting that monsters and mayhem are not an exception to the status quo. It means understanding that they *are* the status quo.

There's something almost noble in Scully insisting otherwise. Besides, even though Mulder is so often right, there are some things Scully knows better than he ever will. When he asks why she missed out on her chance to hear from her father one last time, she tells him, in a callback to an earlier exchange with her mother, that she already knows what he would've said "because he was my father." In an often violent and disturbing hour, it's a lovely reminder of how graceful Scully's faith in the simplicity of the universe can be. —ZH

STARBUCK THE SKEPTIC

Though "Beyond the Sea" is clearly inspired by *The Silence of the Lambs*, it was also influenced by the burgeoning world of Internet fandom. Notes Chris Carter, "It really is a coincidence that *The X-Files* kind of grew up along with the Internet. We started hearing from people in chat rooms. The feedback was immediate. It was enthusiastic. It was heartfelt, passionate. We had a sense that we were striking a chord that didn't have to wait for tomorrow's mail." But the fandom wasn't always so positive. James Wong remembers that, "[We looked on a site called Delphi Forums and all the fans were] talking about how they thought [Scully] was a bitch. 'She never believes anything!' We talked about, in the beginning, that maybe at the end of the first season, we'd have Gillian have an experience that made her believe. Because of the fan reaction, we thought, maybe we should do this earlier, and that's how 'Beyond the Sea' was conceived. Gillian and David switch roles in that episode. We did that earlier [in the season], because of the news groups."

That happy coincidence allowed this hour to deepen Scully's character in having her temporarily become the believer of the duo. Carter notes that the dynamic of Mulder's infallibility on the subject of the supernatural and Scully's logical rationality would have gotten stale if it weren't inverted from time to time: "As people have often pointed out, Mulder is always right, even if there is no explanation for what he believes or wants to believe. His science fiction always trumps her science. If she's wrong all the time, the show could get boring. [So] you do twists on it. You change it up. You have Scully as the believer sometimes and Mulder as the skeptic. Scully is us. She wants to see it, touch it, taste it . . . she wants to smell and apply scientific principles to it. As long as she can do that, you've got at least a plausible position for the character."

Wong, too, echoes Carter's assessment of Scully and remarks that it's actually Scully's position as an audience surrogate that made her such a joy to write for, saying, "I think she is fascinating, because she's the rest of us. David/Mulder has all the answers. But, when you're faced with unexplained phenomenon, she's the rational person who can try to explain what happened. . . . David already knows everything, or he has a point of view that's already out there. She's the one that he can really dig into, and twist, and make her squirm, and make her feel things that she hadn't ever felt before. That character to me is actually richer, or it allows you to do more things with her than David's character."

Though he wouldn't come on board as a producer and writer for the show until Season Two, Frank Spotnitz credits Scully's skepticism, even when it was tweaked by the paranormal such as it is in "Beyond the Sea," as the reason behind the longevity of The X-Files. "I think that's what made the narrative engine of The X-Files work so successfully for so long," he says. "[It] was the classic format of the show in that there's a teaser, characters that you empathize with to some degree, or a situation where something scary and inexplicable happens. Then there's the scene in Mulder's office where Mulder's saying one fantastic fact, another fantastic fact, [and] Scully's challenging each one, she's like the smartest person in the audience, and finally Mulder says one fantastic fact that even smart Scully can't rebut. And then you're off, then there's your argument. So to me, it was justified, because it wasn't so much that she refused to believe, . . . but that she was trying to make sense of it just like the audience would try to make sense of it. That's actually what drove the storytelling."

Scully, then, is not only us—she's the best version of us, always trying to understand and interpret the world around her. Says Spotnitz, "Even if Scully sees things that are fantastic and supernatural, she's going to try to apply science and reason to them. That's her role, to try to make sense of things."

| "GENDER BENDER" | SEASON 1 / EPISODE 14
WRITTEN BY LARRY BARBER AND PAUL BARBER
DIRECTED BY ROB BOWMAN |

ALIEN AMISH

In which the show tries to be "sexy," with mixed results.

"Gender Bender" is an episode whose central conceit has aged poorly in the decades since it aired. The gender fluidity of the "monster" was clearly intended to act as both a shock and an indication of the being's fundamental alienness. The fact that the murderer's shift happens at the very end of the cold open implies that changing from female to male is so inherently disturbing that it will drive our interest for the rest of the hour. The premise is subtly laced with both homophobia and transmisogyny. The horror isn't just that an attractive woman lured a man into her bed to kill him, but that "she" somehow changed into (or revealed herself to be) a "he" post-coitus.

This would be a difficult premise to handle even with a script that was interested in exploring the complexities of gender identity. But here, the concept is used for novelty and gimmick, and as a way to add an element of sexual danger to the story. Horror needs universal fears to be effective, and the fears that writers Larry Barber and Paul Barber assumed would be shared by everyone are telling and unsettling for all the wrong reasons.

This is a shame, because apart from this issue, "Gender Bender" is really quite good; it's an effective mixture of scientific theory, unsubstantiated rumor, and memorable visuals. The club scenes are predictable '90s cheese,[30] but the time Mulder and Scully spend with the Kindred—which includes getting surrounded in the forest, an awkward dinner, and some truly bizarre barn-based funeral arrangements—is *The X-Files* at its best. We see rational people brushing against a bizarre and (quite literally) alien subculture, escaping in the end with only suspicions and the certainty that there is more going on than anyone could ever know.

---

30 Nicholas Lea, who later returned to the show as Alex Krycek, plays one of Brother Martin's seduction targets.

Even the look of the episode represents a step up. As *The X-Files* went on, it developed an increasingly cinematic visual style, but much of the first season has a flat, bland appearance. "Gender Bender" is a comparative feast for the eyes, from its excellent production design (the underground hive Mulder discovers is wonderfully organic and womblike) to a number of strikingly composed camera shots. This was director Rob Bowman's first episode; he'd go on to direct a number of *X-Files* classics, and it's clear to see he's got a strong sense of what works right out of the gate.

The Kindred make for an enigmatic threat, since in a literal sense they aren't really threatening at all; given multiple opportunities to attack Mulder and Scully, they prefer to simply glare and stand aside, which makes them that much more unsettling. One of their number, Brother Andrew (Brent Hinkley), takes a liking to Scully, and tells her the truth about the killer she's hunting; it's Brother Martin,[31] a former friend of Andrew's. One gets the impression that Martin's murders are more an act of indifference than intent; but the Kindred have their rules, and in the end, even though Scully and Mulder track down Martin, it's his people who take him home.

Having Scully be the victim of Andrew's advances sits awkwardly with her characterization to this point; while any human would be vulnerable to the Kindred's seductive touch, her awkward vulnerability and confusion after the fact (combined with Mulder's insensitivity at what is essentially an otherworldy version of a date rape drug) make her seem responsible for what happened in a way that doesn't make much sense. Here, the episode utilizes a complicated concept without bothering to fully take into account its real-world implications. It's still possible to enjoy the hour, but there are an awful lot of caveats to doing so. —ZH

SEASON 1 / EPISODE 15
WRITTEN BY ALEX GANSA AND HOWARD GORDON
DIRECTED BY DAVID NUTTER

"LAZARUS"

THE BANALITY OF PARANORMAL ACTIVITY

In which Scully has an ex-boyfriend all of a sudden.

"Lazarus" is a meat-and-potatoes kind of *X-Files* episode. You're not going to come away from it feeling wildly impressed, and it doesn't really stick in the memory.[32] To its credit, it has a solid hook, some strong performances, and a plot with enough twists to keep you watching. It's remarkable that in the space of a season of television, *The X-Files* went from cranking out pretty terrible mediocre

---

31 Played by both Peter Stebbings and Kate Twa.
32 Between watching it to write this review and sitting down to actually write the review—a time in which about three hours transpired—I forgot almost everything about "Lazarus." My thanks to the unusually detailed Wikipedia entry for jogging my memory.

episodes like, say, "The Jersey Devil" (S1E5) to cranking out slightly less mediocre episodes like this one.

That sounds like damning with faint praise, but a lot of broadcast network television requires producers to turn out north of twenty episodes per season, which means that some are, inevitably, going to be worse than others, and some are going to be *much* worse than others. Often, the difference between a great broadcast network show and a merely good one can be seen in episodes like "Lazarus." It's hard to imagine the episode being anybody's favorite, but if you randomly turned it on during a Friday night in 1994, you would be compelled enough to keep watching. The truly great episodes of *The X-Files* inspire adoration; the ones that are just OK-but-still-watchable inspire devotion.

"Lazarus" definitely qualifies as the latter, thanks to the steady hand of David Nutter, perhaps the show's most important early director. A lot of the episode unfolds in quiet conversations between Scully and her captor (an FBI pal/ex-boyfriend named Jack Willis [Christopher Allport] who may have been possessed by the spirit of a bank robber named Warren Dupre [Jason Schombing]), and Nutter is able to keep the tension ramped all the way up even when Scully is simply trying to deal with the unlikely situation in which she finds herself.

"Lazarus" is also bolstered by a script that turns the scenario into a twisted love triangle. Willis and Scully dated back at the academy, but Dupre carried out his bank robberies with his wife, Lula Phillips (Cec Verrell), and much of the tension of the episode involves Dupre-in-Willis tracking down Phillips, with Scully forced to play witness to the bloody denouement. One of the things that sets apart a good mediocre *X-Files* episode from a bad one is the quality of the guest characters and just how captivating you find their stories. Dupre and Phillips don't *quite* get to the status of the show's finest guest characters, but the show gives their love story enough weight that it's not hard to get at least superficially wrapped up in it.

The real struggle here is something that would bedevil the show throughout its run: Every time Mulder or Scully introduces an FBI colleague from their past, you're forced to just go with it. This isn't an uncommon problem on TV, where we assume characters had lives before we met them, but those lives are often hazy and indistinct. However, *The X-Files* struggled with it more than most, both because of Mulder and Scully's relative youth and because their partnership was so close and so intimate (even by this point) that it's hard to imagine her suddenly introducing an FBI colleague as someone she had once dated without Mulder saying, "Right. You told me all about him when we were staking out the Cigarette Smoking Man."

We also spend so little time with Willis-as-Willis that it becomes difficult to justify developing an attachment to him. He almost immediately becomes possessed by a bank robber, then fixates on pursuing the robber's ends, which means the story is really about Dupre. Thus, we can really only rely on Scully's memories of Willis and her word, and that leaves the whole story line in limbo. It's neither committed enough to Willis to really make Scully's angst play, nor gung ho enough about Dupre to dig into the idea that seeing Willis overridden by such a dark force would give Scully pause about her skepticism.

"Lazarus" was originally imagined as an episode in which Mulder would be possessed by Dupre,[33] an idea that would have been much more potent, even if it would have limited the show in other ways. Mulder couldn't have gone on a killing spree without facing repercussions, even if he used the old "I was possessed!" excuse. Watch this episode imagining Mulder in Willis's shoes, and so much more of it clicks into place. The scenes in which Scully desperately tries to reach the "real" Willis to remind him of who he is would have had more poignancy if it had been Mulder she was trying to contact.

Sure, *The X-Files* often worked best when its guest characters made the most of their opportunities, but the highest heights often arrived in the moments when Mulder and Scully were personally wrapped up in that week's story. Perhaps what's most disappointing about "Lazarus" is that even if you don't know the original concept for the episode, you can still see the silhouette of an hour in which Mulder and Scully have more at stake lurking on the edges of the frame. —TVDW

SEASON 1 / EPISODE 16
WRITTEN BY SCOTT KAUFER AND CHRIS CARTER | **"YOUNG AT HEART"**
DIRECTED BY MICHAEL LANGE

OLD IN SPIRIT

In which Mulder has to track down an old foe.

As Todd notes in his review of "Lazarus" (S1E15), the first season is rife with old colleagues, former nemeses, and ex-flames; it's an unnecessary contrivance that quickly builds to the point of self-parody, especially when you consider that the premise of the show (FBI agents investigating strangeness) already offers a perfect excuse to bring Scully and Mulder to any case. "Young at Heart" has the double whammy of yet another old Mulder foe, as well as a former boss who first lectures Mulder on his weirdness, and then gets murdered.[34]

The narrative device could be overlooked if "Young" was any good, but it's not, really. It's sloppily written and poorly edited,[35] and the first half hour is content to

---

33 As per Brian Lowry's 1995 book *The Truth Is Out There: The Official Guide to* The X-Files. (My thanks to my mother for digging it out of my childhood bedroom closet.)

34 If you've worked with, known, or had the misfortune of being born in close proximity to either Mulder or Scully, your best bet is to fake your own death as soon as possible. If you don't, the writers *will* find you, and they *will* make you pay in the name of dramatic expediency.

35 Several close-ups appear to have been filmed in a parallel universe.

stumble its way through a series of thoroughly unexciting investigation and stalking scenes. The episode picks up some in the last ten minutes, though not nearly enough. The scene in which the mad doctor explains the nature of his experiments and their flaws has a nice, intimate feel, and Deep Throat's brief appearance to tell Mulder that the government is interested in negotiating with said mad doctor helps connect the episode to the show's obsession with conspiracy.

You're left with the sense that *that's* what the episode should have been about, instead of all this killer-out-of-the-past malarkey. Too much of "Young" doesn't go anywhere, from the villain's admittedly cool but not particularly important lizard hand to Mulder's whole "I followed the book and people died!" crisis. *The X-Files* hasn't quite settled on what it does best yet, and as this episode proves, part of the show's process of discovering what works has meant relying on unnecessary cliché. —ZH

| "E.B.E." | SEASON 1 / EPISODE 17
WRITTEN BY GLEN MORGAN AND JAMES WONG
DIRECTED BY WILLIAM GRAHAM |

ON THE GRASSY KNOLL

In which even aliens deserve to live free or die.

"That innocent and blank expression as I pulled the trigger has haunted me until I found you," Deep Throat tells Mulder, recalling the day he killed an alien (or, as the episode's title acronym would have it, an Extraterrestrial Biological Entity) in Vietnam. "That's why I come to you, Mr. Mulder, and will continue to come to you to atone for what I've done."

It's a poignant moment for *The X-Files* at this point in its run. Here's an old arm of the conspiracy baring his soul at last. Even if his answers don't offer Mulder or us anything concrete about the aliens' designs on Earth, they provide something just as important: character motivation. If Deep Throat is telling the truth, his quest to help Mulder uncover the greater truth isn't just as a mechanic of the show's plot. The informant has his own perspective on everything that has happened so far, as well as a deep-seated notion of what justice might look like. He's haunted by the evils he's committed against a species he can barely comprehend, and by his murder of an innocent creature. War makes men into monsters, even if that war is waged in the shadows, against an intergalactic force. Deep Throat is trying to right the scales.

Of course, that's only *if* he's telling the truth. Mulder looks into the room where an E.B.E. had been held mere hours ago. It's empty, and so Mulder tells Deep Throat he's just wondering which lie he should believe.

There's a confidence and purpose to "E.B.E." that really does make a viewer believe the alien conspiracy story line might be headed somewhere. If "Fallen Angel" (S1E10) focused on the human cost of the conspiracy on the random civilians who found themselves in its crosshairs, then "E.B.E." finds a way to humanize the members of the conspiracy itself, to say nothing of the aliens they've confronted over the years. It's a rocket of an episode, zooming from plot point to plot point with a savvy that a show this young shouldn't have. It's that poignancy that hangs with you long after the episode is over. Humanity kills that which it doesn't understand. Why wouldn't it kill aliens too?

This is where things get complicated. While "E.B.E." introduces some important puzzle pieces for the overall alien mythology, much of it seems as though it's setting up some other arc entirely. Deep Throat's mention of the three times a human has killed an alien seems like a placeholder to be filled in later, one that the show doesn't really get around to explaining. Similarly, the idea of the aliens as beings who have landed on our planet accidentally doesn't entirely square with what we've already learned about the government's involvement with extraterrestrials. This makes Mulder's distrust of Deep Throat feel like the smart play because Deep Throat is obviously working him in one way or another. "E.B.E." effectively features all of these tantalizing and contradictory threads, even if the show doesn't entirely tie up their loose ends.

Maybe that doesn't matter, though. Maybe the most important thing about "E.B.E." is the way that it allows the conspiracy story line to zero in on the characters at its center. Above all else, the episode is a great character piece, both for Deep Throat and for Mulder and Scully, who get to have some heartfelt conversations while staking out a mysterious truck that may or may not be carrying an alien.

This episode also marks the introduction of some paranoid pals of Mulder, known as the Lone Gunmen.[36] Mulder and Scully going to check in with them feels for all the world like Starsky and Hutch checking in with Huggy Bear in any given episode of their show, but Glen Morgan and James Wong's script laces the scenes featuring the Gunmen with a nervous energy that practically vibrates off the screen. It's amazing how quickly they come into shape here; you already want to watch a TV show just about them, which is hard to pull off with a bunch of brand-new characters.[37]

---

36 When asked about the impetus to create the Lone Gunmen, James Wong explained, "We just looked around and thought, what fun characters can we put into the show, who are not typically good-looking guys, and just give them quirky, weird things that they're into? They also had this intelligence about them, and they had answers, [and sometimes they] could be wrong answers, but they had answers that aligned with Mulder's worldview, so that's how we approached it. [We thought] 'How can these guys help Mulder in a way that's not [like] Deep Throat?'"

37 Fun fact: Frohike was played by the show's first assistant director, Tom Braidwood.

"E.B.E." also crystallizes the way that the best mythology episodes work, with its relentless forward momentum and focus on action ahead of dialogue. Mulder's defining trait is his willingness to charge headlong into danger if he thinks he will find the answers he seeks, and Scully's defining trait is her willingness to ultimately trust her partner, even when she doesn't *believe* him. Those qualities haven't always been present in previous alien episodes (consider how "Fallen Angel" centers on Scully essentially concern-trolling Mulder about keeping his job), but they're there in nearly every scene of "E.B.E." This partnership might have been one created to keep Mulder down, but in this episode, it's all the more apparent just how much Mulder's quest has also become Scully's, a principle that will animate the show for the rest of its run.

This episode is also tremendous fun. It manages to tap into the show's most important character arcs and thematic concerns, all the while moving at a breathtaking pace. Many latter-day *X-Files* fans hold it as an article of faith that the show's Monster of the Week episodes were generally stronger than its mythology episodes.[38] Does that eventually become true? Perhaps. But in Season One, the mythology has so much more focus and momentum that it's hard not to remember that when the show was first running, plenty of fans wished the series would drop the MOTW entirely, in favor of the conspiracy story line. From this vantage point, it's clear the show made the right choice to keep its peculiar balance. But watching an episode like "E.B.E.," right after lesser hours like "Lazarus" (S1E15) and "Young at Heart" (S1E16), it's almost possible to say, "Less of those other episodes and more of *this*." —TVDW

| "MIRACLE MAN" | SEASON 1 / EPISODE 18
WRITTEN BY CHRIS CARTER AND HOWARD GORDON
DIRECTED BY MICHAEL LANGE |

BELIEF AND UNBELIEF
In which faith can kill.

Religion is a subject that would come up again and again on *The X-Files*, most importantly in connection with Scully's Catholic faith. That faith is only mentioned in passing here, though. "Miracle Man" raises a few interesting issues and has a memorable presence in Leonard Vance (Dennis Lipscomb), the dead man brought back to life whether he wanted it or not. But it's disappointing to see Catholicism here treated like another Monster of the Week: examined, briefly grappled with,

---

38 If you are new to the series, try to track your own reactions to the alien story line versus the stand-alone episodes. This experiment almost inevitably yields intriguing results, which will differ from viewer to viewer.

but ultimately left to its own devices. At least, unlike other early MOTW entries, none of Mulder or Scully's relatives or ex-partners are involved.

Ultimately, "Miracle" skirts around its various premises without ever really engaging them. There's talk about belief, and the internal struggles of Samuel Hartley (Scott Bairstow), a faith healer whose abilities have turned sour, are compelling (even if the goofy Christ imagery is not). The episode's two big villains, Vance and Sheriff Maurice Daniels (R. D. Call), are well drawn. Vance's rage is convincing enough—although more time with him would've been nice, in order for us to fully understand the kind of man who would engineer such an elaborate scheme.

Then there's Daniels, a cynic whose lack of faith becomes its own sort of fanaticism. His wife is an arthritic confined to a wheelchair, and if Samuel Hartley's claims were true, he would be able to ease her suffering. Daniels, however, can't accept this, and he becomes all the more convinced of Hartley's guilt. For Mulder, the visions of his own sister represent his inability to let go of all the questions he can't answer. For Daniels, a blind hatred of an innocent—a hatred so intense it leads him to arrange that innocent's beating and death—represents his inability to accept that there are any questions at all. —ZH

SEASON 1 / EPISODE 19
WRITTEN BY MARILYN OSBORN
DIRECTED BY DAVID NUTTER

"SHAPES"

CLINICAL LYCANTHROPY

In which this show attempts some light racial commentary (uh-oh).

Remember how in our review of "Shadows" (S1E6) we suggested that there would be episodes of the series that struggled in their attempts to present salient racial commentary? Well, welcome to "Shapes"!

"Shapes"[39] handles its "Mulder and Scully investigate a crime in a racial subculture they don't really understand" story line better than most episodes of its ilk. To be fair, it's not immediately and obviously offensive toward the Native American population the agents find themselves investigating.[40] There's a genuine attempt to deal with the discomfort a reservation population would have when confronted with government officials, and *especially* when confronted with two FBI agents, given the agency's history with the Wounded Knee incident in the 1970s. The Native American characters are also given quickly sketched dimensions, even if they tend

---

39 The first episode written by a woman (it would seem).

40 That is, it's not immediately offensive if you know nothing about the term *manitou*, which does not connote a bloodthirsty werewolf-style creature as this episode suggests but is instead about the concept of a more general godlike life force.

to fall into broad character types like "trustworthy local sheriff" and "old man with a dark secret."

In some ways, this is just a typical *X-Files* episode transposed to a reservation setting. When it aired, the episode was derided for its "political correctness,"[41] but from our century's standpoint, the fact that it uses the reservation as the setting for just another *X-Files* episode can be read two ways: It's either surprisingly progressive for its era, or horribly blinkered by the fact that the episode was created in a white-centric writers' room by staff who typically meant well but also never let cultural authenticity stand in the way of a good scare.

Fortunately, "Shapes" has strong acting throughout. In particular, Michael Horse[42] as Sheriff Charles Tskany offers a grounded portrayal of a man torn between his culture and his duty to help the FBI agents solve this perplexing case. Horse depicts the complicated relationship between the U.S. government and the people whom it drove onto reservations so well with his performance alone that you find yourself wishing the episode didn't rely so heavily on exposition about why these Native Americans don't trust the government.

The episode has issues beyond its weak attempts at racial commentary, though. Its biggest problem is one we've encountered many times in this first season: Classic monster stories (in this case, a werewolf tale) don't leave *The X-Files* with much room to maneuver because of how often they've been told. The series partly ran into problems because of how often it insisted on putting its own spin on these classic creatures. As an episode of *The X-Files*, "Shapes" is merely below average. But as a werewolf story, it's an almost complete failure.

The manitou of "Shapes" has many of the classic werewolf tropes, like its bloodthirsty murderousness and its ability to pass its curse through a bite, but it also gets burdened with a bunch of *X-Files*-specific mythology about how it doesn't need the full moon to emerge, but it only arrives every eight years or so.[43] "Shapes" gets so tied up in knots explaining why and how its werewolf knockoff works and explaining all the "rules" of the creature that it leaves itself little room to just tell a simple and scary werewolf story.

That means the reputation of the episode lives or dies based on its portrayal of Native American culture, and while the show would make episodes far more troubling in terms of their depictions of other racial minorities,[44] "Shapes" can never escape the feeling that it's being made by tourists. The episode is fundamentally

---

41 Meaning, I guess, that it used a reservation setting as a quick way to gain diversity points.

42 Another *Twin Peaks* veteran, Horse is best known for his role as that series' Deputy Hawk.

43 The episode concludes with Native American elder Ish (Jimmy Herman) saying he'll see the agents in "about eight years," a promise that must have seemed ludicrous to a show in its first season. Remarkably, the show was still on the air eight years later, but it didn't do a direct follow-up to "Shapes," which is probably a good thing.

44 Chris Carter, for whatever reason, seemed really interested in Native American culture and generally did his research.

about Mulder and Scully acting as government emissaries; they take in a few Native American ceremonies respectfully but with a certain amount of impassive detachment. *The X-Files* would always struggle to deal with race, and "Shapes" provides an early introduction to this blind spot. It means well, but sometimes meaning well still bites people in the ass. —TVDW

SEASON 1 / EPISODE 20
WRITTEN BY CHRIS CARTER
DIRECTED BY JOE NAPOLITANO | "DARKNESS FALLS"

GREEN GLOW THE NIGHTMARES
In which the bugs don't play by the rules.

Buried deep in the back half of Season One is this mostly forgotten classic. An eerie story that sends Mulder and Scully into the remote wilderness, "Darkness Falls" seems to anticipate *The Blair Witch Project*'s ability to turn American forests[45] into a home for almost-primal terror. An episode like this feels less like Chris Carter wrote it and more that he reached deep into some forgotten part of humanity's genetic code and found something that terrified our ancestors but that we've lost memory of entirely.

This is also an episode in which Mulder and Scully spend a lot of time trying to swipe away green glowing bugs, which *should* be ridiculous but somehow never is.[46] The bugs have been unleashed by loggers cutting down old-growth forest without regard for preservation; the insects seem almost to serve the function of nature itself, rising up from the forest floor and devouring whole all those who threaten it. It's telling that the episode doesn't end with Mulder and Scully defeating the monster but instead with them narrowly escaping it, after almost dying at its hand. You can't vanquish nature. You can only battle it for a little while.

"Darkness Falls" seems almost self-consciously styled after the earlier classic, "Ice" (S1E8). Once again, a small group of people in extreme isolation from civilization uncover something unknown with a natural explanation that fails to comfort when people start dying. Once again, the isolation provides a chance for Mulder and Scully to have some heartfelt conversations. And once again, the "monster" isn't a creature so much as a visual effect that gains terror from its utter simplicity. The bugs are just green glowing lights, pouring in through the darkness, aiming to wrap up their prey in cocoons and suspend them in the trees.

---

45 Read: Canadian forests.
46 That said, if you couldn't go with it, I don't blame you. Those effects are pretty chintzy and haven't aged especially well.

The best element of "Darkness Falls" is also the thing that ranks it a step or two behind "Ice." At the conclusion of that earlier episode, Scully's quick thinking and deductive reasoning save the day. At the conclusion of this one, Mulder and Scully lose to the insects. The only thing they have going for them is that they vow to keep going, in hopes that somebody, somewhere, might rescue them. Here, the arrival of the government to save their lives plays as a functional deus ex machina.

But this episode gets away with it because the random intervention of a much larger entity is the only thing that *could* save Mulder and Scully at this entry's end. If "Ice" was designed to underline the fundamental differences between the two characters, then "Darkness Falls" underlines how they're now ride-or-die for each other, devoted to both this weird cause and their strange partnership above all else.

This is also one of the ultimate "Vancouver is scary" episodes. At the time of *The X-Files'* debut, the thought of shooting a series in Vancouver was still something of a novelty, but it was the location's dull, gray tones that helped visually define the show in the public consciousness. "Darkness Falls" takes the characters way, way out into the woods and then leaves them there. That level of isolation was something that could only be provided by such northern climes. The claustrophobic tree cover, the muffling fog, the dampness that seems to coat everything in the episode—they were always central to the series' appeal, and it's these elements that helped create the slightly surreal nature of "Darkness Falls."

In the end, though, this episode has a beautifully constructed script. Chris Carter has really settled into the characters' voices at this point in the first season, and the story twists and turns in unexpected directions. The idea that the monster comes out only in darkness isn't going to win any awards for originality, but the idea that the monster can only be *seen* in total darkness—and that by that point, it's far too late—is a good one. That concept motivates lots of brilliantly simple set pieces that are central to this episode, like the characters cowering in the beam of light provided by a sole light bulb running off a sputtering generator, as they watch the green, glowing bugs flood in from outside.

If anything, this is the rare *X-Files* episode that has actually *improved* with time. When it aired in 1994, the idea of climate change seemed like a far-off theory, like something humanity had plenty of time to prepare for—*if* it indeed existed. The environmental battles of that decade were far smaller in scale, often involving arguments between conservationists and industrialists, perhaps best encompassed by the endless conservative radio chatter about the loggers who weren't allowed to cut down certain trees in order to protect an endangered owl.[47]

---

[47] It is almost certainly no coincidence that the people Mulder and Scully are called in to help are loggers.

But because "Darkness Falls" is an episode of *The X-Files*—and thus must reach for something bigger than merely a conflict between loggers and environmentalists—it instead becomes a cautionary tale about the foolishness of humans who believe they can *ever* control nature. Nature nearly wins in "Darkness Falls," and as the episode ends, the government vows to beat back the bugs with pesticides and controlled burns. But the sense of a momentary cease-fire lingers throughout. We are here at the behest of the planet, and not the other way around. —TVDW

SEASON 1 / EPISODE 21
WRITTEN BY GLEN MORGAN AND JAMES WONG
DIRECTED BY DAVID NUTTER | "TOOMS" |

IT'S A STRETCH

In which our first classic monster meets a monstrous end.

Here's an *X-Files* first: a continuity-heavy episode that doesn't hinge on the series' central mythology. It's rare for the show to have a recurring villain who doesn't work for the government or relate to the alien conspiracy, but this episode even brings back a side character: Detective Frank Briggs (Henry Beckman), the elderly man who provided Mulder and Scully with background info on our monster in "Squeeze" (S1E3). The fact that both episodes aired in the same season makes "Tooms" less like a sequel and more like a concluding chapter, one that is unexpected but nonetheless welcome.

"Tooms" also features Assistant Director Walter Skinner (Mitch Pileggi), in his first appearance on the show. Skinner is a man of divided loyalties. His lectures to Scully and Mulder are far more reasonable than we've yet seen either character receive from their superiors, but the Cigarette Smoking Man is always watching to make sure that Skinner's concern doesn't turn into legitimate support. But we still get the sense that Skinner has at least some of his soul left.

At Eugene Tooms's trial, Mulder takes the stand and makes the inadvisable decision to present the entire history of the case, hundred-year-old murders and all. It's a painful moment for Mulder's pride, but it also, in some ways, defines him; as Mulder later tells Scully, it doesn't matter if the judge listened, as long as Mulder got what really happened on the court record. Much of the episode revolves around both characters making an invested effort to catch their man, from Mulder's one-man surveillance of Tooms post-release, to Scully's trusting the hunch of an old cop in order to link Tooms to his earlier crimes. At the heart of those techniques is Mulder's simple, quixotic assertion that the truth trumps all. Everything else—career, professional regulations, sleep—comes second.

The episode furthers a thematic throughline that's been present in the season from the start, which takes on special significance here. Regular law and order caught Tooms in "Squeeze" but then released him because the system is unprepared to deal with the kind of danger he represents. The mere fact of his existence is arguably a greater threat to the status quo than the murders he commits. It's only through the efforts of Mulder and Scully that such creatures can ever be brought to anything remotely like justice.

The fact that our heroes are driven to work outside usual channels also reinforces the show's core relationship. While Mulder stakes out Tooms in a parked car, Scully visits to try to convince him to let her take over for a while. The conversation between the two of them, with its low-key flirting and honest affection, is charming and gives us a nice character moment when Scully, in a callback to "Beyond the Sea" (S1E13), calls Mulder "Fox" in an attempt to convince him of her sincerity. He laughs and tells her, "I even made my parents call me Mulder," the inference being that Mulder is exactly who he appears to be.[48] When he calls Scully "Dana," it represents a step toward deeper intimacy between the two because for Scully, her two names mean very different things—one represents her professional side, and the other her personal side, and never the twain shall meet. For Mulder, that separation doesn't exist. There is no secret, personal "Fox" whom Scully hasn't seen yet, no private side that he keeps protected from the world. He just is who he is. It's his greatest strength and his greatest weakness. It's also yet another reason he really needs Dana Scully (both versions) by his side.

Mulder and Scully finally track Tooms to a maintenance shaft under an escalator, and for once, an *X-Files* monster comes to a definitive (and definitively nasty) end. It's the rare, unquestionable victory for the duo, but one that may come with a cost by attracting unnecessary attention. In the episode's closing scene, Mulder says that a change is coming to the X-Files. Whether or not that change will be for the better remains to be seen. —ZH

---

48 Fun fact: "Mulder" is actually the maiden name of Chris Carter's mother, which Carter explains is a "common Dutch name."

ANOTHER EPISODE ABOUT REINCARNATION!

In which the series also revisits the "murderous child" trope.

The first season of *The X-Files* is lousy with episodes in which the dead return, in one form or another. It's no wonder "Born Again"—about a police officer reborn as a psychokinetic little girl(?!)—feels so tired, since we recently saw this same basic premise in reverse in "Lazarus" (S1E15), in which a criminal comes back as a cop.

"Born Again" also highlights that although *The X-Files* is, on some level, a cop show, it often struggles when it directly engages with cop-show tropes. The conspiracy Mulder and Scully stumble upon here involves a bunch of police officers who've come up with a scheme to steal a large sum of money, only to find their plot foiled by an idealistic young officer. The young officer is killed, but he returns as a child named Michelle. When she turns eight years old, she starts exacting his revenge.

The fundamental problem with "Born Again" is that its detective story and its paranormal story operate on two completely different tracks. The one time they intersect—when Mulder finds the image of the fish tank decoration embedded in the videotape—is also the episode's best moment, almost entirely because it pulls both threads together. Other than that, Mulder and Scully never really *need* the assistance of the reincarnated cop to solve the case. This leaves the episode piling on plot elements, like psychokinesis, which have very little to do with the fact that Michelle carries the soul of the officer inside of her.

This episode, again like "Lazarus," is one in which you can see the better version lurking just below its surface. "Born Again" is weaker than the previous entry, largely because it feels like a retread and because the acting and directing are weaker here than in "Lazarus." But it's not as though "Born Again" doesn't have its charms. The idea that a cop living in landlocked Buffalo could be killed by being drowned in salt water is a neat little detective-show puzzle, and the ultimate resolution—it was the fish tank that did it!—is satisfying in the way good detective reveals often are.

And yet the episode can't escape its overall sense of déjà vu. Maybe it would have worked if Michelle were a more compelling character, or a better performed one, but the show mostly conveys her inner turmoil by having her shout a lot. Her psychokinetic powers seem to exist primarily so she can have a way to kill people without being cognizant that she's doing so. After so many different riffs on this same story, it's not hard to shrug a little bit at this one.

We're ultimately left with one question: Just why was Season One of *The X-Files* so enamored with the concept of the dead hitching a ride back to our world via the living? Certainly, ghost stories are among the most prevalent and beloved of paranormal tales, and when you're trying to tell a paranormal story that piggybacks on a more conventional murder mystery most weeks, well, a ghost story is a good way to get at that particular blend. But the show so quickly taught its viewers how to watch it—Mulder is usually right, paranormal phenomena are usually involved, and the weirdest explanation you can come up with will often suffice—that it had already run out of useful spins on this particular story by the end of its very first season. It would return to ghosts and spirits reaching out from beyond the grave in the seasons to come, but thankfully, never again with the same frequency. —TVDW

| "ROLAND" | SEASON 1 / EPISODE 23
WRITTEN BY CHRIS RUPPENTHAL
DIRECTED BY DAVID NUTTER |

HIS BROTHER'S KEEPER

In which an innocent man suffers for jet propulsion research.

Here's another entry about spirits, strong wills, and innocent proxies, but luckily, "Roland" is well built enough to be enjoyable despite its familiarity. *The X-Files* always set great stock in giving its secondary characters dignity, and the titular figure in this episode is no exception. As portrayed by Željko Ivanek, Roland himself never seems anything less than authentic, which gives his struggles a real bite and his relationship with another mentally handicapped woman an uncontrived sweetness.

It also helps to have a despicable villain. Dr. Arthur Grable, Roland's twin, is disrupting the life of his still-living brother simply because he wants posthumous credit for his discoveries, and is so driven to succeed he made sure he'd have an outlet for his ambition even if the worst occurred. For once, we have a spiritual will whose motives *aren't* pure, and while that will is eventually thwarted, an innocent still ends up suffering the consequences.

The episode leaves you not with Mulder's frustrated ambitions or Scully's skepticism but with Roland getting taken away from his home for psychiatric evaluation. The situation isn't hopeless, but the final shot of Roland going to brush his hair in the mirror, and then stopping to look at himself, makes you wonder just what the cost of Arthur's machinations truly were. Or if his victims—the living ones—will ever stop paying. —ZH

"THE ERLENMEYER FLASK"

TRUST NO ONE

In which the show pulls back the curtain
just a little bit.

As a cop show, *The X-Files* works best when Mulder and Scully are being good cops, when the suspects they're investigating have complex motivations of their own, and when the mystery they must solve isn't as straightforward as it seems. By the end of Season One, those ideas are more or less cemented, and "The Erlenmeyer Flask" stands as a vivid testament to how completely the show has internalized them. The road to this finale was bumpy, to be sure, but it's such a good episode of television that it retroactively justifies all the weird missteps along the way. It was all worth it if it led to this.

As beautifully as "Erlenmeyer" pulls back the curtain to offer our heroes a tiny peek into the alien conspiracy, what's most thrilling is the way it plays as an amped-up episode of a police drama. At every turn of the episode, Mulder and Scully are confronted with what seems to be a brick wall, until they twist their thinking in a new direction and discover the solution waiting just around the bend. Their innovative solutions are rewarded with big payoffs, as when Scully discovers what appears to be some genuine alien DNA and Mulder finds a giant room filled with human beings in vats (the presumed results of alien DNA experimentation). It's that perfect blend of buildup and release that drives a detective story at its best.

After a full season of pounding on doors in frustration and *just* missing the crucial pieces of evidence, it's also elating to see Mulder and Scully actually catch up to something tangible, even if they have to give most of it up (or have most of it taken from them) by episode's end. Though it's obvious that "Erlenmeyer" is planting seeds for future seasons, the story also convincingly puts a cap on the arc of Season One, right down to the Cigarette Smoking Man hiding away more evidence of his dark dealings, a direct mirror of the end of "Pilot" (S1E1). This perfect balance of tying up loose ends while leaving room for further story development is what makes the episode memorable: More than just a rousing conclusion, it also serves as a statement of purpose for the future of the series.

Consider all of the major changes the episode makes to the show's status quo, some of which will be easily reversed and some of which will reverberate for years to come. The biggest and most obvious example of the latter is the death of Deep

Throat, who seems to give his life to protect Mulder.[49] For a show that, to this point, hasn't established many major recurring roles (to the degree that Skinner—not yet the show's most important supporting player—is only mentioned in this episode but not actually seen), killing off the most recognizable supporting character is a bold move, one that underlines how much danger anyone who's *not* one of our intrepid heroes is in just by helping them out. You can already see how the perpetual vulnerability of those around Scully and Mulder could be taken to comical lengths, but here it's a first-class moment, especially as director R. W. Goodwin stages the shooting of Deep Throat in shadow in a wide shot, so it seems to come out of nowhere, even if you've watched the episode many times and know it's coming.[50]

The more evidently reversible change to the status quo nevertheless gets the weight it deserves: Mulder reveals that the X-Files have been closed down, no longer protected by whatever government forces were keeping its doors open. He and Scully will be split apart and assigned to different divisions,[51] and all of the headway they have made will be for naught. Then again, we know Mulder. We know he's not going to give up on this quest, no matter what's thrown in his way. And we know Scully. We know that she might be reluctant to help Mulder, but she always will. Closing down the X-Files is a real TV contrivance, one we know will be reversed eventually, but "Erlenmeyer" plays it well. We know the twist is less about plot and more about the development of character relationships; Mulder has gotten so close to the truth that he's rattled *somebody*, which will only increase the opposition to him, which will only draw him and Scully closer together, et cetera, et cetera, et cetera. The more the series twisted that unbreakable bond into tighter and tighter knots, the greater its characterization of its two leads became. "Erlenmeyer" is evidence that, if the writers learned nothing else from Season One, they learned that the heart of the show resides with the partnership of its protagonists.

The most decisive statement of purpose offered by the finale is its confident escalation of the conspiracy itself. In earlier episodes, we got a sense that it was big, but never has its scope seemed as vast as it does in this hour. This conspiracy isn't just big—it's massive. It permeates the government at virtually every level, enabling its colluders to carry out dark experiments just behind the locked door you might pass every day on your way to work. It involves men who bleed green and can live

---

49 I'm not sure if this is the official read of what happens to the character, but Jerry Hardin sure plays the moment when he tells Scully that, no, *he'll* make the exchange to bring Mulder back, as if he knows what's coming.

50 Deep Throat's actual death happens in a close-up Hardin milks for all it's worth, especially when he gets to introduce another of the show's big catchphrases: "Trust no one."

51 The producers are already planning to accommodate Gillian Anderson's real-life pregnancy, and the story lines they come up with in the first half of Season Two to write her out of the show in order to make room for her maternity leave will change the series forever and take it to another level. We'll discuss those soon enough.

underwater for days at a time but also very normal scientists who can't help but be subsumed by something awful in the midst of their quest for knowledge. *The X-Files* is a cop show, yes, but it's also one in which you could wake up in a safe, standard reality, then turn the wrong corner and end up becoming a thing that goes bump in the night. No one is safe, and any given door could lead to madness. That's how *The X-Files* sets the stage for Season Two—and the arrival of its golden years. —TVDW

SEASON

TWO

DOUBT: A PARABLE

In which the aliens arrive at long last.

As compelling television, *The X-Files'* second season takes a brilliant leap forward. Yes, the show will continue to make bad episodes throughout its run. Yes, it still has plenty of mediocre hours mixed in with the good ones. But the good episodes in this season go from entertaining to consistently *great*. This is when *The X-Files* becomes the massively beloved series of memory, rather than a mere cult curiosity. The show would have better seasons than Season Two, but it would never have a more important one.

Of course, plenty of series see a surge in quality in their sophomore seasons as the writers, directors, and actors have by then had many opportunities to figure out what works and what doesn't. There's a certain confidence in storytelling that emerges in year two. But what catapults *The X-Files'* second season to a new level of greatness is an unexpected narrative turbocharge in its early episodes. So what happened? Who can we thank for this sudden burst of inspiration?

What happened, it turns out, was something the show couldn't have planned for: Gillian Anderson became pregnant.

Because the series is such a physically demanding one, Anderson would need to scale back her involvement as she neared full term, and she would also need to take time off for maternity leave. However, the series was slated to produce twenty-five episodes in Season Two, which meant it couldn't realistically take even a short production break. This meant the writers would inevitably have to find a way to have Scully recede from the narrative organically, while still providing Mulder with motivation to press onward. The ultimate fruition of this plan won't arrive until later, but even in the first four installments of Season Two, *The X-Files* is planning for Anderson's eventual absence.

In "Little Green Men," we see writers Glen Morgan and James Wong begin laying the groundwork for a solution to Anderson's unavailability: With the X-Files program shut down, Mulder and Scully are left working in new departments, no longer partners. Yet, paradoxically, their bond seems to only grow stronger as they're separated, with Mulder calling Scully constantly to check in. She's teaching at the FBI Academy. He's doing low-level work, monitoring a wiretap. Neither seems particularly thrilled, but they also seem to know their best chance of returning to the X-Files involves laying low for now and keeping their noses clean.

Or, rather, they *should* know that. Scully seems aware, but Mulder (poor, idealistic Mulder) can't abide by the de facto demotion, which means that when he gets a call from Senator Richard Matheson, a patron in the Senate,[1] he leaps at the opportunity to head to Puerto Rico and attempt to make contact with the aliens that are apparently futzing around there, frightening people to death. Despite explicitly being warned not to do this by Matheson, Mulder can't help himself. He hears "little green men," and he races off alone—which strategically centers the show around his experience.

Focusing on Mulder here serves more than just a logistical purpose, however. The true potency of "Little Green Men" lies in the opportunity it affords Mulder to emotionally process the events of "The Erlenmeyer Flask" (S1E24). Without Scully or Deep Throat, Mulder has entered a sort of wilderness period, finding himself tempted to give in to doubt. His belief in aliens is shakier than ever, even if Season One's finale seemed to suggest the best evidence yet for their extraterrestrial presence. Still, you can see where he's coming from. Everything he saw previously might well have been the work of rogue scientists, or a government experiment gone horribly wrong. There might not be actual aliens so much as some random DNA the government acquired from a space rock or something similar, then decided to test on its own citizens.

Of course, we can't have Mulder wallow in doubt for too long. The show wouldn't work if he wasn't intent on chasing every tabloid rumor into the shadows. But what makes this episode so thematically effective is its reframing of *The X-Files* as a religious story more than a sci-fi story.[2] The series has cool bits of fringe science in every episode, to be sure, but its central story is of a man who longs to believe, who is presented with so many reasons *not* to believe but who continues, nevertheless, to hold out hope that his faith will be rewarded. What's twisted about this is that Mulder doesn't really think the aliens are going to bring about anything good! No, he seems quite convinced everyone involved is doing horrible things. But he's built his life around this belief system, ever since his sister was taken,[3] and the only person who can shatter that faith is himself.

Through indulging Mulder's doubts, "Little Green Men" explores humanity's need to not be alone, its desire to keep broadcasting its location to the stars, just in case someone might be listening.[4] We don't have any rational reason to believe anybody is out there, listening for our call, but we persist in believing anyway. The thought of being all alone in the cosmos is too horrible to comprehend.

S2 E1

---

1 Played by the always welcome Raymond J. Barry, probably best known for playing Raylan Givens's father in *Justified*.

2 Mulder's belief in aliens feels even more fervent than Scully's Catholicism, which would become an idea that the show would return to again and again.

3 Samantha's abduction is depicted in this episode for the first time, in a horrifying flashback that haunts the series—even if the child actors chosen to play young Fox and Samantha are disappointingly flat.

4 You'd think watching this show would have disabused humanity of this notion, but there are more Mulders among us than one might think!

So Mulder goes to Puerto Rico, and he hears the Voyager I's golden disk played back, suggesting aliens scooped up this particular bit of space flotsam and traced it back to Earth. He sees a tall, spindly figure in the doorway.[5] He finally, at long last, believes again—wholeheartedly. He has won the war within himself and found his way back to certainty. "Little Green Men" works beautifully as a whole host of things, from an introduction to the show for any curious passersby checking in for the first time to a reassertion of the status quo for any longtime fans who needed help remembering. But what it does best is remind viewers that this isn't a show about aliens as much as it is about our need to believe in something, lest the night become too dark and terrifying. There's so much darkness in the night sky, but there are also so many stars. And maybe one of them is looking back at us. —TVDW

---

5   The first depiction of an extraterrestrial in the series gains power from just how ethereal and strange it seems—a silhouette, blurry around the edges, standing in a door, almost swallowed up by light. It could be an angel if we didn't know better.

THE MAN BEHIND THE DESK

Though he only makes his second ever appearance on *The X-Files* in "Little Green Men" (S2E1), A. D. Walter Skinner and his no-bullshit attitude had already made an impression. Mitch Pileggi traces the genesis of Skinner's hard-boiled personality all the way back to the casting process: "I had gone in and auditioned for Chris twice before for two other roles, two other FBI guys, but at the time I was shaving my head and he thought it was too extreme for *The X-Files*. I was like, 'Uh, really?' So, I grew what hair I had back and went in the third time they called me, and [I] actually was being kind of obstinate and kind of a jerk. I was like, 'You've seen me twice, he didn't need to see me again, he could hire me or whatever.' I was being a total ass. My agent finally talked me into going in for Skinner and I went into the room with that attitude and it's what he wanted for the character, so it worked out."

As for the question of Skinner's trustworthiness, Pileggi sees the confrontation between him and the Cigarette Smoking Man in this episode as a turning point for the assistant director: "I think that was the beginning of Skinner really becoming a champion within the FBI. . . . I think that's where a huge transformation in his allegiance to Mulder and Scully became more and more evident. . . . They started coming to him more and more. . . . I thought that their bond became stronger and stronger as their trust in him developed and . . . their relationship definitely had its ebbs and flows, all the way from the beginning to the end." In Pileggi's mind, Skinner was always a man of integrity and loyalty: "Because of the nature of Skinner and the fact that he's got this incredibly strong moral compass, I think that eventually he was going to see what was right and what was wrong and the Cigarette Smoking Man and his cohorts were not his mode of operation, or the way that he did business, or conducted his life."

NUCLEAR REFUGEE

In which going to the bathroom becomes a terrifying prospect.

In case you were in doubt that Season Two is a big step up for *The X-Files*, consider that it follows a promising premiere with what might be *the* definitive Monster of the Week episode. There are few *X-Files* monsters as iconic, as creepy, and as downright *gross* as Flukeman. And the episode that contains him[6] is a tight little thriller that finds a way to turn the quotidian act of going to the bathroom into something absolutely horrifying. There are so many reasons "The Host" shouldn't work but only one reason it does: It commits, and it commits in a hard-core way.

Flukeman,[7] for starters, is an exquisitely designed character. His little mouth, alternating between a pinched grimace and a perfect circle (complete with tiny toothlike appendages meant for grabbing and latching), walks a line between human and decidedly *not* human, and the episode is wise about how and when we see the creature. (Its first appearance, flowing by in a sewage tube, surrounded by muck, is a great cut to commercial.)

But Chris Carter's script weds this wonderful creature design to one of the most famous urban legends of them all: the idea that there are strange beasts haunting

---

6   Look at me using he/him pronouns to refer to a genderless worm monster. I guess "Flukeman" was catchier than "Flukething" or "Flukeperson."

7   Played by Darin Morgan, who is largely regarded as one of the best *X-Files* writers of all time. Morgan (brother of Glen) will go on to write one of this season's most memorable episodes and several of next season's best before returning to write two stellar episodes for the revival.

our sewers.[8] Granted, those animals are usually alligators or something similar—if larger—but the *idea* of Flukeman is close enough to a story we already know that the episode doesn't have to spend a lot of time explaining why he lives in the sewer. He just *does*.

This is the peculiar alchemy of a great MOTW episode. It has to be a familiar tale but not *too* familiar. It has to remind us of scary stories we've heard before, without becoming a carbon copy of one. A perfect MOTW episode exists in some shadowy zone between urban legend, classic horror movie, and complete original, and it's impossible to say just where that crucial original element will come from in any given episode. An episode like "Ice" (S1E8) leans heavily on its connection to the movie *The Thing*, but it gains its power from how its most original element (the worm that induces rage) tosses the nascent Mulder/Scully partnership into turmoil. By contrast, a standard scary monster episode like "The Host" succeeds because the creature it proposes is just original (and creepy) enough to hook us.

This is also one of the show's grossest episodes. *The X-Files* doesn't typically go in for big gross-out moments—or for gore, even—and in the few times that it does, it tends to be overcompensating for a weak story. But "The Host" is the exception that proves the rule. Flukeman lurks in the sewer system, and even if we never see him lunging up out of a toilet to latch on to a person in a moment of supreme vulnerability, the implication is always there. That's especially true when director Daniel Sackheim's camera races forward to leer down into the Porta-Potty, where Flukeman lies in wait, surrounded by raw sewage.

So much of "The Host" is *set* in the sewers, with Mulder mucking about and trying to figure out what's going on, while Scully hangs back at a safe, less-smelly distance. It serves as an all-too-literal expression of the show's deepest themes. Here are all of the creepy things, lurking in the places we try to pretend don't exist. We *know* the sewers run beneath our feet, but we'd rather not think about that, thanks. It's in those repressed places where horror can best take root, and *The X-Files* starts ruthlessly exploiting this concept in Season Two. "Darkness Falls" (S1E20) had to head all the way out into the woods to find great scares; "The Host" attacks from beneath.

The disgusting coup de grâce is the fact that Flukeman is trying to reproduce—which means biting humans and somehow implanting his Fluke offspring. The image of a man coughing up a giant Flukeworm in the shower somehow hits all sorts of *other* terrifying signifiers for most of us, from the sensitivity of the

S2 E2

---

8   Carter says he combined the idea of a monster who could live inside a transport tanker with a foul story he had heard as a child: "It was one of those unbelievable stories that your parents told you that is unforgettable, and it would occur to me every time I would be at a campground using the toilets. It's that there was a guy who would put trash bags on himself and crawl into the Porta-Potties at campgrounds, and, in the women's toilet, [he would] stand there in the mire while women went to the bathroom on him. I thought that's one of the most disgusting things that I could imagine. And I thought 'I have to do that with an *X-Files* monster.'"

location to the idea of some alien invader being inside of your body. Everything about Flukeman works, even if the idea behind him is basically just, "Oh, hey, what if a worm was also sort of a man?"

The final piece of the puzzle that marks "The Host" as an all-time classic is that it bears a certain degree of sympathy for its antagonist, something we didn't see much of in Season One.[9] There, so many of the monsters—especially the explicitly less human ones—were just embodiments of the dark impulses that drove them. But Flukeman is a creature fighting to survive, just a new step on the evolutionary ladder—albeit one that humanity indirectly created thanks to the Chernobyl disaster. It's telling that the episode shifts tack in its final third, with Scully's acknowledgment and investigation into Flukeman's existence; the story almost pivots to being about her concern for an instantly endangered species of one.

Then again, it's hard to keep a good Flukeman down. Mulder might have cut the creature in two, but the episode ends with his eyes fluttering open again, off to haunt more sewer pipes. It's only appropriate for an *X-Files* episode to end with the monster living to scare another day. "The Host" scores because it makes that moment the sneaky triumph of Flukeman over the species that didn't know it created him. —TVDW

SEASON 2 / EPISODE 3
WRITTEN BY GLEN MORGAN AND JAMES WONG, FROM A STORY BY DARIN MORGAN
DIRECTED BY DAVID NUTTER | "BLOOD" |

KILL 'EM ALL

In which you shouldn't trust what your TV is telling you.

When Mulder gets called in to work up a behavioral profile on a series of seemingly random spree killings, it's Scully he looks to when he needs some science done. There are no tortured confrontations with higher-ups, no late-night conversations about choice and expectations. It's just a solid, straightforward entry—or, at least, straightforward for *The X-Files*.

Poor Ed Funsch. Not only does he have the dullest job in the world—inputting zip codes off of junk mail—he gets downsized *and* a paper cut on the same day. To top it all off, he's played by William Sanderson (best known for his role as J. F. Sebastian in *Blade Runner*), the ideal actor when it comes to playing sympathetic losers. He's the kind of guy whom you automatically like when you meet him but still can't help feeling uneasy around. "Blood" makes the most of this quality; the episode splits its time between Mulder's investigation into the surprising number of murders in Ed's

---

9 There were exceptions, of course. Something about Tooms had a strange, unsettling pathos.

hometown of Franklin, Pennsylvania, and Ed's gradual devolution into a potential killer himself.

Sanderson's built-in pathos imbues his story with a lot of tension. He's reminiscent of Roland from the first season ("Roland" [S1E23]), another innocent driven to violence by forces beyond his control. And like Roland, Ed's descent doesn't happen without a bizarre push: the digital displays on everyday appliances keep telling him to do things. *Horrible* things. The messages would be easy to write off as hallucinations if it weren't for the fact that other people have seen them too, right before they go kill-crazy.

"Blood" is a memorable episode due in no small part to its humor. As *The X-Files* went on, it became more willing to poke fun at itself (sometimes with mixed results), and here it manages to deliver a story that's simultaneously absurd and frightening. The much-welcome return of the Lone Gunmen provides an excellent breather from the tension of the rest of the hour; with Scully's screen time minimized, both the episode and Mulder desperately need the easy camaraderie on display between our hero and his nerdy buddies.

But the nature of the danger is equal parts amusing and disturbing. A businessman slaughters an elevator full of people with his bare hands. A stack of TVs shows Ed a montage of violent images and then tells him to buy a gun. A middle-aged woman visits a mechanic to pick up her car, and a diagnostic display plays on her worst fears: HE'LL RAPE YOU. None of this is ha-ha funny, but the pulpy intensity of each sequence and of the episode as a whole makes you snicker even as you shudder. Someone's sending those display messages and laughing while they do it.

It sounds like the dream of a madman, which is pretty much the point. One of the tools of any effective work of horror is to take the things we dismiss out of hand—the things we *have* to dismiss in order to lead a sane and healthy life—and imagine what might happen if our assumptions are wrong. What if the noise you hear in the middle of the night isn't just the house settling? What if tabloid stories about alien abductions were really true? And what if the crazy person screaming about messages from the microwave was actually on to something?

It makes sense that the version of mind control featured in "Blood" uses technology. The fear that strange emanations come from modern devices—things we've come to depend on, but rarely understand completely—is hard to shake entirely. The idea that some group has found a way to control those devices, to infiltrate displays and screens that most of us have spent our whole lives taking for granted, is as terrifying as it is fun. It's a terror that hasn't lost any of its punch in the years since this episode first aired either. It's a jump from digital watches to Internet security breaches and the infiltration of social media, but not *that* much of a jump.

The conspiracy behind the spree killings is grotesquely absurd, and it's the punch line to Mulder's deepest fears: a group so secret that you can never be sure they exist at all. It's hard to shake the hopelessness of fighting against a cabal that can so readily corrupt an entire town, but this discovery only serves to raise the stakes of the quest at the heart of the show. Something must be done about this, and Mulder and Scully are among the few people who are willing to try. —ZH

SEASON 2 / EPISODE 4
WRITTEN BY HOWARD GORDON
DIRECTED BY ROB BOWMAN | "SLEEPLESS" |

TROUBLE BREWING

In which Mulder needs to wake up.

At first glance, "Sleepless" is a routine Monster of the Week entry. The premise—a government experiment during the Vietnam War created a group of soldiers who could perpetually stay awake—is engaging and appropriately cynical, and Tony Todd is well cast as Augustus Cole, the main antagonist and a man driven by decades of constant consciousness into a vengeful religious mania. Best known for his turn as the titular hook-handed *Candyman*,[10] Todd is a marvelous presence; his voice sounds like something crawling out of the abyss in a really bad mood.

But "Sleepless" is also important for introducing two key characters to the series: Mr. X (Steven Williams), a new informant to take Deep Throat's place; and Alex Krycek (Nicholas Lea), a new partner to take Scully's.

The latter serves primarily to reinforce Scully's importance on the show. We want to believe, and we want the truth, but as Scully has warned Mulder time and again, the former doesn't automatically lead to the latter. Wanting to believe makes Mulder open to "extreme possibilities," but it also makes him vulnerable to manipulation. That's why their partnership is so critical: Mulder opens Scully's eyes to a deeper understanding of the world, while Scully keeps Mulder's wilder flights of fancy grounded.

Unfortunately, Scully is stuck at Quantico, and Krycek is not an adequate replacement. Mulder's eventual grudging acceptance of this outsider both demonstrates his intense need for support and also encourages the audience to trust an outsider, which makes the reveal at the end of the hour all the more impactful. Lea certainly looks the part; clean-cut and handsome, he could've stepped out of an educational short on "Getting to Know Your Government Employees." It also helps that he's not immediately dismissive of Mulder's more outré concepts.

Mulder should've known better, but he's having a busy episode. His new informant is different from the predecessor: more irritable and a good deal more

---

10 A 1992 horror film in which Todd plays the vengeful ghost of a man murdered by a lynch mob for fathering a child with a white woman.

concerned about his own safety. Williams' performance establishes a clear and immediate contrast with Deep Throat's more avuncular approach. It sets the stage for dark times ahead. Mr. X tells Mulder, "The truth is still out there—and it's never been more dangerous," a potentially corny line that works, thanks to the actor's commitment and a general sense of unease.

In the plot of Augustus Cole's activities, we find an answer (of a sort) for why Mulder, who sees conspiracies in everything, would fail to realize he's being conned. During their tour in Vietnam, Cole's insomniac unit went crazy and started killing indiscriminately. Cole decides that it's his job to avenge the deaths of the innocents, starting with the doctor who made the soldiers what they were. Cole has the ability to project dreams into reality. He murders the doctor by showing him a fire in his apartment—no fire exists in the physical world, but when Scully does her autopsy, she finds the man's body reacted as though it believed it were burning.

While the logic of Cole's dream ability is sketchy, the idea that belief itself can be dangerous highlights Mulder's significant blind spot and serves as an indirect warning for what's to come. If you jump too blindly, give in too freely, it can be deadly. This axiom plays out in the final reveal, in which, unbeknownst to Mulder, Krycek reports on his activities to the Cigarette Smoking Man. When Krycek comments, "Scully is a problem," and the CSM responds, "Every problem has a solution," it's clear that Mulder won't be the only one who suffers for his lapse in judgment. —ZH

"DUANE BARRY"	SEASON 2 / EPISODE 5 WRITTEN AND DIRECTED BY CHRIS CARTER
"ASCENSION"	SEASON 2 / EPISODE 6 WRITTEN BY PAUL BROWN DIRECTED BY MICHAEL LANGE

EVERYTHING CHANGES

In which The X-Files *grows up.*

The biggest turning point in *X-Files* history came about thanks to an unexpected, real-life development.

Gillian Anderson's pregnancy necessitated removing Scully from the story line entirely for one episode, as well as mostly taking her out of the proceedings for several more episodes. And that meant Scully had to go somewhere, and on a show in which aliens abduct people regularly, well, there was a pretty logical place for her to go.

I don't in any way mean to chastise Anderson for her pregnancy.[11] Figuring out how to write pregnancies into TV shows is as old as the form itself,[12] and shows have employed all manner of ingenious tricks to either hide pregnancies or incorporate them into the story lines. What's more, the creative team learned of Anderson's pregnancy late in the filming of Season One, when they had the time to plan for how to fold it into the show.[13] This way, the writers could end the season with Scully and Mulder being split up, which would allow Anderson to mostly appear in stories that wouldn't require too many stunts, would frame her largely in close-up, or would have her wearing big coats to disguise her baby bump.

These strategies had the added benefit of giving the season's early episodes a feeling that was *just* different enough to be intriguing. Every time you might start to think, "Boy, I'd like to see Mulder and Scully working together again," the show would introduce another new wrinkle, like the arrival of Krycek. By the time you get to "Duane Barry," you're already a little off balance, which the show exploits to gleeful effect when it turns what seems like a vaguely paranormal hostage standoff into Mulder, Scully, and *X-Files* fans' greatest nightmare.

"Duane Barry" isn't just another great Chris Carter script;[14] it's also his directorial debut. At this point in the show's run, he's second to none on the writing staff when it comes to deploying twists that come out of nowhere but that simultaneously explain what's happening. He utilizes this skill five or six times in "Barry," to major effect. Perhaps the best of these twists occurs when Scully gets a look at Barry's files and realizes that the former FBI agent, who seemingly went crazy after an alien abduction, has been a different, more violent person since his frontal lobe was damaged by a shot to the head in 1982. Scully has every reason to be frightened for her friend (who's closed himself in with Barry), and Mulder has every reason to start doubting himself when he hears Scully's information.

But the twist that changes everything occurs at the end of "Duane Barry," and Carter executes it with incredible precision. The episode has ended! We think we know how it's going to turn out, with Duane Barry (Steve Railsback) suffering in a mental institution, or maybe escaping for another rendezvous with the aliens. But then Scully scans the implant found in his body on a supermarket checkout scanner, which goes berserk, and Duane Barry shows up at her apartment and abducts

S2 E5–6

---

11 Anderson gave birth to a daughter in September 1994.

12 The most famous early example is Lucille Ball of *I Love Lucy*. The popularity of the show allowed its writers to incorporate Ball's pregnancy into the story line, when her network, CBS, was worried her condition might offend viewers. The 1950s, everybody!

13 It's also worth noting that they learned of Anderson's pregnancy at a time when her skill as an actress and her centrality to the series had become apparent. Without those elements, a less-ambitious story arc might have been considered.

14 One for which he would receive the first of several Emmy nominations (though he would never actually win an Emmy).

her. The episode *isn't* over. Absolutely nothing about "Duane Barry" when it aired suggested it was part one of a two-parter, and the episode uses everything viewers know about the show's formula against them. Just when you think you know where everything is headed, it turns out to be Scully who was in danger all along.

Of course, this is *The X-Files*. We know that Barry is, at the very least, working with the conspiracy and is quite possibly a genuine alien abductee (because the opening of the episode named after him certainly seems to depict a classic abduction). But both "Duane Barry" and "Ascension" do a great job of keeping us from learning too much about who took Barry—and to whom he subsequently delivered Scully. You're allowed to believe that she was taken by the aliens, yes, but there's every chance the people who took her were military, as part of their ongoing nefarious experiments. All of the tests we see conducted on Scully in "Ascension" occur in Mulder's imagination, after all—likely inspired by his suspicion of the government.

"Ascension" suffers somewhat in comparison to the episode it's paired with, but it's nevertheless a thrilling showcase of Mulder's dedication to rescuing Scully, even though everything in the universe seems to be trying to stop him. The moment when he climbs out of the ski gondola to ascend the mountain is one of the series' first showstopping stunts. It's impressive and gutsy how "Ascension" lets Scully disappear around the episode's midpoint so Mulder can spend the rest of it in abject horror and desperation at how thoroughly he failed the person he cares about most. It must feel like a dim echo of Samantha's abduction to him, and the series isn't afraid to live in his despair.

As much as "Ascension" is Mulder's action-adventure hour, its second half provides some beautifully orchestrated moments for many of the other characters as well, like when the Cigarette Smoking Man offers the latest rationale for Mulder's continued existence.[15] Plus: Skinner reopens the X-Files! Mr. X turns up just to frustrate Mulder's attempts to get to Senator Matheson! Krycek kills Duane Barry himself, only to have Mulder realize his duplicity! This half hour is like a greatest hits collection of jaw-dropping moments, pivoting to each reveal with exhilarating abandon.

But make no mistake, the most significant thing that happens in "Ascension" is that Scully disappears. This wasn't the sort of thing television *did* in 1994, for the most part. Scully's disappearance isn't as despair-inducing as, say, the death of Laura Palmer on *Twin Peaks*, but it comes close. Instead of ending with a reassurance that everything will be OK, the episode ends with a deeply sad Mulder sitting atop the mountain where he lost his partner and looking to the stars that took her. Yes,

---

15 This one—killing Mulder risks turning one man's crusade into a religion—never made all that much sense. Just how many people in the *X-Files* universe even know Mulder exists?

in the back of your head, you know this won't be forever,[16] but in the moment, it felt like the show outdoing every other series on TV without breaking much of a sweat.

When these episodes aired in late 1994, were there fans who knew that Anderson's pregnancy was going to necessitate her stepping away from the show for a time? Almost certainly. But the show does everything it possibly can to disguise its intentions from the audience, even when Scully is tied up in Duane Barry's trunk and heading for the top of Skyland Mountain. Surely Mulder will catch up, right? Surely Scully won't actually be taken, right? And then when she *is*, it happens with enough time left in the episode to assume that she might be found before the hour is over.

But no: Scully is taken. Mulder is left distraught. The show rises to another level. In "Duane Barry" and "Ascension," *The X-Files* goes from a promising series to one with the potential to be one of the greatest series of all time. Everything that happens in these episodes will fundamentally shape the rest of the series, for Mulder, for Scully, for the increasingly large supporting cast, and for the fans. "Duane Barry" and "Ascension" might now seem less stunning in this age of heavily serialized television and beautifully calibrated twists, but make no mistake: Had these episodes not existed—had the producers not needed to write Gillian Anderson out of the series for a time—you probably wouldn't be reading this book right now. —TVDW

SEASON 2 / EPISODE 7
WRITTEN BY CHRIS RUPPENTHAL, GLEN MORGAN, AND JAMES WONG
DIRECTED BY DAVID NUTTER | "3"

IT BITES

In which something sure, uh, sucks.

"3" finds both the show and Mulder trying to cope in the wake of Scully's absence, and the results are mixed at best. What initially holds charm as a trashy throwback to erotic '90s thrillers takes a turn for the maudlin once our hero gets involved with a new woman and a trio of melodramatic vampires. Mulder, lonely and plagued by guilt, meets Kristen Kilar (Perrey Reeves), an angst-ridden brunette with a hypodermic needle in her purse. The two make some sort of connection. Stupidity ensues.

Scully's abduction is one of the show's most iconic mythology arcs, capitalizing on some of Mulder's (and our) darkest fears. But while the episodes that deal directly with the abduction are excellent, "3"—which is nominally about Mulder struggling on his own—is terrible. The reliance on easy clichés betrays what should've been an opportunity to show Mulder at his most vulnerable.

---

16 And boy, I hope I'm not spoiling anything when I say Scully is coming back.

It certainly doesn't help that the *X-Files'* version of vampires is disappointingly unimaginative. Despite their undisputed place in the horror pantheon, bloodsuckers are a difficult monster to portray effectively. It seems like every possible iteration on the themes they represent—sex, immortality, general paleness—has been done to death. There's nothing particularly scary about whiny Goths with pointy teeth and overheated metaphors.

"3" makes no real attempt to subvert these tropes. The trio of vampires whom Mulder tracks down fails to make any real impression. The only one we get to know at all, John (Frank Military), looks like he just got thrown out of a Creed concert. Kristen, the mysterious dark-haired stranger who serves as the hour's ostensible emotional center, doesn't fare much better. We don't spend enough time with Kristen or her vampire stalkers to get a real sense of their story, and what little time we do spend is full of awful dialogue and heavy-handed attempts at mood. The question of just how far a person should be willing to go for immortality is a good one, but the answer comes across as a series of grunts and yells.

Worst of all is the romance between Mulder and Kristen. You can see what the writers were aiming for: Mulder is lost without Scully; Kristen is caught between the real world and the darkness on the edge of town; together they can heal each other's wounds, and then do kinky stuff involving candle wax. But the writing isn't up to the task, and Reeves's performance is borderline catatonic.

Duchovny is subdued as well, but outside his scenes with Reeves, the low-key approach makes sense. This is the closest we've seen to him bottoming out. The scene of him reopening the X-Files and putting Scully's file in with the rest is a deeply upsetting image, and while he shoots off a few quips during the investigation in Los Angeles, it feels like he's not really all there. At one point he says, "I don't sleep anymore," and it's not hard to believe him.

That's what really makes this episode so disappointing. Scully's disappearance and Mulder's mourning for her are serious subjects, and they deserve better than to be background noise for a by-the-numbers erotic thriller. "3" has a definitive conclusion, with Kristen and the others burned to a crisp. It's the rare happy ending, since you know you'll never have to hear any of them whine again. —ZH

WILL TO LIVE

*In which your enjoyment of this episode will be in direct
proportion to your appetite for '90s mysticism.*

"One Breath" is stuck in time. By that I mean it's one of those works of art that
becomes so attached to the era in which it was released that the further we get from
that era, the harder it is to appreciate why it was so beloved at the time. Everything
that felt adventurous about "One Breath" in 1994 has been so thoroughly improved
upon elsewhere that it's hard not to cringe just a little bit when watching it today.

Nevertheless, it's "One Breath." It's the episode in which Scully comes back.
It's the episode in which Mulder chooses to spend a night at her bedside instead
of exacting his revenge. It's the episode in which she's saved by some sort of angel
nurse, and in which everybody who loves her moves heaven and earth to try to figure
out how to save her. It might be the first "event" episode of *The X-Files*, by which I
mean it's the first to assemble much of the show's increasingly large ensemble of
recurring players in one place. You might roll your eyes at elements of this episode
now. You might find the very 1994-ness of it unbearable. But it's "One Breath." Never,
ever skip past it.

Much of what has aged poorly about "One Breath" is its depiction of the afterlife as a kind of loose, empty dreamscape where Scully can hang out and listen to
other people say nice things about her. When her dead father shows up late in the
episode to tell her that she'll join him someday—but not right now—it essentially tips
the episode's hand when it comes to the story's ultimate resolution. These scenes
are nice and all, but the *Twin Peaks*–inspired dream imagery has been taken to
more beautiful lengths on so many subsequent series that watching this now
feels a little tame. That's to say nothing of the New Age philosophy, which rears
its head here and there and often feels like the show has backed its way into a
crossover with *Touched by an Angel*.

But these moments are too emotionally important to the story to besmirch.
The X-Files is too invested in the trauma and magnitude of Scully's abduction to
just have her wake up one day and be on her path back to wellness. There has to be
a sense that she made *some* sort of journey to overcome the weakened condition the
ordeal left her in, and the scenes set in this hazy halfway place suggest just such a
journey without having to do too much. The purpose of this portion of the episode
isn't to present some wild new vision of the afterlife either, but instead to imply
that not every paranormal phenomenon needs to be scary. Indeed, many of the

supernatural ideas humans cherish most are those that are hopeful, those that hint there is something beyond this earthly plane.[17] So yes, you might find these scenes just a little hard to take (as I do), while still accepting their importance to the episode.

The other half of this episode is some rip-roaring stuff, as Mulder tries to work through his grief by doing anything he can to save his seemingly doomed partner. That "anything" includes having the Lone Gunmen try to ascertain just what's wrong with her,[18] confronting the Cigarette Smoking Man in his lair, and seriously contemplating Mr. X's advice to lay in wait and kill the men who took Scully when they come to search his apartment later that night. It's an episode that very believably pushes Mulder to the point where he might murder someone, and the outrage of his struggle and Scully's condition makes you *want* him to murder someone too.

Certainly, *The X-Files* is not always a show about great moral quandaries, insomuch as it's about the quest to maintain human dignity in the face of dehumanizing forces. But if there's a place where the episode's religiosity is most welcome, it's in the idea that what Mulder needs isn't to seek revenge but to be at the side of his closest friend and beloved partner. The episode doesn't present Scully's recovery as a direct result of Mulder's bedside vigil, but it also doesn't dissuade you from thinking that her revival is at least a little bit his reward for choosing the righteous path. If *The X-Files* is a religious show on some level, then its morality revolves around doing the right thing and being rewarded for those actions.

The rest of "One Breath," silly and ooey-gooey as it is, offers a bittersweet look at what it might mean to die, or even to have a near-death experience. It's an episode with the temerity to pull the old "No nurse by that name works here!" bit but also an episode with the good-natured temperament to actually pull it off. *The X-Files* lives in the shadows, but its darkness is only bearable because it occasionally offers us little glimmers of some other, more hopeful way of living, peeking through that darkness. "One Breath" might be forever stuck in the time it was made, but we take our comfort where we can with the people we love, no matter what corner of time and space in which we find ourselves. —TVDW

---

17 Key to this idea is the frequent motif of Scully's cross necklace, which has been all Mulder has of her since he found Duane Barry's empty trunk in "Ascension" (S2E6). Her Catholicism, which will be explored much more thoroughly in future seasons, first makes a significant dent in the story here (it was first mentioned at all in "Miracle Man" [S1E19]).

18 "Branched DNA," they conclude, meaning human DNA that has been grafted with . . . something else.

INTO THE INFERNO

In which it burns.

After the emotional outpouring of the previous episode, "Firewalker" gets back into the regular swing of things. Apart from a couple of exchanges about Scully's health, the episode could've taken place at any point in the first two seasons. The plot serves as a companion piece to "Ice" (S1E8), another story about an isolated outpost, extreme temperatures, and internal parasites.

The comparison does the later episode no favors. "Firewalker" lacks the intensity of "Ice" and also its convincing threat. The silicon-based fungus's actual effect on its host, apart from its grotesque result, is never made clear. We know that the members of the research team are supposed to be behaving oddly, but the oddness is surface level (mostly just twitching and occasional shouts), without any of the growing paranoia that made "Ice" so powerful.

Still, the episode is competent, and it's a pleasure to see Scully back on her feet. Anderson has settled into her character, and her performance is noticeably more self-assured. The cast is full of talented character actors, including Leland Orser (probably best known as the guy who had fatal sex with a prostitute in *Seven*), Shawnee Smith (pre-*Becker* fame), and Bradley Whitford (best loved as Josh Lyman in *The West Wing*) as the possibly-saner-than-he-looks Daniel Trepkos.

This episode's biggest advantage is context. Regardless of the plot's flaws, it's a relief and a thrill to have the show's central characters working together again. Put anywhere else on the episode roster, this one could've been a write-off; even the conversations about silicon-based life, while intriguing, never go anywhere. But after the sloppiness of "3" (S2E7) and the intensity of "One Breath" (S2E8), it's nice to get back to basics. —ZH

PICKET FENCES

In which the cows are part of it.

"Red Museum" doesn't entirely work, but boy, is it wild! The show throws every-thing it can think of into this one, and it emerges on the other side with a story that doesn't really make a lick of sense but still makes for a whiplash-inducing good time. It's a kitchen-sink kind of episode, in which Chris Carter might have said, "I think we have everything we need in this episode," and someone else, having pried a kitchen sink (probably labeled ALIEN CONSPIRACY STORY LINE) out of the floor, leaving water spewing everywhere, said with a wink, "Not *everything*, Chris."

As such, the episode makes a useful case study for exploring just why the second season is so much stronger than the first. On a purely structural level, the episode most similar to this in Season One is probably "Space" (S1E9), another episode that throws ideas at the audience until we can barely keep up, while relating very tangentially to the alien conspiracy story line. Yet "Space" is a disaster, whereas "Red Museum" is a lot of fun. The latter has similar plotting issues, but it takes its headlong plunge into the alien world with an irresistible confidence. Hold on tight: "Red Museum" knows where it's going.

It's impossible to talk about this episode's abrupt left turn into alien con-spiracy wackiness without talking about its inception as something else entirely. Originally, the episode was intended as a crossover with the CBS series *Picket Fences*,[19] then in its third season. Chris Carter and *Picket Fences* producer David E. Kelley thought it would be fun to do a pair of episodes that would depict the same events transpiring in the CBS series' town of Rome, Wisconsin, from the point of view of the *Picket Fences* characters on their show and the point of view of Mulder and Scully on *The X-Files*. It was an interesting idea, one that might have jazzed up otherwise routine episodes of both shows, but it was one that CBS ultimately nipped in the bud.[20]

---

19 Although *The X-Files* aired on Fox and *Picket Fences* aired on CBS, both shows were produced by 20th Century Fox Television, which is the only reason anyone thought such a crossover had a prayer of happening. *Picket Fences* was one of many *Northern Exposure* clones to air in the early '90s, all centered on weird little towns in the middle of nowhere. This one, however, won considerable ac-claim and several Emmys because almost every episode ended in a courtroom with the characters confronting an important issue of the week.

20 Had the network foreseen just how much *The X-Files* would grow into a sensation in its second season, it might have been more amenable to spending an hour of the perpetually ratings-starved *Fences* essentially promoting another network's show.

Robbed of a connection to another show, "Red Museum" was left with a lot of time to kill, and Carter was left with very little time to revise the script to make it a stand-alone episode. Indeed, it's right around the midpoint—either when Scully spots the assassin who killed Deep Throat or when she says, "Mulder, it's purity control!" of the substance found in a toxicology report—that the episode abruptly stops being about a weird rural cult and becomes about the alien conspiracy's experiments in a small town in Wisconsin. It's a shift that doesn't entirely work, as the alien conspiracy is so much bigger than anything else in the show at this point that it has a tendency to swallow all other story lines whole.[21] But it's certainly an *intriguing* twist.

Injecting a normal Monster of the Week episode with alien-conspiracy DNA makes a certain amount of sense when you start to think about how isolated the MOTW episodes are from the rest of the show. As in "Space," Carter just keeps introducing MOTW ideas—a weird cult, wandering souls that enter other bodies, growth hormones, serial rapists,[22] cows, et cetera—without seeming to have any intention of paying them off.[23] But with such a fleshed-out mythology in its wheelhouse, the show can turn to it in its hour of need. The seemingly random collection of incidents and stories doesn't *cohere* by episode's end, but the presence of the conspiracy suggests coherence wasn't possible in the first place.

This tendency to shrug and say, "The conspiracy did it!" might get the show in trouble eventually, but it's still novel enough to essentially save "Red Museum." You leave the episode dizzied, confused, a little cheated, but wanting to get back on the ride. And besides, not every story can have an easy explanation, right? Somewhere out there in the woods, the Church of the Red Museum is carrying on its services, waiting to return to a story line that's long since passed it by. Maybe it's better that way. —TVDW

21 Unlike most other alien conspiracy stories, the various strands introduced in this episode don't recur with any frequency, so it's tempting to write it off as a weird sidebar to the overall mythology. But shockingly, some of the ideas introduced in "Red Museum" pay off *five seasons later*. That probably wasn't planned, but you can never quite be sure with this show.

22 This episode hasn't aged poorly as much as it's aged *strangely*. The frequent reference to "all of those rapes" from locals is jarringly callous, and the description of the cultists as "diaperheads" is similarly upsetting.

23 To be fair, "a large collection of seemingly unrelated incidents turns out to be part of the same story" was a frequently used structure on *Picket Fences*, and it's entirely possible that series would have made sense of all of these elements with a concluding speech from Judge Ray Walston.

RAGE AGAINST THE DYING OF THE LIGHT

In which little good comes from mushrooms.

Sexual assault is a tricky subject for a show like *The X-Files* because the ugly real-world truth of the act and its aftermath is constantly at odds with the fundamental fiction of paranormal circumstances. "Excelsis Dei" is no exception. The cold open has a nurse raped by an invisible entity, and there's a painful reality to the investigation that follows to which the otherwise silly premise doesn't do justice. The time spent trying to place blame on the victim is both authentic to the prejudice involved in sexual assault investigations and distracting, especially given that the audience saw the event in question. Mulder comes off especially badly, as over and over he tries to dismiss Scully's suspicions due to his own skepticism about "ghost rape."

The assault isn't the subject of the episode but merely a symptom of a larger problem. A number of patients at the home for the elderly suffer from Alzheimer's, but in the past few years they've made incredible progress, thanks to some mushroom-based meds from Gung, the Malaysian orderly who grows the fungus in the basement. The drugs, as it turns out, have also tapped into the spirits of the convalescent home's former residents, which in explaining everything, explains nothing at all.

"Dei" goes for mystery, but when the twist lands, there's no "aha" moment, no sense that all the pieces have finally clicked into place. Instead, it has the reek of desperation, a story relying on exploitative material to pull in viewers, but lacking the depth to redeem the ugliness. Unlike the more sympathetic monsters we've seen, there's no investment in having the audience connect with anyone besides Mulder and Scully, which severely limits the story's emotional impact. In addition, the offhanded manner in which Gung's motivations and history are handled is embarrassing, another example of the show's inadequacies in depicting cultures outside of the straight, white, American mainstream. You don't even find out what country he's from till the final voice-over, leaving us with an episode that feels unsavory from start to finish. —ZH

DNA AND SYMPATHY

In which genes do not work that way.

There's one powerful scene in "Aubrey," and then there's a whole bunch of other stuff. It's yet another episode about a dead person attempting to carry out his bloody plan by possessing the soul of somebody else, but at least this episode (unlike its many Season One forebears) features a "dead person" who turns out to be alive and is thus possessing his offspring via novel means. The downside is that those "novel means" make very little sense.

"Aubrey" is one of the few *X-Files* episodes written by a woman, and its Monster of the Week gains a degree of empathy from Sara B. Charno's script. At its center is the idea of cyclical abuse, the ways in which women carry the scars of violent behavior visited upon them by men across generations. There's probably a version of this story (which is set in rural Missouri, no less) that plays out as a spookier version of a Flannery O'Connor Southern Gothic tale—the woman who inadvertently finds herself a vessel for the continuation of sins of the past and struggles to find a way to keep from committing further sins.

This leads to that powerful scene, in which B. J. Morrow (a very strong Deborah Strang), acting at the behest of the rapist biological grandfather the adopted B. J. never knew, confronts the woman he raped (who is B. J.'s biological grandmother) on a stairwell. The older woman, cowering in the face of what seems like imminent death, slowly talks B. J. out of this rash action and helps her realize that the person who *really* needs to pay is the rapist and murderer himself, who is now living alone, having been released from prison after serving a sentence for rape.[24]

It's a surprisingly moving depiction of two women coming to realize how much they have in common and how much hurt they've both suffered. Instead of turning that rage and anger toward the wrong target, however, B. J. must override her own genetic programming and take down the man whose memories she's suddenly discovered lurking in her subconscious, thanks to the presence of genetic memories that skipped a generation (B. J.'s father is the child that resulted from the long-ago rape). Nestled inside her, these memories have been awakened by her first pregnancy.

Even by the standards of Mulder theories, this one is pretty out there. Charno makes a halfhearted attempt to tie this pseudo-possession to the idea that B. J. is pregnant with a baby boy (the masculine tendency having awakened her dark

---

24 He was never convicted for his murders. Even the most cursory discussion of this plot reveals its messiness.

passenger, I guess), but any power that comes from the concept that these two women can break the cycle of abuse is ultimately defused by the utter strangeness of the explanation for how all of this is happening. The theory behind the setup has the weird effect of weaponizing pregnancy, among other things, and the episode constantly races several steps behind the ultimate reveal, which leads to some painful exposition dumps.

All of the proceedings are meant to lead to the scenes in which B. J. finally confronts the monstrous actions that nevertheless led to her existence. There are hints, here and there, that Charno's script is going to dig into this conflict and into the idea that, once B. J. knows the secrets of her past, she'll be unable to escape their shadow. It's one of those concepts that *almost* works but ultimately runs aground on the rocks of too much plot. Unfortunately, Mulder and Scully also unnecessarily clutter the episode. They're there to investigate the murder of an FBI agent that B. J.'s biological grandfather killed all those years ago (uncovered by B. J. in the early throes of her genetic memory activation), but the murders have almost nothing to do with the action of the episode, beyond offering a creepy flavor and an ostensible entry point to the events.

No one will ever put this on a list of all-time *X-Files* classics, and it's certainly one of the weaker Season Two outings. But it's saved from being completely unnecessary by the presence of strong actors (including Terry O'Quinn[25] as B. J.'s sheriff boyfriend) and that scene on the stairwell. If ghost stories—even ghost stories in which the "ghost" is still alive—are about finding ways to escape the haunted remnants of the past, then "Aubrey" finds a meaningful way to suggest that some of us have more appalling horrors in our pasts than others. —TVDW

| "IRRESISTIBLE" | SEASON 2 / EPISODE 13
WRITTEN BY CHRIS CARTER
DIRECTED BY DAVID NUTTER |

PSYCHO KILLER

In which some monsters are men.

The X-Files is the progenitor of most twenty-first-century cop dramas. Virtually everything about *CSI* (which became the template for so many cop shows thereafter) was borrowed from *The X-Files*, from the muted lighting to the obsession with flashy science to the gallows humor. Indeed, remove the paranormal elements from *The X-Files*, and you'd get a show very much like *Criminal Minds*. Or maybe a show very much like "Irresistible."

---

25 O'Quinn would turn up in a future episode of this show, the first film, and Chris Carter's later series *Millennium*.

"Irresistible," one of Chris Carter's periodic attempts to really push the skills of Gillian Anderson and director David Nutter, is one of the few episodes of *The X-Files* in which there are no apparent paranormal forces at play. Instead, what makes it so terrifying is its restraint. Carter originally intended to make serial killer Donnie Pfaster (Nick Chinlund) a necrophiliac, but the network balked.[26] Instead, he became a man who was obsessed with women's hair and fingernails and was eventually willing to kill for them, which is somehow much creepier.

There's a lot of contrivance involved in the storytelling here. The reasons that take Mulder and Scully to Minneapolis[27] right before Donnie starts killing people are sketchy. The way Donnie happens to see Scully in the jail and feels that he must have a little of that red hair is similarly strained. And the moments when Donnie seems to shape-shift—spurred by Scully's imagination—don't click with everything else, as if Carter got scared the fans would bolt without something paranormal-esque.[28] Scully chickening out right as she is about to escape Donnie's clutches, just so Mulder can ultimately save the day, feels similarly fabricated and, even worse, flies in the face of what we know about her character.

But all of that happenstance leads somewhere legitimately terrifying. *The X-Files* is at its best if it can capture that feeling of racing past the spooky old house where the guy who only comes out once a week to collect his mail lives. "Irresistible" nails that sensation. Chinlund's performance as Donnie suggests a man who isn't inherently suspicious but is still just odd enough to clue in anyone he talks to for more than a minute that something's not quite right. Carter and Nutter take their time revealing the inside of his apartment, or his mother's house (where Scully is imprisoned), which looms in the frame like something out of a John Carpenter movie.[29]

Mulder basically plays a supporting role in this episode, though it's always nice to see him break out his skills as a criminal profiler to zero in on Donnie. But it's Anderson who makes this episode a must-watch. It might be her finest performance in the series so far. "Irresistible" captures Scully's growing sense that the world she knows is sliding off-kilter, and thus works as a microcosm for everything she has experienced while working on the X-Files. It was already a cliché by this point to

---

26 Says Carter, "They basically put a stamp on it that said, 'Not approved for network consumption.' Here I was up against the wall, no other script to fall back on to put into production. The clock is ticking, and I thought, 'How do I solve this problem?' [So] I rewrote the script and just removed the word *necrophiliac* and replaced it with *death fetishist*. I passed the test, and the episode went forward."

27 The city is portrayed, for whatever reason, as only a few degrees removed from Mayberry in *The Andy Griffith Show*. Except it has a red-light district for some reason? Sure.

28 Some victims of Jeffrey Dahmer said the serial killer really did seem to shape-shift, and Carter took this idea from that.

29 Or *Psycho* or real-life killer Ed Gein or . . . take your pick. This hour is a hearty gumbo of serial killer references.

put Scully in danger, especially since she's usually so good at taking care of herself.[30] But it still works most of the time, thanks to her positioning as the series' heart, the one person who can keep the world from tipping over into pitch-black darkness.

With "Irresistible," we get the sense that the show is testing just how elastic its premise can be in the Monster of the Week episodes. It's difficult for horror, especially TV horror, to maintain its punch over time, as tastes change and our sense of what's scary evolves. But "Irresistible" remains legitimately unnerving today, and much of that is thanks to the way the show was pushing itself in new and interesting directions. —TVDW

"DIE HAND DIE VERLETZT"

SEASON 2 / EPISODE 14
WRITTEN BY GLEN MORGAN AND JAMES WONG
DIRECTED BY KIM MANNERS

SATANIC PANIC

In which: witches!

Where "Irresistible" (S2E13) was unsettlingly creepy, "Die Hand Die Verletzt" is good, old-fashioned creepy *fun*. The two episodes couldn't be more different, yet they're somehow parts of the same show. That's impressive.

"Die Hand" is an *X-Files* take on occult goings-on, which pulls off the expected story beats with aplomb. Indeed, most of this is so implausible that Mulder seems briefly confused as to how it could be happening. The steadily building progression of spookiness and the excellent guest cast help the episode overcome the way Mulder and Scully seem to be passengers in the story, shuttled from event to event as they attempt to remain unflappable in the face of all that weird stuff going on.

The fun is evident in the very first scene, in which a school faculty meeting ostensibly called to discuss concerns about the drama instructor having students perform *Jesus Christ Superstar* is revealed not to involve Christian fundamentalists but something else altogether. This sequence is a deliberate, cheeky nod to the Satanic Panic of the 1980s (not so long ago when this episode first aired), when authority figures the country over were suspected to be a part of a sinister conspiracy to harm children.[31] But here, that notion is played for subversive comedy. The faculty members light red candles. They pray to the lords of darkness. The camera pulls back and back and back, until all we can see is the glowing red light creeping around the edges of that closed door.

---

30 Honestly, if she escaped alien abduction, how is a creep like Donnie Pfaster going to keep her down?

31 Certainly not an idea that no longer exists in the 2010s. We just generally no longer believe Satanists are the ones at fault.

Doors are everywhere in "Die Hand," and the episode uses them very well.[32] There's this glowing door in the opener. There's the classroom door Mrs. Paddock[33] (Susan Blommaert) locks herself behind when she kills her victims. There's the door to the basement Mr. Ausbury (Dan Butler) is locked in, the one that clicks open and permits a snake to enter and devour him. And of course, the satanic worshippers are attempting to open a door to some other reality, to let evil into our world.

These physical doors are somehow unable to shield us from wickedness. Monsters rarely let a little wood stand in the way of devouring us whole. Mulder and Scully, usually so on top of things, are largely unable to fight back against the dark forces at work in this town, which leads to them nearly being sacrificed.[34]

The notion that Mulder and Scully could be slaughtered in a locker room shower is ridiculous, but it also feels like a logical culmination of everything that's come before in this episode. Once you've had a fetal pig come to life and scream at a girl, or a woman's eyes shift into those of a snake, it's easy to roll with sacrificial shower murder, even if it's doubtful that Mulder or Scully will actually perish. The episode might have been better served by the demise of guest players whose imminent deaths could have seemed plausible and thus meant something to viewers, but that, again, feels like quibbling with an episode that's such a good time.

The best moment in this episode arrives in the very final shot. Mulder and Scully, drenched from their time in the shower, freaked out by the way the faculty members fell victim to a murder-suicide that was far from self-inflicted, stand alone in the biology lab, the power in the school abruptly coming back on to reveal the humdrum normality of fluorescent lights. Scratched across the blackboard behind them are the words GOOD-BYE, IT'S BEEN NICE WORKING WITH YOU in a neat cursive; the punch line of the episode becomes clear. Mulder and Scully were pawns, yes, but pawns of an emissary of the Devil himself, who used them to push the faculty against each other, the better to rid himself of these unfaithful servants. It's rare that Mulder and Scully get completely played, but they do here, giving the episode the feel of a powerful, very sick joke.

Those words on the blackboard double as a farewell from writers Glen Morgan and James Wong, perhaps the most important producers in the early history of the show besides Chris Carter. The two are famous for writing episodes you might call "Halloween episodes," the kind that you could put on in late October and find the perfect accompaniment to the rattling branches outside. The two left the show for a time after this episode, heading off to produce the short-lived *Space: Above and*

S2 E14

---

32 The director of this episode, Kim Manners, was helming his first hour of the show. He would become one of the series' most important directors, working on episodes right until the end of the original run of the series.

33 "Paddock," meaning an enclosure? Get it?

34 If there's any reason to dislike this episode, it's because Mulder and Scully seem so hapless.

Beyond.[35] It's hard to think of a better good-bye for the duo than "Die Hand," which pours all of the things the two writers love into one big stew. The episode has their sick sense of humor, their outright left turns into demented darkness, their horrifying visuals—and always, always the sense that the darkness is only barely kept at bay, and that even Mulder and Scully would be powerless should it be unleashed. —TVDW

"FRESH BONES"	SEASON 2 / EPISODE 15 WRITTEN BY HOWARD GORDON DIRECTED BY ROB BOWMAN

A VOODOO EPISODE

In which there are zombies.

After a couple of very strong installments comes an episode that's standard-issue. It boasts some eerie ideas and a surprisingly thoughtful contemplation of the plight of a refugee community living in a nation that isn't sure it wants to deal with a refugee community.[36] As always with Rob Bowman's directorial efforts, there are some memorable, disturbing images: someone's fingers coming out of Scully's bloodied hand and grabbing for her throat; the head of the refugee compound, Colonel Wharton, trapped in the casket beneath the earth; the writhing bowl of maggot breakfast cereal; the shot of the corpse in Mulder's hotel-room tub, surrounded by blood. There's a great feeling of Grand Guignol[37] to this episode, a bloody sense that anything could happen. Too bad the plot makes so little sense.

As happens so often with these early, weaker episodes, "Fresh Bones" tries to do too much. Voodoo is a potentially good idea for an *X-Files* episode. Zombies are a potentially good idea for an *X-Files* episode. The clash between refugees who practice folk religions and the American military is a potentially good idea for an *X-Files* episode. But all three of them in the same story leaves the episode rushing from place to place, never taking a spare moment to really let the tension seep into your bones.

Zombies are one of the classic monster types that *The X-Files* hadn't gotten to just yet, and because the very concept of the zombie finds its origins in Haitian folklore, it's a logical leap to center the story on Haitian refugees. (If you guessed this

---

35 They would return—briefly—in Season Four, then shift over to running Carter's *Millennium* in that show's second season. Both would then return for Seasons Ten and Eleven but no longer working as writing partners.

36 Watching today, this story line feels quite prescient, as does the creeping sense of paranoia that stems from the government locking up a bunch of people and making them disappear completely.

37 A long-closed Parisian theater whose name has come to stand in for "super gross, perhaps even immoral, horror."

was yet another episode without particularly stellar racial politics, you win a prize.) Unfortunately, the attempts to splice in the usual Mulder and Scully investigation formula, plus the scenes detailing the highly problematic and uncomfortable conflict between Colonel Wharton and imprisoned refugee Pierre Bauvais, leave the hour feeling overstuffed. It rumbles along in first gear for three-quarters of its running time, then abruptly shifts into high gear for the end, moving toward a completely unearned, apocalyptic finish.

The guest cast saves some of this from completely faltering. Daniel Benzali (later of the short-lived but brilliant *Murder One*) gives Wharton just the right notes of authoritative menace. The lesser-known Bruce Young makes Bauvais into a figure of mystery and suspicion. Future TV favorites Callum Keith Rennie (Leoben Conoy on *Battlestar Galactica*) and Roger Cross (Curtis Manning on *24*) shine in tiny parts,[38] as the groundskeeper and Private Kittel, respectively.

The episode strains throughout to feel important, even resorting at one point to recruit the elusive Mr. X. The series usually brings in Mulder and Scully's informants only when it wants to make sure the audience notices a particular story point, whether it's because said story point will return in the mythology later on or just because the show is trying to more generally underscore something "significant." "Fresh Bones" has the heart of a more political episode, one that examines how Americans treat refugees and other immigrant communities, but its political elements compete with the flimsy voodoo and zombie story at every turn. As happens so often with these thematically cluttered episodes, there are the seeds for four or five really great installments here, but with all of them planted right next to each other, nothing has room to grow. —TVDW

S2 E15

---

38 Both will also later play other tiny parts on the show in future episodes. *The X-Files* was nothing if not efficient with using every single Vancouver-based actor in as many different ways as possible. As Chris Carter puts it, the series managed to amass "a really solid group of actors" local to the city. "It almost became our troupe because we shot so much up there," he says. "We shot well over one hundred episodes. I think we used about everyone in town at least once. We cast an actor in episode 217 who had been in the show five times. [. . .] We were just lucky enough to have these great character actors . . . sometimes people who went on to be stars and sometimes people who were achieving stardom, and we were able to reach out. And because they were fans of the show [we could] get them to come work with us."

"COLONY"	SEASON 2 / EPISODE 16 WRITTEN BY CHRIS CARTER, FROM A STORY BY CARTER AND DAVID DUCHOVNY DIRECTED BY NICK MARCK
"END GAME"	SEASON 2 / EPISODE 17 WRITTEN BY FRANK SPOTNITZ DIRECTED BY ROB BOWMAN

TOO MANY SAMANTHAS

In which Mulder gets sick.

"Colony" and "End Game" are Season Two *X-Files* in top form, with Carter and his writers expertly balancing plausibility against weirdness. The two-parter leaves plenty of unanswered questions in its wake, but this tactic works to the mythology's benefit. Green goo, deadly gases, and an alien bounty hunter[39] stabbing various middle-aged bald men: These are scenes that skate up to the edge of madness but have enough internal cause-and-effect to hold together. The answers we *do* get are inconclusive, offering a series of contradictory justifications that serve to make the danger somehow more real.

None of this would work without a sense of tension, however, so "Colony" smartly begins by jumping ahead in time to show Mulder in the throes of deadly danger. In medias res beginnings[40] are difficult to deploy effectively; they change the way we watch an episode, and knowing that the main threat is still to come can cause all the dangers that precede it to lose their edge. This cold open works thanks to the relentless and growing intensity that follows. The details of the future danger recede from our minds until we face them again in the final minutes of "End Game."

Mulder being at risk fits with one of the most effective parts of the show's approach to serialization: the escalation of nightmarish revelations. *The X-Files* started its run with the procedural comforts of government bureaucracy. Mulder and Scully investigated like good FBI agents. They interviewed witnesses, studied reports, did autopsies, and followed clues, and while they occasionally found themselves at risk, they always got to walk away at the end of the story. As the mythology builds, though, the lack of bigger consequences is revealed to be an illusion. Serialized storytelling gives the audience a sense that bad and impactful things will happen to our characters, that horrible events won't be resolved by the end credits. Chaos eats away at the status quo, until each new bizarre discovery serves to suggest some darker impossibility lurking behind.

Overly simple coincidences abound, like the way one of the alien bounty hunter's first victims runs directly into his arms, or the way an FBI agent comes by

---

39 Played by fan-favorite Brian Thompson.
40 Starting the story in the middle of the action—in this case, near the end of the actual events of the two-parter—before jumping back in time to explain everything.

the house of another victim and interrupts the ABH in the middle of his work. But what could've been sloppy writing instead adds to the sense of larger forces at work, moving pieces in unfavorable directions. Mulder and Scully are unable to contact each other. When Mulder tries to leave a message with a hotel clerk, the clerk's pencil breaks before he can write down the name, and Scully arrives, seconds too late. All of this leads to the exceptional cliffhanger, involving a shape-changing alien, a hotel room, and a last-minute phone call.

The two-parter makes excellent use of Mulder's sister, Samantha, as well, returning a version of her to the Mulder home and then immediately forcing him to choose between his sister and his partner. The conversation Mulder has with his father after this Samantha's death is heartbreaking because there's no comfort in it: Mr. Mulder (Peter Donat) blames his son for the killing, and worse, he blames his son for the fact that Samantha returned at all. The dramatic pushback against anyone who tries to find out what's really going on is a reminder that Mulder and Scully's efforts would have an emotional cost even if people weren't dying. Our heroes aren't just facing a group of villains with plans to take over the world; they're fighting to save a world that's at best apathetic and at worst openly hostile to anyone who tries to force its citizens to see what's really going on. The search for the truth is as lonely as it is fatal.

There are all sorts of games within games at work in these two episodes; they bifurcate and split like the clones that Mulder fails again and again to save, twists and dead ends with the same face, the same plea for protection from an evil that changes forms at whim. And yet the search continues. Mulder is angry when he discovers the multiple Samanthas, and he realizes he's been conned. He claims he'll wash his hands of the whole thing, but in the end—despite the danger, despite the setbacks—he still has the faith to go on searching. He believes. He'll follow any lie no matter how outlandish, because maybe, just maybe, he will find that final thread that will give all this death some meaning. —ZH

SEASON 2 / EPISODE 18
WRITTEN BY STEVE DE JARNATT
DIRECTED BY JAMES WHITMORE JR. | **"FEARFUL SYMMETRY"** |

MAN SAVE MAN

In which Scully helps autopsy an elephant.

For an episode that starts with an invisible elephant wreaking havoc, this is disappointingly middle of the road. Invisible wild animals should be terrifying, but "Fearful Symmetry" ignores its B movie premise in favor of a lot of heavy-handed talk about the rights of animals. The invisibility turns out to be just some kind of bizarre side effect, and it's only used again effectively when an animal-rights activist is mauled. There's some ugly footage of zoo workers abusing their charges, and Lance Guest (as Kyle Lang, the head of a group of "animal freedom terrorists") gives statistics and horror stories about mistreatment. Human cruelty toward nature is a legitimate angle, but it all feels pretty rote.

As usual, Mulder has some theories about what's happening, Scully is skeptical, and Mulder turns to a gorilla to try to prove his point. It's a memorable concept, especially considering that Sophie (the gorilla) is able to confirm his suspicions. Overall, the episode lacks suspense and makes no serious effort to instill concern for Sophie's well-being. While her death is sad, it doesn't justify forty minutes of meandering. Willa Ambrose's (Jayne Atkinson) half-baked backstory and her personal connection to Kyle seem thrown in at the last minute to try to create an illusion of depth.

It doesn't help that this is yet another episode in which Mulder and Scully do a lot of running around, to precious little result. Making our heroes passive observers can work on *The X-Files*, but only in episodes with strong stories.[41] While Mulder and Scully ensure that Willa faces justice, they still know roughly the same at the end about the invisible animals as they did at the beginning. Mulder provides voice-over about how our destruction of the natural world might have negative repercussions, but that's not enough to hold this together. The feeble attempt at conservationist wisdom ironically renders the episode entirely forgettable. —ZH

| **"DØD KALM"** | SEASON 2 / EPISODE 19
WRITTEN BY HOWARD GORDON AND ALEX GANSA, FROM A STORY BY GORDON
DIRECTED BY ROB BOWMAN |

SALTY DOGS

In which Mulder and Scully grow old together
(over the course of a couple of days).

There's something rather lovely about "Død Kalm," provided you can overlook some absolutely atrocious makeup effects.[42] It can be hard to acclimate to the ways in which the episode strays from the show's usual format, as it opts to tell a more emotional story about Mulder and Scully's deep connection. Even though "Død Kalm" sits on many fans' "worst episode" lists, it doesn't blunder in actuality as much as its reputation might suggest.

---

41 See, for example, "Die Hand Die Verletzt" (S2E14).
42 Though, no worries if you can't.

The episode's best qualities are atmospheric. The ghost ship that Mulder and Scully (and assorted guest stars) stumble upon in the far north Atlantic Ocean[43] is deeply haunting—one of the better one-off settings the show came up with. The sense of claustrophobia becomes overwhelming the longer the episode goes on. The screen might go pitch black, with only random sound effects and Mark Snow's foreboding score letting viewers know what, exactly, they're supposed to be following. The exploration of the ship, and the gradual uncovering of what happened to its crew, make for the strongest sustained sections of the episode.

But once the episode reveals that, somehow, the crew of the ship all aged far more rapidly than they should have, it pivots into something almost as fun: Scully and Mulder freestyling various theories, from wormholes to free radicals to whatever else they can think of. As in Season One's "Ice" (S1E8) and "Darkness Falls" (S1E20), the two are in a death trap, one they know they may not escape, which means the whole thing ends up being a test of Mulder and Scully's friendship and partnership. The episode even lets Scully play a role in their rescue,[44] before the sudden, convenient arrival of the U.S. Navy, which is more than "Darkness Falls" (a better episode that nevertheless largely chalked our heroes' survival up to blind luck) could muster.

It's the personal aspects of the story that make it come together in the end. Scully's final monologue about Ragnarök is one of the best she was given in the series. It eschews five-dollar words in favor of a very personal, well-written story of a woman facing down death yet another time. She's more scared than she's letting on, even after her brush with death after her abduction. Mulder and Scully look out for each other, even as they realize the hopelessness of their predicament, in a way that make the two seem less like FBI partners and more like an old married couple.

So why doesn't this join "Ice" or "Darkness Falls" in the pantheon of classic Monster of the Week episodes? Well, the makeup really is that bad. When the army of desiccated, prematurely aged corpses pops up, they look less like they've aged and more like they've been exposed to some sort of strange alien acid. Even worse, the big emotional moments are hindered by Gillian Anderson and David Duchovny having to emote through what appear to be rubber Halloween masks. There's real depth of feeling in the writing and in the performances, but you have to force your way through the laughable makeup to get to that sentiment.

Furthermore, as in "Darkness Falls," the choice to bring in the government as a sudden savior detracts from the story a bit. Where it worked in the earlier episode, thanks to its ties to the themes of man versus nature, the device feels much more convenient and implausible here. The fact that the doctors solved *and* reversed

S2 E19

---

43 It's always nice when the show takes on an international feel. Sure, Mulder and Scully are traveling to help out fellow Americans, but the scene set in the Norwegian bar is a lot of fun and very different from the show's usual approach.

44 She realizes the aging is being caused by the ship's water—a perfectly nebulous but strangely credible solution.

Mulder and Scully's condition, solely from reading Scully's notes, feels less like a triumphant moment of salvation and more like the writers realizing there was no other way to conclude this episode.

If you can find a way to look past those two (admittedly very distracting) issues, this episode works. There are so many nice moments here, like the two ships crunching together or Trondheim (John Savage) drowning as the outer hull gives way. The script is sprinkled with surprisingly poetic little bits of dialogue, like Scully discussing her father's love of the sea or the dying captain's story of how he managed to make it far enough to have a conversation with our heroes. What's most welcome is the way "Død Kalm" pauses from the constant horror the show had been serving up for several episodes in a row just to tell an unsettling but moving tale of two friends who look into the abyss without falling in. —TVDW

| "HUMBUG" | SEASON 2 / EPISODE 20
WRITTEN BY DARIN MORGAN
DIRECTED BY KIM MANNERS |

ASTOUNDING ACTS OF BODY MANIPULATION AND PAIN ENDURANCE

In which The X-Files *is a comedy now.*

Darin Morgan is one of the most acclaimed television writers who ever lived. And for a long time, Darin Morgan was one of the most acclaimed television writers who ever lived based solely on the first six scripts he wrote across two TV shows.[45] His way of thinking about the universe and the show he was writing for twisted *X-Files* fans' brains in knots and left more than a few of them in awe of his considerable skills (your humble reviewer included).

Morgan is pretty much the TV equivalent of an Alan Moore or a Charlie Kaufman, someone who would resurface every few years (whenever his brother Glen could lure him out) with a blisteringly funny script about the cost of living in a world of paranoia before retreating, seemingly because he just didn't like the

---

45 Those scripts, by the way, are this one, then the fellow *X-Files* episodes "Clyde Bruckman's Final Repose" (S3E4, for which he won an Emmy), "War of the Coprophages" (S3E12), and "Jose Chung's *From Outer Space*" (S3E20); as well as the *Millennium* episodes "Jose Chung's *Doomsday Defense*" and "Somehow, Satan Got Behind Me." Then he went on a lengthy hiatus, which he broke to write a few mostly forgettable episodes of a kids' show called *Tower Prep* and an alien drama called *Intruders*, both of which employed his brother, Glen. He also penned two well-received scripts for Seasons Ten and Eleven of *The X-Files* revival: "Mulder and Scully Meet the Were-Monster" (S10E3) and "The Lost Art of Forehead Sweat" (S11E4), and he did uncredited rewrites on a handful of other episodes, notably "Quagmire" (S3E22). But his reputation, such as it is, largely rests on those first six scripts.

pace of television work. Morgan's reputation is so good that he could probably get a series of his own made, but he seems less interested in the business aspects of show business and more interested in following his strange little muses wherever they may lead him.

Like Kaufman, Morgan is obsessed with the idea that every one of us will die alone, no matter how much love there is in our lives. Both men make that idea simultaneously horrifying and strangely poignant. There's a moment in "Humbug" when Scully is talking to the proprietor of a museum focusing on freak shows and other circus oddities and the proprietor tells her the sad story of the end of the famous conjoined twins duo, Chang and Eng Bunker. Chang died in his sleep, and Eng woke to find himself joined to his dead brother. Finally, he died of fright.[46] It's a small moment amid the goofy hubbub of the episode, but it gets at what Morgan is obsessed with—our ultimate, utter inconsequentiality in the face of the cosmos.

Morgan's other obsession is weird arcana. In "Humbug," most of that takes the form of tales of circus folk, ranging all the way back to P. T. Barnum and incorporating the '90s sideshows run by Jim Rose.[47] Morgan has considerable respect for anyone who's been tossed outside of the mainstream; he attempts to get at what's funny about them at the same time that he explores what they have in common with everyone else.

Take, for instance, Michael J. Anderson's[48] trailer park manager, who spends much of the episode complaining about how people regard him as somehow different because of his height and how they judge him solely based on how he looks. He also, in classic Morgan style, undercuts his own point by hypocritically pegging Mulder as an FBI agent based completely on our hero's appearance. Or observe how quickly Morgan sketches in all of these people, creating an entire community of oddballs that other shows might have chosen to mock. Consider how many other episodes of the show have struggled to discuss just these ideas, and then watch how effortlessly Morgan does it.

Morgan is also deeply, deeply funny. All of his scripts are stuffed with joke after joke. "Humbug" begins with the typical *X-Files* teaser (though the gag that the Alligator Man isn't stalking his sons but is, instead, ushering them up to bed gives us a clue that this won't be the same show we're used to), and the idea of a weird monster lurking among the circus folk initially makes "Humbug" feel like it might be a very special *Murder, She Wrote*. But by the time we get to that funeral sequence, crammed full of both wonderful sight gags and dialogue-based quips, we're clearly in some other show entirely, the only links in the continuity chain being Mulder

---

46 That's not quite how the Bunkers really died, but let's allow for some dramatic license.

47 Starring here as Dr. Blockhead.

48 Michael J. Anderson is, of course, yet another *Twin Peaks* veteran. He's perhaps most famous for playing Man from Another Place, who memorably popped up in the Red Room of that show.

and Scully themselves. "Don't worry," the show winkingly says, "We'll get back to the typical monsters next week."

Morgan's scripts constantly bite the hand that feeds. Few TV writers have been as caustic about the show they're working on as Morgan has. It's clear he doesn't hate *The X-Files* or think it's beneath him. He just thinks there are stupid things about the show, and he never tires of pointing them out. His scripts will frequently feature gags about how handsome Mulder is—"Who would want to go through life looking like *him*?"—or take apart the structure of the show and leave it in shambles or deconstruct the entire experience of watching the series.[49] There are fewer of these hallmarks in "Humbug" than there would be in Morgan's future episodes, but that lack may stem from how the very idea of watching a comedic episode of *The X-Files* was such an unusual departure at this point in the show's run.

Here's what's really remarkable: As good as it is, "Humbug" may still be Morgan's weakest script. The pacing at the beginning is a little logy, and the frequent detours into circus arcana are not as neatly tied in to everything as they could be. At the same time, few TV writers would come up with something as haunting and as perfectly understanding of the human condition as this episode's reveal of its killer.

Throughout "Humbug," Lanny (Vincent Schiavelli, turning in poignant work amid the madness) has wandered through various stories, occasionally referencing his conjoined twin Leonard, kept inside a small sack around his abdomen. (In one of the episode's better visual gags, Lanny tries to check out Scully's breasts, as she tries to check out his twin. We're all gawkers in Morgan's world.) But Leonard *can* detach from Lanny. Indeed, he's the one who's been killing everyone. Lanny insists Leonard isn't malicious—he just resents Lanny for being the one who's taken care of him since birth, the one who's kept him from freedom. He's not trying to actually kill anyone. He's simply looking for a new twin to join, a new caretaker, a new perfect double.

It's dark, full of despair, loneliness, and the sense that we're all going to die unfulfilled, no matter how much we accomplish. So naturally, Leonard's killing spree ends only when one of the other denizens of the circus eats him, in a darkly funny and bitterly acidic joke. That's Darin Morgan for you—life's the saddest thing there is, but also the funniest. If you can tell the difference, well, good on you. —TVDW

---

49 For more on this, turn ahead to the piece on "Jose Chung's *From Outer Space*," one of my top ten favorite episodes of TV ever made. Spoilers.

PLAYING FOR LAUGHS

"Humbug" (S2E20) was a landmark episode for the series. It was future fan-favorite Darin Morgan's first script for *The X-Files*, but also the show's first foray into outright comedy. Morgan recalls no trepidation about leading the show into uncharted waters. For him, he was only being true to his own sensibilities as a writer—as opposed to consciously mining elements of the series for untapped comedic potential. "The show has some jokes and stuff in the first season, but it wasn't funny or silly," he says. In Morgan's opinion, there's a terrifying side to the various phenomena explored by the show, but there's also a preposterous side: "It isn't until you really start thinking of, 'OK what stories can you tell based on such things?,' when you tend to either become serious or ridiculous, and I went down the ridiculous route I guess, for better or worse . . .

"It wasn't like, I was going, 'Well, here is how the show could go or how it should go.' . . . I just knew I wasn't going to be able to write the show the way the show [had been written before and] I didn't feel obligated to. . . . It's hard enough doing a good job; [so] the worry about, 'Does it fit in? Is this the right tone?'—all this sort of stuff—I was too inexperienced to really worry about . . . [I just tried to] do a decent job and the decent job just kind of . . . lent itself to go in the direction that I took it."

Frank Spotnitz recalls the genesis of "Humbug," and his and Morgan's first months on the writing staff (which both men joined in Season Two): "Morgan had started on the show a few weeks before I did, and all I knew about him was that he was Glen Morgan's younger brother, and that he'd been the Flukeman in 'The Host' (S2E2). Other than that, I knew nothing about him. He had a very dry sense of humor, and we'd go to lunch every day, but he never went to the writers' room, he didn't really work on the other episodes. He was always in his office, which was right next to mine. I wrote my first episode, it got produced, [and] I was writing my second episode, and [I was like], 'What's Darin doing?' Nobody knew what Darin was doing.

"And finally, one week I notice that Darin is not going home; I leave in the evening, I come back in the morning, and he's still there—he has not left. And after the end of that week, he announces that he's finished his script, and my curiosity was enormous. So, he hands it to me, and the first line—I can't remember what it was, but it was something like, 'It's a dark and stormy night;' it was a very obvious cliché. I just felt my heart sinking, thinking, 'Oh my god, after all that, this is going to be dreadful.' And of course, I kept reading, and it was brilliant. It was beautifully constructed and conceived and so moving and funny and profound and just fantastic. I think everybody who read the script had the same reaction I did, and recognized what a remarkable script it was. However, that didn't mean they wanted to produce it, because we had not done a comedy in any way, shape, or form up to that point, and this was clearly a comedy."

As Chris Carter puts it, "'Humbug' came out of left field, and it was something that the network and studio were terrified of. I remember even at the script level they didn't quite understand what we were doing." The tonal elasticity of *The X-Files* was still largely unrealized at that time, apart from the structural toggling between mythology and Monster of the Week episodes. Spotnitz recalls, "The studio executives came to Chris and said, 'Our advice to you is do not produce this episode, because it will destroy the illusion that you've created here, and people will no longer believe in the world of *The X-Files*, because you're making fun of it.' And I remember talking to Chris, and my recollection was that he said, 'It's a beautiful house, I'm just not sure I want to build it.'

Spotnitz continues, "But then the next day, [Chris] ultimately felt it was just too good not to produce. And somehow the gods just smiled on that script, because it was set in Florida and we were filming in the spring in Vancouver, where by all rights it should have been raining every day; instead the sun shone, and who knew David and Gillian both had fantastic comedic timing! Kim Manners did an amazing job—he was still proving himself in the world of *The X-Files*; he was still relatively new to us as a director."

Carter remembers, "When we finally filmed the episode, [the network] wanted to market test it to make sure we weren't doing something that the audience was going to reject. This was all a fight, as it almost always is in the beginning to push limits and/or limitations on the show." However, despite the network's fears, as Spotnitz declares, "It instantly became one of the most popular episodes we'd done, and created another genre . . . which we kept doing [for] the rest of the series."

A ROMANIAN EXORCISM

In which there are even more evil twins.

Compare "The Calusari" to Sara B. Charno's earlier episode this season, "Aubrey" (S2E12), and you'll find they have one big problem in common: Both land on ultimately nonsensical theories meant to explain their paranormal phenomena. Each episode overcomplicates when it could simplify.

Somehow, Charlie, the murderous child at the center of "The Calusari," is plagued by an evil twin[50] whose soul was never separated from his, so he must be saved by a bunch of old Romanians. And yet the creepy opening scene depicts what appears to be Charlie (Joel Palmer) killing his younger brother. It's not bad when the show leaves this sort of thing open to interpretation, but both "Aubrey" and "The Calusari" feel as if they're a little too welcoming of absolute chaos. At first, Charlie seems to be totally OK with the evil (unseen) twin Michael bumping off his little brother. Then he gets more and more upset with Michael as the episode goes on. The way the story lurches from seeming like a rip-off of *The Omen* to some sort of evil, incorporeal twin story line mostly feels like the writers consciously trying to distance themselves from that movie.

Still, there are beautiful images and eerie moments here, as is typical even in Season Two's less capable hours, perhaps best encapsulated by the way the balloon hangs unsettlingly just over Charlie's shoulder in the icy teaser, which acts as a prelude to a baby dying at the hands of a kiddie train.[51] It's also hard to go wrong with crazy rituals and old men and women who warn that if they aren't allowed to complete these rituals, terrible things will happen. The final exorcism sequence, especially, is nicely handled[52] (though obviously owing a lot to the sequence in *The Exorcist*). Duchovny makes a great acting choice when Mulder's expression goes from one of a passive observer to that of a man freaking out in the face of something paranormal.

At the same time, little of the plot hangs together, which is too bad for an episode that includes a bunch of chickens killing an old woman. There's so much room for backstory about the Calusari and about Grandma[53] and all of her Romanian

---

50 Though this and the immediately preceding episode, "Humbug" (S2E20), couldn't be more different in almost every way, they are technically both about evil twins.

51 This was a gutsy show when it wanted to be. Killing off a baby is something TV generally doesn't do, even today.

52 Though it beggars belief that the Calusari could somehow carry out the exorcism in a *hospital*.

53 Who seems like she regularly accuses people of being the devil and just got lucky this time.

friends, but the episode provides none. The way that Charlie's mom also has a firm command over the magic ritual is also never explained. The theorizing about the true nature of evil seems misplaced, like the show is biting off giant hunks of philosophy it has no intention of chewing. If Hitler was evil because of an evil ghost twin, that certainly explains *something*, but the references to real-life evils feel cheap and insensitive, like the show was worried viewers wouldn't invest in what's ultimately a small-scale family story about a very bad son.

This is yet another episode where Mulder and Scully are mostly just tourists (again, a flaw this entry has in common with "Aubrey"). Yes, "The Calusari" does at least give the two a genuine argument over what's happening. Scully's Munchausen syndrome by proxy theorizing makes so much more sense than Mulder's abrupt "Ghosts did it!" excitement. But the two of them are several steps behind the old Romanians far too often. Instead of facing down ultimate evil ghost twins, and anything else they could find, our protagonists wait for somebody else to do it for them.[54]

Yet there's a propulsion to "The Calusari" that keeps it from being a complete waste. A long string of intriguing moments is barely bound by the episode's messy, chaotic story, but at least those moments are genuinely compelling. Every act has at least one great set piece, like when Charlie's father gets chewed up by the garage door opener or when the social worker comes to see the boy and ends up in a scene from *The Exorcist*. Episodes that toss too much information at the audience tend to feel really disjointed, and "The Calusari" is no exception. But the fact that the story is always galloping forward at a breakneck pace makes it easier to ignore just how often it changes focus. If you let go of hoping for this one to make any sense, then you just might be convinced by its charms. —TVDW

| "F. EMASCULATA" | SEASON 2 / EPISODE 22
WRITTEN BY CHRIS CARTER AND HOWARD GORDON
DIRECTED BY ROB BOWMAN |

GREED IS A DISEASE
In which Scully and Mulder can't find a cure.

"F. Emasculata" is as grim as they come, full of gore and horrible death and tragedy. It's also a good example of why *The X-Files* embraced darkness for so long: When it works, it makes for remarkable television. "Emasculata" is a plague epic pared down to under an hour, with just a hint of conspiracy and paranoia. It includes

---

54 They also seem awfully unconcerned about the dead toddler at the center of the case. Mulder, in fact, seems sort of happy about a cool new case in which a two-year-old was lured onto some train tracks by a death balloon. Then again, haven't we all been excited about new death balloon–related opportunities at work at one time or another?

escaped cons, scientists in hazmat suits, dead bystanders, federal marshals with itchy trigger fingers, and lots and lots of body bags. The result is a tense, gripping mini-movie that hasn't really aged at all.

Chris Carter and Howard Gordon's script does an excellent job of sticking to the essentials, giving us just enough information to follow what's going on. The direction focuses on the most striking and suspenseful sequences to keep us interested—the shots of the supposed CDC men lugging bodies and taking tests, ignoring Scully's demands for information; escaped inmate Paul's (John Pyper-Ferguson) increasingly ugly condition; and the bodies stacked like plastic-wrapped cordwood. Even though there's no serious concern that Paul will get away in the end (a plague-decimated world is a bridge too far for even this nihilistic episode), the manhunt for him is exciting, and the final standoff works as both a thrilling climax and a reminder of the potential futility of Mulder's work. It's not enough just to get to the bottom of what's going on, or even to find evidence that proves your theories; you also have to have a context in which those theories actually matter. Here, even Scully thinks it's a bad idea to bring the answers to the public, for fear of causing mass panic. But when would learning that aliens exist, abductions are real, and a shadow government controls the world *not* cause mass panic? Finding the answers isn't enough; you need to have some way to use them, and Mulder is so fixated on the first part of his quest that he often seems blind to the consequences of his information.

Great guest stars also make the episode work, like Charles Martin Smith as Dr. Osbourne, whose efforts to help Scully get him killed. Smith conveys weak-willed guilt in a sympathetic manner, playing a character who's working for the wrong team but feels just bad enough about it to give his death weight. Pyper-Ferguson[55] is strong as a doomed man, and Dean Norris does solid work as the leader of the manhunt.

There's the usual corruption and greed motivating all these events; it just wouldn't be *The X-Files* if all of this horror came down to chance. "Emasculata" reinforces the necessity of Mulder and Scully's pursuit of the truth, while at the same time questioning if that pursuit can ever hope to bear fruit. Dr. Osbourne explains to Scully that the "prisoner getting infected" plan was concocted by the pharmaceutical company he worked for; that two of the infected people managed to escape was just bad luck. This reality points to another flaw in Mulder's understanding of The Truth. His theories rely on a black-and-white view of the world: There are evil men working behind the scenes to control our lives, and they must be stopped. Yet the world operates in shades of gray, and even if Mulder did somehow manage to defeat the Cigarette Smoking Man and his ilk, we'd still have situations like this one, in which a capitalist system encourages the exploitation of society's vulnerable. Mulder can't be expected to save the world, but who's to say that the people in charge of such systems would want to be "saved" at all?

S2 E22

---

55 Who will reappear as a different character in future episodes.

That's the problem with conspiracies, *The X-Files* claims: They are never as perfect as they need to be. There are always errors, mistakes, random disruptions, and the stakes the conspirators are playing for are so incredibly high that even the slightest misstep can wreak misery and destruction on thousands of innocents. Our heroes need to bring these men to light not only for the sake of justice, but also to stop them from creating even greater catastrophes.

Yet the final confrontation between Mulder and Paul doesn't offer much hope. Mulder thinks he finally has proof that someone, somewhere did somebody wrong, but there's no information Paul can give him. Even if the guy wasn't out of his mind with terror and disease, he doesn't really know anything. "What was in the package," Mulder shouts at him, as if that means something. What if Paul told him? It was just dead meat. It's not enough to know you're being played. You have to figure out the game—something Mulder still hasn't quite realized. —ZH

| "SOFT LIGHT" | SEASON 2 / EPISODE 23
WRITTEN BY VINCE GILLIGAN
DIRECTED BY JAMES CONTNER |

BLACK HOLE SUNK

In which a great writer has an inauspicious debut.

At least the cold open is novel. Chester Banton (Tony Shalhoub) vaporizes another man with his shadow. The effects aren't all that convincing, and we've seen plenty of murders on the show; but the concept is so absurd that it pulls you in, if only because you want to find out what the hell is going on. One of the major flaws of the episode is that its premise can't satisfy that initial interest, relying instead on the audience's ignorance of "dark matter" and quantum physics to justify the scientifically implausible. Once people start trying to explain the situation, the threat turns goofy fast. But it works initially because it's so damn odd.

Shalhoub is a talented comedic and dramatic actor, but he isn't given much to do here beyond looking increasingly desperate. It's a committed performance, but without a chance to get to know the character beyond his immediate plight, the story loses much of its potential power. This is Vince Gilligan's first script for the show,[56] and while he already indicates an interest in the unpredictable repercussions of scientific arrogance, the ideas here aren't well formed. While Banton's horror with what he's become, and his efforts to avoid killing again, set him apart from the show's usual monsters, the episode quickly turns into a circular loop in which he warns

---

56 Written as a freelancer, in fact. Gilligan is best known now for creating and showrunning *Breaking Bad*, as well as its critically acclaimed spin-off *Better Call Saul*.

people not to approach him, they approach him anyway, and the inevitable occurs. There's a lack of humor that makes both the repetitive plot feel even blander and the thoroughly wonky science stand out even more. Gilligan would soon become one of *The X-Files* most accomplished writers,[57] but his debut is disappointingly flat.

Still, there's that striking cold open. The end isn't bad either; in the episode's best twist, Mulder calls in Mr. X to try to protect Banton from the authorities, only for Mr. X to betray him. If Deep Throat was a cheat code to the quest for truth, X is a walkthrough written by somebody who doesn't want to share his secrets, doesn't like you, and might not even be playing the same game. It's important to be reminded of just how dangerous he can be, and his appearance also provides some structural variation for an hour that could've used more variety.

The final shot, of Banton stuck in a room as a light flashes at him, is haunting. In their efforts to save him, Mulder and Scully ended up sticking the poor guy in a different kind of hell. Throughout "Soft Light," there are glimpses of the work Gilligan would do in future episodes; his knack for devising immediately gripping premises and nuanced villains (plus a fine sense of humor) will give us some classics down the road. But sometimes, even the brightest bulbs need some time to warm up. —ZH

SEASON 2 / EPISODE 24
WRITTEN BY FRANK SPOTNITZ
DIRECTED BY ROB BOWMAN

"OUR TOWN"

TASTES LIKE CHICKEN
In which format can only do so much.

"Our Town" begins in the most clichéd manner possible: A couple goes into the woods at night to make out, with horrible results. It's a setup that's been the starting point for roughly half a million horror movies, shows, and stories, and little is done to distinguish it here from those other iterations. The closest this sequence gets to novelty is the fact that the male half of the couple turns out to be the target of an intentional bait-and-switch instead of the woman, which at least distinguishes it from a standard-issue slasher.

The episode title is most likely an ironic reference to the 1938 Thornton Wilder play of the same name. The joke is obvious enough; the play was about small-town life (and death), and that's more or less what the episode is about, only with a sprinkling of cannibalism. Honestly, the joke is a little *too* obvious, which is indicative of the hour as a whole. This is Frank Spotnitz's second script after "End Game" (S2E17), and while his work is consistent, it takes few risks, going through what have already

---

57 See Season Four for a discussion of Gilligan's role as a staff writer.

become standard Monster of the Week motions. Once again, there's trouble in rural America. This time, instead of devil worship ("Die Hand Die Verletzt" [S2E14]) or alien-DNA injection ("Red Museum" [S2E10]), it's man-eating.

The only distinctive element of this story is the chicken factory operated by the main villain, because how often do you see chicken factories on TV? It's not enough to carry the rest, though. The personalities of the townsfolk are generated by casting rather than by the script, and apart from the sheriff's bland geniality (so you know he's hiding something) and the plant manager's icy contempt (so you know he's hiding something), we don't know a lot about any of these people.

To be fair, we do get some information about the antagonist. Walter Chaco (John Milford), the man who started this whole mess, is given some backstory to justify his choices. But that backstory also points to a deeper problem with the episode: yet another use of a native culture as a prop for plot purposes. In this case, it's a tribe in New Guinea who gave Chaco the idea that eating people would allow him and his community to live forever. The offensive stereotype of cannibalism is bad enough, but Chaco and the locals' insistence on wearing tribal masks and keeping sunken heads around smacks of misguided (and tacky) cultural appropriation. It might have been funny, if there was any indication that anyone working on the episode was in on the joke. —ZH

"ANASAZI" | SEASON 2 / EPISODE 25
WRITTEN BY CHRIS CARTER, FROM A STORY BY CARTER AND DAVID DUCHOVNY
DIRECTED BY R. W. GOODWIN

DOUBLING DOWN

In which the truth is inside a boxcar.

"Anasazi" has a lot of strong moments: some great acting work from both leads, an escalation of the major threat, a well-executed cliffhanger, and of course, the sudden and brutal death of Mulder's father. But this episode finds the show at a crossroads. The writers can either begin wrapping up the mythology that's been established, providing some resolution before moving on to other subjects, or they can expand outward from what's been established and add another story to the house of cards. They unfortunately chose the latter.

It's early enough in *The X-Files* run that it would've been easy to believe things could still be satisfactorily concluded. It's also unfair to judge a strong entry like this on the possibility of disappointment down the line. Still, it's troubling that instead of answering any big issues here, the show gives us only new directions. The script broadens the scope, with encoded defense department files, a group of old guys with secrets, and some old-fashioned Native American mysticism. Mulder keeps reaching for what's just beyond his grasp. Scully keeps struggling to make sure they both have jobs, even while her personal life continues to shrink.

"Anasazi" covers for its lack of immediate closure by pushing its heroes even closer to the edge. Mulder's apartment is gassed, and Duchovny plays it to the hilt, nearly alienating Scully and even going as far as to throw a punch at Skinner. For once, there's a plan in motion to get Mulder out of the way for good. First, they gas him, disrupt his mental state, and set him on edge. Then they murder his father and pin the crime on him. If it weren't for Scully, this tactic might have worked. Mulder's first instinct at the crime scene is to wait for the authorities, which certainly would have landed him in jail, where it wouldn't have been too hard to have him shivved.

Mulder's father's connection to the Cigarette Smoking Man is a smart twist because it provides better justification as to why Mulder has been allowed to get as far into everything as he has. It also enriches CSM's character, and his development over time is one of the few aspects of the mythology that never really stops giving. It's great to see him slowly change from a malevolent symbol of control to a flawed, even tragic, character.

Bringing back Krycek, even if only for a few minutes, is another good move, and there's a satisfying scene in which Mulder kicks the living crap out of him, only to get shot by Scully before he can do more permanent damage. The Lone Gunmen cameo is justified and fun, and the final scene sets the high-water mark for end-of-season cliffhangers. We get a train car full of dead bodies, then CSM's arrival, Mulder's disappearance from the car, and a firebombing.

Yet there are hints of possible problems to come. The sudden involvement of Native Americans makes thematic sense, given how long the group has suffered at the hands of the government. But it introduces an element of mysticism, with the promise that Mulder's coming had been "foretold." Mulder works well as a slightly crazed seeker of truth. The character doesn't need "Chosen One" status, especially one who slots so easily into the racist cliché of the "white savior," reducing a native culture to a crutch that only serves to help a Caucasian hero fulfill his destiny. Even if that implication weren't borderline offensive, the idea of prophecy fits poorly with the overall world of scientific and paranormal phenomena that *The X-Files* has built.

In the end, the elements of "Anasazi" don't entirely gel, although that opinion could be tainted by virtue of the fact that it serves as the first part of a much longer story. Even so, it's possible to sense here, in this moment, that this is as good as the mythology is going to get in terms of making sense. Mulder and Scully will keep finding new sources of information, other people will get shot, indeterminate menace will ensue, and we may never have this end the way it really needs to. The outward growth may be very entertaining now, but you also get the unnerving sense that it's not going to stop. —ZH

"THE BLESSING WAY"	SEASON 3 / EPISODE 1 WRITTEN BY CHRIS CARTER DIRECTED BY R. W. GOODWIN
"PAPER CLIP"	SEASON 3 / EPISODE 2 WRITTEN BY CHRIS CARTER DIRECTED BY ROB BOWMAN

A LEGACY OF ASHES

In which this was all done for your own good.

Season Three is the one season of *The X-Files* in which everything works. The mythology seems like it's heading somewhere. The Monster of the Week episodes have the highest hit-to-miss ratio in this show's history (and the hits are *really* big hits). And, as a capper, Darin Morgan turns in three episodes that rank among the best television episodes of all time. It's incredibly consistent, handily taking the show from cult sensation to genuine sensation and major part of the '90s cultural landscape.

And the season premiere is one of its weakest episodes.

When it dealt with the serious compromises the West made to stay ahead of communism after World War II was over, *The X-Files* was at its best, filtering some of the awful actions the United States had taken during the Cold War through the prism of alien conspiracy theories to give them a new spin. Episodes like that—like the season's second episode, "Paper Clip," in fact—are the best the conspiracy story line had to offer. Season Three is chock-full of these mythology episodes (and one that brilliantly sends them up). But when *The X-Files* tried to engage in New Age spiritualism, it tended to completely fall apart. And too much of "The Blessing Way" is pseudo-mystical hogwash.

Scully spends this episode running around, trying to find Mulder and the men she believes killed him. A motivated Scully is one of the very best things *The X-Files* has to offer, and Gillian Anderson makes the most out of racing across the country to try to find Mulder, facing off with Skinner, and just generally being a pain in the ass to the Syndicate,[1] which gets its proper introduction in this episode.

But every time we drift over to Mulder, lying in the midst of some sort of Navajo ritual, the episode feels like remnants from Chris Carter's college diary. At the time, no other show on TV was doing sequences like the one in which Mulder's father delivers lengthy monologues about how the quest for truth and justice is a holy one, so it was easier to forgive them. But they have aged incredibly poorly. Mulder languishes between life and death, in a weird purple-y afterlife, and it turns out to be a lot like that mid-century show *This Is Your Life*, with Deep Throat and

---

1   The Syndicate refers to the group of men who are running the alien conspiracy.

Papa Mulder and the whole gang showing up to talk to Mulder about his deepest motivations. The answer to "How did Mulder get out of the burning boxcar?" turns out to be "Don't ask any questions!"

To state my position up front here: I have a higher tolerance for the mythology than a lot of fans do. If the story just keeps getting bigger and bigger and more nebulous, fine by me. Pile mysteries on top of mysteries until the groaning weight of the artifice topples in on itself. As long as the character stuff and the plotting are generally tight on an episode-by-episode level, I don't mind that the central mysteries can get so big that they seem to encompass all of human history.

But smaller questions of how or why certain moments happened to our characters need to be answered. Did we need to see Mulder climb through the flames only to get buried by a rockslide? Not necessarily, but it would have been one amazing scene, and it would have handily redramatized the lengths he's willing to go to for his quest. It's not an egregious cheat that we don't really figure out how Mulder gets out of the boxcar, outside of the suggestion that he did so painfully, but it's a cheat nonetheless, and when taken together with the series' penchant for half-baked mysticism, it makes for an episode that's half deflating after the ramp-up of "Anasazi" (S2E25).

It is, luckily, then, a great Scully episode. It's the episode in which Mulder's mission really becomes her mission. Scully starts to lose damn near everything to this cause. She gets fired from her job! She pulls a gun on Skinner! She plays games with very dangerous men to avenge her partner's near-death! Her sister[2] gets shot by Krycek and a goon who've mistaken her for Scully! Scully may not believe everything she hears, but she's finally reached a point where she needs to know just what in the world would be worth so much destruction.

Ultimately, "The Blessing Way" is caught in limbo, seemingly designed to keep us in suspense about a bunch of things we know won't happen. Mulder's not going to die and become Scully's spectral adviser, nor is the Syndicate going to catch up to Scully and eliminate her. And yet "Blessing Way" *does* suggest a greater sense of danger. Maybe Mulder and Scully won't lose their lives, but they can certainly lose everything else.

The mythology arc is much more successful when it focuses less on the mystery out there beyond the stars and more on the very prosaic evils men can do to each other by their own hands. If "The Blessing Way" demonstrated the former, then "Paper Clip," perhaps the best mythology episode of them all, more than proves the latter.

---

2 Melissa Scully (Melinda McGraw) is an intriguing addition to this two-parter, as her New Age spirituality stands out as a sort of nonconfrontational faith within a world in which belief systems are often incredibly combative and dichotomous. Her beliefs don't really *fit* within the world of the show, which may be why she was killed off, but Carter will offer a sort of riff on this type of character with the female lead of his next TV series, *Millennium*. (Though no one on that show ever figured out what to do with that character either. Maybe TV just isn't built for this sort of mysticism.)

"Paper Clip" works because it understands that a conspiracy theory is a way of reordering the universe, a kind of religion. Things will never go the right way because the people in control make sure of it and you cannot stop them. They're the ones who keep the populace cowed and ignorant. They killed JFK. They're hiding the truth about the aliens. They know about zero-point energy or alternative biofuels or cars that get six hundred miles to the gallon, but they're keeping these things from you to keep the old order in place. They, they, they. Despite the powerlessness inherent in such thinking, a conspiracy theory is comforting. If you can blame someone else for everything that happens, then there's no need to take responsibility for your own actions. Bad things don't happen because the universe is terrifying and random. Bad things happen because the men in the shadows are doing them for their own nefarious purposes. We're all pawns in a much larger plan.

But real conspiracies are prosaic, often carried out in the open. Operation Paperclip[3] was a real-life and horrible government secret, but people eventually found out about it. The people involved all had to say, "Well, we did it for the good of our country. Would we have won the Cold War without those scientists?" For the most part, Americans shrugged and took the government at its word. They felt there was nothing to be done about it.

"Paper Clip" is one of the defining episodes of *The X-Files* because it somehow expands the conspiracy into the kind of omnipresent, colossal force you could never hope to fight and simultaneously brings it down to a more practical level. The Cigarette Smoking Man is a many-tentacled monster with hands in every possible government plot, but he can also be defeated by a resourceful FBI assistant director and a bunch of people with top-notch memorization skills.

The smartest thing "Paper Clip" does is tie the larger alien conspiracy in to things that actually happened. The bargains that the United States and other Western nations struck in an attempt to defeat communism during the Cold War should have made those nations' citizens take pause and stop to think about the moral cost of their lifestyles, but we almost never did. The Soviets had their own versions of these concessions, as two superpowers engaged in an intellectual arms race designed to make sure that both sides would keep their eyes open in a gigantic staring contest. When you need to stay one step ahead of an enemy who could wipe you off the face of the planet, you do some pretty bad things. Very bad things happened. Operation Paperclip is just the tip of the iceberg.

The fact that even now we still can't see the rest of the iceberg is precisely what keeps conspiracy theories alive. "Paper Clip" works because it never suggests anything below that visible tip that would give the conspiracy's members super-

---

3   Operation Paperclip involved the United States recruiting Nazi scientists, some of whom were very high up in the Nazi government, to work for the Americans post-World War II. The most famous scientist recruited in this fashion was the rocket genius Wernher von Braun.

human powers. The Syndicate members are men and nothing more. Every deed carried out in this episode could be executed by any man with the will and desire to do so. Alien/human hybrids? Plausible in a science-fiction universe like this one and something that could be handled by Nazi doctors who'd tested the capabilities of the human body in the Holocaust. A giant warehouse containing tissue samples and medical information from everyone who received a smallpox vaccination?[4] Eminently plausible, if you're willing to assume the government would want such a thing. A UFO hiding out in a mountain base? If the government's going to have one, where else would they keep it? The CIA being called in to clean up a problem involving U.S. citizens? Pretty sure we've been doing this for a while now. Once you accept that one dark thing has been done "for the greater good" and kept secret, it becomes easy to believe that the world is full of insidious evil, guarded by powerful men but slowly seeping its way into the cracks of everyday life. And it's out to get you.

One of the best things about this episode is the way it suggests that all of the men Mulder has been gobbling up information from are, indeed, just messing with him, dressing up sharply and leaking him information that will keep him within spitting distance of the truth but never quite in reach of it. Scully is able to see through their lies, to see that much of it could very well be designed solely to keep her partner away from the more prosaic truths that would really infuriate him. This is neatly encapsulated in the single image of Scully staring down that long mining tunnel at the tiny figure of a hybrid that seems to grow before her eyes as the ship's light stretches its silhouette. The conspiracy becomes something normal and comprehensible but still frightening.

The story of the United States after the Cold War is the slow, dawning realization that we aren't who we said we were. We as a nation aspire to ideals that are good and worthy, but the failures of our particular system, and of the men and women who run it, have led to a long series of trade-offs between our better angels and our selfish pragmatism. When you make compromises, it's inevitable that horrible things will happen around the edges of those decisions. Like all humans, we have a poor view of the big picture and a focused eye on what's in our immediate vicinity. Mulder discovers a photograph of his father standing next to a monster of a man, smiling. We are not who we think we are. The iceberg looms in the dark, and nothing is scarier than what we can't see just below the surface. —TVDW

S3 E1-2

---

4   Scully and Mulder discovering a giant room full of files—"Lots and lots of files!" Scully breathlessly intones—is one of the most chilling moments of the series, precisely because of how *normal* it all is.

SEASON 3 / EPISODE 3
WRITTEN BY HOWARD GORDON
DIRECTED BY KIM MANNERS

PINBALL WIZARD

In which power falls into the wrong hands.

When it first aired, "D.P.O." was greeted with a certain amount of scorn from the fan community. After three episodes in which the show's continuing story line seemed to take off into the stratosphere, how could the show simply return to Monster of the Week episodes? How could *Mulder and Scully*? Weren't there bigger fish to fry? Yet here we are in the middle of nowhere with a disaffected teen who can control the lightning.

But "D.P.O." suggests, in its own way, why *The X-Files* exploded in popularity in Season Three: The show's direction, always good, made the leap from consistently interesting to look at to consistently cinematic. This is probably the result of Fox, the network that aired the show, giving the series a larger budget, allowing it to take its time with more intricate and intriguing shot setups. Even in future seasons, when *The X-Files*' scripts would start to become more variable in quality, the direction was almost always top notch. The series took chances on big, cinematic sequences and moments, and they would usually pay off.

You can see the difference in quality in the opening of "D.P.O.," which introduces us to Darin, our MOTW, a teenager who's killing people by conducting lightning. His attack on a fellow teen who hogged his favorite video game at an arcade is told almost entirely through visuals, with a rock song rising on the soundtrack. It's appropriately paced, cleanly edited, and briskly shot. Few of the teasers in Seasons One and Two were as well constructed as this one, and this level of cinematic verve quickly became the show's norm.

The guest casting, always good, also reaches new heights in Season Three. "D.P.O." stars Giovanni Ribisi as Darin and Jack Black as his closest compatriot, Zero. Black here plays a younger, less fully developed version of the same guy he often does. Ribisi perhaps leans too heavily on a vacant-eyed stare toward the camera to convey the horror of what Darin is doing, but there's something very true to the way he depicts a teenager thrilling at being able to use his powers for destruction.

"D.P.O." also indicates how the show had gotten better at having Mulder and Scully drive the action forward. The duo is solidly one step behind Darin, instead of being shuttled from place to place like they're observers in a travelogue. They come up with a good theory on what it is that makes Darin tick, find him via his initials in the arcade game, and have a series of standoffs with him. It's not the greatest police work in the world, but in Season Two, the agents would often seem like they were guest stars in their own series. Now, their crime solving is a little more active.

In many ways, "D.P.O." is a well done but garden-variety episode of a show that could do so much more, which can't help but make it feel just a bit disappointing after two episodes in which the series' mythology broke itself wide open. But there are so many sequences that confidently walk the tricky line between horror and broad comedy[5] that the episode suggests the series was closing in on a firmer sense of its best self. The willingness of the episode to push up against the fourth wall in its conclusion also speaks to its experimentation; Darin psychokinetically flipping through TV channels only to land on the episode's closing credits suggests that he, too, is watching this show alongside us. *The X-Files* had every reason to rest on its laurels at this point in its run, but instead it's pushing into new territory and seeing what new ghouls and goblins it can turn up. That "D.P.O." appears to us—then and now—as a middle-of-the-road episode indicates just how good the show had become. —TVDW

<table>
<tr><td>SEASON 3 / EPISODE 4
WRITTEN BY DARIN MORGAN
DIRECTED BY DAVID NUTTER</td><td>"CLYDE BRUCKMAN'S
FINAL REPOSE"</td></tr>
</table>

ALL THERE IS

In which it's possible to know too much.

Heart attack. Car accident. Heart attack. Car accident. Lung cancer. Going out for cigarettes at 3 A.M., crossing the street when a drunk driver makes an illegal left. Bowel cancer. Heart attack. Drowning. Car accident. Slipping in the tub and breaking your neck and nobody knows until the neighbors notice the smell. Cancer. Cancer. Cancer.

It's not much, is it? The way our worlds end. Bangs for some, whimpers for most, but the circumstances only matter in the moment. And yet, because our consciousness allows us the questionable luxury of knowing it has a conclusion, we keep asking why. What causes cancer? Was there ice on the road? Is a secret government conspiracy hiding the truth about aliens from a gullible public? "Clyde Bruckman's Final Repose" is a remarkable episode because it's funny, suspenseful, does well by Scully and Mulder, and creates some indelible one-off characters. It also addresses our mortality without blinking, balancing an almost unbearably brutal pessimism with just enough hope to be honest. Or maybe it's not hope. Maybe it's the understanding that, miserable or not, this is the life we get, and we might as well try to live it.

---

5 The cow barbecue is a particular highlight.

Clyde Bruckman (Peter Boyle) isn't a happy man, and his unhappiness stems from a curse he's lived with all of his adult life: He sees how things fit together, but only because they all wind up in the same place. Boyle's innate charisma and humor help to soften the horror of Bruckman's circumstances, but the longer the episode goes on, the more obvious the man's despair becomes. Anyone who has lived with clinical depression might recognize the signs of such hopelessness, but whereas a person suffering from mental illness might have recourse to therapy or medication to ease their suffering, Bruckman has no such option. His problem isn't a question of his brain chemistry, but of the power of his own thoughts, and it's the sort of thinking that's impossible to undo. His life has lost all mystery. Without the element of surprise, existence becomes mechanical and routine. Have you ever tried to unopen a Christmas present?

Time spent with his character could've been agonizingly miserable, and yet "Clyde Bruckman" is brutally funny throughout, finding humor in death, gore, and just the regular foolishness. Darin Morgan's script[6] finds the writer moving further off-format than his debut; the structure nominally follows the Monster of the Week tradition, with a monster, a handful of unsettling kill scenes, and a confrontation that ends in gunshots. But the "monster" here is hard to pin down. The obvious answer is the murderous bellhop (Stuart Charno) who kills psychics because he believes he has no control over his actions. But the longer the episode goes on, the harder it becomes to shake the idea that the bellhop is just a symptom of some deeper inevitability.

Morgan accomplishes what the show had to do if it ever wanted its MOTW episodes to be more than pulp, repurposing familiar tools to unexpected, soulful ends: He questions its very premise. While Mulder has been the butt of jokes before this hour, "Clyde Bruckman" is the first episode to ever call his search for answers—the search at the heart of his and Scully's work, and of the series as a whole—into doubt. Mulder has given up so many years to uncovering secrets, and in some ways, he's as pathetic as Bruckman, isolated from family and nearly all of his friends, squandering any potential for an existence outside of work. Perhaps the only difference between the two men is that Mulder hasn't actually found the truth he so desperately covets. Mulder is smart enough to realize that there's more going on than he knows, but not smart enough to understand that if he ever found exactly what that "more" was, he could end up like Bruckman—a man trudging through life like a corpse waiting for a coffin. Or perhaps he'd just crack, start working as a bellhop, and murder strangers because he thinks he's destined to.

---

6 His second (!!!) for the show after "Humbug" (S2E20), and arguably his best; this is my favorite episode of the series.

Is there any hope? Well, there's Scully. While Bruckman ribs Mulder throughout the episode,[7] Scully's calm, sensible presence makes a strong impression on the older man, and he on her. Their conversation in the hotel room is wonderful, as Boyle makes potentially embarrassing lines sound sincere, abashed, and slightly amused, and Anderson strikes just the right tone between amusement and irritation. When she breaks down and asks him how she dies, he simply tells her, "You don't." It's an exchange that could be taken literally, but it works best here as a beautiful and merciful untruth. In "Clyde Bruckman," Scully represents the best of us—not perfect, but someone whose sanity and compassion keep Mulder from going off the deep end. She realizes that life is as much about living as it is about understanding. While that knowledge doesn't always make her happy, it at least lets her be present in a way Mulder rarely is—and in a way Bruckman, trapped in the only future he can see, can never be.

The episode ends with Bruckman's suicide. It's a death he predicts earlier in the hour, in perhaps the script's most effective (and elegant) story beats. He and Scully are killing time in a hotel room, and she asks him about *his* death; and he tells her he sees them ending up in bed together. It's an exchange that could have felt inordinately lecherous, were it not for Boyle's measured, wry delivery and Anderson's dismissive but not unkind response. But it plays as a joke regardless. It's only at the very close of the episode, in which Mulder and Scully find Bruckman's corpse in his bed, and Scully sits down beside him and takes his hand, that the joke turns in on itself and becomes something much more meaningful.

The scene breaks me a little, every time I see it.[8] The older I get—and the easier it is for me to see the pieces of my life behind me—the more I'm able to relate to Bruckman's dilemma. I'm not a psychic (thank goodness), but anyone who has lived long enough can understand the exhaustion that comes out of seeing the same patterns repeating themselves, the same routines done over and over with less and less of the original magic. I cling to unexpected moments like a miser clings to gold, knowing that every year brings fewer of them, and the longer this goes on, the more likely it is that any surprise will be a bad one. Bruckman leaves a note but no explanation, but why would he need to? The entire hour has given you all the explanations you'd need. Who'd want to stick around if this was all you had left?

All that said, this episode always makes me happy. I can't explain it. After all, if a heart attack, or cancer, or a plastic bag over your head are the only ways this thing can end for any of us, what's the point? There's no moral here. It's unlikely that

---

7 Bruckman: "You know, there are worse ways to go, but I can't think of a more undignified way than autoerotic asphyxiation."
   Mulder: "Why are you telling me that?"
8 The whole episode does, really.

any of us will have to suffer Bruckman's particular curse, but we still know we're going to die no matter what we do. And yet we keep going anyway. We keep going because there's still blank space on the calendar. We keep going because we need to see and experience things to believe them. Hell, maybe we keep going because there really is some riddle we can solve that will make all of this better. Maybe we can save everyone, and ourselves, and the sun will shine tomorrow and those lotto numbers will come in. Maybe Scully never will die. It's a lie, of course. But there are worse ones to believe. —ZH

| **"THE LIST"** | SEASON 3 / EPISODE 5
WRITTEN AND DIRECTED BY CHRIS CARTER |

DEATH ROW

In which violent men meet violent ends.

The X-Files has recurring characters and basic continuity, but non-mythology episodes are closed circuits. The bland ones are bland because they never develop beyond their original conceit. "The List" is a good example of this kind of episode. A prisoner is executed but swears he'll come back from the dead to avenge himself on five people who wronged him. Mulder and Scully show up and try to stop him. They fail. That's pretty much it. The side plots have so little effect on the main narrative as to be basically padding.

What makes "The List" interesting at all is that it really nails the *look* of a great episode. The set design and cinematography are the highlights here; beyond that, there are a couple of good lines and a few scary moments. There are nice touches to be found, with creepy maggots and some shockingly gory deaths. Because the set design is as good as it is, the thinness of the episode is easier to accept. The unnerving prison setting and rain forest–level humidity are almost enough to compensate for the lack of interesting writing.

Ultimately, though, the fact that the dead man is able to rise up and kill from beyond the grave just because he's smart and found some religion isn't enough. There's no second act to that. The concept isn't distinctive, and the episode leans too heavily on amassing a standard body count with uninteresting characters dying horribly. This one might get good marks for style, but it barely scrapes by on its content. —ZH

SWIPE LEFT

In which it sucks to be single.

This episode's take on online dating isn't as relevant as it used to be, but some things never change. There will always be predators like Virgil Incanto (Timothy Carhart) aiming to take advantage of lonely women by telling all the right lies. But it takes more to elevate such a premise to above average. Although the episode's depiction of single women as targets is chillingly plausible, it feels underexplored, like a writer taking advantage of a trope without digging into its origins or underlying mechanisms. We see this especially in the two-dimensional characterization of the female victims; they aren't given much personality beyond insecurity and shyness.

Still, Virgil is wonderfully gross, draining his victims of their fatty tissue and leaving corpses in his wake like masses of bloody pudding. Carhart is polite and nonthreatening enough to be believably appealing to someone who doesn't want to get hurt, and it's fun watching him transition between seduction mode and contempt for all living things. It's interesting, too, how Virgil takes refuge in the home of a woman he dated when Mulder and Scully close in. There's something very vampirish about needing your victim to let you in before you can murder her.

Worth mentioning, too, is the resistance Scully faces from a sexist cop who doesn't think that women should be allowed on cases where a killer is specifically targeting women—which seems in its way as dated as the chat rooms and email conversations. Again, the routine misogyny that a woman in Scully's line of work would face in the office is worth talking about, but the script relies on throwing out men who are obviously in the wrong in a way that doesn't force audiences to confront these issues with enough nuance.

The overall surface-level approach here keeps the episode from being particularly effective. Virgil's M.O. is certainly distinct, but he engages in such an elaborate process to kill someone that once he's finally uncovered, he's not much of a threat. The reactionary take on the horrors of computer technology here is too knee-jerk to be insightful. But at least the effects are fun!! —ZH

| "THE WALK" | SEASON 3 / EPISODE 7
WRITTEN BY JOHN SHIBAN
DIRECTED BY ROB BOWMAN |

PHANTOM LIMBS

In which astral projection is used for murder,
because what else would you do with it?

"The Walk," the first script credited to John Shiban,[9] is meat-and-potatoes *X-Files*. A ghost seems to be killing people at a military hospital. Mulder and Scully get called in to try to stop said ghost. The real answer is, of course, what no one would have expected. Along the way, there are some strikingly shot sequences, a few legitimate scares, and some pretty poor acting. Naturally, that makes this a good point to talk about the way the *X-Files* writers' room was shifting and changing.

In the first two seasons of any show there are usually a few iconoclastic voices within the room that are gradually shifted out of the way or moved on to other projects. The staff will also tend to be whittled down as time goes on to a smaller core group. The bulk of the writing in the first season of *The X-Files* was done by Chris Carter, the team of Glen Morgan and James Wong, and the team of Alex Gansa and Howard Gordon.[10] The same dynamic prevailed in Season Two, though Morgan and Wong left midway through, and Darin Morgan, Vince Gilligan, and Frank Spotnitz each made their first contributions to the series that year.

The third season of a show is often when the writers' room solidifies into the one that will shape the overall voice of the show for seasons to come, and *The X-Files* is no exception. Whereas the writing staff throughout the first two seasons played around with many different styles and premises in order to figure out what the show should be, Season Three's staff (undoubtedly one of the best of the era) was designed to rein in the experimentation and instead boil the show down to its essence.

Carter is there for the big-picture stuff and any detour into mysticism. Spotnitz will become Carter's right-hand man for the alien conspiracy plot, though he'll also branch out by taking the paranoid ethos of the mythology episodes and injecting it into more mundane tales. Gordon (who will leave the show after its fourth season) will be the one most dedicated to crafting the kind of vaguely pretentious, horrifically scary MOTW episodes common to the first two seasons. Gilligan (who finally becomes a staff writer in Season Three) is capable of writing a tense monster tale or a goofy comedic episode, and he's most interested in creating interesting and compelling monsters and examining the Mulder and Scully relationship. Shiban is a utility infielder, filling in on any and all types of episodes, always solid, rarely transcendent.

---

9 Shiban would stay with the series through to its ninth season.
10 Though Gansa left after Season One, Gordon continued with the show by himself.

Darin Morgan is around this season as resident iconoclast, a role that would be filled in future seasons by the Morgan and Wong team, then by Gilligan and Carter.

At this point, yes, *The X-Files* is a hit show, but it's also a show that keeps winking toward its origins, seeming less formulaic than it actually is, particularly when you don't consume episodes one after the other. More than any other drama in its weight class, *The X-Files* is always a collection of individual voices coming together to form a greater whole.

And while this approach can make for a more colorful and dynamic series, it can also lead to weaker episodes like "The Walk," which feels as if it stemmed from an early draft of Shiban's that simply didn't get the love and care it might have on a series in which the writers worked much more closely together as a unit. The amputee who's revealed to be the villain is far more intimidating as a shadow than he is as an actual flesh-and-blood character. When he's just a shadow, astrally projected outward to drag a woman to the bottom of the pool, he's a terrific villain. But when he's overacting in his hospital bed, he loses his menace.

Still, plenty of stuff here is fun in that *X-Files*–Mad Libs way. The setting of a military hospital is well realized, and the other characters around the edges[11] are all quickly and neatly sketched in. Rob Bowman's direction is terrific throughout, whether it's backlighting the very real meeting of the men who were injured in the line of duty, such that they all appear as weird, shadowy ghosts; or the swimming pool scene, which is an excellent scare sequence, thanks to the way the image of a man who isn't there darts through the water after a swimmer.

If the script has problems, its storytelling at least offers some refreshingly thoughtful political commentary. There's a frank consideration in this episode of the way the government fails its veterans, often abandoning young men to suffer death or worse instead of providing adequate support when the fighting is over. It could be more pointed, perhaps, but even so, with a better villain, this might have been an all-time classic. —TVDW

| S3 E7 |

---

11 Who include a man played by talented character actor Willie Garson (from *NYPD Blue*, *Sex and the City*, and *Friends*—to name a few).

DRAFTING THE TEAM

Chris Carter is known for nurturing up-and-coming talent, not only by who he casts, but also who he brings on board to write alongside him. At the beginning of "the adventure," as Howard Gordon calls it, the core writing team consisted of James Wong and Glen Morgan, Gordon himself and Alex Gansa, and Carter. By Season Two, Carter had tapped another key player to join the show: Frank Spotnitz.

Spotnitz remembers reconnecting with Carter, whom he first met when he joined a book group in Los Angeles: "[I'd] never written professionally for anyone, [and was only just] out of film school, [when I came] on to the show. I was incredibly green, incredibly ill-prepared, but it was the perfect show for me; it was exactly the show I would have watched when I was a kid. I understood something about it right from the beginning, and Chris saw that and he threw me right in.

"The first week I was there, I was in the editing room, and two weeks later I was mixing sound; [Chris] didn't respect hierarchy, and he just gave me responsibility right away. I think within three years I went from staff writer to executive producer of that show, and it was because I was stronger as a producer first, and he gave me the time and the shelter to grow as a writer, and I did. It was my second film school those first two years."

Chris Carter explains the show's writing process as, "[First] the writers would come up with their stories. They would pitch them to the room, and then Frank Spotnitz, most often, would sit and work with the writers, and plot the stories. Basically, the idea would be refined, explored, synthesized through that process." And through this process, as Howard Gordon describes it, Carter facilitated a creative atmosphere in which many distinct voices and visions could thrive: "Glen [Morgan] and Jim [James Wong] had a filmography that was much more steeped in horror and B movies. I had more of a character-based approach. [Alex Gansa and I] always started with 'Who is a character who might live in this universe? Whom we might want to tell a story around?' We all brought something different.

"Chris, of course, who created it, had this mythology and this relationship which he kind of ultimately is the steward of. It was interesting, and to Chris's great credit, he let each of us have our process and also our autonomy on our respective episodes. That kind of cooperative and competitive—in all the best possible ways—environment, where we learned to think from each other and I think there was always a great deal of respect all around [. . .]

which was so cool, because in some short order it would [become] this hit, and this international phenomenon. . . . It was fun. Kind of felt a little bit like a garage band that suddenly became this thing."

Another writer who cut his teeth working on *The X-Files*, and whose voice would become integral to the continued success of the show, was Vince Gilligan. Spotnitz recalls how impressed he and Carter were with Gilligan's freelance contribution, "Soft Light" (S2E23): "His episode . . . which did not go untouched, was nonetheless extraordinarily good for somebody who wasn't in the writers' room and didn't know where all the trip wires were. And so, Chris asked him to join the show in Season Three. And I think for [Gilligan], having been living alone in Virginia writing movies, he loved being in a collaborative environment and loved being in that writer's room. He was a terrific writer on the page, his dialogue and characterization and cinematic vision were always remarkable, but I think his sense of structure and plotting . . . all of those things grew. I think for all of us [they] did. We were doing twenty-four episodes a year. That's a lot, and every one had its own set of rules, that had to track internally, and I think that's why [Gilligan] blossomed on *The X-Files* and was able to go on to do *Breaking Bad*."

A wild-card addition to the group was Darin Morgan, whose inimitable voice lent an exciting and irrevocable new dimension to the series. Darin's brother Glen Morgan was the one who first roped him into working on the show. Darin says, "Between the first and second season, [Glen] suggested I work on a story idea, that he could maybe give me a job. And that was the episode called 'Blood' (S2E3), which was his story. He had told me to try to develop the premise, and I didn't get far at all, and then he called up and said, 'We need to use that story,' because some script had come in and it wasn't usable. And, so Jim [James Wong] had to crank out a script quickly, so the deal was if I came up and helped them break the story they'd give me story credit, but they would have to write it.

"After that I was offered a part on the staff, right after that, which—none of that made any sense. There was no reason to hire me because [Chris] hadn't read anything I'd written. . . . But Howard Gordon and Chris seemed to think I'd kind of gotten the show from the limited time that they [had spent with me]." Darin felt he was "ill-suited" to write for the show since he was mainly interested in being a comedy writer, and at first his brother agreed with his assessment, because as Darin puts it, "I've always had a problem meeting deadlines, which is all of television right? Television writing on staff is basically just meeting deadlines; that's the main kind of requirement."

As it turned out, Darin was afforded some time to settle in, without too much pressure to churn out script after script. Darin remembers: "I've never asked Chris about it, [so] I don't know if this is intentional or not. But I joined right after the beginning of the second season and then I only had to write [one episode] that first year, and it came right at the end of the season. So, I had kind of an entire season to just sort of watch and participate. And then the next season Chris did the exact same exact thing with Vince Gilligan, since he'd written ["Soft Light"] at the end of Season Two, [before joining] right after the beginning of Season Three, but then only did one episode that season and it was at the end of the season. And so I don't know if that was Chris's plan of not wanting to put too much pressure on a new writer who had never been on staff. Because, shows now don't do that. . . . The shows now really take their young writers and really kind of crack the whip. I've never asked Chris about it, but I've retroactively looked back and I'm so thankful [for] not having that immediate pressure."

Carter, for his part, refuses to accept all the glory when it comes to the success of the series: "[Although] I'm the creator of the show, it's really [been] the showcase of so many great talented storytellers."

| "OUBLIETTE" | SEASON 3 / EPISODE 8
WRITTEN BY CHARLES GRANT CRAIG
DIRECTED BY KIM MANNERS |

UNDERGROUND

In which future sci-fi favorite Jewel Staite gets kidnapped.

Watching *The X-Files'* early seasons is often watching some of your favorite actors of the future get an early break. Take, for instance, the always welcome Jewel Staite, who would go on to become a favorite of genre TV fans (thanks to her work in *Firefly,* among other cult series) but is here just a little kid who gets kidnapped by a creepy department-store photographer and locked in an underground dungeon. What's more, watching "Oubliette" is a lesson in why an actress like Staite went on to a bright career, while Tracey Ellis, who plays the woman she becomes psychically linked to, didn't, really. So much of the reason "Oubliette" works—and it works quite well—is thanks to Staite, who never lets her character, Amy, devolve into a generic damsel in distress amid a fittingly moody episode, all shadows and camera flashes.

The photographer villain kidnaps Amy from her bed at night; meanwhile, one of his former victims, a woman named Lucy, starts to feel whatever is happening to

Amy as it happens. Mulder and Scully somehow discover this and use Lucy to track down Amy before anything bad can happen to her. What none of the above conveys, however, is just how impressively dark and occasionally moving this episode is. It's about people who have had their lives cruelly interrupted, whose forward progress is stalled by a past that keeps returning to haunt them. Mulder's sister, of course, could fit the same description, but "Oubliette" is much more interested in the way her abduction affected *Mulder*, who was left amid the ashes of Samantha's disappearance and reordered his own inner world to make sense of them. Neither Lucy nor Mulder are able to escape the trauma of abduction, even if they see it through different lenses.

"Oubliette" belongs to a subcategory of *X-Files* episodes that are consistently satisfying—episodes in which the monster is a human being, and the paranormal element is used to catch him, not to facilitate his vile tastes. The villain is a very human, nonparanormal kidnapper, and the show feels almost no need to give him the sympathy it gives its greatest paranormal monsters. He deserves that bullet in his back at episode's end. He's a creep, and the show suggests the link between his victims is a kind of karmic comeuppance for the bad he's done over the years. Indeed, the scene in which he shoots photo after photo of Amy in the dark may be one of the most genuinely unsettling sequences in the series. Other episodes provide safe horrors. This one gets under your skin and fills you with dread.

"Oubliette" matches its thematic darkness with visual darkness. All of the scenes inside the dungeon[12] where Amy is held may as well consist of complete blackness with a soundtrack. Few shows that followed in *The X-Files'* wake were this comfortable with shutting off all of the lights and letting your brain fill in the gaps. It is this kind of cinematic boldness that consistently set even a standard-issue *X-Files* episode like "Oubliette" apart from any number of knockoffs that aired around the same time. There's nothing particularly new or different about the story of locating a kidnapping victim, outside of that psychic link, but the cinematography, editing, and overall storytelling here are truly exceptional. Mulder and Scully's increased agency also plays a huge part in the episode's effectiveness. Instead of simply following Lucy around wherever her intuition leads her, Mulder and Scully actively piece together the clues she gives them, assembling a large enough picture to find Amy's prison.

The weakest link here is Ellis's performance. Instead of appearing to relive the worst days of her life, she seems like she's been heavily dosed with Valium. This acting choice makes for a dreary heaviness that threatens to take the episode down with it. Otherwise, Staite does nice work with a thankless role (one that mostly consists of screaming), and Michael Chieffo is very good as the show's latest all-too-human monster.

S3 E8

---

12 Also known as . . . drum roll . . . an oubliette.

It doesn't help, though, that this is yet another episode to go to the well of "violence against women is the best way to provoke audience sympathy." *The X-Files* has more latitude to tell these sorts of stories than other, similar shows,[13] thanks to how vibrant and interesting Scully is, and because the show is stronger at characterization on the whole. However, an overreliance on "women in peril" stories can be cheap and borderline indefensible. "Oubliette" toes the line but manages to be effective, thanks to the characterization of both Amy and Lucy (at least on the page, if not in the performance of the latter).

This episode is another sign of how thoroughly the show had figured itself out in Season Three. It blends the things the show already does well and constructs an emotional core at its center by so vividly showing how Mulder will grasp at any straw he can find to save Amy. Then, just when you think things might have become too bleak, it adds just a touch of heart. *The X-Files*, while not sentimental, has a romantic soul. Episodes like "Oubliette" bare this soul in full force. —TVDW

| "NISEI" | SEASON 3 / EPISODE 9
WRITTEN BY CHRIS CARTER, HOWARD GORDON, AND FRANK SPOTNITZ
DIRECTED BY DAVID NUTTER |

BABY, YOU ARE GONNA MISS THAT TRAIN

In which the mythology almost seems like it
will make sense at some point.

Season Three is the last season in which the mythology is wholly rewarding. There are good mythology episodes in every subsequent season of the series' original run, up until Nine.[14] But, for the most part, this is the last season in which it still feels like things will eventually make sense, even as it becomes obvious that the story is getting too big to ever resolve satisfactorily.

Interestingly, throughout the original run of *The X-Files*, most of the buzz around the show was specifically about its mythology. You can chart the series' rise and fall based on how successful the mythology episodes were—these episodes even had higher viewership numbers than the stand-alones. Today, while some of the mythology episodes remain entertaining, the prevailing consensus is that the stand-alone episodes are the ones that have stood the test of time. Generally, that's true, but there's still something to be said for the way the mythology episodes shaped our experience of *The X-Files* then and now. We were really invested in this

---

13 Think *Criminal Minds*.

14 The less said about what the mythology becomes in the two revival seasons of the 2010s . . . well, we'll get to that.

stuff back in the day. We had theories and ideas. We speculated about how all of the pieces fit together.

It's not hard to see why. In episodes like "Nisei," *The X-Files* has the drive of a big-budget action film. These episodes were bigger than pretty much anything else on television, and they featured our protagonists at their most motivated. The three central questions of *The X-Files*—"What happened to Mulder's sister?" and "What do the aliens want?" and "What happened to Scully?"—were all so personal and pressing to our characters that they always pushed harder for answers in mythology episodes than they might when investigating a stand-alone case.

At their best, the mythology episodes also played off a particular tension not always indulged in the rest of the show. They pushed the viewer to accept that much of what Mulder believed might be completely inaccurate, specifically fed to him to keep him away from the actual truth, which was more prosaic but more damaging. Season Three is the last season in which you can say that maybe the aliens aren't actually aliens but rather, frightening government creations, birthed out of mad science and the U.S. government's collusion with Nazi and Japanese scientists after World War II. These conclusions, which Scully reaches, are, if anything, even more horrifying than the conclusions Mulder always lands on. That sense of government betrayal gives Season Three's mythology episodes a moral center that makes them immensely powerful.

Even beyond thematic concerns, "Nisei" is endless fun. There's great wit in the script.[15] There are some solid action scenes. And the whole episode builds relentlessly. By the stunning cliffhanger, when Mulder jumps on top of a roaring freight train, the plot has almost as much momentum as that charging locomotive. "Nisei" starts from a very small incident—Mulder buys an alien autopsy video and wants to find out who's distributing it—and turns into a nation-spanning story line very, very swiftly. Everything in this episode feels like it fits with everything else, thanks to the way Mulder keeps pushing and pushing until things finally break.

"Nisei" also works in a way earlier mythology episodes didn't because Mulder's quest is now becoming Scully's as well. She might be separate from him, but she's still chasing the truth and making progress. Whereas Mulder's story line is more action packed, Scully's introduces her to a group of abductees who tell her she's one of them and serves up flashbacks to her time as a helpless captive. Her scenes give "Nisei" the emotional core that keeps it from feeling hollow.

To be sure, the show will give Scully a plausible explanation for what she and Mulder are up against and allow her to pursue the "truth" in her own way, but it's still decidedly on Mulder's side.[16] We see aliens, after all, and a piece of a UFO. No

---

15 Especially when Mulder talks about the alien autopsy video he bought from a magazine ad.
16 He's kind of a jerk about it too. "After all you've seen!"

matter what Scully says, we know that Mulder's the one who's right.[17] *The X-Files* seems heavily influenced by the story of the doubting apostle Thomas. Whether or not you require proof, everyone's going to end up believing.

When it comes down to it, the central story of *The X-Files* is embedded in the mythology episodes. Some fans will disagree; you can make the argument that the true story is how a series of unusual cases bond an unlikely couple into friendship, or that the true story is the gradual exhumation of the weird underbelly of America. But if the element that made *The X-Files* so unique was the fact that it understood it needed to have compelling, non-extraterrestrial stand-alone entries, the decision that kept it from being merely a cop show with monsters were these overarching mythology episodes. It's here that the show most thoroughly engages in its portrayal of post–Cold War America as a place full of secrets waiting to be uncovered, and it's here that our two leads follow the threads they can—not because it's their job, but because they have no other choice. —TVDW

| "731" | SEASON 3 / EPISODE 10
WRITTEN BY FRANK SPOTNITZ
DIRECTED BY ROB BOWMAN |

TILTING AT FLYING SAUCERS
In which the truth may not be what you're looking for.

"731" is fantastic. The stakes are personal: Scully finds some of the answers she's been looking for, Mulder gets as close as he's ever gotten to the truth, and both of them are the driving forces behind the story. In the end, when all is said and done, neither can walk away from what happens here.

The central plot of "731" has Mulder holding an assassin at bay while Scully tries to talk some sense into him. It's a marvel of construction, as the bomb in the train car is both a logical safeguard and a great device to spur Mulder's quick decision making as the clock runs out. This sense of urgency is the marker of a good mythology episode, the feeling that there are so many possible answers, but there's never enough time to process them all. It's like trying to read a burning letter that was lit from the bottom.

The crux of this episode comes when Scully learns the possibility that the truth Mulder's been working for years to uncover is nothing but a kind of double bluff to hide the *real* truth: The government has been kidnapping and running tests on humans and hiding it under the cover of "alien abductions." It is a far more

---

17 Even his craziest conclusions—"There's a secret government railroad!"—are usually right.

cynical explanation for the events they've witnessed. No aliens, just vile, arrogant men exploiting their power in ugly ways. There's a grim satisfaction to this theory, sure, but it is ultimately a gut-wrenching invalidation of Mulder's quest for far more profound answers; it doesn't change the way we view our universe to learn that bastards remain bastards behind closed doors. This version of the truth is a mockery of Mulder's struggles, turning his belief in the occult and the supernatural into his greatest weakness. To find he's been a patsy all these years would destroy any faith in his own discernment and rob his life of the greater meaning he so desperately desires.

Rendering Mulder as a Don Quixote–like figure delivers an intense emotional impact and exemplifies *The X-Files* mythology writing at its finest. This episode introduces just enough doubt—in spite of all the strange things we've already seen—to make even the audience question what's real and what's illusion. Mulder finds his answers but is forced to accept they weren't what he was truly looking for. His plight speaks to a potential tragic end for his quest. The longer you search for the truth, the more you believe you know what that truth is—but the less likely you'll be able to accept what you actually find. —ZH

SEASON 3 / EPISODE 11
WRITTEN BY KIM NEWTON | **"REVELATIONS"**
DIRECTED BY DAVID NUTTER

ON A MISSION FROM GOD

In which Scully stands with the angels.

Mulder is a nerd. He doesn't look like a nerd because he looks like David Duchovny, but underneath his chiseled exterior beats the heart of a socially maladjusted, bitter misfit. He chastises Scully for not believing in the absurd when it's a question of aliens or Flukemen or werewolves, but as soon as Scully starts exploring ideas that fall out of the *Tobin's Spirit Guide* realm, he gets snippy. How dare she like *Star Wars* more than *Star Trek*! How dare she believe in a higher power and angels and demons when everybody knows it's Cigarette Smoking Men whom you really have to worry about!

The tension in Mulder and Scully's relationship in "Revelations" is organic and dramatically effective, demonstrating how dysfunctional their partnership could sometimes be. Mulder needs Scully because he needs someone he can trust completely. And yet when Scully needs someone she can bounce ideas off of, Mulder can't handle it. It's easy to dismiss Scully's skepticism as evidence of a closed mind, but Mulder has just been lucky enough to live in a world that confirms his beliefs. When he encounters an experience that doesn't fit into the patterns he believes in, he dismisses it.

The idea of Scully as a mystical protector is both goofy and perfectly sensible. Her role as a calm, rational center in an insane world has long been established, perhaps most notably in "Clyde Bruckman's Final Repose" (S3E4). That earlier episode also suggested Scully might be immortal, and while that suggestion was intended as a joke, it's hard to think of a universe that *wouldn't* benefit from her having eternal life. It's also a nice change for this episode to put her in a situation in which Mulder doesn't come to her rescue in the final minutes. Simon Gates's (Kenneth Welsh) is a fine monster. There can be no surprise in a character who goes to the Holy Land and experiences a religious conversion, but the idea that Gates's conversion has him playing for the Devil's side deserves more explanation than a throwaway line.

"Revelations" strains plausibility at times. Mulder and Scully's rapid response to a boy's stigmata doesn't fit with their usual work because a single occurrence doesn't seem to merit that kind of attention that quickly. It would've been nice if Kevin (Kevin Zegers) had an actual personality beyond generic boyhood. The structure of the episode is odd as well because Scully doesn't really step in to protect the kid until the very end; I can't help but wonder if it wouldn't have worked better if the two had paired off sooner.

Still, this entry works best as a Scully episode. Given her track record, she makes a much better quasi-divine protector than Mulder does, and Anderson's honest, slightly appalled amazement at each new discovery makes the premise easier to swallow. Her skepticism is at its most dramatically effective in "Revelations," as a way to ease us into the story instead of solely being deployed as a wall for Mulder to butt against. Positioning her as the believer breaks with the established formula of the show in a way that deepens our understanding of her character. The episode's final scene has Scully in a confessional booth, despairing that no one is listening to God. It's a powerful moment and an effective reminder that her partner isn't the only one concerned with finding the truth. —ZH

"WAR OF THE COPROPHAGES"

SEASON 3 / EPISODE 12
WRITTEN BY DARIN MORGAN
DIRECTED BY KIM MANNERS

A BUG HUNT

In which there is less than meets the eye.

Miller's Grove, the name of the town where "War of the Coprophages" takes place, is a riff on Grover's Mill from Orson Welles's *The War of the Worlds* broadcast. Just as some listeners of that real-life broadcast were certain that alien invaders were touching down on Earth, the citizens of Miller's Grove go crazy because of a series of events that appear to have a malicious connection but don't have any connection at all. For once, skeptical Scully is right: The cockroaches are only cockroaches. Everyone here just draws the wrong conclusions, which inspire them to make bad decisions. This is one of the few *X-Files* in which the implications *don't* add up to something more sinister. In the end, it's all smoke and mirrors.

"Coprophages" represents the most extreme example of Darin Morgan's early efforts to deconstruct the series. The show's willingness to satirize itself is one of the reasons it came to be as great as it was, but you can only go so far with self-parody before it becomes impossible to go back. It's not just that "Coprophages" presents a possible conspiracy and then fails to deliver on that promise. It's that, in the world of this episode, even if there *were* a conspiracy, it wouldn't justify the stupidity, greediness, or selfishness of humankind. The discovery that there are no dark forces at work here isn't disappointing because it doesn't seem necessary. Who would need an elaborate scheme to take down this bunch of rubes?

The ideas in this episode don't come together as effectively as they did in Morgan's "Clyde Bruckman's Final Repose" (S3E4), as there's no Bruckman-like emotional center or Morgan-esque viewpoint character to hold everything in place. The main question of the hour is how humans might deal with other species when those other species aren't particularly attractive. Morgan is, as always, not optimistic. We can aspire to greater understanding and compassion, but when it comes down to it, most of us are like Mulder, dropping everything to embrace the hot doctor and killing the ugly bug that wanders into our personal space, because—*blech!*—ugly.

This theme isn't completely realized, but "Coprophages" is tremendous fun to watch. The dialogue is great, the pacing is sharp, the leads are at their best. It's great to see Mulder actually turning to Scully for answers, listening to what she tells him, and even agreeing with her. His sudden infatuation with Dr. Bambi (Bobbie Phillips) and bug-killing show him almost as much at the mercy of his base impulses as the rioting townsfolk, but while the story once again pokes fun at his obsessions, the jokes here aren't quite so pointed.

Even Scully isn't completely invulnerable. There's no conspiracy that could stand up to her calm, occasionally snarky, rationalism. She'd point out how implausible the whole scenario was, and the Cigarette Smoking Man would simply collapse before her like a house of cards. Yet, even with her commendable sanity, she gets sucked into Mulder's story.[18] No matter how logical you are, you want there to be a pattern, and you want it to be a pattern you can somehow influence. I doubt Scully would be wearing a cross around her neck if she felt otherwise.

There's something exciting about watching or reading a story that's willing to throw out big ideas and mix them together without slowing down, that aims for a balance between black comedy and pathos without overplaying either.

S3 E12

---

18 She also gets sucked into what appear to be feelings of jealousy over Mulder's relationship with Dr. Bambi.

"Coprophages" shows us how easy it is to convince yourself you know what's going on, even when you don't. It's nicer for us to believe in a bunch of bugs from outer space coming down to Earth to mess with our minds than it is to accept the actual truth that bugs like manure—and, as the episode hilariously reminds us, there's always plenty of bullshit to go around. —ZH

| "SYZYGY" | SEASON 3 / EPISODE 13
WRITTEN BY CHRIS CARTER
DIRECTED BY ROB BOWMAN |

SURE. FINE. WHATEVER.

In which Chris Carter can be funny too.

"Syzygy" is a textbook example of the limits of certain *X-Files* writers. The quality of this episode is also hurt by the fact that it immediately follows a Darin Morgan script. The writers most able to write like Darin Morgan were his brother, Glen Morgan, and James Wong, who were not quite as effortlessly funny as he was but often exuded his same sense of black humor.[19]

Series creator Chris Carter took a while to find his own imitation-Morgan voice. Carter was great at some things at this point in the show's run. He kept the mythology episodes humming. He came up with some great Monster of the Week episodes. Most of all, he created and defined the show itself. But *The X-Files* is an anomaly in the landscape of television in that its creator was never its sole major creative force. Many voices jostled for room in establishing the series' voice—the writers, the directors, the actors—and Carter's was always present in the conversation but never rose above to dominate it, unlike his TV contemporaries. It's easy to identify *NYPD Blue* as a David Milch production or any David E. Kelley series as a David E. Kelley production. But outside of the central concept of the show itself, it's a lot harder to find the stamp that Carter put on *The X-Files.*[20]

Carter spent much of the midsection of the show trying to write off-format hours. A few of these episodes would become classics.[21] But "Syzygy," his first crack at something off format, is an entertaining hour that never feels vital. In this episode,

---

19 Vince Gilligan would prove himself an apt mimic as well, as the show would learn in several subsequent seasons.

20 I used to find this a flaw of Carter's, but I've come to think of it as a strength. He empowered his staffers to become their best creative selves.

21 My favorite being the oft-derided "Post-Modern Prometheus" (S5E5), for my money one of the best episodes the show ever produced. But you might also include "Triangle" (S6E3) or "How the Ghosts Stole Christmas" (S6E6) in your calculations, and Carter has continued to tinker with the format of the show into the series' later seasons, particularly with "Babylon" (S10E5), a misfire but an endlessly interesting one.

Carter doesn't yet grasp that what makes Morgan's funny scripts so funny is how very sad they are.

A certain alignment of the stars and planets (the "syzygy" of the title) causes two girls born on a certain date to have an immense amount of power, which they, being teenagers, are abusing.[22] And whether it's the girls, or the return of that celestial alignment, something is causing people to act out of character, often to the ends of broad comedy. The episode is most notable for the way that same something has Mulder and Scully at each other's throats as they struggle to keep their cool, professional demeanors.

Is it funny to have Mulder tell Scully he assumed her "little feet could never reach the pedals" when she asks why she never gets to drive?[23] Absolutely. But there's also a sense that the laughs here are emptier than they were the week before in "War of the Coprophages" (S3E12), an episode that's also broadly comedic, full of goofy, edgy Mulder/Scully banter, and that features a flirtation between Mulder and a gorgeous woman. Because that episode was written by Darin Morgan, it belongs in the series' pantheon. This one can only suffer in comparison.

It feels unfair to compare "Syzygy" to the episode that immediately comes before. But it's so clearly trying to be a Darin Morgan episode[24] that it invites the comparison, and having two comedic episodes come between "Revelations" (S3E11) and "Grotesque" (S3E14), both of which are among the season's darker hours, makes the similarities even more pronounced. When watching the entire series on a streaming platform, it's easier for us now to accept "Syzygy" as a weird, occasionally funny experiment and just flip right on to the next. But in 1996, it felt like the show had turned into a comedy and briefly lost its mind. If you removed "Syzygy" from its place right after "Coprophages" and had it air several episodes later (maybe after the upcoming mythology two-parter), it might hold its own a little better.

Or it might not. It might just be an episode that is trying too hard to push its way out of Carter's own wheelhouse and wander off into a new landscape. While Morgan blends comedy with a pessimistic sense of impending doom, Carter was always best when he could blend comedy with an earnest, optimistic sense of the universe's limitless possibilities. But "Syzygy" is too broad and too mean to accomplish this, a teen-slasher movie parody[25] that never finds a way to put all of its cards on the table. It's like a shadow of some other episode we'll simply never get to truly see. —TVDW

S3 E13

---

22 Asshole teenagers abusing their power is a theme this season. See also: "D.P.O." (S3E3).

23 This line and others address criticism of the show then popular on the Internet, and it very well may be one of the first episodes of any TV show ever to have a script expressly respond to online discussions. So it is certainly notable for that reason.

24 Also evident in how the structure of the episode essentially mirrors that of Morgan's Season Two outing, "Humbug" (S2E20).

25 Those teens, we're contractually obligated to note, include a young Ryan Reynolds.

SEASON 3 / EPISODE 14
WRITTEN BY HOWARD GORDON
DIRECTED BY KIM MANNERS

THE ABYSS (INTERNAL)

In which: Nietzsche.

"Grotesque" is, in many ways, pretentious and self-serious.[26] The subject matter—Mulder and Scully track a serial killer who may have demonic help, possibly endangering Mulder's psychological well-being—essentially invited the series to indulge in its own worst tendencies. Written by Howard Gordon (probably the only writer on the series to give Chris Carter a run for his money in the self-serious sweepstakes), it's a moody, logy hour, far too thrilled with its own importance.[27]

However, the hour also unquestionably works for one big reason: It's disturbing in a superbly scary way. That commitment to terror carries the episode over the finish line, even when it seems to be falling down a self-constructed rabbit hole. "Grotesque" ends with an unattributed quote from Nietzsche applied without any deftness whatsoever, but it bizarrely feels as though the episode has earned it. The plot has holes, and the story's logic doesn't always make sense, but its dark moodiness casts an engrossing spell.

"Grotesque" belongs to that category of episode in which Mulder and Scully are tipped off to a non-supernatural criminal for one reason or another, then use their particular prowess and talents as a duo to capture said criminal. Usually, they're dragged onto the case because there's a sense that something paranormal may be involved, but in these episodes, it often turns out that Man Is the Real Monster. "Irresistible" (S2E13) is the show's first instance of this trope, and "Grotesque" occupies a similar place within this season that the earlier episode occupied in Season Two. This episode is essentially an inverted version of that story—again, a serial killer is the target, and again, one of the central duo is imperiled. But this time, Mulder is the one in danger, and the threat is psychological.

Mulder and Scully join a case involving a man who's been attacking and killing male models who pose for his art class. The case has obsessed Mulder's former mentor, Agent Bill Patterson (Kurtwood Smith), for years, and now that it's almost over, Patterson seems almost let down. Plus, no one can seem to find the artist's victims. Mulder discovers that the artist is hiding his victims within his gargoyle statues, and from there, everybody's favorite paranoid FBI agent tries to prove there's

---

26 In that sense, it feels like a dry run for *Millennium*, the Chris Carter–created series that would debut in the fall of 1996, alongside *The X-Files'* fourth season.

27 It also features an incredibly serious performance from Kurtwood Smith, who would later go on to be much better known for his comedic work on *That '70s Show*.

a demon pushing the artist to kill. At the same time, the evidence starts to mount that Mulder may have taken the killer's knife himself, driven mad by the horror on display.

The final twist—Patterson is the killer's accomplice—feels ingenious the first time you watch the episode but makes less sense the more you think about it. It's interesting, in the sense that it suggests men like Patterson or Mulder are drawn to the darkness because it exists somewhere within them already. It helps that Smith really sells the twist, but the show barely bothers to explain Patterson's motivations, even as Smith[28] and director Kim Manners imbue every bit of menace into the final shot of Patterson protesting his innocence behind bars. He just got in too deep, and that's apparently all we need to know.

The ponderous nature of the episode, often a demerit on this show, ends up reflecting the themes of "Grotesque" beautifully. The slow, painstaking uncovering of the depths of the brutality on display lets us get a good sense of how awful the killer was and gives credence to the idea that Mulder or Patterson might have been driven over the edge by his savage violence. It's not only a useful reminder that Mulder and Scully do, in fact, make a crack crime-solving unit but also a nod to the idea that not all of the darkness in the world comes from strange creatures and aliens. We humans generate darkness easily enough on our own.

"Grotesque" falls just a hair below the thematically similar "Irresistible." The later episode is better directed and relies on fewer contrived coincidences, but there's also nothing as visceral in it as Scully's need to free herself from her captor in "Irresistible." The stakes here seem less palpable because it feels hard to believe that Mulder would ever become a killer. Cold and aloof, "Grotesque" distances itself from the viewer, but it effectively makes you consider the toll our heroes' work might have on them. Maybe the ultimate difference between "Irresistible" and "Grotesque" is the difference between Scully and Mulder themselves. The former is an episode that takes place in a world of nightmares, but ones that can be punctured by a smart, incredibly capable woman; the latter suggests that nightmares breed further darkness, and that the only way out is for a determined man to dive deeper and hope he doesn't get lost somewhere in the depths. Sound like anybody you know? —TVDW

28 Who maybe has a Bryan Cranston-esque career turn in him, if this episode is any indication of his talents!

A MAN'S CHARACTER IS HIS FATE

"Grotesque" is yet another example of a stand-alone X-File that nonetheless touches on the personal lives of our two agents. Many of the show's writers noted that involving Mulder and Scully more intimately in a case made for a stronger episode. Chris Carter recalls that the show's fans seemed to agree. Carter says that as far back as Season One, "I had gotten a letter from a passionate fan telling me what she felt worked best and what worked least on the show. She felt that the episodes that worked best were the episodes that Mulder and Scully were personally invested in. She was right. You see that everything that came out of that letter, including 'The Erlenmeyer Flask' (S1E24), we're taking it to heart. You had to fight a tendency to do the stand-alone episodes as simply X-Files case files. You had to find a way to get the actors or the characters and ultimately the actors to care about the case they were involved in."

Howard Gordon says that inventing the character of Patterson for "Grotesque" came directly out of that impulse. "It is always good to find what about the case was personal," Gordon says. "Mulder got to have so many mentors and it was fun because I do remember it was a bit of a land grab in the early seasons where we got to expand [Mulder and Scully's] stories beyond just the two of them and meet Scully's parents: her father who died, and her mother." Hence the many Season One hours in which new characters were introduced to fill in the backstory of our two protagonists and implicate them more directly in the cases at hand.

As for influences behind the tone of "Grotesque," Gordon credits the works of writers like Edgar Allan Poe and Dostoyevsky more than horror films. In fact, when he was first writing the script, he says, "I couldn't tell if I was writing something supernatural or not." He ultimately settled on a "kind of a possession, in a civil kind of way. . . . I think the wellspring of that idea was the nursery rhyme—I'm going to massacre it—'He who seeks monsters risks becoming one.' . . . [Patterson] was gifted. That was his gift. He'd actually . . . fallen into that black hole." And so Gordon, in showing us that Mulder is similarly gifted, gives us a story that works not only as a deeply unsettling horror story, but also plumbs the depths of our hero's mind in new and enlightening ways.

THE ABYSS (EXTERNAL)
In which we meet some very strange oil.

Which is the better *X-Files* mythology two-parter:[29] "Nisei"/"731" (S3E9/10) or "Piper Maru"/"Apocrypha" (S3E15/16)? Honestly, it might be easier to flip a coin. "Nisei" and "731" are two halves of a gigantic action thriller, with ticking time bombs and runaway trains. "Piper Maru" and "Apocrypha" are a more emotional duo, episodes that allow time for Scully to grieve her sister while simultaneously bringing back the villain who helped kill her and who has become Mulder's most immediate nemesis: Alex Krycek.[30]

The difference between the pairs of episodes can be explained by the differences between the main alien antagonists of both two-parters. The alien villain of "Nisei" and "731" is the alien bounty hunter, a mysterious figure, but one that we now know is also easily dealt with. Take an ice pick to the back of his neck, and he's not a problem anymore. He's not a bad figure. He's just a horror-movie monster.

In "Piper Maru,"[31] however, we get our first look at the black oil, which may be the most original and frightening creation of *The X-Files*' mythology. The black oil is far more insidious than the alien bounty hunter, who acts like a blunt object, hammering at a closed door. The black oil turns people you trust against you. It keeps people alive at the bottom of the ocean for decades, waiting to strike. It overwhelms and converts you.

Ironically, the biggest problem with the black oil is also what makes it one of the coolest inventions of the show to this point: It basically removes any possible logical explanation for the alien conspiracy. The earlier mythology episodes often have Scully explore more mundane possibilities for what the government was covering up, possibilities that were often much more terrifying than little green men. It's just as scary to imagine that the government has gone to great lengths to cover up an atomic bomb on the ocean floor as it is to imagine that aliens are out there, waiting to invade our planet. But the black oil renders moot Scully's skepticism. There's just no way it could be a government creation.

---

29 Not to be confused with the best single mythology *episode*, which has to be "Paper Clip" (S3E2). However, in that case, the weakness of "The Blessing Way" (S3E1) keeps the season opening two-parter from taking the "best two-parter" crown. In the cases of the other episodes discussed here, both halves of the two-parter are vital.

30 Who pops up trying to sell the contents of the digital tape from "The Blessing Way" (S3E1) and "Paper Clip" (S3E2). Continuity!

31 Chris Carter reportedly named this episode after the daughter Gillian Anderson had during the show's second season.

Yes, there's an ABH who can change his face, but crucially, our heroes have had limited contact with him, and Scully is always able to write off sightings of him as people merely seeing what they want to see. However, the moment we meet the black oil, we see it in the eyes of a World War II pilot who's been kept alive at the bottom of the Pacific since his plane crashed there. There's no way to explain this as people hallucinating. As the black oil infects more and more people—starting with the crew of the French salvage ship that finds the World War II plane, then spreading to one of their wives, then, ultimately, spreading to Krycek—it gets even harder to dismiss as some kind of hoax.

It's at this point that the onus of the mythology subtly shifts from Scully coming up with alternate theories of what's going on that make just as much sense as Mulder's ideas to the show desperately trying to keep her from knowing things so that she can still fit into the "skeptic" role the show has predetermined for her. It mostly works in these two episodes because she's busy grieving her sister, but it becomes more and more of a problem as the series goes along, because it becomes more and more obvious that Mulder is right. "Piper Maru" is a hell of an episode. It also marks a shift within the mythology and, eventually, the show itself toward embracing Mulder to the detriment of Scully.

Still, this shift was inevitable. It's preferable to have our two leads on equal footing, but this has always been a show in which it was going to eventually become obvious that, yes, aliens exist and have been visiting our world, and yes, they intend to colonize it. That's simply a more viscerally interesting and paranormal story than "The government did bad things, and now it's trying to keep them covered up." The black oil is thrilling because it's a solid indication that the show is definitely going ahead with its interest in extraterrestrial life. There's pretty much no reason for the oil to exist, unless it's a way for the aliens to turn humans against each other. Humans can try to control the black oil, but it is a force almost unto itself, an alien monster that comes from within.

"Piper Maru" belongs to the rapidly diminishing period of time when the mythology episodes are exposing viewers to more pieces of the puzzle, fitting in various ideas meant to make up a greater whole. There's always a sense of the camera pulling farther and farther out in these episodes, revealing more and more of the picture. That's thrilling—right up until it isn't. —TVDW

SOMETHING IN YOUR EYE

In which Krycek gets screwed.

The end of this mythology installment has Krycek locked in a silo with the alien ship, screaming for help to an abandoned building. Even from a show that traffics in dark endings, this is high-quality nightmare fuel. It feels like the closing beat to a great, epic story line, and it sort of is—but it also sort of isn't. Mulder and Scully have risked their lives to get closer to the truth, and they know more than they ever did before, but each new piece of information sends them down another rabbit hole, falling through space as they search for the ground. *The X-Files* creates grand import out of eerie moments and a lack of closure. Eventually that lack of closure would become a detriment, but in the third season, images like Krycek pounding on a door where no one can hear him still have the power to haunt you.

It's not as though the show couldn't end story lines when it needed to. The biggest emotional payoff of "Aprocrypha" comes in the resolution of the murder of Scully's sister. The episode does a fine job of both "solving" the mystery and yet showing the complete lack of satisfaction that the solution provides our heroine. Melissa is still dead. A scene at the cemetery drives the point home, and it's during that scene that we learn that Melissa's killer died in his jail cell. There's no vengeance or catharsis or relief, and the forces that ordered the hit remain unpunished and unidentified.

The mythology episodes are driven by Mulder and Scully's determination to create order out of chaos, to merge all the pieces together into an arrow pointing toward the guilty—to reduce the shifting sands of plot into something coherent and easy to prosecute. Yet scenes like the one described above suggest a potential hollowness to their efforts, a hollowness that only grows more pronounced with each new chase, each new grave, each new lead. It's a writer's problem, in a sense, because it's always easier to introduce a mystery into a narrative than it is to find a satisfying way to resolve it. What makes "Apocrypha" so affecting is how it finds a way to incorporate that meta-textual dilemma into the text itself.

There's a great scene in which the Lone Gunmen team up to get the envelope Krycek left in a locker; there's ice-skating, and it's hilarious and suspenseful. It doesn't really matter that the envelope they get is already empty. The sequence is enjoyable enough that the means justify the ends. That's not a trick you can pull off forever—no matter how pleasant a Sunday drive is, you eventually get sick of looking at the road, and the more empty envelopes and just-missed discoveries there are, the harder it is to shake the feeling that you're being led by the nose and told to like it. Yet it's an approach that continues to work in the third season, because the show is just starting to interrogate the efficacy of its heroes' goals while still allowing us to believe in them. That balance of self-awareness against idealism is often as compelling as it is frustrating.

As Todd notes in his review of "Piper Maru" (S3E15), this two-parter does a great job of expanding the scope of the conspiracy, allowing for a sort of paranoid vertigo to endanger our heroes and the audience. The opening scene has Mulder's dad and the Cigarette Smoking Man interviewing a burn victim in 1953. There's such a sense of dread in the reveal of their identities, in knowing how long and how thoroughly those in power have been working to hush up what's happening. There's also tremendous potential in Mulder struggling to make right the errors of his father, and maybe even finally doing what his father always wanted to do himself. As absurd as Mulder's growing list of connections to the conspiracy can sometimes seem, it serves the purpose of anchoring the global to the extremely personal.

And again, there's that ending. After all his scheming, Krycek finds himself worse off than ever, and while it's possible to argue that he deserves his plight—given the various betrayals and horrors he's been a party to, surely he had some piece of this coming—there's also a creeping knowledge of the many deaths that haunt this hour. Like it did to the man who killed Scully's sister, we here see the conspiracy doing what it does best: using someone for its own dark ends, and then casting that person aside when he's served his purpose. In fighting back, in refusing to play along, Mulder and Scully might have a chance at survival. But the deeper they dig, the more dirt they uncover. You can't shake the feeling that they might just be burying themselves. —ZH

"PUSHER"	SEASON 3 / EPISODE 17
	WRITTEN BY VINCE GILLIGAN
	DIRECTED BY ROB BOWMAN

CERULEAN BLUES

In which our heroes meet a samurai without a master.

"Pusher" is Vince Gilligan's second script for *The X-Files*, but it's his first script on staff, and his first great one.[32] The episode is a return to the traditional MOTW episode after a run of aggressively stylized variations on the formula. In "Pusher" there's a bad guy, and Mulder and Scully have to stop him before he kills more people, plain and simple. There's no commentary on the major themes of the

---

32 Gilligan's first script for the show being "Soft Light" (S2E23). According to Gilligan himself, "Pusher" was written in the midst of him "having a terrible, six-week-long bout of mononucleosis."

series here, and no attempt to deconstruct clichés. In many ways, this episode is the platonic ideal of an MOTW entry, and when the mythology started losing steam, it's solid tales like this that kept the show on its feet.

"Pusher" has a superb villain, whom the script uses to great effect, never getting too much into exactly how Robert Patrick Modell's (Robert Wisden) powers work on a biological level. Nevertheless, the basic scope and danger of his abilities are quickly made clear. If he can talk to a person, he can make them do things. It's mind control, but it's mind control that can be expressed through dialogue, making it that much more dynamic on-screen. It's also a simple, clear premise that's immediately easy to understand, one that isn't diluted by unnecessary explanation or complication, but which allows for enough variation to stay interesting and suspenseful.

Wisden does excellent work as a complete bastard, the actor expertly capturing arrogance and petty rage and ensuring that the character is always compelling, but never falsely sympathetic. Throughout the episode, Gilligan makes creative use of Modell's abilities, effectively subverting the "investigate, monster attack, investigate" formula that most MOTW episodes follow, without making him too powerful. In particular, there's an intensely thrilling scene in which Modell forces a cardiac arrest on the agent who's been tracking him by taunting him over the phone about his high cholesterol. Modell is formidable enough that the stakes are quite high, and the possible solutions seem very limited.

The climax is a marvel. Mulder strides into a hospital, shots are fired, and Mulder's camera goes dead. Scully runs in after, and she finds Modell and Mulder in a staring contest, about to engage in a game of Russian roulette. By now we know that Modell isn't long for this world, and that his powers most likely stem from a brain tumor. He wants to win, but he already has a death sentence. What's fascinating is how this episode speculates on just how much of a death wish *Mulder* has. Given the intensity and desperation that often characterizes his work, there's a certain despair buried in all of his efforts, the fear that nothing he does could ever be sufficient. It's enough to give Modell an in—and if it weren't for Scully and a nearby fire alarm, who knows what might've happened.

This face-off serves as an apt culmination of the battle of wits Mulder and Modell have engaged in throughout the hour. Modell's power is an extension of his will, and he uses that will as a tool to break others; for him, every victory is a confirmation of his own innate superiority. Mulder's entire life has been defined by *his* will, his refusal to bend or break in the face of overwhelming odds. Scully is just as strong, but Scully would refuse to play Modell's game. Mulder already knows half the rule book.

This is smart, well-paced, and exciting, and Modell is wonderfully memorable. *The X-Files* gets a lot of mileage out of the tragic killer, but Modell stands out as an underdog who may have deserved all the abuse he received. It's his rage, really. That when-is-it-my-turn rage. That why-won't-these-idiots-pay-attention-to-me fury. We have a habit in our culture of rooting for the little guy, but it's important to remember that in some cases, we'd all be better off if the little guy stayed small. —ZH

"TESO DOS BICHOS" | SEASON 3 / EPISODE 18
WRITTEN BY JOHN SHIBAN
DIRECTED BY KIM MANNERS

ME-OW

In which little is purrfect.

If "Teso Dos Bichos" had dropped earlier in *The X-Files'* run—in Season One, or even Season Two—it would have been considered a minor misstep, an avenue to explore before moving on to better and brighter things. It's straightforward, not particularly scary, and makes no attempts to subvert its B movie setup. But to get this now, after such a strong season thus far, makes it worse than just forgettable.

It doesn't help that the premise is almost irredeemably silly. There are some bones, and they belong to an ancient medicine woman, and they get moved. And wouldn't you know it, this turns out to be a bad call, because some crazy point-of-view shots start killing people. Mulder and Scully are called in to investigate. They do some poking around and find a herd of murderous cats. Cats can be great harbingers or mood setters, but they are not, in and of themselves, frightening. Not even when you have a whole bunch of them at once.

There's some decent Mulder and Scully banter, and a name-dropping of Val Lewton, who produced (the far superior) *Cat People* from 1942. But while there is at least something clever in a group-based threat instead of just having one big cat–type monster, the reveal of our heroes batting away a bunch of orange tabbies is too ludicrous to be effective. Plus, there are no winks to acknowledge the absurdity; the episode is straight-faced from start to finish. This is paint-by-numbers at its most tedious, and while it's nice to have proof of how far the show has come since it started, that doesn't make the episode any easier to claw through. —ZH

FORGET IT, FOX; IT'S CHINATOWN

In which it's time for another racially insensitive episode.

Vaguely boring and borderline racist,[33] "Hell Money" should be more awful than it is. That it's not speaks to the heightened cinematic quality of third season episodes. It also helps that the central idea of the episode is actually a pretty engaging hook: A gambling ring that plays for body parts instantly draws the viewer in, playing on any number of very basic fears and horrors. It's not a natural idea for an *X-Files* episode, but it fits into Season Three's newfound philosophy that "anything dark and weird can be an X-File."[34]

Unfortunately, "Hell Money" can never overcome the feeling of being a series of shocks strung together across a standard story setup. *The X-Files* usually excels at depicting communities that are part of the larger American community, technically, but also completely separate from it. The best of these use their American sub-communities—and associated monsters—to examine what it means to be outside the mainstream. The worst are like "Hell Money," where the San Francisco Chinese community never feels like it exists outside the show itself, not even with great actors like Lucy Liu,[35] James Hong, and B. D. Wong.

"Hell Money" commits one of *The X-Files'* cardinal sins: sidelining our two heroes. The episode is far more concerned with Wong's corrupt police officer Glen Chao, leaving Mulder and Scully to watch the chaos unfold around them. To its credit, the story does give Scully the rare chance to crack a case that's non-supernatural in nature, but so much time is spent on the guest cast that it ends up being a wash in that regard. Mulder and Scully's process of plunging through the layers of the mystery feels less like them uncovering a dark conspiracy and more like them just getting lucky. Setting a story like this in an American immigrant community is at least a break from the cop-show usual. But there's nothing terribly compelling about either the depiction of Chinatown or the story line. This feels like a story about other characters that Mulder and Scully just happened to wander into in order to receive

---

33 It really tries to be respectful, which keeps it from fully tipping over into racism in the end, but it's very, very obviously an episode about Chinese culture written by people who've read about it in a book.

34 It's also worth noting that the episode's use of subtitles is groundbreaking for 1996, when networks had a hard time imagining viewers would be willing to follow along with a story they had to look up from their laundry-folding to read.

35 Here playing Kim Hsin, before she was famous ("before-they-were-famous" is a recurring theme for Season Three guest stars).

the exposition the audience needs to piece the story together. It's a flaw that Season Three has otherwise mostly avoided.

"Hell Money" probably isn't as insensitive as it could be, considering the time and method in which it was written. But too many of the Chinese characters are simply there to introduce weird overtones of mysticism to the proceedings. Plus, simply setting a premise like this in a part of the country where the dominant population is full of foreign-born residents bumps up against notorious xenophobic urban legends about well-off white Westerners having their organs removed in foreign countries. A thinly disguised overtone of cultural invasion permeates the episode, and while "Hell Money" thwarts it in the end, thanks to the more nuanced portrayals of the Hsin family and Chao, who's simply a corrupt cop like any other, it verges on that xenophobia.

That being said, there's still quite a bit to enjoy in "Hell Money." There are plenty of great, freaky images (like a frog emerging from a corpse), and the whole idea of gambling with your body parts is kind of genius.[36] But the story here is just too big for forty-five minutes of television. There's no real room to develop the Chinese community *and* give Mulder and Scully something to do, but in its best moments, "Hell Money" feels like a half-hearted adaptation of the greatest *X-Files* tie-in novel ever, rather than an episode undone by its own ambitions. —TVDW

| "JOSE CHUNG'S FROM OUTER SPACE" | SEASON 3 / EPISODE 20 WRITTEN BY DARIN MORGAN DIRECTED BY ROB BOWMAN |

WE ARE ALL ALONE

In which everybody's got a point of view.

"He's stealing my memories." —Chrissy Giorgio

Think of yourself as a baby, perhaps in a parent's arms or playing with a favorite toy. Do you recognize yourself in the eyes of that child? Do you remember those experiences directly, or do you remember photographs, stories others have told you? Now think of your first memory. There's a difference between the stories you're told about your infancy and the stories your earliest memories tell you. Thoughts of your pre-aware self are in the third person, filled in by others who knew you then. The you who existed for the first few years of your life feels like another person entirely, an alien inside of your skin, looking out through your eyes,

---

36 The episode gives you just enough sense of how it's played that you, too, could set up your own body-part gambling ring tomorrow if you wanted to.

waiting for you to take control. But that first memory—*that's* your first experience of yourself as an "I." The divide between those two perspectives—between first and third person, between seeing your life as a movie and remembering it as a memory—is the uneasy land where "Jose Chung's *From Outer Space*" resides.

"Jose Chung" is often described as a *Rashomon*-style episode,[37] meaning we see the same series of events through the eyes of multiple witnesses, with each new perspective offering an alternative view of reality. Whatever the real truth is, it's elusive, simply because of the inherent subjectivity—and thus inevitable unreliability—of each narrator. Nevertheless, Truman Capote-esque writer Jose Chung[38] is determined to record the truth about what happened to two kids who may or may not have been abducted by aliens. Although he starts out by talking directly with Scully about the case, the story twists and turns, allowing us to learn additional bits and pieces of information from other characters. The episode's second cruelest joke is that what happens to the two teenagers is never satisfactorily answered by any of the other characters, whether due to bias, apathy, or just a dearth of information.[39]

Darin Morgan's script wanders and loops into some weird, wildly inventive territory, but at every turn, he introduces instantly identifiable characters. The terrific humor of "Jose Chung" comes through in the stark differences between these characters' version of events, and what their stories reveal about their perception of the people around them and the way they interpret their own reality. When Blaine (Allan Zinyk) recalls his encounter with Mulder and Scully as though the two were Men in Black, it's funny precisely because it nails how a regular person coming across Mulder and Scully out in the field might perceive the two to be. When Scully sanitizes Detective Manners's speech patterns[40] for her discussion with Chung, it's funny because we know it's a sly dig at the limits of television's capacity to portray reality. And when Roky (William Lucking) tries to share his message from Lord Kinbote, it's funny because Chung and Scully know the story has gone off the rails and been turned over to a complete fantasist, yet everyone else keeps treating it as something worth talking about. All of this is wonderful fun, but what grounds it is each character's genuine quest for answers.

Much of the discourse around "Jose Chung" over the years has focused on two questions: one, how much of what happens in the episode really happened as depicted, and how much is created by either the influence of hypnosis or the wild

---

37 After the famous Japanese film of the same name, directed by Akira Kurosawa.

38 A tremendous Charles Nelson Reilly, in one of the show's very best guest performances.

39 The cruelest joke is that the girl, Chrissy (Sarah Sawatsky), insists she was raped by the boy, Harold (Jason Gaffney), but he's such a nice boy that people find it easier to believe aliens abducted them than that he raped her.

40 "A bleepin' alien!" Morgan here is also sliding in a joke about *X-Files* director Kim Manners, who was infamous on set for swearing like a sailor.

conjecture of men like Fox Mulder; and two, how much of the episode is intended to mock *X-Files* fans for their passion for the show?

Regarding number one, I've watched this episode dozens of times over the years and would argue that there's a clear explanation for what happened. Chrissy and Harold were abducted by U.S. government operatives with a flying saucer, who then implanted them with memories of being abducted by aliens via hypnosis.[41] That's really about it.

Sure, at some point, both operatives and both teenagers may have been abducted by an actual alien, but the episode leaves room for doubt. The only person who claims to have seen the alien monster is delusional, and the only person to take him halfway seriously is, of course, Mulder. The only place in the episode in which the two stories blatantly contradict each other is when the diner owner says that Mulder dined alone, while Mulder maintains he talked to one of the two operatives and got the full story before returning to the motel to be interrogated by the two Men in Black.[42]

There's enough haziness here to conform to the series' original mission statement—you can believe or you can maintain skepticism—but most of the fun comes from the way that reality flits around the story like a trapped insect, frantically beating its wings as Chung tries to pin it down. The episode isn't as hard to understand as its reputation makes it out to be. There are two solid interpretations of events, and both are remarkably like each other, with only a few key divergences.

As to whether this episode is meant as a slam against *The X-Files* fan base, there's certainly the temptation to read the episode as such, particularly when it comes to Blaine and Roky, both of whom exemplify fans of the show who were more willing to engage with the sci-fi craziness than any sort of human story at its center. The episode's overall dismissive attitude toward Mulder's theories has certainly been interpreted by some as a strike back against the fans.[43] However, I have to disagree. Morgan may affectionately nudge the fanbase in the ribs, but he also implores us to stop searching for weirdness in fiction or UFO research circles, to embrace the fact that we are, all of us, lonely and weird and standing outside of where we'd really like to be, looking in.

---

41 Again, words—and the stories we tell with them—drive perception.

42 Played, in what might be the most famous *X-Files* gag, by Jesse Ventura and Alex Trebek. Says Darin Morgan, "I wrote the part for Jesse 'The Body' Ventura, because he was my favorite wrestler as a kid. I originally wanted Salman Rushdie [as the other Man in Black] which I thought was funny at the time. Nobody was willing to go along with that. Glen [Morgan suggested] it should be Johnny Cash—which is perfect cause he's the original 'man in black.' So in the script I believe it's Johnny Cash, and we tried to get [him to come in but] he just wasn't available. And then it was like, 'OK, who do we get?' [. . .] I was brainstorming with Jeff Vlaming, who was one of the staff writers, and he goes, 'Alex Trebek.' And I go, 'There we go.'"

43 Though the episode is for sure a big ol' love letter to Scully, as a patron saint of science-driven skepticism.

Thus, at the end of the day, if we're getting at the heart of what makes "Jose Chung" a classic, I think both questions are barking up the wrong tree. The genius of this episode can be summed up by its final monologue, which I'll quote in part:

Then there are those who care not about extraterrestrials, searching for meaning in other human beings. Rare or lucky are those who find it. For although we may not be alone in the universe, in our own separate ways, on this planet, we are all alone.

Here, Chung (a proxy for Morgan) offers the true meaning of the episode. All this time, what we thought we cared about most was aliens, and the unraveling of a giant government conspiracy. But Chung's closing words remind us that what we're identifying with when we watch *The X-Files* are the people—people who are desperate and lonely and aching for something more, whether it's to get out of their hellhole town, to find a connection with another person, to learn the truth, or to simply move past a traumatic night.

The relationship forged by the two people at the heart of the series is its most powerful element. It's also crucial to the episode's success, even as Morgan seems to hold Mulder in withering contempt. *The X-Files* inhabits a world of loneliness, a world in which everything from modern technology to shadows in the night stand in the way of human intimacy. The fact that Mulder and Scully are still able to connect in spite of all these negative forces is deeply affecting. It's Morgan's awareness of this potency that makes his scripts so moving, and so funny; they're filled with indelible characters who long to make connections and then do, briefly, before seemingly forgetting how to do it again. Clyde Bruckman reaches out to Scully ("Clyde Bruckman's Final Repose" [S3E4]). The freaks in "Humbug" (S2E20) build a community with each other. But whatever bond Chrissy and Harold once shared is destroyed by Harold's actions—or by aliens, or by the government; whatever the cause, it's left them both distraught and alone.[44]

Also key to the episode, and to Morgan's philosophy, is the way identity shapes memory. In other words, we are our memories. When Chrissy says the doctor is trying to steal hers, it underlines Morgan's belief that what is most important is the contents of our minds, not some crazy government plot to fake alien abductions. If the government agents steal Chrissy's memories, no one is around to clean up the emotional aftermath. The case simply remains unexplained, leaving her to pick up

---

44 Throughout "Jose Chung," the episode often seems to most sympathize with Harold, when he very well might be a rapist and the *best case scenario* to argue he isn't is that his ex-girlfriend was sexually experimented upon by aliens or the government. But the episode seems to sympathize with Harold because he can't find a way through what happened, whereas it finds Chrissy's ability to become a survivor somewhat awe-inspiring. This, incidentally, is how Morgan approaches writing the characters of Mulder and Scully too.

the pieces on her own. If your memories are sucked out of your head, do you cease to exist? Or does a central truth remain, even after everything is stripped away and we're left alone, throwing rocks against the window, trying to reconnect?[45]

"Jose Chung" has more to say about the human condition than any other episode of this show. And although it's probably one of the very finest episodes of television I've ever seen, period, I'm not sure it's a terrific episode of *The X-Files*. If *The X-Files* were a *Lord of the Rings*–length novel, then "Jose Chung" would be its first appendix, a source that is at once in love with the main text and critical of it, a place where real human concerns creep around the edges of the show's chilly implausibilities. But the very best episodes of television are like this sometimes. They push so far and press so much against the constraints of the series to which they belong that they cease to be episodes of that show and become something else entirely.

If Jose Chung's final monologue is the episode's emotional Rosetta stone, then the elegant opening shot is its intellectual counterpart: The camera softly glides past what appears to be a Star Destroyer from *Star Wars* until we see it's merely the undercarriage of Roky's crane lift. It seems the world is strange enough without us pinning further strangeness onto it. Our fellow travelers are far more interesting than any ghosts or monsters ever could be. We do not have to be alone. —TVDW

S3 E20

---

45 Needless to say, what you come to believe "actually" happened will drive how much sympathy you can feel for Harold at the end. I really do think the government abduction hypothesis makes the most sense.

MONSTERS OF THE WEEK

AN ODE TO DARIN MORGAN

Darin Morgan's episodes are renowned for both their hilarity and ingenuity. Frank Spotnitz recalls taking a decidedly hands-off approach to Morgan's work in the writers' room because, "Darin was such a unique talent and such a strong individual voice." Looking back on Morgan's contributions to the series, Chris Carter ruminates, "Well, 'Clyde Bruckman's Final Repose' (S3E4) is, of all Darin's episodes beyond 'Humbug' (S2E20), the most 'X-Fileian'; it really works for an X-File. Whereas, 'Jose Chung's *From Outer Space*' (S3E20)—it's something else completely, entirely. You read the episodes, and you laugh at them. I remember reading 'Humbug' to my wife, actually, in bed, and both of us laughing out loud at it. Darin's scripts are laugh-out-loud; they're such twists on the show, and they're such thumbs in the eyes of the show. They make fun of the show, and of the characters." As Vince Gilligan put it, "Darin Morgan really paved the way for the comedic episodes . . . dark comedies but comedies nonetheless. [Having a comedy writing background myself], when I got to *The X-Files* one of my great fears was I wouldn't be able to write drama, [but] Darin Morgan showed us all that *The X-Files* was elastic enough to allow for great leaps of humor. When I saw that opportunity, I ran with it as soon as Chris Carter would let me."

Besides being funny and delightfully idiosyncratic, Morgan's scripts also poignantly explored themes of sadness, loneliness, and isolation. Where did these melancholic tones come from? "Well, you know, that's me. I mean, that's sort of been my life," Morgan says. He points out that *The X-Files* is, after all, a dark show in and of itself, centered as it is on strange deaths, unsettling predators, and dastardly conspiracies. "And, so even though 'Clyde Bruckman' [is supposed to be funny]—[although] some people don't even know that it's supposed to be funny, they look at it as a tragedy (which it is)—the trick is that you have the jokes [but] it's still as dark as the show is. I mean, I've always felt I could argue that 'Jose Chung,' which a lot of people think is just a silly, goofball episode, is the darkest episode the show has ever done—pretty easily." Whereas most would emphasize the influence of *Rashomon* on the episode's exploration of subjective viewpoints, to Morgan the far more potent and altogether demoralizing idea is that of memory manipulation. Morgan explains, "If someone has the ability to manipulate your memory—all your memories—then, what are you? You don't even know who you are, if say, your happiest memory or your most depressing memory are all fiction. Who are you as a human being? And, to me that was much darker and more disturbing than the usual kind of conspiracy stuff."

| SEASON 3 / EPISODE 21
WRITTEN BY HOWARD GORDON, FROM A STORY BY DAVID DUCHOVNY AND GORDON
DIRECTED BY JAMES CHARLESTON

SKINNER'S LAMENT

In which Mitch Pileggi gets his time to shine.

"Avatar" is the story of Walter Skinner and how he came unhinged. It's also the story of how Vietnam made him a different man, and how his marriage fell apart, then came back together at the last possible moment.

This episode is remarkable for its embrace of personal narrative. The series had been building toward an episode about Skinner for the entirety of Season Three, and even if it arrived largely because David Duchovny wanted a lighter week,[46] it remains a vital episode within the context of the series. Here, finally, the writers realize that the supporting cast is rich and varied enough to support episodes on its own. This experiment bore fruit; the show would go on to do more Skinner-centric episodes, as well as entries centered on the Lone Gunmen, the Cigarette Smoking Man, and even a former X-Files investigator.

It's important to remember just how much of an oddity *The X-Files* was when it aired, and especially how much of an oddity it is now. If you were going to air the show today, Skinner would absolutely be a regular, and the CSM, Mr. X, and possibly even Krycek might be regulars as well. The show would also be more heavily serialized; there would be little bits and pieces of the alien story line threaded through every episode, and the Monster of the Week episodes would keep getting interrupted by the supporting players. But this odd little show did none of those things, and it still works because at its heart it's a simple series that chooses to expand only when it really wants to.

Even in the less successful episodes that revolve around the non–Mulder and Scully characters, the show gives off a sense of being grateful to have a moment to step in a different direction. It makes sense for the first extracurricular hour to be about Skinner, simply because he's the character who has the closest direct connection to Mulder and Scully. Thus, the two agents turn up frequently throughout "Avatar," but the story line is undoubtedly about Skinner dealing with the fallout from his crumbling marriage.

---

46 Note that "Story by" credit! Of course, Mitch Pileggi was elated at the opportunity to both expand his role as Skinner and give David and Gillian a bit of a break: "I was very thrilled about it. It was very exciting to see that they were doing something with [my] character, and also David and Gillian were working their asses off every day, so anytime they could get some kind of relief . . . and I know that David was pushing for a long time for Skinner to have even more involvement with them because then it gives them a little bit more time off."

In true *X-Files* fashion, it turns out that Skinner has been seeing an apparition of an old woman most of his life, and she pops up again when he's having sex with a prostitute he claims to not remember hiring. When the prostitute turns up dead in bed next to Skinner, Mulder quickly determines the old woman may be a succubus.[47] For Mulder and Scully,[48] the race is on. If they want to save their boss, they're going to have to unravel yet another paranormal mystery. In many other episodes, this setup would merely be the jumping-off point for further spooky happenings and would let Skinner fade into the woodwork. Instead, "Avatar" chooses to pivot in another direction.

To be sure, the sudden appearance of the old woman is an out-of-nowhere conceit. We've been given no occasion to speculate that Skinner had such an affliction in the past, even though the show does a mostly elegant job of writing around it (being the logical person he is, he just assumed she was a drug-induced hallucination in Vietnam). The strange woman also solves a different problem because the writers probably weren't even sure at this point if they *could* do an episode without Mulder and Scully at the center. Placing Skinner in the middle of a very traditional X-File must have seemed like a way to make "Avatar" feel more like an episode of the show, even as it relegates our heroes to the sidelines. That Mitch Pileggi is able to shoulder the burden and never make you miss Mulder and Scully is a testament to how much both the character and the actor have grown.

The episode has a surprisingly domestic story at its core. Skinner's marriage falls apart and his wife falls into a coma before quickly recovering—a plot that should feel like *thirtysomething* wandered in and took over *The X-Files* for one week. But it works, which is not only to the credit of Pileggi but also to the subtle and nuanced writing of these scenes. The writing on *The X-Files* could sometimes be ham-fisted, but the scenes in which Skinner is contemplating the end of his marriage are surprisingly deft (even when they take brief pauses[49] to all but shout, "In case you hadn't guessed, Skinner might get a divorce!").

There are some good scares in the episode, mostly stemming from the apparition of that old woman.[50] The image of her popping up where she's not supposed to and taking the place of Skinner's wife is always creepy, thanks to unsettling but low-key special effects that make her look more demonic than anything else.

"Low-key" is a good descriptor for "Avatar" as a whole. It could be a grand hour of Skinner's flashbacks to Vietnam and the slow dissolution of his marriage,

---

47 Scully seems almost fine with this theory. "Whatever," she seems to say, "It's late in the season."

48 Both of whom immediately believe Skinner when he says he didn't murder the woman, which speaks to the new strength of the relationship between the three, as they probably wouldn't have had the same response in Season One.

49 Likely network-mandated.

50 Who feels strongly like an homage to Nicolas Roeg's *Don't Look Now* (complete with red raincoat).

but it makes the choice to tell the story all in real time, to trust that many of the big emotional moments can be struck entirely by Pileggi delivering a monologue. The series would turn out a better Skinner episode later on, and its experiments with episodes centered on other characters would also yield positive results, but "Avatar" is an important and successful first step for the show. —TVDW

| "QUAGMIRE" | SEASON 3 / EPISODE 22
WRITTEN BY KIM NEWTON
DIRECTED BY KIM MANNERS |

RIDDLES IN THE DARK

In which an alligator has its lunch (and Queequeg meets his end).

One of the hallmarks of *The X-Files'* third season has been the show's repeated interest in poking holes in its own style and fixations. "Quagmire" takes that same Darin Morgan-esque approach[51] but uses a softer touch. The episode deals with some of the show's serious and central ideas—like the danger of looking too hard for answers and the potentially destructive nature of Mulder's idealistic search for the truth—but it also ends on a hopeful note, with the suggestion that our protagonists might eventually find what they're looking for. It allows for the possibility that *The X-Files* itself might have some kind of happy ending.

That added warmth is evident in the scenes between Mulder and Scully from the start. Instead of the usual professional attire, we see both characters dressed in casual weekend clothes because (as Scully mentions to Mulder with frustration) it's a Saturday. Scully is annoyed because Mulder, as always, hasn't really explained himself, but she's *there*. Of course she is. The only justification for why Scully would devote so much of her time to Mulder's cause, and why Mulder would trust her so completely, is that they belong together, in the only sense of the phrase that matters. Their interactions throughout "Quagmire" speak to this dynamic, framing it as a complex, but ultimately positive, connection. There's a reason that it's two of them stranded on a rock near the end of the episode, and it's not just because their boat sinks.

That long dialogue scene is what sets "Quagmire" apart from all the other standard Monster of the Week procedurals. To get to that moment, we have the usual run of idiots-about-to-be-corpses, including a scuba diver who's hanging out

---

51 Morgan did some uncredited work on the script; thus the return (and demise) of Queequeg and an appearance from Tyler Labine and Nicole Parker, who both appeared in "War of the Coprophages" (S3E12) in similar roles as druggy teens.

with those surviving druggie teens. Mulder believes it's all the work of Big Blue, the local Loch Ness–type creature that's rumored to live in the lake, and with each discovered corpse, he becomes more vehement about proving Blue's existence. Scully does her reasonable explanation run, and the locals keep dismissing him, but Mulder refuses to listen. He's right that *something's* going on, but it's a lot more everyday than a cryptid dinosaur.

After some further misadventures, the pair gets stuck in the middle of the night on that rock in the middle of the lake. The setting is eerie: just them and a rock and a lot of water and darkness as far as the eye can see. If you've ever been swimming in a lake, you know how creepy it is to look down between your legs and see what could be miles of blackness below you. Anything could be down there. That sense of isolation and uncertainty helps to make the exchange that follows between the characters all the more impactful. Saying intimate things in broad daylight is very well and good, but nighttime conversations when there's no one else to hear them always mean so much more.

Both characters get good speeches: Scully calls Mulder an "Ahab,"[52] and Mulder talks about his dreams of a peg leg. The bond between them is a lovely mix of humor and affection, something that feels legitimately sustainable. Later in the episode, after the mystery has been chalked up to an alligator and everyone heads home, Big Blue briefly surfaces, to give us some small hope, however absurd, that Mulder might someday find his answers. But the real hope is in that previous scene with just Mulder and Scully, being honest in the dark. Sometimes, the people we're closest to don't always make sense, and sometimes they drive us crazy. But then it's just the two of you, alone in the night, and that's when you know that the person you're with is the only one you need. —ZH

---

52 The same nickname she had for her father, oddly enough.

TELEVISION KILLS

In which there are fifty-seven channels and something strange is on.

This episode starts with an unforgettable cold open: A guy buries a corpse, muttering, "Your killing days are over!" to the dead body. The guy goes home, tries to relax, and then the supposedly dead killer appears in his kitchen. The guy kills him *again*, jams him in the trunk of his car, and then the cops show up. Both of the cops look like the twice-murdered killer. The cops subdue the guy, and then one of them (who now looks like himself) checks in the trunk. The guy looks in and realizes he's made a horrible mistake. It's not the dead man he's stuffed in the trunk. It's his wife.

Nothing in the rest of "Wetwired" is as shocking as that first reveal. The episode is, in many ways, an echo of "Blood" (S2E3). Once again, the government is running experiments on unsuspecting townsfolk, once again those experiments have a body count, and once again Mulder makes it through the experience without succeeding in bringing those responsible to justice. It's well made and it has moments of brilliance, but the familiarity of the concept somewhat dulls its impact.

Somebody's sending signals through televisions, subliminal advertising that clouds viewers' minds and drives them to commit violent acts against those closest to them. The Lone Gunmen help take apart a device Mulder finds in a cable box, and there's a conversation about signals and control and whatnot, but the actual conceit lacks the craziness of "Blood" or the hook suggested by the episode's opening scene. There's no commentary on the way media can define our reality, nor is there much exploration of Scully's suggestion about how violent videos can drive the viewer to commit violence themselves—a hotly debated topic at the time this episode aired. The closest the episode comes to inventiveness is the way everything gets scrambled like a bad TV screen right before something bad is about to happen.

Episodes in which characters have been brainwashed always have at least one of the leads fall under the spell. "Wetwired" is no exception, but in a smart change of pace, Scully is the one who succumbs. She gets suspicious of Mulder, thinking that he's working with the men responsible for abducting her and murdering her sister. This might seem more like Mulder's deepest fear than Scully's, but it serves to illustrate how much adopting Mulder's worldview has changed her own. More effort to tie her fears into her abduction and the death of her sister might have helped, though; she gives a speech spelling out the connection late in the hour, but it feels like more of an intellectual connection than an emotional one.

Regardless, it's dramatically effective to have Scully lose her cool every once in a while. Her hallucination of Mulder and the Cigarette Smoking Man laughing together is terrific, an image that's both hilarious and unsettling, and one of the few times that this episode's mind-bending potential is fully realized. It's chilling to imagine the show's moral and ethical compass led this far astray.

The episode also puts tension on Mulder's relationship with Mr. X, to the point where Mulder pulls a gun on his informant, insisting that *someone* pay the price for all this death. Mr. X manages to talk his way out of the situation (unsurprisingly), but it's a dangerous game he's playing, as highlighted by his final scene with the CSM. It's a lot of chainsaws for him to juggle, and eventually, one of them is going to drop.

If there had been a greater sense of the tragedy here, of lives and families destroyed by the government's arrogant interference, then we might've had a more compelling episode. Given how much of *The X-Files* is already about how we're all programmed to act by the people who think they know best, "Wetwired" would have done well to focus more on that central concept. —ZH

SEASON 3 / EPISODE 24
WRITTEN BY CHRIS CARTER, FROM A STORY BY CARTER AND DAVID DUCHOVNY
DIRECTED BY R. W. GOODWIN | "TALITHA CUMI"

MOM KNEW EVERYTHING

In which smoking can be hazardous to your health.

The cliffhanger ending of "Talitha Cumi" is one of the best the show has done because it knows whom to convincingly threaten. While Mulder and Scully are nominally in danger from the alien bounty hunter, it's really the nice guy alien we're worried about. Jeremiah Smith (Roy Thinnes) heals the wounded and preaches calm, and he's more than willing to finally provide our heroes with definitive answers. On *The X-Files*, being a friendly freak suggests you may not last long, but promising the truth guarantees it.

We're back in the land of heavy mythology, and even better, we're coming to a rise in the action. There are more connections to be made and the impression that some awful scheme is coming to a head. For once, Mulder and Scully have an ally who isn't incompetent or corrupt. Jeremiah Smith is a powerful, morally righteous figure, someone who knows what's going on and who isn't trying to hide from it. One of the defining characteristics of Mulder's quest is its isolation. Scully's presence keeps him sane. Who knows what another ally might bring?

There's another game-changing twist here: Mrs. Mulder (Rebecca Toolan) knows the Cigarette Smoking Man. If there's always been something vaguely

Freudian about conspiracy theories, this episode takes that concept and runs with it. Powerful figures with impenetrable motives controlling the lives of the innocent—from a certain skewed angle, that pretty much describes parents, too, setting rules and structure for children who rarely have the ability to decide for themselves. The discovery that both of Mulder's parents were involved with the CSM on some level makes the metaphor literal and adds new psychological depth to our hero's efforts. Mulder is not just trying to find the truth; he's rebelling against a plot that has defined his life long before Samantha was taken. Before, in fact, he was even born.

Teena Mulder is clearly not too fond of the CSM, but it's the kind of antipathy that can only come from betrayal and more than a little self-loathing. She's conflicted by her past, by the death of her ex-husband, and by the damage that her and her ex-husband's choices have done to both their children. The conversation between her and the CSM, jagged and off-putting, is wonderfully done, especially the climax, in which we shift to them being photographed from a distance and see how quickly their barely restrained politeness changes into shouting and arm-waving and turned backs. It's hard to blame Mulder for his obsessions when his entire family has been corrupted.

The plotting here does an excellent job of bringing us to that final confrontation, raising the stakes and building suspense out of the potential death of a sympathetic character. Scully and Mulder are often in danger, but there's never really a chance of either of them getting killed; the fact that it's not just possible but likely that Jeremiah will die gives the ending a substantial kick. The main threat to our heroes is that the destruction of everything they hold dear might finally break them, and Mulder is closer to the edge than ever before. Mulder has been unhinged and demanded answers before, but here his anguish is driven by the involvement of his mother—by both a concern for her safety, and the horrible knowledge that nothing in his life is entirely free from the CSM's clutches.

The conversation CSM and Jeremiah have while Jeremiah is locked away is also a highlight of the hour. We don't know much about the CSM, but the more we learn, the more we see a man whose only goal in life is control. Yet even he can't escape the inevitable ends of his own biology, a fact that Jeremiah is more than willing to point out. The alien's transformations—first into Deep Throat, then into Bill Mulder—are powerful, as is Jeremiah calmly telling the CSM that he's riddled with lung cancer. The CSM can deny it, but no one believes *this* denial.

After everything that's happened this season, it's remarkable how effective the show still is at drawing the audience in and leading them on with the perpetual promise of resolution. Anyone who's watched the show to this point must know that any answers the fourth season might offer will be temporary at best, and yet it's hard to deny the pull. In its third season, *The X-Files* questioned the sanity of its leads while still committing more fully to their search for truth. "Talitha Cumi" is a fitting conclusion, pushing the story forward while showing the rot inside Mulder's family tree. —ZH

SEASON 4 / EPISODE 1
WRITTEN BY CHRIS CARTER
DIRECTED BY R. W. GOODWIN

ANOTHER SERIES OF SAMANTHAS

In which the fourth season opens with the by-now
standard mythology episode, and it's not bad.

"Herrenvolk" has some chase sequences, pathos, horror, and death. Lots of death, actually; Jeremiah Smith meets his, and Mr. X finally pays the price for trying to live two lives at once. Mulder gets more information on the alien/human conspiracy, and Scully finds evidence that suggests that the government has been tracking each and every one of its citizens for the last fifty years. Just as important, the episode lacks the silly mysticism that plagued last year's season premiere. No magical Native Americans or monologues full of vague, portentous imagery here, thank goodness. We don't even get narration.

Yet even with all that incident, nothing actually *happens*. This is the sort of mythology episode that would ultimately give the show a bad name; it's more about moving around familiar elements than providing any real progression. We're stuck in *Gilligan's Island* mode: Mulder and Scully can find new clues and make new friends, but God forbid one of their coconut rafts ever stays afloat for more than a second or two.

Last season ended with a good cliffhanger: Just as Jeremiah offers to tell all he knows to Mulder and Scully, the Bounty Hunter arrives, and he does not look pleased.[1] This episode opens with a utility guy dying from a bee sting while a bunch of creepy duplicate blond kids watch. The established structure for mythology episodes is to start with misdirection; the cold open is almost always a sequence that doesn't involve our main characters, focusing instead on some piece of the puzzle whose relevance won't become entirely clear until later on. This is effective because it catches us off guard, and because these scenes play out like short horror films—even without the reveal about the drones and the killer bees and so forth, the utility guy's death is unsettling.

But there's something about the teaser that doesn't work here. The show has reached a point in its run in which we're so used to misdirection that it has become the norm. The first scene, while pertinent to the plot (it makes Mulder's position more perilous later on because we know what happens if he gets stung by one of the hundreds of bees floating around his head), hampers the momentum that ended Season Three.

---

1 Even when Brian Thompson does look pleased, he does not look pleased.

There are all sorts of weird hiccups like this throughout the premiere. We get a well-constructed chase scene in the factory, which ends when Mulder manages to get the drop on the Bounty Hunter and stabs him in the back of the neck with that needle-knife our hero found last season. It's immensely satisfying. After all the setup with the blade, all of Mulder's agonized confusion, we get something dangerously close to results. For once, it seems like the good guys can make actual, positive change. For a brief second, it's possible to believe that the endless armies of obfuscation and manipulation might be stopped.

But lord knows, we can't have that! So when Scully comes across the fallen Bounty Hunter and bends down to check for a pulse, the ABH comes back to life. It's possible to justify this scene: This was, to be fair, Mulder's first time using the needle-knife. And the scene is admittedly suspenseful—putting Scully in the hands of the ultimate badass is terrifying, and Mulder's abandonment of her gives us another glimpse into the cost of his desperation for the truth.

The scene is still disappointing, though. The episode's unwillingness to permanently resolve any threat makes the tragic conclusion to Jeremiah a little less tragic. That's the kind of series this is, after all. We're operating on conspiracy story logic, so it's natural to assume that for every step forward, we get thrown half a dozen back. We've seen all this before. We knew Jeremiah was doomed from the moment he told Mulder and Scully that he could explain everything. While inevitability usually lends tragedy greater emotional weight, here it has the opposite effect; the knowledge that a character is certainly going to die makes all the noise leading up to that final moment much harder to care about. The Bounty Hunter should've died, but he didn't, so what does it matter?

Mr. X's death is another side of the same coin. We learn early in the episode that the Syndicate is getting suspicious about an information leak, and we also see their attempt to flush out the leak. This is compelling, and when Mr. X tells Scully that Mulder's mother is in danger, it's the first time in the series that we know more about what's going on than X does, which means he isn't long for this world. His execution is appropriately shocking, and the terrific editing, with Scully telling Mulder how she thinks that X can help them right before we cut to X bleeding out as he crawls down the hallway toward Mulder's apartment, makes it one of the most memorable deaths in the series. And yet, by the end of the episode, Mulder has followed X's cryptic last note ("SRSG") to the Special Representative of the Secretary General, where we meet Marita Covarrubias (Laurie Holden), our newest informant. The vacuum of conspiratorial information left by X's death is filled almost immediately, and while this new contact is a little different from the others, her appearance on the scene deflates the importance of X's loss. The more things change, the more they stay the same.

Scully doesn't get a whole lot to do in this episode beyond play catch-up; her discovery of the list of smallpox vaccinations has some power (her fury that other agents won't listen to her is well played), but haven't we already seen how the government tracks its citizens? The thrill is gone, so to speak. It fits in with the slowly unfolding colonization plot, but it's also a lot of familiar ground reinforced.

"Herrenvolk" has some amazing moments too. When Jeremiah leads Mulder to the fields and Mulder sees a clone of Samantha, no older than she was the day she was abducted, it's both moving and disturbing. Mulder's desperate need to take her away, despite her inability to communicate and despite the obvious fact that this isn't really his sister, makes sense. Her death, at least, is shocking, occurring offscreen after the Bounty Hunter finally tracks Mulder down. For all these surprising moments, though, much of this episode feels like the show just running in place to seem like it's keeping up with the moving scenery. The ending demonstrates the show's attempt to feign new developments while really remaining constant, with the Cigarette Smoking Man convincing the Bounty Hunter to heal Mrs. Mulder playing as both a step too far and yet another refusal to commit to permanent change. By the end of the episode, it's impossible to shake the sinking sensation that we're getting nowhere, slowly. —ZH

| **"HOME"** | SEASON 4 / EPISODE 2
WRITTEN BY GLEN MORGAN AND JAMES WONG
DIRECTED BY KIM MANNERS |

WONDERFUL, WONDERFUL

In which Mulder and Scully come across a spooky house and a family
with some . . . interesting ideas on keeping the bloodline going.

If you wandered far enough into the countryside surrounding the tiny town I grew up in, you'd find people who desired the absolute minimum of human interaction, people who put signs up on their farms warning that trespassers would be shot, people who collected abandoned sheds and set them up in a lonely cow pasture in some semblance of a small ghost town consisting almost entirely of chicken coops. If you talked to these people, they were almost always friendly but terse, able to interact with others but attempting to end that interaction as soon as possible. It's not so hard to imagine twisting this terse emptiness into horror.

"Home" is twenty-two years old, but it feels part of a different world entirely. In the 2010s, small towns feel like part of a much more homogenous whole, thanks to the wonders of modern connection. If you go for a drive in even the most isolated parts of the nation, you're still connected to the rest of the country. "Home," like its central figures, the Peacock family, is a remnant. Like so many *X-Files* tales, it's both a sterling example of a certain kind of horror story and a last-gasp effort within the subgenre, a sort of sad farewell to the weird America that was rapidly smoothing over.

"Home" is the first episode of four this season written by the returning Glen Morgan and James Wong,[2] and every one of those episodes is a notable break from the form the show had established up until that point. "Home," in particular, is among the finest episodes the show produced, a reminder that *The X-Files* could do brutal, scary episodes even as it was crossing over into a mainstream hit.

The setup Morgan and Wong exploit is a simple one: There's a creepy house at the edge of a small town in the middle of nowhere. That house holds a family that doesn't want anything to do with anyone who might disrupt them. This is, basically, the show's *Texas Chainsaw Massacre* episode, only here the family are three inbred brothers, products of generations of incest, attempting to beget another child with their own mother.[3]

Morgan and Wong were fantastic at taking old horror movie templates and updating them for the show's universe, as they did when they turned *The Thing* into "Ice" (S1E8) and folded any number of '80s Satanism chillers into "Die Hand Die Verletzt" (S2E14). Morgan and Wong understand both what makes *The X-Files* work and what makes those old horror movies work, and they understand where and how the two intersect. "Home" is somehow both a creepy house horror movie and an episode of *The X-Files*. That the two overlap so comfortably is proof that the show's template was so elastic as to incorporate almost anything the writers and producers could throw at it, but it's also evidence that the weirdness and wildness of America was becoming almost commonplace. The rise of mass communication (and especially the Internet) made little local monsters and urban legends into well-known national figures, the best spreading and choking out more localized phenomena. In earlier decades, you had to be road-tripping through the Texas wilderness to run across a family of chainsaw-wielding freaks. Now, Mulder and Scully could pop in and out of a small town[4] to hang out with an inbred sideshow for just a few days' time.

Two touches set "Home" apart from other episodes. One is Morgan and Wong's sense of grim humor. One of the common fan complaints against the episode when it first aired was that Mulder and Scully's jokes destroyed any mood the episode had built up to that point, but the jokes actually enhance the atmosphere. The humor builds on the realistic rapport between our two protagonists because by now, we know that Mulder and Scully stare directly into the face of awful, awful things and find a way to keep going. Plus, the writers had a terrific sense of when, exactly, a dark

| S4 E2 |

---

2   Morgan and Wong had left to create and run the enjoyable sci-fi series *Space: Above and Beyond*, but Fox had canceled the show, deciding its expense wasn't worth the critical acclaim.

3   Much of the episode's infamous reputation rests on the fact that Fox didn't re-air it for years, and perhaps that general plot summary will give a sense as to why the network blanched at it.

4   In Pennsylvania no less, not a state known for its extensive collections of wild, empty areas like West Texas is.

wisecrack would lighten the mood just enough to break the tension—and to deepen the next plunge into utter terror.[5]

And why does the episode need those tension-breaking moments? Certainly much of that suspense is due to Morgan and Wong's script, but this is also possibly the most evocatively directed episode of *The X-Files*. Director Kim Manners proves equally at ease with the gentle domesticity of small-town life (particularly in a small town with a sheriff named Andy Taylor, played by Tucker Smallwood) as he does with the chilling horror sequences. In particular, this might literally be the darkest episode of the series,[6] with shots emphasizing narrow slits of light to highlight, say, Mrs. Peacock (Karin Konoval) lurking underneath a bed.

The killing of the Taylors is where everything good about "Home" comes together. Directorial flourishes like a zoom in on a door lock that remains open, the careful tilts up from the looming headlights of the Peacocks' stolen car, or the way the camera simply takes in Mrs. Taylor's (Judith Maxie) fingers just coming into contact with the pool of her husband's oozing blood help underline that this is, as much as anything else, a clash of societies writ small. Manners finds a way in this sequence to distill the essence of that nightmare in which someone is in your house, but you can't quite find them, and he even manages to include a slight rumination on the word *home*.[7] Is *home* what the Peacocks inhabit in their insular, closed-off world? Or is it the quiet, pleasant life of the Taylors, all cozy porches and silent moments together? Does it mean what Mulder and Scully share, a life spent endlessly on the road, building a home in each new city?

Maybe that ambiguity is why a sense of intense melancholy pervades "Home." Just before he's killed, Sheriff Taylor sits on his front step and looks out over his little town, talking about how he wants to take one last look before it all goes away, and it seems almost as much a mourning for the death of the great, weird America that *The X-Files* so obsessively chronicled, the local subcultures that were both a part of the larger national community and separate from it. The Peacocks have existed separately from the rest of the country since the Civil War, but the encroachment of the modern world has finally reached their door, and they react in the only way they know how: by lashing out.

Which is, in its own way, understandable. "Home" is spine-tingling, terrifying television, but it's also something that's harder to pin down. Mulder and Scully are our heroes, but they also represent the world that threatens to homogenize all of that weirdness. We're not meant to sympathize with the Peacocks in the way we are other monsters on the show, but there's a melancholy here all the same. The old ways of life are dying, as high-speed electrical cables smooth out our differences, one

S4 E2

---

5   Scully attempting to move some pigs by using the "Baa ram ewe!" chant from the movie *Babe*—and Mulder's bafflement at the same—is the best moment in this regard.

6   The only real competitor is "Oubliette" (S3E8).

7   A bonus: The name of the town itself is Home, Pennsylvania.

connection at a time. So, yes, Mulder and Scully are our heroes—but they never met a place they couldn't make a little less wild, a little more tame. The eldest Peacock and his mother escape at episode's end to continue the Peacock way of life, but the abandoned country roads and bizarre little byways that they once thrived on are now disappearing. The world may be better for it, but it is no longer as unknowable. —TVDW

YOU CAN NEVER GO HOME AGAIN

What was the inspiration behind what many fans have dubbed the scariest X-File of all time? According to James Wong, he and Glen Morgan drew from many sources. One was a book, whose title escapes Wong's memory, about the nature of evil in the animal kingdom: "It was about how we have this rosy-eyed view of nature. Nature is really the mother bird who, [if she saw] anything wrong with her baby bird, would kick it out of the nest and let it die. There's a lot of examples of nature being more harsh and ruthless than humans."

A second font of inspiration came from an idea Wong and Morgan had while reading a biography of Charlie Chaplin: "[Chaplin] was doing vaudeville back then—it was early in his career. This family took to him, and they invited him back home to have a meal with them. He went back, and they said, 'Would you like to see something special?' and he said, 'Sure.' They pull this kid out from—maybe not out from under the bed—but from somewhere. He had no arms and legs, and he was on a trolley, like what we had in the [episode]. They sat him up, and sang music or played music, and then he started to just wiggle around dancing. We thought that was really horrific, so we wanted to do that with 'Home' (S4E2)."

Another influence was a story told to Wong by a dentist he met while on vacation in Hawaii: "[The dentist] told me about this guy, a patient that came in, . . . and the patient said, 'I don't want any Novocain or anything.'" The dentist told Wong, "Usually, when you start working on their teeth, everybody says, 'OK, I need something,'" but the man never did. Wong says, "What he discovered was that this guy basically had no pain receptors in his body."

The last ingredient came from watching the 1992 documentary *Brother's Keeper*. As Wong remembers, the film "was really creepy, and alluded to homosexual incestuous relations." These elements all came together to form a deeply upsetting episode that Fox refused to re-air for many years. Wong describes the initial response to the episode when it was first being made:

"We wrote the script and we started getting reactions from people, from [employees in] Broadcast Standards, and even from our head of production. He would call us, 'You guys are sick.' We go, 'What? What's going on?' I thought we had done worse stuff before.

"Kim Manners directed the episode. We were showing Broadcast Standards [the teaser], and we knew that it was pushing the envelope. Broadcast Standards was [there to hear] the sound mix, [which] had these horrific baby cries that [were] almost too much for us. [So] we showed the teaser, and you can just see it, [an employee from Standards] was in the room with us, and you see her face was just—she was in shock. Then you hear Kim and all he said was, 'That was fucking great!' We had to take out the baby sounds . . . . Broadcast Standards was really—we were trying to ease them through, and [Kim's] exclamation just made it worse."

But "Home" wasn't the end of the Peacock family for Wong and Morgan. When the writers departed *The X-Files* to work on Chris Carter's new series *Millennium*, they considered bringing back the Peacocks for an encounter with the main character Frank Black. "We pitched it to the head of Fox at the time, who was Peter Locke, [and] he says, 'Never. The Peacocks are never going to be on the air again.' He says—I don't know if I believe him, I sort of believe him, because he said it to me—[but he says], 'The reason why we have the V-chip is because of your show!'"

| "TELIKO" | SEASON 4 / EPISODE 3
WRITTEN BY HOWARD GORDON
DIRECTED BY JAMES CHARLESTON |

A MONSTER WITHOUT, A TERROR WITHIN

In which Mulder takes a bad trip, and Scully shoots a pigmentation vampire.

It's impossible to talk about "Teliko" without bringing up the issue of race; stripped of its commentary (intentional or otherwise) this is just a standard Monster of the Week episode. The setup is similar to "Squeeze" (S1E3): A creature who can hide anywhere kills people to acquire the crucial biological material it needs for survival.[8] *The X-Files*' ability to vamp on familiar structures is one of the reasons the show survived as long, and as well, as it did, and much of the enjoyment of these mid-series episodes comes from the twists and adornments the writers tack on to predictable material. Watching a great entry of *The X-Files* can be like

---

8 See also: "2Shy" (S3E6).

listening to jazz music—the melody is just the starting point. What matters is what you do with it.

You can't strip away the racial element, though. All of these characters we're introduced to in the cold open are African American—or, as we learn, just African. Which shouldn't be a problem; just last week, that nice black sheriff and his wife were horribly murdered in "Home" (S4E2), and—while it's possible to read racial overtones into their deaths—it didn't feel like they were killed *because* of their race. In "Teliko," though, the series attempts a story about governmental cover-ups of minority deaths (alongside its usual obsessions with science versus faith and creepy dudes engaging in creepy behavior).

Theoretically this could work, but the message here isn't exactly progressive. All the major roles played by people of color are either victims or the villain himself, and in many ways, this plays out like an othering horror film from the '50s: *Beware the Terror from Dark Shores!*[9] Though "Teliko" is more awkward and ham-fisted than outright unpleasant, this is ultimately an episode about a frightening foreigner who comes into our country without any difficulties whatsoever, a creature who can barely communicate with others and still benefits from our social systems, a monster who sprung from the tribal myths of the Dark Continent. Sure, it's not running around stealing white women out of skyscrapers, but it has a seriously questionable premise. It certainly doesn't help that the episode keeps drawing attention to its own uncomfortable politics.

Like, for example, how the only character on the show who tries to stand up for immigrants and their rights is nearly murdered for his kindness. Carl Lumbly plays Marcus Duff, a social worker assigned to help Samuel Aboah (Willie Amakye) assimilate into American culture. Duff is enthusiastic in his work, and when a pair of FBI agents come around the office asking questions about Aboah, he goes on the defensive like a good social worker should. He even delivers a speech about how Samuel's attempts to avoid the officials stem from growing up in a country where the police routinely torture suspects to get the confessions they want. It's just too bad, then, that the person he's standing up for happens to be a horrible monster who's murdered at least four Philadelphians in the past few months. Even worse, Duff's good nature and trust isn't just used to block Mulder and Scully's path; it puts him directly in harm's way, as he offers Aboah a ride home after the creature escapes from a hospital. He would've ended up like the Teliko's other victims if it weren't for a police officer's timely intervention.

A white police officer, by the way, just as it's the very, *very* white Mulder and Scully who finally manage to take the baddie out in the climax. Again and again the episode raises thorny issues—the way minorities are treated in America, the difficulties immigrants face when trying to integrate into a society that

S4 E3

---

9 Although if it was the '50s, we'd need some white people getting attacked, because . . . well.

automatically views them with suspicion—but settles for the easiest possible outs. "Teliko" speaks to a certain narrowness of perspective from the primarily white male writers' room—a perspective which, while not intentionally malicious, lacks the diversity of viewpoints necessary to draw out the script's more troubling (and potentially fascinating) subtext. It would be hard to argue that the episode isn't about race on some level—the fact that Aboah drains the pigmentation from his victims' skin isn't exactly subtle—but it would be equally difficult to draw some coherent point from any of it. It is precisely because the subject matter is so weighted that the thematic incoherence is so troubling.

In some ways, the episode's attempts to shoehorn real-world problems into a silly story are more misguided than intentionally harmful, and "Teliko" certainly has some strong scenes. The final moments of the fight between Mulder and Aboah, for example, are wonderfully tense, as we watch Mulder frantically signaling to Scully with his eyes that the creature is coming up behind her. It serves as a metaphor for their larger situations: Mulder's crazed plunge toward the answers has a habit of leaving him stunned and shaken, while Scully's cooler, more measured approach means it often falls on her shoulders to interpret what her partner can only suggest, doing what needs to be done. It's a smart conclusion. It's just too bad that so much of the rest of the episode is incurious. —ZH

| **"UNRUHE"** | SEASON 4 / EPISODE 4
WRITTEN BY VINCE GILLIGAN
DIRECTED BY ROB BOWMAN |

HOWLERS

In which psychic photography cracks the case and
Scully is menaced by a very, very tall man.

The best episodes of *The X-Files* feel like little urban fairy tales, bits and pieces of the American cultural scene that pull together into a cohesive narrative of dread. And the writer on *The X-Files* who was best at crafting that kind of tale was always Vince Gilligan, who took things you might see in everyday life and made them incredibly terrifying (when he wasn't making them weirdly humorous).

Season Four of *The X-Files* served as Gilligan's coming-out party, with three stand-alone-episode scripts that bear his name as the sole credit and two mythology scripts that count him among a team of writers.[10] He loved everyday monsters,

---

10 As a freelancer Gilligan had written one episode in Season Two, "Soft Light" (S2E23). Though hired on staff during Season Three, he only contributed one script—"Pusher" (S3E17)—to that season. From "Unruhe," he was a vital part of the writing staff and he would stay with the series until its very end.

normal people who were tormented in some way that tilted them over into becoming an X-File. Here, for instance, the "howlers" that mark the killer's photographs aren't tangible monsters—instead, they're psychic projections of the killer's pain.

"Unruhe" was the second episode of Season Four that was produced, but it made sense to bump it to fourth in airing order, simply because it was a good way for the show to put its best foot forward in a new time slot.[11] While not the finest *X-Files* episode ever, "Unruhe" embodies the show's ideal self. It features a paranormal mystery on the sidelines. It features a monster who was taking helpless women hostage. It features Scully in danger. It features great Vancouver location work. "Unruhe" is a nicely nasty piece of work but a good calling card for the show at the moment it found a new audience.

The episode flirts with blandness here and there, but it proves to be one of the most solid Monster of the Week episodes of the season. In particular, I'm taken with how tied "Unruhe" is to a technology that has now almost completely disappeared: film processing (and film cameras). Though the nation is dotted with the remains of those little parking lot kiosks where you could take your film to be developed, how many of them are open today? Had *The X-Files* launched in 2003, instead of 1993, it would have been almost impossible to do an episode like "Unruhe," because the central idea—the killer's psychic torment is so intense that it imprints itself on film—wouldn't make nearly as much sense with a digital camera. There's something spookier about analog technology, and this episode's perch on the cusp of the digital era is reminiscent of the way "Home" (S4E2) suggests a world of local urban legends being dragged, kicking and screaming, into the light.

"Unruhe" is also pretty damn terrifying when it wants to be. Gilligan plays off of a whole host of common fears, and he was always *The X-Files'* most obviously *visual* writer. He's got the killer (played by the always engaging Pruitt Taylor Vince) lurking under Scully's car. He's got drugs that paralyze the person who's injected and leave them helpless. He's got a long ice pick extending toward someone's nostril. He's even got the way the killer's eyes do that little flutter when the darkness overtakes him.[12] Gilligan never met a mundane visual he couldn't make creepier, and his talent for taking ordinary objects—like construction stilts—and making them the stuff of nightmares or tense action sequences works so well because he never calls more attention to these devices than absolutely necessary.[13] Gilligan understands that horror isn't confined by the limits of logic, not precisely, but it does play by its

| S4 E4 |

---

11 "Unruhe" was the show's first episode to air on Sundays, in the time slot it would occupy until the end of its initial run. While the show had become a sizable hit off in the hinterlands of Fridays (a poor night to launch a big series even in the 1990s), Fox could sense it had even more room to grow. Thus did it land on Sundays, where it, *The Simpsons*, and *King of the Hill* (which debuted later) would build one of the best lineups of the era.

12 This is partly due to actor Pruitt Taylor Vince's nystagmus, a condition that causes involuntary eye movement.

13 Zack has called him the show's Stephen King, and that's dead-on.

own rules all the same, and he's ruthless at inventing and subverting those rules to inspire deeper terror.

But the episode also struggles here and there. The idea of putting Scully in danger is already offering up diminishing returns at this point in the show's run, which makes it all the more wearying that the series continues to rely on that device. Gilligan gives her some good dialogue with the killer before she's nearly lobotomized, but there's always a sense that the show tosses her into danger simply because of how enamored it is with Mulder and his impossible quest. Despite the fact that so many of the show's best episodes were Scully-centric—and so many of its best writers (including Gilligan, who goes on to write some incredible Scully episodes in later seasons) were invigorated by writing for her—you'd think the series would have skewed toward writing for her far more often.

But, as I mentioned, "Unruhe" at its core is, like so many great *X-Files* episodes, an urban fairy tale. There are these beautiful princesses, see, and they keep getting taken in the night by a tall man who's very strong. The man speaks magic words in another language, words that they will repeat for the rest of their lives, after he manages to steal their souls. And when he grabs hold of you, he's able to keep you from moving. But this man didn't realize his fatal error: He was always leaving the good guys magic clues as to what he would do next. And one day, he took a princess who knew just enough to buy herself some time, until the prince was able to rush in at the last moment and save her.

It's easy to scoff at some of the more eye-rolling moments of "Unruhe," the moments when it falls prey to some of the worst clichés of *The X-Files*, but at a base level, Gilligan understands just how deeply the series conforms to fairy-tale logic. The screams are there because the fear is primal. —TVDW

| **"THE FIELD WHERE I DIED"** | SEASON 4 / EPISODE 5
WRITTEN BY GLEN MORGAN AND JAMES WONG
DIRECTED BY ROB BOWMAN |

DON'T LOOK BACK

In which Mulder takes a trip down memory lane.

We form our lives out of rituals. Call Mom on Sundays. Sleep on the left side of the bed. Television is one of those rituals, made easier because networks (even in our current age of streaming and binge-watching) dictate when our favorite series air. Every week you tune in, you're following a ritual and building a routine to hold on to, to make yourself more "there."

"The Field Where I Died" is about past-life experiences, and in a way, past-life theory is the end point of our fondness for rituals. If I've done this a thousand times, that's a thousand moments connected in a chain that brings me to now, a chain that makes me something more than a collection of impulses and regrets. And if I've lived before, if I were once a citizen of ancient Greece, or if I fought and died in the Civil War, that's even better than a chain. That's a history, and it's a history that means when I die, I won't be gone forever. That's what the need for permanence is, really: the hope that if we make a deep enough mark on the world, then, when we go, we won't be completely gone.

Speaking of rituals: *The X-Files* is the first show I can remember making an effort to watch. I missed a couple of episodes,[14] but it was always accidental. "The Field Where I Died" is the first episode in which I sat down, excited, saw the first five minutes, and decided, "Screw it; I'm going to go read."

Watching it now, I'm not sure what turned me off so suddenly. In the cold open, Mulder's standing in a field, staring intently at a pair of old photographs. There's something terribly sad about this scene, about the expression on Mulder's face, and his mournful voice-over. Cold opens on the show are usually either stalk-and-kill scenes or sideways references to the mythology plot. But this one is obscure and direct at the same time. It signals a different kind of episode.

The plot isn't that unusual: a joint raid by the ATF and the FBI on the Temple of the Seven Stars in Tennessee yields up the David Koresh–like Vernon Ephesian (Michael Massee), his six wives, and a cult of the devoted. Unfortunately, it does not turn up the illegal weapons the authorities were looking for, and because of their X-Files experience, Mulder and Scully are asked to help in the investigation to locate the missing weapons. (Ephesian is a religious nut, and Fox is a master profiler, after all.)

Things get spooky[15] when Mulder feels an intense connection with both the land on which the temple is built, and one of Ephesian's wives, Melissa (Kristen Cloke). Mulder believes that Melissa's apparent multiple personality disorder is actually a manifestation of her past lives,[16] past lives that he comes to believe coincided with *his* past lives. Mulder has a history of diving headfirst into whatever strangeness he finds, and this belief is a logical extension of that commitment. Mulder finds cases he connects with so strongly that he makes himself *part* of the case, whether it makes sense to or not.[17]

What sets "Field" apart is its approach. There are no flashbacks here, no shots of Mulder or Melissa reliving their past experiences. The only real camera

---

14 Weirdly enough, I first saw "Jose Chung's *From Outer Space*" (S3E20) when I watched it for these reviews.

15 Zing!

16 Cloke is mostly strong in this episode, but there's some unintentional comedy in her depiction of Melissa's various selves: one persona, "Sydney," sounds a bit like Billy Crystal doing vaudeville under stress.

17 See also: "Grotesque" (S3E14).

effect in the episode is the *Vertigo*-esque shot in which Mulder and Melissa see a particular window that looks out over the field. The episode relies almost entirely on music and performance to sell the idea that these two characters are spiritually connected. There are long conversations and monologues and a sustained intensity of emotion. If I had to guess, I'd say the reason I bailed when I was a kid was that I found the episode too ponderous. There are few jokes,[18] and a story line that works only if you're willing to take it at face value. If you think past-life experiences are ridiculous, and if you find Melissa's sudden personality changes laughable, well, you aren't going to find much comfort here.

Thankfully, whatever inspired me to abandon the episode when I was younger, I'm now able to appreciate the episode's striking mood and how its intensity builds to a tragic climax. The finale has a thudding inevitability that makes it difficult to forget. Cloke is a strong actress,[19] and her multiple-personality shtick is fearless and committed; it's also inherently absurd, and if we'd had more Scully and Mulder banter here, it would've been nearly impossible to watch her work without snickering. But there is no banter, so it's possible to believe, if only for a little while, that she and Mulder really might be some kind of soul mates.

S4 E5

Still, there's a little too much suspension of disbelief going on here. I have no problem accepting that Mulder would go in for past-life experiences. His willingness to believe makes him both open and vulnerable to any possibility; the only thing that separates him from being just another sucker is the fact that he's so often *right*. I just don't buy how immediately he commits himself to Melissa and their shared past. "Field" rests its power on the strength of that relationship, and the only tool it has to sell it are shots of Mulder and Melissa looking through that strange window and having themselves a moment. It's too easy to detach from Mulder's experience here, and this is an episode that really requires you to believe along with him. That's easy to do when there are monsters or aliens or any kind of tangible threat. Here, it's all about feelings, and the episode spends most of its running time perilously close to self-parody.

I liked it more than I was expecting, though. I rolled my eyes when Mulder called in a hypnotist to access Melissa's past-life experiences, but it's a great scene, and Mulder's own regression is some of the best work Duchovny has done on the series. The finale, too, with Mulder arriving just a few seconds too late to stop Melissa from joining her cult's mass suicide, is haunting. The episode doesn't quite earn its conclusion, but it works enough to qualify as a moderate success. You have to be willing to go along for the ride, and back when this first aired, I wasn't. I won't say I'm sorry I missed it, but I am glad that I finally got the chance to come back. —ZH

---

18 Scully's reference to the Flukeman is a hilarious exception.

19 She's also married to Glen Morgan!

I'M A MEDICAL DOCTOR!

In which Mulder and Scully happen upon the ol' "plastic surgery
outfit as a front for some serious witchcraft" gambit.

"Sanguinarium" is one of the worst *X-Files* episodes ever, but to discuss why it is bad, we have to discuss the circumstances under which it was made.

Until very recently, the way to break into the TV script–writing game was to write something called a "spec script." You watched a whole bunch of episodes of a particular show, outlined them to figure out that show's particular formula, then wrote your own take on said formula, while also not cribbing anything the show had ever done. You were writing, in other words, the ultimate fan fiction. The spec had to be scarily plausible as an episode of the show, but not so plausible that it actually *had* been an episode of the show. It had to be a show that people in Hollywood were watching and aware of, but it couldn't be a show *too many* people in Hollywood were watching and aware of.

In that regard, *The X-Files*, a cult show with pretty good ratings and Emmy recognition, was a godsend to spec script writers, and it seems like everyone who was working in the game in one way or another in the '90s had a spec *X-File* in their back pocket. Spec scripts were the best way to land a job on a series, but writing a spec script of the show you wanted to write for rarely worked. If you wanted to work on *The X-Files*, you couldn't just write an *X-File*. You had to write a spec for some other sci-fi show and hope Chris Carter liked that show.[20] *The X-Files* generally employed freelancers for a couple of episodes per year, and those episodes were inevitably among the worst of that season.[21] "Sanguinarium" is a freelance episode of *The X-Files*, but it also feels like somebody's spec script that just happened to be accidentally produced, with nobody on hand to offer quality control.

The central idea of "Sanguinarium" isn't a bad one. It's fun to watch the show dabble in the iconography of witchcraft, and blending that world with the world of plastic surgery is a cheeky way to riff on the medical shows that were so popular at the time. The guest acting is strong, particularly from John Juliani and Richard Beymer.

---

20 And what did this lead to? Usually not a staff-writing gig. Most TV shows were in the habit of employing freelance writers, people who would come in for just one episode, but not join the staff full-time. The Writer's Guild of America had rules in place about how many scripts per season had to be written by freelancers (usually two), and rather than pay a fine, most shows would bring in someone else for a few weeks to work on a script with the staff .

21 The grand exception to this rule is Vince Gilligan, who went from a freelancer on Season Two to full-time staff writer by Season Three.

Duchovny and Anderson seem to be having a bit of fun with their arguments about whether the murders are thanks to witchcraft or just a bad sleeping pill addiction. This episode also ranks as one of the goriest *X-Files* ever, with disturbing depictions of plastic surgery and blood and guts memorably filling up almost every scene.

But at every turn, "Sanguinarium" is just too much. The voices for the characters are too flat and on-the-nose. The scares are both predictable and too self-consciously edgy. The story doesn't make a lot of sense and puts much more focus on the paranormal stuff than the show usually does. The dialogue is ludicrously bad. Everything is turned up to eleven, where the show usually leaves things at about a seven or an eight. So much of the strength of *The X-Files* stems from the way that it suggests, rather than directly shows. The series is almost always about getting somewhere too late to really see the monster— about the proof Mulder seeks and Scully questions so often slipping out of their grasp—and its best episodes put the audience right in their shoes. The monsters are always already the next block over.

Not so with "Sanguinarium." Director Kim Manners tries to preserve this integral element of the show, but the script doesn't give him a lot of room. There's no way Manners can leave anything to the imagination in the scene where Dr. Lloyd performs a horrifyingly violent liposuction, say, or the scene where Dr. Franklyn peels off his face with a fork. Blood seeps out of seemingly every frame in this episode, but in disappointingly straightforward fashion. There's no hint here, no tease, just the arterial spray, and it feels jarring compared to the show's usual style. Consequently, Mulder and Scully's quest to prove what's happening feels a little silly. Why can't they catch the villains? The bad guys are right there!

Maybe excess gore was the best way to cover up the fact that the story here doesn't really make a lick of sense. It requires us to believe that a hospital has been infiltrated by dark warlocks and witches who are able to use their magic to perform medical miracles but also have to make the occasional blood sacrifice of a patient or a fellow coven member. The people who die in the episode were all born on the holiest of witches' feasts. "Sanguinarium" requires us to believe that an evil doctor is successfully able to pull off this ruse, keeping it not only from the patients but also from many of the other doctors. With such a thin premise, it's easy to see why the show overcompensated by pushing the graphic content to the limits of what TV could show at the time, but more often than not, it makes the episode seem desperate and cheap.

At every turn, "Sanguinarium" disappoints by shouting when a whisper would do. All that blood ends up feeling cheap. Rather than merely suggesting great feats of witchcraft, as "Die Hand Die Verletzt" (S2E14) did so effectively, "Sanguinarium" shows us a dude floating in midair. Rather than have Mulder come to a hypothesis, the episode just has him skip straight to witchcraft, while Scully regresses to her Season One self, tossing off pithy asides and telling her partner how wrong he is, over and over. The episode reduces the two to talking heads who comment on their stated positions but don't say anything that would suggest how seeing this strangeness affects them. "Sanguinarium" ultimately mimics the superficial beats of *The X-Files* but captures none of its soul. —TVDW

<table>
<tr><td>SEASON 4 / EPISODE 7
WRITTEN BY GLEN MORGAN
DIRECTED BY JAMES WONG</td><td>"MUSINGS OF
A CIGARETTE
SMOKING MAN"</td></tr>
</table>

NOT TODAY

In which life is like a box of chocolates: a cheap, thoughtless,
perfunctory gift that nobody ever asks for.

For years now, *The X-Files* has spread the news that something very bad is happening. The men in power have plans, and they are willing to go to any lengths to ensure those plans are executed, even if that means bumping off civilians, covering the truth, and cozening with alien forces. They have lied, obfuscated, inveigled, and denied the facts, and through it all there has been one individual—one particular bastard—standing at the edge of every curtain, whispering the words that got the trigger pulled. He is nameless. You can call him the Cancer Man, the Morley Man, the Cigarette Smoking Man, but while all of these titles are true, none of them get to the heart of the matter. That is his power. He knows who you are, but to you, he's just another shadow in the back of the room.

Until tonight.

We don't really learn anything new about CSM in "Musings"; it's been obvious from the start that he was a key figure in the show's cabal of old white dudes, and knowing that he may have killed at least two very important public figures isn't really a surprise. We don't find anything more about the colonization project, CSM's role in it, his plans for (and real relationship to) Mulder. All we really get is that he's been pulling the strings for a long time, and that despite being arguably the most powerful man in the country, he can't get a short story published. That's enough, though.

Of course, none of this is canon. The episode starts with CSM setting up eavesdropping gear in an abandoned building. Mulder, Scully, and the Lone Gunmen are across the street, and Frohike has a story to tell. Most of the episode is a visualization of Frohike's narrative, apart from a handful of scenes set in the present to remind us that CSM is listening and that he has a sniper rifle in case he doesn't like what he hears. At the end of the episode, Frohike admits that everything he's just said came from stories in a magazine he subscribes to; this is both a joke about Frohike subscribing to a porno mag (when CSM finally gets his work in print, the only place that will accept it is a *Hustler* knockoff that changes the ending), as well as a nod to fans to let us know that none of what we've seen is meant to be taken verbatim. The facts are irrelevant; it's the spirit that matters.

And it's the spirit that gets me, the humanization of a character who was, until this episode, just an amalgamation of every paranoid fear about government power. Sure, he had a relationship with the Mulders, and he may be Fox's father. Sure, he had cancer, and he could be insecure and afraid of his position. But this is the first time we've been asked to see everything that's happened from his (possible) perspective and maybe find some sympathy for the devil.

CSM is stoic throughout; his younger self says he doesn't like movies and doesn't smoke, but after he's recruited to shoot the president, he takes up both. In the next section, he assassinates Martin Luther King Jr., after the man makes potentially dangerous comments about communism. CSM says he admires MLK so much, he'll do the job himself—which proves, if nothing else, that he's invested in a warrior's dignity. Already he's writing stories and getting rejection letters. Already he's a villain, but there's something tragic in him as well, largely thanks to William B. Davis's mournful performance; the actor's perpetual hangdog expression adds nuance to otherwise purely evil acts. We don't really understand what he was before all this happened or what's driving him to act now, beyond an abstract sense of duty.

In the final two flashbacks of the episode, William B. Davis takes over the role from Chris Owens (who plays the younger version). The thrills have gone from the job, and we see him dealing awkwardly with his staff, rejecting their attempts to invite him over for Christmas, and trying to quit smoking. The Evil Russian Empire has finally collapsed, which means CSM has won his battle to defeat the Reds . . . but what now? Deep Throat makes a cameo appearance here, as the two men face their first direct contact with an alien life form. CSM talks Deep Throat into shooting the creature, even though "a living E.B.E. could advance Bill Mulder's project by decades." CSM takes up smoking again. In the next chapter, he listens in to the first few scenes of *The X-Files*, smiling.

What does any of this mean? There is a point here, and it's not just making fun of a line from *Forrest Gump*. We've known for a long time now why Mulder does what he does; his quest to uncover the reality behind the plotting and plans that have controlled his life is both the noble dream of a hero and a desperate scramble for meaning. Conspiracy nuts exist because people want to believe coincidence and catastrophe make sense. It stands to reason, then, that the actual conspirators would go about their work for much the same reason.

CSM gets his cause when he shoots JFK. It's not a cause he truly believes in, as evidenced by the fact that he starts smoking after he pulls the trigger (because cigarettes are a great way to let God know you wouldn't mind dying). But, as Frohike says, he feels like he has no choice. He does what he does because it gives him a purpose, because it builds a world that he can live in, if not be happy in. He allows Mulder to continue his work; he smiles when Scully and Fox hit it off, maybe because he's happy to have the X-Files contained—but maybe it's just another version of those cigarettes, another slow route to his inevitable death.

And as for the stories he writes? That's the best part. A man who's spent his life creating history can't get work writing fiction. "Raul Bloodworth" and his ridiculous tales are CSM's attempts to express himself, to be human in a way his government work will never allow him to be. Yes, this episode doesn't fit smoothly into the show's mythology. Yes, using the two most infamous assassinations in recent history is a little obvious. And yes, removing the helmet of *The X-Files*' Darth Vader to reveal the insecure Anakin underneath is arguably undercutting his impact in later episodes. It works, though. By this point in a show's run, either you give your villains a little breathing room, or you risk them becoming stale caricatures. "Musings" is great because it transforms CSM from a living ghost into the walking dead—still horrifying, still dangerous, but pitiable just the same. —ZH

SEASON 4 / EPISODE 8
WRITTEN BY FRANK SPOTNITZ AND CHRIS CARTER | **"TUNGUSKA"**
DIRECTED BY KIM MANNERS

SEASON 4 / EPISODE 9
WRITTEN BY FRANK SPOTNITZ AND CHRIS CARTER | **"TERMA"**
DIRECTED BY ROB BOWMAN

PARANOIA, AMERICAN STYLE

In which Mulder goes to Russia and Scully testifies before Congress and the black oil is in the Mars rock and . . . it's all weirdly complicated, OK?

Just what was it about the Clinton era that made over-the-top paranoia creep ever closer to the American mainstream? In the wake of the 2016 election, and the endless onslaught of stories suggesting (but never proving) that Bill and Hillary Clinton have been responsible for dark deeds, returning to the Clinton-era overheated flop sweat of *The X-Files* feels even stranger. At the time of its original run, the show was giving some extreme fringe a voice; now, it plays like the shape of things to come, dressed like someone from another world.

In the '90s, though, paranoia took odd routes to the surface. Occasionally, it broke through in an act of shocking violence and tragedy, like the Oklahoma City bombing.[22] More often, though, paranoia had to push its way through undiscovered channels, whether via the late-night ramblings of *Coast to Coast AM*, assorted attempts to reignite the conspiracy thriller at the multiplex, or a little TV show called

---

22 This horrifying event shook Chris Carter and actually became a reference point later in the series.

The X-Files. To be sure, the looming year 2000 played into these fears, as did the fact that the United States was now the world's sole superpower and, as such, was able to finally show doubts about its exceptionalism. Without the evil Commies to whom we could favorably compare ourselves, some things Americans on both sides of the political aisle took for granted seemed more questionable. But for as much as TV reporters at the time tried to credit *The X-Files* with driving the paranoid zeitgeist, it was never really in control. Chris Carter had just latched on to something in the body politic, and he seemed more and more alarmed by it with every passing year. But the fact that the show's paranoia was so *American* in nature also explains why "Tunguska" and "Terma" don't work as well as they might have.

In interviews at this point in the show's run, Carter will sometimes muse about the Oklahoma City bombing, trying to say that he was not encouraging Timothy McVeigh's brand of skeptical paranoia. And yet he really does believe that the government should be questioned at all times. That itself is not an objectionable idea, not really. Indeed, the idea of being skeptical of the government is central to America's foundational myth of itself.[23] The purpose of an engaged citizen, at least in a democracy, is to question every aspect of his or her country and make sure it lives up to its own principles.

At the same time, Carter struggled to square that with the darker heart of America he'd accidentally tapped into. Carter was saying that questioning things was good; McVeigh was saying the system was broken and needed to be burned to the ground. The problem with healthy skepticism is that if it's not watched carefully, it can tip over into paranoia, and paranoia has a tendency to approach everything as though it were concealing secrets.[24]

It's worth thinking about all of this because "Tunguska" is one of the first really unfocused mythology episodes in the show's run. Just as Carter and company were alarmed by America's growing paranoia, "Tunguska" makes incredibly clear that the show itself—and its mythology in particular—had become sprawling and unmanageable. All involved were simply trying to hold onto the tail of twin dragons of their own creation. The first was a mythology story line rapidly spiraling out of control and the second a country that had grown addicted to its own paranoia.

It doesn't help that "Tunguska" and "Terma" are inextricably of their time. There are references to the possible alien life discovered in the Mars rock aplenty. There's a certain immediate post–Cold War paranoia about just what

---

23 Boston Tea Party and all that.

24 See also: Fox Mulder. (Incidentally, can you imagine trying to plan a surprise party for the guy? He'd be digging through your belongings about five seconds after he came to think you were hiding something from him.)

experimentation the Russians might still be up to in their gulags.[25] Even the government hearings Scully has to attend—by far the two-parter's weakest scenes—feel very much of the era's constant Clinton investigations. Mark Snow's score is one of his clunkiest, piling on the sustained tones he was known for, then giving way to some funky electronic beats every so often, particularly in the scene closing out "Tunguska," in which the black oil threatens to infect Mulder.

Now, of course, much of this just feels silly. The Mars rock's "alien life" was revealed to be hokum. Our Russia fears have gone on to take very different forms. And the most any of those congressional subcommittees could ever even attempt to pin on the president was the idea that he'd conspired to cover up an affair. Worse, this episode marks a point in which the mythology begins to be less certain of itself.

Here's a simple example: Back in Season Three, the black oil was like a disease, passing from one person to the next. But here, it seems more like a sentient being, infecting many or just whomever happens to be closest at the time. To be sure, some of these sequences are chilling, like the scientist somehow getting infected even though he's in his biohazard suit or the infection of Mulder.[26] But it feels like the show is using a cool new villain to vamp for time.

The plot is similarly messy. Mulder's been getting tips from an informant, who's turned him on to a group of right-wing militia members. After taking in the militia members with the help of Scully and other agents, Mulder discovers his informant is Krycek. Krycek knows all about a certain courier who's carrying something in a diplomatic pouch and due to arrive at Dulles airport. If Mulder and Scully can stop him, they might be that much closer to the next piece of the puzzle. So far, so good.

But after this point, the two-parter collapses under its own weight. There's very much a sense of the show gathering all of the major *X-Files* players to go through the motions of a mythology episode, as if that's merely what's expected of it in episodes like this. The Cigarette Smoking Man turns up, and so does Skinner, and Krycek gets a lot to do, and even Marita shows up for a scene.[27] Scully briefly goes to jail, and then Mulder storms into a congressional hearing to save the day.

Up until this point, the mythology had always been driving forward to some new goal, always doling out new bits of information. Mulder has to get on that train. Scully has to escape from her coma. The story goals are usually simple, and the plot payoffs seem more complex than they actually are. Most of what we've learned about the conspiracy deals with its construction at present because the show is

S4 E8-9

---

25 This paranoia leads to the episodes' most memorable image, of Mulder, pinned down, the black oil (dubbed the "cancer" by the Russians) seeping toward him. It's how "Tunguska" cliff-hangs, and its resolution in "Terma" doesn't quite work, filled as it is with the sorts of narrative inconveniences the show often used to prolong the heroes' peril. But it's a cool image!

26 Or the reveal of how Krycek is involved in all of this.

27 Weirdly, Mulder has sexual tension with all of these people. Well, maybe not the CSM.

not yet at a place where it can delve too deeply into backstory or the organization's ultimate plans.

But "Tunguska" and "Terma" adopt a holding pattern. Instead of moving forward with another development, the show moves laterally. It's not a bad idea, really. Finding out how other countries, particularly the remnants of the Soviet Union, are dealing with the alien menace makes a certain amount of sense. But for the first time, Mulder feels less like he's driving the action and more like he's a messenger boy.

And yet, there's still a lot to recommend in the two-parter. That sequence in "Tunguska" where Krycek dangles from a balcony by one handcuffed hand and drags the courier over the edge is fraught with tension, and every time the CSM does anything in either episode, it's good fun and filled with portent. The various encounters with the black oil have a certain level of spooky charm, and the action set pieces are terrific, underlining just how much the show's budget has increased. Everything with Mulder and Krycek in Russia is fun, almost in spite of itself. These two actors are having a great time running from men on horses and getting locked up in a gulag together, and even if the truck chase in "Terma" is a little silly[28] it's at least staged thrillingly.

In particular, the shift of the conspiracy's various players toward the story's center yields the most dividends. The few scenes between the Well-Manicured Man (John Neville) and the CSM in "Terma" are the most intriguing. One of the reasons "Musings of a Cigarette Smoking Man" (S4E7) works so well is that it offers a peek behind the curtain in Oz's palace. There's so much about the cabal of codgers we don't know, and as the conspiracy wears on, the biggest mystery becomes what drives these men to behave the way they do. It's not just a quest for power; on some level, they believe they have humanity's best interests at heart. There's potential tragedy in that, in watching good intentions corrupt and decay into cruelty. It's a shame we only get to peer around the edges.

Really, the two-parter should have been about the Syndicate's machinations all along. A nursing home full of dead people oozing black gunk? The WMM's fury over the murder of his friend? The CSM's arrogance? These are the exciting beats, whereas the other story lines are just running us down familiar tracks in slightly new settings. This repetition is the heart of the problem and signals the beginning of a new direction for the mythology episodes.

"Tunguska" and "Terma" are a lot of fun, but they're not groundbreaking or eventful in the way every other mythology episode has been up to this point. There's a lot of tap dancing in the episodes, as though the show is unsure of where it's going and how it can stretch this story line out to an uncertain future. By this point, the series was successful beyond anybody's wildest dreams. If there was some sort of

---

28 The brakes on the truck being out feels almost completely random and unmotivated.

plan, it had to be extended indefinitely. In that regard, the lateral move into geopolitics made sense, but it also robbed the show of some of its urgency.

Maybe, ultimately, this two-parter just doesn't work as well because it abandons the central idea of the conspiracy's Americanness, the idea that the American government is out there, ready to snatch you at a moment's notice and do nasty things to you, and that said government has been up to this for a long, long time. Much of the action takes place in Russia, and the two-parter begins shifting the Syndicate from a uniquely American organization to one with its roots in every country. The move to make the conspiracy a global one must have seemed smart at the time, but it also robs the series of something essential, of a sense that the worst monsters are the ones who purport to have our own best interests at heart. Global paranoia is all well and good, but *The X-Files* always succeeds best when it indulges in paranoia, American-style. —ZH and TVDW

SEASON 4 / EPISODE 10
WRITTEN BY VINCE GILLIGAN
DIRECTED BY ROB BOWMAN | **"PAPER HEARTS"**

AMONG THE MISSING

*In which Mulder discovers an alternate explanation
for his sister's disappearance.*

"Paper Hearts" spends its entire running time trying to get you to believe a lie. More than anything, it wants you to think the show will throw away one of its most important structural underpinnings in the service of a Monster of the Week episode that seems cribbed from a more earthbound detective show. Chiefly, it wants you to believe that Mulder will uncover that his sister's disappearance is due to a man—a monstrous man, but a mere man nonetheless. Not aliens. Not a conspiracy. Not a shining light in the sky. A man.

There's a term for this kind of move: "schmuck's bait." TV writers use it to signify any kind of ostensibly series-changing moments that they've tossed in the middle of a story line, moments you know will never actually produce change but which they dangle in front of viewers like candy anyway. Schmuck's bait promises a fundamental shift in the show so seismic that it wouldn't really be the same show if the series went through with it, and it takes a fairly bold sense of purpose to stick the bait-and-switch. The reason Samantha being kidnapped by a serial killer named John Lee Roche (Tom Noonan) qualifies as schmuck's bait is because if Mulder ever learns what truly happened to Samantha, the show will lose a principal driving force and emotional throughline. Samantha's abduction is the central idea that tethers Mulder's physical quest to uncover the conspiracy's machinations to his psychological quest to be whole.

Thus, "Paper Hearts" is ultimately an episode that respects the viewers who know that the show, like Mulder himself, will never give up on the idea that Samantha was abducted by aliens. But, to the episode's credit, it also wants to tell a really powerful story about the idea that maybe she wasn't.

Yes, by this point, Mulder has met clones of his sister and read government files on her, so it beggars belief just a bit that he would buy an alternate version of Samantha's story. Because the plot pivot deals so explicitly on Mulder's backstory in ways that could fundamentally alter it, and because it's so achingly emotional, "Paper Hearts" is more fundamentally a mythology episode than the two that precede it, even if it has basically nothing to do with aliens or government conspiracies.

The central plot is remarkably simple: Mulder's dreams start nagging him about an old case, one that he thought solved.[29] In the case, Mulder and the FBI took down Roche (undoubtedly one of the show's most recognizably—and disturbingly—human monsters), who had taken thirteen little girls, molested and strangled them, cut a cloth heart from their nightgowns, and then buried them. Of the victims, thirteen were accounted for, and Roche confessed to thirteen murders.

But the hearts were never found, and when they finally are,[30] Mulder instead finds *sixteen* hearts and has a dream in which, instead of being taken by aliens, Samantha is taken by Roche. It's an idea Roche does nothing to dismiss, and the sort of mania that often grips Mulder in mythology episodes overtakes him here. How does Roche know so much about Mulder's sister's disappearance? Will Mulder finally find the answers he seeks?

Of course, those of us watching along at home know that the answer to the latter question is "no" because to take away the question of Samantha's abduction would rob the show of something it needs to function. Without Samantha's abduction motivating Mulder, the show would be much less powerful.[31] The mythology episodes would come to feel more and more poorly motivated, and eventually, you'd start to wonder how Mulder could believe in *any* of this bullshit. Thinking he might find Samantha at the end of everything is occasionally the only thing that makes him a sympathetic character. His paranoia has destroyed so many innocent lives—including, arguably, his own—that we need to believe he's on the right track, need to understand he's chasing a massive, global conspiracy and not just a single, horrible man.

---

29 These sequences are indelibly playful, with a terrifically whimsical score from Mark Snow and a dancing laser pointer providing all the special effects the show could ever need.

30 After Mulder's dreams help lead him to a previously unaccounted-for fourteenth victim.

31 And, in some ways, less enjoyable to watch. Duchovny as Mulder is rarely more compelling than when his motivation is to find out the truth about Samantha.

Yet Roche is oddly convincing! You're waiting for the show to toss off a lackluster explanation for how Roche could know so much about Mulder's past, and it more than delivers when it suggests that Mulder focused so intensely on the case that it opened up some kind of dream nexus between him and Roche—one that Roche used to his own advantage in trying to get our favorite agent to snap.[32]

So how does "Paper Hearts" avoid becoming just another example of writerly schmuck's bait? Despite all the healthy skepticism the episode engenders, there's a power to its final moments. Mulder has gone so far around the bend in his attempts to discover if his worst fears about Roche are true that he's taken the killer to Martha's Vineyard, forcing him to stand in the middle of the Mulder home and tell him how he took Samantha. Mulder pulls a nifty trick here,[33] as he eventually reveals that the home is not the home Samantha was taken from at all but rather the home his dad moved the family to after Samantha's abduction, thereby revealing that Roche knows a lot of the surface details but has fabricated the undercurrent of his story. But in his sleep, Mulder dreams of Samantha being taken again, and somehow frees Roche as a consequence. It's a moment in which Mulder's mania makes him breathtakingly—yet believably—stupid, made even more horrifying by our knowledge of its effect. When Mulder has something go wrong with the conspiracy, the consequences of his actions are not immediately clear. But if he doesn't catch up to Roche in time, a little girl's life will be over, and it will all be his fault.

Mulder, of course, catches up to Roche in time, in a nicely shot sequence in a graveyard of abandoned buses that suggests the ghosts of childhoods long past. He saves his reputation, as he must, but he never does get an answer about that sixteenth heart. He's pretty sure it doesn't belong to Samantha, but now there's enough doubt to leave his brain mulling the possibilities. The episode ends, as all *X-Files* episodes must, with Scully and Mulder talking about what just happened, and then she leaves the room to let him have his thoughts.

The look on his face, held over an astounding amount of wordless screen time, suggests that he knows he did the right thing by killing Roche, but that he's haunted enough by doubt now to wish he hadn't, to wish he'd gotten the answer he's looking for. In this moment, Mulder is very much a man who has lost his faith and a piece of his reason for being.

Absolutely none of this works without David Duchovny or writer Vince Gilligan. Gillian Anderson may have given the greater performance of *The X-Files*, but Duchovny gave the more iconic one. His role often gets boiled down to a few moments or scenes, ones in which he seems to stand in for the show itself, a

---

32 Personally, I prefer Scully's explanation that Roche got all of this information from the Internet. Though it only explains how he knows so much about, say, Samantha and Mulder playing Stratego if you make the leap that he's somehow reading *X-Files* fan sites.

33 As does Gilligan, who executes a cool little switcheroo on the audience (inverting the idea of this episode as schmuck's bait).

larger-than-life figure of everything it hoped to achieve. Think about his work as Mulder, and you remember a random mix of shots of the guy heading down darkened corridors with his flashlight held high, or chasing after alien spaceships, or screaming at an informant about what's just happened as the informant smiles bitterly in his face.

Even in Season Four, the idea of Mulder needed some puncturing, so self-righteous had the writers made him. They accomplished this later in the show's humorous episodes, but "Paper Hearts" is a serious take on the idea that Mulder is less a man than he is a manifestation of paranoia wearing a human suit. To his credit, Duchovny (who could coast when he was bored) steps up his game, and this episode might boast his finest overall performance of the series. The look on his face when he digs into the ground in West Virginia to find the girl who might be his sister is a testament to his expressiveness. He is wounded, haunted, driven by impulses he can't bury after nearly thirty years.

Gilligan, meanwhile, firmly reminds us why he became the best writer on the show for its midperiod. Both "Pusher" (S3E17) and "Unruhe" (S4E4) suggested Gilligan as someone who could do great, terrifying things with the show's formula. "Paper Hearts" at some level follows that formula as well, but it pushes past it, taking the show's central ideas and using them in service of a story that feels personally fraught for us because it is personally fraught for one of our heroes. This sort of emotion-driven plotting is common in the mythology episodes, but much less common to the Monster of the Week episodes, and it's frustrating how rarely the show would try something like this again. The overall impression is that of a very good X-Files episode haunted by something more, a thematic depth that transforms it from solidly entertaining into a top-tier hour.

There are still fans who reject "Paper Hearts" vociferously, who think it's worthless (despite its many virtues) because they always knew that Roche wouldn't be responsible for Samantha's disappearance. Gilligan knows this too, and he knows that you know it. His job is not to convince you that Roche took Samantha. His job is to introduce doubt in both your mind and in that of our protagonist, if even for a moment.

The comforting idea of a conspiracy theory is that it removes all room for random chance, that the death and misery that greet our time on Earth can be written off as machinations of the devil or a secret cabal that controls everything that happens. The boldest move of "Paper Hearts" is that it takes away the certainty that some sort of evil order prevails and replaces it with the idea that it *all* could be random chance. In real life, most of us eventually come to accept this fact of life. But in fiction, particularly in fiction like *The X-Files*, where there's a place for everything and everything has its place, it can be disconcerting.

"Paper Hearts" lives in that uneasiness. Its suggestion that sometimes it's not your dad turning you over to aliens, that sometimes it's just a nut with an El Camino and a horrible secret, is almost radically simple for the show. The possibility that there could actually be a reasonable explanation becomes a doubt that nags and can never be entirely dismissed, even as you know the lie for what it is. *The X-Files*, for all its feints toward ambiguity, exists in a universe driven by an almost godlike conspiracy that can do whatever it likes, and there's a comfort in having that kind of certainty in our fiction. But there's a power in embracing the mystery, the idea that life is a scary, random place. "Paper Hearts" isn't the only episode in which *The X-Files* explored that concept, but it's probably the best example of an entry that suggests the truth might be too difficult to know. —TVDW

SEASON 4 / EPISODE 11
WRITTEN BY JOHN SHIBAN | **"EL MUNDO GIRA"**
DIRECTED BY TUCKER GATES

EL CHUPACABRA

In which The X-Files *becomes a telenovela.*

"El Mundo Gira" never hits the heights of whimsy or cynicism *The X-Files* can reach in its greatest hours, but it *is* more interesting than it initially appears to be. Two brothers are feuding over the same woman in a migrant workers' camp in California. One afternoon, there's a flashing light, a yellow rain, and then the woman winds up dead, her eyes missing and the skin around her mouth shredded away. A goat lies dead next to her, so the locals start panicking about El Chupacabra, a gray monster with black eyes and a bulging forehead who sucks goats. Those who don't automatically believe in monsters assume Eladio, one of the dead woman's suitors, is responsible, but due to the bizarre nature of the crime and the so-called Fortean Event that precedes it, Mulder and Scully fly in, and we're off to the races.

The first half of "Gira" plays it straight. Mulder and Scully wander around; we learn about the plight of the immigrant community; Mulder pairs up with local cop Conrad Lozano (Rubén Blades); Scully does an autopsy . . . that sort of thing. Where "Gira" disappoints is in its surprising choice of villain: rather than a Chupacabra being responsible for the run of mysterious deaths in the community, it is Eladio (through no fault of his own) who is infecting those around him by secreting an enzyme that inspires fatally aggressive growth in whatever fungal material he touches.[34] That's all neat and science-y, sure, but it's no goat-sucking beast.

---

34 One poor bus driver dies from the worst case of athlete's foot in history.

Plus, while the episode goes to great lengths to try to connect the illegal aliens we see here and the ones Mulder has spent most of his life tracking down,[35] that connection has no weight beyond the pun. The ETs who've been causing all kinds of crazy on planet Earth don't flourish because white people ignore them; they flourish because they have magical space alien powers and because they've made deals with the U.S. government to stay hidden. They have actual power. All poor Eladio has is an unfortunate skin condition and a nasty handshake.

Yet as the episode wears on, something strange happens. It gets . . . looser, somehow. The Mulder/Scully banter is solid as ever.[36] The music turns playful, almost mocking Eladio's sweaty desperation. "Gira" looks neat, too, thanks to some nifty direction from Tucker Gates; there's a great shot of Eladio stumbling down a hallway that could've been just filler, but is so full of blinking shadows and gloom that it stuck in my head for the rest of the hour.

Then there's the bizarre ending. We don't see the final confrontation with Eladio and his brother because Mulder and Scully don't see it. First, we hear an account from an immigrant who firmly believes in the Chupacabra myth, mistaking men in hazmat suits for aliens and telling the community that Eladio turned his brother into the same kind of monster he is, and that the two have gone off to some special place in the sky. Then we hear the official version Mulder and Scully tell Skinner; it isn't much better. Lozano is dead (his sudden shift from world-weary apathetic to someone who gives a crap about the immigrants' customs doesn't really work), and the brothers have vanished. The fact that Scully isn't freaking out about the disappearance is odd, seeing as how earlier, she was stressing the importance of apprehending Eladio before he stumbled into a city and killed hundreds, if not thousands. I guess because they're headed back to Mexico, she doesn't care anymore?

None of this holds together—it's mostly the appearance of deconstruction without the wit or pathos to mean anything—but it's nevertheless entertaining. Eladio's gradual transformation into a monster helps bring together the aliens/aliens connection better than any dialogue. (At least the visual pun forces us to do our own homework.) And the last shot of the brothers, both now full Chupacabra, wandering down the highway at night, is undeniably haunting, if also undeniably silly. If we aren't going to get a classic episode, I'd prefer to get a bananas one, and unlike the plodding mediocrity of "Teso dos Bichos" (S3E18), "Gira" actually had a few moments of nutso joy. I can't really defend it, but it partly won me over in the end. —ZH

---

35 The episode loses any pretense toward serious reflection when Blades literally says, "To most people, they're aliens in the true sense of the word." How does that even make sense?

36 "Purple rain?" "Yeah. Great album. Deeply flawed movie."; "Scully, I've been thinking. I know that's dangerous, but just bear with me."

SOMETHING I NEED

In which Scully gets some bad news.

"Leonard Betts" has become so much about its incredible final five minutes that it's easy to forget how awesome the rest of the episode is. It's positively filled with chilling moments, goofy (but cool) science, and gross-out bits. It's easy to see why Fox chose to air this episode after the 1997 Super Bowl; "Leonard Betts" is a stellar example of the show at its most thrilling. This coveted time slot led to the episode being the most-watched episode of *The X-Files* ever, exposing the show to its widest possible audience—29.1 million people in its initial broadcast. You have to wonder what all the people viewing the show for the first time thought. Subsequent ratings in the months to come would indicate that most of them must have liked what they saw. For all of the unsettling images, the viewers of "Leonard Betts" seemed to take what the episode was selling in stride.

Try to think of this as your first exposure to *The X-Files*. Imagine finishing the big game, only to have the next thing you see be a headless body roaming around. The show's usual aesthetic is in full force and then some, so whether you've seen it before or not, there's a significant shock factor. All the scenes in which we see the more monstrous aspects of Leonard—like his resurrection sans head, or the way his eyes and mouth open on Scully's autopsy table, or his horrifying regeneration—are shot with the series' sense of dark foreboding. The cool blacks of the show's color palette, as well as the distinctly moody Vancouver location work, are highlighted to the utmost. "Leonard Betts" is an eminently accessible episode of *The X-Files* for new viewers, while still staying true to the show's quintessential nature.

Even more remarkable, this hour is far from a stand-alone. Indeed, it launches the show's single most sustained story arc to this point. Unlike the alien conspiracy, *The X-Files* couldn't simply look away from Scully's cancer. It became something that informed many episodes to come, even Monster of the Week episodes. When Leonard tells her she has something he needs, one of the most chilling lines of the entire series, we suddenly understand the dark implications. This is an episode that is designed to draw in as many new fans as possible, but it's also one that pays off in a big way for longtime fans. If you're watching for the first time, Leonard's line is just a disturbing suggestion. But if you've been watching from day one, this is the culmination of a plotline that began in Season Two. That's a remarkable feat of storytelling, any way you slice it.

Here's another reason "Leonard Betts" works so well: It moves like a rocket. It's often dangerous on a show like this to introduce too many new ideas. Pile on too many crazy notions, and you threaten to lose much of the audience. "Leonard Betts" is *technically* a straightforward MOTW story. But the revelations are so crazy that any single one of them could be the basis of an entire episode, and the show just keeps piling them on.

First we find out that Leonard—his name isn't actually Leonard, but it's his alias for long enough that we should probably just go with it—can somehow walk around sans head. Then we find out that his decapitated head can open its eyes and mouth. Then we find out that for whatever reason, Leonard keeps his tub full of iodine. Then we find out that he can regrow his entire head and break off his thumbs to escape from handcuffs. Then we find out he's willing to kill to keep his mutation under wraps. Then we find out that he's not only made entirely of cancer but that he needs to feed on cancer to survive. Cancer is what lets him live, but that means he has to kill others to get those tasty, cancerous cells, including his mother.

This is a giant, rolling ball of plot revelations that drives the momentum of the episode. In most *X-Files* episodes, Mulder and Scully will happen upon some sort of crazy situation, then Mulder will say, "I think it was a ghost!" and Scully will say, "I think it was electromagnetic interference from the moon!" And it will turn out to be a ghost. But the show is often more compelling when Mulder is trying to figure it out along with everybody else.

When the episode starts, he's certain that a headless Leonard Betts walked out of the morgue and headed home. While he's right about that, he doesn't even begin to grasp the entirety of what's going on. The series works best when it's a conversation between Mulder and Scully, when her skepticism drives him to greater heights of pseudoscientific lunacy and his lunacy drives her to try to come up with more scientific rationales for what's going on. Here, it becomes clear very quickly to both characters that Leonard is something special. This is a MOTW episode in which Mulder and Scully are scrambling to keep up with just what the hell is going on.

The show plays this trick on the audience too. Usually, we know slightly more than Mulder and Scully. Mulder will often have a theory or two that puts him on the same level as us, but we've generally seen the monster up to its business before Mulder and Scully do, which gives us an advantage over our heroes. To a degree, we usually know if this is a vampire story or a werewolf story, and it's just a matter of waiting for Mulder to get on the same page as us. But in "Leonard Betts," we're lagging behind, along with the agents, and that makes everything feel even more off-kilter than usual. *The X-Files* was endlessly inventive with its basic formula, but it rarely tweaked it as effectively as it did here. We don't quite know what to expect next, and that makes the episode have a greater sense of fun than it might have had if Mulder wandered in at the start and said, "Cancer monster!" The flow of information among the show, its characters, and the audience is all messed up, and it makes the episode work incredibly well.

It also helps that Leonard's so understandable. He just wants to survive, and he's not happy about what he has to do to be able to survive. By its fourth season, *The X-Files* had reached a level of success that allowed it to attract top guest stars, and the character of Leonard wouldn't be nearly so haunting without Paul McCrane[37] playing him. McCrane makes Leonard a regular guy who hides a terrible, terrible secret that drives him to do horrible things. He's a monster, sure, but he's also recognizably a human being, and as everything starts coming down around his ears, he reacts like most of us would, if we needed to periodically devour a tumor to keep our regenerative powers.

But let's also not ignore that final moment, in which Scully's nose begins to bleed and the show pulls together a whole bunch of strands it's been developing for much of the season, letting us know that Mulder and Scully are never going to be out of the woods. This has always been a show in which the MOTW episodes and the mythology rarely, if ever, intertwine, but here the show breaks its own rules, in a way that first-time viewers won't really catch on to.[38] It's ingenious, and it still packs its punch all these years later.

However, "Leonard Betts" deserves to be remembered for a whole host of other things as well. This is the kind of episode that only a show at the top of its game could produce, an episode that takes everything the series has built to an entirely new level. "Leonard Betts" isn't the best episode of *The X-Files*, but it signifies the dawning of a golden age for the series, and it does so with an electrifying confidence. It puts a punctuation mark on one chapter and begins a new one in style. —TVDW

SEASON 4 / EPISODE 13
WRITTEN BY GLEN MORGAN AND JAMES WONG
DIRECTED BY ROB BOWMAN

"NEVER AGAIN"

OUROBOROS

In which Scully gets a tattoo, and Mulder goes to Graceland.

The X-Files has made playful jabs at alien conspiracy theories before, but I can think of few starker examples than the exchange that starts this episode (post-title sequence). Mulder is talking with an informant in front of the Vietnam Memorial, but we don't see him or the informant. We see Scully, bored out of her mind. The boredom is funny enough, but what's really striking is the slightly lost look on her face, the one that inspires her to wander to the wall, read some of the names, and pick a rose petal off a dying flower. She's probably thinking about her father,

---

37 Best known for his wildly different work on *ER*.

38 The episode it's most similar to is "Duane Barry" (S2E5), another episode of surprise Scully peril.

which connects to her monologue later in the episode about her issues with the demanding men in her life.[39] It's a scene of deep loneliness, made all the more effective because it's asking us to empathize with one lead at the cost of our respect for another. The informant's story *is* ridiculous, and spending a cold night lurking by the names of the dead just to chase down another empty absurdity can't be satisfying.

"Never Again" is colored by an overwhelming sense of deep dissatisfaction, a feeling that organically drives the story to new and exciting places. It is an excellent entry for many reasons, including its wonderful direction—full of the kind of stylish cinematic touches that have come to define the series in its third and fourth seasons—but the best part about "Never Again" is its critical examination of the Mulder/Scully dynamic and its complex portrayal of the two as flawed individuals. In particular, we are given a chance to see Scully acting like a person with wants and needs instead of the strong and endlessly competent agent she so often seems to be.

I don't think I've ever hated Mulder quite like I hate him in the last scene of this episode. The show has mocked him before; it has poked holes in his arrogance and in his obsessive quest for the truth, and it has criticized the collateral damage his quest has done—both to him and the people close to him. But "Never Again" shows him at his absolute worst, and it's even more damning because his behavior here isn't that unusual. It's in his nature, much the same way that Scully's complicated relationship with authority figures is in hers. There's a sullen self-absorption—a little-boy-ignored feel to his dialogue at the end, and more than a fair bit of condescension as well. "Congratulations for making a personal appearance in the X-Files for the second time," he tells his partner. That moment, the gulf between them is made clear, and potentially irreparable: Scully may want more from her life than chasing X-Files, but for Mulder, it's everything. If Scully is not wholeheartedly committed to the X-Files, then who can Mulder trust? Conversely, why should Scully always be expected to fall in line and make Mulder's pursuits her own?

"Never Again" lets Scully be flawed in a pretty unprecedented way. Generally, Mulder's the screw-up. He rushes in without thinking, he gets in over his head, and he's so righteous that he forgets that simply being right isn't enough to keep you from getting killed. Scully hangs back, gathering data, providing support, and more often than not, she's the one left to clean up the mess. As the series has progressed, it's become more and more obvious that Scully is the grown-up in this partnership. The show has done a decent job of never letting either character off the hook for their complicity in the dysfunction laid bare by this episode, but Scully is typically the sensible one, and there's something one note in always letting her be the paragon of

---

39 The connection Scully makes here between men like her father and men like Mulder is echoed in "Quagmire" (S3E22), when she called Mulder "Ahab"—the same affectionate *Moby-Dick*–inspired nickname she used for her dad.

logic. Sure, her skepticism means she's nearly always wrong (which is funny, seeing as how the main reason a person becomes a skeptic is that skeptics are nearly always *right*), but her solid, unshakable professionalism makes her a little too perfect.

Here, we see Scully being more impulsive and reckless than we've ever seen her,[40] and her relationship with Edward Jerse[41] is doomed from the start. Before they've even met, Ed has already murdered someone, driven by the disembodied voice[42] of his new pinup girl tattoo to near madness; worse, Ed's fury is propelled by his recent divorce. Women bring out the worst in Ed, the audience is told, and this creates a tremendous tension as we see Scully being further drawn in by him.

Nevertheless their pairing—and its intensity—makes sense. Ed is attracted to Scully from the moment he sees her, though his overtures are clumsy—but it's that very clumsiness, that raw and fumbling sincerity, that pulls Scully in. There's a directness to his approach that offers her something new, something that at first seems completely different from Mulder and his X-Files. It's the immediacy of his flirtation that does it, I think, and the fact that Ed isn't interested in Scully because of some conspiracy but because of who she *is*. We know he's dangerous, but that danger appeals to her. Justifying Scully's decision to get involved with a stranger is tricky business, but it works because she's clearly trying to break old patterns.

"Never Again" is a departure from the typical *X-Files* formula. Mulder's gone for most of the running time, and given the strained relations between him and his partner, we don't get as many back-and-forth phone calls as we usually would in episodes in which the leads are apart. Ed is the Monster of the Week, but the threat he poses is not a particularly paranormal one. He's just a deeply screwed-up guy who gets a tattoo and fails to cope with his misogynistic impulses. Sure, the tattoo has a special kind of ink that's known to cause hallucinations, but as Mulder says at the end, there's not enough in his bloodstream to justify what he's hearing. This is the closest we've come to a nonparanormal episode since, what, "Grotesque" (S3E14)? Jodie Foster's voice-over is unsettling, and the direction is stylish enough that the episode feels of a piece with everything else, but a friend of mine dismisses "Never Again" as an "erotic thriller knockoff," and while I disagree about the quality, plot-wise, he's not that far off.

Then why does this work so well? Giving Scully a chance to vent some of her frustrations about her life with Mulder is an important step, for one. One of the strengths of *The X-Files* is its willingness to challenge its own core values, and it's

---

40 After the big twist in "Leonard Betts" (S4E12), it would be easy to see Scully's behavior in "Never Again" as a response to the death sentence she hasn't quite finished reading. But there's no mention of an illness, and Scully never coughs or appears physically drained. Ascribing her motivations to some desperate need to spit in the face of mortality would be selling the character, and the episode, short.

41 Played by Rodney Rowland, another *Space: Above and Beyond* alumnus.

42 Of Jodie Foster, herself!

hard to imagine the show ever getting much darker than this one does in its final scene: Mulder's inability to understand that Scully might want a life outside of the world of the X-Files; that final, brief shot of the two seated; Mulder behind his desk, Scully a few feet away; and all the empty space around them. "Not everything is about you, Mulder. This is my life." "Yes, but it's . . ." That final exchange is so slight, and yet it's impossible to shake. Mulder's refusal to accept that there are priorities outside of his is such an ordinary monstrosity. We've all known people like that; we've all *been* people like that. And we've all been like Scully, sitting on the other side, unable to leave. The real monster of "Never Again" is the way our need to connect with others makes us vulnerable, how sometimes it seems like the only response to that vulnerability, the only way to be safe, is blind, senseless rage. Scully, as always the sanest person in a mad world, doesn't have that recourse. Her sense of responsibility and obligation to maintaining order defines her, but it also prevents her from the sort of indulgences that Mulder takes for granted. She's left with a cold and clear comprehension of exactly the position she's in and with no way to change it. Never again, indeed. —ZH

"MEMENTO MORI"

SEASON 4 / EPISODE 14
WRITTEN BY CHRIS CARTER, VINCE GILLIGAN,
JOHN SHIBAN, AND FRANK SPOTNITZ
DIRECTED BY ROB BOWMAN

THE LIFE OF THE WORLD TO COME

In which Scully has cancer, and Mulder thinks it's caused by aliens.

I have an atheist friend who believes in Heaven.

He doesn't believe in floaty clouds and angels playing harps or anything like that. Nor does he believe in anything like reincarnation or another life on this Earth. He cheekily calls the idea "atheist Heaven" because it's a way to live again without actually having to believe in some grand force tugging the cosmos around. Billions upon billions of years from now, the long process that began when the big bang turned an infinitesimal ball of matter into the whole wide universe will end, and everything will start pulling back together.[43] Stars will collapse into each other, planets will be burned to dust, and everything that is will end, drawn back into the tiny place it all began. And then there will simply be nothing—an endless expanse of colorless, shapeless impossibilities. The only thing that will exist in it will be something too small to see with the naked eye yet something that somehow contains everything.

---

43 Scientists differ on if this will happen or if the universe will expand indefinitely or something else, but this isn't an astrophysics book, and can you please just go with me here?

And then it begins anew. The pressure of that tiny object will cause it to explode again, spitting forth everything that ever was or ever will be all over again. Stars and black holes and planets and France and aliens and doughnuts and sandstone and palm trees and giraffes will all exist again, if you give them time. Some versions of the universe will be completely different. Some will have slight differences—I'll have black hair here, you'll be a superintelligent cat there—but there will be some that are the same, or the same with minor changes. And since time is infinite, we've done all of this before. I've written these words before, you've read them before, and you've probably decried my self-indulgence before as well.

This is only one possible interpretation of how the universe could end and begin all over again, and one of the less likely ones at that. But it's the one my friend chooses to believe in because he likes to have something to imagine as the end approaches, even if it's just the prospect of doing all of this over again, making the same mistakes and celebrating the same successes. Ultimately, the idea that animates faith, that animates most belief, is the idea that death can't just be it. For so many of us, death is a gaping canyon that swallows everything we had hoped to be, no matter how long it takes for it to take us.

The twin ideas that animate "Memento Mori" seem at cross-purposes on a casual watch. The first idea is that Dana Scully is ill with cancer. She is going to die. There's treatment, but the hope it will work is slim at best, and the doctor who thinks he can treat her turns out to not have her best interests in mind. There is no way out of this for her.

At the same time, the second idea is that she's a television character. She's one of two regulars on a TV show that would be deeply harmed by either of the regulars being written out of the show. So she can't die. As Clyde Bruckman said back in Season Three, Scully is more or less immortal, as she's a fictional character who's integral to the success of the story she's a part of. We know that she will come out of this, perhaps a better and wiser person but still a *living* person. The experience might change her on some level. She might really ail and struggle with the disease and get to win an Emmy for her troubles. But she will undoubtedly live. And since it seems her cancer was caused by the implant that was placed in her head when she was abducted, and then later removed, someone within the conspiracy must know how to make her cancer get all better. Hey, what about the Cigarette Smoking Man? He seems pretty plugged in!

And these two ideas even create a fundamental split within the episode. On the one hand, you have Scully starkly confronting her mortality, the fact that she will die sooner rather than later and deciding what she wants to die doing is the work, the work that has come to define her life. This is the kind of realistic grappling with actual, physical death we rarely see on the show, the kind that leads so many of us to invent an afterlife even if we don't quite believe in it. On the other hand, you have Mulder wandering the eastern half of the United States, trying to find the answers he needs, the one key that will unlock the question of just how Scully will get better and get back to working at his side. And that's not to mention Skinner cutting a devil's deal with the CSM. These events take place in a TV show—a very good TV show, but a TV show nonetheless.

This is a famous, Emmy-winning episode, one that routinely settles into lists of the best *X-Files* installments of all time. And I can see why! It's an occasionally beautiful, occasionally haunting, often overwritten story about one woman confronting what her life has come to mean, with an action-packed, propulsive mythology episode, one that advances the human/alien hybrid plot and fills in a few key puzzle pieces, clumsily grafted onto it. Coming right after the moving, self-assured "Never Again" (S4E13), an episode that does pretty much the same thing but mostly leaves Mulder out of the proceedings, it seems even more ridiculous.

But then I started thinking about my atheist friend and his atheist Heaven, about faith and the reasons we cling to it, even when reason keeps battering at the doors we use to close it off from the rest of our brains. Scully is facing the end of her life, and she has nothing. What does she do? She tries to help a fellow woman suffering from the same kind of cancer. She writes a lengthy, perhaps intentionally pretentious message to Mulder in her diary. She finds another doctor who might be able to treat her. When all else fails, she returns to the mission, to the work that is now her life's work as well, even though it was given to her by a long succession of men and not actively chosen by her. The answer to what gave her and the other abductees cancer just might be in the X-Files somewhere. She has to have faith.

But this is what Mulder's doing too. Mulder's not a believer in God. He's a believer in the conspiracy, in the notion that a group of men in shadowy rooms are dictating the terms of the playing field he's scrambling around on. When Scully gets sick, it makes Mulder feel powerless, and he figures that to beat death, to cheat death, really, he's going to need to get out there and make the conspiracy listen to him.

This is exactly what he does, of course, finding out about Betsy Hagopian's death and the man trying to download the information she had on her Mutual UFO Network computer, then tracing that information to a strange medical facility (government-owned!) that ostensibly works to help women with fertility problems but is actually a front for the human/alien hybrid program. The facility contains frozen ova from abducted women and is growing more versions of Mulder's new MUFON friend, who turns out to be the grown version of the little boy from "Herrenvolk" (S4E1).

The mythology has, again, been stripped down to a very human complication: How are we going to get Scully better? And, as always, having that human story at the center gives everything the drive that it needs.

"Memento Mori" could turn terrible so easily. The two halves of the episode never feel like they belong in the same space. Indeed, making this a "Never Again"-esque character study and following it up with an episode about Mulder's investigation, effectively turning "Memento Mori" into a two-parter, might have worked slightly better. Scully's narration is the purplest of purple prose, and the way it keeps popping up, sounding like something a really pretentious kid writes in the high school yearbooks of his really pretentious friends, is always jarring. It's all one can do to remain engaged with the episode when that narration rears its head again and again and again. The episode was written over a single weekend (when a different episode fell through), and it shows.

Yes, there are beautiful, understated moments here, like Mulder not being able to tell Scully what happened to all of those women she met last season, or Scully trying to sit with Penny (Gillian Barber) as she slowly slips away, or the fragile look on her face as she restates her dedication to the cause at the end, but those moments almost get swallowed up by the action-heavy mythology stuff that's also going on.

And yet they don't, not quite. And that's because Gillian Anderson, who won an Emmy for her work in this episode, even though she's not on-screen nearly as much as you'd expect, and David Duchovny play absolutely everything in this episode like raw nerves. Both Scully's desperation and the way she tries to bury it deep within herself, only to have it emerge at unlikely moments, are written all over Anderson's face. This was one of the high points for both the Scully character and Anderson's work as her.

What's easier to forget is how drop-dead terrific Duchovny is here, as Mulder's jokes stop being able to cheer Scully up and he realizes that there's no way out of the predicament the two are in, that he's going to lose his best friend, the woman he's more attached to than anyone on Earth, the arguable love of his life. (This is perhaps the most forthright episode about the deep, abiding love these two have for each other to this point in the series.) Duchovny plays all of this as a man who's simply unable to fathom that any of this is happening and, thus, plunges himself neck-deep into the one thing he believes in—an all-encompassing conspiracy to ready the world for alien occupation. The actors commit so thoroughly that they are able to overcome any amount of purple narration or terrible dialogue.

Or maybe it all works because, on some level, the notion that every one of us will die and none of us quite knows what to do with that knowledge permeates every level of the episode, right down to its title. Chris Carter's shows have always been terrified of the notion that, no matter how much you can possibly understand the secret workings of the world, no matter how much you can make sense of the senseless, you can't make sense of death, not without doing some mental gymnastics and inventing a place to go once it's all over, be that place a city in the sky, or this world—the world as you know it with potholes and grocery stores and pudding cups and your next-door neighbor's mail in your mailbox and the sound of rain on a Sunday morning—all over again. —TVDW

A CURE

The creative impulse behind Scully's cancer, one of the more significant plot points in the series, was actually more pragmatically motivated than it might appear. Frank Spotnitz explains: "In Season Four, Darin [Morgan] had left the show because he found the whole process of writing television deeply painful: getting notes, and all the frustrations of actually making a TV show. But [Darin] said, 'I'm gonna come back and I'm gonna write one more episode,' [so we thought], 'Fantastic, Darin's gonna write one more episode in Season Four.'

"He was due to deliver the script in December, and my recollection . . . is that three days before prep he called and said, 'I'm really sorry, I couldn't crack it . . . I'm not going to be able to deliver a script.' And [unfortunately] we had zero things to put in its place. At the beginning of the season, there had been some discussion about Agent Scully getting cancer, because we'd had these other female abductees in Season Three who had cancer. Some people [thought it would be] a bit cheesy and melodramatic and beneath *The X-Files*, [but] when Darin said, 'I don't have a script,' we turned to each other and said, 'That's it, Scully's getting cancer.' And in one day, Vince, John Shiban, and I [devised] an episode where Scully got cancer, and then in the next day, the three of us [each] wrote a third of that episode, and then we stitched those three things together and it was a pretty rough Frankenstein monster at that point. Fortunately, the Christmas vacation followed, and during his vacation Chris rewrote that script, which became 'Memento Mori' (S4E14). So, it had four writers, which I think was a record for *The X-Files*, but it was also the only episode that the four of us got nominated for an Emmy for writing."

Interestingly, "Leonard Betts" (S4E12), which teased the revelation soon to come in "Memento Mori," was conceived *after* the latter episode was written. Spotnitz recalls the thinking behind selecting "Leonard Betts" for the coveted, post–Super Bowl slot: "We wanted one that would lead into Scully's cancer, and that would be a great monster show, so that was really designed to be [what] we knew would probably be the highest-rated episode of the show ever. There was a lot of debate actually, about whether it should be 'Leonard Betts' that [aired in that slot], or 'Never Again' (S4E13) which Glen and Jim had written. And we won!"

'TIL DEATH DO US PART

In which mourning takes an unexpected form.

"Kaddish" isn't amazing, sad to say. The *Tales from the Crypt*–style "justice from the beyond the grave" plot has been done so often it's hard to get too excited watching a victim track down and finish off his attackers, and we're never given much reason to care if the victim in this episode is stopped. The bad guys are one note; Mulder and Scully's confrontation with a creep who prints delightful pamphlets like "How AIDS Was Created by the Jews" is too much like a lecture about the dangers of hate.[44] Yet there are intimations of deeper themes here that occasionally resonate. There's precious little comedy to be found, outside of a few quips from Mulder, and that melancholy—that feeling of something precious irrevocably lost—permeates the episode's best moments.

At heart, "Kaddish" is a supernatural gloss on how acts of great horror and violence echo into the future, turning people into living golems, forever driven by a dead past. Ariel (Justine Miceli) loses her fiancé, Isaac (Harrison Coe), to a group of neo-Nazis. To avenge him, she raises a monster, who causes more death, ensuring the cycle of violence continues. Ariel's father, Jacob (David Groh), is a Holocaust survivor, and his experiences made him protective of what family he had left, sometimes to extreme degrees. But these powerful pieces don't combine into an effective whole, and it's hard not to feel as though Judaism was brought into the episode solely for the purpose of creating a new spin on an old story.

"Kaddish" works best if you enjoy it for its style and presentation without getting too caught up in the script. The revelation that Ariel is responsible for Isaac's golem is a good one, and the final confrontation in the temple is one of the more beautiful sequences I've seen on the show. We don't really know Ariel very well, and her relationship with the dead man is more a fairy tale than anything specific enough to be invested in. Nevertheless, the last shots of the two completing their vows, of their embrace, of her wiping off the symbol on Isaac's hand, finally ending his unlife, are haunting. At this point in the show's run, *The X-Files* has gotten very good at making even the worst scripts look cinematic on-screen, and "Kaddish" benefits greatly from this. It's also a fine twist: The Isaac golem wasn't just created for revenge. But sometimes love, too, can be monstrous. —ZH

---

44 Check out Mulder's "one-up" moment when the creep makes a snide comment about resurrection: "A Jew pulled it off 2000 years ago," our hero says, and then he *nods*, like, "Aw yeah, suck on *that*, Mr. Hater-ade."

| SEASON 4 / EPISODE 16
WRITTEN BY HOWARD GORDON AND CHRIS CARTER
DIRECTED BY MICHAEL LANGE

INVISIBLE MAN

In which there's an invisible assassin.

Vietnam did a number on America.[45] That war inspires the paranoia of Oliver Stone (whose films are an obvious touchstone for *The X-Files*), and it helped kindle the growing distrust of the government that proved to be the series' central belief system. So naturally, *The X-Files* has dealt with the Vietnam War on a handful of occasions, but it has rarely done so as directly or as succinctly as it does in "Unrequited." Here, the echoes of the war haunt us out of the corner of our eye, and the soldiers who fought in the conflict become literally ghostlike, returning to their homeland to enact a revenge they barely understand.

Sadly, this isn't a very good episode, but it's a potent one all the same. The assorted mysteries of the story never coalesce in a way that allows the entry to pack a punch. And yet "Unrequited" is hard to shake.

The biggest problem is structural, which is apparent in the opening scene. The episode opens at a speech about the Vietnam War (given just feet from the Vietnam War Memorial) being delivered by a general who is being stalked by an assassin out in the crowd. Neither Mulder nor Scully can see the assassin, and just when he draws his gun and Mulder finally locks eyes on him, the assassin vanishes into thin air, seemingly whooshing out of existence. It's a neat effect, and it immediately establishes the paranormal aspect of the episode. It would be a great starting point for an episode. Instead, it's actually the end point.

A TV storytelling device that needs to be retired posthaste is the idea of starting an episode at a point of maximum conflict, then flashing back to, say, a day earlier, so that we can learn how the plot came to that point. It rarely works as a way to goose drama because it reduces everything to a series of equations that need to add up to the scene we saw earlier, inherently negating any element of surprise the plot may have held.[46] While *The X-Files* is old enough that the device was still pretty new when the series utilized it, this episode doesn't utilize the tactic in a clever way. The rest of the episode literally just confirms what we learned in the opening, and the final scenes involve replaying the five-minute opening almost shot-for-shot, meaning that roughly ten minutes of the episode are taken up by showing the same scene twice, for no real discernible reason.

---

45 I am almost certainly the first person to have ever had this idea. Don't @ me.

46 For an episode that contradicts this argument and uses this device to maximum effect, see "Colony" (S2E16).

As the episode plays out, we learn that the man Mulder and Scully are trying to capture is Sergeant Nathaniel Teager (Peter LaCroix), a Vietnam vet who was a presumed POW, before his charred remains were ostensibly returned to the United States. Is Teager a ghost? Some sort of brainwashed robot? Both?

The episode weaves a fairly convoluted story, involving Teager joining forces with a militia group to take out Vietnam War generals, employing techniques of disappearance he learned from observing the Viet Cong while he was in captivity. At the same time, he's acting at the behest of the government, which wants the generals dead to keep them from exposing embarrassing information about the country's assorted military adventures. Or so Marita Covarrubias says, but who can trust her? The episode, scripted by the show's two biggest government paranoiacs, suggests a lot of great ideas without really bringing those ideas home. For instance, Teager says that there are many other POWs still in Vietnam, an old conspiracy theory that could have helped anchor this episode. Similarly, the idea that Teager learned his disappearing tricks from Vietnamese soldiers is a cool one that never gets fleshed out, and the episode never really bothers to settle on an explanation for why Teager can disappear from view (outside of suggesting he somehow creates floating blind spots in people's eyes . . . ?). The ideas seem trapped in a never-ending quagmire, which might be the point, given the episode's suggestions that Vietnam was something these men could never leave behind, while many of their fellow citizens preferred to stop thinking about it (and them) altogether.

The episode doesn't have time to make Teager anything more than a boogeyman, able to pop up wherever he wants at any given moment, putting bullets into the heads of heavily guarded generals with impunity. The first time we see him chronologically, he appears opposite one of the generals in the backseat of a car, while the car is moving. It's a great idea, a great image, and a great moment. But the impact of it is muted by the fact that Teager remains a barely sketched character throughout the episode. Look at Teager entering the Pentagon without anyone noticing him, or talking to a veteran who later recognizes him at the general's speech. There's potential here for an intriguing spin on a classic monster type: the invisible man. Instead, Teager is a generic almost-ghost. The scene in which Teager repeats his name and rank over and over after he's shot is supposed to serve as emotional catharsis, but the lack of character development means the moment has no true impact.

But "Unrequited" can't be dismissed out of hand either. In terms of great, scary visuals, the episode offers us only one: the scene in which Scully stands outside a compound for a separatist militia group, scanning the tree line, and the camera barely picks out . . . someone just standing there, even though Scully can't quite see him. It's a good episode for Skinner too, since it gives him a mission (keep the generals safe) and alludes to his past as a soldier in the war without diving too far into it. Here, Mitch Pileggi is allowed to do something other than just be the gruff boss who still

S4 E16

cares deeply for his agents. And while Mulder and Scully don't get a lot to do, the scene in which she's forced to share his crazy theory (at least in part) is a lot of fun.

The best thing about the episode is the way that it uses Vietnam—a national wound that felt even fresher when this episode aired—as a sort of point A in a long line of national calamities, a natural beginning for a country that became controlled more and more thoroughly by "them," whoever "they" may be. *The X-Files* was always a show for free-floating conspiracy theorists, people who really believed in the Roswell cover-up *and* the JFK cover-up *and* any other number of cover-ups. Here, Vietnam fits into that picture readily, as a sort of lie we all can agree on—a war that occurred at a time when the government didn't tell the whole truth and pretty much everybody knows now that it didn't. For a show featuring an escaped Vietnam POW who can make himself invisible, "Unrequited," with its sense of fraught paranoia and concern about the disregard of veterans, feels almost believable. —TVDW

| "TEMPUS FUGIT" | SEASON 4 / EPISODE 17
WRITTEN BY CHRIS CARTER AND FRANK SPOTNITZ
DIRECTED BY ROB BOWMAN |

FLIGHT 549

In which time stops for 134 people.

A plane flies through the night sky. One of the passengers keeps looking over his shoulder at the intimidating bald man sitting a few rows back. The bald man returns the glance, goes to the restroom, and puts together a plastic gun. Assembled gun in hand, he leaves the restroom, and it looks like things are about to take a turn—and they do. It's just not the kind of turn we're expecting. A wash of light floods every window on the plane and the cabin shakes, and as the poor guy (who was probably about to get shot) stares on in horror, something sucks at the emergency door next to his seat. It's something beyond comprehension, and it's coming for *him*.

The man being chased here is a familiar face, although we haven't seen him in a while. We met Max, an epileptic alien abductee, back in "Fallen Angel" (S1E10), and at the end of that episode, he was abducted again. At that point in the show, Max's repeated abduction was one of the first clear indications that all of Mulder's crazy talk had both real-world foundations and human consequences. Max's life story in "Fallen Angel" was a sad one, presented to us as he was an innocent man tormented by forces he could barely understand, let alone escape. Since the end of that episode, he has apparently been working undercover, and he's come up with some terrifically important information that he needs to get to Mulder. It's during his journey to see Mulder than Max dies in the plane crash. *The X-Files* has always been ruthless with its secondary characters. It's as much a horror series as it a science-fiction one, and the show's high mortality rate helps to create a mood of ever-encroaching doom. Plus, in order for the show to keep the conspiracy plot going, anytime anyone collects a crucial piece of the puzzle, he or she also gets a bull's-eye on his or her forehead. Knowing things on this show is a bit like, well, smoking too many cigarettes. Sooner or later, it's going to catch up with you. But still, it feels hard to stomach the fact that the show decided to pull poor Max out of an ambiguously unhappy ending only to write him into an unambiguously tragic one.

And Max's ending is not only tragic but predestined. The bald man chasing him is a government agent, and the flashing light that shakes the plane right out of the sky is from a UFO. The show's mythology is now so complex that it feels incredibly welcome to have such a primal, immediate conflict in the cold open. The triangle of action is easy to draw: Someone is being chased, and two forces are chasing him. Filling up the spaces in between are all of the people on the flight who are about get a literal crash course on the concept of collateral damage.

"Fugit" is a strong episode throughout, full of iconic set pieces and a clear sense of purpose. Mulder and Scully find out about Max from his sister, and they join forces with the team investigating the wreck of Flight 549. Mulder is immediately convinced something sketchy went down, and the stopped wristwatches at the crash site—and the way those wristwatches all mysteriously "disappear"—confirm his theory. Mulder comes up with his craziest (and, by the logic of the series, truest) theory: that Flight 549 was shot down by a stealth plane sent by the military to shoot down the UFO that was a attempting to swipe Max out of his seat midflight. Or else the stealth jet was intending to shoot down 549 all along to get rid of Max because they didn't trust the intimidating bald man to get the job done. Whatever the specifics, there must be another wreck out there, and the corpses on this one aren't going to be human.

"Fugit" draws much of its emotional force from the 549 crash site, first show-ing the wreckage from high overhead, and then following Mulder and Scully as they pick their way through the mess, sticking flags in the ground to mark the location of bodies or limbs. There is a real power in that moment. It's impossible to deny the reality of those 134 yellow body bags lined up in a hangar, and their corporeality effectively grounds the show's abstract conspiracy paranoia in the real world and its real-life consequences.

There are smaller, more personal moments that similarly function to root the mythology by giving the emotional life of our two leads room to grow. This episode features a nice mixture of Mulder at his most infuriating and his most charming. In one of my favorite Mulder/Scully moments, he takes her out to dinner for her birth-day and gives her a medallion commemorating the Apollo 11 landing. It's a sweet, believable exchange, and it goes a long way in reminding us why they work so well together. For most of the rest of the episode, Mulder is as bullheadedly dick-ish as always, and Scully's expression of pained embarrassment seems practically frozen on her face, but because they had that birthday dinner at the top of the hour, I didn't mind so much.

The "stealth plane shot down the alien plane that was going after Flight 549 and wrecked them both" story is more than a little convoluted. Still, "convolution" is a hallmark of mythology plots, and what works best about "Fugit" is its simplicity. There's a clear mystery to solve, with a clear human cost, and—while it may not fit in quite yet with all the other info we have on the black oil/shape-shifter craziness—it works well on its own. For all its moving pieces, "Fugit," as embodied by its cold open, is refreshingly direct. The aliens are up to their inexplicable happenings again, the government men are murderous and unmerciful, and Mulder is . . . well, Mulder.

"Fugit" ends with our heroes separated and in over their heads (literally, in Mulder's case). Mulder finds at least one alien body (which may mean the writers will have to come up with some way for him to lose the corpse in the next episode). But we can at least briefly hope that this might change things. Some things, however, are immutable. Agent Pendrell returns briefly,[47] only to die for no reason he would ever understand. And Max is still dead. Mulder found the man's body in one of those anonymous yellow bags, and he found his own business card tucked into Max's pocket, bloodied but legible. Maybe we can see in that moment why Fox is so driven. He needs to believe there is some way to justify all these corpses. —ZH

| "MAX" | SEASON 4 / EPISODE 18
WRITTEN BY CHRIS CARTER AND FRANK SPOTNITZ
DIRECTED BY KIM MANNERS |

LOOK, UP IN THE SKY

In which we see the last moments of Max Fenig.

It must be exhausting to believe in the grand conspiracy behind everything. Doing so means pretty much that you never accept the "official" truth and are always looking to see exactly how you're being lied to, poking around the corners of the stories you're told to find what you believe to be the truer facts. When you can't believe anything anyone says, why should you believe anything at all? Couldn't it all be a massive charade put on by the lizard people? Well, couldn't it?

Yet in most Hollywood stories about paranoid people—people who believe the conspiracy is coming for them—the most paranoid people are right. Fox Mulder and Max Fenig certainly are. The aliens are out there, and they're working with

---

47 Last seen in "Terma" (S4E9).

the government (and select military contractors, it would seem) to abduct several individuals, wreak havoc on their lives, and eventually reduce people like Max to tatters. Why? We still don't know.

Obviously, it's good to be informed and get engaged about government goings-on. But there's a line, and sometimes it's impossible to know when that line has been crossed. When do you go from arguing that the U.S. government will continue to perpetuate civil liberties abuses because it has no vested interest in the freedom of its citizens to living in a trailer in the middle of nowhere, trying to pin down the phantoms in your nightmares on paper, and being certain that if you can get the proof you need, the dominoes will start to fall. What separates the people skeptical of the government from the people who push right through to believing the truly nutty things?

This is all complicated, as mentioned, by the fact that Mulder and Max are, in the world of *The X-Files*, right. The government *is* working with aliens; we even see an alien corpse. That military contractor *does* want the alien technology in Max's bag. Aliens *are* stopping planes in midflight to abduct the people with their tech. What makes all of this work, somehow, is the fact that "Max" manages to be a paean to the many, many lives lost in this fictional war while, at the same time, a very real story about someone who could very well live on the edges of our society, driven mad by visions that are only real to himself. Reality and fiction intertwine, and it's difficult to discern where Real Max—the social outcast and conspiracy nut who could live in a trailer park in any city in the world—begins and the Conspiracy Chess-Piece Max—just another pawn in the aliens' game—ends.

This makes the "Tempus Fugit" (S4E17) and "Max" two-parter oddly melancholy, even if the story line doesn't need to be split over two parts. This second hour takes its time futzing around, and—outside of the truly impressive abduction sequence around the midpoint and the wonderfully chilling scene in which Mulder realizes time has stopped for him too—there's a lot here that could have been easily condensed.

But to its credit, where other alien conspiracy episodes might have filled this time with scenes of the conspiracy members acting conspiratorial, "Tempus Fugit" and "Max" fill the time with mourning. The episode is permeated with an overwhelming sense that the people on that plane, including Max, didn't have to die. There's a shot, shortly after Mulder has finished telling his story to the crash investigator, in which we pull back and see the entirety of the re-created plane in that empty hangar, a once real and tangible thing resketched via connect-the-dots. It's one of the best shots the series has come up with to express the deeply intangible idea of lives lost in an ultimately incomprehensible struggle.

That notion is explored, too, in the humanization of Max. His video monologues mark him as either crazy or one of the few who really "gets it," and the emotion he displays in the scene in which he awaits what he knows is coming during the abduction—part nonchalance, part terror—is chilling. He doesn't want to go, but he knows he will, and then his eyes roll back in his head, and he's drifting out across the inky black sky into the bright light that draws the eye of the other passengers.

Mulder is undoubtedly more put together than Max, but he feels a sort of kinship for him, something intense enough that even Scully mentions it during that visit to Max's abandoned trailer. There, but for the grace of God, goes Mulder. I sometimes hate how the show always allows Mulder to be right, and it's a low moment for the narrative of the episode when he tells the crash inspector that there's only one explanation that accounts for all the facts, and it (of course) involves UFOs. But it helps to set Mulder's quest back on track here, when it had started to feel slightly ill-motivated earlier in the season. Moreover, there's a sense that in *The X-Files* universe, at least, things like UFOs and aliens can come true if you just believe hard enough. Mulder and Max need the aliens to be real, and so they're real.

To be clear, though, this two-parter is just more tap dancing, as the show tries to extend the mythology story line further and further, via a pair of episodes that would have fit in Season One, had the show had the budget to pull them off. But I find "Tempus Fugit" and "Max" to be terrific little episodes nonetheless. The image of Max being taken from the plane is hard to shake, and the plotting is largely comprehensible because it doesn't try to do too much. The new villains are interesting, and the episode is filled with smart, small touches, like Scully's visit to Max's friend in the mental institution or the sick moment in which Mulder realizes he's possibly about to be abducted.

This is the kind of dread *The X-Files* specializes in, that sense that you are powerless in the face of something so much larger than yourself, something that wants to toy with you like a cat toys with a mouse. The aliens don't really want Max. They want the experiments they can perform on him. They want to see how far they can make him bend until he breaks. And because that is all the aliens see him as useful for, that is all the Syndicate sees him as useful for too.

Max has come up against so much beyond his scope of understanding, so much more powerful and awe-inspiring than he can imagine, that he can't find his way through the maze back to the person he was before he first encountered that white light. Even though Max is barely in "Max" (he is dead, in fact, before this hour begins), his ghost and legacy haunt these two episodes, while the spirit of who he was haunts the series as a whole. Even without aliens and UFOs and grand conspiracies, Max's story resonates. We all have known someone who got lost in the dark and never came back out. —TVDW

FROZEN IN TIME

In which things cool down before heating up.

"Synchrony," which has all the pieces of my favorite kind of episode, is too cold to work. I don't mean literally; the frozen bodies that dot the landscape of the episode like so many tragic snowmen are a fine visual, and the idea that they aren't exactly dead is an interesting twist. I mean that the episode is detached, with a chilly, removed perspective that views characters as less than people but slightly more than insects.

The best time-travel stories are grounded in regret. If alien conspiracies are fundamentally about our fear of what we don't know, time travel is about the tragedy of what we know now that we didn't know then. Time-travel stories need this sense of missed opportunities, a sense of stakes beyond vague portents of doom. The science in "Synchrony" plays out mostly in the background; we hear about fantastic compounds and see a creepy penlike injector that turns people into Popsicles, but that's all window dressing. That's mostly fine because time travel doesn't need to be about the means. But it does need to be about the ends, and unfortunately, that's where this story sort of falls apart.

Jason (Joseph Fuqua) and Lisa (Susan Lee Hoffman) are in love, and they are scientists, which means no good can come of this. The two are working together to create a freezing compound, but they're still years away from perfecting it. One day, an old man (Michael Fairman) shows up, and things get complicated. The old man is actually a future version of Jason, who's traveled back in time from a future in which Lisa successfully used the freezing compound to do something with tachyons and create practical time travel. This was a terrible discovery, as Old Jason alludes to a world "without history," and so he has traveled back to the present in order to prevent the compound from ever existing. He fails to save someone who might have exposed the technical flaws in Jason and Lisa's work, then he kills some other people, and, after a lot of pained looks, tries to kill Lisa. In the end, he sacrifices himself to murder his younger self, but, as the closing stinger reminds us, it won't change much.

This episode could have been fascinating, but it fails to make you care much about any of these characters. Jason's younger self is a cliché of an arrogant academic, and he spends most of the episode in jail. Lisa, who I think is supposed to come across as the "real" villain (in addition to eventually perfecting the time travel that causes all the trouble, she also falsified some research when test results weren't conforming to her expectations), feels icy herself, and while Old Jason does his best to convey an emotional throughline, he isn't given enough to work with. There are stabs at pathos here. Old Jason clearly loves Lisa, even though he knows that killing her is probably the only way he can accomplish his goals. While I can appreciate this idea conceptually, there's nothing all that moving or upsetting about it in the execution. Much like the pseudoscience the episode espouses, the plot is just a series of variables.

To make matters worse, the plot doesn't make very much sense. Old Jason's actions are easy enough to follow, but he seems to be going out of his way to fail in order to provide the episode with conflict. For example, he needs the successful freezing agent to survive the trip back in time to our future, but why, if the whole point of this journey was to prevent that compound from ever being invented, does he keep using it as a murder weapon? Did it never occur to him that leaving samples of the compound laying around might not be the best way to erase it from history?

If "Synchrony" had its emotional core in place, these questions would be beside the point; a warmth of feeling throughout the episode could have easily compensated for the various plot holes. But because Jason and Lisa and Old Jason are never more than concepts, we're left to focus on the details, which can't handle the strain. Mulder teases Scully a few times in the episode about a paper on time travel she did as student, and near the end of the episode, he quotes that paper in one of the show's most deterministic moments ever: Despite the possibilities of infinite universes, each individual universe can only ever arrive at one outcome. It's a fitting dissertation for a woman who defines her life by logic and faith in God (neither of them flawed), and one of the few times the episode connects back to our heroes. It's also the truth of all stories. No matter what happens, there's only one ending for everybody. The trick is to make the journey worthwhile, which "Synchrony" never quite manages. —ZH

| "SMALL POTATOES" | SEASON 4 / EPISODE 20
WRITTEN BY VINCE GILLIGAN
DIRECTED BY CLIFF BOLE |

LIVE A LITTLE

In which Mulder learns he is no Eddie Van Blundht. (The H is silent.)

When I first met my wife, one of the first things we talked about—before we were dating, even—was our mutual love of *The X-Files*. We talked favorite episodes, favorite recurring characters, and even favorite moments and lines. I tried to make my defense for how the alien conspiracy arc made sense.[48] We talked about those VHS tapes that came in packs of three, putting all of Chris Carter's personal favorites onto tape for posterity. Both of us had come to the show after Season One's

---

48 I've always been one for a lost cause.

"Ice" (S1E8). But whereas I launched into my lengthy and rather tiresome explanation of why "Jose Chung's *From Outer Space*" (S3E20) is dearest to my heart, she simply said her favorite was "Small Potatoes" and left it at that. I certainly wasn't going to call her on it. She didn't need to say anything more.

I think you'll find that's the case for most *X-Files* fans. Besides my wife, I don't know many fans who'd rank this one at the absolute top of their list, but I don't know any who'd outright dismiss it either. Even those of us who don't love it like crazy still really, really like it. "Small Potatoes" may not feel as grandly important to the plot or character development or emotional growth as many other episodes do. It may not seem as wildly ambitious. But it is, in some fundamental way, TV comfort food. Nine times out of ten, if I'm just going to turn on an *X-Files* episode to watch, it's this one.

The plot is deceptively simple. Mulder has learned of a woman in West Virginia who has recently given birth to a baby with a tail. The tabloid report that intrigues him mentions four other women in the same town have had similarly tailed babies, and what's piqued Mulder's interest is a throwaway mention at the bottom of the tabloid's front page: Were these women impregnated by men from outer space? As it turns out, that's exactly what the first woman (the one we see giving birth to her baby girl in the teaser) claims. In their interview, Mulder leans toward her, going in for the kill. Was she abducted? No. Was it an alien? No, but he is from another planet. It was Luke Skywalker! Apparently, he came to her place one night and they had a passionate evening together.[49]

Upon hearing this explanation, our heroes are at first ready to just chalk all this up to run-of-the-mill delusions. But the other four women make both Mulder and Scully think there's something more going on here. Scully deduces that all of the babies must have the same father. But why would four happily married women all seemingly dally with the same man? It turns out that all four were going to the same doctor for artificial insemination, and when our protagonists go to see the doctor in question (who's being berated and threatened with lawsuits by all four couples), Mulder wanders down the hall to find a janitor at work. When the janitor bends over far enough (as janitors are wont to do), Mulder notices the scar where a tail might have been removed. The janitor runs. Mulder, with a perfectly timed eye roll, gives chase. Such is our introduction to Eddie Van Blundht, would-be lothario and all-around loser (played by former *X-Files* writer and all-around favorite Darin Morgan). Eddie can shape-shift. And Eddie's obviously been getting around. So much so that, late in the episode, Eddie decides to imprison Mulder in the basement of the hospital where Eddie works and assumes Mulder's identity—primarily, it seems, to put the moves on Scully.

The central idea of "Small Potatoes" is a good one: Are you who you are because of how you choose to live your life? Or are you who you are because of how other

S4 E20

---

49 Scully, with pitch-perfect comic timing: "Did he have a light saber?"

people treat you? Assuming Mulder didn't eventually get free, burst in on Eddie attempting to seduce Scully, and reclaim his rightful place in the world, would Eddie eventually get so comfortable in Mulder's life that he would functionally become Mulder? Are our identities so fixed and constant that we would remain fundamentally the same even if we somehow physically became someone else? Or would the very act of having everyone else treat you like a different person eventually make you fundamentally a different person?

Eddie sees Mulder as someone who chooses to be a loser. He simply can't understand why such a tall, broodingly handsome man would have only geeks for friends and no love life to speak of. Eddie, a schlubby janitor, longs for an escape from the life he's been given. So he becomes the more handsome husbands. He becomes Luke Skywalker, the true love of the girl he dated all through high school. He becomes the best-looking FBI agent on Earth.

Here's what's fascinating to me about Eddie: He always returns to his old life eventually. Some of this is just motivated by practicality since sustaining the appearance of another person puts quite a physical strain on him. He's also not willing to kill any of those husbands and, thus, can't assume their identities on a more permanent basis. And he certainly can't live his life answering to the name Luke Skywalker. Sure, he seems ready to become a permanent occupant of Mulder's life, but when he gets found out, he seems resigned to the idea that it would all be over eventually anyway, that this was always just a vacation from the rest of his life.[50]

Ultimately, Eddie is resigned to being Eddie. He's willing to escape into other lives for a little while, and what he does is clearly wrong and lands him in jail. But his sad-sack resignation to his lot in life makes him one of the show's saddest monsters. He just wants to be happy for a little bit, to feel whole in someone else's skin, and he aims to give other people what they want while he does it. As he puts it, if those women wanted kids and nobody got hurt and everybody was happy, where's the crime in that? The issue here, of course, is that Eddie—and the episode—try to pass off Eddie's crimes as more harmless than they are. This is another *X-Files* comedy episode about rape, which was an unsettling theme for the show.[51] In reality, he'd have sowed even more physiological destruction than depicted here.

Yet this episode works because it makes Eddie sympathetic by expressing a universal truth: Very few people are wholly happy being themselves. Almost everyone would change something about themselves if they could, or rather, they *believe* they would change something about themselves. One of the appeals of fiction—either consuming it or writing it—is the chance to step into, just for a little while, somebody else's shoes. But in the end, Eddie doesn't escape for the same reason I don't or you

---

50 Surely someone would catch on eventually. Even Mulder wouldn't misspell "Federal Bureau of Investigation" in a report—twice.

51 See also my favorite episode: "Jose Chung."

don't: He can't. At some level, he's so fundamentally Eddie that he would never be completely comfortable as Mulder, even if he got used to the job and won the girl. Eddie can be anyone he wants, but he's intensely bound to the life he was born into. The episode wants to raise these ideas of identity as a question, but it essentially sets out a hard and fast answer at the hour's close: Even when you're someone else, you're still yourself.[52]

What's interesting is that Eddie didn't have to be a complete loser. The world certainly perceives him that way, but in the episode's pivotal scene, when he's romancing Scully as Mulder, he's not bad. Sure, when he moves in for that kiss, the look on Scully's expression is more "Wait, what?" than "Thank God this is happening after so long!" but he's still a good listener, letting her open up in the time he spends hanging at her apartment, talking about her lousy prom night. Perhaps—just perhaps—the episode cheekily argues, Eddie is a loser because he bought into the hype. He looked and sounded like a loser, and everybody said he was a loser, so he just went along with it. His alternate personae suggest he could have found a way to be charming, had he worked at it.

"Small Potatoes" also marks a romantic hallmark for the show's central relationship. David Duchovny, who submitted this episode for Emmy consideration, plays two different roles and gets a number of incredibly funny comic set pieces, but Gillian Anderson is also warm and amusing throughout. Indeed, for much of the first half of the episode, she's the one with the funniest lines and comic beats. Anderson and Duchovny's sexual chemistry was undeniable, but up until this point, the show has kept any possible passion at arm's length. In many ways, Mulder and Scully are more connected to each other than to any other people in the whole world, including to their own families, and yet they know basically nothing about each other's pasts and hidden secrets. As Chris Carter intended, they're more like courtly lovers, bound together by a shared quest but kept separate in almost every other way. Letting Eddie-as-Mulder go in for a (doomed) kiss is a way of indulging the chemistry while keeping the relationship pure, but it also marks the first time the show would engage in such an overt tease to the Mulder/Scully fanatics known as shippers.

All of the above philosophizing is ultimately just the underpinning for an episode that is, at its core, a lighthearted lark. Vince Gilligan has written many, many scripts since "Small Potatoes" (some of which are much better than this one), but he's never written one as effortlessly playful and inventive. In Morgan's guest turn as Eddie, you can almost sense him passing on the mantle of "the guy who writes the funny episodes" to Gilligan—a title Gilligan would hang on to for much of the rest of the show's run. Gilligan's episodes aren't as dense or as intrinsically tragic as Morgan's. "Small Potatoes" is no "Clyde Bruckman's Final Repose" (S3E4), with

---

52 If it weren't so playful, the script might feel oddly deterministic about both genetics and identity.

its darkly comic reflection on mortality. There's instead something almost wistful and whimsical in this episode's tone.

Morgan, in keeping with the spirit of the thing, turns in a solid and funny performance and, as usual, seems to get the most enjoyment out of tweaking Duchovny's image as the world's handsomest man. Gilligan's script gestures to bigger ideas while deftly landing golden comic moments (watch Eddie-as-Mulder wandering Mulder's apartment and tossing out in-jokes for fans, as well as clumsily dribbling a basketball). Even the score and the cinematography seem more relaxed. This is a big hit show, late in a dark and stressful season, just having a good time. This is the show letting its guard down to chat after a few drinks. This is the show learning to just let go and have fun with what it can do.

In the end, that self-assuredness is what makes this a perfectly comforting entry for *X-Files* fans. There's enough here to dig into if you really want to. Or if you just want to sit back, have a laugh, and remind yourself of why you love this show so much, there's plenty of space to do that too. "Small Potatoes" isn't the very best *The X-Files* has to offer, but it's perhaps the easiest episode to call your favorite. As long as the show exists, *X-Files* fans will be tentatively saying to fellow fans, "I really love 'Small Potatoes,'" and then, with a rush of smiles and shared memories, they'll hear in return: "I do too." —TVDW

| **"ZERO SUM"** | SEASON 4 / EPISODE 21
WRITTEN BY HOWARD GORDON AND FRANK SPOTNITZ
DIRECTED BY KIM MANNERS |

HIVE MIND

In which Skinner tries to save the day by pretending
it never happened.

"Zero Sum" is a mythology episode, which means it's already playing fast and loose, structurally speaking, with a handful of recurring villains and a greater sense of personal involvement for our heroes. At first, this one looks like a standard Monster of the Week episode: A postal worker sneaks off to the bathroom for a smoke break, the bathroom fills with bees, and the lady dies screaming. While bees have a certain history on this show, our first real confirmation that *something* strange is going on (beyond, you know, that instant bee swarm in the women's restroom) is when we cut to Assistant Director Walter Skinner deleting the woman's case file off someone's computer. A ray of light illuminates the nameplate of the office's true resident (there's a musical sting here, and a couple other places through the episode, that is hilariously overwrought); this is a case Skinner doesn't want FOX MULDER to see.

Roughly the entire first act of the episode follows Skinner as he attempts to cover up the postal worker's death. He's one of the few reliable foundations in a show full of shifting sands, which means there are only a handful of reasons for the cover-up, and if we've been paying attention, we already know the right one: He's trying to save Scully's life. This is the price Skinner has agreed to pay to the Cigarette Smoking Man in order to cure Scully's cancer.

Given the number of lies and half truths the conspiracy has parceled out over the years, it's almost charmingly naive that Skinner, who's even more of a pragmatist than Scully, thinks he can trust the CSM to save everyone's favorite redhead. But it works, and even though Scully doesn't appear once in this episode (she's at the hospital having tests done, which is possibly the most mundanely terrifying phrase I've ever heard on the show), her presence looms large. The sheer force of Skinner's commitment to protecting his agents helps drive the point home. The episode is told largely through his point of view, another change in structure that serves the neat trick of making Mulder nearly as much of an antagonist as the CSM is.

Which makes you start thinking about slippery slopes and how the CSM himself started off with good intentions but went to hell soon enough. (Admittedly, going by "Musings of a Cigarette Smoking Man" [S4E7], the CSM's first big assignment was shooting JFK, which is a little more . . . intense than what we see here. But still.) Skinner's worst mistake during his cover-up gets a cop killed, and it isn't even really his "mistake," as much as just bad timing. Once Mulder is on his trail, Skinner has to balance staying a step or two ahead of one of his best agents with trying to figure out just what he's gotten himself into, and that can't be easy. By the end of the episode, he's learned that he's been protecting a conspiracy that just got half a school's worth of ten-year-olds infected with smallpox. Oh sure, he isn't directly responsible for that, but standing in a hospital surrounded by innocent victims isn't the easiest time to split hairs.

"Zero Sum" is utterly badass. Skinner is always angry,[53] and "Sum" gives us a good reason to understand *why* he's so pissed. He's dedicated his life to upholding the law and protecting the people he works for, but he's risen to a level of power, through skill and drive, that forces him into a position in which he's endlessly dancing around the potential compromise of those goals. And there's not a damn thing he can do about it. He confronts the CSM at the episode's climax—has a gun at the guy's face—and any hope he had that his actions will help obtain a cure for Scully are nearly gone, but when it comes time to pull the trigger, he fires into the wall. There's still a chance the CSM could save Scully, and he can't afford to lose that chance. He put his soul on the line for it. —ZH

S4 E21

---

53 He's like a high school football coach whose team is always six points down.

BOWLING ALONE

In which she is me.

"Elegy" mostly centers on an autistic man named Harold (Steven M. Porter), who can remember every single score at the local bowling alley where he works (going as far as to hole out a small space in the back in which to keep his scorecards)—and who also sees the dead at the instant of their deaths. Somehow, this ability spreads out to other people in Harold's immediate vicinity. But we'll get to that in a moment.

The biggest problem with "Elegy" is that its portrayal of autism is offensive at worst and just plain idiotic at best. The second biggest problem is that the whodunit makes absolutely no goddamn sense, unless you conclude that writer John Shiban decided he simply had to copy the film *One Flew Over the Cuckoo's Nest* as much as possible. The portrayal of Harold is ridiculous, and the other patients at the psychiatric hospital where he lives fare no better. For one thing, the idea of the magical mentally handicapped person is one of the most cringeworthy and problematic of clichés. Because we get to know Harold for only a very short while, he doesn't get to be anything *but* a magical mentally handicapped person. And when you get to the part in which the episode explains the crimes, it utterly falls apart.

Let me explain: The portrayal of Howard is idiotic, but it stays on the right side of offensive for most of the run time. But then Scully abruptly realizes that the evil nurse (Nancy Fish)—yes, the evil nurse, just like in *Cuckoo's*—is the one who's responsible for the killings, because she was taking Harold's pills or something and trying to eliminate the beautiful love he had from his life *or something* to take away his happiness. She goes from a nobody character to Nurse Ratched in about five seconds simply because Shiban needs a villain and didn't bother to build up any of the other characters. He can't make it another patient, nor can he make it one of the more caring psychiatric hospital workers, nor can he make it one of the random bowling alley patrons, who are all good, salt-of-the-earth folk.

This brings us to the third huge problem with this episode: It collapses under the weight of its ideas. You've got the psychiatric hospital, full of patients and doctors and nurses. You've got the bowling alley, full of workers and bowlers. You've got the beautiful girls, all ghostly and unable to talk. You've got Scully's cancer, menacing and unknowable. You've got the idea of an autistic man keeping such perfect track of scores at a bowling alley that he builds a connection to the bowling alley's dead. You've got *ghosts*. And you've got an old-fashioned murder mystery supposedly underpinning all of this. It's too much.

Any one of these ideas would have made a great basis for an *X-Files* episode. The depiction of the bowling alley, especially, works as a kind of mundane time travel, a way to step into a bygone era without anything so out of the ordinary as opening a door. But everything smashed together creates a script that inspires whiplash. There are great, great *X-Files* episodes that toss this many ideas together, but most of them are written by Darin Morgan or Vince Gilligan.[54] Those two were able to keep fifty different plates spinning and then provide the one piece of information that made everything instantly crystallize. The other writers were usually better off when they did fairly straightforward creature features, Monster of the Week episodes that didn't try too much or too hard. As such, Shiban's script for this one tries a bunch of tones—weirdly campy comedy, grim melancholy, slasher film—while succeeding at none of them.

And yet I give this episode the slightest of passes. Why? Well, it all comes down to a series of beautiful little scenes that let you see the weight of everything Scully's been carrying around with her. As mentioned, up until the climax, this is an episode with enough good stuff to overlook some of its more ridiculous elements, and so much of that good stuff runs straight through Gillian Anderson and her remarkably raw performance as Dana Scully. The writers often seem to have forgotten that Scully has cancer, but Anderson never has, and I like the way she clings to variations on the phrase "I'm fine" as a way of warding off further illness. She's not fine, not really. She's seeing ghosts in the bathroom and ghosts in her backseat and weird signs of the darkness waiting for her in what could be weeks. She's succumbing, and she knows it, but she presses on. She has to. That's who she is.

Simplify "Elegy" just a bit—cut it down to, say, Scully in the psychiatric ward with the ghosts haunting her and Mulder consulting by phone—and you have an all-time classic, an episode that forces her to confront her own mortality with the most direct symbol of that mortality. As it is, the Scully scenes are just enough to grant this episode an authentic emotionality it doesn't really deserve. After the ludicrous, far-too-grim finale (in which Harold collapses in an alley and dies of respiratory failure), Mulder takes Scully aside and tries to find out if she's OK. She says she's fine one last time, and she heads out to her car. She's crying, realizing how un-fine she is, when she sees Harold in the backseat. She turns, and he's gone.

The thing I love about ghost stories, my favorite horror subgenre, but one *The X-Files* has rarely handled well, is the same thing that lends an unearned power to "Elegy." Nothing is ever really gone. The past echoes, in ways only a few—maybe those closest to death themselves—can hear. And even when you no longer believe in ghosts, you can still believe in being haunted. —TVDW

---

54 Or they were written by a team—see "Leonard Betts" (S4E12).

| SEASON 4 / EPISODE 23
WRITTEN BY R. W. GOODWIN
DIRECTED BY KIM MANNERS

FUGUE STATE

*In which Mulder asks someone to drill a hole in his
head so he can remember something.*

In "Demons," Mulder wakes up in a hotel room, covered in blood, with no memory of how he got there. All he knows is that he's in Rhode Island, and that he's probably involved in something that went south in a very bad way. So he calls Scully, and over the course of the episode, the two piece together just what happened in that missing time. Rife with effectively disorienting flashbacks, the episode reveals that a voluntary psychiatric procedure is responsible for both his amnesia and the aggressive hallucinations of his past—as well as the deaths of three other people.

"Hero with amnesia who may have committed a horrible crime" is a standard genre plotline. I've seen it on *Star Trek*, film noir, and probably a few *Twilight Zone* episodes. It's reliable because it has a hook built in and because it provides writers with a very clear objective. Even the blandest versions of this can't help but have some slight existential crisis to them. If you forgot a weekend, how certain would you be that you didn't do something awful in that lost time? And how easy would it be to convince the people closest to you of your innocence?

"Demons" largely forgoes the obvious suspicions. Yes, the cops have some serious questions for Mulder, once he and Scully find a pair of bodies with bullet wounds in an abandoned house. And yes, those cops arrest Mulder once they establish that the blood on his shirt came from those bodies. But once Scully does some digging, and finds evidence of hallucinogens, it's not that difficult to get Mulder out of his cell. (It doesn't hurt that a cop who also took part in the treatment kills himself seemingly minutes after Mulder is officially incarcerated.) The blood spatter on Mulder's shirt, and the angle of the entry wounds, clear him of wrongdoing; and if that sounds a little convenient, well, maybe it is. But this episode isn't about whether or not our favorite Ahab is a killer. It's more interesting than that.

Some of the details around Dr. Goldstein's (Mike Nussbaum) experimental memory treatment don't entirely hold up. Why does he lie when Scully and Mulder come to see him? Is he trying to cover up the treatments, due to the fallout? He also seems surprised when he learns that Amy and the cop are dead, but he could just be a good actor. We get a sense of why Amy and the cop killed themselves by the end, but we don't know why Mulder was there to get his shirt covered in blood, or how he survived. Scully suggests Amy suffered from Waxman-Geschwind Syndrome (a real thing). Was this induced by the Goldstein treatments? And if it wasn't, why did the cop and Mulder have similar experiences? It'd be a stretch to think they *all* have the syndrome.

Questions aside, what does work here is great. The doomed cop is effectively disquieting, as is the reveal that Amy had been painting pictures of the house where she would meet her end—a lot of pictures too. (Though that begs the question, why? Is this where she was abducted? Is her abduction connected to Samantha's? Because . . . that actually makes a chilling degree of sense.) And Mulder's memories of the past are wonderfully unsettling, jumbled recollections of an argument between his parents that may or may not have ever taken place. The way those memories hit him—randomly, but so powerfully he falls to his knees—are as good a metaphor as anything about the way his past refuses to let him go, and how his pursuit of the truth threatens to obliterate the world of the present.

Ultimately, "Demons" is about Mulder's need to understand what happened to his sister and how that need drives him to *expect* betrayal. At least with betrayal, the world makes some kind of sense. He remembers his mother and father fighting; he remembers his mother shouting "Not Samantha!"; and he remembers the Cigarette Smoking Man lurking behind every door. So he goes to his mother and starts asking all sorts of uncomfortable questions. When his mother refuses to give him the answers he believes he is owed, he goes back to Goldstein for another treatment, nearly losing himself in the process.

There are potentially devastating revelations here, but there's nothing solid in the end. After a certain point, one's determination to find the truth overwhelms whatever truth there might be. *The X-Files* gets a lot of justly deserved criticism for muddling its ongoing plotlines, but it also deserves credit for being the rare show that is more than willing to acknowledge that its central premise is fundamentally flawed. Just because the truth is out there doesn't mean it's worth finding; maybe the truths we want, and the truths we need, aren't the same thing. There's a chance Mulder and Scully could defeat the CSM and his cabal, but if they ever want a chance of doing so, Mulder will need to find a way to stop looking backward for the answers. —ZH

SEASON 4 / EPISODE 24
WRITTEN BY CHRIS CARTER | "GETHSEMANE"
DIRECTED BY R. W. GOODWIN

THE HOAX
In which Mulder is pronounced dead.

Scully apparently identifying Mulder's corpse is a reasonable way to inject suspense into a season finale's opening scene. It's a trick, though, and on some level, most viewers will recognize that. The show isn't going to kill off one its stars, and knowing that makes the scene more obviously manipulative. There's tension, but it's the sort in which you spend half your time watching to see where the strings are attached.

Far more effective, at least on a dramatic level, is the sight of Mulder alone in his apartment, watching old videos of science conferences as tears stream down his cheeks. It's moving because it speaks to a crisis that can't be resolved through fake cliffhangers. Mulder needs aliens to be real not just because it's cool, or because he has a distant, aching hope that he might see his sister again. He needs to believe it because without it, he thinks his life will have no meaning.

This whole season has been building to a final test of Mulder's faith. *The X-Files* has been willing to poke holes in itself for quite some time, and "Gethsemane" feels like a logical end point for that poking, the final statement that we've been waiting for. A shadowy government operative sits Mulder down and says, Yes, all this ridiculous stuff is a lie, created by the government to allow them to continue the free rein they had during the Cold War, and here's how they did it. It's not a new idea—the show first raised the possibility that Mulder was chasing lies back in "Nisei" (S3E9) and "731" (S3E10). But when the "there are no aliens!" theory was first introduced, it added a welcome note of ambiguity, twisting our assumptions without outright contradicting them. "Gethsemane" attempts to double down on this, with mixed results.

And yet this version of events isn't all that more probable than alien invasion. It's asking us to believe in an even more complicated web: a conspiracy created largely to give the illusion of another conspiracy. Not only are they hiding the truth, they're hiding it with a lie that must be ever so traceable—never too obvious, because that would give the game away, but never completely hidden because then, people like Mulder might lose the scent.

Of course, if *The X-Files* really had decided to make its core mystery one giant Scooby-Doo adventure, it would've pissed off a lot of fans. However, from a dramatic perspective, it might have given these first four seasons of the show a powerful unity, channeling so much of the mythology's dead ends and dropped leads into a rich statement on how we struggle for meaning in our lives, and how bad men can exploit that struggle for their own ends. The problem is, there have been too many scenes of shape-changing bounty hunters and mystical alien healers for this to be even remotely plausible.

When the critique and deconstruction of Mulder's quest was just a theme in Monster of the Week episodes, that was fine. The anthology nature of this series allows considerable thematic flexibility for stand-alone entries. But to try and bring that hole-poking into the central mythology, to introduce it as though it's a question of practical suspense—as opposed to a meta-textual criticism of the series' core ideas—doesn't work. Hearing Scully talk to her superiors about her belief that Mulder had been led astray in the same pseudo–poetic speak that Carter has used throughout the show robs what should be a bombshell—everything we've been told is a lie—by reducing it to just another plot point. In order for this reversal to work, the show would have to feel like it was heading in a new direction; because it doesn't, it becomes that much harder to believe in anything, which makes it nearly impossible to care about what's actually going on.

Trying to balance possible truths while maintaining the plausibility of both is incredibly difficult to pull off on a long-running show, and after dabbling in existentialism for so long in Season Four, "Gethsemane" comes down on the only side of the fence it really can. Everything here has a ring of familiarity to it, and the repetition is getting old, no matter how cool the lighting is, or how much we see of that alien corpse. It's not terrible, and there are scenes here I liked quite a lot. But "Gethsemane" confirms what I should've known long ago. When it comes to doubt, *The X-Files* is willing to spend only so much time asking questions before it gets back to telling us what it thinks we want to hear. —ZH

YOUR HOLY GRAIL

Mulder and Scully's dynamic is often reduced to a dichotomy of belief, but ask the writers and they'll acknowledge that the question of faith in *The X-Files* was always more complicated than it appeared. To Chris Carter, in fact, Scully's skepticism was much more than a prop for Mulder to grapple with. "Scully's science is really the heart of the show," he muses. "If it weren't for her science, there would be no good science fiction in the show. Oftentimes [a script] started with science, and the monsters came out of that idea." Still, Carter wanted to be sure that Scully was given more depth than a stoically skeptical scientist: "It was always my idea with her that she had a strong religious faith. . . . I think that sometimes it gets buried under X-Files cases, and the science fiction. But, when necessary, we need[ed] to go back and reestablish that she has a much-conflicted life, and that she believes in something real and tangible—science—and she believes in something that can be considered irrational, which is her faith."

The complexity of belief and faith come to a head in "Gethsemane," in which Mulder's faith in the supernatural and the existence of aliens is tested in a new and devastating way. Frank Spotnitz says that, even before this episode, he began to understand the contradictions Carter had laid out for his two main characters: "The thing that I came to realize about the mythology of the show, and about actually the search for extraterrestrial life, is that it's really akin to religious faith, and that's what's so interesting about the design of the show that Chris created. Mulder, the man—contrary to gender stereotypes—was the character of faith, and Scully, the woman, was the character of reason and science. And yet she was a Catholic, and Mulder seemingly an atheist. And this was his religion, this searching for alien life."

Perhaps "Gethesemane," in this respect, doesn't break new thematic ground, but Spotnitz credits the conversation Mulder and Scully have on the stairway with illuminating Mulder's character and his relationship with Scully in a whole new way. When Mulder asks Scully, "If someone could prove to you the existence of God, would it change you?," Scully replies, "Only if it were disproven." According to Spotnitz, this moment summarized the arc of the show. "I thought, 'That's actually the heart of *The X-Files*' mythology and what made it tick: Mulder is trying to prove God exists.'"

"REDUX"	SEASON 5 / EPISODE 1 WRITTEN BY CHRIS CARTER DIRECTED BY R. W. GOODWIN
"REDUX II"	SEASON 5 / EPISODE 2 WRITTEN BY CHRIS CARTER DIRECTED BY KIM MANNERS

I DON'T WANT TO BELIEVE

In which Mulder learns it's all a lie and Scully lives.

The fifth season of *The X-Files* was the height of the series' popularity. Suddenly, the show was everywhere, on the tip of everybody's tongue. Even your older friends and relatives could be counted on to have seen an episode or two and have a vague notion of what the show was about. Questions about the alien conspiracy's ultimate goal had filtered into the mainstream, and the show's actors—and even writers—were becoming superstars.

But something else happened in Season Five: It was made immediately after the show had completed production on its first feature film, which meant the season needed to follow an unusually rigid structure in order to arrive at the events that occurred in the film.

In particular, the movie's mere existence undercut Season Four's big cliff-hanger. It was really, really obvious in the gap between Seasons Four and Five that Mulder wasn't dead. Why, Duchovny was off filming the movie! Even without the movie, the show likely wouldn't have fooled anyone, and without showing viewers the corpse (and, instead having Scully tell us about it), the show was indulging in one of the oldest TV tricks in the book. If you say someone's dead but don't show us the body, it means they're not dead, as turns out to be the case here.

Still, combine all of these factors, as well as an uncharacteristically late November premiere date,[1] and the anticipation leading into "Redux" was more heated than at any time in the show's run. Even though Mulder's death made for one of the show's weaker cliffhangers, it had the benefit of lots and lots of public scrutiny.

All this excitement made "Redux" a pretty good episode back in 1997. But watched now, it pales in comparison to how good it seemed when it first aired; the "Redux" duo is the rare *X-Files* two-parter with one weak half and one incredibly strong half ("Redux II" is much stronger on the whole). Watching now, it's much more evident than it would have been then that the show's producers were highly constrained by the need to stretch out the alien conspiracy story line without utterly

---

1   This reflected both Fox's need to air the baseball playoffs and the fact that the show shot only twenty episodes for Season Five, so as to have time to produce the film in the same year.

damaging the show, in order to build to a movie whose plot was chiseled in stone since it had already been made.

There's something to be said for this two-parter's Oliver Stone envy, always present on the show but particularly palpable here, as the show tries to convince us that maybe everything Mulder has believed in for so long is an elaborate con game, carried out by a conspiracy that wants to keep funding a never-ending war, the better to make the U.S. economy hum. Chris Carter and R. W. Goodwin wed an endless speech, delivered by the government lackey Michael Kritschgau (well played by John Finn), about the true reason for the government's interest in UFOs, with stock footage of nuclear bombs and historical moments. The implications couldn't be clearer: Carter wants to take this mini arc, in which Mulder loses his faith and has to regain it, into something like Stone's *JFK*.[2] It's an impressive job of salesmanship. The collage of sounds and images becomes oddly powerful, and it almost makes the viewer want to believe that all of the alien shenanigans we've seen over the years were meant to mislead both Mulder and us. (This is despite the presence of, say, the shape-shifting aliens, who would seem to completely disprove Kritschgau's thesis. But it's a good effort!)

If all of this is in fact a game carried out by the Syndicate, a dark but homegrown conspiracy inspired by aliens but not driven by them, it has the power to seriously rejuvenate the mythology. In some respects, the least interesting thing about the show is that the aliens are behind it all, and they probably want to invade Earth. It's exactly what you'd expect, which goes against the way the show often works, where Mulder and Scully are often proved wrong and confronted with something even more ridiculous, even weirder than they'd initially thought. So if the government is perpetrating an awful shell game designed to test out new bioweapons and destroy more and more lives via the vacuum at the conspiracy's center, well, that's something more interesting. It could rattle Mulder and test Scully. It could be something soul-shaking and great. This new version of the conspiracy is a lonelier one, but it's also, potentially, a better one.

The premiere delivers its highly anticipated cliffhanger resolution: Mulder faked his own death after killing Ostelhoff, a man positioned in an apartment above his to listen in on Mulder's actions.[3] Mulder kills Ostelhoff, then decides to have Scully help him fake his own death, so he can infiltrate the Department of Defense, both to get some answers and to find the cure for Scully's cancer. Scully distracts

---

2   It almost makes you wonder what the movie would have been like with this approach—all free-form editing and cross-cutting in an attempt to tie fifty years of American history together into one unified theory.

3   The shot of Ostelhoff's monitoring equipment showing Mulder leave his apartment, then transitioning to the sounds of Mulder rushing upstairs, followed by the camera panning over to reveal Mulder kicking open the door, is one of the episode's few thrillingly cinematic moments.

government agents from where Mulder is, there's a lot of talk about lying, then Mulder gets into the DOD and sees some very weird stuff. Finally, he finds the cure he's looking for—even as Scully collapses—but the Lone Gunmen tell him something awful: It's just deionized water.[4]

It's thrilling, to be sure, but not enough for a full hour of TV, so Carter turns to a trick that has gotten him through plenty of other episodes: endless, endless monologues. And not just Kritschgau. Mulder and Scully both get lengthy voice-overs, making for one monotonous episode. Worse, the voice-overs usually explain exactly what we're seeing on-screen, when it would be a lot more compelling to piece together the whole "Mulder fakes his death" plot on our own.

What's most frustrating is that there are moments that point to how the show could have truly made this "Mulder is a skeptic; Scully is a believer" arc—so transparently a TV-writer cheat—really work. That moment in which Scully discovers the material in the ice cores that contains a new life form is filled with the kind of scientific wonder that marked the show's best episodes in the early days. No, it's not little green men (though we get that here, too, in a mournful image of dozens upon dozens of them lying on cold slabs in an endless DOD room), but it is something new and wonderful, and even Scully seems taken aback by it. But there's far too little of that sense of discovery and far too much of the show explaining itself, over and over.

Fortunately, then, "Redux II," the far stronger half of the season-opening two-parter, does a good job of reinvesting us in the show's ideals, returning to the status quo but also tweaking it slightly, in a way that's exciting, emotionally powerful, and satisfying. The Cigarette Smoking Man is killed—supposedly. Mulder meets his "real" sister, Scully's cancer goes into remission, and Section Chief Blevins, the man most visibly responsible for Scully's X-Files assignment back in the pilot, is discredited and murdered. Mulder has faith in Skinner again. And Scully goes back to religion, which lays the groundwork for her next big story arc.

But this being *The X-Files*, nothing *really* changes. Scully's cancer is "cured" in the most ambiguous, indefinite way possible. Apart from that, the CSM's death is the biggest game changer, and the character beats in this episode are powerful in direct, clear ways that the mythology so rarely manages. Scully wasn't going to die, but her scenes in the hospital are still effective. Her conversations with Mulder are some of the best the show has ever done: two people trying to communicate the immensity of their feelings without succumbing to them.

Scully's mother and brother show up, lecturing Mulder on the cost of his quest, and reminding him how terrible he should feel about everything. But for once, these accusations help to put Mulder in a more sympathetic light. Everything Bill says is basically true, but Mulder's resigned response, and his struggle to maintain the bare minimum of composure throughout the episode, make him a hero again. After

---

4   This is a marvelous gut-punch of a closer.

the recriminations of Season Four, the second part of "Redux" does a tremendous job of making its hero righteous again. It comes down to belief, in how wanting to believe means as much as believing itself.

In "Redux," Mulder's faith takes some heavy blows. Like any of us who, when lost or lonely, decide that the only way to be happy is to compromise ourselves and become what others want us to be, Mulder is offered a chance to give up in the second half of the two-parter, to surrender to whatever lie comes next. Here, Mulder, the universe says, believe in aliens. Now believe in black oil. Believe in vampires, believe in mutants that can stretch and kill, believe in fluke monsters, believe in a world in which reality teems with undercurrents and wonders that the rest of us only dream about. Now, stop believing in that. Give up your little green men. It's all shadow and mirrors and distraction to hide the cold clinical lust for power that drives the vilest men to do their vile deeds. There is no magic, despite what your eyes have told you. There's just a Cold War made by colder hearts, and you were their fool all along.

It's possible to imagine a version of this show in which Kritschgau's version of the truth works. But when Mulder decides to stay true to himself, when he refuses to fall for the next game, and when he stands up for Skinner—well, we're glad to be watching *this* show. The aliens don't really matter, just as it doesn't matter if Scully's god is God, or just her faith in the essential meaning of her own suffering. What matters is that true belief, the best sort of belief, is the belief that takes us closer to who we want to be, to our best selves. —ZH and TVDW

WRITING THE MYTHOLOGY

When Chris Carter first pitched *The X-Files*, he imagined the plot would be largely driven by investigation into the existence of aliens. Carter says he knew even then that "Mulder's entry into the X-Files was specifically about the disappearance of his sister. That was the thread that we followed from the beginning, and literally right to the end. . . . I'd like to tell you I knew exactly where it was going, but I didn't. It was a discovery. But I can tell you this, when you start making choices and start laying down, I'll call it a mosaic, laying down pieces and tiles, pretty soon the story takes on a life of its own. It starts to, because you've made so many choices, it starts to kind of tell itself. The mythology was kind of amazing to me, because while you give it direction in the beginning, it starts to take its own direction."

Although Frank Spotnitz helped break the story in the writers' room for nearly every episode from Season Three on, he came to play a special role in developing the mythology alongside Carter for the series: "I stumbled into a role in the conspiracy, because when Gillian got pregnant, they'd written her abduction as a way to cover for her absence, and we just discovered you can't have that happen, and then leave it alone. [So I ended up being] involved in the first mythology episodes after 'Ascension' (S2E6), which were 'Colony' (S2E16) and 'End Game' (S2E17), and they were deemed to have gone well, so Chris kept returning to me whenever we had to have these big event episodes. [At first] I didn't realize that all of these episodes were meant to lead to one thing, that they were one narrative; they just felt like they were bigger aspects of alien life. It became clear after a couple years [however, that these episodes would have to form] one single narrative. We were really feeling our way forward and making it up as we went along, and it's only by around Season Four that we started to realize [we should] try and make this more cohesive."

At the start of each season, Spotnitz and Chris Carter would sit down to a long discussion about what the serialized story line for that particular season should be. Spotnitz recalls, "Chris was always resistant to nail it down too specifically; he wanted an endgame or a target, but he didn't want to be obligated. He always felt like if we came up with a better idea, we should take it and use it right away. He always wanted to be collecting things from the news, and making it as immediate as possible. That was why we had the alien autopsy tape in 'Nisei' (S3E9), [for example]." In addition to borrowing plot elements from current events, Carter was also heavily inspired by fringe history—such as Roswell and Area 51, and Cold War conspiracy theories—as well as the mysticism of indigenous American cultures.

Carter wanted the writers to both know the show inside and out and push themselves to generate new and exciting ideas to fold into the mythology. He recalls, "I always said to Frank, 'Lay it all out there because there will always be more.' I think you make a mistake in a show if you say, 'Hold back, hold back, hold back.' Because it's almost like you're not taking advantage of the radioactive material that's lying there to be exploded. I always said, 'Don't be afraid. Just put it all out there and there will always be more to draw.'"

Carter's openness in this regard likely contributed to the mythology reaching a somewhat unwieldy size later on. Spotnitz remembers: "The other thing that was incredible to me, looking back on it, is that Chris refused to have a series bible, because he felt that writers who came on the show would just consult that, and they wouldn't be forced to watch the show. We had no document, nothing in writing we could look at to remind ourselves of what we'd said or done, which became increasingly challenging after seven or eight seasons."

Hindsight is, of course, twenty-twenty. Spotnitz muses, "I think looking back on it, if I'd known in the beginning that it was only going to be one thing, I probably would have been more disciplined about all the elements we had. . . . I think if we'd known in the beginning how long the show was going to last, we would have designed something that had [far more of] a character journey for Mulder and Scully in mind. But really, that was impossible, so I say that wishing we could, but there's no way on earth we could have done that."

SEASON 5 / EPISODE 3
WRITTEN BY VINCE GILLIGAN
DIRECTED BY KIM MANNERS | "UNUSUAL SUSPECTS"

ALUMINUM FOIL MAKES A LOVELY HAT

In which the Lone Gunmen first meet.

The one hundredth episode of *The X-Files* to air (though the ninety-eighth to be produced), "Unusual Suspects" is a love letter to the very idea of paranoia, to the idea that believing the absolute worst of the institutions around you is the proper attitude to hold at all times. It's about a group of men who encounter a femme fatale and find themselves losing all sense of bearing. They wake up one day as ordinary men. They go to bed the next day as men who firmly believe the U.S. government is out to spy on every single one of its citizens and control them via drugs and other forms of psychological manipulation. It also doubles as an origin myth for three of the show's most beloved characters (as well as, arguably, Mulder himself), and it's often very funny but in a slyly unexpected way.

Fittingly, "Unusual Suspects" was produced under unusual circumstances. Thanks to production on the first feature film, which preceded Season Five, the writers quickly realized they would not have access to David Duchovny and Gillian Anderson for as much time as they might have liked for the first episode filmed that season. Thus, the writers decided to give the two a rest and pursue an idea that had surprisingly not yet been done: a Lone Gunmen–centric episode.

Roughly speaking, the hour is structured as a conspiracy noir, complete with femme fatale, late-night meetings in hotel rooms, and bad guys who let the heroes live because they know there's no way said hero could make a difference anyway. It's a little too pat here and there, but I love the way that it, like the Lone Gunmen themselves, seems like a kind of tribute to old-school nerdery, to the way that people used to get on the Internet before you could just use a Web browser, when technical know-how was a kind of arcane magic.

It's this low-fi, analog vibe that's always appealed to me about the Gunmen. Their spinoff, launched late in the show's run,[5] never worked as well as it should have, simply because the world had caught up to their brand of nerdery.[6] The Web had become so prevalent that what had at one time made them so fringe and geeky cool—computer hacking and weird zines—by the turn of the century seemed mainstream.

"Unusual Suspects" almost acknowledges this passage of time, setting the entirety of its action in 1989. Yes, it's an origin story, and origin stories have to go back to the beginning, but it also allows the show to mine humor out of just how much the world had changed between 1989 and 1997. When Mulder pulls out a ridiculously huge cell phone, it's a sight gag, where it once would have been a sign of how well connected and technologically with it he was.[7] The computer hacking in the episode mostly involves common passwords used to get around security systems, and government computers seem laughably easy to break into.

"Unusual Suspects" has enough charm and old-school fun that it's impossible not to like, but it's also not an episode that inspires the absolute love this series does at its best, despite the best efforts of Gilligan, especially. The episode opens brilliantly: Byers, Frohike, and Langly are all apprehended by the police at a warehouse, where a man endlessly screams such lunacies as "They're here!" The twin reveals—the Gunmen are the culprits the police are looking for! Mulder is the screaming man!—are fun, and everything is heightened just enough. I even like the giant "1989" that opens this segment.

From there, we cut to Detective Munch (Richard Belzer[8]) interrogating Byers about what happened, and we get the full story. Byers bumped into a woman named Holly Modeski, and after he pursued her, she told him she was being stalked by an ex-boyfriend, the father of her child who had taken said child from her. He was a psychopath, she said, so Byers resolved to help her out, recruiting Frohike and Langly

S5 E3

---

5   *The Lone Gunmen* premiered in March 2001, at the tail end of *The X-Files'* eighth season.

6   That said, this episode is far too fond of "Heh, heh *nerds*" gags as punch lines.

7   And now, of course, Mulder and Scully's 1997 phones look cumbersome and preposterous.

8   Belzer's appearance as Munch ties the series into the endless "Tommy Westphall Universe Theory." To explain: the 1980s series *St. Elsewhere* was revealed to be a hallucination conjured up by a child named Tommy Westphall in that show's series finale. If there's one thing *St. Elsewhere* loved during its six-season run, it was crossing over with other TV shows. So if you accept that *St. Elsewhere* is all Tommy's dream, then all of the shows it crossed over with are too. And since those shows crossed over with many *other* shows (including *Homicide*, where Munch got his start), eventually, much of American television is being dreamed up by Tommy—including *The X-Files*.

for the hacking operations.[9] And who does that boyfriend/baby daddy turn out to be? Why, Fox Mulder, of course! Most viewers will see this reveal coming from a mile away. Doesn't make it any less effective.

True to its noir roots, the episode's plot is needlessly convoluted. Holly Modeski is really named Suzanne Modeski (the name she gave for her daughter), and she's wanted for killing a bunch of people. Mulder's on her trail because he works for the FBI and needs to bring her in for those murders. But once the group runs across Suzanne again (or, more accurately, she runs across *them*), she lays out an even more improbable tale: She was working for the government when she was part of a team that discovered a chemical that would inspire mass paranoia, a chemical the government aims to test on the population at large. She begins ranting about government surveillance bots in Gideon Bibles and eventually rips out her own tooth when the file she's been trying to decrypt all episode says there's some sort of tracker that was implanted the last time she went to the dentist. It all concludes in that warehouse, where the Gunmen come across the men behind the plot—led by the still-alive-in-1989 Mr. X—and Mulder is doused with large quantities of the paranoia drug.

It's perhaps all a bit too conveniently plotted. The Gunmen start out as believers in the government and its righteousness; it gave us Amtrak, after all! Mulder is just a typical FBI agent, pursuing a woman as a part of his work with the violent crimes division. By the end, they're all raving paranoiacs, thanks to the events of the episode and (in the case of Mulder, at least) the influence of the drug. In true femme fatale fashion, Suzanne Modeski is the one who disillusions Byers and his cohorts, the one who shows them how the world *really* works.

When Mr. X improbably lets the Gunmen live after they saw as much as they did, it becomes clear that little of this is meant to be taken seriously, just as "Musings of a Cigarette Smoking Man" (S4E7) is more about who the CSM wished he might have been than the person he actually was. Similarly, "Unusual Suspects" isn't a true story; it's a manifesto. Sure, there may be elements of the truth in there, but every time the Gunmen tell the story of how they met and got their start in bringing down the government, one conspiracy theory at a time, it probably gets wilder and wilder, until it starts to resemble not so much the truth as it does a story in which all of them were firm believers in the government until proved wrong, like recent religious converts, or the people who say they *never* believed in Bigfoot, until . . . And of course, their friend at the FBI was there from the start, and yeah, maybe he got dosed with some of the stuff, and that opened his eyes, man. Or, at least, that's how the Gunmen would tell the story.

S5 E3

---

9 Frohike's disgust with Byers—who works for the FCC!—is a highlight.

Taken as a literal part of the story of *The X-Files*, "Unusual Suspects" leaves a bit to be desired. Taken as a portrayal of how the Gunmen see themselves, it's weirdly winning, a great pilot for a funky flashback series that (sadly) never came. —TVDW

| "DETOUR" | SEASON 5 / EPISODE 4
WRITTEN BY FRANK SPOTNITZ
DIRECTED BY BRETT DOWLER |

TEAM BUILDING

In which Mulder and Scully take a left turn at Albuquerque
and meet some (sort of) invisible men.

With "Detour," the show takes a break from E.T. paranoia and government conspiracies, giving us a straightforward Monster of the Week episode. It's a terrific example of the platonic ideal of an *X-Files* stand-alone: a funny, well-paced, and thrilling entry that doesn't try to reinvent the wheel.

The first shot of this week's threat, two red eyes in a face seemingly buried in the ground, sets a disturbing tone that lasts through the whole hour. As with many of the show's best monsters, it's easy to pity the threat here as well as fear it: They're dying out, and their land is being taken away, and all they want is to be at peace and steal a kid whom they can raise as their own. Ironically, it's the very adaptation to their environment that's made it impossible for them to exist outside the natural world.

The effects work in "Detour" can look a little ridiculous, but that's more of a feature than a bug in this case. Goofy effects in horror can often be *more* unsettling because we're presented with the absurd and told to accept it as a credible threat. The way the Mothmen keep popping up out of fallen trees or bushes creates a constant feeling of uneasiness. It's like the forest itself grew eyes and arms to grab you. That feeling lasts all the way up to that absolutely stellar final shot: Mulder and Scully leaving a motel room, while something lurks under the bed, just missing its chance for revenge.

The plot of "Detour" follows the standard MOTW structure: A mysterious crime or phenomena occurs; our heroes are assigned to (or stumble upon) the case; they face increasing danger as they try to understand and defeat the threat before it's too late; and finally the crime that started it all is resolved (though there may be one last shot of the monster still lurking, lying in wait for the next opportunity to strike). Despite its familiar territory, "Detour" never feels tired or rote. Even when we know roughly what will happen next, it doesn't make it any less scary to see Mulder and Scully once again stuck in the wilderness at night, outmatched and exhausted. And that last, brief scare sequence when Mulder realizes that Scully could still be a target, is a terrific, off-kilter closer. If *The X-Files* was always willing to throw a curveball at its viewers when the mood took it, the show also knew the importance of giving us the familiar to hold onto every now and again. That might be the best recipe for a great TV show: risk and exploration mixed with a healthy respect for comfort food.

Another highlight of this episode is the fun to be found in Mulder and Scully's dynamic. We've seen the show explore the dark side of Mulder and Scully's partnership before,[10] and as in the "Redux" two-parter that started this season (S5E1–2), we've also gotten a sense of the deep emotional connection that keeps them together. In "Detour," we get to see them at their most playful and charming. The comedy of Mulder and Scully begrudgingly hitching a ride with a pair of woefully bland FBI agents in order to attend a team-building seminar is perfectly deployed, with the eponymous detour occurring when Mulder jumps at a chance to bail at a road block—and thus the impromptu MOTW case begins. Not even Scully can blame him for seeking some excitement elsewhere. As grim and dangerous as it can often be, *The X-Files* is also about the curious joys of finding monsters in your closet, of turning weather balloons into UFOs. "Detour" taps into that feeling. It's a sunny day, and there are dragons outside. Time to play hooky from the school of reality. —ZH

SEASON 5 / EPISODE 5 | **"THE POST-MODERN**
WRITTEN AND DIRECTED BY CHRIS CARTER | **PROMETHEUS"**

PUT ON MY BLUE SUEDE SHOES, AND I BOARDED THE TRAIN

In which it's alive.

A dream I keep having:

I'm back in the town where I went to college, a solid, small Midwestern city, filled with brick buildings and tree-lined avenues. For some reason, everyone I've ever met has gathered in some sort of amphitheater, like we're coming up on the end of a long-running TV show and the producers have brought everybody back for one final bow. But as the night stretches on and I see more and more faces of people I haven't seen in years, I start to realize something: Not everybody is here. I take leave of my friends to find everybody else. I board a train (because in this dream I only travel by train, for some reason), and we head west, deeper into the past, toward a camp I

---

10 Most notably in "Never Again" (S4E13).

attended as a teenager. Along the way, I find more and more people, some I've forgotten about but remember the faces of, tucked away in some small corner of my brain. And then, inevitably, before I get to the source, to the beginning, the dream stops.

And I wake up lacking.

I've always had a hard time with the notion that people can't hang onto each other forever. I'm not even talking about death here. Death has always struck me as an inevitability that's not worth worrying about. I'm talking about the fact that to make anything of your life, you have to, necessarily, leave a good number of people behind. I grew up in a small town where I knew everybody in my graduating class as well as I knew anyone I'd ever meet, but now, those people are all very far away from me, both physically and emotionally. Could I call on them if I were back home? Probably, but it wouldn't be the same. Eventually, you have to move on, and that leaves little gaps, little holes that, if you're lucky, get filled by new people. If you're lucky, you meet someone to spend your life with. Maybe you have some kids. And you have your parents until they die. But that's about it. That's really all you can count on. And so, if you're like me, you hang on too tightly, even if it's only on a subconscious train.

For this reason, I've always had an odd affection for small-town stories, particularly on television, where the people of the small town inevitably become a kind of surrogate family for each other and, arguably, for us. These series use the small town to capture just what's so seductive about living in a community where everybody knows everybody and at least professes to care for them. (In real life, this is not always the case.) The fantasy is, in many ways, more potent than the reality. And even though it breaks a lot of my preferred methods of handling a small-town story, "The Post-Modern Prometheus" is such a wonderful expression of this particular idea that it's always been one of my four or five favorite *X-Files* episodes, hands-down. But it wasn't until watching the episode again, in a spate of time when I was having the dream over and over, that I realized why. But we'll get to that.[11]

"Post-Modern Prometheus" is a weird mash-up of a bunch of things Chris Carter (who wrote and directed, and received Emmy nominations for both) found interesting, including genetic engineering, *Frankenstein* (as both novel and movie), old Universal horror movies, comic books, metafiction, and sympathetic monsters.[12] It is, roughly, a very direct adaptation of *Frankenstein*, but it's been skewed to make

---

11 We're also going to get to the fact that this episode is . . . shall we say . . . problematic? I promise.

12 According to Carter himself, the episode "was an amalgam of many little pieces of inspiration," in addition to those aforementioned influences. Carter says that prior to writing the episode, "I had been contacted by two people who said they were fans of the show: one being Roseanne Barr, the other being Cher. I thought, 'I'm going to write an episode that features both those actresses. I'll put them both in an episode and it'll be great fun. I'll do something that has a character like the kid from *Mask*.' Then, you know, I started building [. . .] I had seen a Tim Burton short called *Frankenweenie*, which was done in black and white, which was great. I thought, 'I'm going to do a black-and-white episode. But do it with a touch of inspired madness and craziness.'" Ultimately, neither Roseanne nor Cher could clear their schedules to appear. But the episode stuck.

sense in modern times, and it's been tossed into the middle of a broad example of the *X-Files* comedy episode.

But like all of the best *X-Files* episodes, there's a deep sense of loss at the center of "Prometheus," a sense of loss that manifests in the fact that Mulder can't find a happy ending to the story without purposefully asking the writer to concoct one for him, an ending that's probably not even real. Loss and loneliness are the twin emotional engines that drive *The X-Files*, whether it's a grand example like Mulder losing his sister to dark forces, or something far subtler like the teenager who gets her life taken from her in "Jose Chung's *From Outer Space*" (S3E20). Even on the broadest possible level, the show is about the loss of regionalized myths, replaced by an all-consuming national myth.

Mulder and Scully have been called to a small town in the middle of nowhere, a small town that may as well be a Hollywood small town, for how it seems to consist entirely of small-town stereotypes and standing sets on the studio backlot.[13] The reason they've been called is an unexpected pregnancy. Shaineh Berkowitz (Pattie Tierce) discovered an intruder in her house one night, a horrifying, lumpy-headed kind of monster. She passed out—perhaps because of drugs pumped into the air—and when she woke up three days later, she was pregnant. But that's not the weird part. The same thing happened to her seventeen years ago, resulting in her son Izzy (Stewart Gale). And even *that's* not the weird part. Because after that event, Shaineh had a tubal ligation. She shouldn't be able to get pregnant. Yet here she is. She's thinking aliens. Mulder says he's not sure he believes in that anymore.

Carter piles on silliness and story elements. He's got a comic book written about a local legendary creature. He's got a mad scientist. He's got a scene in which Mulder and Scully have a conversation, and the same extra is raking leaves over each of their shoulders (a marvelous joke on TV's tendency to shoot everything in a long succession of close-ups and mid-shots).

But he's also got a story that's positively filled with the kinds of things I usually hate. For one thing, this is a story that is entirely about women getting pregnant with hybrid creatures when someone invades their house and uses a knockout gas to get them to fall asleep. This means that, yes, this is another one of the great *X-Files* comedy episodes that features rape, alongside "Jose Chung" and "Small Potatoes" (S4E20). It's the sort of thing that didn't ping as many radars in 1997 but is far harder to ignore given more modern conversations about consent. Yes, this was a series focused on body horror, but by putting rape in a comedic context, the show seems to ignore how troubling it is.[14]

---

13 Like all episodes from the first five seasons, it was filmed in Vancouver, which makes the ability to evoke standing sets on a Hollywood backlot even more impressive.

14 That said, I think "Prometheus" is occasionally smarter about this than "Jose Chung" and especially "Small Potatoes," which I'll explain.

Also troubling is the fact that every member of this little town is portrayed in as condescending a fashion as possible. These aren't characters so much as they're stereotypes, but Carter, crucially, doesn't seem to realize this. He's got Scully spouting nonsense about how people in the middle of the country see fit to pattern their lives after Jerry Springer and tabloid covers, and outside of the Berkowitzes—who have a certain kind of idiotic dignity—and the monster and his father, the show doesn't really bother to contradict this.

Certainly, Carter has fun playing around with the idea of a mad scientist living in these people's midst, and John O'Hurley, then best known for playing J. Peterman on *Seinfeld*, is a marvelous choice for the part. There's a scene in which he has a conversation with Mulder and Scully about his experiments; every line is punctuated with thunder and lightning, and it goes on for so long that it becomes tiring and then wildly funny again by the end. But where Carter understands very specifically what he's doing, comedically, with the mad scientist, the other townspeople are often portrayed as, "Gosh, people in the middle of the country are weird."

To a degree, he has to do this to make scenes like the one in which the town forms a mob bearing pitchforks and torches believable (and that scene is necessary for him to really get the Frankenstein story right). But *The X-Files* has always been a show that's at its best when it's celebrating how weird and wild the United States can be, how it's a big, strange place where the only things odder than the monsters hiding in the night were the oddballs terrorized by them.

In "Prometheus," Mulder tells Scully that she was right, and she says, "That these people can be reduced to cultural stereotypes?" and, again, the show doesn't really call her on it. There's a discomfiting sense that Carter views the entire middle of the country (or maybe even America or humanity in general) as thickheaded lummoxes who can be led to just about any conclusion and tend to behave as giant collectives that don't really think through their actions. Maybe he's right about that. You can certainly point to as many real-world examples as you want. But it's still a little disconcerting to be asked to laugh at the lunkheaded idiots without really questioning that reaction, as the comedic scripts by Darin Morgan and Vince Gilligan always ask us to do.[15]

And yet "Prometheus" *works*. Part of it is the fact that the Frankenstein tale has such an inherent momentum that Carter can't go wrong in melding it with the MOTW formula. There's a kind of wonderful purity to Mulder and Scully coming to town and thinking they've stumbled upon a silly joke, perpetuated to sell a comic book, then finding, as time goes on, that there really is a monster here—who's not the monster at all. It's an old, old story, but Carter manages to bring something vaguely new to it. There's the usual pretentious Carter-babble, but there's also that wonderful

---

15 "War of the Coprophages" (S3E12) and "Bad Blood" (S5E12) being good examples of this.

sense you get sometimes while watching *The X-Files*, the sense that what's hiding under the bed is stranger than you'd ever be able to imagine.

Through gorgeous black-and-white cinematography, and expert shot selection and editing, the episode deftly pays homage to its twin influences of Universal horror movies and comic books. One of the strengths of *The X-Files* is its capacity to make all kinds of episodes and call on all kinds of influences, and this might be the episode that went the farthest afield of the show's standard repertoire. The confrontation between the monster's father and O'Hurley (who is later revealed to be the old man's son) is gloriously filmed, the final betrayal of the son killing the father shot entirely in shadow for extra heightened terror. Even better, the actors, including Duchovny and Anderson (both of whom are positively luminous in black and white), get into this spirit. The episode's general condescension toward its characters, especially, is easier to swallow when couched in homage.

But the episode wouldn't work without that emotional core of longing and loneliness. I'm not someone who strongly desires to see Mulder and Scully get together. I tend to agree with Carter's idea that the two are a kind of perfect platonic partnership, a duet in which the two people so perfectly complete each other that to have sex would be sort of unnecessary. But one of the things that drives the show, I think, is that so many of the people Mulder and Scully meet—monsters and normal folks both—are people who lack that essential other half, people who are constantly searching out something compatible and not finding it. Now, in many episodes, this leads them to kill, but in "Prometheus," it leads an old man, no matter how unethically and immorally and haphazardly,[16] to create, to try to build something better, even as he always fails.

Which brings us to the core reason this episode is so troubling to watch: It's about a man who medically impregnates women in order to create a mate for his son. Even worse, it doesn't regard this behavior as anything but a quirky turn of events, just another strange thing about this oddball town. When the episode focuses on the monster, who is himself a failed experiment and who has lived his life in the shadows, it is on firmer ground, and it actually starts to scratch the surface of the deeply horrifying implications of the old man's work. But it also tries to make the old man himself a figure of sympathy, despite the fact that he effectively sexually assaulted many, many women *and* locked his son away from the world at large.

Whereas "Jose Chung" kept what actually happened to Chrissy Giorgio in the dark, and whereas the sexual assaults in "Small Potatoes" were ostensibly consensual at the time they occurred,[17] there's no way to write around the violations at the heart of "Prometheus," try though Carter might. *The X-Files* was always on shaky

---

16 And let me reiterate that his methods are *really unethical, immoral, and horrible.*

17 Though I would argue that whereas "Prometheus" at least knows what the monster has done is wrong, "Small Potatoes" has next to no interest in seeing Eddie's actions as anything other than goofy.

ground when it tried to tell stories involving rape, pregnancy, and other horrors traditionally accorded to women. "Prometheus" is, in many ways, another egregious example of this sexist trope.

Even on a storytelling level, the idea that this old man created most of the town (to find a mate for his son) by impregnating women with farm animal–human hybrids is not just morally repulsive but also completely ridiculous. The episode's attempt to let the monster off the hook when he admits to everything he did—with the exception of killing his father—shouldn't work because you can't believe the townspeople would just be OK with this, no matter how gullible they may be.

But the episode remains one of my favorites for two big reasons. One is that sense of pervasive loneliness. No matter what happens, the monster will never find a mate. His father doesn't know what he's doing with his experiments, and the two of them will inevitably be caught.[18] The monster, like monsters since the dawn of time, is an easily made scapegoat for whatever anyone wants to blame on him. Sure, he might be a fun local legend and the basis of a comic book, but once he steps into the light, well, he's hideous, and even if he wasn't directly part of his father's experiments, he aided and abetted them. He was just as complicit.

And yet the character of the monster complicates the episode's horrific elements in a way that ultimately works and makes "Prometheus" a richer experience than you might expect. The monster lives in a basement and can't show his face at night. He loves Cher and peanut butter. He's a monster, but if only he could find his own Mulder, his own Scully, he might not feel so monstrous. It's not an excuse, but it's—maybe—an explanation.

I would also argue that the episode owns up to the horror of what these men did. The mad scientist is arrested for the old man's murder, the old man having paid for his own horrible actions with his life, and the monster is arrested as well. He's still guilty of helping his father invade houses and impregnate women against their wills.[19] He's carted off to jail, and that's that. In attempting to stave off isolation, these men only invented further isolation for themselves. "Prometheus" is an episode that starts out as a goof and ends up becoming deeply sad and weirdly horrific, a story in which everyone is cruel to each other, almost as a matter of course.

Except, of course, that it *doesn't* end that way. Sort of.

The monster's about to go off to prison, sitting in the back of a car, head hung in shame. But Mulder isn't satisfied by that. The monster's supposed to escape

---

18 It makes no sense that they don't get caught anyway, with those giant striped exterminator tents they keep using. You'd think someone would say something. (The image of exterminator tents covering up something dastardly was one Vince Gilligan would reuse in the final season of *Breaking Bad*.)

19 You might argue that the monster was so sealed off from the world at large that he didn't really have a moral framework per se, and that he was a de facto victim of parental abuse. That probably stretches the episode to its breaking point, and I highly doubt Carter thought about any of it. But it's certainly something worth considering.

imprisonment. He's supposed to run off into the night to seek his mate. The monster can't die, because the monster, no matter how well developed as a character, is about something more elemental, something pure. Mulder asks to speak to the writer, who just so happens to be Izzy Berkowitz, who's written a comic book about the monster after all. From there, the episode abandons all logic and reality and, for lack of a better word, *transcends*.

I should reiterate that none of this really happens. The townspeople don't come together and attend a Cher concert. Cher doesn't really perform "Walking in Memphis" for the monster and dance with him. Mulder and Scully don't really dance together at the end. Shaineh and the scientist's wife don't really go on *Jerry Springer* to express how much they love their little Mutatos.[20] The show hasn't just left the reality of this episode; it's left reality, period. We're not in the realm of fiction but in the realm of metafiction, the only place where a truly happy ending can occur, because metafiction is constantly commenting on its own unlikeliness. And even though it's theoretically a happy ending, it's also very sad and empty in its own way. Because Mulder and Scully—all smiles for what must be the first time ever—are just a drawing in a comic book. Once the book is shut, we can't get back into it, no matter how much we might want to.

One of the aims of writing, in addition to reflecting the world as you see it, is to perfect the world as you want it. And here we circle back to the beginning, both of this piece and of *The X-Files*. I don't know what, exactly, Carter and his writers experienced in their lives, but the show often seems an elaborate attempt to combat a crippling loneliness, to fill in gaps that shouldn't have been opened in the past. And even though none of the end sequence actually happens, the end of "Prometheus" is one of the most beautiful expressions of this desire to re-create the world, to make something better of it, that I've ever seen. The monster doesn't have to move on. He's surrounded by people who, no matter how absurdly, love him. He's seeing Cher—*live*! It doesn't really happen, but if someone writes it down, and if it comes alive for enough people, then it does. And he doesn't have to be alone.

Don't we all sort of hope this? Don't we hope that we'll get to the end, lying on our deathbeds or facing down the firing squad or tucked in the back of a car en route to life in prison, and get a reprieve? Don't we hope that someone will turn to the writer and ask for something better, even for just a little while? And then maybe we'll all

S5 E5

---

20 The babies on *Springer* are often taken as evidence that the monster physically raped these women, but they're in a fictional construct, presented as evidence that the experiment the old man could never get right has finally worked, and the monster will have a companion. The monster is complicit in his father's acts, but not actually a direct part of them, except in a fantasy sequence. You can (and probably should) argue that this is a weird thing to present as a great part of a closing fantasy, but it doesn't actually happen, which reflects the episode's ambiguity about the monster's motives and crimes. If this is a happy ending, it's a hollow one, because it's a fantasy.

get in a chain of cars—or maybe a train?—and head through the flat, Midwestern afternoon toward a better place, a better day. And we'll open the doors to the club, and everyone we've ever known or cared about will be there, and for just a moment, we'll all have a single, perfect moment of happiness.

And then, maybe, we'll be able to look up and face what inevitably comes next. —TVDW

| "CHRISTMAS CAROL" | SEASON 5 / EPISODE 6
WRITTEN BY VINCE GILLIGAN, JOHN SHIBAN, AND FRANK SPOTNITZ
DIRECTED BY PETER MARKLE |

LONG DISTANCE

In which Scully is visited by the Ghost of Christmases Past.

It's a little frustrating how often Scully story lines revolve around things being done *to* her. Mulder is trying to find his sister and save the world. He's the one doing the searching, forcing the government to react to *him*. Scully just showed up for the ride, and then Duane Barry stuffed her in the trunk of his car, changing her life, and forcing her to deal with the aftermath ever since. Mulder chose his path; Scully had hers forced upon her. It makes sense from a character perspective, but it would be nice if she were given some autonomy down the road.

The problem, of course, is that while Scully and Mulder are both leads on the show, it's Mulder's world that *The X-Files* spends the vast majority of its time exploring. Mulder is the obsessive whose paranoid assumptions so often prove right; Scully—introduced initially as a skeptic sent to discredit his work—was intended as an audience identification figure to ease us in to the show's weirder flights of fancy. While this dynamic has evolved over time, it's still rare to see an episode from Scully's perspective that gives her the room and autonomy to be her own distinct person, as opposed to just half of a partnership.

This emphasis on Scully is part of what makes this episode so welcome. "Christmas Carol" spends considerable time building up Scully's family life in a way that it hasn't really explored with much depth before. While not all of that exploration is fun to watch, it's character work that's been long overdue.

The plot revolves around Scully spending time with her nearest and dearest at Christmastime, when she receives an anonymous phone call. The voice on the other end says, "She needs your help. She needs you, Dana." Scully recognizes that voice as her dead sister, Melissa, and has the call traced back to it source: the Sim household, where Mrs. Roberta Sim has apparently committed suicide. Who was calling Scully? And why on earth does the phantom caller want her to get involved in such an open-and-shut case?

The answer to the first question is, unsurprisingly, never answered, but the answer to the second becomes clear soon enough. Roberta Sim's suicide wasn't much of a suicide, and her husband isn't much of a husband. To make matters worse, they have an adopted daughter, Emily, who's just old enough to be horribly scared by all of this. Like so many kids on *The X-Files*, Emily is a little spooky; she doesn't say much, and she's always stone-faced and staring, as though she doesn't quite understand what language everyone is speaking. Scully finds a picture of her at a birthday party: The kid's got a huge smile on her face, and she has a cake and party favors, but she's the only one in the shot. No friends, no loving parent standing next to her. Even before her mother's death, she was alone.

Scully does some investigating and discovers that Emily shares DNA with Melissa Scully. Throughout the episode, Scully has dreams of her own childhood. In the first dream—the best of the lot—lil' Scully sees a little girl watching her from the basement stairs. Since the little girl on the stairs and Emily are played by the same actress, it's natural to assume that Emily was invading Scully's dreams. But the girl in Scully's dreams is actually Melissa, a fact we don't realize until we find out how similar the two children look. It's a trippy, eerie beat that helps add to the sense of interconnection throughout the episode. Perhaps, we're led to believe, Scully's involvement with a conspiracy is even vaster, if more benevolent, than Mulder's.

Scully can't resist getting drawn into the case—especially after she gets another phone call from beyond the grave—and, of course, it turns out that things are not as they seem. Roberta was drugged when she died, and while there's some indication that she'd ingested the sedatives herself, skeptical Scully isn't buying that explanation. A second autopsy reveals a small needle prick on Roberta's heel where the drugs were injected. But who would want to kill her? And who are those strange men that keep following her husband around?

While Scully gets to the bottom of it all, she also has to fight off her family's constant interrogations. This works as a clever reversal of Scully's usual position; for once, she's the believer, having to constantly fend off the skepticism of others in order to get to what she knows in her heart is the real truth. Gillian Anderson does her characteristic terrific work here, and it's great to see her basically kicking ass and taking names.

Still, it's hard to stomach her brother, Bill, and her mother in this episode, both of whom spend seemingly every moment on-screen being judgmental, dismissive, and just generally unhelpful. It's possible to justify their attitudes here. Scully *should* take some time off from her job, and, under any other circumstance, claiming that you've been getting calls from your dead sister would be a clear indication that you're not entirely over her death. It's not like working with Mulder is a regular 9 to 5 position; in her hunt for the truth, Scully has sacrificed not just career opportunities and peace of mind, but has lost both her sister and her old family connections.

S5 E6

While Mulder's life has been tied up in conspiracy even before he was born, Scully is becoming involved in this world at a time in her life when she might have otherwise been developing relationships and working toward a more conventional future. Instead of moving up the career ladder and finding someone to share a normal life with, she's chasing aliens and various other monstrosities. It's a loss that deserves to be noted, especially by the people who care about her.

Even still, it's frustrating to watch these conversations, because it feels like scene after scene of Scully struggling to defend herself to people who refuse to respect or support her decisions. While that exasperation is certainly intentional—an argument with people you love that isn't frustrating wouldn't be all that credible or dramatically effective—these scenes also get repetitive very quickly, and suffer from being more about Scully's family denying what she's telling them and overriding her concerns than it is about them expressing their genuine concerns for her. The friction makes for some tough scenes in an otherwise great episode.

In the end, we don't know exactly what's going on with Emily. She has some rare diseases, and there's a pharmaceutical company that's been paying Roberta Sim for permission to run drug trials on the kid. That same company is probably responsible for Roberta's death (and it's certainly responsible for the death of her husband). The stakes are undoubtedly high for Emily's life, so there's no way Scully could leave this alone—especially after learning that Emily isn't Melissa's daughter but her own. While it's hard to care too much about the stakes here (I can't imagine the show saddling Scully with a kid at this point in the run), the episode works to effectively convey excitement and shock. Whoever expects to get a call from the dead, only to find someone living on the other end? —ZH

| "EMILY" | SEASON 5 / EPISODE 7
WRITTEN BY VINCE GILLIGAN, JOHN SHIBAN, AND FRANK SPOTNITZ
DIRECTED BY KIM MANNERS |

IT BEGINS WHERE IT ENDS

In which the conspiracy (or the status quo) always wins.

"Emily" is an episode that's difficult to invest in, even if its heart is near the right place. Somewhere inside of it is the story of a woman who has given up on having children but has nevertheless been given a gift, before having it roughly taken from her. But the episode fails to commit to the degree it needs to if it's going to find this core story and make it sing. It feels almost as if the show doesn't think a deeply personal story like this one can work as an X-File. It shouldn't have worried. "I Want to Believe" is, ultimately, an optimistic yet deeply personal mantra. Scully wants to believe that she can pick up with Emily like no time was left off and that nothing strange has happened, that she can simply raise this little girl as if she had known her all her life. Scully should know by now that it has never been that simple.

The X-Files writers paint themselves into an impossible corner here. To kill Emily at the end of this hour suggests a story line that exists solely to have something awful happen to the characters we care about so we can watch them be tortured by it. Gillian Anderson is superb enough to pull it off, but this a character who has survived an alien abduction *and* cancer. You'd hope the show would let up on her for a little while at least.

The writers also couldn't very well let Emily live. She's a special-needs child, who would need Scully far more than Scully could possibly provide, given the circumstances of the agent's life. To abruptly give Scully a little girl—a lasting, positive consequence of her abduction—would have been interesting, but it ultimately would have gotten in the way of the show's primary dynamic. You can't send Scully out into the field to battle monsters when you're constantly wondering if the nanny's doing all right with the kid at home.

The powerful idea that Scully temporarily has everything she wants, then has it all taken from her, gets lost in the story's convolutions. It's as if the show doesn't trust itself to do another completely emotional hour, coming right off of "Christmas Carol" (S5E6). That episode is a beautifully evocative portrayal of Scully's attempts to move past all of the death that's surrounded her since she joined the X-Files. It's a more overtly emotional key for The X-Files to play in than usual, and it works. "Emily," however, wants to be Season Five's "Memento Mori" (S4E14). It features overwrought Scully monologues, Mulder chasing down conspiracy phantoms, and a plotline in which Scully stands in a hospital and looks sad a lot. It's true what they say about diminishing returns.

What's most frustrating is how this all *almost* comes together. Anderson finds some of the raw sense of hope and loss that comes with having a possibility you thought was closed off to you abruptly spark back to life. The last ten minutes of the episode, when Emily has slipped into a coma and the Mulder story dovetails more neatly with the Scully story, work well, despite hitting many beats the show has hit before. Emily, at the very least, gives us a more human and personal connection to the havoc the conspiracy wreaks. The problem is that we've only just met her.

Where "Christmas Carol" centers on Scully's connection to her dead sister and the things the X-Files have taken from her, "Emily" is about an ordeal surrounding a little girl we didn't even know existed. This two-parter reminds me of the Max Fenig two-parter "Tempus Fugit"/"Max" (S4E17/18), but those episodes relied on our affection for a character we'd met way back in "Fallen Angel" (S1E10). Emily is a cipher, a child more interesting for what she represents than for who she is. Indeed, that's who Emily literally is to Scully, but like so many other little girls on TV,[21] she functions more as a symbol of innocence than as an actual character.

Thus, the most interesting thread here is Scully wanting to adopt Emily, but it's also a thread you immediately realize (because of Scully's centrality to the plot of the show) will have very little bearing outside of these episodes. The Mulder story line is basically just his story line from "Memento Mori" all over again, only his rage reads like reheated leftovers. The show could have found a parallel between Emily and Samantha—a girl connected to Scully and created by the conspiracy for nefarious purposes contrasted with a girl connected to Mulder and taken by them for the same reason—but it doesn't really bother. The mythology threats here are the usual mishmash of experiments, weird shape-shifters,[22] and unethical medicine. Had Emily *been* someone, instead of just another example of the conspiracy at work, her loss would have been felt more deeply. Instead, she's mostly an X-File and barely a person. We're supposed to find the proceedings more involving because they personally affect Scully and because we see an innocent face that gives the human toll more tangible weight.

But we don't, not really. When Scully opens Emily's coffin at the episode's end and finds only sand, it's supposed to be a sad reminder of how much the conspiracy has taken from our heroes, but it feels too heavy-handed. A lighter touch overall, one that really made you feel how Mulder and Scully had fallen for this kid and were going to do anything to make the world safe for her, could have pulled the disparate parts of the episode together. Anderson conveys through her performance that Scully knows that Emily, ultimately, was only sand, slipping away from her before she had a chance to grab hold. But everybody else involved plays it like the kid was a solid statue made of clay, one that simply got misplaced somewhere along the way.

The grief at the core of this episode here stays buried because no one's quite sure how to react, quite sure how to mourn something that now exists only in stories and dreams. The "Christmas Carol"/"Emily" two-parter is strongest when it confronts this understanding of Emily's ephemerality. It's at its weakest when it turns that notion into just another episode of *The X-Files*. —TVDW

---

21 The "good-hearted teenage daughter who shows the antihero protagonist how much they have to lose" is now a total cliché. See also: Meadow Soprano from *The Sopranos*, Dana Brody from *Homeland*, Sally Draper from *Mad Men*, Paige Jennings from *The Americans*, Grace Florrick from *The Good Wife*, and on and on. Some of these characters are more complicated than others (particularly *The Americans'* Paige), but they all began their series as symbols of something that might be lost, rather than actual people.

22 You'd think that Mulder, especially, would be hip to the shape-shifters by now, but he seems perpetually flummoxed by them, perhaps because the plot requires him to be.

ON THE HUNT

In which he had to go.

"Pusher" (S3E17) is a great episode, and Robert Modell was a great monster: arrogant and terrifying but still recognizably human. *The X-Files* hardly ever gives its non-mythology episodes sequels,[23] but even though the last time we saw Modell he was a zombie dying of a brain tumor in a hospital penitentiary, the show has decided there's enough wiggle room to bring him back. Maybe this unexpected follow-up was conceived of as a way to revitalize and expand the world of *The X-Files*, by connecting story lines and different episodes that don't include aliens and government conspiracies.

Or maybe this attempt is just a sign of creative exhaustion. I can't know for sure, but I can tell you that "Kitsunegari" isn't nearly as good as its predecessor. In fact, it's a mess; the story repeats many of the same basic ideas from "Pusher" without adding anything truly new, and Scully is here at her most frustratingly skeptical and close-minded.[24]

The episode never really justifies its existence. It tries to provide us with a new angle on Modell by giving him a twin sister named Linda, but we never really get any sense of what Modell's relationship with his sister is like, or who she is, or how this relates to Modell's obsession with Mulder. Besides including this ridiculously contrived twist, the episode makes that horrible mistake that so many sequels seem to stumble over—bringing back a great villain, and making him . . . less great.

There are ways "Kitsunegari" could have worked. Maybe Modell's relationship with Linda wasn't an entirely happy one. They were separated at birth and barely knew each other, so maybe she grew up just as self-centered and conceited as he did, and when she found him, maybe she was less interested in who he was as a person and more interested in what she could make out of him, or what she could use him as—an inspiration, a cause to fight for, a path to follow. Maybe the reason Modell is behaving so strangely throughout the episode is that his brain really isn't working properly due to that tumor we learned about in "Pusher." Maybe Linda has actually

---

23 The only examples I can think of to this point are "Squeeze" (S1E3) and "Tooms" (S1E21) (a few more are coming).

24 Which is especially frustrating, considering the episode is a sequel; she's literally seen evidence of Modell's abilities before, and yet the writers refuse to allow the character to build off those ideas. It's a perfect example of one of the show's most notorious flaws: the reluctance to move beyond the Believer vs. Skeptic dynamic upon which it was created.

had to use her push on him to get him to escape so that she can pin her husband's murder on him.

It's impossible to say if changing (or clarifying) the characters' motivations would make the episode a good one, but at least it would be easier to understand why Modell seems so confused and half there throughout the hour, and why so little of what he does here gels with what we know about him from his first appearance. As is, this is a well-shot episode that goes through a lot of the familiar motions of a Monster of the Week entry: weird assaults (including that dramatic cerulean blue-paint murder of Linda's husband), Mulder getting suspicious, Scully doubting him, and a confrontation in which Mulder and Scully's trust for each other is tested (albeit in a somewhat off-kilter fashion).[25] But any deeper thought reveals how little the story makes sense. In the end, this is just more evidence of how sequels fail when they attempt to build on a story that was already complete. —ZH

| **"SCHIZOGENY"** | SEASON 5 / EPISODE 9
WRITTEN BY JESSICA SCOTT AND MIKE WOLLAEGER
DIRECTED BY RALPH HEMECKER |

SOMETHING IN THE TREES

In which M. Night Shyamalan, regretfully, gets some ideas.

Here's the most damning thing about "Schizogeny": At this point in its run, at the height of its powers, *The X-Files* shouldn't have let an episode this crappy air. Most shows use their fifth season for resting on their laurels and growing too comfortable with mediocrity, sure, but something this bad? That's usually a Season Seven or Eight kind of thing. Because this episode is truly, truly bad.

Like Season Four's worst hour, "Sanguinarium" (S4E6), the credit for this script goes to a couple of freelancers.[26] And like that prior episode, right from the earliest moments of "Schizogeny," its tone is off. Mulder is far too callous about the twelve pounds of mud Scully digs out of the episode's first victim (a man dragged down into the mud by living trees because . . . why not?). "Is it possible he took the term 'mud pie' literally?" he says. It's such a howlingly bad line that David Duchovny seems intent on milking every bit of awfulness out of it, his deadpan curiously enlivened by it.[27]

---

25 Linda pushes Mulder into thinking that Scully has shot herself, and when the real Scully shows up, he sees her as Linda. It's disorienting, and it doesn't entirely work the way it should.

26 Flip back to that episode to read more about the role of freelancers on '90s TV shows.

27 Later, when he comes across a desiccated corpse with tree roots sticking out of it in the wall of someone's cellar, he'll say, "Talk about puttin' down roots." Thank you for your service, David Duchovny.

On top of the tonal imbalance, this episode might feature the most uninspiring troupe of guest actors the show ever assembled. We've got Bobby, whom Chad Lindberg occasionally plays with an incredibly terrible accent. We've got his crush, Lisa, played by Katharine Isabelle, who at least seems to be trying. We've got a mysteriously accented man who wanders around with a hatchet and babbles about the trees. Then we've got Karin, played by Sarah-Jane Redmond, who was good over on the Chris Carter drama *Millennium* but is here given something that's not entirely a character, and she doesn't quite rise to the challenge.

Karin is the bad guy here, and it's the way in which she's a bad guy that ultimately dooms this mess. Karin, see, was terrorized by her father as a young girl, and somehow, this gave her *power over trees*. There are some hints as to how this is possible, and there are occasional nods in the general direction of why all of this could be happening and Karin's dad being a "very bad man" who damaged the trees or something, but for the most part, the show just doesn't even bother to explain why this might be happening. One imagines the writers came up with "trees kill people," realized how dramatically uninteresting that was, then tried to come up with a human antagonist while still keeping the tree thing. In the final act, which involves Karin and Bobby facing off and Mulder getting snared by a tree root, you almost want all of them to get dragged down into the mud, then have the next episode begin with Mulder striding into his FBI office to the shocked expression of Scully, with him saying, "What? I had an extra life."

Sadly, the more the episode tries to tie the "killer tree" premise into the idea of child abuse, the less it acquires any of the power or tragedy the subject is supposed to bestow. Karin has the town's teens relive her trauma with her father, thus giving them the idea that their parents were hurting them, thus giving her and the trees license to kill. This abrupt shift into an examination of the long-lasting legacy of child abuse on its victims (with killer trees!) continues, with the show doubling down both on the plant mayhem and the ostensibly tragic core. Maybe this would have worked better if the tree effects were more convincing, but they aren't in the slightest.

Damaged teenagers (or adults damaged as children) were the stock-in-trade of *The X-Files* for a while,[28] but "Schizogeny" treats these broken characters as nothing more than bizarre tree puppets in a half-realized story. By the time the weirdly accented groundskeeper has chopped off Karin's head with an ax, sending both pieces of her body sinking into the mud, you won't just be wondering why you decided to watch this episode; you'll be wondering why you decided to watch a show that could produce an episode this bad at all. —TVDW

---

28 Think "D.P.O." (S3E3) or "Oubliette" (S3E8).

LET'S HAVE FUN

In which Scully does not do the hokeypokey, as that's not what this is all about.

On paper, it's a brilliant idea for an episode: bring in Stephen King, a best-selling pop-horror juggernaut, to write a script for *The X-Files*, a sci-fi–horror megahit. King is the reason I became a writer. I've spent most of my life reading and rereading his work, but even I wouldn't go to bat defending his abilities as a screenwriter. It's not a medium that plays to his strong suits. Great screenplays use structure and dialogue to tell their stories, and King is too intuitive a prose writer to be much good with the former, and too much a sucker for dopey catchphrases to be adept at the latter. He's capable of creating worlds populated by terrifying monsters and sympathetic heroes, but when he tries to translate those creations into a different medium, he runs into some problems. Thus, it's no surprise that this episode might look great on paper and be a total mess in practice.

Even putting King's screenwriting shortcomings aside, it's no easy thing for any writer to jump into a long-running series and nail the feel of the show and the character dynamics. If anything, the offenses against Mulder and Scully here are even worse than in "Schizogeny" (S5E9). The writing credit on "Chinga" is for Stephen King and Chris Carter; the word is, Carter stepped in to rewrite King's work because he wasn't happy with the Mulder-Scully interactions. If that's the case, I shudder to think what the original draft looked like.

The episode plays like someone doing a broad parody of King tropes. The first thing we see is a Maine license plate, and the local color comes on strong for the remainder of the hour. Some of it's cute; I won't say I didn't feel a twinge of state pride seeing Scully wearing a MAINE: THE WAY LIFE SHOULD BE T-shirt. But somewhere around the tenth time the local sheriff says "Ayuh,"[29] all that color goes from charming to caricature. There are close-minded townsfolk, including a shrewish religious zealot who could have stepped out of half a dozen King books. Scully has a lobster dinner that's about twice the size of her head. It's all too silly for words, and while I suspect much of the humor was intentional, it's never all that funny.

The story itself is the worst kind of lazy, as the script simply pulls together a few creepy ideas, ladles on the gore, and calls it done. We've got a killer doll, which (as Mulder points out) is a conventional horror-fiction trope—so conventional that it's surprising to realize the show had never done it before. We've got an autistic (and

---

29 He stretches it out to the point of absurdity each time: "eehhhhh-Yeaaaaah."

possibly telepathic) daughter, as King loves his mentally "different" characters like nobody's business. We've got grotesque deaths, another favorite of the author. We've got the silly catchphrase, which has the perverse effect of turning a monster into a commercial for murder. It's all very lurid, and, in its defense, "Chinga" is rarely boring. Instead, it's empty, kind of dorky, and generally ridiculous.

Then there are those Scully and Mulder scenes. "Chinga" plays like a love letter to our favorite redheaded heroine. Nearly everyone around her is an idiot, and her occasional communications with Mulder show him to be the biggest buffoon of the lot. It gets especially weird when the script has our protagonists swap places on the skeptic-believer spectrum, with Scully theorizing that the deaths she's seeing might have a supernatural origin. While it's welcome to see her try on a different perspective, the shift is so sudden and unmotivated that it feels shockingly out of character. We never get a sense that she's exhausted other, more rational possibilities first, as we know our Scully would. This whole endeavor comes across as Scully fan service, which is only exacerbated by one scene's slow pan up of Gillian Anderson in a bubble bath.

Is there anything unequivocally good about "Chinga"? Gore fans will be pleased, and if I'm honest, I'll admit I get a kick out of how unrepentantly fevered this all is. A few of the jokes land,[30] and the episode at least retains a sense of King's work, however ill-fitting and clunky that sense may feel.

But overall, this feels thin. There's no plot here. There are just a bunch of folks dying horribly, and a climax in which a woman bashes her head with a hammer. Scully doesn't learn anything, doesn't discover the doll's history, doesn't use some secret trick to stop the threat. She just gets the doll and nukes it in the microwave. "Chinga" has a few freaky shots, and it's bizarre enough to avoid dullness, but it's ultimately a waste of two great flavors—which, it turns out, taste horrible together. —ZH

S5 E10

---

30 We get our first glimpse of Mulder's pencils in the office ceiling here, as well as a quick origin story for the I WANT TO BELIEVE poster.

DISCONNECTED

In which the Internet comes alive.

Remember 1998? Remember people freaking out about how the Internet was going to reach into all of our lives and utterly change them? Or Y2K, and how everybody briefly thought our overreliance on computers would plunge us back into a Dark Age? "Kill Switch" is most certainly a product of the "The Internet will ruin our lives!" era, but it's also more than that.

Sure, it's got a killer computer virus that's been evolving online and can take over Department of Defense satellites to fire plasma beams. But it's also a story in which a woman eventually finds a kind of literal paradise within the labyrinthine walls of the Internet, a story in which she essentially becomes immortal. It's dated, in that it's very much an episode about virtual reality and the Internet from the late '90s, but it overcomes that datedness by being fun. This is one of the more exciting, fast-paced *X-Files* episodes, and it's a nice respite after a long string of solemn episodes with good intentions, alongside some outright duds.

"Kill Switch" is the second episode in a row featuring a script by a famous genre author, in this case science-fiction superstar William Gibson. Gibson's cyberpunk milieu wouldn't necessarily seem to be the best fit for *The X-Files*, particularly since cyberpunk tends to nestle a week or so into the future, rather than in the present where *The X-Files* resides. Most monsters on this show tend to be of the past, rapidly being paved over by modernity. But the monster in "Kill Switch" is emphatically of a few years from now. That probably should unbalance this episode and rip it to shreds, but Gibson and cowriter Tom Maddox (also an acclaimed novelist) keep the whole thing tumbling along.[31]

"Kill Switch" is also the third episode in a row written primarily by someone who wasn't on the show's writing staff. However, unlike its predecessors, "Kill Switch" weirdly benefits from less staff oversight.[32] It's very entertaining TV, and it's entertaining in a way *The X-Files* rarely was. And here's the key to why it succeds: It doesn't really give you much time to think.

"Kill Switch" is a rare example of an *X-Files* episode that works, despite trying to do too much. Over the course of the hour, Gibson and Maddox keep introducing

---

31 Perhaps their foremost achievement is crafting a suspenseful episode in which the "villain" could probably be stopped by pulling the plug.

32 Chris Carter and company almost certainly helped Gibson and Maddox break this story, and they had final script approval. But the whole thing feels a bit like it sneaked by the usual gatekeepers.

idea after idea, and rather than overcrowding the episode, the ideas all bounce off of one another, collectively depicting the Internet as a wild frontier, where new life forms can gallop along and evolve inside RVs parked behind abandoned chicken farms in Fairfax, Virginia. Now, of course, this whole idea seems preposterous, but that naïveté is also a part of the episode's charm. There was a time we really thought this stuff could happen!

In short order, the episode cycles through all of these ideas: There's a computer virus that can control Department of Defense satellites and use them to track down those who would eradicate it, then fire weapons at them. Said virus can also track just about anyone to anywhere (using the phone network, naturally) and has all sorts of tricky ways of identifying its enemies. It can use the Internet to build itself a perfect habitat. There's a countermeasure virus that a computer genius (who invented the original virus) was building to dismantle the original, embedded on a CD with a copy of the song "Twilight Time." The virus has built a virtual reality world, catered to the whims of whomever falls into it, designed to extract information. The virus was apparently built initially to allow people to download their consciousnesses into computers, and Invisigoth (the woman tracking the virus) was working to download herself.

It should be too much. It almost is. The VR world, especially, is the sort of premise you'd build an entire episode of the show around,[33] but when you come down to it, all of these ideas are the same idea at a base level: We've eliminated the actual frontiers and explored all of them, but now we've invented a brand-new one—one that we can keep expanding indefinitely. That's more William Gibson than *The X-Files*, but the author understands the show enough to know that the best way to stop Mulder is a squadron of sexy nurses, so it all works by the skin of its teeth.

Kristin Lehman is not the greatest casting choice for Invisigoth. True, the role as scripted might be impossible for anyone to play. It's also entirely possible that the further we get from 1998, the less this seems like a believable character and the more it seems like the old stereotype of the computer hacker's dream girl, a touchy but gorgeous woman with raccoon makeup around her eyes and a wizardly way with a keyboard. Gibson can make this kind of character work on the page, but it's much harder to embody on-screen without seeming forced, and Invisigoth seems less like a scared kid being stalked by an all-powerful computer virus and more like a snotty tour guide to the wonders of the World Wide Web.

Luckily, none of that matters—for two reasons. First, things are moving so quickly that Invisigoth's characterization and the episode's many logical problems and plot holes are beside the point. Gibson and Maddox pace the action sequences well and space them apart perfectly, and they are similarly good at dropping in

---

33 Gibson and Maddox would in a later episode.

revelations and intriguing tidbits whenever things seem like they might be about to flag.

Second, this is one of Season Five's best Scully episodes.[34] While Mulder gets trapped by an evil A.I. and vivisected by sexy nurses, Scully drops plenty of skeptical bons mots and great one-liners as she's forced to hang out with Invisigoth, then gradually comes around to her new companion's way of thinking. Even better, we get to see Mulder's imaginary Scully, who storms into a room and starts delivering roundhouse kicks to those nurses. Both Scullys are variations on the proactive, sarcastic Scully we love best, and she's a relief to see after so many somber episodes.

"Kill Switch" portrays the Internet as place of both boundless possibilities and boundless terror. But could anyone involved in the episode have predicted the Internet would become perhaps the most important yet ordinary thing in many people's day-to-day lives? Would the citizens of 1998 be pleased that the Internet didn't turn into a lawless wasteland? Or would they be sad that instead of a paradise, we built a giant strip mall? —TVDW

| "BAD BLOOD" | SEASON 5 / EPISODE 12
WRITTEN BY VINCE GILLIGAN
DIRECTED BY CLIFF BOLE |

GETTING OUR STORIES STRAIGHT
In which Scully says po-tay-to, and Mulder says po-tah-to.

Four and a half seasons into *The X-Files*, the characters of Mulder and Scully are pretty static and predictable. With each new episode, we know Mulder will believe everything he hears and have a crazy theory that explains all of it; we know that Scully will cling to rationality and common sense in the face of all evidence; we know that Mulder will almost certainly be proved right; and we know that Scully will put up with pretty much anything. One of the strengths of a long-running series is the way the audience's familiarity allows the writers' room to play with our assumptions. What must it be like for Mulder to have to put up with a partner who never agrees with him? And what must it be like for Scully, working with a guy who seems to believe in everything?

"Bad Blood" is one of my favorite *X-Files* episodes. It's goofy in the best way possible, offering a welcome respite from some of the heavier subject matter of the season. Like many of the series' strongest comedic entries, "Bad Blood" is a genial self-parody, lovingly pointing out our heroes' flaws in ways that only serve to make them more human. The humor derives from how Mulder and Scully see themselves

---

34 And by now we should all know the Scully episodes are generally better, right?

and each other, and how both of their versions of the truth work to reinforce their ideas of who they really are. It doesn't hurt that their latest investigation reveals that some monsters are just as invested in self-image as the rest of us.

After learning about a series of cattle exsanguinations that escalated to the murder of a tourist, Mulder and Scully head to Cheney, a small Texas town. There they meet Sheriff Hartwell (Luke Wilson, at his Luke Wilson-est!), Mulder tries to prove his wild theory about vampires (which is correct), and Scully does autopsies, firm in her belief that they're dealing with a killer who's read *Dracula* one too many times (this is also correct). Mulder is attacked, Scully arrives just in time to save him, and then Mulder chases his assailant—a teenage pizza delivery boy—into the woods, where he stakes him in the chest. This leads to a horrifying moment for both our heroes (and the audience) when Scully removes the kid's fake vampire teeth.

It's one of the best cold opens in the show's history, one that plays on our expectations and our automatic assumption that Mulder ultimately knows what he's doing. While in medias res beginnings don't always work, the surprises this one holds—from the sudden twist (those plastic fangs!) to Mulder's "Oh sh-,"[35]—it's clear that we're in for something different from the normal hunt for monsters and ghouls.

It all turns out OK, of course: the kid, Ronnie, really *is* a vampire, and when the local coroner removes Mulder's stake, he pops back to life. He's part of a community of bloodsuckers (a community that includes Sheriff Hartwell), and when Mulder and Scully return to Cheney to investigate the disappearance of his "corpse," that community pulls together to protect one of its own. Ronnie may be an idiot, the sheriff explains to Scully, but he's *their* idiot, and the episode ends with the vampires driving their RVs off into the night, leaving behind a pair of dazed, possibly wiser, and undeniably relieved FBI agents.

It's not the most dynamic of plots, and Mulder and Scully are even more irrelevant to the action than usual. But the idea that all this happens because a kid vampire breaks the rules of his kind is a creative premise. Throughout the series, Mulder and Scully spend much of their time hunting creatures that are essentially anomalies in the social order, viruses in the system, and purveyors of bizarre deaths. They typically aren't "pleasant people who pay their taxes on time," so it's nice to see ones that are, and do.

Like "Jose Chung's *From Outer Space*" (S3E20), "Bad Blood" is a *Rashomon* episode, in which multiple characters explain their version of the same events. Unlike *Rashomon*, however, Mulder and Scully's accounts don't differ much on facts—the differences are in the details, and "Bad Blood" gets a lot of laughs out of exaggerating how far each character will go to make themselves look good. In Scully's version,

---

35 The full curse helpfully (and hilariously) cut off by a smash cut to the opening titles.

Mulder is an endless trial, while Scully is the long-suffering grown-up forced to put up with his foolishness, even as she makes eye contact with the dreamy local lawman. In Mulder's version, Scully is dismissive and close-minded, ignoring his insight while she flirts with the bucktoothed idiot sheriff.[36]

While it would've been possible to make this episode as brutal and conceptually terrifying as *Rashomon* really is (if there's no such thing as objective truth, how does anything mean anything?), "Bad Blood" keeps things light. What comes across most clearly is the sense of how long-term relationships settle into routine over time. Like any couple, Mulder and Scully have formed narratives of how they fit with each other, and those narratives affect how they see the rest of the world, which can be healthy—we need the continuity—but can also be limiting. In Mulder's mind he is the enlightened and noble seeker of truth (and tired of being doubted); in Scully's she is the ever-patient (ever put-upon) heroine, logical and competent. Mulder and Scully might've put together the case faster if they weren't so busy editing events in their head to fit how they want to see themselves.

Mulder and Scully aren't the only ones trying to make themselves look good. Ronnie puts in vampire fangs and menaces cows and tourists, clinging to horror movie clichés about what it means to be a vampire because he thinks it makes him look cool. The kicker isn't that he really *is* a vampire; it's that the whole town is made of creatures just like him, bloodsuckers smart enough to know that the only way they can survive in the modern world is by making sure the world doesn't see them as a threat. The locals who keep Mulder from killing Ronnie in the end are arguably the clearest thinkers in the whole episode—they've figured out the only story that keeps them alive, and, occasional idiots like Ronnie aside, they're doing a great job telling it.

You could go the despair route with this. If we're all our own main characters in our stories, then on some level, we're never going to see eye to eye on anything. But maybe that's not so bad in the end. I don't argue that "Bad Blood" is trying to make some profound existential statement, but I do think there's something to be said for the pleasure we get in seeing how those separate stories collide. That's the real joy of art: the attempt to communicate your own, specific, unique, never-to-be-repeated view of the world to others. And maybe that's the most we can hope for in real-life relationships: that we agree on the basics but take pleasure in noting the discrepancies. That's how I see it, anyway. —ZH

---

36 Scully's version feels a little bit closer to the truth, if only because we've had ample opportunity to see her putting up with Mulder's antics in the past. Yet Gilligan makes the smart choice to have both of them look equally foolish by the end; Anderson's been stuck playing straight (wo)man for so long, it's a relief to see her just as silly as her partner.

HE SAID, SHE SAID

When asked what made Mulder and Scully such compelling characters to write for, Vince Gilligan says he was interested primarily in their dynamic: "To me, it was the tennis match that occurred between them. These were two really smart characters who had their own view[s] of the world and their own various areas of expertise but they were both whip-smart and both respected and even loved each other. . . . There was always a deep respect and affection between them and they were both just really interesting to write for in the sense that on the best days and in the best episodes, there was a real argument going on between them. Mulder would have his point of view about what was going on and it would be . . . an otherworldly explanation . . . and Scully would have her explanation, which was much more grounded in reality.

"Keeping that tension, that romantic tension—that tension of argument, so to speak—going was one of the hardest parts about the job, in that you wanted them in a perfect world to both have equally compelling arguments. . . . You wanted that tennis match between two excellent tennis players, where the ball gets lobbed across the net and then it gets returned beautifully and it's always in play, back and forth, back and forth, your head is going left and right and left and right watching this ball get knocked back and forth—this argument gets kicked back and forth, and you're impressed with it at every turn. That was easier said than done; we [the writers] had a real hard time doing that in practice, keeping that argument going, because a lot of the time the plot at hand in any given episode was so out there that there really was only Mulder's explanation.

"Of course, when you're watching as a viewer, the whole thing is weighted toward Mulder being right, which is why some of my favorite episodes were ones where Scully, at least in the short term or in some sense, turned out to be right. Those were the most successful to me. But that's what was always great about writing for them: you loved both of them. . . . As a writer, sometimes when you're really tuned in to your characters, you're listening to them talk and then you're writing it down. You're listening to the conversation in your head and then you're just transcribing it. Those moments late at night on the Fox lot back in the mid-'90s where I was listening to Mulder and Scully talk and then typing down what they said on my computer were wonderful moments."

"PATIENT X"	SEASON 5 / EPISODE 13 WRITTEN BY CHRIS CARTER AND FRANK SPOTNITZ DIRECTED BY KIM MANNERS
"THE RED AND THE BLACK"	SEASON 5 / EPISODE 14 WRITTEN BY CHRIS CARTER AND FRANK SPOTNITZ DIRECTED BY CHRIS CARTER

REVERSAL

*In which Mulder doesn't believe in aliens, Scully sort of
does, and cats and dogs become best friends.*

The problem with altering the status quo on a TV series is that your audience is always going to know in the back of its head that the shift is temporary. The best shows poke and prod at the limits of the central setup to see what can happen. But changes to the status quo usually work best when they push the characters in new directions and reveal new things about them. And in the end, Season Five's attempt to make Scully the believer and Mulder the skeptic just doesn't offer enough fresh information to convince the audience of this somewhat unbelievable reversal. This ultimately bogs down this two-parter.

Sure, this is where the mythology gets moving again, after chasing its own tail throughout much of Season Four and reaching a sort of climax in the opening episodes of Season Five. We meet new, important characters in Cassandra Spender (Veronica Cartwright),[37] a multiple abductee who uses a wheelchair, and her son, Jeffrey (Chris Owens),[38] an FBI agent who'd rather Mulder and Scully not be talking to his mother, honestly. We learn that there's yet another alien faction, composed of strange, faceless men with no eyes or mouths, and we see Krycek[39] playing some sort of long con on the Syndicate. Plus, we get those horrifying images of mass gatherings of abductees that turn into mass immolations, carried out by the faceless men.

If you could combine these two episodes into one hour, it would be one of the best hours of Season Five. But as a two-parter, both halves are a little slow and clunky. Even though "Patient X" involves a bunch of faceless men burning people, there's simply no urgency to it until Cassandra and Scully are in danger at the end. With the

---

37 Best known for her work in Alfred Hitchcock's *The Birds*, *Invasion of the Body Snatchers* (the 1978 version), and *Alien*.

38 You may recognize him from "Musings of a Cigarette Smoking Man" (S4E7), in which he played a young CSM. And you might not recognize him from "The Post-Modern Prometheus" (S5E5), in which he played the Great Mutato himself!

39 At this point in the series, Krycek seems to surface exclusively in locations that could best be described as "dank."

Cigarette Smoking Man no longer around, the show lacks a single iconic villain,[40] which leaves things feeling scattered, in ways that might have been sharpened with a shorter running time.

There's still a lot to like here. The Syndicate is still cryptic as all get-out, but it feels, finally, like we're zeroing in on an explanation, with all the talk of timetables and the like. The Emmy-nominated Cartwright grounds the two-parter, too, as someone who knows she's a pawn in the conspiracy's game but dearly wishes she wasn't any more. That gives her plenty in common with Scully, and Cartwright and Anderson's pairing offers some juicy material.

The larger problem, then, is Mulder's arc from belief to skepticism, back to belief, which has felt arbitrary all season long, particularly because he's still willing to believe in so many crazy things that *aren't* aliens. It seems sort of silly that he'd be totally fine with mad-scientist genetic experimentation, descendants of the Ponce de León expedition who ended up evolving into super forest predators, and somebody with the power to control trees, but he'd draw the line at alien visitation and abductions, particularly because within the world of *The X-Files*, he's got far more evidence for aliens than he does for anything else. Duchovny plays the bored cynicism of someone who's lost his faith well, but the whole thing feels like the writers vamping as they try to write their way to the movie.

Plus, we in the audience have seen enough in other scenes to know that the aliens really are around. With a stronger, better-defined arc (one that popped up in the Monster of the Week episodes too), Mulder's turn toward disbelief could have defined both his character and everybody else's, building to a scenario in which everything around him was falling apart, and we realized that his need to believe in this new theory was driven just as much by his desire to believe in a giant conspiracy as the alien theories were. But because the story really only pops up in the mythology episodes, it feels grossly truncated, appearing only when the show remembers, "Right, Mulder's a UFO skeptic now."

None of this reveals anything new about the character. Mulder used to believe in this stuff; now he doesn't. It's like the show flipped a switch and reversed its central character paradigm, simply because it could. By this point in the show's run, Anderson and Duchovny would have been looking for new angles to play on their characters, and certainly the writers would have wanted to explore new permutations of what they could do. But without the time necessary to really explore this arc, it feels so abrupt that it hardly registers.

Yet this is one of the better post–Season Three mythology two-parters, if only because it uses almost every character in the show's arsenal very well. The best thing about the mythology episodes at this point is that they're able to draw on the

S5 E13-14

---

40 Though it tries to turn the Well-Manicured Man and Krycek into mini-bosses in this two-parter.

entirety of the show's increasingly massive ensemble of recurring characters. And these episodes dig deep, bringing in old friends[41] and introducing new characters like the enjoyably single-minded Agent Spender.[42]

"Patient X" also features that slow crane down onto the group on the bridge at its end, one of the show's best single shots. Director Kim Manners captures the wonder and awe in that group when the UFO appears above them, thrilling everyone. This is a show that always worked best when the threats were both wondrous and terrifying, and the mass abductee gatherings and the faceless men give a sense of both sides of that coin.

That big shot underlines one of the two-parter's strengths: It feels epic. There's the international sweep of some of the messier Season Four mythology episodes in this two-parter, as nearly everyone eventually comes together on the Eastern Seaboard. There are the stunning set pieces that mark the mythology episodes at their best and a strong sense that the show's fragments are coming together when Cassandra starts marking a constellation on her window with her fingerprints. If Season Five's mythology felt like a big stall so far, "Patient X" and "The Red and the Black" start it moving with purpose all over again.

Of course, none of this directly matters to our heroes. The conflict introduced in "The Red and the Black" is never more than window dressing for dark rooms and shadowy plots. You could argue that's cheating, that the show was making promises it couldn't keep, but at this point, it works, and works brilliantly. There's something terrible and chilling about always being just on the edge of the abyss. By the end of this episode, Mulder has regained his faith, but he's no closer than he was before to the answers, and it's possible to criticize the show for still, nearly six seasons into its run, pulling the same "nothing ever changes" crap. But it's so thematically fitting. The climax of the episode has him screaming "No!" into a flashing white light and firing his gun, and it doesn't matter in the slightest.

Still, more finesse would've been nice. Mulder's twist of faith has been a running theme through this whole season, and his return to his original beliefs by the end of this is a decent restatement of purpose. Unfortunately, due to a lack of consistent serialization, it wasn't as powerful an epiphany as it should've been. A character arc doesn't have to be constantly explicit, but here, it's barely detectable at all, popping up a few times before it is finally concluded, for good or for ill. Often, *The X-Files'* anthology approach can work to the series' benefit. But it also makes it difficult to get too worked up over character arcs, unless they're handled with more commitment than this one.

---

41 Like Dr. Werber, the hypnotic regression specialist who was in "Pilot " (S1E1) but then didn't appear again until this episode.

42 A lot of contemporaneous fans hated Spender because he represented, to them, the show toying with the idea of someday replacing Mulder and Scully. Heresy!

If Mulder's journey is undercooked, Scully's is . . . also undercooked. For the first part of "The Red and the Black," while she never comes out and says she's a believer, it's clear that she trusts her experiences as an abductee. And yet as soon as Mulder starts wondering if he's been too quick to doubt, Scully is back on the skeptic bandwagon. Gillian Anderson commits enough to make it pass muster, and you could say that Scully is just retreating back to what makes her the most comfortable in a stressful situation, but it's obviously a mechanism for bringing us back to the status quo.

So is the return of the Cigarette Smoking Man, whose identity isn't revealed until the final shot of the two-parter. He's hiding out in Canada, pulling strings and writing letters to his son, who turns out to be (gasp!) Agent Jeffrey "Stay away from my mom!" Spender. Spender is less a character than an irritant at this point, and learning that the CSM misses him enough to mail him stories of Navajo war gods (which may or may not be subtle justifications of certain deals made with certain nefarious extraterrestrials) isn't a major stunner.

Really, the big surprise here is that the biggest bad guy to die during the show's run so far is not, in fact, dead. We've been given no reason to care about Agent Spender, and thus, no reason to care about who his father is, and no reason to care that the CSM is calling in favors to protect him. It's like the return of the Joker in a Batman comic. No matter how long the absence, you figured he'd be back eventually.

All of this sounds like we're overly critical of "Patient X" and "The Red and the Black," and we are, from a long-view, here-are-some-fundamental-flaws-in-the-show standpoint. But as actual episodes of television, these are terrific hours. It feels like a show with a purpose, and what excites us is how vital this all seems even knowing the criticisms we mentioned above.

It works because the performances are great, and because the second part of this two-parter rarely feels weighed down or draggy. It works because it's often eerie and beautiful, like the shot of the former abductees raising their hands to the sky as small bits of ash float upward. Even if we're still not convinced that all that much happened,[43] emotionally, we're satisfied. This sort of approach, this sideways, ground-level view of a picture that can only fully be perceived from above, makes ridiculous or convoluted story lines come off as more realistic because we only ever catch things at the edges. While we have more information than Mulder, it's still not that hard to empathize with him, hoping to find answers in a lifetime of glimpses. —ZH and TVDW

---

43 The "rebel aliens," while a fine visual, are just another card stacked on top of an increasingly precarious house.

WHERE WERE YOU IN '52?

In which we first meet Arthur Dales.

Of all of the episodes of *The X-Files* that felt like pilots for abandoned spinoffs, "Travelers" is the one that seems like it might have made for the best actual show.[44] It's set in the 1950s, and it takes us back to the formation of the X-Files, with minimal involvement from the show's regulars. Indeed, most of it is a story told to Mulder in 1990 (a few years before the show begins) by one Arthur Dales, who turns out to be one of the show's best Easter eggs.

See, Dales, when elderly, is played by Darren McGavin, who played Kolchak in the short-lived '70s series *The Night Stalker*, which was one of the most significant influences on Chris Carter's creation of *The X-Files*.[45] Having him play the spiritual father of the whole department Mulder works in nods and winks toward the show's spiritual roots. And the episode functions as an origin myth, giving us hints about where the X-Files were before there was an official department set up to investigate them, and giving us a better idea of how Mulder comes to be associated with these kinds of cases. It doesn't overexplain these things, instead trusting the audience to let the answers snap into place.

The bulk of the episode takes place in 1952, when Dales is a young man, and he confronts the strange case of a man accused of being a communist, who's something else entirely, something Dales doesn't really understand. But you know who does? A young Bill Mulder! Plus, our villain goes around killing people with an alien spider that he keeps vomiting up, which is a wonderfully creepy notion.

The '50s flavor adds quite a bit to the episode, in a way that reminded me of the underrated, '60s-set *X-Files* rip-off *Dark Skies*. As Dales investigates, he's drawn further and further into a conspiracy that has ties to the House Un-American Activities Committee (HUAC) and the hunt for communism (a young Roy Cohn briefly pops up) but is mostly all about rooting out the aliens in the early days of a war the United States was barely prepared to fight. Cold War paranoia makes just as addictive a mixer for the alien conspiracy as post–Cold War paranoia does.

If there's a problem with the 1950s setting, it's that it feels a little generic. It's good to find out how Bill was drawn into the conspiracy back in the day, and lots of care is put into establishing the world of the series. But this emphasis on exposition

---

44 Actually, if someone wants to reboot *The X-Files* on a more permanent basis, without having to worry about the schedules of David Duchovny and Gillian Anderson, it could do far worse than doing a period-set version of the show.

45 See more about this in the introduction.

means that the story line suffers. HUAC is all well and good as a cover for alien activities, but it feels a little easy, like it was the first idea everybody landed on and they didn't try to think of anything else. As such, it's the same old "the aliens are behind it all" rigmarole. It doesn't help that, while the actors cast as the young Agent Dales and the young Bill Mulder are adequate, they lack the requisite charisma to carry a whole episode. It's not hard to wish that Dales had his own version of Scully, especially because this is one of the few episodes Gillian Anderson completely sat out.

There's a reason Season Five is likely the most inconsistent season of the show's golden age (which spans roughly from Season Two to Season Six), and "Travelers" exemplifies this. Because the movie was taking up the time of so many involved in the show, the writers tried to fill in the story around the edges of the series, more than the story of the series itself. We've seen all the beats "Travelers" hits before, and that makes it feel much more retread-y than it might have had it actually been a pilot for an *X-Files* prequel.

Still, *The X-Files* is great at overlaying its own version of history over actual history, drawing weird connections between assorted events and coming up with little links that most viewers wouldn't think of on their own. Dales is a fascinatingly enigmatic character, particularly as an old man played by McGavin. *The X-Files* was always adept at showing something seemingly idyllic and normal, then pulling the rug out from underneath you, and "Travelers" does a great job of transplanting this attitude to the 1950s and its attendant nostalgia.

And, if nothing else, it's a reminder of the show's unique willingness to break with its typical format. Episodes like this one or "Unusual Suspects" (S5E3) may have been born out of necessity, but you can tell the writers relished the challenge and looked for ways to expand the show's universe by following its characters into new arenas.[46] Even when the show was at its most uneven, *The X-Files* was more inclined than just about any other show in TV history to try something completely new. Even if "Travelers" doesn't always work, it rests comfortably enough in that tradition to be worth a recommendation. —TVDW

---

46 That said, we really should have gotten an all-Krycek hour.

| "MIND'S EYE"

BLIND SPOTS

In which what you see isn't always what you get.

"Mind's Eye" is a Monster of the Week episode that could have fit quite easily into any of the earlier seasons of the show. The only truly memorable element here is Lili Taylor's guest star turn as a blind woman who, as it turns out, isn't *exactly* blind. The concept has potential, but the execution is not all that well thought out. Scully is back to her usual not-quite-convinced self, and Mulder is slinging crazy like always (albeit with maybe a bit less verve than usual). It's a step up from the weaker MOTW entries this season (no killer trees!), and it's nice to take a breather from all the experimenting, but without any cool scare sequences or clever twists, "Eye" feels a little too familiar.

The hook is an interesting one: Somebody was killed in a motel room, and the police have a suspect in custody. Unfortunately (for the cops), the suspect is a small blind woman named Marty Glenn (Taylor). The detective in charge of the case brings in Mulder and Scully (because that's just what you do). Mulder immediately suspects something is up, so he gives Marty a lie-detector test and notes that the only time the machine catches Marty in a lie is when she claims she didn't "see" the murder. After many more events, Mulder finally realizes that Marty *does* see. She's just not seeing with her own eyes, but instead through the eyes of the killer. The killer who murdered her mother before Marty was even born. The killer who also happens to be Marty's father.[47]

"Eye" doesn't put much effort into explaining how this could've happened; the closest we get to a reason is that Marty's dad stabbed her mother to death, and that the resulting loss of blood and premature birth robbed Marty of her sight, so her senses worked to compensate in other ways. This is, to put it nicely, total nonsense. Taylor is convincing in the role, and Duchovny does a good job of making his lines sound more logical than they actually are, but it doesn't work because there's just not enough justification for the viewer to maintain a suspension of disbelief. Whereas the mythology episodes can suffer from too much information (conspiracies building off conspiracies building off conspiracies, until it's impossible to remember which way is up), bad or mediocre Monster of the Week entries often fail because of too little. A writer will come up with a clever premise, but can't find a satisfactory way

---

47 The theme here—sins of the father shaping the lives of the child—is one the show has used before, perhaps most notably in "Aubrey" (S2E12). If you wanted to stretch, you could say the idea is built into the core mythology as well: Mulder was, after all, born the son of a man deeply entangled in the very alien conspiracy that would come to define his life.

to explain or justify that premise, resulting in an episode that feels incomplete or insufficiently thought through.

For example, there's the issue of Marty's evident sanity. Sight is arguably our most dominant sense, and (were this explanation of her powers accurate), Baby Marty would have been dealing with visions that had no bearing on her own life before she'd had a chance to start establishing her own place in the world. But the episode makes no effort to explain or clarify how she managed to negotiate a life in which she wasn't just blind but actively receiving visual information that had no bearing on her surroundings or actions. It simply uses her ability as a clever way to connect her to a series of murders and leaves it at that.

However, that ability does at least give Marty a strong motivation for stopping her father's crimes. The character is smart and resourceful, and the connection between her and Mulder over the course of the episode is deftly accomplished. The ending, too, saves this episode from being completely mundane. For once, an X-File ends in neither triumph nor tragedy. It depicts a woman who merely made her choice and is willing to pay the price for it.

Yet, despite Taylor's best efforts, the writing of "Eye" reveals the flimsiness of its logic—a shame, given the striking premise. "Eye" has some interesting ideas, and a great actress, but it can't quite pull these pieces together into anything memorable. It's certainly not the worst episode we've seen this season, but if we're going to go back to an old routine, it would be nice to add a few new steps. —ZH

SEASON 5 / EPISODE 17
WRITTEN BY FRANK SPOTNITZ AND JOHN SHIBAN,
FROM A STORY BY BILLY BROWN AND DAN ANGEL
DIRECTED BY ALLEN COULTER

"ALL SOULS"

TRUE BELIEVER

In which God sends Scully another message.

The idea that God controls everything that happens on Earth and often uses minor events to communicate his control to believers can become awfully self-centered if you're not careful. Free will, which most Christian denominations suggest humans have, is in this way incompatible with the notion that God is up there, in charge, making things happen. But we want to have free will so badly, so we invent reasons for why God might be trying to tell us something, why God might be nudging us toward the right path. We give ourselves agency even if we maybe didn't have it to begin with.

This is the conflict that resonates at the end of "All Souls," an occasionally too-slow episode that nonetheless soars due to yet another Emmy-worthy Gillian

Anderson showcase in a season full of them. The episode centers on an intriguing mystery that builds in power and horror over the course of the hour, and it features a very good villain, played by the very good Glenn Morshower. But it all boils down to the fact that Scully is pretty sure that God sent four mentally handicapped girls with the souls of angels into her life so that he could burn out their eyes, take them to Heaven, and let her know it's OK to let go of any residual sadness she has about the death of Emily earlier this season. It works because Anderson sells once again the idea that she really, really loved a girl she knew only for a couple of weeks. Just don't think about its somewhat nihilistic theological implications too much, and you'll be fine.

The episode drags the most when it hews too closely to the show's classic skeptic-believer formula. Its attempts to come up with some sort of scientific rationalization for what is quite obviously divine intervention feel even sillier here than they usually do. But then the episode forgoes any attempt at earthly explanation and simply starts giving Scully visions of Emily and a four-faced man/monster, and the whole enterprise gets much, much better. At this point in its run, the show has realized that the best way to tackle these occasional "Scully struggles with her religion" stories[48] is through vaguely expressed symbols of her devotion, like her ever-present cross necklace. This tactic serves to better underline the fact that Scully doesn't think about her faith all of the time. It just is a part of her. Scully's Catholicism could easily have tipped over into facile irony—"She's a skeptical scientist, but she's religious too!" Instead, the stone-faced seriousness with which *The X-Files* here treats this aspect of Scully's characterization heightens the contradiction to beautiful effect.

The episode's emphasis on explicit religious symbolism also allows it to offer a great villain, when it reveals that social worker Starkey (Morshower, playing both sides of the character to perfection) is a demon in human form. His sudden apparition in the locked room at the police station is a great scare in an otherwise somber episode, and his appearance as a full-on devil at the end pulls out all the stops, with glowing hellfire, shadowy horns, and a distorted voice. It's a welcome change to have a purely evil antagonist, one for whom the episode doesn't try to offer any explanation other than, "Well, we're dealing with seraphim and nephilim here, so just try and keep up."

The choice to frame the story around Scully giving confession believably builds her feelings of guilt, despair, relief, and contrition throughout the hour while still maintaining a slight sense of dread. When the episode concludes with the stark idea that faith is sometimes just about gritting your teeth and getting on with your life after a tremendous loss, Gillian Anderson sells Scully's entire season arc with a handful of words and a smattering of tears. The Emily story line has up to now

---

48 Including this season's "Christmas Carol" (S5E7) and "Emily" (S5E8) two-parter, as well as Season Three's "Revelations" (S3E11).

seemed like a convenience, a way for the writers to wring more pathos out of Scully following her abduction and cancer. But when Anderson starts crying over this little girl, it feels like a punch in the gut.

With every season, the show seems to increasingly relish the idea of giving Anderson big episodes that hinge entirely on her performance, and even though a lot of them feel like the writers are repeatedly poking Scully with a stick, the actress always surpasses whatever the writers have given her. Perhaps most remarkably, nearly all of these episodes work, sometimes *solely* because of Anderson's nuanced performance. Mulder-centric stories tend to lean more heavily on the show's science-fiction tropes, but Scully showcases tend to be much more about the human and emotional cost of constantly peering into Pandora's box. Though it's Mulder who actually goes through the trials and tribulations of investigating the conspiracy and trying to find his sister, almost all of the human toll is foisted onto Scully. She's the one who was abducted, after all. Her many crises could turn her into a walking punching bag, if it weren't for both the writers' sense that her punishments only increase her resolve and Anderson's beautiful performance.

Scully's position as the emotional core of the show is why the ending of "All Souls" works, despite its preposterousness. Of course God would want to tell Scully to proceed with her work. Of course he would contrive an elaborate scenario wherein he sends four of his angels down to Earth in the form of endangered young girls, purely so he could call them back at some point in order to teach Scully a lesson or two about letting go. And of course he would let this entire cosmic battle play out before her very eyes as a way to let her know which path to follow. Scully, you see, is just that important. She's not just a rational skeptic, there to give Mulder the support he needs. She is *the* skeptic, the woman who stands between the mundane and the unexplained and sees demons and doesn't get her eyes burned out. She's on the front lines, and that's exactly where the almighty wants her. —TVDW

SEASON 5, EPISODE 18
WRITTEN BY JOHN SHIBAN
DIRECTED BY ROB BOWMAN | "THE PINE BLUFF VARIANT"

PLAYING CLOSE TO THE VEST

In which Mulder robs a bank.

The more you believe in something, the easier it is to see how that belief impacts every aspect of your life. If you believe in God, then everything you do and everything that happens to you is affected by God. If you're in love, every sigh or vocal inflection is part of some secret language only your heart can truly understand. And if you're Fox Mulder—conspiracy enthusiast and fervent follower of little gray men—every calamity is just the latest iteration of a government dedicated to crushing its citizens and consolidating power in the face of a potential alien invasion.

At first glance, "The Pine Bluff Variant" seems to have nothing to do with Mulder's usual fixations. In the cold open, Scully finds out her partner is aiding and abetting one Jacob Steven Haley (Daniel von Bargen), the second in command of an anti-government militia group. But all is not as it seems. The group contacted Mulder because of a speech he gave at a UFO convention, and Mulder is now working as a double agent, on the order of Skinner and U.S. Attorney Leamus (Sam Anderson).

Skinner and Leamus instructed Mulder not to tell *anyone* of his work to protect his cover, which explains why he hasn't let Scully in on what was going on. While this is never made explicit in the episode, Mulder might be feeling some shame that's keeping him quiet as well. This hasn't been an easy season for his relationship with Scully; the two-part season premiere had him enlisting her help in covering for a murder, and while his efforts managed to find a cure for her cancer, he's also indirectly responsible for making her vulnerable to the forces that infected her with the disease. Perhaps in trying to keep this current mission to himself, he's doing what he can to give her some space for a change, and punish himself in the process.

In fact, Mulder here seems to be attempting to pay penance for something. This sense owes as much to the placement of "Pine Bluff" in the season as to anything in the actual script, but one can read his reticence and double-dealing here as an attempt to make up for his earlier confusion. At one point, Jacob has one of his men torture Mulder by breaking his pinkie, in order to establish Mulder's commitment to the cause. Duchovny plays this scene very close to the edge, at one point head-butting the pinkie-breaker to get him to back off, and while his fury makes sense in context, you have to wonder just how close what we're seeing is to the *real* Mulder. How much of his emotion here is fear and pain and anger in this moment, and how much of it is just him being so close to the forces that have been driving him his entire life?

Even if you're not inclined to read that much into Mulder's state of mind, "Pine Bluff" is an excellent episode, notable for both its tension and the way it tells a story that has ostensibly little to do with the X-Files—right up until its final twist. For most of the episode's running time, the bioweapon that Jacob and militia leader August Bremer (Michael MacRae) have at their disposal is the only thing that separates this story from a well-made but quotidian cop drama.

That's not a critique. This is a tight, smart hour of television that never lets the audience get too relaxed with Mulder's position and manages a number of terrific suspense set pieces with aplomb. There's even a bank-robbery scene, in which all the militia members wear monster masks and Mulder is ordered to shoot a bystander but can't bring himself to do it. When Bremer tells him Mulder's gun "can be traced," and shoots the bystander himself, it seems like a cheat, allowing Mulder to get off the hook in a way that just barely makes sense. But then we find out that it's all part of the episode's endgame.

That intention connects back to the bioweapon, which is a very nasty piece of work indeed. *The X-Files* has gotten a lot of mileage out of a variety of lethal toxins over the years, but this one stands out from the rest, as it eats the flesh off a person's bones and leaves them looking like the Tarman from *Return of the Living Dead*. Bremer tests the virus out on a small-town movie theater, and the result is pure horror.[49] Initially, Scully is told that the militia most likely purchased the bioweapon from the Russians, but when she looks deeper, she learns the virus is homegrown. This whole thing is a government setup. Bremer is working for Leamus (who's working for who only knows), and he's using the militia to do field tests on a virus that can be sprayed on money and passed around the world to infect whomever they see fit.

Most of the time, believing that everything is connected is a paranoid fantasy. On *The X-Files*, assuming that everyone is out to get you is the only way you can survive. And while it may be comforting to believe that everything happens for a reason, and that you understand what that reason is, it can also be unsettling. It means that nothing is without meaning, that any hiccup or snag has dark implications. That's exhausting, which may be why most of us don't live in that world. Mulder believes he knows what's going on—and the more he learns, the clearer it becomes that he may actually be *right*. Pity him, then. —ZH

SEASON 5 / EPISODE 19
WRITTEN BY VINCE GILLIGAN
DIRECTED BY KIM MANNERS | **"FOLIE À DEUX"**

A MADNESS SHARED BY TWO

In which there are bugs in the system.

There's something crazy-making about holding an opinion no one else shares, or believing in something no one else believes. You feel just a little paranoid, just a little insane. You believe in it so strongly, but no one else does. The rest of the world just brushes by and shrugs its shoulders, and as much as you may scream in their faces, no one seems to pay you any mind.

The greatest argument *The X-Files* ever made is that Scully is pretty much the only person who keeps Mulder clinging to sanity. Sure, when we (and she) meet him in the pilot, he's a reasonably together guy. But it's easy, over the course of the series,

---

49 A small audience who paid to see *Die Hard with a Vengeance* meets a fate worse than Bruce Willis.

to see where the wheels could come off the truck, where this guy could just start shouting to the stars in the dead of night with no one talking back. When Mulder lands in a mental hospital in this episode, there's a grim inevitability to it, and David Duchovny plays that irony for dark laughs.

Scully is a tether, the person who holds Mulder back while he spins his madness. Even if she doesn't believe what he does, she at least willingly listens. "Folie à Deux" literalizes that idea, which is what makes it one of the show's best episodes. The "folie à deux" of the title—the madness shared by two—seems, at first blush, like it will refer to Mulder and Gary (Brian Markinson), the vinyl-siding company employee who teaches him to see giant man-bugs in our midst. Instead, the phrase ends up describing Mulder and Scully, and the dynamic at the core of the show. Scully may not share Mulder's madness, but she's in close enough proximity to have just a little rub off on her.

The episode's structure perfectly illustrates exactly how this happens. "Folie" starts out as what seems like a Mulder-centric episode, then slowly racks focus to become a Scully-centric episode, before finally reasserting itself, in the end, as an episode that argues that these two characters only work as a duo. It's not a romantic pairing, not exactly. Mulder and Scully share a kind of perfect professionalism, as though Sir Thomas Malory designed a courtly romance of government bureaucracy, with knights carrying cell phones and maidens doing a fair share of the saving.

Start "Folie à Deux," and you might assume it's going to be a "hostage situation" episode, one in which the protagonist stumbles into a crisis and then has to persuade the gunman to abandon his plan. Instead, Vince Gilligan immediately starts breaking the rules. Gary kills a man who tries to disarm him. He discovers that Mulder is an FBI agent much sooner than he would in a typically structured episode. And, in the hour's greatest trick, Gary passes his madness along to Mulder right before the SWAT team bursts through the wall and shoots him. Ostensibly, the problem at the start of this episode is over. But now Mulder has, quite literally, been infected by the bug.

How refreshing, too, that this deep into its run, *The X-Files* could still come up with a great monster. Barely seen, the giant bug-man is mostly suggested through sound and half-glimpsed shadows that . . . could be trees or plants? They must be, right? But, no, then there's some strange shape lurching across the ceiling, about to drop down, suck out your life force, and turn you into a zombie. The few times we look at the monster head-on, we only see a blurry motion in front of the camera.[50] Even better, the episode doesn't bother to explain what the monster is or where it came from, beyond the idea that it can somehow mask itself by making us see it as a normal middle manager in a major corporation. The episode shows us the effects

| S5 E19

---

50 Fittingly, the best look we get comes from Scully's point of view.

and lets us draw our own conclusions, based on what we already know of both the show and American corporate culture.[51]

As is so often true in Vince Gilligan episodes, the monster here works just as well as a metaphor made manifest as it does a literal horror. Gilligan and director Kim Manners particularly play up the hivelike aspects of working in a giant call center, the camera drifting over the throngs of workers buzzing on the phones, the managers roaming the aisles like soldiers who are dedicated to keeping the worker bees hard at work. Then there's the leader, off in his office, rarely emerging, the workers readily sacrificing themselves to him when he asks. After all, who hasn't sometimes felt like a mindless drone while at work?

The penultimate episode of an *X-Files* season often featured Mulder questioning reality. It was a device that the show turned to often because it grew so naturally out of the premise: What if Mulder is just flat-out crazy? It is a pretty obvious place to go when you move outward from the fundamental concept of the show, and some of *The X-Files'* very best episodes wrestled with this question. What makes this entry the best version of that type is that Mulder subsequently passes the bug onto Scully, who is resistant at first but ultimately becomes infected herself. It's a potent, metaphoric comment on Scully's place within the series. She doesn't believe, but she also can't *not* believe.

Consider the moment when the camera pushes in on Scully's face ever so subtly as she looks at the nurse at the hospital and sees that the nurse has become a zombie. Gillian Anderson's expression perfectly flashes between incredulity[52] and acceptance, as she realizes that the person she cares most about in the world is utterly screwed. So she takes matters into her own hands and unloads a couple of bullets into bug-man Greg Pincus (an eerie John Apicella) before he can turn Mulder into one of the unquestioning zombies who will follow Pincus to an unfulfilling job somewhere in the great American heartland.

See, madness is always better when shared by two. The second you find out that someone else shares the same crazy opinion as you—the second you find someone on your wavelength—you come out of the darkness just a little bit. It's telling that Mulder only gets out of the mental institution once Scully also comes to believe. Maybe she doesn't believe in the entirety of the Pincus mythos, but she certainly believes in *something*. Just having her come that far is enough to make him get better, to start to come back into the light, even as they both know that Pincus is still buzzing around the country. "Folie à Deux" knows that Mulder and Scully are something more important than lovers: They're soul mates. —TVDW

---

51 By implication, the episode also suggests that everything Mulder and Scully have investigated (conspiracies and otherwise) is part of the horror of bureaucratic corporate culture, of the idea that you can control anybody if you give them the right incentives. Like Gary, they, too, see what no one else does.

52 Love Scully's attempt at keeping her skeptic cred in this episode: "Well . . . it was dark?"

STALEMATE

In which we are all just pawns.

Ah, chess. It's a game of strategy. Two men enter[53] and vie for mental dominance by moving small statues across a field of squares. Only one may emerge victorious from the struggle unless there's a draw. But let's focus on the titanic struggle of minds, the manipulation of control, the sacrifice of pawns to draw out your opponent, the brilliant endgame strategy. Chess symbolizes so many things, mainly because it functions as rather lazy shorthand for "War, but smartish."

"The End," the finale of *The X-Files'* fifth season, has a lot of chess talk in it. The episode opens with a match between two masters: one a grown man, the other a child who looks barely old enough to read. The Cigarette Smoking Man, having been dragged back into the thick of things by Krycek, is responsible for the bulk of the chess metaphors, spewing analogies about giving up pieces and forcing opponents to move where *he* wants them, and so on and so forth. It's not unusual for the character, who has always been defined by his tendency to speak in heavy-handed terms of prophecy and portent,[54] but the desperation in his manner here makes clear that his position is no longer as secure as it once was. The problem, though, is the show's isn't either.

The episode has some fine moments, and the climactic shot of the X-Files office going up in flames is one of the most iconic visuals in the run of the series, but too much of its running time is spent trying to raise stakes in ways that are hard to take seriously. Mulder has finally found the evidence he needs to prove that the phenomena reported in the X-Files are real! A psychic kid named Gibson Praise (Jeff Gulka) is the key to all of the universe's mysteries! *Something something* aliens! There are revelations here that should hit the ground like seismic explosions but instead barely register on the scale. The mythology building has now reached a critical mass in which each new major story line has to somehow top the previous one, while simultaneously never quite explaining everything or delivering on what it has promised. The routine nevertheless has some power to shock, but the novelty is gone; it's still possible to enjoy much of the mythology, but harder to believe in it as an actual coherent story.

---

53 Or two women, or one woman and one man, or maybe there are kids.

54 Like this humdinger from "Talitha Cumi" (S3E24): "Men can never be free. Because they're weak, corrupt, worthless and restless. The people believe in authority. They've grown tired of waiting for miracle and mystery. Science is their religion. No greater explanation exists for them. They must never believe any differently if the project is to go forward."

The Mulder/Scully/Diana Fowley (Mimi Rogers) love triangle may be the episode's single worst sin. It's not as integral to the larger problems as are the mythology plot holes here, but it feels cheap and off-putting. Scully has been jealous of Mulder's relationship with another woman before,[55] but here that jealousy is both out of character and forced—a reaction devised solely to build tension but which doesn't take into account everything we know about the show's most central relationship. We're five seasons in now, and the Mulder/Scully dynamic has weathered far more serious blows than the sudden appearance of A Woman from the Past. It feels almost insulting to suggest that Diana Fowley would be the person to ultimately fracture this foundational relationship, especially given the fact that she's never been mentioned before.

Even without the Fowley story line, the mythology here leaves something to be desired. We have Gibson, the psychic boy who just might be an alien-human hybrid. He's likable enough, in the eerie, slightly "off" way that the episode utilizes well, and the idea that Gibson has risen so high in the ranks of the chess world not because he is good at the game but because he can read his opponent's mind is clever. As a Monster of the Week hour, this premise really could have worked. But as a "key to everything" in a mythology episode, Gibson is not impressive. After waiting so long to finally make some progress—after hearing so much innuendo and rumor about the alien colonization project and all the terrifying and fantastic creatures that come with it—a telepathic preteen just doesn't feel that exciting (even if he is kind of dorkily adorable).

The sense of anticlimax that pervades "The End" isn't Gibson's fault.[56] The episode utterly fails to provide sufficient justification to back Mulder's pompous pronouncements about Gibson's importance. You could view the child as simply another piece in the puzzle, an indication of the mythology's new direction, but the episode simply doesn't generate much excitement about the story line at the ostensible core of the show. It just seems like another standard myth story, which makes it hard to shake the sneaking suspicion that the normal state of affairs will soon return.

In its defense, "The End" has some good scenes, nearly all of them driven more by character than by plot, like the lovely moment in which Mulder explains to Fowley how Scully's skepticism has helped keep him grounded and made him a better agent. Gibson has the dubious honor of being a memorable tragic figure with the unfortunate luck of appearing on a show with a long history of memorable tragic figures, and even if Mulder's insistence about his value rings hollow, there's something chilling and sad about seeing someone so young and vulnerable in the center of the chaos. The CSM's triumphant (?) return to action is also swell, and the

S5 E20

---

55 See "Fire" (S1E12).

56 When Mulder told Skinner and a roomful of colleagues just how important he believed the golden child was, I laughed out loud, because . . . come on, *really*?

sense that he's still at odds with the Syndicate, and that any member could turn on the others at any moment, has potential. There is also, of course, that iconic ending, in which the CSM returns to the FBI, grabs Samantha's file and torches Mulder's and Scully's office and all the X-Files inside.

It's a bold ending but not quite bold enough to save the episode from feeling lackluster. There really isn't anything here to capture the thrill of the show's best mythology story lines. "The End" desperately wants you to believe that all bets really *are* off, and that things really *are* changing. The thing is, though, that all those chess metaphors work only if you believe the person using them is utterly unpredictable and really does see four or five moves ahead of everyone else. Here, however, it's easier to believe that the only reason the writers know the next move is because it's been pulled so many times before. —ZH

THE X-FILES

FIGHT
THE
FUTURE

WRITTEN BY CHRIS CARTER,
FROM A STORY BY CARTER AND FRANK SPOTNITZ
DIRECTED BY ROB BOWMAN

THE X-FILES TAKES THE MULTIPLEX

In which The X-Files *gets a movie so big it has its own Foo Fighters song.*[1]

TODD: Whether you love or hate it, whether you love or hate what follows it, *Fight the Future*, the first *X-Files* movie,[2] is a major dividing line in the history of the series. It clefts the original run of the series in two almost exactly,[3] and it serves as the high-water mark for the series' cultural presence. It was the biggest the show would ever be, but it didn't launch the show into the sphere of cultural omnipresence claimed by franchises like *Star Wars* or *Harry Potter*. Indeed, watching the film now, completely removed from the *X-Files* mania of the mid-'90s, it's a little crazy that anyone thought this effort would win over multiplex dwellers who had never seen the series,[4] so steeped is it in the ongoing tales of the alien conspiracy. It feels like you have to take an extended lecture course just to understand the plot.

All that said, I don't hate *Fight the Future*. Yes, it's hokey. Yes, it's ridiculous. Yes, it writes the show's main narrative into a corner it can't hope to escape. But if this were a mythology two-parter, its streamlined plot would be most similar to Season Three's "Nisei"/"731" (S3E9/10) duo, which were among the show's finest hours. The movie is not quite at the level of those episodes, but in the way that it depicts Mulder's obsessive quest as taking him to the ends of the Earth,[5] *Fight the Future* comes close to scratching the same itch as the best mythology episodes. The truth is out there—maybe it's just over that next rise. But if you find it, someone will surely take it from you at great cost.

Given the movie's similarity to classic mythology plots, it's not immediately clear why this is a feature-length story instead of two or three episodes of the series. The huge scope of the film (as evidenced by its budget) is the most obvious justification for its big screen status, but exploding buildings and eerie desert encampments will get you only so far when the basic story remains: "Mulder gets a lead, Mulder

---

1   OK, *technically* the Foo Fighters—a band named for an early term for UFOs—didn't record a song "for" this movie. But the most famous version of "Walking After You," one of their better-known songs, *was* a rerecorded version used over the closing credits of the film. Dave Grohl, a longtime *X-Files* fan (who even has a small cameo in "Pusher" [S3E17]) probably relished the opportunity
2   Which is also referred to as just *The X-Files*, the better to confuse people.
3   If it were an episode of the show, it would be number 118 of 202.
4   The movie had the impossible task of having to break out beyond the core fan base, which was large enough to merit a film but not so large as to turn said film from a modest hit into a world-dominating blockbuster.
5   Like the *literal* ends of the Earth—our heroes go all the way to Antarctica.

chases the lead, Scully gets dragged along." The movie is too indebted to the show to suddenly break off from it entirely, but there's something a little timid about it all the same. Even Rob Bowman's direction succumbs to the "TV, but bigger" ethos that seems to be behind many of the decisions made here.

Despite this struggle to warrant its own existence, there's still plenty to enjoy (and lovingly mock)[6] in *Fight the Future*. The narrative here snaps many of the mythology pieces into place in a way that mostly makes sense. If the show had then pivoted from here into Mulder and Scully racing against time to stop colonization (as in, *ahem*, fighting the future), the mythology would have been much better for it. But the movie does a reasonably good job of detasseling its corn and stinging its bees. By its final moments, you have a feel for the scope of the mythology, which is deeply necessary at this point in the series.

Fight the Future, in many places, explicitly wrestles with the show's status as a big enough hit to actually benefit from the production of a movie. The ingenious early sequence—which does a remarkably good job of introducing Mulder and Scully to curious moviegoers who may have never watched the show—even grapples with the show's paranoid legacy, embodied at the time by Timothy McVeigh's bombing of a federal building in Oklahoma City.[7] *The X-Files* was never supposed to be this big. *Fight the Future* is a clear, if sloppy, attempt to capitalize on the show's unexpected success.

ZACK: I too do not hate *Fight the Future*. In fact, I was pleased to discover on my latest rewatch that I'm actually rather fond of it. It has all the flaws you mention, Todd, and maybe a few more; it's hard to ignore that the movie doesn't so much expand the show's horizons as it does place the same small handful of characters we know and love on larger sets. The climax in Antarctica is a particularly egregious example. It looks great, but it's mostly just a vast expanse for Mulder to wander through. The whole enterprise feels weirdly empty, like Carter decided to augment the breadth of the show but forgot to provide the narrative and character depth needed to justify the expansion.

It's not surprising that Carter would keep major plot and character developments to a minimum here; any movie looking to adapt a TV show to the big screen has the challenge of finding ways to provide exposition to a new audience while not belaboring the premise for diehard fans. Moreover, *Fight the Future* also has

---

6 I'll start: Mulder and Scully's would-be first kiss is interrupted when she gets stung by a bee that has ridden out on her person on a flight from Texas to Washington, D.C. It already strains credulity, but the film makes it worse, somehow, by doing an insert shot of the bee ominously crawling around on her.

7 An event that weighed heavily on Chris Carter in promotional interviews at the time.

to remain roughly consistent with the show's ongoing continuity.[8] The result is, unsurprisingly, something that doesn't work that well for newbies *or* devotees—a compromised, "same-thing-but-louder" version of *The X-Files* that, as Todd noted, never makes a case for itself.

TODD: The Syndicate's willingness to use Scully's accidental bee sting[9] as an excuse to imprison her aboard an alien spaceship, before deciding to kill Mulder is a big part of why this movie gradually deflates after the almost-kiss. Everything up until that point has a propulsive conspiracy-thriller vibe to it, and it's easy to see why critics of the time who weren't watching the show still sparked to what they saw on-screen.[10]

But after that romantic anticlimax, things start to just sort of happen, from Mulder not quite dying several times to the way he sneaks out of the hospital alongside the Lone Gunmen, which really betrays the movie's roots as a TV show.[11] Reportedly, the movie went through a rather extensive reshoot process; the specter of studio notes looms large throughout its increasingly dull second hour. Beside these plot failings, the curiously empty quality you point out, Zack, feels even more vacant than some mythology episodes of the show. I'm not saying that dropping in Krycek or Marita Covarrubias (or even Flukeman) would have made the movie better, but the fact that it all boils down to Mulder, Scully, and the Character Actor All-Stars[12] makes the world feel curiously small. That's an issue the series almost never struggled with, perhaps due to its ever-evolving format and rotating cast of monsters and villains.

ZACK: Keeping all of that in mind—including, yes, that hilariously awkward near-kiss[13]—there's still a fair amount to enjoy here, even if most of it is for people who are already invested in the original series. Though the story really is just a streamlined version of a couple of mythology episodes, it's nevertheless satisfying

---

8   It's rare for a show to make the jump to the big screen while still airing new episodes, which only adds to the strain on this movie.

9   Which *has* to be accidental, right? That's all a bit unclear.

10 Even Roger Ebert was into it! "I liked the way the movie looked, and the unforced urgency of Mulder and Scully, and the way the plot was told through verbal puzzles and visual revelations, rather than through boring action scenes," he wrote in a three-out-of-four-star review in the *Chicago Sun-Times*.

11 That shot of Skinner wandering around, pretending to be on his phone to fool the bad guys, is pretty awful. It's the sort of thing that can work on TV, where narrative expediency is everything, but up on the big screen, where every storytelling decision is blown up as big as possible, you start to fixate on these little conveniences.

12 And they *are* all-stars! There's Terry O'Quinn! And Jeffrey DeMunn! Glenne Headley cameos as a bartender! I don't know why Blythe Danner is here, but I'm glad she is!

13 It's incredible how awkward that scene is, given how strong the Mulder/Scully chemistry is throughout the rest of the film.

to see the familiar routine performed with shinier and flashier accessories. There are visuals from this movie that have stuck in my head for years, like the scene with Mulder and Scully fleeing the bee hanger, or that alien ship in the finale. Watching these moments again, I find myself appreciating that they exist at all, rather than being disappointed at how little they add up to.

I'm also delighted at how well Duchovny and Anderson handle themselves. Their first scene together manages to summarize their multiple-season relationship both efficiently and amusingly, traits the rest of the movie struggles with.[14] Both actors seem perfectly at home in the new format, and while the movie doesn't ask much of them performance-wise, their evident comfort is an indication that trying to adapt *The X-Files* into a movie wasn't doomed from the start. Mulder and Scully are, after all, the show's biggest assets. Yet, the fact that our protagonists remain just as charming and fun on the big screen as on the small one makes it hard not to watch this movie and wish that the script had just been a tad bit stronger.

Despite a concerted effort to make Mulder and Scully's connection the focal point of the finale,[15] and despite how worried everyone looks throughout the film, the stakes never seem all that high, nor the emotional beats all that consequential. Once again, there's that frustrating refusal to enact any substantial or permanent change that has become the hallmark of the mythology. Boiled down to its essence, *Fight the Future* is just another story of Mulder pulling Scully in over both their heads and escaping without the definitive proof he's so desperate to find. Sure, there's that dead bee, and sure, they apparently (and inadvertently) stopped an alien invasion, but this still plays more like an amusement-park ride tour through *The X-Files* than an actual event.

Even judged on those terms, though, this movie isn't bad at all. It's slick and well-paced and goes down easy enough—the sort of thing you can find on TV and not regret giving over a Sunday afternoon to. There's something to be said for competence, and even at its worst, this movie is competent, especially considering what a disaster it could have been. Not particularly original,[16] and rarely inspired, but still not an embarrassment to the legacy of the show.

---

14 Although I'm fond of Mulder's drunken confession to the bartender. Both that speech and the Mulder/ Scully exchange are intentionally funny, which goes a long way to making them seem more natural.

15 The sinister conspiracy decides to punish Mulder by taking away something he can't live without, which not only centers Mulder by reducing Scully to just a figure in his life but also doesn't really square with the revelation later that the Well Manicured Man was supposed to kill Mulder.

16 I'm not sure we needed yet another doomed informant for Mulder, even if he *was* played by Martin Landau.

TODD: And speaking of, it's hard to escape the tendrils of the show that pervade throughout *Fight the Future*. I wonder if the film would have been more effective as a stand-alone horror tale, if it should have instead stranded Mulder and Scully in the ultimate Monster of the Week story, with contributions from all of the show's major writers.[17] But by the time all involved would try such a thing,[18] it (ironically) would have made more sense to continue the alien conspiracy story line. *Fight the Future*, hitting theaters when it did, was instead doomed to be that most dreaded thing for any media property hoping to hit the next level of sensation:[19] a middling and hollow exercise for a franchise that could have reached higher.

There's a lot to like here, but you have to already be primed to like it. Still, if you *are* primed to like it, it's a lot of fun to learn more of the Syndicate's plan,[20] and it's lovely to watch Mulder and Scully treat each other so tenderly. Plus, that early fake-out with the bomb is as twisty and thrilling as anything the show ever did. I like *Fight the Future* for what it says about the show as it stood in 1998, on top of the world and leading the cultural conversation, aware of its role in helping to turn America into a more paranoid place, but not quite sure what to do about it. It's telling that the bomb sequence is so memorable because it's the movie in a nutshell: The thing you thought it was turns out to be hidden in another place entirely. To find it, the show would have to return to television.[21]

ZACK: I appreciate the movie for similar reasons. It's a snapshot of the show's cultural impact—a sort of CliffsNotes version of the mythology arc—and a modestly entertaining two hours. I can even imagine it still bringing new fans to the show, considering how easy it is to find *The X-Files* online these days. It's an inherently absurd idea to try to carry a serialized story over from one medium to an entirely different medium and then revert back to the original medium; maybe it's even a little disappointing that the final product isn't as crazy as that notion itself. *Fight the Future* sprang more out of brand extension than creative necessity, so—without

---

17 This would be the approach eventually taken by *The Simpsons Movie*, which is one of the better "we made a movie while the TV show was still on" films, though that's admittedly a very small sample size.

18 If you're curious about how that turned out, flip forward ten years later to the second movie, *I Want to Believe*.

19 Though you could argue *The X-Files* couldn't have gotten any bigger than it did; it was always just a bit too weird and esoteric to breathe the rarified air of an unqualified phenomenon.

20 And to see Armin Mueller-Stahl, then a recent Oscar nominee, turn up as the Syndicate's seeming Big Boss!

21 Though it would carry over one major thing from the movie: Los Angeles. *Fight the Future* is the first *X-Files* installment shot partially in Southern California (though the sequence set in the ice field was filmed near Vancouver), and the four following seasons would be shot in LA as well, about which: keep reading.

the fully realized story and complete cast of characters really needed to make the jump to the big screen—it's hard to get tremendously excited about the result. But it absolutely could've been worse.[22]

---

22 As we shall (unfortunately) see!

SEASON SIX

| "THE BEGINNING" | SEASON 6 / EPISODE 1
WRITTEN BY CHRIS CARTER
DIRECTED BY KIM MANNERS |

CALIFORNIA, HERE WE COME

In which we mostly ignore the major motion picture.

Plenty of fans point to Season Six as the moment *The X-Files* jumped the shark. It certainly made enough changes that noticeably altered the show's rhythms. The show had, up until now, been shot in Vancouver, which lent the series its moody atmosphere; the Canadian forests, drizzle, and perpetual mist gave those first five seasons a sense that *The X-Files* was like nothing else on TV. Beginning with Season Six, production on the show moved to Los Angeles; *The X-Files* was now shot in the same city as almost every other TV program. The show started doing lots of episodes seemingly designed to revel in its new, sunny locale. The mythology had long ago ceased to make much sense to the layman.[1] For the first time ever, the ratings, season-to-season, were down slightly. The movie was a hit, but not a massive one. *The X-Files* briefly became a comedy for several episodes in a row. It's no wonder fans nearly mutinied.

Season Six, however, is underrated. It's not up there with the series' best years, but it's only a slight step down from its highest heights. While the mythology has mostly run out of gas by now, the Monster of the Week episodes are still as inventive and wickedly funny as ever. There are a few by-the-numbers stand-alones, but that's been true of every season. Yet it's also the season when the show's ambitions seem aimed at getting its audience to question not just the government, but the very limits of reality itself.

"The Beginning" is yet another lackluster season premiere, though it moves more energetically than the last season premiere, "Redux" (S5E1).[2] This episode does have a few points to recommend it. The idea of a chest-bursting monster that erupts from within will always be terrifying, for example, even if the series here is ripping off the concept from *Alien*. The ending revelation—that the hungry monster alien is just the pupal stage of the gray aliens—is also intriguing, if a touch

---

1   Though basically all of the mythology episodes in Seasons Four and Five have their pleasures, they also mark a sort of downward slide in that they either neglect to clarify the various forces involved in the conspiracy, or cannot offer the simple enjoyment that comes from Mulder and Scully discovering new layers to this massive mystery. There's no single turning point, so much as there is an overall sense of diminishing returns.

2   "Little Green Men" (S2E1) is probably one of the best premieres the show aired, as "The Blessing Way" (S3E1), "Herrenvolk" (S4E1), and "Redux" all disappointed in one way or another.

predictable.[3] Plus, the monster attacks are stylish and ghoulish, and the series is clearly having a lot of fun with its new California climes.[4]

But this episode is also burdened by the need to tie up the loose ends of two separate story lines. The fifth-season finale, "The End" (S5E20) was only tangentially connected to *Fight the Future*, via a few oblique references in the film to the X-Files being closed (and/or burnt to a crisp) and Mulder and Scully being reassigned.[5] And while the movie was somewhat close-ended with regard to its story line, it left unanswered the giant question of whether Scully would remember her infection by an alien virus, the spaceship buried beneath Antarctica in which she was held captive, being saved and cured by Mulder, then falling unconscious beneath said ship rocketing toward the stars. Since this is a show that never met a reset button it couldn't press, the outcome of these theoretically character-changing events is that Scully has only the vaguest memories of what happened. On the one hand, this makes absolute sense, because Scully was sick with a disease that was hollowing her out to be the incubator for an alien monster. On the other, it's incredibly frustrating to see her harping on about how science doesn't explain what happened to her because there's simply no logical explanation for it other than "aliens did it."

The writers—wedded as they are to the series' "skeptic/believer" conceit—need Scully to constantly question things she (being the no-nonsense person we know her to be) probably would have admitted were real ages ago, given the chance. It's one thing to have Scully say, "Hey, Mulder, werewolves seem like a pretty crazy thing to believe in," but it's altogether another to have her continue to deny that aliens and the Syndicate are behind a (completely ludicrous but utterly real in the world of the show) conspiracy to overthrow the Earth. The conceptions the writers have of Scully have become too limiting at this point in the show's progression, and those predetermined notions hurt the character in these mythology episodes.[6]

To be fair, though, "The Beginning" is partly proof of concept, designed to demonstrate that *The X-Files* could still be recognizably itself even while filming in Los Angeles; Scully's rigid characterization here helps it to pass that test. Filming in the TV capital of the world certainly has its benefits too. The foot chases through murky locations (in this case, a nuclear power plant) have a brisk handsomeness to

S6 E1

---

3 It makes no sense that a being would evolve so its larval stage is a virus, its pupal stage is a flesh-rending monster, and its adult stage is a sentient being, but, also: Who cares?

4 This episode is set in Phoenix, and boy, does it look like Phoenix!

5 Gibson Praise, so important to "The End," doesn't feature in *Fight the Future* at all, in yet another example of the disconnect between the two stories.

6 This is one reason the MOTW episodes continue to work well past the point the mythology has given up the ghost. There, Scully's skepticism can be taken on a case-by-case basis, and if she doesn't want to believe in, say, a marauding bug monster disguised as a man (as in "Folie a Deux" [S5E19]) it's easier to be on her side. When she refuses to believe in aliens with dark designs for planet Earth at this point in the show's run, it feels wildly out of character. Hasn't she seen enough??!!??

them. The guest actors pulled for this episode are strong. Nothing was left behind in Canada either. The show's supporting players are all present and accounted for, and if the mythology feels totally ludicrous now (which it does), at least all involved are still dedicated to making it scary. The "world conquest" narrative has completely gone off the rails, but it's hard to be too mad when there are space monsters literally eating us from the inside out, so that they might evolve into higher life forms in our nuclear power plant reactors.

What's more, the idea that Mulder and Scully's work at the X-Files is finally being questioned not for how it has hurt the Syndicate but for how it has hurt the FBI's bottom line is a surprisingly durable idea. In the past, the series had marginally acknowledged how bonkers the duo's expense reports must be, but here it's given fuller consideration. Plus, the impromptu audit gives David Duchovny something to play with in an episode in which Mulder might otherwise be going through the motions. Here, when the X-Files are taken from him, he looks suitably gutted, and when he's trying to imagine a world in which he works for Assistant Director Alvin Kersh (James Pickens Jr., later of *Grey's Anatomy* fame), it seems like all the air has gone out of him. The audit, and the idea that the X-Files are just too expensive and ineffective or irresponsible, are great ideas for an interconnected story arc—especially because they can mostly run along in the background and resurface when needed.

On the other hand, making Spender and Fowley the new heads of the X-Files Department doesn't work nearly as well. Fowley doesn't really make sense as a character. She seems to exist in order to do solely whatever the plot needs her to do, and the show so insists on her undeniable villainy that every action she takes feels inherently ridiculous. Spender fares slightly better—and the reveal that he's working for the Cigarette Smoking Man is telegraphed but still effective—yet he's still a rote antagonist. The idea of other people working in that famous office is a very potent one, but making these characters the bad guys feels like the easy way out.[7]

"The Beginning" has so much to overcome in terms of plot and expectation that it's not a surprise that it didn't quite manage to. It's still a grimly effective little episode of television when it needs to be, even if it feels stitched together from leftover pieces of other mythology episodes.[8] Yet notice just how much better the

---

7   I always hesitate to tell artists how to do their job, but imagine an X-Files office staffed not by Syndicate stooges but by people who don't question the bureaucracy they're involved in, who are more easily cowed by the conspiracy because they just want to work a "nine-to-five" job and get home to the family, who don't have Mulder's all-consuming passion for uncovering "the truth." It would offer a different *kind* of conflict, and it would tie nicely in to the season's overarching ideas about Mulder and Scully's irresponsible investigations.

8   Even other non-mythology episodes, honestly. Reducing the aliens to ravenous monsters (at least at one stage of their life cycle) makes them into just another werewolf or vampire out of a MOTW entry, instead of strange and complex life-forms from beyond the stars.

episode is when focused on the monster and not the man and woman chasing it. That's never a good sign of things to come. —TVDW

DON'T STOP

In which Mulder tries to prove that he's a real hero.

At its most basic level, plot is just a pretext for momentum. The Vince Gilligan–created *Breaking Bad*[9] is one of the purest examples of this concept in the television pantheon, a show whose protagonist's greed and ambition serves as a constant pressure to keep things moving forward. The obvious reason to watch "Drive" is that the episode is how Gilligan met Bryan Cranston, the man who would go on to star as the cancer-ridden, meth-cooking chemistry teacher Walter White; the less obvious reason is that this hour is a great example of the engine that keeps great TV moving. It's a principle so simple it would fit on a bumper sticker: Keep moving, or you die.

Cranston plays Patrick Crump, a roofer and a bigot with a very bad headache. After Crump's wife's head explodes in the cold open, Crump takes Mulder hostage and sends him speeding down the road. There are no scenes of the Crumps' lives before things went south for them, and we don't get much backstory of them or their relationship. That's fine, because we don't really need one; who Crump is doesn't matter as much as what happens to him.

Gilligan doesn't go out of his way to make us feel bad for the man, but Cranston is excellent in the role. His monologue about what happened to his wife the morning she got infected is haunting in a way monologues of that type rarely are. Six seasons into the show, audiences have come to expect collateral damage with each new threat, and the bodies that fall in stand-alone episodes rarely mean much outside the moment. Yet Cranston invests the character with an unexpected amount of dignity, one that acknowledges his racism and anger while still forcing you to give a damn. His final moments, as he begs Mulder to go "Just a little bit faster," make for one of the more affecting deaths I've seen on the show.

The script manages to wring a tremendous amount of tension out of its premise. The episode's most nerve-racking moment has Mulder forced to make a pit stop for gas in the middle of the night. It's a short scene but it works because the lack of contrived threats makes those practical concerns all the more effective. You can

---

9   As well as its less gripping but still fantastic prequel spin-off, *Better Call Saul*.

quibble with the episode's explanation of events, which is so thin as to be transparent; something to do with low-frequency radio broadcasts and the weapons potential thereof, and the possibility that this all may have been an accident, or maybe not. But that flimsiness is actually a strength. The show would often struggle with underexplored threats, but here, the ambiguity makes sure that nothing distracts us from the main story. Gilligan earns the simplicity of his script by making sure the effect of what's happening is so intense that all our attention is held by what's right in front of us.

Both Mulder and Scully are in top form in "Drive," doing what they do best, but Mulder's characterization here is what holds everything together. Duchovny is excellent, building a relationship with Cranston that starts off with mutual suspicion and frustration before circumstances force them together. It's a compressed arc that requires real sincerity to be effective; since we know deep down that Mulder isn't going to die, we need to believe that *he* believes he might, and to also care about what happens to Crump. This only works because Mulder's efforts to save a man he doesn't know and doesn't much like seem like the most important thing in the world to him. Duchovny makes the most of the strong part he's given here, allowing him to help build the hour to a sense of real tragedy at its close.

The episode doesn't force the connection, but the fact that the plot only gets going when Mulder chooses to get involved in a case that has nothing to do with him is telling. This is who Mulder is: He has to act, and in his way, he is as damned to forward motion as the poor bastard in his backseat. Mulder's compulsion to find the truth has been heralded, undercut, mocked, and vilified, but "Drive" presents his compulsions as simple and necessary fact. While we may regret the trouble they cause him (and feel bad that Scully gets dragged along for the ride time and again), we can't deny how essential they are—both to him, and to the show. "Drive" works perfectly well on its own, without striving to find deeper symbolic significance, but it also elegantly summarizes both Mulder's character—his inability to stop—and how that character, in turn, defines *The X-Files*. The truth is out there. But it won't stay still for long. —ZH

BETTER CALL MULDER AND SCULLY

By introducing Bryan Cranston to Vince Gilligan, "Drive" made television history. But how exactly did Cranston end up playing Patrick Crump? "I just wrote the episode as you always do: you come up with an idea and you write it," Gilligan says. "[Only when] Rick Millikan [the show's casting director] and his team started to set about casting it did I realize what an impossibly hard part I'd written in terms of finding the right actor for the job. Rick, as I recall, brought in actor after actor after actor for the role of Patrick Crump, and none of them quite fit the bill. There were plenty of very scary guys who came in who could just terrify you, make you afraid to be alone in a room with them. But they had a sort of animal magnetism or animal repulsion and you'd be frightened of them, but you wouldn't feel for them—you wouldn't have any sympathy toward them. We all realized you have to kind of feel bad for this guy at the end of it all; as bad as he's been, you want to feel sorry when he dies.

"We got to a point [when] it was real desperation time; I think we were only a day or two before the start of photography for the episode, and we didn't have anybody to play the part. Then, lo and behold, this guy I'd never heard of walks in the door, Bryan Cranston, and he just crushed it. . . . I looked over to Rick and the other producers and I said 'OTW,' which is short for 'off to wardrobe.' He was so clearly the guy, we didn't even discuss it in the room. We just pulled the trigger and left it at that. . . . Watching Bryan work in that episode, it became very clear to me very quickly that this guy is a major talent. [I saw that] he can do it all, and I want[ed] to work with him again."

And, were The X-Files to take place in the same universe as Breaking Bad and Better Call Saul, who would fit best into Mulder and Scully's world? "Gus Fring," says Gilligan. "There's nothing supernatural about him, but he would be a hell of an arch-villain for Mulder and Scully to go up against. I can see Gus Fring ultimately being the guy who runs the entire government or government conspiracy. I can see him as the guy at the top. I think he could give Cigarette Smoking Man a run for his money."

IN CASE WE NEVER MEET AGAIN

*In which Mulder and a 1930s-era Scully fight Nazis,
and it's much better than it sounds.*

"Triangle" marks an ending, of sorts. It's a terrific episode of television, the sort of episode only this show could have done at this point in its run, alive with possibility and experimentation. But "Triangle" marks the endpoint of the media's intense fascination with the show, a fascination that began somewhere during Season Three.[10] "Triangle" got that last gasp of *X-Files* hype. Critics offered glowing reviews. Chris Carter was hailed as having a great shot at winning an Emmy. The use of "real-time" takes—shots that seemed to last the eleven minutes that take up an act of running time—was held up as the latest innovation on a show that was always pushing boundaries. "Triangle" was one of the "fun" ones, one of the episodes that gave in to the sheer, geeky joy at the show's heart, rather than the dour conspiracy-thriller elements. Yet the "fun" here was very different from that of the comedy episodes, instead tilting over into outright pulp adventure.

"Triangle" very much remains a triumph of production values and sheer craft. Few episodes of television—before or since—have been as well executed at every technical level. After the first few minutes (in which Mulder is dragged belowdecks on the mysterious *Queen Anne*), you stop waiting for the camera to cut away and start just going with the flow. This is partially because the story, equal parts *Twilight Zone* and *The Wizard of Oz*, is such a goofy joy. But it's also partially because Carter and his crew keep coming up with good reasons for Mulder and Scully to keep moving, and for the camera to keep following right alongside them. What's more incredible is that "Triangle" lacks the dark, melancholy heart of many of the show's other experimental and innovative hours.

"Triangle" may be pure candy, but there's been so much darkness and angst in the episodes leading up to this one that it's not hard to allow for forty-four minutes of unadulterated, brassy momentum. It helps that in some ways, this doesn't feel much like an episode of *The X-Files*, yet it manages to remain a recognizable part of the show's world. There's some silly, general backstory about Mulder attempting to find a ship that disappeared in the Bermuda Triangle in 1939—a ship that Scully

---

10 What ended it was less anything to do with the series itself and much more to do with *The Sopranos*, which would debut in January 1999 and steal almost all of *The X-Files*' "intelligent drama for adults" thunder. But it's rare for a show to occupy such a central place in the TV hype machine for as long as *The X-Files* did.

and the Lone Gunmen later find while looking for him—but for the most part, this is an excuse to abandon the show's usual formula by folding it into another genre altogether.

That genre is perhaps best understood as a strange but breezy amalgamation of classic Hollywood romp and time-traveling sci-fi. The villains of the episode are "movie Nazis," those comical goons who are always ready to meet the business end of an American or British fist. The "Scully" of 1939 is a sharp-talking dame who packs a mean punch.[11] The soundtrack features swing music[12] prominently, and the big set piece involves a bunch of British and Jamaican sailors getting into a brawl with those Nazis (and includes an older woman bashing a Nazi over the head with a bottle). 1939 Scully and Mulder just happen to meet again while crawling around amid that brawl. It's all super pulpy, super entertaining, and super glorious.

That it works at all speaks to just how self-aware and capable the series is at this point in its run. The use of long tracking shots[13] gives the whole thing a sense of urgency that propels scenes that shouldn't be at all interesting. For instance, the best sequence here is probably the one in which Present Day Scully attempts to figure out just where Mulder's gotten off to this time, while she's at work at the FBI offices. The camera follows her all around the building, just a few paces behind, as she goes up and down in the elevator, ducks out of the way of the Cigarette Smoking Man, and threatens Spender with death.

There's nothing inherently dramatic in these scenes. Scully is just trying to get a small piece of information. In a normal episode, we'd hear the Lone Gunmen tell Scully that she needed to get this information to save Mulder, and then we'd cut to her having it. The gimmick of the episode can't allow for that shortcut, so the *process* has to be more entertaining than the result. This is a tough challenge the show has set for itself, but we're so familiar with its rhythms that it works. Here's all the stuff we normally *don't* see, and because Carter's direction is so buoyant, it carries us through what amounts to Scully very dramatically doing some paperwork while racing around to save Mulder's hide. It obviously also helps that Gillian Anderson is so delightful throughout, here racing all over the building and even kissing Skinner full on the mouth when he gets what she needs.

All the threads come together in the episode's fantastically entertaining final act, when the two timelines converge and that brawl breaks out. The use

---

11 Carter writes her like the hero of a radio serial about a tough-talking girl reporter, which is sort of great.

12 Written, of course, by Mark Snow, who's clearly enjoying setting aside the droning synths for a while. It's amazing he didn't win an Emmy for this episode, as it feels like something the Academy of Television Arts & Sciences would have adored.

13 Which have gone from incredibly rare on TV to incredibly overused in just the last five years. Now even the *best* examples of the form, on shows like *Mr. Robot*, are greeted with a slight eyeroll and a grumble of, "Show-off."

of split screen here is perfect, and when the two Scullys pass each other in the hall—separated by decades—and then turn and frown, as if sensing the presence of the other and trying to figure out what the hell just happened, the moment is both playful and thoughtful at once. It makes you grin at the idea that maybe time itself is just a suggestion.

Hell, "Triangle" even has Mulder and Scully kiss! Sure, he kisses the Scully of the past, but it nonetheless feels like a significant moment in this very slow burn of a relationship. The moment feels for all the world like Mulder finally admitting what he really wants, even if the Scully of 1939 isn't truly the woman he really wants to be with. The final scene at his hospital bedside—in which he tells Scully he loves her—is surprisingly moving, given the light tone of the rest of the proceedings. She's all he has, and is often the only thing standing between him and death. Don't think he doesn't know it.

In the end, it was all a dream. Or was it? We're meant to think *some* of the events happened, or happened enough to somehow give Mulder both a sore eye (where 1939 Scully slugged him) and an emotional breakthrough (where Present Day Scully saved his ass, yet again). But holding the possibility of the cheap "it-was-all-a-dream" twist against an episode that is this much fun—and has this much visual invention on display in every corner of every frame—would be churlish. The "dream" suggestion lets the show have its cake and eat it too—and works in a great number of *Wizard of Oz* references,[14] to boot.

If "Triangle" was one of the show's final attempts at total experimentation, it certainly went out with a bang. To watch "Triangle" now is to remember a time when this was the most daring show on television. It's not deep in the sense of making grand philosophical statements, but it's fizzy and fun and invested in the idea of Mulder and Scully as two halves of a perfect duo. Maybe, then, this is the show at its best. Once, there was a show that attempted big, bold things like this, and it was beautiful. —TVDW

---

14 Simply the idea that everybody in Mulder's visit to the '30s is also one of his pals in the '90s allows for some great gags in this regard. "And you were there, Scarecrow," indeed. (Also, 1939 is the year *Wizard* was released.)

OVER THE RAINBOW

According to Chris Carter, the idea for the experimental format of "Triangle" came partially from the physical medium of film. "We were shooting on film at the time, and I was looking at a film magazine," Carter recalls. "I said, 'How many minutes of film are in this magazine?' They said, 'eleven.' I said, 'Our show is forty-four minutes long. . . . what if we just used one magazine for every act?' . . . It was a four-act show then [and I thought, maybe] we could do one long take on [each] magazine. Everyone laughed at me. Then I started thinking about it, and . . . I had seen *Rope*, I knew that you could do what I was talking about. I thought, 'This would be a really clever thing to do for television.'"

Of course, Carter is the first to admit he wasn't immediately aware of what it would take to shoot an episode all in long takes. He says, "[I was] not thinking about the practical considerations, which were that to do a five-minute scene, nonstop, you would have to rehearse it for hours and hours and hours. It took the actual making of the show into a direction we had never gone before, [because before] we had always shot the show in bits and pieces. That we were going to shoot it in big chunks takes a completely different approach. I think it scared the hell out of the head of production at Fox, because we would be rehearsing until lunch, and we would get our first shot off six hours after we had begun the day. Usually you get your first shot off after the first hour."

Filming wasn't the only aspect of the episode's production that didn't go exactly as planned. Mitch Pileggi remembers being handed the script for his part as the Nazi turncoat version of Skinner: "Some of my dialogue was written in German, and I went to school in Munich back in the '70s for three years, so I spoke German. I got the script and I look at it and I say to Chris, 'This doesn't make any sense,' and he goes, 'Why?' and I said, 'It just doesn't make any sense,' and he goes, 'Then rewrite it so it makes sense!' because he knew that I spoke German. So I did. I got to make up my own dialogue in those scenes."

But the spur-of-the-moment and out-of-the-box nature of the episode worked in its favor, and Carter credits the expansive thinking of the cast and crew to making both "Triangle" and the series thrive. "Like many things on *The X-Files*, it was basically, 'Let's try this!'" he notes. "I would say *The X-Files* succeeded because we didn't know what we *couldn't* do, which means we tried everything."

BODY-SWAPPING BLUES

In which Mulder has a freaky Friday.

Wouldn't you like to take someone else's life for a spin, if only for a little while? Sure, most people are content to be themselves, and most people wouldn't want to change *everything* in their lives. But one of the chief appeals of fiction is that we get to take turns living vicariously through other people or animals or space aliens. We all carry a little curiosity around what it would be like to be someone else, and fiction helps to satiate that desire.

The "Dreamland" two-parter is the first overtly comedic story of *The X-Files*' sixth season. The cold open is so familiar that it verges on self-parody: Mulder and Scully are driving out to the desert surrounding Area 51 at night, so Mulder can meet one of his informants.[15] Scully's reaction to the whole escapade makes it obvious that the writers understand just how ridiculously self-referential this sequence is, helping to ensure that the audience is in on the joke from the start. She raises the issue of a "normal" life, which serves as the thematic crux of the episode: Is Mulder missing out on the possibility of domestic bliss by giving everything to his cause? Wouldn't he be happier if he settled down and stopped wasting his life on an endless pursuit of little gray men?

The answer we get to that question by the end of the first half of this two-parter is a resounding "no," although the episode isn't exactly playing fair. There are a lot of great jokes in "Dreamland," but the best might be the fact that the Man in Black with whom Mulder swaps places (Morris Fletcher, played by the always great Michael McKean[16]) has a dull, completely uninteresting little life. After years of being thwarted by forces he can barely understand, Mulder finally gets behind the curtain and finds nothing of note whatsoever; just the life of a disaffected middle-management type with an unpleasant home life. The best joke of both episodes is that it turns out that at least some of the forces Mulder has been fighting against are just as eager to get out as Mulder is to get *in*.

Meanwhile, Fletcher is having the time of Mulder's life. His attitude toward becoming Mulder is similar to that of the pathetically endearing Eddie Van Blundht

---

15 All that's missing is a reference to Samantha Mulder's abduction, and we'd have *X-Files* bingo.
16 McKean would end up working with Gilligan again on the *Breaking Bad* spin-off *Better Call Saul.*

from "Small Potatoes" (S4E20), but unlike Eddie, Fletcher is a jerk whose boorishness serves mostly to make us appreciate all the ways Mulder isn't just a "normal" guy.[17] And unlike that earlier episode, Duchovny and McKean continue to play the same characters even after the body switch—we as the audience can see Mulder standing in as Fletcher, and vice versa, even though everyone else around them sees them as their switched selves. It creates a dynamic different from that of "Small Potatoes" in that it keeps us seeing things through Mulder and Fletcher's perspectives, and allows both actors to get a lot of comedic mileage out of their respective reactions to their situation. Gillian Anderson's double takes throughout are hilarious, and her increasing frustration over Fletcher's antics make some of the episode's padding bearable.

Still, there's no reason this logy two-parter couldn't have become a much tighter single episode that dealt with the same themes and issues. The best gags are all crammed into part one, the revelations made over the course of the two hours are minor, and the whole thing is basically an excuse to let Michael McKean[18] and David Duchovny screw around for a couple of episodes. There are worse reasons to make television, and both McKean and Duchovny are very funny. But at some point, there should be something more in order to justify the whole endeavor. The sheer fun of seeing these two actors goofing off carries the first episode along, but the pleasure isn't enough for the second.

Not all of the comedy in the first episode lands either. Nora Dunn does what she can as JoAnne Fletcher, Morris's long-suffering wife, but the script does her no favors in its insistence on her role as a suspicious shrew; even the small attempt to humanize her near the end of the first hour turns into a Viagra joke. The episode's take on the *Duck Soup* mirror gag also falls flat—like the two-parter as a whole, it's a cute bit that wears out its welcome by dragging on for too long.[19]

A lot of the humor works, though, and—while these flaws keep the episode from being a classic—the surreal jokes give it a loopy vibe that ensures everything goes down easily. There are also some solid moments of comedy when Fletcher is hanging out around Mulder's apartment and reveling in jokes designed for fans.[20] Plus, the scene in which Mulder is tossed into that holding cell that's seemingly miles

S6 E4–5

---

17 Mulder may be an obsessive nerd, but at least he isn't a sexist brownnoser.

18 Who is very good as both Morris Fletcher *and* Fox Mulder, it should be noted.

19 It's also missing a crucial element that makes the *Duck Soup* gag such a classic: suspense. In the Marx Brothers movie, one character is pretending to be another in the context of the story, which means that we're waiting to see how long he can keep the ruse up. In the "Dreamland" version, since Mulder is just looking at an actual reflection of himself, even if that reflection is being played by a different actor, there's no tension. A small complaint, but one that's indicative of the two episodes' larger issues; the unnecessary running time makes for less immediate stakes, which gives the jokes nothing to build off of.

20 "Where does this guy sleep?!" cries Fletcher. And thus, the eventual arrival of Mulder's waterbed, which is something to take note of (and all we will say about that for now).

below the Earth plays like a confirmation of Mulder's worst fears and is a nicely ironic reversal of his position. This guy always sees his evidence disappear into some warehouse somewhere; now, he *is* the evidence that's disappearing. Some of the emotional territory the episode toes around is unexpectedly effective too. It's a fascinating twist that the Fletcher marriage is repaired by Mulder's time as Morris, and it's poignant to think that neither Fletcher will remember their reconciliation.

Yet the pair of "Dreamland" episodes doesn't tell us anything, not really. There's no new information here about the characters, or about the show's version of the U.S. government, or about the culture built around this version of the shadow military. Perhaps that's just fine for a comedy episode that isn't, after all, a mythology episode, but there's also a vague sense of the show tilting off-center, toward some other series entirely, about the Fletchers. After all, the emotional climax hinges on the Fletcher marriage, and while that's alright in theory, it relies in practice on getting us to care about two people whom we've only just met and whom we haven't seen share significant scenes together before this point. The more we realize that so much of these events happen just to offer gags about, say, elderly Native American women talking like hotshot fighter pilots, the more the whole exercise starts to seem pretty slight.

Ultimately, "Dreamland" is what's called an up-and-back—a story in which we go on a journey, then end up right back where we started, with the events having effected no changes in the status quo, nor provided new knowledge about the world. Television thrives on the up-and-back, and the best shows—including this one, occasionally—turn that innate pointlessness into part of the joke. People *think* they have learned things by the story's end, but in actuality they're just as clueless as they were at the start. "Dreamland" forces a bunch of emotional resolutions and tries to get us to care about them, then immediately creates a reality in which those scenes don't exist, thus rendering those emotional resolutions moot. The episodes don't really bother to do much else; the puncturing of the Mulder-as-hero bubble, the insistence that he's a lost and lonely guy without a center, feels a little emptier every time the show goes to that well. Besides, since the primary emotional payoff is for the Fletchers for an event they won't remember, it's harder to argue the pointlessness is all part of the fun. Scully[21] finds the two coins fused together again in a desk drawer, and that's that.

There's a lot of rich comedic and dramatic potential in having Mulder swap lives with a man who works in the one place he wants information about—only to realize that the man knows as little about what's really going on as Mulder does. But the episode works to make sure none of this really matters. It even gets the central idea of the body-swap story—realizing your old life wasn't so bad after all—mostly

---

21 Who, it should be said, gets nothing to do throughout these episodes beyond those excellent reaction shots.

wrong because it gets lost in tangents.[22] In the end, you might wish this episode would swap with "Small Potatoes." That one would have been fun to see again. —ZH and TVDW

HOLIDAY SPIRITS

In which Mulder and Scully are together for Christmas.

Once again, Mulder and Scully find themselves in a crisis that challenges the ties that bind them together. If all this episode had going for it was its examination of the Mulder/Scully dynamic, it would be perfectly adequate, if not exactly essential. What elevates and complicates the formula is the villains themselves: ghosts who don't care why Mulder is who he is, and why Scully does what she does. They just want them dead.

Rather than having Maurice (Ed Asner)[23] and Lyda (Lily Tomlin)[24] tailor their torment to the psychology of our two heroes, Chris Carter, who penned this episode, reveals the ghosts' mischief is simply a part of a game they like to play with intruders. Carter has a lot of fun with the haunting, and with the characters of the ghosts themselves. It takes about fifteen minutes of running time before the ghosts finally show up, and Carter makes the most of the buildup, throwing in all sorts of spooky tricks: front doors that close and lock themselves, creepy shadows, lights apparently turning themselves on, and a pair of corpses under the floorboards wearing Mulder and Scully's clothes. Worst of all is the room our heroes can't get out of, no matter how many times they walk through the door.

The episode fits with the usual Monster of the Week setup: Mulder wants to investigate something, Scully thinks he's crazy, they poke around, *BOO!*, and end credits. The difference here is that everything happens over the course of a few hours. There are no autopsies and, apart from Scully's brief monologue about how the idea of "ghosts" really says more about the living than the dead, there's no effort made to explain what's going on. Mulder isn't even visiting the house because he wants to stop the spirits or get proof of the supernatural. He just wants to see something strange.

---

22 Again, in part because the whole thing runs two full episodes, which is really not necessary for this particular story.

23 Asner holds the record for most Primetime Emmys awarded to a male performer (seven). He's probably best known for playing Lou Grant on both *The Mary Tyler Moore Show* and its spin-off, *Lou Grant*.

24 Tomlin is a multi-award-winning actress and comedian of stage and screen, best-known for her performances in such films as *Nashville*, *The Late Show*, and *9 to 5*. She currently stars as Frankie on Netflix's *Grace and Frankie*.

The real draw here are the two guest stars, and Asner and Tomlin are more than up to the task. At around the midpoint of the hour, there's a subtle shift of focus, and the audience starts to see the story from their point of view. They discuss their plans with each other, they kvetch about the way things are now: It used to be they had decades to work their destructive magic on a couple, now they just get a single night; "kids these days," et cetera. Interestingly, Carter makes no attempt to show us anything about who Maurice and Lyda were when they were alive, apart from Mulder's story. We don't even really get an explanation as to why they're so much older than they're supposed to be. (The lovers in Mulder's tale offed themselves in the bloom of youth.) Do ghosts age? Or maybe in the "real-life" version, Maurice and Lyda saw themselves getting older and losing touch, and decided what the hell, it's better to go out with a bang.

Who knows? Who cares? Asner and Tomlin fill in the blanks on their own, creating a lived-in, cranky relationship that's as warm as any we've seen on the show. While they don't succeed in getting Mulder and Scully to shoot each other, they don't seem particularly upset by their failure. They're just playing around. A good ghost story reminds you to value what matters the most: the people you love, and the fact that you're still breathing.

Things get scary for a while, and the sequence in which Lyda pretends to be first Mulder shooting Scully, and then Scully shooting Mulder, is terrific black comedy; the sight of Mulder and Scully dragging themselves toward the door, convinced that they've been fatally wounded by their partners, is appropriately bizarre. But there are no consequences, no deaths that aren't already decades old.

In the end, Scully comes by Mulder's apartment and they exchange gifts, while at the same time Lyda and Maurice muse over another year gone by. Happy endings are rare on *The X-Files*. Usually the best we can hope for is a return to normalcy, and although that's exactly what happens here, it's rarely been so sweet and satisfying. The ghosts hold hands and fade away, while Mulder and Scully open their presents. Survival is reason enough to celebrate, but our heroes did more than survive; they once again found a way to defeat a threat trying to tear them apart by finding strength in each other. In such a mordantly comedic hour, it's a surprise to get a lesson this hopeful. There are dangers and monsters and mocking spirits in the world, but maybe, in the end, love (or something like it) finds a way. —ZH

BRUCE CAMPBELL'S BABY

In which a demon just wants a nice, normal life.

With all of the horror movies *The X-Files* has subverted, turned inside out, and outright ripped off, it's amazing that it took the show this long to offer a direct take on *Rosemary's Baby*. The series has had pregnancy fears and demonic motifs before, but it's never really combined the two into one episode. And if you're going to argue *Rosemary's Baby* is such an unimpeachable horror classic that the show would never dare touch it, remember that the show did a lackluster riff on *The Exorcist* all the way back in Season Two.[25] Maybe the show was waiting to break out *Rosemary's Baby* for when Bruce Campbell could come along and play the demon baby's dad.

It's safe to say Campbell is the best thing about this episode. The episode is aware of the most famous version of this tale, so it's constantly looking for unpredictable ways to undercut that story. Campbell's character—Wayne Weinsider—is played mostly sympathetically. He's a demon, sure, but he's a demon who just wants a normal life and a normal kid. He keeps falling in love with and impregnating women so he can finally have that towheaded little boy or girl he's always dreamed of without having to worry about covering up the horns. Once Wayne's plot is revealed, it's so amusingly prosaic that the whole episode takes on a veneer of melancholy. All this guy wanted was a normal life, and the involvement of Mulder has completely derailed his plans.

Yes, Wayne was causing women undue stress and hardship—and he was framing some of them for his crimes. Because this is *The X-Files*, you're constantly aware that the demon Laura Weinsider (Lisa Jane Persky) saw standing above her bed and reaching between her legs to "deliver" her demonic child was real and probably Wayne. But at the same time, there could have been a very compelling story here about an otherwise normal man carrying around some sort of genetic defect, so desperate to have a child that he turns to medieval abortion methods to remove the ones who don't stand up to scrutiny. It's a horrifying tale, but it's also one based in recognizable human motivations. The fact that these machinations are being carried out by a demon adds a bonus twist.

Campbell sells the part too. He has an authentic-seeming connection with both of the actresses who play his lovers, as well as with David Duchovny, as Wayne's normally tight-knit, happy-go-lucky persona begins to unravel in the face of Mulder's

---

25 See: "The Calusari" (S2E21).

doggedness. Check out Wayne driving his sports car and listening to Garbage when Mulder pulls up alongside him with that cocksure grin on his face. It's one of the best examples of how Mulder would be a thorn in the side of monsters everywhere.

After four straight episodes that have been more concerned with comedy and stylistic invention than with anything like a "traditional" episode, this one gets back to the straightforward Monster of the Week format. Yet underneath its surface, "Terms of Endearment" is almost as experimental as some of the others that came before. Has any episode to this point spent this amount of time hanging out with the monster as this one does, or tried as hard to make him sympathetic? When Wayne is finally bested by a fellow demon, the moment is meant to play as somewhat tragic, despite his crimes.

Yet those crimes are *substantial*. Wayne might not be magically inducing pregnancies, or tricking women into having children with him (as we've seen occur in previous episodes[26]), but he's causing women to miscarry without their consent, which is essentially the other side of that same coin. "Terms of Endearment" is more aware of the horrors of what Wayne is doing than previous hours, and paying homage to *Rosemary's Baby* necessarily involves riffing on the idea of pregnancy as a horror show. But Wayne's real actions clash tonally with the darkly comic vibe the episode aims for, and the reveal that Betsy, too, is a demon can't quite put right all of these unpleasant implications.[27]

In part due to this episode's focus on the monster, its biggest flaw is that there's too little Scully involved. She sits back at FBI headquarters, apparently waiting for Mulder to call in what's happening. It's a weird return to the way the character was written back in the show's first couple of seasons, before she was given more depth and allowed to carry her half of the series' stories. Sure, Mulder and Scully are still *off* the X-Files at this point,[28] and Scully is less amenable to risking her career by chasing demon fathers. Thus, she too often ends up stuck on the sidelines when, in many ways, she's the series' most dynamic character. When Scully disrupts the Wayne and Mulder duet, it's almost as if the series' writers have remembered, "Oh, right, we have this *other* character to work with."

The episode's final twist also undercuts the proceedings slightly. Finding out that one of Wayne's paramours is also a demon and is hoping to have a demon baby to raise is too coincidental and pat. The final image of Betsy driving off with her new

---

26 Most notably "Small Potatoes" (S4E20).

27 "Terms of Endearment" is at least *aware* of its issues in regard to women, and I'd guess the Betsy reveal is meant to mitigate those issues somewhat (which it does in part). But this is yet another episode that suggests the show could have used more female voices in the writers' room, to say the least.

28 We do see Spender lean back and shred the case brought to him by the sheriff. He may as well cackle and twirl a mustache. The character is a huge missed opportunity, shoehorned into the role of "evil toady" when that was the most predictable and least interesting thing the show could have done with him.

S6 E7

demon spawn is a great dark joke, and it's nice that Wayne gets his comeuppance thanks to being outsmarted, rather than having Mulder catch up to him. Maybe finding out that Betsy was a demon far earlier would have helped. But that would require giving over even *more* time to the episode's monsters, something the show wasn't yet comfortable with. —TVDW

SEASON 6 / EPISODE 8
WRITTEN BY JEFFREY BELL
DIRECTED BY KIM MANNERS

"THE RAIN KING"

RAINY-DAY WOMAN

In which it can't rain all the time.

"The Rain King," is a soppy, relentlessly adorable story about unspoken devotion, everlasting friendship, and unstable weather patterns. When did this show start filming in the land of sunshine and lemon drops? In earlier seasons, the more lighthearted episodes worked because they were rule-proving exceptions. A quick and sudden turn into comedy offered a respite from Mulder and Scully's normally horrific and murderous world. Every once in a while, it was nice to see the heroes get what they really wanted.

Now, though, it seems like every week everything is made of hugs and good news. It's too much. None of these episodes are outright bad, but so many of them bunched together at the start of the season sets a tone that makes each successive happy episode seem just a little too familiar. There needs to be darkness to balance out the bright, to make the victories seem important. It's like Mulder and Scully got transferred to the Hallmark Department.

As if that wasn't bad enough, the show is also leaning far too heavily on jokes about the Mulder/Scully relationship. In "The Rain King," they're mistaken for a couple numerous times, and at least two characters go to great lengths to explain how amazed they are that Fox and Dana aren't going at it. At first, this was a cute way to acknowledge that, yes, David Duchovny and Gillian Anderson are both very attractive people with a lot of chemistry. Now, though, it's overbearing and indicative of the writers' unwillingness to effect permanent change.[29] Either make them a couple or get over it.

"The Rain King" isn't terrible, thankfully. The episode's essential sweetness has enough snarky asides from our heroes that it never goes completely off the rails. A lot of the humor comes from "Boy, these hicks sure are dumb"-style jokes, but

---

29 Another example of this: Mulder and Scully being ordered off the X-Files has in no way impacted their ability to work on X-Files.

none of those jokes come across as mean-spirited. Everyone comes out OK in the end. Jeffrey Bell's script manages to generate at least one good red herring, and the episode never drags. David Manis as Holman and Victoria Jackson as Sheila are both charming in their roles, and it's a pleasure to see Mulder finally get a chance to talk to one of the "freaks" he's been hunting his whole life. His inability to give helpful dating advice is a good gag made better by Scully's reaction, and it's lovely when everything turns out well for everyone.

"The Rain King" is gently amusing, but at times, its twee-ness can be hard to take. If this episode had popped up in an earlier season, it might have been a cockeyed classic, a rare respite of levity in an otherwise horrific universe. Placed here, it's like trying to get to the bottom of a pint of Ben & Jerry's. It never stops being delicious, but at some point, you start to wonder if you're going to throw up. —ZH

| "S.R. 819" | SEASON 6 / EPISODE 9
WRITTEN BY JOHN SHIBAN
DIRECTED BY DANIEL SACKHEIM |

SKINNER BOX

In which Skinner has to die to save his own life or . . . something.

Walter Skinner is a great character, all hard-boiled and ready to leap into attack if need be, yet also possessed of a rich sense of morality. Even if the trope in which Skinner warns Mulder and Scully not to pursue something but ultimately has their back is pretty predictable,[30] it hasn't gotten stale just yet. Other Skinner-centric episodes suggest how the conspiracy story line might have played out if its central hero didn't necessarily believe any of this bullshit but still knew he had to dig deeper. Sadly, "S.R. 819" is a bit of a dud.

For one thing, there's surprisingly little Skinner for a Skinner-centric hour. He stumbles around for a while, trying to figure out why he has a weird blood disease, then Scully and Mulder[31] leap onto the case while he slowly expires in a hospital bed. The episode has a terrific ending, one that suggests a new twist in the relationships between the characters, but the path there is full of narrative dead-ends. The episode wants us to believe that Skinner will die, but there's just no good reason to suspect the show would do such a thing (at least, not like this). The show has proven

---

30 The series even poked fun at this notion in "Triangle" (S6E3), in which Skinner seems like a Nazi but is really working for the good guys.

31 Who are still technically not on the X-Files beat and get involved in the plot because Mulder stops by Skinner's office for no real reason.

remarkably bad at writing people off on a permanent basis,[32] so when Skinner "dies," you're just waiting for the twist.

Say what you will about the show's Monster of the Week structure, but when it can really get you to care about a guest star of the week, then bump them off, it often makes for the show's finest episodes. There's just not as much peril surrounding Skinner, even if the rest of the cast does its damnedest to make us think this is Very Important Stuff.[33]

A major structural choice also proves key in leaving the episode undramatic and turgid: It opens by showing us Skinner's death, then flashes back twenty-four hours to show us how he got to this point. Since we suspect that Skinner will ultimately survive, we're just waiting to get caught up. Yet the episode takes almost all its running time to return us to the point in which the doctor regretfully says, "Let him go" as Skinner passes away, the nanobots in his bloodstream constructing the walls that will cause a heart attack more rapidly than the doctors can cut through those walls. The stuff we don't know is coming—which is much more exciting than anything else—takes under five minutes of screen time. The episode ends up running in place.

Shift the story line so it legitimately opens with Skinner's death (and he spends the episode searching for the means of his resurrection), and you might have something more structurally sound. Skinner ultimately drops out of the episode for too long, when it's ostensibly his story. Part of the fun of the conspiracy episodes in these later seasons comes from watching characters *other* than Mulder and Scully deal with the massive plot they're caught up in. And to be sure, watching Skinner chase down his poisoner and get involved in a gunfight in a parking garage is riveting. But there are too few of these sequences, which makes the excess of Mulder and Scully scenes feel rote by comparison.

Now, the idea of a conspiracy being enacted to ship nanotechnology out of the United States and into other countries, for presumably nefarious ends, is a nice break from the alien story line, and it's always interesting to see people who are on the extreme edges of the story line, like Senator Matheson. One of the great things about conspiracy stories is the way that they reinforce the belief that humanity isn't to be trusted, that most people will immediately give in to their own self-interest when push comes to shove. The scenes in which Matheson steadily sells out everybody in order to keep his life effectively captures some of that "Season Three mythology" sense of deep and inevitable corruption.

Then there's that ending! In retrospect, it should have been obvious that Krycek was the man behind Skinner's poisoning. The character hasn't been featured in

---

32 See also: Krycek, who pops up again in this episode despite having been left for dead in the middle of nowhere countless times.

33 David Duchovny, for example, races through this episode, shouting loudly like he can save the entire premise through his acting presence alone.

Season Six, and he was going to come back sooner or later. He's the ultimate cockroach on a show full of them; the guy who keeps being left for dead, then pulling his way back from the brink. Every single time the eternally committed Nicholas Lea pops up on-screen, sinking his teeth into whatever the series has given him this time (no matter how ridiculous), you understand why nobody ever wanted to completely kill him off. Krycek is so fun! And so, so fun to *hate*!

Yet the closing moments play as a shock, and the idea of Skinner having something that could instantly kill him in his bloodstream, something that puts him under the conspiracy's control, is a smart way to restore the old status quo of Skinner's allegiances being in question without assassinating the character. "S.R. 819" is worth it for that final moment, which reveals the minor demon who has clawed his way back out of the abyss to make life hell for everybody else. —TVDW

| "TITHONUS" | SEASON 6 / EPISODE 10
WRITTEN BY VINCE GILLIGAN
DIRECTED BY MICHAEL W. WATKINS |

DEATH AVOIDS HER

In which Scully doesn't die.

Crime-scene photographer Alfred Fellig (Geoffrey Lewis) is under suspicion for murder, and Scully, sans Mulder, is on the case. The FBI hits a wall in the investigation, which leads to a stakeout in front of Fellig's apartment building. But when it's Scully's turn to sit in a car drinking stale coffee, she breaks protocol. Realizing that whatever is going on is a lot weirder than the other agents will ever admit, she goes into the building and confronts Fellig directly.

It's a bold move that galvanizes the story, changing the relationship between the protagonist and the latest Monster of the Week into something more intimate and dangerous than the usual cops-and-robbers routine. It also helps that Fellig isn't a monster, at least not in the usual sense, and while he is on the run, it's in the opposite direction you'd expect. He's not trying to escape anyone. He's trying to catch Death.

At times, Gilligan's script plays like an homage to "Clyde Bruckman's Final Repose" (S3E4); but whereas Clyde was tormented by an unshakable understanding of the machinations of fate, Fellig doesn't know *how* his subjects will die, just *when*. For all his weary cynicism, Clyde Bruckman had a soul; Fellig's seems lost. "Final Repose" leavened its grim fatality with dark wit, but "Tithonus"[34] is rarely funny. Nothing ever feels safe enough to laugh about.

---

34 In Greek mythology, Tithonus was the mortal lover of Eos, Titan of the dawn. When Eos asked Zeus to make Tithonus immortal, she forgot to ask the god to grant her boyfriend eternal youth. He can live forever, but all the joy in life is gone.

Lewis's hangdog expression is the face of a man with nothing left to lose. Fellig is resentful of the people he photographs, jealous of their mortality. Ever since he turned away from Death a century ago, he's been doomed to wander the Earth, unchanging and wholly alone. Denied his eternal rest, he is obsessed with finally looking Death himself in the face. Fellig's decades of torment still don't make him any easier to pity. In fact, one of the episode's subtler points is the suggestion that Fellig's immortality, his exclusion from one of the two things that must happen to every living being, has made him something less than a man. He's a monster not for what he does, but for what he *is*.

The episode also makes good use of Death as the ultimate monster, positing that our deaths cannot be forestalled, merely exchanged. The seeming random chance that leads to each fatality is far creepier than death at the claws of some slavering beast would be. Scully isn't trying to track down a threat that can be neutralized or defeated. Fellig is dead by the end of the hour, but even if he'd died ages ago, the people in the elevator would still be goners, just like the mugging victim and the sex worker who gets hit by a truck. People will still die tomorrow, and the day after that, and the day after that. Fellig just happened to get a glimpse of the underside of it all, and, like a protagonist in an H. P. Lovecraft story, what makes him awful is the knowledge he brought back.

Yet the episode isn't entirely despairing. Scully's efforts to understand Fellig belie the frequent criticism that her character's skepticism is static or close-minded. She may be a sane observer in an insane world, but her struggle to reconcile her faith in the solidity of life with Mulder's lawless visions is one of *The X-Files'* most powerful dramatic arcs. Scully is driven by a need to uncover the truth completely, to reveal all its complexities and inner mechanisms. She doesn't understand Fellig's misery, his listlessness, his barely veiled contempt. She says, "I think you're wrong. How can you have too much life? There's too much to learn, too much to experience." It's simply stated, but it tells you everything you need to know about who Scully is: She believes in the inherent value of living, and she has a boundless curiosity for all there is to know and encounter. That's why it is so horrifying when we see through Fellig's eyes that Scully has turned black-and-white; by the story's logic, she's doomed.

The climax of "Tithonus" is a fine example of misleading suspense. We know Fellig has watched countless people die; we assume he's planning to do it again. When that doesn't happen—when Fellig takes Scully's death on himself—it doesn't redeem him, but it does make him more than just a ghoul.

It also makes Dana Scully technically immortal. In "Clyde Bruckman," Scully asks Clyde how she'll die, and he tells her, "You don't." It was a lovely exchange, and almost certainly just a good-natured lie, but "Tithonus" makes it real. That's a bold choice, and if this weren't Scully, it would probably be too much. But, going by Mulder's last line ("I think Death only looks for you once you seek its opposite"), Scully is probably just as mortal as the rest of us; after all, she's still reaching for life. But I'd rather believe she'll go on forever. —ZH

"TWO FATHERS"	SEASON 6 / EPISODE 11 WRITTEN BY CHRIS CARTER AND FRANK SPOTNITZ DIRECTED BY KIM MANNERS
"ONE SON"	SEASON 6 / EPISODE 12 WRITTEN BY CHRIS CARTER AND FRANK SPOTNITZ DIRECTED BY ROB BOWMAN

ANSWER UNCLEAR. ASK AGAIN LATER.

In which some things are maybe explained . . . ?

Heavily promoted as the two-parter that would tie up the current block of *The X-Files'* mythology and begin a new chapter, "Two Fathers" and "One Son" aired among a great deal of advance buzz and garnered kind reviews. Yet the more time that passes from its original airdate, the more this two-parter feels like a frantic attempt to keep a top spinning, even as it's clearly running out of momentum. These are episodes that almost completely sideline the protagonists in favor of the supporting characters, many of whom are people we don't really know that well. These are good showcases for the Cigarette Smoking Man, but there are not many other characters who shine here.

In some ways, the two-parter—in which the old men who hold the world's future in their hands quibble over what to do—acts as a sort of series-within-the-series about the pointless, irritating office politics of working for the Syndicate. The Syndicate always works best when it comes across as a group of men who really think they are doing the right thing, even if they are probably doomed to failure. The revelations of this two-parter almost entirely focus on the Syndicate's endgame, and while their strategies include things most fans have already figured out by this point, it's nevertheless fun to hear William B. Davis croak them out.

Sadly, the story hinges almost entirely on a character the show has failed to make interesting: Jeffrey Spender. These two episodes are pivotal moments for the *entire series,* yet the writing can't be bothered to give its main two characters much to do beyond hang out at Mulder's apartment. This overarching story at the show's heart was ostensibly about Mulder's quest for the truth about his sister, then Mulder and Scully's quest for the truth about what happened to Scully, then Mulder and Scully's gradual realization of what their country had done in the name of "security" in the post–World War II world. By now, the story has become an elaborate shell game, in which the "truth" has gotten more and more distant from our heroes.

When the Syndicate was introduced in earnest[35] the only real question about the group was what it ultimately planned to do with the various experiments it oversaw. The most obvious answer was that it was helping to prepare the world for an alien invasion, in the hopes that the lives of its members would be spared. This was too obvious a conclusion, and many fans had guessed it online before it was confirmed. However, the show never came up with any alternative long-term plan.

In the fourth and fifth seasons, the mythology began stalling in earnest, introducing characters that were meant to be important to the overall structure of the serialized story and then trying to build up each one as *the* clue to the whole conspiracy.[36] This tactic allowed the show to get away with moving sideways within the mythology instead of advancing it. This cloak-and-dagger routine certainly kept the story from getting entirely too cumbersome, but, in addition to being an obvious attempt to delay answers by asking more questions, it gradually created a new problem: The mythology became insanely cluttered.

In "Two Fathers," the series pretty much just picks Cassandra Spender (the returning Veronica Cartwright) to be the "answer" to a lot of questions and its trump card, in the hopes that we'll forget about all of the other cards it had in its hand. Cassandra is the former wife of the Cigarette Smoking Man, the collateral he sent away with the aliens in exchange for the Syndicate's cooperation (which, in turn, bought them time to develop a vaccine to the alien virus). She's also the first successful alien-human hybrid, the creation of which marks the beginning of the colonization process.[37] She's *also* a cantankerous woman whose presence seems to inspire everybody who's *not* her family. Jeffrey Spender, Cassandra's son, is embarrassed by her, and he doesn't believe in aliens in part because of his mother's insistence on her abduction experiences.

There's something thrilling about boiling the whole of the Syndicate story line down to a single family's struggle. This move gives the whole story line a quasi-Shakespearean patina, suggesting that the Spenders and the Mulders have been trapped in a never-ending cycle of misery by the knowledge they had of the alien race. As is so often the case with the deeper mythology, this idea is planted more by implication than by anything we actually get to see, but it's the closest the episodes come to making this story about people as much as it is about galactic empires. Stories like this often need to take the general and make it hyper-personal in order

---

35 Via revelations trickled out in Seasons Three and Four, starting with "The Blessing Way" (S3E1) before getting expanded to the international level in the "Tunguska" (S4E9) and "Terma" (S4E10) two-parter.

36 Characters who fall into this category include Jeremiah Smith (technically first introduced in "Talitha Cumi" [S3E24]), Michael Kritschgau ("Gethsemane" [S4E24]), and Gibson Praise ("The End" [S5E20]).

37 One thing Mulder and Scully do get to do in these episodes is hang out with Cassandra, then contemplate killing her, to stop colonization. They don't seem to ponder whether an advanced alien race bent on conquering the whole universe might be able to get DNA samples from a recently deceased corpse.

for the proceedings to feel effective, and—despite all of the cheese and hokum on display here—that idea rings loud and true in this episode.

Yet we're not nearly as invested in the Spender family dynamic as we are in the stories that more directly affect Mulder and Scully, so the show frantically tries to fill in exposition about the colonization plans *as well as* the backstory of the CSM and Cassandra's marriage of convenience that produced a son who's not sure where he fits in the food chain. Clearly, there are whole seasons of material in this story line, and one of the issues here is the attempt to condense it all into one two-parter.

But for all of its problems, "Two Fathers" is still held together by Chris Carter, frantically hanging onto various strands of the story as they jet off into space, and damned if he doesn't do his best to keep everything constantly moving forward. This is grand and entertaining (if dumb) TV. The villains are worthy of our disdain, the heroes worthy of our adoration, and the story moves along like a rocket. *The X-Files* is better when it's not quite this frenetic, but there's just enough here for you to enjoy the show—as long as you don't think too hard about all of the ways what we're being told now doesn't match up to what we thought we knew before.

There are striking moments too, in "One Son": Mulder's shocked realization that he's too late, and that he's finally lost; Cassandra's knowledge that her very existence throws the whole human race into jeopardy; the Syndicate gathering with its families, expecting to have the children and relatives they lost earlier to the aliens finally come home—only to be surrounded by a mob of alien rebels.

But not everything works. The CSM shoots Jeffrey, his son, in one of those twists that should be powerful and shocking but instead stands there, shuffling its feet and trying not to make eye contact. Agent Spender was always a drag, and his sudden moral awakening (and subsequent murder) feels like nothing more than a convenient way to justify Mulder and Scully's return to the X-Files. That he'd be shot seemingly moments after coming over to the light side isn't surprising; that his dad would pull the trigger is dramatically preferable to having him offed by some faceless thug, but it still plays as the payoff to a story arc that never moved past insinuation.

As is so often the case with later-season mythology episodes, "One Son" mixes the compelling with the absurd, and the results are . . . well, mixed. Every time you might give up on the episode completely (like, say, when the writing contrives to have Scully's supposed issues with Diana Fowley reemerge), there's some burst of forward motion, or some wild action sequence, to pull you back in. If nothing else, this two-parter thrives on its ability to keep everything moving at a breakneck pace.

It's difficult, if not impossible, to make sense of the mythology at this point. The aliens are still intent on colonizing the planet through black oil, and the alien rebels are still running around being terrifying and lighting people on fire. The idea of Earth as a pawn in a fight between two baffling and otherworldly forces—neither of whom appear to give a damn about humans—is powerful, but only works as background noise, which the series never completely grasps. By now, the conflict is so big that our heroes barely register in it at all, and yet we still spend four to six episodes a season watching Mulder and Scully hear things, put on serious expressions, and then watch Earth live to fight another day—through no real effort of theirs.

In its early seasons, *The X-Files* got a lot of power by taking the ridiculous at face value. Devil-worshipping schoolteachers, liver-eating Stretch Armstrongs, Flukemen, and, of course, alien abductions are all terrifying because of how much they sound like scary stories for the gullible and foolish. It stops being funny when there's a hand, or worse, around *your* throat. This is, in part, why the Mulder/Scully dynamic works so well. Mulder's theories always *sound* absurd, and by arguing against them, Scully gives the audience's natural disbelief a voice—which makes it all the more powerful when Mulder turns out to be right.

But this approach to the absurd is only effective if it can make the silly stories *just* plausible enough that we can't help but believe in them a little. The urban legend about the ghostly hitchhiker is frightening because driving alone at night is frightening, and hitchhikers are already mysterious, so anything could happen, right? But give that hitchhiker a backstory, make him part of a coven that's at war with a different group of hitchhiking ghosts, and have them struggling to gain dominion over the Earth via a special cemetery in Nebraska that has a tombstone made out of solid gold, and the thrill is gone. "Two Fathers"/"One Son" explains events to death without really explaining itself at all. The episodes have their moments, but the entries are undone both by the refusal to come to any serious conclusions, and by the inherent limitations of the mythology's approach to storytelling. It spends all its time describing the trees without ever paying attention to the forest. —ZH and TVDW

SEASON 6 / EPISODE 13
WRITTEN BY DAVID AMANN | "AGUA MALA"
DIRECTED BY ROB BOWMAN

OCTOPUS'S GARDEN

In which there's an octopus monster that's actually living water.

The worst thing about "Agua Mala" is that it comes so very, very close to working that it's frustrating to see just how little it does.

The idea of a monster killing people in an enclosed space—in this case, an apartment building during a hurricane—isn't bad. It's basically just a variation on Season One's "Ice" (S1E8)—a premise the show really should have returned to more often because it almost always paid off.

Unfortunately, this episode isn't content to simply tell the story of Mulder and Scully battling a weird tentacle monster in an apartment building isolated by a hurricane. No, the episode lurches all over the place, going out of its way to incorporate several elements that don't really belong. One is former FBI Agent Arthur Dales, the first X-Files agent from last season's "Travelers" (S5E15). "Agua Mala" finds him living in Florida, from where he calls Mulder down to save the day. Dales is fun but feels completely tangential to the proceedings. He turns up at the start to make fun of Scully, pops up randomly in the middle when he's listening in on a radio, then comes back at the end to tell Mulder and Scully about how the world is full of weirdness.[38] It's a glorified cameo, and it's a broad, hammy one at that. He basically stands on his porch and yells at the neighborhood kids about the good old days.

The episode also takes a long while to isolate Mulder and Scully in that apartment building, and once it does, it doesn't have nearly enough running time left to establish the people who live there, so they're instead broad stereotypes.[39] The script works to make these people into more than monster chow, and Gillian Anderson does her level best to act like the characters are the sorts of fascinating people Scully might enjoy chatting with on other occasions. But the episode is simply unable to do much of anything with these characters when it counts most. There are too many of them and too little time to flesh them out. So inevitably, we wait for them to start dropping like flies.

If the script had eliminated Dales entirely and gotten Mulder and Scully to the condominiums right away, that might have streamlined things enough to give time to fill out the secondary characters beyond the broad strokes stereotypes. Hell, if Dales had just been living at the complex, that would have improved the episode immensely and made better use of Darren McGavin. It's rare to have an episode in which the solutions to the flaws are as obvious as they are here: Just condense the events!

Similarly, the monster is far too complicated for its own good. Amann's original idea of a sea monster that washed up on land might have felt stupid if he had gone the usual sea serpent route, but what he came up with instead is flat-out bizarre. The idea of "living water" is hard to wrap one's head around, and the mechanics of how it works are hand-waved away by Mulder saying a few things about how there are weird and creepy things at the bottom of the ocean. Water somehow forming into a solid mass with tentacles makes less and less sense the more you think about it. How would this even happen? And why, exactly, would freshwater be the thing that would defeat it?

---

38 He also offers them some water, which could have been a funny closing moment were it part of a better episode.

39 Including a stereotypical Latino couple—because we haven't had an uncomfortable, racially charged episode in a while.

The effects for the monster tarnish the episode further. The show has historically used its budgetary restrictions to its advantage when making low-budget monsters, but here, it can only get so much mileage out of suggesting tentacles through writhing shadows and sudden bursts of movement. When we get a sustained look at the monster, it's laughable. Pull all of these lackluster elements together, and you get the rare *X-Files* episode where nothing—story, characters, or technical aspects—works.[40] —TVDW

SEASON 6 / EPISODE 14
WRITTEN BY VINCE GILLIGAN AND JOHN SHIBAN | **"MONDAY"**
DIRECTED BY KIM MANNERS

TIME AND TIME AGAIN

In which it's just another Manic Monday. And another. And another.

By the time "Monday" starts, it's almost over. A bank robbery has gone horribly wrong. Mulder has been shot, and Scully is holding him while he bleeds to death. The bank robber (Darren E. Burrows, who here looks like Shaggy crossed with Charles Manson) is twitchy and on edge. No matter what Scully says to get him to calm down, it doesn't matter. The SWAT team is coming in through the front doors—the robber sees them—and he's got a bomb. *KABOOM*! Then it cuts to the opening credits.

And so we discover that this is a time loop episode in which one morning will get replayed over and over again until someone gets it right. It's a storytelling frame movies and other shows have used before,[41] but "Monday" is not a gimmick for the gimmick's sake. Writers Vince Gilligan and John Shiban here use the repeating hours to play around with grand ideas about character, destiny, and free will. Their script flatters our intelligence, showing its cards slowly and depending on its audience to work out the story without much hand-holding. This is a puzzle with a soul, and one so entertaining that it's easy to forget how dark the central message is: Some people are doomed no matter how hard they try, and the best they can hope for is the chance to make sure they can do some good on the way out.

---

40 Here's an interesting sidebar: In her 2018 memoir *Just the Funny Parts*, longtime writer Nell Scovell (perhaps best known as the creator of the *Sabrina the Teenage Witch* TV series) talks about a prospective *X-Files* episode she almost sold during Season Five, which was to be about a diverse apartment complex that is driven to rage by a strange alien scent carried through the air vents. It's not *exactly* like "Agua Mala," but it's close enough that I note it here for curiosity's sake.

41 Some examples include the Bill Murray comedy *Groundhog Day*, the *Star Trek: The Next Generation* episode "Cause and Effect," and the *Twilight Zone* episode "Shadow Play."

Pam (Carrie Hamilton), the only person aware of the time loop at the start of the episode, is having a rough time. Stories like this consist of half-nightmare, half-perfectionist fantasy, but Pam doesn't get the chance to enjoy the second half. She doesn't have the freedom necessary to make the most of her repeating time. Her loop lasts six hours at most, and from the little we know about her, she doesn't have the money to take advantage of the lack of consequences the situation affords. All she really wants to do is stop the bomb from going off. Which, of course, is the one thing she *can't* do.

There's also the fact that each iteration of the loop is slightly different than the one before. Every Monday has certain basic requirements for Pam: Her boyfriend has a bomb, he attempts to rob the bank, the FBI agents (Mulder and Scully) intercede, and it all ends in an earth-shattering *KABOOM*. Aside from those elements, nothing is certain. This clever, cruel structural trick makes it impossible for Pam (or the audience) to predict events with enough specificity to change them. She knows it'll all end badly, but she can't do any of that thrilling, video game–esque memorization to alter things that fictional recurrence generally allows.

The fact that the episode also picks up long after the time looping first started[42] creates a challenge for the actress playing Pam, as she's robbed of getting to play much of a range of emotion beyond pure, elemental despair. For us, this is all new; for her, it's a personal hell. Hamilton does a great job of conveying misery and frustration and a bone-deep sadness, enough to make the reality and the scope of the situation clear very early on. The script spends more time with her than the show usually gives to its victims and supernatural devices, and this time is critical to making sure this episode amounts to more than just a clever thought exercise. There's significant tragedy *and* redemption here, and Hamilton makes sure both elements register.

For all the sadness implicit in the recursive plot, this is also a surprisingly fun hour, as Gilligan and Shiban make the most of the chance to take multiple approaches to the same settings. As long as certain beats occur in every iteration, they can riff on them with new angles and new jokes without having to worry about repeating themselves. While the main tension of the episode is concerned with how the time loop will be resolved, smaller moments of suspense come throughout in seeing just how things might fall apart in each successive run-through.

While Pam is the center of the loop, this is a Mulder episode. He's the one who suffers through the horrors of the whizzing waterbed,[43] and it is Mulder's need to deposit his paycheck that sends him—and Scully—to the bank. Mulder is the only one aside from Pam who realizes something strange is going on, although he doesn't

S6 E14

---

42 Judging by what Pam tells Mulder near the end of the episode, this is only the tail end of a long run of agonizing repeats.

43 A great callback to "Dreamland" (S6E4) and "Dreamland II" (S6E5).

have Pam's level of awareness. It's never explained how he's able to slowly piece together the problem over the many versions we see in the episode, but then, it's never explained why any of this is happening. The closest we get to a reason is that somehow, something went wrong along the way, and now the day keeps skipping until Pam can get it right.

That works on a meta-level—Mulder and Scully die in the original explosion, but because they're the protagonists of an ongoing TV show, they *can't* die. This fact also makes it even more tragic that Pam's death is what ultimately breaks the cycle. She doesn't have the same protection of primacy. At one point, Scully and Mulder debate the nature of free will and destiny, and while Mulder believes that everything is blind chaos, Scully (as befits her religious upbringing) believes there's more sense involved: "I think that it's our character that defines our fate," she explains.[44] Pam is doomed because of who she is. Her end, like the end of every monster and victim on the show, was always certain. The rest was just details. —ZH

SEASON 6 / EPISODE 15
WRITTEN BY DANIEL ARKIN
DIRECTED BY MICHAEL WATKINS | "ARCADIA"

MONSTERS, TOO, ARE IN PARADISE
In which Mulder and Scully are married! Squeeeeeeee!

"Arcadia" is a fan-favorite episode that might be the most overrated episode of the series. Yes, it's a solid example of the show's mid-period form, when it would give in to its comedic tendencies as often as it would its horror or dramatic impulses. It starts out well and has some strong moments. But the episode's monster is weak, at once too obvious a symbol for suburban rot and not particularly compelling on a visual level, and it's easy to sense that the production team wasn't sure what to do with the idea of sentient garbage held together into a human form by an old man's thought. That's to say nothing of the overly broad suburban satire.

It's easy to see why this episode is so beloved, though. It allows us to see what it would be like if Mulder and Scully were a happily married couple and still working on the X-Files, which is a fun concept for an episode. The writer has fun with it, Gillian Anderson and David Duchovny have fun with it, and it's easy to sense the fans having fun with it too, even as it plays out. The flirtatious marital banter between the two agents, undercover as couple Rob and Laura Petrie, is only present in a handful of scenes, but it's always light and enjoyable. It's fan service, but it's

---

44 An idea Vince Gilligan would return to in his later work!

the good kind of fan service, where everybody involved knows just how far they can push things.

"Arcadia" exists as a very real argument that the show might have been improved if the writers had let Mulder and Scully just have sex already somewhere in Season Three or Four, if only to clear the air of their sexual tension. David Duchovny and Gillian Anderson have an undeniable chemistry, and while the conventional wisdom holds that getting two characters together will ruin a show irreparably, *The X-Files'* episodic structure was strong enough to have weathered such a thing, as long as the show just kept the pairing on the down-low and in the background. It could have been a case of the show having its cake and eating it too.

At the same time, Chris Carter's initial idea for the characters as two people in a sort of chaste, courtly romance probably fits the show better on the whole. Mulder's quest is straight out of an epic poem anyway, what with all its unlikely twists and turns, its constant slew of archetypes for him to fight and befriend, and its underlying pure motivations and goals. Having him be accompanied by a woman with whom he shares a clear affection but no real sexual activity fits directly into that dynamic. Plenty of people in life will share some sort of spark with you, but that spark doesn't always have to be sexual. Duchovny and Anderson have great sexual chemistry, yes, but they also have great friendship chemistry, the latter of which is consistently underrated.

"Arcadia" tries to have the best of both worlds. The fake marriage stuff allows the show to tease the fans who are desperate to see the two get together. But our heroes also put their heads together to puzzle through a seemingly unsolvable mystery. This is best evidenced in a moment in which Mulder and Scully are pretending to be lovey-dovey for the neighbors as they move in, then immediately snap into detective mode the moment the neighbors leave. At this point in the show, sex would be a distraction for these two, and they already have every other form of intimacy. The work is all that matters.

The mystery is the problem. Right away, it's obvious that the community members are doing some sort of weird thing to make sure they get rid of those who don't conform to the specifications in the community rule book, but when the reveal is made that the monster is a *tulpa,* a Tibetan thought-form held together by the mental abilities of community leader Gene Gogolak (Peter White), and that it's made out of garbage, it makes for yet another half-baked monster in a season full of them.[45] The horror is as silly as the fake marriage stuff, but the episode depicts it as terrifying.

What's really lame here is the satire on planned communities.[46] The idea of someone violating the rules and having something comically over-the-top and awful

S6 E15

---

45 Though the idea that the suburban community has some of the same social dynamics as a tribal society (implied by the documentary Big Mike is shown watching at home) is compelling, even as the episode does too little with it.

46 Arcadia Falls is built atop a landfill. Get it?!

happen to them was already played out in early 1999, and the episode doesn't do much with it otherwise. There are clever ideas here, particularly the idea of the owner of a Pier 1 Imports–style chain coming into possession of mystic knowledge during his travels abroad, but much of the humor in this section is meant to stem from Mulder failing to fit in among the Arcadia Falls residents. This could have worked with some sharper comedy, if it had followed more thoroughly from the notion of Mulder putting a pink flamingo in his front lawn and cockily intoning, "Bring it on!" Instead, we get Mulder kicking over a mailbox and playing basketball at night. It's too tame to really work.

What's more is that Mulder and Scully are weirdly pointless for an episode that features them so much. Most of their action throughout the hour has little to do with solving the mystery and everything to do with playing at being married. When the monster is defeated, it's because it killed its own creator and died when his thoughts ceased to give it life, at which point, it collapses into a heap of trash all over Mulder's shoes. "Arcadia" isn't bad, but it's mostly a pleasant diversion. Nothing more. —TVDW

SEASON 6 / EPISODE 16
WRITTEN BY JEFFREY BELL | "ALPHA"
DIRECTED BY PETER MARKLE

BAD DOG

In which someone other than Mulder wants to believe.

This episode feels like a throwback, in that its structure hearkens to the show's early years: Mulder and Scully are tracking the inexplicable in between standard stalk-and-kill scenes with doomed guest stars. Unfortunately, there's a reason the series has moved away from this approach. By now, it's less like a story than a checklist of death. Here's the cold-open kill, here's the first-act kill, and so on. *The X-Files* has spent so much time thinking outside the box since its early seasons that going back inside feels reductive and disappointing.

The rudimentary nature of this episode's structure wouldn't matter so much if the story were better. There's a twerpy villain (Andrew J. Robinson) who's a sort-of werewolf, but we never get to know him beyond knowing that he's the twerpy villain. There's also Karin Berquist (Melinda Culea), a dog-loving shut-in who calls Mulder in on the case after meeting him on the Internet. Her crush on Mulder makes Scully suspicious and jealous of her intentions, but it's never a dynamic that makes much sense; the idea that a new character with no history with Mulder apart from some online interaction would make Scully feel threatened really just seems like something the writer cooked up to add drama. For an episode with a relatively straightforward premise, "Alpha" is often muddled, with a script that dictates twists instead of developing them organically.

This is made all the more frustrating by the parts of this episode that work quite well. Culea gives a low-key, convincingly uncomfortable performance as a woman so wounded she can barely stand to be around other human beings. Her conversations with Mulder and Scully show glimpses of a much more interesting story. Karin giving her life to kill the doomed doctor is treated like the conclusion of some awful tragedy—but while the scene is well-handled, there's nothing in the rest of the episode to really justify that sense of sacrifice. Robinson is a fine actor, but he isn't given much to do beyond standing around and looking suspicious. There are pieces of compelling drama in here, but none of them fit together the way they should.

Still, the final scene manages to rouse some real feeling. The discovery that Karin mailed Mulder a gift before she died—a copy of the I WANT TO BELIEVE poster that has so long been his character's hallmark but has been missing from the X-Files office since it went up in flames in last season's finale—serves to end the hour on a bittersweet note. It's too bad everything that comes before it is such a mess. —ZH

| **"TREVOR"** | SEASON 6 / EPISODE 17
WRITTEN BY JIM GUTTRIDGE AND KEN HAWRYLIW
DIRECTED BY ROB BOWMAN |

WALKING THROUGH WALLS

In which he wants what's his.

"Trevor" has a strong idea: a killer who can walk through walls. It's got an emotional hook. It's got a great performance at its center from John Diehl.

Yet the script from first-timers Jim Guttridge and Ken Hawryliw makes the same mistake lots of first-time *X-Files* writers' scripts do: It focuses so much on a not particularly original "monster" that it leaves no room for Mulder and Scully. This approach requires getting the audience to sympathize with a character to whom we have no attachment. It fails often, and it's highly subject to the ability of the actors cast in these parts. Diehl tries his level best, but he can't fight off the fact that by the end of this episode, there's a heavy "Who cares?" factor.

This problem afflicts plenty of the Monster of the Week episodes in the period after the show left Vancouver to shoot in Los Angeles. To be sure, there are some *great* MOTW episodes in the remainder of the original run, but it was clear that the writers often struggled to come up with new variations on the same forms. When struck with writer's block, the show would often go for broke on a single image—in "Trevor," it's the wall that breaks out roughly into the shape of a man—and then hope that was enough to carry the day. These are episodes assembled in compliance with the instructions that came in the box.

Diehl plays a man named "Pinker" Rawls, a hardened convict who is presumed deceased after a tornado destroys the solitary confinement box he's been placed in. In the immediate aftermath of the storm, the prison's warden is found inexplicably dead, split in half, with both halves burned off, as if he were set on fire or struck by lightning.[47] Then more people with connections to Pinker turn up dead, scorched to ash, sometimes with faces burnt off. Now made from electricity, Pinker works as an effective boogeyman in the episode's first half.

Here's where knowing too much about an episode—even its title—can hurt you. This episode is called "Trevor," and by the halfway point, there haven't been any characters named Trevor. But the episode has checked in with an old girlfriend of Pinker who has turned her life around, and Pinker is clearly motivated by something more than money. Who could Trevor be? Perhaps a son, a son who's going to get a limited amount of screen time to try to make us care about whether he and Pinker can bond? Yep, you guessed it! By the time Trevor's in the middle of the story, things have flown off the rails, as the episode scrambles to make Pinker an object of sympathy, not terror.

When something like this is done well, there's nothing quite like it. An episode of TV getting us to reconsider something we've held to be true about a character is wonderful indeed. But the episodes that do this often feature characters we've gotten to know over time[48]—or else it steadily deepens a newly introduced character as the episode goes on, such that what at first seems simply scary ends up being much more complex. "Trevor" mostly tries to get us to sympathize with Pinker by insisting that he's sympathetic, and even though Diehl gives it his all, he can't overcome the sheer predictability of the story, the laziness of the character development, or the way the story falls apart once Trevor is introduced to it.

Southern Gothic is a genre *The X-Files* turned to often, but it almost always struggled to pull it off for reasons that are unclear.[49] Perhaps the genre itself invites trafficking in broad stereotypes, of the sort that require a Flannery O'Connor or William Faulkner to make believable. There's a haunting, eerie core to "Trevor," and the rules that govern Pinker's powers are ingenious, if arbitrary. (Why, for instance, is glass[50] the only thing that can stop him? Wouldn't wood also have same effect on him?) There are several good ideas here, but they never cohere, and even Mulder and Scully seem bored. —TVDW

S6 E17

---

47 It's enough to make the usually sensible Scully suggest spontaneous human combustion.

48 Think of when we learned Scully was a devout Catholic, which was discussed early in the series but finally delved into in "Revelations" (S3E11).

49 The best examples are either comedic—like "Humbug" (S2E20)—or not set in the true South, like "Home" (S4E2), or have Southern Gothic elements which are largely tangential—like "Detour" (S5E4).

50 That said, the moment where Scully locks herself in a phone booth to avoid Pinker and he starts bashing the glass with a rock is a highlight.

DEATHLY PROSE

In which Scully meets a heartless writer.

"Milagro" is a self-serious, intermittently insulting chunk of television. John Hawkes's[51] performance as Phillip Padgett and the absolute batshit weirdness keep this from being the write-off it probably deserves to be. But it's still not very good—because it's pompous, and because it treats Scully with a sort of ill-defined contempt and exhausting male gaze that forces the viewer to ask some really uncomfortable questions about just what the writers think of her. Admittedly, Carter didn't come up with the story. It's bad enough that Scully is once again relegated to victim status; even worse, the episode makes her a puppet of Hawkes's creepy infatuation before he gives up upon realizing she's already in love with Mulder.

None of this makes much sense. Things pick up a bit in the final act, when an actual plot that's more than just "creepy guy is creepy" emerges, but so much of this episode rests on the supposed poetry of the script that it's hard to take any of it seriously. And we're clearly supposed to take it *very* seriously. Any fan of *The X-Files* is willing to put up with baroque prose, but there are scenes in this hour that are severely cringe-inducing, most notably a pair of ill-advised voice-overs in which Padgett narrates a third-person view of Scully's inner monologue. It's full of weird insinuations about her being weak and womanly, which somehow leads to Scully's initial dislike of Padgett being translated into burgeoning attraction.

It's like watching someone's fan-fiction getting brought to life, played with such agonized seriousness that it's perilously close to camp. There are all sorts of interesting things you could say about a man who makes up a story to woo a stranger, but this episode is fixated on the sort of vague philosophizing that always makes Carter's monologues so goofy. At least in a mythology episode there are aliens and conspiracies and flying saucers. No such luck here.

The worst is how Scully is reduced to a damsel in distress waiting to find out which handsome man will rescue her. There is some precedent for Scully being attracted to potentially dangerous or unstable men,[52] but that attraction shouldn't rob her of her identity. In "Milagro," her motives are continually being defined by others, and her lack of agency throughout the hour undercuts any commentary. She's just not present, to the point where I honestly don't know if Padgett's writing

---

51 Known for his work in *Deadwood*, *Winter's Bone*, and *Martha Marcy May Marlene*, among others.
52 See "Never Again" (S4E13).

actually influenced her, or if she was legitimately attracted to him. Ambiguity is fun, but not when it's this half-assed.

Yet in spite of all of this, the episode's commitment to its own skewed vision makes it oddly compelling. Hawkes is excellent, finding the center in a character whose obvious symbolism threatens to send him floating off into the margins. He's interesting and nearly likable even when the script isn't. There's at least one good twist here, and, as ever, Kim Manners's direction gives the whole thing a veneer of credibility even at its most distasteful. The result is something hypnotic, intermittently captivating, and frequently horrid, with all the profundity of a late-night jam session between two stoned (male, single) philosophy majors. But it's just so disorienting that I can't help but marvel that it exists. —ZH

SEASON 6 / EPISODE 19
WRITTEN AND DIRECTED BY DAVID DUCHOVNY | **"THE UNNATURAL"**

NO CRYING IN ALIEN BASEBALL

In which that which fascinates us is by definition true.

"The Unnatural" shouldn't work whatsoever, but it gets by on a sense of nostalgia and an almost aching sincerity. It's a reminder that at the height of its powers, *The X-Files* used the very elasticity of its premise to become all manner of things. Can you think of a series on the air today that would devote nearly an entire episode to a 1940s-set flashback about black baseball players of the era, interwoven with a story about aliens in a way that feels mostly elegant? In addition, neither of the show's regulars would appear in the flashback, relegated instead to the story's sidelines. It's a big gambit.

Let's get this out of the way first. "The Unnatural" is a little—OK, a *lot*—corny. The script, by David Duchovny, tries too hard, particularly when he has the characters in the 1940s talk in a folksy patois that's meant to denote they have great wisdom or what have you. The early banter between Mulder and Scully is clumsy, and when we meet Arthur Dales (M. Emmet Walsh),[53] he spends all of his time talking like an old man in a movie. Also, apparently, all great baseball players were actually aliens, which is a ridiculous idea on its face, though at least the episode doesn't take Dales too seriously on this one.

---

53 A different Arthur Dales than the one we already know. The original Arthur Dales, Darren McGavin, suffered a stroke and could not reprise his role. This led to the addition of a quirky anecdote about them being brothers to explain why both Arthur Dales-es, clearly two different men, share the same name (though it doesn't bother to explain why the same actor played both the young Dales ["Travelers" (S5E15)] and the other Dales featured in flashbacks in this episode).

However, none of the above is the episode's biggest problem. For that, look to how "The Unnatural" leans *heavily* on the magical-black-man trope, in which a black person with special powers arrives to show white characters what they have to live for. Baseball player Josh Exley (Jesse L. Martin) is such a good player that his home runs seem to travel for miles. He's impossibly caring and warmhearted and fun-loving. He's the best friend a guy could ever have, able to overcome both a racial and species barrier through his simple, loving ways.

And, oh yeah, he's *literally magical,* in that he's an alien who loves baseball and can shape-shift. He apparently becomes an actual human being through sheer force of will. Duchovny's script does some interesting things with the idea of how the gray aliens might feel like outsiders in our society, but it's not hard to feel just a touch uncomfortable with the whole endeavor.

And yet . . . "The Unnatural" somehow *works.* It's the fact that the episode turns mournful in its last quarter that finally saves it. The stuff about the Cactus League baseball teams is entertaining enough, but it also feels as if it's been transported in from another series entirely.[54] Once the episode reaches its emotional core, however, and once Exley and young Dales (Fredric Lane) are becoming friends and Exley is sharing with Dales the secrets of his species, it becomes remarkably warm. *The X-Files* was such a chilly show that it's easy to forget that it could do something sweet and lovely and moving, and "The Unnatural" ultimately works because it embraces this side of the show's profile.

As Exley, Martin is terrific. The script asks him to play more of a saint than a person, but with his wide grin and "aw, shucks" demeanor, Martin finds the dignity in Exley that Duchovny's script can't always locate.[55] Lane is a bit stiff as the young Dales here, but the scenes in which Exley and Dales can finally be honest with each other show off Martin and Lane's easygoing chemistry. So many episodes this season struggle to make the audience care about characters we've just met. "The Unnatural" is not among them.

Duchovny has a keen visual sense. He sometimes overplays his hand—as in a slow pan to a television that is showing what will be the next scene in black and white—but he mostly lets this all play out like a weird American folk tale, with the images of Exley's alien reflection, or those baseballs Mulder and Scully hit at episode's end turning into winking stars, making for some lovely little motifs that he doesn't call too much attention to. He even finds the needed weight in the image of the Ku Klux Klan galloping toward a baseball field without losing the whimsy of the whole "aliens playing baseball" thing. It's a tricky balancing act, and even if the script sometimes veers too far into cornpone humor, Duchovny's direction always saves it.

---

54 It even messes up some of the particulars of the mythology.

55 The scene in which Exley reveals his true self to Dales works only because of Martin's voice acting. That's impressive.

"The Unnatural" eventually just goes whole hog, but it's better for it. It has a choir performing a spiritual, Exley sacrificing himself, and anything it can think of that might provoke an emotional reaction. It's shameless, but it works, particularly since Duchovny knows exactly when to puncture the weightiness with a joke. He also knows exactly how to leave the episode, with Mulder and Scully at the ballpark, hitting baseballs into the night. It may have nothing to do with anything, but it still connects them to a noble man the episode has just improbably made us care about.

Most of all, "The Unnatural" works because it just feels so utterly itself. It's hard to think of another X-Files episode like this one. It's hard to think of another episode of television like this one, period. That it somehow draws us in to its improbable story, well, that's the icing on the cake. —TVDW

SEASON 6 / EPISODE 20
WRITTEN BY VINCE GILLIGAN AND JOHN SHIBAN
DIRECTED BY BRYAN SPICER

"THREE OF A KIND"

SCULLY GETS THE GIGGLES

In which the Lone Gunmen save the day.

This is the second part of a story that didn't really need one, a follow-up to "Unusual Suspects" (S5E3) that changes that episode's unsettling conclusion into something more fuzzy and life-affirming. Filmed in order to work around David Duchovny's absence—the actor was busy prepping for "The Unnatural" (S6E19)—the hour undermines its predecessor's strongest choices, bringing back Susanne and even giving the Lone Gunmen a totally unexpected win. Yet it looks great, and the whole production has a laid-back, "let's just hang out and have some fun" vibe that makes it very easy to watch. There are valid complaints to make, but it's hard not to enjoy the winning cheeriness of it all.

The high point is Gillian Anderson's turn as "Agent Scully Golightly." After a series of convoluted events, the Gunmen call Scully for help, and after doing yet another autopsy, she gets drugged by a government operative. Scully is such a reliably sober presence that the sight of her holding court to a room full of half-drunk, lovestruck businessmen is hilarious even before she starts gurgling about cigarettes and lighters and slapping Michael McKean (returning here as Morris Fletcher from "Dreamland" [S6E4/5]) on the ass. Anderson plays it big enough for the cheap seats, and it is glorious.

The episode is also helped by the fact that it's impossible not to like Byers, Frohike, and Langly. "Three of a Kind" does a decent job keeping up the suspense, offering up some clever fake outs before the end. It's probably too convenient that the super-evil government-assassin guy is taken down this easily, but it plays into the wish fulfillment that makes this story so charming in spite of its flaws. Usually the nerds don't get to be the main characters, not unless they look like Mulder, and it's hugely entertaining to watch someone like Byers get to pretend he's a badass. There are definite diminishing returns, but this episode is hard to hate.

Besides, the cold open and the conclusion have a certain resonance, a sense of just what it might feel like to be someone like Byers—someone who really did believe America was pure and just and perfect, and then lost his faith. Mulder has his quest, and Scully has science and God, but characters like Byers and Langly and Frohike are just little people stuck outside the vast machinery of a world much darker and more insidious than they ever thought possible. However clumsily, this episode shows us what it's like to be one of the pawns; perpetually stranded, nearly defenseless, but hoping, with a little luck, to become something more. —ZH

"FIELD TRIP"	SEASON 6 / EPISODE 21 WRITTEN BY VINCE GILLIGAN AND JOHN SHIBAN, FROM A STORY BY FRANK SPOTNITZ DIRECTED BY KIM MANNERS

A FUNGUS AMONG US

In which all that we see or seem is but a dream within a dream.

Is there any twist more unsatisfying than "It was all a dream"? Maybe that's a twist that can work once or twice when you're a little kid, but once you get past those first couple of uses, it starts to feel like a cheat. If the storyteller isn't going to take their story seriously, then why should you?

"Field Trip" is one of the best episodes of *The X-Files*' sixth season, but it's an episode that sets such an impossibly high bar for itself that it's surprising the show was able to cross it. Much of the sixth season has been about the relationship between what's real and what's just in our heads, and this is the ultimate examination of that, as our two protagonists are trapped inside of an active hallucination, one that's working as hard as it can to keep them from moving, so that they might be digested by a giant fungus.

On one level, the episode plays mind games with viewers—the twist at the very end when Mulder realizes that he and Scully *haven't* escaped the fungus is beautifully executed. But if it was just that twisty, complicated bit of business, it wouldn't have the resonance it does. No, what makes "Field Trip" work is that it's as much an examination of the Mulder and Scully relationship—and the way they complete each other in a nearly mystical way—as any episode in the show's run. This is an episode explicitly *about* the show and its central characters, in a season occasionally lacking in that.

The best choice the script makes is to isolate Mulder and Scully from each other, the better to ask just what each would most want, then giving it to them. That's fairly easy for Mulder: He wants proof that the aliens are real. It's more difficult for Scully, but the episode zeroes in on something tragic about her: She just wants to be right.

This whole time she's been on the X-Files, Mulder's crazy theories have almost always proven to be true, while she's been forced to ride along and realize the world is weirder than she gave it credit for. Scully is trapped not just by her own rational brain or by having to watch her partner's theories proved correct. She's trapped *by her own show,* forced to play a certain part by the series she stars in. And when the hallucination is giving her what she wants, it doesn't just involve people buying one of her theories; instead, it involves Mulder's death.

This is a marvelously complicated bit of business. By this point, we've figured out that some strange goopy thing is making Mulder and Scully see things that aren't there, just like the young couple did in the opening scene. The fact that Mulder's skeletonized remains turn up just clinches this fact: The show isn't going to kill off its male lead so unceremoniously. But this is what's smart about "Field Trip." It gets the "it was all a dream" winking out of the way early on, so that we might get down to the knottier business of how dreams can reflect our worst fears and greatest hopes. For anybody to take Scully seriously, Mulder must die, because he's always been what's standing in the way of her theories. Yet his death, understandably, all but guts her, and the way that the coroner, then Skinner, then the Lone Gunmen parrot her theory about ritualistic murder right back to her becomes terrifying.

But roughly the same thing happens in Mulder's hallucination, when he brings Scully over to his place to meet the presumed dead couple and the little Gray that he abducted and kept in the spare room. These hallucinations reveal, on some level, that both Mulder and Scully crave being proved *right.* But where Scully's hallucination reveals that to be proved right would involve such a change to her status quo that she doesn't want to contemplate it, Mulder's hallucination reveals that, on some level, he needs the skepticism, needs people to think he's crazy. When Scully says that, yeah, he's sure proved the existence of aliens all right, he seems a little hurt. He enjoys always being right, sure, but he almost seems offended at the idea that Scully would give up on the fight. He needs the push back. So does the show.

"Field Trip" is also about a series approaching the end of its sixth season and looking for new stories to tell. Season Six was filled with these sorts of hallucinations and dream sequences, and I suspect that's because this far into the show's run, there was simply no way to keep playing out the string of these weird mysteries without understanding, on some level, that it was all bullshit.[56] There's no way that Scully would keep questioning Mulder this long once she realized he was always right. There's no way Mulder would always be right. These things only happen because the story of the show requires them to.

In a lot of ways, Season Six is an artful dodge of many of these questions. Through comedy and twists and structural experimentation, *The X-Files* spent much of this season both questioning why it was still going and why we kept watching it. "Field Trip" is the ultimate expression of both of those questions.

Yet it answers those questions perfectly with its final shot. Mulder and Scully, pulled from the ground before getting eaten by the fungus, lie in the back of the ambulance, exhausted, but alive, almost a tacit acknowledgement by the show that these people shouldn't keep getting so lucky, yet they do. He reaches out for her hand, and she finds it, and in that connection, the show is supported. The hallucination hypothesis is one Scully arrives at, but it's one Mulder bolsters. These mysteries can only be solved if *both* of these people are working to solve them. In its sixth season, *The X-Files* wandered away from its own increasingly constrictive formula, heading out into the hinterlands in search of new pulp myths to exploit. The thrill of "Field Trip" is that there are still blank spots to write "Here be monsters," as surely as there are still these two people to head into caves and fight them together. —TVDW

| "BIOGENESIS" | SEASON 6 / EPISODE 22
WRITTEN BY CHRIS CARTER AND FRANK SPOTNITZ
DIRECTED BY ROB BOWMAN |

WHO MADE WHO?

In which Scully has to go back to where it all began.

The theory that humanity's consciousness is a gift from an alien race doesn't make much sense in the real world. It's an unnecessary complication in a universe that already has enough mysteries, existing solely to satisfy that itch in our brains that usually only gets scratched by contemplating the grassy knoll.

But as a starting point for science fiction, it's not the worst concept for *The X-Files* to take on. By now, the mythology has gotten so convoluted that I'm honestly not sure if the black oil story line is supposed to be resolved, or if this just yet another iteration on the original idea. "Biogenesis" is a stab at a new beginning.

---

56 Mulder firing a gun into Skinner's chest is another thing that would really only happen on a show that had run this long, in which dream sequences might give the series a chance to do all of the things it had always wanted to try but had been kept from by the boundaries of reality.

It's an exciting episode, even if most of it is just Mulder and Scully wandering into places where things have happened, asking questions, and then not being around when people get killed.

Unfortunately, it's hard to shake the suspicion that this episode is going to include a lot of cool hints that never go anywhere. It's difficult for any show to introduce a major story line at the tail end of its sixth season; the challenge of finding a new plot that's both fitting to the series and original enough to not just be old ideas in different clothes is immense. And that's not even getting into this particular show's fitful history with promising more than it can deliver. Each new mythology development requires an investment of faith on the part of the audience—the belief that a mystery will have some sort of satisfactory resolution in the future. But given the way the show's overarching stories have played out this season, it's harder to make the leap of faith that "Biogenesis" requires.

As for what we're leaping for with this latest installment: we've got a mysterious artifact, Mulder's fugue states, and a return of the dreaded Mulder/Scully/Fowler triangle. We also get the return of Albert Hosteen (Floyd "Red Crow" Westerman), last seen all the way back in the third season episode (and mythology high point) "Paper Clip" (S3E2). Hosteen's return at least offers a sense of continuity, and a crucial impression that the episode is as much about uncovering information already inherent in the show's world as it is about introducing new ideas. While there's an implicit risk in that gamble—pretending major events were always part of the plan even when they weren't can make for some confusing, tangled plotting—the nod to the past helps to keep this entry from feeling entirely disconnected from what's come before.

Still, too much of the character drama is overheated and forced, and while there are creepy scenes, the actual plot behind them risks moving away from the tenuous science fiction the show has generally stuck to and into something more akin to magic.[57] We're asked to take too much at face value too quickly, without any of the slow build that made earlier mythology episodes so effective. As a result, the seams show too obviously, robbing events of their dramatic impact.

So what does this episode have going for it? More immediately, sidelining Mulder with paper-rubbing-inspired headaches puts Scully in the more active role for most of the hour, a comparative rarity for mythology episodes (which are more often driven by Mulder's compulsions) and a welcome opportunity to give the character more agency in ongoing story lines. Finding a way to make the mythology less about the struggles of the Mulders and the Spenders and more about the history of the entire human race is ambitious, to say the least. The craziness makes for a good cliffhanger. Most of "Biogenesis" is just building up to the final couple of scenes,

---

57 A move reminiscent of Mulder's "chosen one" status from back when Hosteen was introduced, a plot thread that would, unfortunately, be better off left behind.

although, as of yet, there's no clear indication of what the bigger picture is, or why anyone would want to kill to keep all of this secret. Maybe that's the real problem. Our heroes are just wandering through backstory, taking notes on events that keep happening to someone else.

I appreciate the episode for its willingness to take huge risks, and there's a sense that the show is trying to redefine the stakes at its core. We've gone from "aliens are working to colonize the planet" to "aliens are responsible for our existence," and that's a pretty big deal. But it's not enough. The end of the hour has Scully discovering an alien ship resting on the shore, a huge reveal that is somewhat undercut by strange editing (parts of the beach don't match up between shots). It's ambitious, to be sure, but it doesn't always make sense, which could be said for the mythology as a whole as the series heads into its seventh season. —ZH

"THE SIXTH EXTINCTION"	SEASON 7 / EPISODE 1 WRITTEN BY CHRIS CARTER DIRECTED BY KIM MANNERS
"THE SIXTH EXTINCTION II: AMOR FATI"	SEASON 7 / EPISODE 2 WRITTEN BY DAVID DUCHOVNY AND CHRIS CARTER DIRECTED BY MICHAEL WATKINS

THE END IN THE BEGINNING

In which Mulder faces temptation.

The "Sixth Extinction" two-parter is a real test of a viewer's *X-Files* fandom. It indulges many of the series' most lambasted tendencies, wanders down tangents that no longer really matter, and gorges itself on awful, awful dialogue and voice-over. It's an elaborate homage to the central premise of *The Last Temptation of Christ*[1] for no particular reason, and it's obvious at all times that the show's writers are frantically scrambling to keep the alien mythology plots spinning without all of their usual go-to tricks. Killing off the Syndicate in "One Son" (S6E12) was the right move for the story, as it gave the series the room it desperately needed to maneuver out of some hopelessly convoluted territory. But by delving into stories of ancient aliens in these episodes, the series wanders into another narrative cul-de-sac, checks out the location, then wanders right back out.

The premise that ancient aliens deliberately influenced human civilization, the markers of which can be found throughout our oldest art and religious texts, is fundamentally inert as drama. If Bigfoot's out there, he's out there *right now*, Bigfooting around and making giant footprints. If aliens influenced our evolution, that's *interesting*, sure, but there's not really anything a story can do with that information. Bigfoot can be tracked and trapped. Ancient astronauts are a theory that can never be proved, a bunch of backstory when what's more interesting is the idea that aliens might be visiting us (and abducting us and spying on us) right now. It's more mythology in a world that doesn't need more.

The X-Files seems to realize this, largely dropping this aspect of its story after this two-parter. And even these episodes don't seem all that interested in it. The vast majority of the material here is a weird attempt to pull back in as many long-missing guest stars as the series can think of. There's Albert Hosteen! There's Deep Throat! There's Mulder's mom, who's been weirdly absent for a couple of seasons. There's Kritschgau, for some reason! The only thing the episode's missing is a scene in which Gibson Praise throws a wild party and dances the Charleston with Alvin Kersh.

---

1   In which Satan gives Jesus a vision on the cross of what the world would be like if he just abandoned his calling.

These two episodes are ridiculous and so, so pretentious, but . . .

(Yes, there's a but . . .)

They're so over the top that it doesn't really matter. There's a sequence in which Fowley walks toward Mulder in the middle of his "last temptation"—he's moved into a pleasant suburban neighborhood with everyone else from the conspiracy,[2] and she tells him all about what a pleasure it is to a man to have a woman around, to have her taking care of him, to have her take him into her arms every night, and it's impossible not to start giggling. Somebody thought this was going to be a serious attempt to get Mulder to abandon his quest! The whole two-parter is filled with the purplest of prose, and Chris Carter delivers what might be his most overwrought script since the glory days of "The Blessing Way" (S3E1).[3]

Most of the excitement happens in "The Sixth Extinction II: Amor Fati," while "The Sixth Extinction" (part one) ends up serving primarily as a continuation of the Season Six finale, "Biogenesis" (S6E2)—fairly typical of *The X-Files*' transitions from one season to the next. For example, whereas in "Biogenesis" we saw Mulder getting sick, in "The Sixth Extinction" we see that it's gotten much worse, and his telepathic abilities have gotten stronger, and so on. There are no real complications. Instead, things keep getting worse along a linear path, until the second episode drops in the other big idea of this trilogy of episodes: Mulder entering his fugue state.

It's surprising that more shows don't come up with ways—even figuratively—to have their characters get a chance to see what life would be like if they just abandoned their holy quest to live a normal life. "Amor Fati" is the better of the two episodes precisely because it suggests that Mulder could have lived a happy life, could have given away the quest in favor of turning a blind eye to what he knew to be coming, and, crucially, he might have been happier that way. When the Cigarette Smoking Man talks about how he admires Mulder's capacity for suffering, it seems as if that's what the *writers* most admire about him. Thus, showing him the possibility of a normal life, then showing us how the world would eventually crumble anyway, feels like the show itself wondering what it would be like to be some other show entirely.

"Amor Fati" also succeeds thanks to the connection between Mulder and our favorite nicotine addict. If you can overlook the florid dialogue and David Duchovny's absolutely atrocious old-age makeup, which seems to reduce all of his facial expressions to that of an old woman looking over lunch meat at a deli counter, the scenes in which the two of them watch the world burn in Mulder's coma dream are powerful. And it's fitting that Mulder is saved by his strongest connection of all: Scully (who finds him, with some help from Fowley, of all people). When push comes to shove, she's the one he wants to be around. Aw.

---

2 A couple of doors down from Deep Throat and just down the block from the Cigarette Smoking Man.

3 He has help in this department from David Duchovny himself.

Despite its obvious flaws, this two-parter still manages to be ludicrous fun. It takes a certain kind of show to make an episode this entertainingly bad, this over-the-top—and *The X-Files* was definitely that kind of show. By this point in its original run, the series was trying so hard to impress you with every trick in its bag that it feels churlish not to be a little impressed. "The Sixth Extinction" parts one and two are ridiculous television, but dammit, they're *our* ridiculous television. —TVDW

"HUNGRY"	SEASON 7 / EPISODE 3 WRITTEN BY VINCE GILLIGAN DIRECTED BY KIM MANNERS

CONFESSIONS OF A BRAIN-EATER

In which we see how the other half lives.

There's a tragedy at the center of every great monster story, even if we don't always want to see it. Frankenstein's monster didn't ask to be created; King Kong didn't ask to be taken away from his home to die in a strange land; even Dracula, for all his old-world charm, was an anachronism, doomed to be crushed under the wheels of progress. While they are often terrifying, bloodthirsty villains, the very thing that makes monsters so unsettling—their abnormality—is what ultimately destroys them. Monster stories usually end with the monster defeated, because that's what monsters do: they show up, they menace us, and then they die. There's no support for them, no place they can go for help when the world turns against them. Most of them have as little control over their fates as their victims do.

It's a story *The X-Files* has told many times before,[4] and in terms of plot and theme, "Hungry" isn't anything new. There's a creature who eats brains; he eats some brains; Mulder and Scully track him down; Mulder shoots him. Were this episode structured like most Monster of the Week entries, it would make for a perfectly fine but not particularly memorable hour. What makes it a standout is how Vince Gilligan takes this familiar routine and changes our perspective. Instead of following our heroes as they track down a killer, we follow the killer as he tries to avoid getting caught. This shift results in a compelling episode, noteworthy both for what it is—a funny, creepy, and unexpectedly sad tale about a kid who is trying his best—and for the way it encourages us to take pity and find empathy for all those crawling creatures under the bed.

For years, MOTW episodes have operated under a simple premise: There are nasty things in the world, and many of those nasty things view humans as only slightly smarter than cows. Rob Roberts (Chad E. Donella) is operating on the same

---

4 Heck, it even gave us a title for this book!

biological urge that drove, say, Eugene Tooms[5] to kill, but whereas Tooms was a sullen, animalistic creep, Rob's only wish is to fit in. He has a decent job at a fast-food place, gets along with his co-workers, and is nice to his neighbors. The only problem is that he has a biological imperative to eat people's brains. It's an urge he's largely powerless to resist—the episode begins with him devouring an overly aggressive customer at work—but it's an urge he clearly wishes he *could* resist.

About that cold open: Part of what makes "Hungry" so effective is how little it needs to change the established MOTW template in order to get its message across. By now, starting an episode with a murder in order to introduce a threat is such a familiar trope for the show that it barely registers, and Gilligan makes sure to include the expected number of creepy set pieces. There must have been a temptation to cut down on the body count to make Rob more sympathetic, but over the course of the hour, multiple people die at Rob's hand; the only real major concession to audience investment is the way those murders start with unpleasant or deserving victims—the rude customer, the creep in the car across the street, the jerk at work who decides to blackmail him—before building to the death of the friendly lady living downstairs (Lois Foraker), with whom Rob has a real connection.[6]

Gilligan also makes sure to include the requisite Mulder and Scully banter, despite the fact that we see the agents from Rob's perspective throughout the hour. Our two FBI agents show up at the Lucky Boy where Rob works, and Rob manages to eavesdrop on them[7] as they chat about their next move, with Mulder doing his usual theorizing routine.[8] Mulder pops up repeatedly throughout the hour to menace Rob whenever he starts to relax; it's clear that Fox has more or less figured out the killer's real identity early on and is just waiting for enough evidence to make his assumptions stick. By showing us Mulder through Rob's eyes, the script essentially reverses the traditional protagonist/antagonist role, turning Mulder The Hero into something of a menace.[9] It's less a deconstruction of the character than a sidestep, giving a glimpse of what it would feel like to be hunted by the person who comes closest to understanding what you actually are. The tragedy being that when Mulder sees Rob, all he sees is the monster.

---

5   The show's very first monster, featured in "Squeeze" (S1E3) and "Tooms" (S1E21).
6   This last murder is the one we see the least of; all we get is a shot of Rob removing his teeth before going into Sylvia's apartment. While it's obvious what happens next, the episode doesn't rub our noses in it, making sure our sympathies are still with Rob for the final scenes.
7   With the drive-through microphone, no less!
8   This time, he brings up brain fetishization.
9   The reversal here is more than a little similar to the premise of *Columbo*, a murder mystery series starring Peter Falk as the titular rumpled detective. On that show, each episode started by following that week's killer as he or she plotted out and committed their crime, before bringing Columbo in to investigate. While Rob doesn't really resemble the arrogant, wealthy murderers that Columbo typically sparred with, Mulder's knack for showing up at awkward moments and needling Rob without ever flat out stating what he knows is very much like Columbo's method for badgering suspects into making mistakes so that he can catch them out.

None of this would work without a sympathetic lead performance. As Rob Roberts, Donella is friendly and well-meaning, but just a little bit off—not enough to make it implausible that he could've hidden in plain sight for as long as he did, but enough to make it impossible to ever completely forget he's an outsider. Part of what makes the character so affecting is that while Rob is pretty good at covering his tracks, he's not some Machiavellian super-genius.[10] Rob's normalcy in this regard only serves to underline just how unsettling it is when Mulder comes into his life; after years of going unnoticed, Rob is suddenly discovered by a government-enabled Van Helsing.

Rob is a memorable lead most of all because, ultimately, he just wants to be like us. He watches self-help videos; he recognizes his compulsions as a form of addiction; he even tries to make a connection with the company-mandated therapist who comes the closest of anyone (much more so than Mulder) to understanding him. In the end, he commits suicide-by-FBI-agent because he decides that he can never be anything but what he is. Given the number of bodies Rob has left in his wake, it's impressive just how mournful that final shot is; how it makes it possible to acknowledge both that maybe Rob was right—maybe there is no place in the world for someone like him—and that you wish things could have worked out differently. It makes you wonder about all those other monsters out there in the dark, waiting for their next victim—or maybe just hoping for someone to say hello. —ZH

---

10 If the episode has a fault, it's that we never get a clear idea of why Rob is the way that he is; he mentions at the Overeater's Anonymous meeting that he's had the cravings to eat brains his whole life, but only found those cravings irresistible starting a month ago. The character is so well-realized you can't help wondering where he came from, and how he decided to wear a wig, fake ears, and false teeth every day to fit in.

FRIEND OR FOE

As the series continued, devising a new Monster of the Week episode was an opportunity for the writers to invent complex and even sympathetic characters and monsters, and to find original ways to subvert the tried-and-true formula first established in "Squeeze" (S1E3). Howard Gordon considers himself to be a very character-driven writer. Besides the pleasure of creating unique three-dimensional characters, Gordon likes to consider, "Why this moment, and [how will this character's] interaction with Mulder and Scully . . . change their lives forever? What questions will it answer? What conclusions will it [draw]?" Usually, as Gordon puts it, "Mulder and Scully [turned] out to be the people who were champions of these . . . underdogs and misfits." Especially Mulder, who in seeking "answers no one else was willing to [look for]," became an advocate for these characters on the fringes of society.

In "Hungry" (S7E3), however, penned by Vince Gilligan, we see—for the first time—the exact opposite of this dynamic. As Gilligan says, "I think it surprised all of us how elastic the show could be, [but] at a certain point, even writing on it five, six, seven years . . . you kind of get the formula down and then you're looking to extend the formula, and sometimes you're looking to subvert it, so I was always looking for those kinds of opportunities.

"'Hungry' was definitely a situation where I wanted to subvert the formula, so to speak. That was an episode in which I set out to tell a story where you absolutely were on the side of the bad guy, the killer, and you were rooting for him 100 percent and you were troubled by the fact that Mulder and Scully kept popping into the story. . . . When they stopped him in the end, in theory, in a perfect world, I wanted the audience to boo for Scully and Mulder and root for the bad guy."

SEASON 7 / EPISODE 4
WRITTEN BY VINCE GILLIGAN AND FRANK SPOTNITZ | "MILLENNIUM"
DIRECTED BY THOMAS J. WRIGHT

AN EPILOGUE
In which Mulder and Scully finally kiss!

"Millennium" is an odd one: an hour-long fan tribute to an unpopular show. *Millennium*, Chris Carter's short-lived television series, aired from 1996 to 1999 and centered on Frank Black (Lance Henriksen), an ex-FBI agent-turned-consultant for a secretive organization known as the Millennium Group. Grim to a fault, the show dealt with serial killers and end of the world cults, exploring much of the same paranoia-laced conspiracy theory as Carter's most popular work, minus the crucial charm and chemistry of Mulder and Scully.[11] In this crossover episode, *The X-Files* aims to give the cancelled series an appropriate send-off. Unfortunately, although the hour boasts some effectively creepy zombie sequences and the always impressive Henriksen, its hybrid nature dooms it to footnote status.

---

11 Henriksen, a terrific character actor (*Aliens, The Terminator, Near Dark*), lacks Duchovny and Anderson's easy charisma, although he brings his own world-weary gravitas to the role.

To their credit, writers Vince Gilligan and Frank Spotnitz have done their homework. "Millennium,"[12] at least on a surface level, covers all of the original series' big obsessions. The bad guy, Mark Johnson (Holmes Osborne), is constantly reciting Bible verses about resurrection and belief, exemplifying the threatening mysticism *Millennium* so loved. Similarly, Johnson's plan to bring about the end of the world by resurrecting dead men to take on the roles of War, Famine, Plague, and Death is appropriately apocalyptic and absurd.

Regrettably, the script's efforts at more specific continuity don't make a lot of sense. In the *Millennium* finale, Frank Black and his daughter Jordan (Brittany Tiplady) were driving off to brighter days; when this episode picks up, he's in a mental institution, fighting with his dead wife's parents for custody of Jordan. If you're a fan of the original series, it's frustrating to see characters you care about put through the wringer for no good reason. And if you're not a fan, you won't understand how important Jordan was to Frank, nor what it means that his wife is dead. At least everyone alike can appreciate Henriksen, whose performance makes the most out of the uneven material.

Either way, from a story perspective, it doesn't offer effective closure, and that's not a huge surprise. *Millennium* ran for three seasons, and while those seasons often retconned and/or contradicted each other, it still wove an expansive mythology, much too complicated to try to tie up in a single hour of another show. It's hard not to see "Millennium" as doomed from the start, a hopelessly quixotic enterprise which, in wanting to satisfy everyone, accomplishes nothing.

The only scene in "Millennium" that comes close to justifying the episode's existence as a tie-in comes at the very end: Frank is reunited with Jordan. The sight of the two of them together again is sweet, especially considering that this is the last we'll see of either character. Given that the original series already provided a similar conclusion, it's questionable if this was actually necessary to see on *The X-Files*, but at least the writers don't leave things worse off than they were before.

Still, the biggest draw here is in the final scene: Mulder and Scully watch the ball drop in Times Square on TV and share a kiss for the start of 2000. It's their first on-screen kiss in the series,[13] a sweetly modest romantic moment that plays more like an afterthought than a payoff to over six seasons of romantic tension. Putting it at the end of such an otherwise undistinguished episode is an odd choice that diminishes the potential impact even further, as though the creative team was trying to keep the relationship status ambiguous while offering a sop to fans who'd been patiently wating to see the characters' obvious affection consummated for years. It's

---

12 Apologies in advance for the number of times you'll have to read the word "Millennium" before this recap is through.

13 Well, the first Mulder and Scully kiss; Duchovny and Anderson also smooch in "Triangle" (S6E3), but Scully wasn't actually herself in that encounter.

a lovely exchange in its own right, though. As is so often the case with this season, there are pieces worth watching, even if they never quite add up to a whole. —ZH

SEASON 7 / EPISODE 5
WRITTEN BY DAVID AMANN
DIRECTED BY ROBERT LIEBERMAN

"RUSH"

BACK TO BASICS

In which the kids are getting faster, and the adults are getting slower.

Early in its seventh season, *The X-Files* had one goal: produce some seriously scary episodes, all the better to respond to critics who thought the sixth season had gotten too humorous and soft. The best way to push back against criticisms of this sort is often to get back to brass tacks, back to what made everybody love the show in the first place. In the case of *The X-Files*, that meant taking aim, dead center, at horror again.

The problem with going back to basics, usually, is that once you've evolved, it's hard to return to the place you started. Once *The X-Files* moved past the old-school Monster of the Week format into more experimental stuff, it was hard to revert to something more straightforward. We saw this a bit in Season Six's later episodes, but we're really seeing it here in the early portions of Season Seven, particularly in "Rush." It's largely watchable, and it has a few truly horrifying and dark murder sequences. But it's also hard to appreciate, given the context of where it came in the series' run. At least when you watch something like "Hungry" (S7E3), you can see the series still trying to stretch its wings. In "Rush," it's much harder to race from the ghosts of *X-Files* past: all those other, better monsters of the week.

The premise of the episode isn't bad: Teenagers have found a mysterious light in a strange cave that gives them superspeed, and since they're all so hopped up on hormones, that superspeed is being used in nefarious ways.[14] Mulder and Scully are called in to investigate when one of the teens bashes in a local deputy's face with a flashlight, and the gruesome, telling detail is that said deputy's glasses were embedded all the way in the *back* of his skull, from a single blow. It turns out these superspeed powers wear off after a bit, *and* the human body isn't built to withstand such velocity. The kids become more and more desperate for their next hit.

By far the best thing about this episode are the scenes in which Max (Scott Cooper), the first kid to discover the light, kills somebody; in particular, when he kills the teacher who dared accuse him of cheating. The effect used to indicate that

---

14 This very premise became the mostly solid 2012 movie *Chronicle*. Whether this episode somehow inspired it remains a matter of debate.

Max is moving quickly—which mostly consists of his body blurring in an otherwise standard, head-on mid-shot of him—is simple and subtle. What's more, the growing horror the students feel as the teacher is first tripped in the cafeteria, then sliced up by glass, then rammed against the far wall by a table, then clobbered with a chair, is felt by the audience as well. This is a visceral sequence, an oasis of brutality in an episode that can feel by the numbers.

As you might expect, "Rush" wants the kids' superpower to be symbolic for all manner of things. When it starts out as a metaphor for the way that teenagers feel like they move more quickly than the slowpoke adults around them, it's a nicely elegant piece of storytelling, especially when we see one of the kids just *waiting* for the clock to inch forward, that she might be done with the boredom of her day. But the episode works a little too hard to drive this point home, until everybody in the cast is remarking on how teenagers sure are different from adults, and the whole idea starts to feel trite. Once the episode starts mixing in parallels to drug abuse, the whole thing crumbles. Sometimes a mysterious energy found in a cave is just a mysterious energy found in a cave.

The ending—which offers no definitive explanation for why the weird light in the cave made the teens all The Flash-y—keeps the episode from completely falling apart,[15] especially coming as it does at a point in time in which the show sometimes tried too hard to tie everything up in a neat little bow. The teens losing superspeed winks broadly toward the fact that they can't turn back time and stay young forever. They, too, are going to grow up and get older and move at the same speed as everybody else. You can only feel young and fast and free for so long. You're never invincible, but you might *feel* invincible a little while there—until the first injury, the first crack, the first break. Which leads to the inevitable slowdown. And then you'll be trapped forever by your own body. Better to get your kicks and die young. —TVDW

"THE GOLDBERG VARIATION"

SEASON 7 / EPISODE 6
WRITTEN BY JEFFREY BELL
DIRECTED BY THOMAS J. WRIGHT

THE INCREDIBLE MACHINE

In which everything balances out in the end.

Do you feel lucky? Not in the Clint Eastwood sense. In the genuine sense.

Luck is such a weird concept, such a strange little thing on which to hinge so many of our belief systems. Nowadays, nobody really believes in a literal personifi-

---

15 As does an admirable performance by future Emmy winner Ann Dowd (known for her work in *The Handmaid's Tale*, *The Leftovers*, and much more) as Tony's mother.

cation of luck, smiling down on us and arbitrarily deciding to reward or punish us. But it's still such a strange framework for explaining the terrible whims of fate. The lucky get good things, and if they get those good things in an improbable fashion, well, then, they're *really* lucky. The unlucky get dumped on.

And yet don't we all sort ourselves, broadly speaking, into the categories of "lucky people" and "unlucky people," even as life is just as likely to dump good stuff on our heads as it is bad? Maybe making your own luck—an idea we've all heard—is as simple as mentally taking yourself out of the unlucky box and placing yourself in the lucky one, reframing your worldview.

"The Goldberg Variation" plays around with the ideas of luck being a giant system you pay into, then make withdrawals from. It's a charming, enjoyable episode, but it never moves beyond its initial premise to become one of the truly great *X-Files* episodes. There's a man named Henry Weems (played by the always excellent Willie Garson, who also appeared in "The Walk" [S3E7]), and he appears to be the luckiest man who's ever lived.[16] Everything he touches turns to gold, and when mobsters try to kill him, they invariably end up dead instead. But there's a tragic offshoot to his luck. Whenever something really good happens to him, something bad has to happen *around* him, be that a bunch of small, inconvenient things happening to a bunch of people, or one big, awful thing happening to one person.

As an illustration, think about when Henry buys a lotto ticket, hoping to win $100,000. He does, but when he finds out he won't get the money as quickly as he needs it, he tosses out the ticket. It's useless to him. Another man dives into the trash can after the ticket. Henry tries to warn him about what will happen, but he doesn't listen (because this is a fairy tale, and people never listen in fairy tales). The man races into the street to celebrate his good fortune and is, of course, hit by a bus. Henry never makes deposits in the bank of luck. For him, it's all withdrawals.

Henry was trying to get that $100,000 because Richie, a little boy in his building[17] needs an expensive operation, and he's running out of time. Henry is altruistic, and it is implied that's why luck keeps rewarding him. If he were attempting to use his luck to benefit himself, he would be punished, perhaps. Instead, he very quickly realized that his good luck has an adverse effect on the people around him, so he holes up and hides out, trying not to hurt anybody too much. He's a good man, and that makes him a good character to build a heartwarming episode around.

The problem is that a "good man" doesn't make for a particularly effective Monster of the Week. Think, for instance, of "Clyde Bruckman's Final Repose" (S3E4), in which Bruckman is a decent fellow, whose ability to see everybody's death has marked him with loneliness and melancholy. But to make that episode

---

16 Mulder theorizes endlessly in this episode, but it's Scully who gets it right when she shrugs early on and says, of Henry Weems, "Maybe he just got lucky?"

17 Played by a young Shia LaBeouf!

the masterpiece that it is, Darin Morgan's script brings in a murderer as well, a bad guy for our heroes to catch.

Such a compelling plot device is missing from this hour. Sure, there are some mobsters who want Henry dead because they think he cheated them out of a bunch of cash, and yeah, the FBI finds Henry's extreme luck suspicious and assumes it stems from criminal activity. Garson gives Henry exactly the right blend of "good guy" and "guy who just wishes this would all be over with already." Yet at the same time, it's not hard to imagine what the third or fourth season *X-Files* writing staff might have done with this character and idea, how they might have teased out the philosophical implications of a good person who causes bad things to happen by his mere existence. Jeffrey Bell's script is solid and funny and full of nice ideas and exchanges, but it never quite finds another gear besides "clever and whimsical."

Yet who wouldn't take "clever and whimsical" over "strained and self-important" at this point in the show's run? Somewhere at its core, the episode offers an intriguing rumination on cause and effect, or the hidden systems that dictate so much of our lives, particularly whenever it makes this subtext into text and brings in one of Henry's homemade Rube Goldberg contraptions. The mobsters' deaths in incredibly unlikely fashion offer some great laughs. This late in the show's run, "Goldberg" comes close enough to being a great episode that it's tempting to say, "Good enough!" and give it a pat on the back.

It all works out in the end. The mobsters take Henry, but they all die in the process of doing so, and it just so turns out that one of them has a liver that is a match for little Richie, which will mean that he doesn't have to die. Mulder and Scully get to have some of the playful interaction that enlivens their partnership. The whole episode toys with some big ideas in a way that doesn't push too hard—because pushing too hard might have made the whole featherlight conceit at the episode's center fall apart. "The Goldberg Variation" starts down many paths—funny and philosophical and spooky—but it never commits to any one of them in a way that might make it better than "pretty good." It's sweet, sure, but also a little cloying. —TVDW

| "ORISON" | SEASON 7 / EPISODE 7
WRITTEN BY CHIP JOHANNESSEN
DIRECTED BY ROB BOWMAN |

DON'T LOOK ANY FURTHER

In which an old monster returns with older tricks.

The last we saw of serial killer Donnie Pfaster ("Irresistible" [S2E13]) he was headed off to jail. Nick Chinlund's performance in the role was appropriately off-putting, but apart from a shot or two of him morphing into a demon (which could've been Scully's exhausted brain trying to cope with the situation), he was just a normal, incredibly sick human being. No conspiracies, no mythos, no supernatural powers. Why bring him back?

"Orison" doesn't sufficiently answer this question. Although it's spooky and has some haunting sequences, the hour never comes into its own. So much of the entry plays like reheated leftovers from other episodes, including Mulder once again attacking Scully for her belief in God. The first few times this happened, it was a smart way to show the limits of Scully's skepticism and Mulder's beliefs, but now it's just tedious.

The scenes of Reverend Orison (Scott Wilson) hypnotizing people are eerie and mesmerizing, and we hear enough of his backstory to make me wish the script had spent more time on him. Donnie's presence is necessary for the final confrontation, but the reverend could've supported an entire episode by himself, and mushing the two together makes for messy results. Still, Rob Bowman's direction is as stylish as ever, and "Orison" is more of a *Millennium* episode than "Millennium" (S7E4) ever was, soaked in portent and omens and God.

The climax has Scully shooting Donnie after Mulder has him in custody. It's a shock, and the ambiguity of her motives at least offers some interest. Either she wanted closure, or Orison had hypnotized her into pulling the trigger, or maybe everything that happened was the work of some higher power making her end the life of a monster who deserved to die. It suggests a mystery that almost, but not quite, ties everything together: Who's pulling our strings? And why? Ultimately, though, "Orison" is a jumble—an example of the show's late-period tendency to incorporate too many elements in one story. —ZH

SEASON 7 / EPISODE 8
WRITTEN BY VINCE GILLIGAN, JOHN SHIBAN, AND FRANK SPOTNITZ
DIRECTED BY THOMAS J. WRIGHT | **"THE AMAZING MALEENI"** |

PURE MISDIRECTION
In which: abracadabra.

In a season already characterized by charm over substance, it makes sense to have an episode about con-men magicians. It helps that one of the magicians, the title character, is played by Ricky Jay, real-life stage performer, card-thrower, actor, and raconteur.[18] Springing from an apparent freak accident on the boardwalk, the plot leads Mulder and Scully into a strange world of low-rent prestidigitation, bitter feuds, and Mexican car accidents. The audience sees just enough of what's

---

18 If you enjoy Jay's work here, he's great in *House of Games*, a considerably darker version of the "con men playing games" story.

going on to know that there's a plan, but never enough to figure out what that plan is. That's enough to generate curiosity, but the stakes here are so low that the curiosity never tightens into suspense. Still, it's all so fun and good-natured that it never wears out its welcome.

That good-naturedness is due in no small part to Mulder and Scully's chemistry. It's no new thing to say the actors play off each other well, but there's a fantastic ease to their banter here. Mulder spends as much time trying to impress Scully as he does trying to solve the case, and Scully is clearly enjoying herself. The two take such obvious pleasure in each other's company that it's infectious. No one's worried about aliens or murderers or government conspiracies. They're just goofing around in the sun.

The script is well-paced, doling out secrets in a way that never makes either the magicians or our heroes come off as idiots. In both mysteries and magic, the trick works best when the audience thinks it knows more than it does, and several times through the episode, our heroes believe they've solved the case only to come up empty-handed. The result is something that continually pulls us forward along with Mulder and Scully, promising new and greater mysteries with each new discovery. At its best, the episode plays like a challenge the writers came up for themselves: How can we pull this off? And where can this go next?

Mulder does figure it out in the end, though, and he lets the foiled thieves go. This is slightly ridiculous: FBI agents aren't generally in the habit of letting criminals escape, no matter how charming they may be. But it's hard to object too much in this case. Throwing the con men into the slammer would have been at odds with the tone of the rest of "The Amazing Maleeni," which is both a compliment and a criticism.

To its credit, there's something to be said for taking a break from the murder, mayhem, and existential horror that the series typically traffics in. As both Todd and I have noted, one of the great strengths of *The X-Files* is the elasticity of its premise, the way "investigating strange phenomena" allows for stories in multiple genres—from gruesome body horror to goofy buddy comedy to just about anything else—without ever feeling inappropriate or out of place. The lightness makes the darker entries all the more unsettling.

But there's a slightness to "The Amazing Maleeni" that makes it a little *too* disposable. Apart from the head-turning opening, there's not a strong hook that justifies Mulder and Scully's presence investigating the case; just because the show's premise is flexible doesn't mean you can just throw our two leads into *any* plot. What's more, there's never a chance to understand the con men or their perspective because they spend the entire hour lying about their motives. They never rise to anything more than plot facilitators. Without any greater depth, the geniality on display here sometimes curdles into something closer to self-satisfaction, as though the writers expect that the sight of Scully in a top hat will be enough to tide us over.[19] But maybe, in the end, my frustration is due less to the episode than to a season that seems content at settling for more immediate pleasures. —ZH

"SIGNS AND WONDERS"

OPHIDIOPHOBIA

In which you might start to wonder why there hasn't been a snake-handling episode yet.

In "Signs and Wonders," scary, serpentine moments abound: A woman[20] is killed by a staple remover that abruptly morphs into a rattlesnake, snakes pour out of the sleeves and pant legs of Mulder's suit, and, of course, who could ever shake the moment[21] in which Gracie (Tracy Middendorf) gives birth to dozens of live snakes on the floor of a ramshackle church, surrounded by snake-handling devotees. However, the last ten minutes of the episode scuttle so much of what came before that it's impossible to parse what happened. The basic idea here—the villain we think is the villain is actually a good guy—isn't a bad one, but when we find out who the ultimate villain is, the story stops making any sense.

Set in rural Tennessee, the episode opens with the death-by-rattlesnake of Gracie's boyfriend. We come to understand that the catalyst for this and all that follows is the pregnant Gracie's decision to leave the snake-handling fundamentalist church run by her father, pastor Enoch O'Connor (Michael Childers), in order to join a more progressive congregation. The leader of Gracie's new church, Reverend Mackey (Randy Oglesby), is exactly the sort of kindhearted local preacher Bing Crosby might have played in the '40s, but Childers's brilliant, scenery-chewing performance as O'Connor steals the show here.

The most powerful ideas at work in "Signs and Wonders" emerge through a particularly artful sequence around the episode's midpoint. The camera crosscuts between the hollering, tongues-speaking snake-handlers at the Church of Signs and Wonders, led by O'Connor, and the comparatively tamer Bible study circle in Mackey's house of God. The folks at the progressive church are saying the things we who profess to live in a more tolerant world want to hear coming out of the mouths of ministers. But the people at the snake-handling church look like they're having a

---

19 Though, to be fair, Scully in a top hat *is* terrific.

20 Played by beloved character actress Beth Grant, who so often portrays religious and/or conservative women.

21 Perhaps one of the scariest ones this season.

much more exciting experience. Yes, they're playing around with poisonous snakes, but there's a real fire and passion there that seems to have been completely leeched out of the other form of worship. Fanaticism is always going to have a certain lure to it—the lure of complete commitment, of surrendering oneself to someone who claims to know all the answers. To its detriment, the episode muddies these contrasting visions of religious devotion when it reveals that Mackey is the man behind the snake attacks, not O'Connor or his daughter Gracie, as Mulder and Scully have supposed.

Why? Mackey's motivations are never made clear. Mulder gives us some hooey about how it's all an attempt to cloak a more devilish religion in the guise of a more tolerant one, and Frank Spotnitz has confusingly described the theme of this episode as "Intolerance can be good!"[22] But why is Mackey doing any of this? The monsters on this show often have a simple objective: a need to feed. But what Mackey is doing is more complicated than that, and the fact that we don't get *any* explanation of how his powers work or where they come from muddies the waters even more.

Ultimately, the intriguing contrast of religious expression, the scary snake sequences, the compelling guest performances, and a scene in which Scully very nearly finds herself judged by snakes before being saved by Mulder,[23] cannot save the episode from being completely undermined by its final reveal. —TVDW

| **"SEIN UND ZEIT"** | SEASON 7 / EPISODE 10
WRITTEN BY CHRIS CARTER AND FRANK SPOTNITZ
DIRECTED BY MICHAEL WATKINS |
| **"CLOSURE"** | SEASON 7 / EPISODE 11
WRITTEN BY CHRIS CARTER AND FRANK SPOTNITZ
DIRECTED BY KIM MANNERS |

ONE TINY PIECE OF THE TRUTH

In which Mulder stops looking for his sister.

"Sein und Zeit" and "Closure" are episodes that only a show in its seventh season could offer. Despite promising—at long last—definitive answers to one of the show's biggest mysteries, this two-parter lands in a place that seems to suggest that no answer will ever be satisfactory—that what's more important is finding emotional closure. They're wise episodes in that they understand that life doesn't always give you the answers you want. They're also maddening. Seriously, *what happened to*

---

22 This doesn't really come across, unless he means we should be intolerant against magic snake people, in which case, agreed.

23 The snakes don't judge Scully worthy of biting but *do* judge Mulder worthy of biting. Exactly so, snakes.

you the answers you want. They're also maddening. Seriously, *what happened to Samantha*?! The answers we get are simultaneously devastating and confusing.

The first episode of this two-parter, "Sein und Zeit," is an impressively grim piece of business. It takes the story of Mulder's loss of his sister about as seriously as the show ever has. The disappearance of Samantha has been gradually receding from the show's center for some time now, which makes this return to the question of her fate surprising. Really, it hasn't been central to the show since Scully's abduction gave *both* main characters a reason to pursue the conspiracy. Truth be told, the show probably doesn't *need* to give an answer better than "Aliens did it." Samantha's absence—her ability to serve as a beacon for Mulder to move toward—was always more compelling than her abduction. On television, the journey is more compelling than its catalyst, and Mulder's search for his sister was all journey.

"Sein und Zeit" plays like a lesser version of the great Season Four episode "Paper Hearts" (S4E10), another story in which the disappearance of a young girl leads Mulder to consider a more prosaic end for his sister than an alien abduction. But where "Paper Hearts" was a straightforward procedural about one case that had greater bearing on Mulder's state of mind, "Sein und Zeit" seems a concerted effort to inflict misery upon our hero, implying that he must suffer for the sin of trying to topple the system.

These are not fun episodes. Stories like this had an air of escapism to them in the early days of the show, but now this is a deadly serious quest, something that Mulder must trudge through to make his way to the next heap of misery that will be visited upon him.

As the two-parter continues, it becomes more and more clear that Samantha is probably dead, not just missing, and the effect this realization has on Mulder is pronounced.[24] If she's still out there somewhere, she can be found. What's wrong can be made right; Mulder can *do* something. If she's just dead, that's a different kind of closure altogether. It's a matter of accepting utter powerlessness, and it throws the meaning of Mulder's life's work into question.

Letting Samantha stay lost forever would certainly be the safer choice, as it would keep Mulder's core motivations wholly intact. But the drive toward upending Mulder's hope of rescuing his sister is obvious. There are so many signs Mulder will never find her: We discover that the little girl, whose disappearance reinvigorates Mulder's search for Samantha, was abducted not by aliens but by a man who has apparently murdered many children; children who appear as ghosts, which implies they are, in fact, dead, and not off in outer space; and when Mulder's mother dies (because Mulder's punishment must be total), Scully confirms that Mrs. Mulder

S7 E10-11

---

24 There's an honest-to-God "Mulder cries" scene in this episode, and for as sleepy as David Duchovny has seemed this season, here he brings the kind of intense mania to Mulder that has always been a staple of his best character work.

killed herself, and was not assassinated by the conspiracy for nearly revealing something Mulder needed to know about his sister. This is an episode about a man having his very belief system eradicated before his eyes.

However affecting Mulder's emotional journey is, these are narratively messy episodes, to be sure. The introduction of the Santa Claus killer comes out of nowhere, essentially, and the concept of the "walk-ins,"[25] children who are taken out of life before they're forced to suffer extreme pain, is hard to buy as a definitive answer. The actual mechanics of the phenomenon are mystifying at best, convoluted at worst. The connecting of the dots feels forced and often too grim for the sake of being grim, even as the effects of these revelations are surprisingly moving and occasionally beautiful.

"Closure" is the no-question, no-wiggle-room, "we're completely serious about this" final resolution to Samantha Mulder's disappearance. Sort of. Given the number of times Samantha's story has "ended" before, it's hard not to approach this with Scully-levels of skepticism. Yet it's played with a compassion that makes it hard not to trust. This show has never been afraid of putting itself out there when it comes to absurdity. All those purple prose monologues are a kind of warning sign that what follows requires a commitment to belief. The commitment isn't always worth it, but we wouldn't still be talking about the series if it didn't hit more than it missed.

This one hits, although it requires a willingness to meet it more than halfway. For one thing, Samantha's true fate is too convenient, mortality as a kind of deus ex machina: "She's dead, but it's OK." That's fine thematically, but it's asking a lot on a story level. After all the dead ends and detours, it's difficult to just accept that Samantha Mulder was kidnapped, tested by scientists, and ultimately ascended into a non-denominational heaven where she'll be eternally black-and-white, translucent, and fourteen years old.

Also forced is the throughline between the two episodes, which are bound only by the fact that the little girl in "Sein und Zeit" left this earth the same way Samantha did. But Samantha wasn't kidnapped by the same man, and her body isn't in the cemetery Mulder, Scully, and Skinner find. This is less one big story than it is two smaller stories tenuously connected.

Despite its flaws, "Closure" does offer some compelling elements. The police psychic Mulder and Scully consult, Harold Piller (Anthony Heald),[26] sits at just the right point between ridiculous and plausible; his position and purported abilities are seemingly a joke, but Piller's calm, unruffled confidence make him hard to dismiss. Duchovny's performance is also excellent—half devastated, half hopeful, like he thinks he might see an end, but can't quite allow himself to accept it.

S7 E10-11

---

25 An idea that reaches all the way back to Season Two's "Red Museum" (S2E10).

26 Whom you may remember from *The Silence of the Lambs*, in which he portrayed Dr. Chilton.

The two best, most redeeming scenes in "Closure" are as follows: First is the unsettling sequence in which Mulder reads aloud from Samantha's journal. The powerful simplicity of the entries is heartrending. As often as the show has used Samantha as a motivation for Mulder's actions, we've rarely had a chance to hear from her directly. To do so now, if only for a moment, changes the narrative in a small but important way. It's not just Mulder who's lost something. There are consequences behind all the black-oil, alien-abduction, alien-human-hybrid insanity, and those consequences can be as simple as a teenager forced to participate against her will in the mad dreams of old men.

Second is the ending itself, the "closure" Mulder is so desperate to find. What he gets is something more emotional than factual, the mystery not so much solved as deeply felt. It's beautiful; a bit sappy, a bit surreal, a bit lovely. Samantha's absence isn't going to be important to the show anymore, and while this may be narratively unsatisfying—even infuriating to some—it's not a bad way to move on. For the first time, *The X-Files* grants Mulder some peace. —ZH and TVDW

SEASON 7 / EPISODE 12
WRITTEN BY VINCE GILLIGAN
DIRECTED BY MICHAEL WATKINS | **"X-COPS"**

THE ONLY THING TO FEAR

In which Mulder and Scully come for you.

Our heroes have faced down aliens, vampires, Flukemen, cannibals, and government bureaucracy, but "X-Cops" pits them against their greatest foe to date: reality television. It's a brilliant twist on a familiar formula, taking all the standard elements of a Monster of the Week episode and placing them in a context most viewers will immediately recognize even if they aren't intimately familiar with the show being referenced. The monster's fear-based yet imperceptible method of attack meshes well with the "live action" aesthetic and provides enough of a structure to make sure that the fun doesn't stop even after the novelty dies off. The episode is lively, light-footed, and funny, riffing off the core of in a way that reminds us once again of just how resilient that core can be.

For any readers who may not know, *Cops*[27] is a popular reality series that follows police officers around on patrol. Violence and obscenity ensues, most often featuring some blurred face, shirtless drunk and/or high dude screaming bleeped curses at the police while his wife/girlfriend sobs in the background. "X-Cops"

---

27 Not coincidentally, *Cops* debuted on Fox in 1989 and was still on the network when this episode aired. As of this writing, the show is still being produced.

imagines what might happen if a standard episode of *Cops* somehow wandered into an episode of *The X-Files*. Everything is shot on video, events unfold in real time, and the opening theme song (as with *Cops*) is "Bad Boys" by Inner Circle. The whole thing feels authentic, right down to the bits of dialogue that play over the title screen that introduces commercial breaks.

Gilligan's script makes excellent use of the *Cops* format. The video footage, flat and ugly as it is, breaks past the barrier between serialized and reality television; the brain reads the cinema verité–style as "real" even though it clearly isn't in this case. Watkins does a masterful job of pushing important events to the background or on the edge of the frame, forcing us to engage more actively with what we're watching. This choice fits perfectly with the logic behind the monster Mulder and Scully are chasing, a creature that manifests as its victim's greatest fear. The *Cops* visual aesthetic makes the idea both more real and quite literally harder to spot; the episode takes place over the course of a single night, and scenes are often a mix of harsh fluorescent street lighting and stark shadow. The presentation works much the same as found-footage horror movies like *The Blair Witch Project*:[28] it gets past our defenses by mimicking the panicky, confused camera movements of people trapped in actual events. For much of the episode's running time, considerable tension is generated by the fact that it often seems like were just about to see something absolutely horrifying, even though we never do.

The format also creates some great opportunities for humor, of which Gilligan and the cast take full advantage. Putting Mulder in front of a group of people not used to his particular belief system makes his theories seem even more outlandish than usual, and his attempts to use the camera crew as a way to get his message to the masses is entirely in character. Scully spends most of the episode trapped between frustration at being caught on camera and the knowledge that, as a representative of the FBI, it's part of her job to present as professional and competent a front as possible. Her growing irritation at both the absurdity of the situation and the fact that she, unlike Mulder, knows exactly what it sounds like to actually listen to Mulder, gives Anderson a chance to do some absolutely fantastic barely-controlled irritation.

The format also allows the show to sneak in subtle but effective social commentary. The popular conception of *Cops* is a mixture of redneck violence and inadvertent black comedy; the "reality" angle allows viewers at home to judge the various suspects from the safety of their living rooms, content in the knowledge that they themselves would never behave so idiotically on camera. But by and large, "X-Cops" avoids the shriller aspects of the material in its homage; while not every

---

28 A 1999 movie that more or less jumpstarted a genre through its canny mixture of clever advertising and raw filmmaking (and which had only come out a year prior to this episode airing).

character who appears has depth and nuance,[29] it's impressive how much personality Gilligan is able to work into the script given the limited running time and gimmick of the *Cops* format. The episode feels as sympathetic to the various locals the camera crew comes across as it does to the cops they're following around, which helps keep the episode from falling into mean-spirited parody.

There's also the idea that the creature Mulder and Scully are hunting feeds off of mortal fear—and where better for it to hunt than in a high-crime urban area? Making sure that the people we see are sympathetic adds a level of unease and even tragedy to what is, at first glance, one of the goofier threats our heroes have gone up against. That's not the only poignant thread to be found in the hour either. Steve and Edy (J. W. Smith and Curtis C. respectively), a black gay couple who witness some deaths, are flamboyant and performative in a way that could be read as camp. Yet they survive the episode, and there's a heartfelt implication that their relationship protects them from mortal fear. Just because they're camp doesn't mean they aren't sincere.

The only real flaw here is in the monster's ultimate design. It acts more like a disease that jumps from body to body rather than a tangible being; it feels like no coincidence that the one death we actually see is when a morgue attendant convinces herself there is a threat of contagion and promptly catches a case of instantly fatal hantavirus. But while that's an intriguing concept, there's a lack of concrete detail that robs the episode of a lot of its scares by the end. Apart from Mulder's theory of "mortal fear," there's little to connect the attacks, and there's no sense of the physical creature behind any of it. After all the buildup,[30] the episode reaches the least imaginative conclusion possible in that it gives us a mild scientific gloss: "Well, it's just this *thing*, y'know?"

In a more conventional episode, these flaws would be more of a concern, but it's easy to overlook them here thanks to the all-in-one-night format. A more conventional episode would also have allotted more time to our heroes for investigating crime scenes and questioning witnesses.[31] The immediacy of the *Cops* format makes for an entry that's more about the rush of the moment than about trying to determine the logic of the threat. With its entertaining, nuanced view of inner city life, strong humor, and great visual style, "X-Cops" is the sort of gimmick episode that gives the concept a good name: one that takes a premise and makes the most out of it. —ZH

---

29 Chantara (Maria Celedonio), a prostitute eyewitness to one of the monster's murders, probably gets the shortest shrift, due mostly to the fact that she dies fairly soon after meeting with Mulder and Scully. In a clever, morbid touch, her face is blurred throughout, since she dies before she can sign the release form to appear on the show.

30 Including a funny but surprisingly creepy sketch artist drawing of Freddy Krueger from *Nightmare on Elm Street*.

31 Thankfully Scully still finds time for an autopsy.

	SEASON 7 / EPISODE 13
"FIRST PERSON SHOOTER"	WRITTEN BY WILLIAM GIBSON AND TOM MADDOX
	DIRECTED BY CHRIS CARTER

DOOM

In which it's all in the game.

Every season of *The X-Files*, it seems, has a legendarily bad episode, and "First Person Shooter" is Season Seven's entry in that rotten sweepstakes.[32] The only thing notable about this episode is that it just keeps *getting worse*, until it ends in an utterly hilarious confrontation within a virtual reality world that's somehow stored in a warehouse in California's Inland Empire. At every given moment, "First Person Shooter" follows the precise path a viewer would expect it to, and it does so in ways that often peddle sexist attitudes toward women *and* men. Some feat, if you'd like to call it that.

Incredibly, "First Person Shooter" is the rare terrible episode of television that's also completely worth watching. It's unusual to see an episode of TV *this* bad that has still been made with such evident care. The episode won two technical Emmys,[33] and Chris Carter's direction has solid moments throughout the hour. It's also an episode that really wants to have *scope*, and it's scripted by William Gibson and Tom Maddox (also responsible for the much better "Kill Switch" [S5E11]) to be the sort of over-the-top action showcase this series rarely indulged in.

The overall experience of watching "First Person Shooter" is akin to watching the show slowly but surely let the air out of its own tires. The central conflict—revolving around retrograde sexual politics that argue men indulge exclusively in aggression and bloodlust whereas women just don't cotton to such things—is meant to be embodied in Mulder and Scully (though such characteristics run contrary to everything we know about these characters). To make these traits even remotely applicable to our heroes, the episode must perform some logistical gymnastics in order to make it seem as if Mulder is the sort of guy who would really be into first-person shooters, only to have Scully save the day in the end. You can see the problematic structural bones that were meant to make this endeavor an examination of male bloodlust and how it's tempered by the soft, warm, caring women of the world. This idea is both predictable and reductive, resulting in an episode that reaches its nadir when a bunch of cops stand in a hallway and bite their knuckles in excitement over the sight of an attractive woman.

---

32 What will tell you everything you need to know about this season is that there are, unfortunately, multiple candidates for that loathsome spot this season.

33 For Sound Mixing and Visual Effects, for those curious.

The central conceit of the premise is what literally everyone first thinks of when they hear the words "virtual reality": Hey, what if people were going into a virtual reality world and they started getting *killed*? It's the basis of many a cyberpunk tale, in addition to being the basis of *The Matrix* and Carter's own *Harsh Realm*.[34] Virtual reality worlds have primarily been of interest to fiction writers insofar as people can go into them to mysteriously die. So when people start getting vivisected by a sexy woman in the middle of a new VR game, you can bet that we're going to learn a lesson about the dangers of machines, or of turning our lives over to video games (or something).

What makes "First Person Shooter" even more pointless is that we *don't* end up learning a lesson. Mulder and Scully get involved in the case because of the Lone Gunmen, but they're very quickly sucked into the game world itself. The moral of the story is ostensibly that men need to have their aggression stoked because male aggression is exactly what the sexy-woman-within-the-game-world monster feeds off. The episode possesses no real stakes because it just keeps turning guest stars into obvious cannon fodder. The Lone Gunmen briefly get stuck inside the game, as do Mulder and Scully, but there's never any doubt that all five characters will survive. Other people die, but those deaths don't have any weight, and the point the episode tries to make is too unwelcome and backward to really care about.

To their immense credit, everybody here is really trying to make this work, in ways that are not always evident in other episodes this late in the show's run. Both David Duchovny and Gillian Anderson[35] are more dialed in than they have been for much of this season. Anderson especially seems to relish playing an action hero version of Scully as she starts gunning down multiple versions of the villain in an Old West setting. It's going to take a woman to defeat a monster that thrives off machismo, so why not our hero, Scully?

Questions about video game violence and how it enables toxic masculinity have been with us since video games became sophisticated enough to portray approximations of real brutality. But "First Person Shooter" raises complicated questions it's not smart enough to fully answer, instead offering ideas that are too pat, a plot that's too predictable, and a villain who is, literally, a two-dimensional video game character. It all adds up to a nothing episode that concludes on what's meant to be a shocking image of a sexy Scully striding through the middle of the virtual reality world that manages to be completely uninteresting. For an episode featuring this much talent,[36] "First Person Shooter" shouldn't make a viewer giggle so much at its dopiness. —TVDW

---

34 And for that matter a good portion of "Kill Switch"!

35 Who do *not* look cool in the outfits they wear to enter the VR world.

36 Including a then-still-mostly-unknown Constance Zimmer, in a bit of a nothing part.

THAT HOODOO THAT YOU DO

In which backwoods voodoo takes on modern medicine. Guess which one wins?!

When the subject of underrated Monster of the Week episodes comes up, you might not hear "Theef" bandied about, even though this understated and creepy hour is a bit of a kick in the teeth. It's no unheralded classic, but it is probably the strongest straight-up "scary" episode of Season Seven. It's incredible what having the show's A-team working on an episode can do to an hour even as meat and potatoes as this one.

The X-Files always works best when it introduces the strange and mystical into otherwise ordered communities. The idea of a very modern doctor and his carefully constructed life being disrupted by an ancient hoodoo rite that seems to have arrived straight out of the year 1886 is so perfectly in the show's wheelhouse that it's surprising it took it this long to pop up. The horrors throughout the hour stem from our villain, Orel Peattie (Billy Drago), striking back at his victims remotely, and the murder sequences in this late MOTW are particularly inventive.[37]

The biggest strike against the episode is how it depicts Peattie as the broadest possible stereotype of a backwoods hick. It beggars belief that Peattie would spell "thief" the way he does (the misspelling of which lends the episode its title).[38] Though the episodes remembered with derision from the first few seasons usually included some broadly stereotypical players, *The X-Files*, even at its least subtle, used to exhibit a little more care than this when coming up with its antagonists.[39] "Theef" instead has moments in which the characterization of Peattie borders on embarrassing.

What saves the episode—and the character—is Billy Drago's performance, which is shot through with both a foreboding menace and a strange sort of dignity. The episode never condones Peattie murdering the family of the doctor who took his daughter, but it does position his power such that you start to believe that he might have been able to save his girl if he'd managed to get to her soon enough. "Theef," in short, allows viewers to understand and empathize with Peattie's pain. The show is always at its best when it lets us see monsters who have something sympathetic

---

37 Notice how Peattie uses a microwave to kill Mrs. Wieder (Kate McNeil) while she's getting an MRI. The ancient practice of this folk magic meets some very modern appliances.

38 Though he *was* working in blood, which is admittedly not the most malleable of mediums.

39 Even the show's "other" voodoo episode, "Fresh Bones" (S2E15)—while not particularly good and bedeviled by its own stereotypes—is interested in the political pressures that spring up around refugee communities in a way that's more thoughtful than anything here.

at their core, monsters about whom we care—even if we don't agree with what they do. Peattie might be a stereotype, but he's one driven by impulses that are recognizable and human, which, coupled with Drago's performance, helps him transcend the other problems with his character.

It's worth comparing "Theef" with the previous entry, "First Person Shooter" (S7E13), just to see how much more effective this episode is at making death count. Whereas "First Person Shooter" kills a bunch of people to whom the audience has no attachment, "Theef" skillfully yet quickly sketches in a little family the viewer begins to care about, before picking them off one by one. The casting helps here,[40] certainly, but the strong sense of characterization from the get-go makes the audience concerned about why Peattie would be targeting this particular family with his strange hexcraft.

This isn't a particularly good episode for Mulder and Scully. Mulder is allowed to spew exposition about voodoo and spells before saving the day at the end. Scully comes to half-believe that Peattie really is capable of such feats, and she gets a particularly unexpected moment in which she's blinded and taken out of the climactic battle via Peattie's tricks. But the two of them are largely there to frame the proceedings by talking to the guest characters and investigating the assorted creative murders Peattie visits upon the Wieders. Since the guest characters are so interesting to be around, the lack of activity for Mulder and Scully isn't a huge demerit to the overall quality of the episode. But great *X-Files* episodes offer good material for the guest players *and* the regulars. This one comes close to fulfilling the latter criterion, but doesn't ultimately succeed.

Still, "Theef" forces viewers to feel the anguish both Peattie and the doctor feel at having people they consider precious taken away from them. Horror works best when it's rooted in both the psychological and the emotional, when it gets past the basic fear response and makes the audience sympathize with the monstrous on some other level before bringing down the hammer. That "Theef" comes as close as it does to hitting that sweet spot at this point in the show's run is something to be impressed by—warts and all. —TVDW

---

40 Especially James Morrison (who would become well known just a few years later for his work as Bill Buchanan on *24*) as Dr. Wieder, the family patriarch who finds his life torn asunder.

DINE WITH THE DEVIL

In which the Cigarette Smoking Man and Scully go on a road trip.

"En Ami" is William B. Davis's only script for *The X-Files*, and an odd duck: a piece of fan service written by someone to themselves. The episode pairs the Cigarette Smoking Man with Scully for a road trip to discover the cure for all diseases. It's a team-up that at least has the benefit of novelty. Typically the CSM is either lurking in the shadows or threatening Mulder, so to bring him face-to-face with the woman whose life he's so repeatedly damaged has inherent dramatic possibilities. But while the episode at least references Scully's cancer,[41] it suffers from a certain tonal blindness, trying to tell one story while inadvertently revealing another.

The most immediately obvious problem with this hour is that Scully needs to be a fool in order for the story to work at all. William B. Davis's hangdog sincerity can make the CSM seem very convincing, but our protagonists have fought him for too long—and he's been presented as too sinister—for him to be believably trustworthy. Yet Scully accepts what he tells her more or less at face value, making a token effort at fulfilling her own agenda[42] but still managing to stay a step or two behind him the entire time. She goes where she's told, her one act of rebellion quickly and easily stamped out. Anderson sells Scully's choices here as best she can, but it's an impossible job, as the script essentially reduces her to a passive observer and dupe for the CSM's manipulations.

What makes this setup even more unsettling is the creepy mixture of paternalism and seduction that characterizes the CSM's behavior here. Early on he tells Scully he has a special affection for her—he hastily adds that he cares for Mulder as well, but it's hard to miss the subtext. The implication gets even more difficult to ignore (and even grosser) when he drugs her (offscreen), undresses her, and puts her to bed. Later, he gives her a nice dress and takes her to dinner. The problem isn't just that the CSM is behaving in a predatory way; it's that the episode seems to have no real understanding of just how predatory all of this is. If Scully had gotten a chance to fight back, if she'd actually managed to accomplish anything at all, her treatment here might have been easier to take—at least then she'd be allowed some agency. But the CSM bests her at every turn.

---

41 The cancer that the CSM gave her, remember.

42 She brings along a recording device with the mic strapped to her bra, of which we get a close-up for some reason.

These issues are further compounded by the way Davis's script completely buys into the CSM's self-constructed mystique. He comes off as a tragic antihero here, though the character works best as a kind of preternatural vulture, plotting at the edges of history to pick off the vulnerable bits. The reason "Musings of a Cigarette Smoking Man" (S4E7) worked so well is that it showed how little CSM's control means in terms of his actual happiness; for all his success, he's a perpetually lonely old man who's always just a few steps ahead of the chopping block, someone who can't really exist in actual daylight. While much of "Musings" is arguably non-canonical, the core dramatic principle—that it's the writer's job to see characters as they actually are and not as they see themselves—is something that could've made "En Ami" more bearable.

Instead, it plays like a fantasy sequence without a framing device. Sometimes it works, largely thanks to Anderson's ability to make the most out of lesser material. It's both darkly hilarious and deeply sad to watch the CSM try to chat up Scully as they drive across the country or share a meal. For Scully, this is agony, a frightening glimpse directly into the heart of darkness. For the man formerly known as C. G. B. Spender, it's very likely the most human contact he's had all year. The actors have a history together, even if they haven't shared this many scenes before, and both Davis and Anderson are able to find a nuance in their interactions that's arguably not present in the script itself.

Still, "En Ami" is a waste of a good premise, with a script that could definitely have used a few more drafts.[43] If nothing else, a better understanding of what the episode's conclusion actually says about the Cigarette Smoking Man would have been nice. The bad guys win again, and the final scene finds Spender basking in his victory with a glass of wine. But as nice as that cabin is, and as comfortable as it looks sitting by the fire, there's only one person in the room—the house—for miles around.[44] —ZH

S7 E15

---

[43] In addition to the other problems, it would've been nice if someone had pointed out how many times people say "science," and how it sounds a little dumber every time.

[44] Like "Red Museum" (S2E10), "En Ami" sets up a story that won't be paid off for several seasons. Unlike "Red Museum," this story setup is completely horrifying.

SEASON 7 / EPISODE 16
WRITTEN BY DAVID AMANN
DIRECTED BY CLIFF BOLE

A THING OF IMMORTAL MAKE

In which a woman does everything she can to protect her family.

How much do we need to know about our monsters? Too often in these later seasons, it feels like the writers come up with the sketch of a creature and leave it at that, trusting the stars' chemistry and a few well-directed scare sequences to carry the hour. The effect is comparable to reading a lesser short story from a prolific genre writer: All the signs of quality are there, but some crucial part is missing.

"Chimera" at least makes the effort to give its monster some sort of psychological justification. The monster here has an agenda that adds pathos to the horror—a combination necessary for creating the series' most memorable creatures. The killer is a very nice lady named Ellen (Michelle Joyner) who's so obsessed with protecting the sanctity of her home that she turns into a hideous beast and murders the two women her husband had affairs with. This premise is more than a little sexist, failing to give its antagonist more than generic motives for her actions, but "Chimera" at least tries to depict its characters as sympathetically as possible. Joyner is likable as a monster in human clothes, her maternal warmth just barely masking a desperate need to maintain familial normalcy. Yet, apart from her overly solicitous nature toward Mulder, a trembling voice, and a few troubled looks, we don't know much about Ellen.

Despite the best efforts of its cast, "Chimera" fails to completely hold together because we never really get a sense of how Ellen went from frustrated housewife to murderous beast. There doesn't need to be a rigorous scientific explanation for how she came to be possessed by a homicidal monster, but merely insinuating that Ellen needed her marriage to succeed isn't enough. The episode refuses to dive deep enough into all of the societal or psychological pressures Ellen herself could be under as a mother and housewife.

Holding back the reveal of who the killer is helps to hold our interest throughout the hour, but it also means that, once the truth comes out, there isn't enough time to develop it into anything significant. The script tries to parallel Ellen's murders with a series of prostitute killings in the big city,[45] but as with the main plot, there's no depth to the connection beyond its simple existence. The speech about multiple personality disorders Mulder throws out at the end doesn't really explain much of anything beyond playing to some stereotypical (and misguided) ideas about mental

---

45 Scully is sidelined by this subplot, unfortunately.

health. The pieces for an interesting take on a woman driven to monstrous acts by the demands of suburban life are there, but they never come together in any revealing or particularly interesting way.

These assorted issues result in a decent hour of TV that disappoints as both a small-town satire and interesting creature feature. The monster may be frightening, but the scares don't linger long. —ZH

SEASON 7 / EPISODE 17
WRITTEN AND DIRECTED BY GILLIAN ANDERSON | "ALL THINGS" |

SO MUCH DEPENDS ON A CURTAIN CORD

In which Scully gets a couple days to herself.

"all things" is an episode of television in which Scully is briefly enamored of a curtain cord thunking against a wall. It's the kind of big, bold, experimental hour that the series should (and, in other episodes, did) nail. Instead, it's mostly a confounding affair, one that's interesting to watch but not particularly successful in its aim of drawing viewers into Scully's exploration of her own consciousness.

It's also the writing and directing debut of Gillian Anderson,[46] and her courage to construct such a small-scale hour that deviates so thoroughly from the show's formula is admirable. But at the same time, "all things" is mostly impenetrable, disjointed, and hard to understand, if beautiful to look at. Anderson is obviously trying to share with us some concepts that are very important to her, but the episode makes it difficult to get on her wavelength.

Scully decides not to join Mulder on a journey to England to check out some crop circles.[47] After he leaves, she just so happens to be drawn back into the circle of a former lover, whose daughter still hates Scully. Scully and the former lover—Daniel Waterston (Nicolas Surovy), a man who taught her in medical school—have a bunch of stilted conversations that sound like no dialogue anyone would ever speak. Our heroine eventually gets a call from Mulder to go and get some information from a woman Mulder has been working with. She brakes to avoid hitting a woman, thus averting a car accident. Then things get even stranger.

---

46 This is, improbably, the first *X-Files* episode directed by a woman. Seven seasons into the show's run. Yeesh.

47 Many Scully-centric episodes suggest this is the way their dynamic operates most of the time, and that the cases we see in which Scully joins her partner in the field only constitute a handful of X-Files.

None of this rudimentary plot summary[48] sounds all that strange. But the way it all plays out—with a hazy gloss of mysticism overlaying everyday occurrences—is defiantly, maybe even commendably, outside the norm of both this show and, quite honestly, television in general. By the time Scully is dropping piles of papers in slow motion so that she can see a helpful sheet about the "heart chakra," or entering a temple and then having a surreal vision of everything in her life flying by her eyes, the whole episode feels like it's completely wandered off the *X-Files* road and is headed toward open pasture. But while its unique sensibility might be honorable, the episode contains no real story progression. Every event comes completely out of nowhere and feels mostly like a lecture from Anderson about various tenets of Buddhism. That might be valuable in another context, but as an episode of *The X-Files*—even a deeply experimental one—it never manages the leap.

But it's still worth watching "all things," particularly if you can get into its rhythm. The episode circles profound notions of fate and those cyclical journeys that keep bringing us back to the same people who hold meaning in our lives. Unfortunately, it expresses those notions in as bald-faced a way as possible, with no attempt to hide the subtext about human connectedness and our own evolution and maturation as we grow.[49] It's an episode of people sitting around and talking about big concepts, followed by scenes in which Scully walks around—occasionally scored by Moby—and just happens into bizarre coincidences that drive the story forward, rather than driving the story forward herself. It's a curious one, and it might be better if the script had really dug into how Scully really feels about these existential questions, or if her epiphanies were treated with a little more weight. Instead, the episode just dawdles along, raising a lot of issues but never settling anything. Then again, these issues are so massive that it would be impossible for any hour of television to do so much as glance off of them, a rock skipping across the surface of meaning. The most frustrating issue with "all things" is that it sometimes seems to realize this, but also sometimes gets caught in a spiral of surface-level interpretations and thunking curtain cords.

And yet! The episode is strangely impressive. Like "The Sixth Extinction II: Amor Fati" (S7E2), this is an entry that dives deep into all the esoteric weirdness

---

48 I've skipped over the most famous part of the episode, in which Mulder is revealed to be sleeping, shirtless, in Scully's bed. The episode never really returns to the idea that Mulder and Scully's relationship may have become sexual offscreen, and it instead just ends with Mulder talking about fate while Scully gently falls asleep beside him. Viewer, you can fill in the blanks (and, if the amount of Scully-Mulder fanfic that exists is any indication, I'm sure many of you already have).

49 One of the things that *does* work here is the way these ideas of change and maturation play against the simple fact of the episode existing in the seventh season of a TV show in which the characters *haven't* changed as much as we might like. In its best moments, "all things" makes it seem as if Scully herself shares these frustrations about her and Mulder's arrested development.

and bizarre lack of subtext that made *The X-Files* so good at its peak.[50] There's no way to truly classify "all things" as anything other than a curious failure, but its willingness to be unconventional and bracingly different marks it as an essential episode of the series all the same, one that might not meet all its aims but is worth watching to get a better sense of the show's willingness to chase down big, *big* ideas. It doesn't always catch them, but the attempt is still worth seeing for yourself.

"all things" is beyond the scope of *The X-Files*, ultimately, but in its defense, it would be beyond the scope of *most* TV shows. It wants to be a poem; it settles for being a riddle. —TVDW

SEASON 7 / EPISODE 18
WRITTEN BY STEVEN MAEDA AND GREG WALKER
DIRECTED BY KIM MANNERS

"BRAND X"

A FEATURE, NOT A BUG
In which the smoke is full of bugs.

"Brand X" is a weird throwback to the era of TV in which shows would fill out their seasons with loose revamps of lesser-known genre movies from the '30s and '40s.[51] Except this episode isn't adapting a little-known movie. In fact, its source material comes from a movie that had just been nominated for Best Picture when this episode aired: *The Insider*, Michael Mann's tale of how *60 Minutes* ran into gigantic trouble when it tried to air an exposé of the cigarette industry. "Brand X" isn't a carbon copy of *The Insider*—for one thing, Mulder isn't going to expose his beetle-riddled lungs on prime-time television —but it shares so much DNA with the movie that it's impossible to ignore the fact that it aired just a few weeks after the film lost at the Oscars.

The episode also has much in common with another red-hot entertainment property of the same era: *Law & Order*. In many ways, *Law & Order* and *The X-Files* were vaguely similar shows at the turn of the twenty-first century. They both mostly told stories that would be closed by the end of the episode, and they both thrived on the kind of terse dialogue that was a hallmark of classic film noir and '70s cop shows.

---

50 This has never been a show to shy away from purple prose or too much exposition or over-explanation, especially in the best mythology episodes. And in some ways, "all things" is a mythology episode, given that it values the lives of the main characters over its stand-alone plot.

51 For an example you might possibly have heard of, consider the cult adventure series *Tales of the Gold Monkey*, which ran for one season and ripped through episodes inspired by a wide variety of Howard Hawks films, most notably *Only Angels Have Wings*.

But where the stories of *The X-Files* were ripped from the headlines of *Weekly World News*, the cases in *Law & Order* were increasingly ripped from *actual* mainstream headlines. Obviously, "Brand X" is an episode about the cigarette industrial complex and the lengths to which the tobacco industry[52] will go to keep its product going and its profits flowing. Sure, it also involves people being devoured alive from within by tobacco beetles, but there's undoubtedly a nugget of truth at the center of this episode.

The story revolves around a type of super-cigarette that was originally meant to provide all the addictiveness of smoking without the cancer-causing side effects. Unfortunately, the genetic engineering process *also* genetically engineered tobacco beetles so that their eggs can be spread in cigarette smoke. People begin dying because the beetles find themselves in a person's lungs and try to eat their way out.

"Brand X" has a hodgepodge of various elements that have worked in the past[53] but feel incredibly tired at this point, what with Mulder in peril by contracting the tobacco illness spread by Brand X in the last couple of acts.[54] The episode's central conceit—bugs devouring people from the inside—*should* be terrifying. Instead, the prosthetics used look fake, and the story never conveys any real danger or suspense about what might happen. By now we know that Mulder is not going to die![55]

Worse, the villain is far more charismatic and interesting than any of the people he might kill.[56] As Darryl Weaver (the man who's spreading the disease through his genetically engineered super-cigarettes), Tobin Bell has a lot of fun with the part. Weaver is the only person to survive the tests of said super-cigarettes, and quickly realizes that because he didn't die, he's much more useful to everybody else if he's alive, which buys him the ability to act with impunity. It's a big stretch that he'd want to keep smoking these obviously horrific cigarettes, but beyond that quibble, it's fun to watch him puff smoke in people's faces, relishing the knowledge that he's spreading something far worse than secondhand smoke.

The rest of the episode can't match up to its central idea or to Bell's performance. Once Mulder is in a hospital bed, the momentum of the plot grinds to a halt, and the other guest characters are singularly dull. There are some nice sequences here and there,[57] and the episode is at least crafting an original "monster" in the genetically engineered beetles, complete with nightmarish imagery. But the episode

---

52 The (fictional) tobacco company in this episode is Morley, the CSM's favorite brand (and a brand that lots and lots of TV shows and films have used because it's never been the name of a real cigarette and is, thus, easy to legally use).

53 Large portions of the plot feel like they were left blank with "Insert Conspiracy Here" in the script until the very, very late sections of the writing process.

54 But this choice does give us two Scully-centric episodes in a row, which hasn't happened in ages.

55 How many times have our protagonists come down with the plague of the week, only for it to gestate more slowly in their bodies than the bodies of other victims, thus giving them more than enough time to be saved?

56 Including maybe even Mulder! David Duchovny seems a little sleepy in this episode.

57 I kind of like the way Gillian Anderson plays the revelation that nicotine just might save Mulder's life.

gives off a desperate sense of trying like hell to be relevant and exciting. Instead, it tells a story that's been told many times before, with the added benefit of its creepy crawlies.

Many great *X-Files* episodes are about relevant and relatable human concerns, but featuring the tobacco industry in this episode feels, more than anything else, like a last-ditch effort. "Brand X" has some good pieces and at least one great performance, but they're not enough to save this one from feeling as insubstantial as a puff of smoke. —TVDW

| SEASON 7 / EPISODE 19
WRITTEN AND DIRECTED BY DAVID DUCHOVNY | "HOLLYWOOD A.D." |

DEALING WITH THE RESURRECTION OF THE DEAD
In which Garry Shandling makes out with Téa Leoni.

As an episode of television designed to tell a cohesive story, "Hollywood A.D." is a total failure, muddled as it is and so in love with being strange for its own sake that it never takes the time to make any sense. None of that really matters, though, because this is a hard episode not to love. The theme of Duchovny's script is difficult to pin down—something about how fiction helps us to achieve a kind of bizarre immortality—but that doesn't stop the funny parts from being funny, and the sweet parts from being sweet. It ends with the murder-suicide of two of the episode's main characters, but they die offscreen because nothing of real emotional consequence can happen in "Hollywood A.D." There's no depth to be found here, but there's so much generous goofiness throughout that it makes it easy not to care.

In effect, "Hollywood A.D." illustrates the difference between parody and satire. Parody has genuine affection for its target, while satire is interested only in going for blood, affection be damned. Scenes of Garry Shandling and Téa Leoni running around a fake cemetery fighting the vegetarian dead in some insane version of *The X-Files* could be seen as a riff on the entertainment industry's excess, but more likely they're there just because Duchovny wants to get some laughs. And he does, really. Garry Shandling asking Mulder about his personal anatomy because he "builds character out of wardrobe" is great. Téa Leoni getting notes on how to run in heels from Scully—also great.[58] It's impressive that Duchovny and the rest of the crew are able to be this self-indulgent without ever becoming too smug or laughing too much at their own jokes.

---

58 The shot of Leoni running back and forth in the background while Mulder chats with Shandling is the funniest the show has been all season.

are able to be this self-indulgent without ever becoming too smug or laughing too much at their own jokes.

If you can accept the screenplay's messiness, there are plenty of these delights to be had. Scully's anecdote explaining the idea of the Lazarus Bowl—a mystical piece of pottery that just happens to have a recording of Jesus Christ ordering a man to rise from the dead—is a highlight, as is Mulder and Scully's laid-back, "Well, we've deconstructed our relationship a dozen times now, so whatever" pleasantness. It feels like such a relief, and both actors are at their most charming throughout. Scully smiles a lot;[59] it's infectious.

And how can she not smile? There's Skinner in a bubble bath. A corpse jumps up off the autopsy room table and asks for his heart back. Ghosts rise from the dead and boogie down to the music of the ages. Mulder has apparently seen Ed Wood's famously terrible *Plan 9 from Outer Space* forty-two times. (Cue Scully: "Doesn't that make you sad? It makes me sad.")

If "Hollywood A.D." contains anything approaching a skeleton key to its message, it's in the scene in which Mulder explains to Scully that the absurd awfulness of *Plan 9* helps him achieve a kind of Zen state of consciousness, which allows him to make connections and deductive leaps he wouldn't normally be able to propose. Tellingly, the cemetery set in *Plan 9* and the one we see in this episode's Hollywood aren't very different. For all this episode's talk about Jesus, about faith and meaning and the power of film to re-create history, Duchovny's real heart is with Ed Wood and all those paper-plate flying saucers and plywood sets. If there's any serious message to be dug up from all this chaos, it's that we have stupid minds, stupid! Thank God Duchovny loves us anyway. —ZH

S7 E19

---

59 It's impressive just how much life Duchovny brings out of Anderson in their scenes together (which is possibly due to his directorial attitude, because Anderson's delightful performance in "The Unnatural" [S6E19] seems akin to her high spirits here). Scully has been warm and funny before, but she's practically glowing throughout this hour. Their dynamic makes you want the show to run forever just so you can spend more time with these two, sitting on the couch, watching bad movies.

DON'T TALK ABOUT IT

In which there are two Kathy Griffins, and little else.

"Fight Club" is dire stuff, the script lazy and repetitive, the music score irritatingly overbearing. Mulder and Scully spend most of the time apart from each other, and in exchange we get endless scenes of Kathy Griffin (playing identical sisters Betty Templeton and Lulu Pfeiffer) wandering into places, hanging around, and then another Kathy Griffin showing up and all hell breaking loose. There's a plot (sort of), but it's so uninteresting that it hurts to think about. It feels like the season finished up an episode short and the producers just grabbed a random spec script off the slush pile—which makes it all the more unpleasant when you remember that Carter wrote it himself.

Griffin is terrible as the sisters who cause havoc whenever they're in proximity of each other. It's hard to blame the actress too much, because the script doesn't give her a damn thing to do. That's a shame, because there's a germ of a real idea in their plight—something fascinating and cruel about the fundamental underpinnings of our biology. However, the characters are so badly written and underserved that they're impossible to care about. How can we care about idiots who have only the barest idea of the damage they incessantly inflict on the lives of others? And so, there's no emotional center to the story at all.

There's something rancid about forced quirkiness; it's rotten and smug, like a dead clown left in the sun too long. "Fight Club" is full of that kind of stink, and you might find yourself wondering (as I did) if the show has run out of ideas.[60] Nothing is resolved, nothing changes, and in the end, the sisters are still out there screwing everything up. No real explanation, or theory, or point to any of this at all.

The last joke of the hour involves the camera panning over to show first Scully, and then Mulder, with severe face lacerations, bruises, and apparently dental repairs. Because there was this huge fight, and they got involved, and . . . that's it. Like nearly everything else in the episode, there's no real joke here, just a joke-shaped hole where comedy could have theoretically existed. This episode is ugly inside and out; it's not easy on the eyes, and it's embarrassing for everyone involved. Let's just not talk about "Fight Club" anymore, OK? Let's make that a rule. —ZH

---

60 Carter is also responsible for "Syzygy" (S3E13), another darkly comic look at a pair of women who wreak havoc whenever they're in the same room together.

THE PERFECT WISH

In which you get three wishes.

"Je Souhaite" is the best episode of Season Seven. You could make a compelling argument that it should be the series finale, even though there are many fine episodes that follow.[61] But there's a warmth and tenderness to "Je Souhaite"[62] that the show will soon lose. This episode, more than anything, beautifully depicts the soul of a show on a cusp of a major shift.

An uncomfortable strain of "Let's make fun of the yokels!" humor runs through nearly all of *The X-Files'* comedic episodes, and unfortunately, "Je Souhaite" is no exception. But to be fair, we meet only two Missourians, as most of the story line centers on the adventures of Anson and Leslie Stokes (Kevin Weisman and Will Sasso, respectively), two dumbasses who somehow get hold of a genie who's been rolled up in a rug lo these many years. The first indication we get that Anson has met a genie is genius: The guy's irritating boss suddenly has his mouth disappear, that he might yell at his employee no longer. That's when it becomes obvious this is a Vince Gilligan episode, and, even better, a comedic one.

Gilligan's greatest talent when writing for *The X-Files* was his ability to reveal the weirdness that might lurk in otherwise normal parts of the American dream. He was great at combining something mundane—a rug in a storage locker, for example—with something utterly fantastical—say, a genie. Since that was such a central part of the thesis of *The X-Files*, he became as crucial to the show's success in the latter portion of its run as were Chris Carter and Frank Spotnitz. Initially, Gilligan developed this hour (which he knew would be his first directorial effort) as a spare, scary story about something unleashed from a storage locker. Instead, he chose to make a story about human frailty and the power of hope. And it's wonderful that he did.

Now, "Je Souhaite" isn't on the level of Gilligan's finest work. There's not really a story here, particularly once Mulder figures out that "Jenn"[63] is a genie. Scully doesn't get nearly enough to do, and though we have just the two yokels here, they're almost unrealistically dumb. Sure, the sequence with Mulder's three wishes is gold, but there's not much else under the hood, plot-wise. This is just a slyly comic outing

---

61 SEASON EIGHT IS MOSTLY GOOD, AND I'M GOING TO PROVE IT!!!!!!!

62 French for "I wish," by the way.

63 Paula Sorge's portrayal, all sardonic snark and wry deadpan, hides the raw sadness at the core of Jenn. It's a lovely little character turn. Her first wish back in the day being for a "stouthearted mule" is the sort of precisely worded joke Gilligan writes so beautifully.

that lets Gilligan play around with the idea of wishes granted ironically, like when Leslie wishes that his brother would be alive again, and instead gets a zombie version of Anson who blows up his trailer.

Gilligan grasps that no wish can be wholly altruistic, that Mulder's desire for "world peace" stems from his own desire to be smug and self-satisfied about what a good guy he is. The ultimate "solution" here—the only way to win at genie is not to play genie—is obvious from the moment Jenn tells us what she'd really want.[64] But while Gilligan has some interesting ideas about wishes and our need to hope for something more, he has something even bigger on his mind.

To wit, this episode feels like the ultimate *X-Files* fan love letter. There's so much stuff in this hour that should feel like fan service but somehow doesn't, like that final scene where Mulder and Scully settle in on a couch to talk about nothing in particular. In some ways, Jenn acts almost as a mirror for Mulder; she, too, is a person whose life has been consumed by something beyond her understanding, to the point where she seems almost to be living on autopilot. But thankfully for Mulder, he has Scully, whereas poor Jenn just has whoever demands they be granted wishes, be that Benito Mussolini or Richard Nixon or Anson Stokes. There's a rich humanity to every Gilligan script, and that sense comes through in every moment here, even when it seems like he's being unrealistically cruel to the Stokes brothers.

The genius of "Je Souhaite" lies in how it utterly embraces the inherent strangeness of the world of this show. Mulder and Scully find a genie, but they end up sitting on the couch with popcorn and *Caddyshack*, the genie released to build her life anew. Everybody on Earth disappears for an hour, and it's no big deal to the man who made them disappear. A man turns invisible, gets hit by a bus, then wanders out of a locked lab, and it's just another day at the office. When *The X-Files* began, it was precisely this sense of possibility, of anything happening, that made the show seem so wondrous and new. But over time, it siphoned off that possibility, that wonder.

"Je Souhaite" has its fair share of problems, but it still takes place in a world where what you don't know is weirder than what you do, where a genie can pop out of a rug, where a man can be reinvigorated by just how little he knows, where the constant struggle to build a better world is the greatest mystery of all. So, if we must leave *The X-Files*, why not leave it there, with our heroes sitting on the couch, reveling in the mystery. —TVDW

---

64 As is true of all genies, Jenn is sick of being a genie.

A RETURN

In which the series redefines itself.

During production of "Requiem," all involved proceeded as if this episode might be the series finale. Though the show's ratings were still solid, it was clearly on the downward slope of its Nielsen trend, and it was beginning to suffer creatively. It was also obvious that David Duchovny was ready to move on to something—anything—else,[65] and it was nearly impossible to imagine the show without Mulder. And then came "Requiem," which reinvigorated and reinvented the show with what might be the series' best season finale cliff-hanger ever.

How to explain just how incredibly difficult it is for a seven-season-old show to accomplish such a transformation? How to tell, too, if any of this was at all intentional? After all, the series would likely have preferred to have Duchovny return as a regular in Season Eight, for even more alien-and-weird-beastie hunting adventures. Instead, Mulder went off into the sky with the little gray men, and the show found itself backed into a corner it would have to write its way out of. But, you know *The X-Files*: It loved to write its way out of a corner.

The best cliffhangers have a finality to them, a sense that nothing will ever be the same—and if they *are* the same, the show has cheated. On a program with only two core players, the death of one of those players (as was teased in "Gethsemane" [S4E24]) never held all that much weight. Yet the idea that Mulder could be tricked into being abducted by aliens—then sort of find himself amenable to that idea until the bounty hunter shows up—was a well-executed fake on the audience. To be sure, Mulder might have known what he was getting himself into. But when the audience realizes what's about to happen, it's a wonderfully dramatic moment.

What's more incredible is that "Requiem" piles a bunch of other huge changes on top of this ultimate twist, just to make the events feel even more momentous. Skinner sees the UFO that carried Mulder away! Krycek and Marita kill the Cigarette Smoking Man by pushing him down some stairs! Scully out of nowhere reveals that she's pregnant! The show skillfully and precisely unleashes a bunch of plot points

---

65 He was also embroiled in a lawsuit against 20th Century Fox, in which he alleged the company had cheated him out of millions of dollars he was owed from the massive success of *The X-Files*. Though Duchovny didn't sue Chris Carter, he *did* allege in the suit that Carter conspired with Fox to keep the profits from Duchovny. The suit, filed in 1999 near Season Seven's start, was settled out of court in 2000.

it had obviously been holding onto for a while. The mythology has been without a singular purpose for a few seasons now, but reconfiguring it as a search for Mulder makes all the sense in the world. That Duchovny left the show as completely as he did, thus allowing for the series to more fully explore this new direction, ended up being a surprising asset.

"Requiem" isn't just its final ten minutes. The episode evinces some clumsiness on the way to that climax, exacerbated by the fact that the series can no longer figure out just what it wants its mythology to be about anymore. The first thirty minutes of the episode don't do much to fix the problems that plague the mythology, or tie up any of its many loose threads. The staid quality of the mytharc is even more pronounced because "Requiem" keeps working in references to "Pilot" (S1E1)—something that increases this episode's sense of series-wide finality—and the story here is not functionally all that different from what went on in the first episode. The characters have learned so much about the alien menace, but they've also learned very little. There's an alien ship that's crashed in Oregon—back on the site of Mulder and Scully's first case—and everybody wants that ship because it could lead to the formation of a new Syndicate. It doesn't make a ton of sense, but honestly, it's not as bad as whatever was going on in "The Sixth Extinction" (S7E1).

To its credit, this episode's nods to the pilot[66] ultimately highlight just how far the show has come from its humble roots. It's fun to remember when the show was all about Mulder explaining concepts like missing time to Scully (and by extension, the audience), and it's a kick to remember just how small-scale the series was way back when. The plot of the pilot would be dealt with in about five minutes by this point in the series, but the central things that made the pilot work—a sense of mystery, the connection between two FBI agents, an overall spooky vibe—remain ever-present. The fundamentals are still strong, even at this point in the series. It's just that everything else is different now.

To watch "Requiem" is to see a show that became something almost totally separate from what it had been originally. To watch "Requiem" is to be viscerally reminded of just how much bigger this show became between Season One and Season Seven. To watch "Requiem" is to be shown just how extraordinary it is that this show became a hit at all.

The differences are noticeable in smaller ways too. Big Bear Lake might look vaguely like the Pacific Northwest, but it's still recognizably Southern California. Those two actors who seemed so fresh-faced and dewy-eyed back in the pilot now seem much more brazen and blasé. Thankfully, "Requiem" wasn't how the show

---

66 Including the return of Billy Miles (Zachary Ansley) himself! Billy, as we knew him in "Pilot," acted as an unwitting accomplice to an alien force abducting teens in his hometown.

ended, in part because ending on a cliff-hanger is always a disappointment.[67] But you can certainly see where the impulse to do exactly that came from. In "Requiem," it's easy to see everybody involved taking a step back to marvel at just how far they've come, whispering to themselves, "Can you believe *this show* got *that big*?" —TVDW

---

67 Also, as mentioned, Season Eight is pretty good! And so is Season Eleven! And there are good-to-great episodes in Seasons Nine and Ten! Don't stop watching! There's so much more! Keep reading!

LOST AND FOUND

The finale of Season Seven—in which Mulder vanishes—changed the course of the show's mythology forever. But the show's overarching story line had already shifted course halfway through this season, when Mulder finally discovered what happened to his sister, Samantha. Chris Carter notes that his original vision for the show dictated that "the mythology would be the place to explore the personal stories of the things that affected [Mulder and Scully] most directly."

Frank Spotnitz recalls that Carter originally had a closed plan for the show, not anticipating its huge success: "I remember when I started, which was a few episodes into Season Two, Chris said that he thought the show was going to last five years, and that the final episode would be Mulder finding his sister. That's what he thought. You can see, that's not at all what happened."

Of course, David Duchovny's departure from the show threw a wrench into the plan to prolong the story of Mulder's search for his sister. Spotnitz credits the actor's leaving as the motivation to finally tie up the thread in "Sein und Zeit" (S7E10) and "Closure" (S7E11). "It was clear to us," he says, "that David wasn't going to come back for Season Eight, but that the show was going to continue—whether we wanted it to or not, it was going to continue. And so, not knowing if we would ever see David Duchovny again on *The X-Files*, I remember saying to Chris, 'I think we have to find a way to resolve the Samantha story line before we lose David.' And it felt like the more honest and unexpected ending to that story line—that she was dead and had been for a long time. It felt like that would be more resonant for people who've lost loved ones for extended periods of time. You're not going to find them alive twenty years on. So that was—we knew that was a deeply unexpected and probably unpopular choice, but [it] felt more honest."

The uncertainty of the show's status in its later seasons also provided a unique challenge for the writers in wrapping up other story lines while balancing the potential of the show to continue into the future. The shocking ending of "Requiem" (S7E22) is only one example. Spotnitz says, "Aside from all the cast changes and the feature film, the last three seasons—Seven, Eight, and Nine—we didn't know whether they were going to be our last seasons or not. So we had to write the season finale for both Season Seven and Season Eight knowing it's either the season finale and we'll be back, or that's it, that was the series finale and we're done. That's incredibly challenging, trying to make the narrative work for both scenarios."

A NEW HERO

In which . . . wait, where's Mulder?

The first shots of "Within" are disorienting. Murky, out of focus, and unsettled, they show us things we aren't yet ready to see. Objects move, voices mutter in the background, and it becomes increasingly obvious that whatever's happening here is deeply unsettling, even if it's impossible to pin down exactly what's going on. This confusion seems to go on forever. Finally, we see something that might be Mulder's face. We see bright lights. We hear screams. Then Scully jerks awake in her bed, and we realize that she's been dreaming of Mulder, dreaming of him suffering at the hands of his alien abductors. The episode begins with a sense of doom, and that feeling never dissipates.

It's an engrossing way to begin after the cliffhanger of "Requiem" (S7E22), and the pair of episodes that open Season Eight work well as an introduction to the new narrative status quo. Unlike so much of the mythology arc of the previous season, the search for Mulder has a strong central purpose with an obvious goal in mind, and that implicit urgency is evident from the start. While the various alien factions and cabals and conspiracies became difficult to keep track of, "Mulder is missing!" doesn't take much time to parse. The simplicity is a godsend in a show that's been in danger of getting lost in the clouds.

"Within"/"Without" finds *The X-Files* struggling to take its new shape in the absence of its most prominent star. Since the show's inception, Mulder was the driving force behind the narrative. His absence has created a vacuum that must be filled, and "Within"/"Without" goes about doing so in two ways: first, by introducing a new mythology arc in the hunt for Fox; and second, by giving us a new male protagonist to serve as Scully's foil. It's successful in both those aims.

Once again, Scully is at odds with her superiors, but—in a nice inversion of the trope—she's now the one shouting down her opponents and refusing to step back even when her opinions make everyone else avoid eye contact. Skinner tries to hold her back as best he can, which works roughly as well as you'd expect. He's been struggling against the bureaucracy for so long that there's not much charm in seeing him going through the motions again; the real thrill to be found here is seeing Scully in action-hero mode. Though she spends some of "Within" moping about, once she shrugs it off, she's full of rage, and it is a sight to behold.

Yet the structure of the show dictates that it has two protagonists, which is where John Doggett (Robert Patrick) comes in. He's introduced as the head of the hunt for Mulder, who tries to con his way into Scully's trust. The conversation doesn't go the way he planned,[1] but while Scully may not be impressed, Doggett comes across as a smart, likable guy, as driven in his way as Mulder is in his, yet equipped with the mind of a cop. He believes in cause and effect, and crime and perpetrator, and it's his job to solve the former and stop the latter. God help you if you get in his way.

Robert Patrick brings a distinct, charismatic energy to the role. He's best known for his iconic turn as a shape-shifting killer robot in *Terminator 2*; here he shifts that icy, indomitable will into a much more human context. He spends most of the first two episodes not really knowing what's going on and trying to convince Scully to trust him, and it's a measure of just how good Patrick is that even in a series based on elaborate, and near omnipresent, deception, you want her to accept him as an ally. Doggett[2] represents a new kind of presence in the world of *The X-Files*, someone who refuses to put up with the double-talk, hints, and insinuations that typically dog our heroes. Sure, he's set up to be the skeptic to Scully's newly converted believer,[3] but his skepticism is different than Scully's was at the start of the show, just as her faith isn't the same as Mulder's is. It's a great way to maintain the back-and-forth dynamic so key to the series while still finding new ways to reframe the old arguments.

Not that there's a lot of time for in-depth arguing in "Within"/"Without." Whereas the former introduces Doggett and puts everyone on the hunt for Gibson Praise, the latter brings back the shape-shifting alien bounty hunters, still more than willing to put on a friendly face to achieve their ends. "Without" builds on the chaos and the paranoia, using the bounty hunters as a literal symbol of the world that Doggett is now a part of, one in which everyone you know might turn out to be someone else entirely. The episode also takes the inevitable, necessary step of assigning Doggett to the X-Files office. Between Scully's bad dreams, the Mulder fake-out,[4] and Doggett getting a new job, it's obvious that for once, things really have irreversibly changed.

In terms of plot, the episodes are solid, but not spectacular; they mostly serve to provide faithful viewers with just enough to tease us with Mulder's disappearance without resolving anything. A Duchovny-free *X-Files* could've easily come off as a stunt, or worse; Mulder's absence could've robbed the season of both the chemistry between its leads *and* its urgency. The shots of Mulder in captivity, however, tell a different story. He's not being kept inside some gooey cocoon, or a hazy peaceful

S8 E1-2

---

1   Scully quickly catches on and throws a cup of water in his face.
2   The last name is a pun!
3   Scully's realization that she's now spouting Mulder's rhetoric is the funniest joke in either episode.
4   Duchovny pops up a few times outside of Scully's visions in both episodes, but each time it's just one of those tricky shape-shifters throwing us off the scent.

oblivion. He's being studied and tortured and sawed open. The aliens have the technology necessary to keep him alive, but who knows how long they'll bother? And if he survives, who knows what will be left of him? —ZH

ASSIGNED TO *THE X-FILES*

Robert Patrick remembers when *The X-Files* came knocking. "The way it went down was, I got a message from my agent that Chris Carter was interested in me for *The X-Files*. . . . At the time, I was still considered a get, because I was a film actor, and I had only done *The Sopranos*; I hadn't done network TV yet. . . . I was under contract to NBC for another show [for which] Kelsey Grammer was executive producer, [so] I called him. He is a friend of mine, and I said, 'You got to let me out of my contract to go do this *X-Files*.'"

When asked what drew him to the character of John Doggett, Patrick says he liked "that he was a skeptic. He doesn't suffer fools. He was a Marine. He was a little bit more urban, a . . . blue-collar guy that fought his way up, put himself through school and got into the FBI. He was a no-bullshit guy, straight to the point; thought Mulder was a bit of a kook. That was it . . . Chris was really, really wonderful, and gave me free rein to do with the character as I saw fit. I wanted him to be a cop from New York, because by that time, I'd done *Cop Land*, and I wanted to bring a little bit of that street with me."

Of course, Patrick was stepping into the show at a pivotal time in the series' run. With David Duchovny withdrawing his involvement considerably, there were a lot of viewers who were prepared to dislike this new lead character. At the time, Patrick was unaware of the negative rumblings among fans: "I was more excited about the fact that I'd found a nice gig in TV, being filmed in Los Angeles. I had seen *The X-Files*, of course. I was a fan of it, but [I hadn't] seen every episode. I wasn't that kind of a fan, but I certainly was aware of what great quality it was. . . . I didn't quite understand why the role had opened up [and] I didn't know David yet, at that time. . . . The Internet was a new deal, and I wasn't a computer guy, so I wasn't aware of what was being said online, and how angry people were. I know that Mr. Carter took real care to make sure that we were not in any way implying that we were replacing Mr. Duchovny. It was a new character created to prolong the life of the series. I was onboard with that, and was committed to making it the best show I could, and was excited about the new opportunity, the new adventure—and I'd never been a lead in a two-handed drama before. It was exciting. Exciting for me, so that was more of the emphasis for me when we agreed to do it."

Patrick remembers the exhilaration he felt about the two-parter that would introduce Agent John Doggett to the show: "Chris assured me that ['Within'/'Without'] was going to be directed by Kim Manners, and just raved about Kim and [how] the first two [episodes would be] like a movie. As a matter of fact, when the first two were finished, they presented it over at the Academy of Television, and put it up on the big screen. . . . It was a two-hour presentation, which was exciting. The thing really did play like a movie. It was great. . . . I have to tell you that Chris knows his fans. He knows his audience. He knew that there were going to be some people that wanted to throw water in my face." In fact, Patrick recalls being asked to perform that very scene in which Scully throws water in Doggett's face for executives at Fox after he had been cast. "It were the first scene I shot with Gillian, if my memory serves me correctly. It was terrific, because it was what people wanted. 'Who are you, and how dare you think that you can come on this show?' [But] I'm just an actor, man. I'm just an actor. You got to go where the jobs are."

SEASON 8 / EPISODE 3
WRITTEN AND DIRECTED BY CHRIS CARTER | "PATIENCE"

A GOOD PLACE TO START

In which maybe a guy could have evolved from a bat.

"Patience" is a necessary episode of *The X-Files*, but it's not a very good one. It is, in some ways, the real premiere of the season, taking us out from under the mythology and settling us back into a comfortable Monster of the Week format. The show likely could have made Season Eight a 21-episode search for Mulder, and there are certainly traces of that approach in "Patience." But devoting the entire season to the mythology would have removed one of the most pleasurable and beloved things about the show: watching two FBI agents heading off into the American hinterland to discover that things are not as they expected them to be. After the high stakes of the past few episodes and the game-changing loss of Mulder, it's honestly a relief to see the show executing its solid formula with interesting variations.

However, the episode has one major problem: its monster. The creature is, apparently, a man who evolved from a bat instead of from an ape. The show has had far more stupid concepts for monsters that, nonetheless, made for pretty great episodes of TV, thanks to how well the show used them. The man-bat in this episode is not in that category. Its design is bland and generic, and its attacks devolve into a series of jittery, blood-soaked jump cuts. It attacks people by pouncing on them from above, then sinking its teeth into them, which is about what you'd expect from such a beast. The man-bat is simultaneously too weird and not weird *enough*.[5]

As Ernie Stefaniuk—the hunter whose actions in the '50s led to the man-bat hunting *him* in the present—Gene Dynarski is sadly the weakest link in a cast filled with actors hamming it up. The scene in which he explains to Scully and Doggett what's going on and how he made his wife live away from society for forty years because of the man-bat is incredibly silly. A lot of this is on Carter's script, but there was probably a stronger approach to take than going full ham.

Other than the flaws of its central creature and some of its guest stars, "Patience" is solid. Yes, it's a very, very slow episode, but that's forgivable because of where the episode falls in the run of the show. The series needs to reestablish how *The X-Files* is going to work with Doggett as a co-lead instead of Mulder, and how Scully can be the "believer" and Doggett the "skeptic." What's more, both characters here are more than willing to blur the lines between their two ideological positions, instead of being rigidly trapped in the boxes designated to Mulder and Scully.

Scully, for example, makes all sorts of crazy leaps about what's happening and suggests that an ostensible animal attack might instead be the work of a human being. She also looks at autopsy results and concludes that she might have been wrong, that an animal might have been involved after all—a conclusion Mulder, with his fervent beliefs, never would have drawn. For his part, Doggett may have his doubts about human involvement, but he backs up Scully at every turn, regardless of his personal opinion. He's committed to playing his good cop part, and he has read all of the X-Files to prove his interest in his new role, so he has the archival knowledge to haul out an old newspaper article that establishes the man-bat as the episode's villain.

In short, the show is having a lot of fun with its new, more flexible dynamics. Shocking, then, that this old dog, improbably, can learn new tricks.[6] The scene in which Scully gives the kind of slide show presentation Mulder traditionally gave her nods to how much she is now trying to suggest supernatural theories in order to compensate for her partner's absence. Yet the moment when she finally puts Mulder's nameplate in a drawer and assumes command of his desk achieves the same, if inverted, effect. Scully must carry on Mulder's legacy, even if she's not interested in entirely replacing him. These moments are important and necessary character beats to help ease the transition to seeing Doggett as our male hero. The audience needs to be given permission to let Mulder go for a little while and to begin embrac-

S8 E3

---

5 One element of the man-bat that really works, though, is its lonely wait to punish the man who killed its mate. It nicely parallels Scully's wait for Mulder to return.

6 To put it mildly, it's really rare for a show to switch up its core dynamics this late in its run and have it actually work, instead of feeling like a desperate retool.

ing Doggett; Scully, by closing the drawer on Mulder (if only for a while), is yet again acting as our surrogate. To an extent, the series accepts that some people will never forgive Doggett for not being Mulder, but the script here is also doing its best to give him every opportunity to persuade us and allow him to catch up.

In the end, the most important thing "Patience" does is underline how much respect Doggett has for both Scully and the job. It would have been easy for the series to introduce a character who came in to the X-Files office guns blazing, complaining about all of the stupid stuff he had to put up with in this job. It would have been easy for the series to introduce a character who blanched at the thought of the other agents making fun of him for all the insanity that would be recorded in his reports. Thankfully, John Doggett isn't that guy. He might know that this is a weird job, and he might think that this is not really the job for him, but as long as he's assigned that office, he's going to do the job as well as he can; he's going to respect and honor the woman who has made this the work of the last seven years of her life. In so doing, the show indicates to the audience that this is a character worth investing in. Sure, he's not Mulder, but he's also not someone who's *trying* to be Mulder—and the show can be reinvigorated by that fact. —TVDW

SEASON 8 / EPISODE 4
WRITTEN BY VINCE GILLIGAN | "ROADRUNNERS"
DIRECTED BY ROD HARDY

YOU WILL BE SO LOVED

In which Scully is going to be Jesus! Hooray!

Even this late in its run, there's something stark and beautiful about the way *The X-Files* can leave behind the urban cityscapes of so many crime shows and end up in a menacing little town in the middle of nowhere. At its best, the show bottles the unsettling feeling of coming across a town that's six or seven buildings at most, thinking it's abandoned, then seeing someone come out of one of the houses, step onto the porch, and watch you drive through, following you with their eyes the whole way.[7]

"Roadrunners" is the only episode of Season Eight scripted by Vince Gilligan, who would head off soon after to head up *The Lone Gunmen*.[8] It comes close enough to classic greatness to indicate that after the bland Season Seven, Season Eight

---

7   Once again, this is an episode in which the characters find themselves trapped in some remote location, forced to simply survive until help can arrive. Unlike its closest cousin, "Ice" (S1E8), however, "Roadrunners" is a solo hour, which gives it some added punch.

8   The show's first proper spin-off (since *Millennium* was retroactively made a spin-off with the Season Seven episode "Millennium" [S7E4]). I'll give you three guesses as to what it was about.

SEASON EIGHT   361

will have more to recommend it. This is a terrifically scary hour, but its attempts to solidify the partnership between Scully and Doggett don't work as well as you'd hope. Regardless, it's one of the season's finest stand-alones and a wonderful examination of just who Dana Scully is at this point in time. Even when she's being held down by the townspeople who mean to implant some sort of slug parasite along her spinal column, even when she starts screaming about how she's pregnant and they can't *do* this to her, even when she's about to have her mind wiped by a Christlike slug, Dana Scully and the woman playing her find a way to push through the horror to a place of determined survival.

Like "Patience," the relationship between the protagonists in "Roadrunners" is dedicated to helping us move past the Mulder era. Unlike that previous hour, this episode accomplishes this aim by tossing Scully—the character to whom we still have a strong connection—into a pot of boiling water before turning up the heat. She constantly tries to find some way out of the situation she's stumbled into—one she very quickly realizes could lead to her death. Though she's been tied down to a bed so a parasite can meld with her mind and destroy her body, our heroine tries to escape by attracting the attention of Doggett (who is right outside) by kicking over a lantern and starting a fire. This is our strong, capable, intelligent Dana Scully, struggling and largely succeeding against overwhelming odds. Moreover, she's bolstered at every turn by the woman playing her. Gillian Anderson is never less than committed to any story she's asked to enact, but here she turns Scully into someone almost feral, barely clinging to her survival and self. It's a side of the character she's rarely asked to play, and she's extraordinary at it.[9]

Gilligan's scripts often gain strength from how little they explain, which is true in "Roadrunners" too. We get just enough clues about the grotesque process we witness—the cultists find hapless folks out in the desert, then stone the former brain slug hosts to death in order to extract the slug and place it in the new host—to put together what really happened after Hank (David Barry Gray) got onboard that desert bus and rode toward his doom. But no character ever sits down with a monologue of exposition that will tell us precisely what's going on or why it's happening. And why would they, given the unblinking creepiness of the episode? Even better, the script lets us think that maybe that slug *is* some sort of incredible, supernatural being, easy for a cult to mistake for the second coming of Christ. There's an undercurrent here of a possible empathy toward the desert weirdos who just want to worship their brain slug in peace. If that means they have to commit a few murders—well, so be it.

The fact that the script is otherwise fantastic makes its failure to believably bond Scully and Doggett all the more frustrating, as that flaw stems almost entirely

---

9   Notably, just before Season Eight debuted, Anderson's work in the Terence Davies film *The House of Mirth* earned her critical acclaim and Oscar buzz. She didn't get the nomination, but that film remains the highpoint of *X-Files* alums receiving praise for big-screen work.

from the final scene. As Scully and Doggett leave the hospital where Scully recuperated, she apologizes to him for not letting him know that she was taking on this case, which started out as a consult on an unidentifiable corpse found in the desert. He tells her how stupid she was to go without him. Doggett's intention is to let Scully know he has her back, but the scene plays instead like he's being kind of a jerk to her after she nearly became a brain slug cult leader in the Utah desert. The fact that Doggett is largely sidelined in the main story line doesn't help to strengthen their dynamic—but he *is* trying to find Scully throughout the hour after he stops hearing from her, which makes him marginally more sympathetic.

The best episodes of *The X-Files* have a weird wildness to them that many, many shows have tried to copy, though few have succeeded. "Roadrunners" unfolds like a long, horrifying nightmare, possessed of logic that makes sense while you're in it but that dissipates as soon as you're roused from its spell. A bus pulling up in the middle of the night in the desert and letting someone on shouldn't necessarily be scary. But it is here. That image shouldn't fit together with cults that stone people or slugs that may or may not be Jesus. But it does. "Roadrunners" is what happens when a confident writer and a confident actress boil the show down to its essence and find out that the barest basics still work well. —TVDW

SEASON 8 / EPISODE 5
WRITTEN BY DAVID AMANN
DIRECTED BY RICHARD COMPTON

| **"INVOCATION"** |

A NEW (OLD) BACKSTORY
In which a lost little boy comes home but stays lost.

Introducing a new lead character eight seasons into a show's run is a risk as well as an opportunity. While it's difficult to quickly and effectively build audience investment in a stranger, fresh blood like Doggett can offer a fresh start. So far, *The X-Files* has made the smart choices that keep that opportunity vibrant and new, starting with casting Robert Patrick. Patrick's portrayal of the character shows a man determined and unrelenting, but not humorless. Doggett's skepticism is different than the sort we're used to from early-seasons Scully. Doggett's view of the world is informed by his cop street smarts and sturdy common sense more than by an overreliance on logic. The character is a great choice to fill Mulder's absence; he's less a replacement for our lost protagonist than a startlingly different and welcome take on a story we've been watching for years.

The fact that Doggett has a tragedy in his past doesn't change his status as a new kind of main character, but it does push the character in directions that undermine some of his strongest traits. The introduction of the man's backstory is deliberately low-key: In one scene, Doggett pulls a picture of a smiling boy out of his wallet, reminding himself of something we don't yet know about. Still, the implication of the boy's picture in Doggett's wallet is clear enough, and it's disappointing to see the character falling into the cliché of the hero inspired to heroism by a tragedy in his past so early on. It's an unnecessary touch, one that diminishes much of what makes him so compelling in the first place; while the tragedy doesn't reduce the character completely, it feels like the easy way out when it comes to characterization, providing a shorthand for motivation instead of finding something new. It wouldn't be so much of a problem if the show hadn't already spent so much time delineating Mulder's quest for his missing sister. After years of searching, that plot was resolved,[10] and there's something exhausting in having a variation of that old idea coming up again, especially during a season which is ostensibly about new beginnings.[11]

"Invocation" works better while watching it than it does on reflection. The premise of this hour is effective, as the idea that a missing child could reappear and turn out to be a threat to the people who've suffered his absence the most is horrifying, especially when that threat seems to be targeting the only sane child his family has left. The story is heavy with portent while managing to stay mysterious for most of its running time. This is crucial, because when the actual answer is revealed—something muddled about ghosts—it lands with a heavy thud. When it comes to the inexplicable, the less the writers explain the better, but there needs to be at least some form of clarity in the last act, especially for a story that spends most of its time setting you up to assume it's zig one way, only to zag in the final minutes.

Overall, this is a mediocre entry that's saved from being completely forgettable by some memorable shots, decent Scully-Doggett banter, and the first suggestion that Doggett has a deeper private life and past than we realized.[12] Patrick is a good enough actor to do well with the material he's given, so it doesn't fall completely flat. But given how hard the show has tried in other respects to distance its new leading man from its old one, did we really need another sad tale of lost children? —ZH

---

10 In a somewhat unsatisfying fashion: See "Sein und Zeit" (S7E10) and "Closure" (S7E11).

11 Funnily enough, Robert Patrick claims that Doggett's backstory sharing themes with that of Mulder's was coincidental more than anything else, as Patrick's wife was pregnant with a boy when the show started shooting. Patrick says on the subject, "All the writers knew that I was welcoming a son into the world, and I think they thought it would make a good story and give me something to work on."

12 As for specific details of that past, we'll just have to wait and see!

SEASON 8 / EPISODE 6
WRITTEN BY STEVEN MAEDA AND DANIEL ARKIN,
BASED ON A STORY BY STEVEN MAEDA
DIRECTED BY PETER MARKLE

"REDRUM"

ALL WORK AND NO PLAY

.gnorw tnew ecno tahw thgir tup ot sah notroM eoJ hcihw nI

As another example of an episode that starts off strong only to falter in the final act, "Redrum" is more successful than "Invocation" (S8E5) for two reasons. Its main asset is guest star Joe Morton. Never a showy actor, Morton makes Martin Wells—a lawyer accused of murdering his wife—the calm, desperate center of an absurd situation, and his performance helps to compensate for the rougher parts of the script. He somehow makes the insanity make sense, even if it doesn't really.

The other strength of the episode is its premise. "Redrum" gains ground by finding a fresh angle on time travel. Wells isn't just jumping to the past or stuck in a loop: He's moving backward chronologically day by day. The way Wells's confusion mirrors the episode's unfolding structure is cleverly done, and the script does a good job of establishing the rules of the game early in the hour. The downside to this dense premise is that, once it finally becomes clear exactly what's happening, the story behind the time travel isn't nearly as compelling as the concept itself. Wells's wife is murdered, and he's been wrongly accused of a crime he inadvertently helped bring about by some earlier shady dealing. Wells finds himself trapped in a backward chronology for reasons that are never truly explored or explained.

Though it's smart that the script makes Wells partly culpable for his wife's death, the reveal of his responsibility only confuses things. There's a disconnect between Wells's guilt and the events of the story that makes the supernatural element less palatable. Why does Wells get a second chance to make amends? Why not help the people whose lives he ruined instead? We don't necessarily need specific answers to these questions, but without any sort of explanation for Wells's experience, his ability to time travel comes across as kind of divine intervention—maybe not from God, but from some force that has decided *his* redemption was more important than someone else's.

It doesn't help that while Danny Trejo's Cesar has considerable presence, the role never really coheres into a real person. He's a rage-filled monster willing to kill an innocent person to get his revenge, but he's also highly articulate and able to quote court cases when needed. It's not that Cesar is an impossible type, but he's so poorly sketched in that he comes across as plot spackle, there to fill holes and little else. It's a problem similar to the issues raised by the lack of explanation for the time loop, something that maybe a few additional rewrites might have cleared up.

Despite the flaws of the script, Morton performs admirably. There are respectable choices here beyond the casting; the shot of Wells still in a jail cell at the end, for example, having saved his wife but needing to confess his sins to Doggett in order to do so, is appropriately ironic. Still, it is frustrating how little the beginning of the episode matters to its final twenty minutes. The nature of the premise means that there is inherently no chance for Wells to accomplish any real action until he's out of jail. Instead of building suspense, much of "Redrum" feels like it's waiting around until the appropriate time. But there are worse characters to wait with. —ZH

| "VIA NEGATIVA" | SEASON 8 / EPISODE 7
WRITTEN BY FRANK SPOTNITZ
DIRECTED BY TONY WHARMBY |

BREAK ON THROUGH

In which Doggett sees the other side.

The story at the heart of "Via Negativa" is about Doggett struggling to come to grips with the darker side of working on the X-Files. He slowly starts to become aware what we—and Mulder and Scully—have long known: The world you thought you understood is no longer a world you can trust. It's unfortunate that Doggett's creeping realization necessitates that he spend more time apart from Scully. While the distance between them has resonance by the episode's conclusion, their partnership remains underdeveloped at this point in the season.

A large part of what made *The X-Files* so riveting was the relationship between its two leads, and while there's no sense that Doggett and Scully should be paired off romantically, keeping them apart robs the show of its core dynamic of co-workers leaning on each other to make sense of an insane world. Given how much Scully has come around to Mulder's point of view in Season Eight, this episode might have given Anderson a chance to reference her character work near the start of the series; Doggett is going through much the same journey that Scully did, and allowing her to share her own experiences might have given both actors more to work with.

Instead, Doggett spends time with some of Mulder's other old friends. With Scully absent, Skinner steps in to fill the gap—with mixed results. The more time he gets on-screen, the more Skinner seems like a shadow of his former self. In becoming an official part of Team Mulder, the character has lost much of his autonomy; his status as an ally with his own agenda gives Pileggi more to do, but the actor seems disappointingly subdued. The Lone Gunmen fare better. Appearing only for a scene, they serve to connect Doggett more deeply to the show's world. The three boys show up, joke around a bit, and demonstrate their almost immediate admiration of the new guy. Their willingness to accept him would be almost too obvious an attempt to ingratiate us with the character if it weren't for the fact that Doggett's transition from good cop in the normal world to good cop in crazy town has its consequences.

The specific X-File Doggett finds himself at the center of is thin on details. There is a lot of plot vagueness, and no elucidation of what the villain's powers actually are, or why they're manifesting in such a relentlessly homicidal way. There are ways to justify this opacity, but the episode doesn't seem interested in getting too deep into the reasons behind it all. There are magic drugs, a freaky third eye, and dream murders. Just roll with it, OK?

Fortunately, the atmosphere—heavy, doom-laden, and frequently surreal—makes up for any shortcomings in the script. "Via Negativa" is less interested in tracking down a monster than it is in expressing what it might be like for an outsider to stumble upon things that Mulder and Scully now take for granted. Doggett—a man for whom common sense and rational thinking are foundational—is now faced with a danger that he can't protect himself from, much less explain. That his final dream climaxes with an attempted attack on Scully isn't really a surprise. Now that he's faced with a universe in which all the closet doors stay open, why wouldn't he blame the woman who opened his eyes to all this monstrosity? —ZH

SEASON 8 / EPISODE 8
WRITTEN BY GREG WALKER
DIRECTED BY TERENCE O'HARA | **"SUREKILL"** |

X-RAY VISIONS

In which Randall is looking through you.

After the deeply creepy proceedings of "Via Negativa" (S8E7), we move to the thoroughly mundane, as "Surekill" presents us with the case of a hit man who can see through walls. There's a glimmer of an idea here, but the more the premise unfolds, the less interesting that idea becomes. It's not terrible, but nothing in this hour—from the sad, close-mouthed "monster" (Randall, played by Patrick Kilpatrick) to the abusive older brother (Dwight, played by Michael Bowen) to the low-rent femme fatale (Tammi, played by Kellie Waymire)—ever rises above its circumstance. It's the kind of story that really depends on the effectiveness of its hook to work, and in this case, its hook just isn't enough.

There isn't much reason to watch this overly familiar setup. The script's misconception that Randall's infatuation with Tammi is indicative of a deeper connection is ludicrous and borderline offensive. Someone who grew up with no conception of privacy would have a skewed idea of what was and wasn't appropriate, but the script implies a profundity to Randall's attentions that just doesn't ring true. He fixates on Tammi in the same way that any lonely (and slightly creepy) straight guy would fixate on an attractive woman who is occasionally nice to him. It's marginally plausible, but not worth building a story around. "Surekill" isn't terrible, but there's really nothing to see here. —ZH

MR. ROBOTO

In which there is a man of steel.

The best thing about "Salvage" is also what makes it a rather weak episode of *The X-Files*. By now, you've surely realized that on this show, the regulars sometimes take a backseat to the adventures of the guest characters. However, it's rare to have the guests take over to the degree that they do in this episode.[13] Scully and Doggett are mostly incidental to this story. It's as if this episode has grafted an *X-Files* structure onto an unused script for *The Outer Limits*.

In fact, that's sort of what happened. "Salvage" is very loosely based on *Tetsuo, the Iron Man*,[14] and you can almost see the bones of that story here. There's the man who becomes more machine than man and loses his humanity to said machine. There are those who made him the way he is, who must be punished. There are the few remaining attachments to his old way of life, like a wife who still loves him and friends who still miss him. And there's the pitiless forward momentum of the story, in which it becomes obvious that he probably should stop his killing spree but can't because of the darkness pushing him forward. Scully and Doggett land somewhere in the middle of all of this, present in the story only because this is an episode of *The X-Files*, and they're supposed to be there.

Thankfully, the main guest character is compelling. Wade Williams animates Ray the metallic man's rage and pain at the realization that it will be impossible for him to ever get revenge because his transformation was accidental. He strikes out in anger at anyone who might bear the blame for his condition, but there's ultimately no villain to blame, no bad guy to kill. Ray is simply a monstrosity, and there's nothing to be done about it but take his own life in a car crusher. The episode is surprisingly soulful, especially once Ray reconnects with his wife, and the moment toward the end of the hour in which he realizes that the guy he's dragged out into the street to kill for what happened to him is just an accountant is potent and moving. The gravitas "Salvage" brings to its subject matter is not exactly what you'd expect from an *X-Files* episode about a metal man, and it's honestly a pleasant surprise.

In most *X-Files* episodes that deal with experimental science, the scientists (on some level) deserve the punishment that the monster metes out to them. "Salvage"

---

13 Though it was fairly common in the show's early going, what with all those Season One and Two episodes that saw Mulder and Scully visit some isolated community going through some deep-seated trauma. The tactic returned in Season Seven with episodes like "Hungry" (S7E3) and "Signs and Wonders" (S7E9).

14 A Japanese cyberpunk horror film from 1989.

instead makes Ray into something that came to be because of an awful accident, which generates some degree of audience pity, while still maintaining that his appearance is utterly terrifying for those he's killing. If this were an episode that focused solely on the guest characters, it would probably be more successful because it could keep us surprisingly interested in the grand tragedy of Ray.

But "Salvage" isn't that episode. This is an *X-Files* episode, which means Scully and Doggett are our ties to the show's universe. Yet most of the scenes with Scully and Doggett investigating the case are *boring*. There's nothing wrong with boring moments in a story that has more compelling things going on (like a metallic man), but for a show that's in its eighth season, scenes that feel particularly formulaic can be deadly to whatever is going on. That dullness is probably to be expected of any show in the middle of a twenty-plus-episode season, more than three-fourths of the way through its series run (and yes, every season of *The X-Files* has an episode or two that feels especially by the numbers). What makes the disparity of engagement so apparent in this episode is that what's going on with Ray is so much more vital and interesting than what's happening with Scully and Doggett.

There's fun to be had with Robert Patrick having played a deadly metal man before,[15] and Gillian Anderson (bless her) will always bring her all to even the dumbest of stories. But you don't need the FBI agents to tell this tale, and yet they keep getting shoehorned into the hour's events. In the past, the show could coast on the chemistry between Anderson and David Duchovny in weaker episodes, but that's simply no longer the case. Patrick and Anderson have chemistry too, but it's much more workmanlike than the sort of grand flirtation that existed between Anderson and Duchovny. Doggett and Scully are respectful co-workers, whereas Mulder and Scully are a coupling that should have epic poetry written about it. The season found some creative ways around that discrepancy in the first handful of its episodes, but the difference in chemistry proves too much to overcome in a tale that leaves less for the agents to do. —TVDW

S8 E9

---

15 As the T-1000 in *Terminator 2* (duh).

THE WORST WAY TO GO

In which there is a guy who crawls into and out of people's butts.

"Badlaa" has a bad reputation, perhaps even a downright putrid one. It's absolutely disgusting, hard to watch, and not terribly well-plotted. But few shows could carry off this bad an episode with as much panache as *The X-Files*. "Badlaa" might be filled with bad ideas, but at least it has style. It also brings Mulder back into the story in the most preposterous way possible, and it features a great guest star in Deep Roy as a man who crawls into and out of people's butts. It's *magnificently* bad. That should count for something.

The foremost problem with "Badlaa"[16] is one of power creep, which is to say that the villain's "superpowers" are never particularly well-defined, and that they just keep increasing in number and strength whenever the plot demands. Not only can the character played by Roy crawl into and out of the corpulent (killing them in the process), but he also uses their corpses to spirit his way across international lines. He can make people think he looks like a normal janitor and cast all other sorts of illusions to distract from the fact that he's a legless beggar who must wheel himself around on a little cart. He's identified within the episode by an old pal of Mulder's as a Siddhi mystic.[17] But there's no real connection between those powers and the fact that he transports himself around by crawling inside of people and operating them like a puppet (or so it seems?). The latter automatically becomes the most memorable thing about the episode, so it gets harder and harder to take the former at all seriously. The character starts to feel like a combination of five hundred better *X-Files* monsters, who could control other people via strange and ill-defined means[18]—and that's *before* you get to the fact that the inherent premise of the episode overflows with racist exoticism.[19]

Yet there's something that *works* about this episode all the same. For one thing, Scully and Doggett affect this story, with Scully's increasingly outlandish theories pushing more and more of a wedge between the two, even though she's ultimately correct. Roy may not have much of a character to play,[20] but he seems to get an almost

---

16 Which roughly translates to "vengeance" in Hindi.

17 John Shiban based the beggar on stories of Indian fakirs with tremendous power.

18 And/or attacked their victims via incredibly delicate, horrifying means. See also: Flukeman from "The Host" (S2E2).

19 Though unlike a lot of the show's other visits to such racially queasy territory, this particular trip is so stupid that you might forget to find it offensive.

20 He's basically playing the menacing and mysterious foreign "other," which marks another racially charged episode with a not-well-thought-out character of color at its core!

vicarious thrill out of all of the crazy shit he gets to do. The other guest characters are weak, and it's bizarre how the episode ends up boiling down to two boys discovering that it would be best if they were friends. But the episode isn't afraid to go for the big gross-out moment, a mode *The X-Files* has occasionally made work in the past.[21] There's something wholly committed in these scares—and there are some great moments, like the one in which the beggar's hand pokes up out of the fresh incision Scully had made in a man's distended stomach.

"Badlaa" also digs into Scully's attempts to be Mulder, which have evidently caused some degree of strain on her. The episode nods toward Mulder's absence by bringing in his old friend who knows so much about mystics,[22] but it's the final scene that hammers home just how hard it is for Scully to channel Mulder. Mulder's wild theories go against every bone she has in her body, but here she is, making the kinds of leaps of logic her former partner would have made and simply hoping for the best. It's a little hard to believe that she would jump from thinking that a legless Indian man is rolling around Washington, D.C., and killing people to figuring he was getting revenge for a chemical spill that killed his son, but she disappears right up into one of Mulder's fever dreams as surely as Roy's character disappears into . . . well . . . you know.

This is a messy episode, in all senses of the word, and it's got way too much going on in it to ever be wholly successful. If you've got a weak stomach, it's probably not the episode for you. "Badlaa" feels at times like it's trying to be seven or eight episodes at once, but in Roy, it has a charming, smiling monster who never speaks but who still creates an eerie atmosphere all his own. The sequence in which he makes a boy's mother believe that her son has drowned, then reveals himself as he drowns her, is incredibly dumb, yet the moment when she turns over her son's body and suddenly sees the face of the beggar is effectively creepy, as is the sound of those squeaky wheels echoing through an airport bathroom. It's understandable to view "Badlaa" as a catastrophe, and it's certainly not an episode to add to your perennial rewatch list. But a catastrophe told with assurance trumps a boring story executed with lifelessness any day. —TVDW

---

21 Whither ist thou, Flukeman?

22 If you've been paying close attention, you'll realize we've met Chuck Burks (Bill Dow) before in a handful of episodes, most recently in "Hollywood, A.D." (S7E19).

| SEASON 8 / EPISODE 11
WRITTEN BY FRANK SPOTNITZ
DIRECTED BY KIM MANNERS

ON THE QUESTION OF THE SOUL

In which Doggett gets chewed up and spat out.

A monster is an exaggeration of a preexisting condition. A vampire, our hunger; a werewolf, our rage; a zombie, the death that lies encoded in each strand of our DNA. If fiction is a way for the mind to cope with the inadequacies of the natural world, then monsters are how we externalize the horrors we can never truly be rid of. It's never as simple as running in the dead of night from something with a cape and fangs. A great horror story realizes that there are costs worse than death involved, and that sometimes surviving means leaving behind a piece of your soul.

"The Gift" is a great monster story. After a cold open establishing Mulder's involvement in a case before his disappearance, Doggett takes the lead, and there's something refreshing about how he handles such a twisty and bizarre investigation. Whereas Mulder's crazy theories always put him on the losing side of any fight with authority, Doggett is practical and thoroughly unromantic. He's not invested in some larger quest for a mysterious absolute "truth." He knows something happened, and he knows the stories he's getting from the sheriff and townspeople of a tiny Pennsylvania town don't add up. And so he starts pushing.

Skinner is convinced that the main reason Doggett is pursuing the case so hard is to help his career; if Doggett can prove that Mulder's disappearance isn't an X-file, he can get back on the fast track at the Bureau. As the events of the rest of the episode demonstrate, there's more to Doggett than that. While he may be motivated by ambition, his primary drive is a deeply rooted sense of justice—which means he's better suited to working X-files than his no-nonsense exterior suggests. He is, like Mulder, deeply driven by a need to know what's going on, though he may articulate that need differently than his predecessor. And if the reality he uncovers is built on an injustice, he will move heaven and hell to rectify it.

Of course, to tell a great monster story, you also need a great monster. "The Gift" finds such a creature in Native American folklore,[23] conjuring up a "soul eater" who exists solely to consume sickness and disease. It eats a sufferer alive, and then vomits his or her body back up, allowing the sick person to return healthy and free of illness. But there's a price: The soul eater exists in a condition of constant agony, burdened by the sickness of every person it helps. Yet people are still willing to go forward with this method if it means protecting their loved ones or themselves,

---

23 A theme which has come up on the show before, although it's arguably better used here than it was in the mythology.

especially because it's a price they themselves are not paying. It's a direct and horrifying form of exploitation, and one that rings especially true considering the original source of the soul eater legend.

Part of what makes this episode so effective is the inversion of the monster/person dichotomy, and the way it helps us get a clearer sense of the show's new leading man. This is the first time Doggett has been involved in a case that has him turning on the people he's been called in to protect, and it's a necessary step in his character development. Mulder was an established outsider from the start, but Doggett has been introduced to us as someone who always worked within the system to achieve his ends. If he's going to keep working on X-Files, we need to see that he can reject that system if it violates his greater sense of morality. His actions here demonstrate he can; once he realizes what's going on, and that the soul eater is actually the victim of this community, he immediately steps in to try and protect the creature from further harm—putting himself at fatal risk in the process.

Which brings us to the other part of what makes this episode so powerful. "The Gift" is terrific because of its willingness to follow its premise through. When Doggett is shot, the soul eater takes his injuries onto himself, essentially dying in Doggett's place. But in order to do that, he has to literally eat Doggett alive, as he's done with each of his "victims" in turn. It's a fantastic visual, simultaneously metaphorical—the creature is consuming the suffering of another—and agonizingly real—the creature is eating a person alive, then vomiting them back up to be reborn. The fact that the actual process of "soul eating" is so explicit and direct makes it extremely effective as horror while also increasing our sense of pathos for a creature who has gone through this painful ritual over and over again. It's a great inversion of the typical predator/prey model to boot. Typically, the thing doing the eating is the thing you have to be afraid of, but here, it's the society that's found a way to turn that consumption to its own ends that's the real threat.

On the surface, the episode's conclusion seems surprisingly pat for an *X-Files* episode. The humans are saved, and the monster winds up in the ground, this time for good. But the closer you look at it, the more that ending feels appropriate for a Monster of the Week entry. While the immediate crisis has been resolved, the real villains remain free, their only punishment the fact that they'll be forced to watch their loved ones die like everyone else. They learned nothing from their experience, but Doggett is forced to go forward knowing what regular, everyday people are capable of, and how much suffering they're willing to create if they aren't the ones who have to endure it. He was also eaten alive, but maybe that hurt less. —ZH

| "MEDUSA" | SEASON 8 / EPISODE 12
WRITTEN BY FRANK SPOTNITZ
DIRECTED BY RICHARD COMPTON |

DON'T LOOK AT IT

In which nobody gets turned to stone, dammit!

"Medusa" takes place largely in the tunnels of Boston Metro—a dark, dank, spooky kind of place. The plot of this one relies heavily on a time limit, darkness, and a crack team of experts working together who you just know are going to fall apart at the first sign of trouble. Scenes of characters wandering around gloomy tunnels are always going to generate atmosphere regardless of what happens next, and "Medusa" is so good at keeping things moving that it takes a while to realize that it doesn't have much else going for it.

There's some fun to be had in watching Scully watch Doggett and his team slowly work through the closed-off subway tunnels and find bodies wrapped in plastic. Scully decides early on to sit this one out, and it's a nice, subtle character choice: She's obviously choosing to stay away from any possible contamination because of her pregnancy, but since she's keeping the pregnancy a secret, she doesn't share this information with Doggett.

The buildup to the actual threat is strong, but once it becomes clear that the "monster" isn't a conscious entity, and more of environmental threat, there isn't much story left to tell. The episode's guest characters aren't interesting enough to carry the hour themselves, and without intent, the "monster" becomes just a prop that waits around for people to stumble over it and die screaming. The climax of the episode has Doggett zapping the creatures via the third rail, and it certainly looks exciting, but it's also silly.[24] "Medusa" ultimately has a few decent ideas and a wasted setting, but not a lot else. —ZH

---

24 Congratulations, you defeated a puddle of goo!

THE NEW GUY

Robert Patrick reminisces about the whirlwind of joining *The X-Files* family: "The whole two years of that show was some of the most intense work I've ever done in my life, and I loved every minute of it. I mean, I was fatigued. I was tested, challenged. I loved it. It was like, for the first time in my life, getting to spend a long time with a character that I loved, and I felt like a factory worker going to punch a clock at the Fox lot. I'd never really done that. I was a movie guy. I was always off on location doing movies somewhere, and very little time on studio lots and soundstages. For me, it was such an exciting experience . . . [getting to work with] the wonderful crew and all the people involved that were committed to making it such a great show. Gillian, when I got the job, sent me flowers, and the flowers were beautiful, and the card read, 'Get some sleep—G.A.'

"[Gillian] became a great friend to [my wife] Barbara and I, and still is. . . . She really was very gracious and welcoming, and invited me to her house, and Barbara and I would go over and have dinner, and she was just super. Wonderful, wonderful gal, and I really, really enjoyed working with her. I will tell you that some new things started to happen to me as an actor that doing a one-hour TV show with the onslaught of dialogue and whatnot, I began, for the first time in my career, screwing up dialogue. I wasn't used to doing that. I was used to always nailing my stuff, and that was a whole new deal, but it's just that there's this continuous flow of dialogue that you finish one script, you get another one, and you just got all this stuff. It's a load. It is work, but incredibly fun.

"Mitch Pileggi became a dear friend, and we'd go to Mitch's house, and he and his wife Arlene, and Jim Pickens—I love Jim. I loved working with him. All the rest of the cast and crew, everybody was cool. Everybody was really hip to the fact that I was doing a whole new character. It wasn't in any way trying to replace Mr. Duchovny. Personally, I think that Gillian and I had our own kind of chemistry.

"I was very aware of how respectful [the show] was to Fox Mulder and his character, and I thought they nailed it. They allowed me to take care of [Gillian's] character in a way I thought was a great way to endear me to the audience, eventually, and make them realize that, 'Oh, yeah. Wait a minute. Doggett's okay. We can trust him.'"

"THIS IS NOT HAPPENING" | SEASON 8 / EPISODE 14
WRITTEN BY CHRIS CARTER AND FRANK SPOTNITZ
DIRECTED BY KIM MANNERS

REUNITED

*In which Scully's baby may not be her own, and the
man who may be the father returns.*

"Per Manum" and "This Is Not Happening" aren't really a two-parter. "This Is Not Happening" is actually the first half of a two-parter with "Deadalive" ([S8E15], which didn't air for five whole weeks after the gut-wrenching cliffhanger of "Happening"), while "Per Manum" is on an island by itself. But it's useful to look at these two hours together, because they both dance around the season's central story line of the search for Mulder and the status of Scully's pregnancy, and they're both key examples of how *The X-Files* utilized serialization and story arcs late in its run.

The serialization the show had practiced in its first few seasons—in which the alien mythology would be trotted out to general acclaim every few months—felt revolutionary at the time. Not only did the character stories continue (as they did on other workplace dramas) but there was also a huge central mystery for Mulder and Scully to uncover, one that would impact every aspect of their lives.

By 2001, when "Per Manum" and "This Is Not Happening" aired, that kind of serialization felt quaint. *The X-Files'* clean demarcation between the Monster of the Week episodes and the larger mythology episodes felt even more frustrating in light of the popularity and storytelling tactics of shows like *The Sopranos* or *Buffy the Vampire Slayer*.[25] As good as "Roadrunners" (S8E4) is, that Jesus slug wasn't going to play into the show's larger alien invasion story. In fact, the separation between its two modes is part of why *The X-Files* remains so watchable today. The show's sense of experimentation and fun in the MOTW episodes remains palpable, and even the lamer examples of the form can be a great time. A fan doesn't have to love the mythology story line to love *The X-Files*.

But in 2001, that wasn't as clear. The fans who had hung with the show through all eight seasons wanted some satisfying resolutions to the mythology, even if they suspected such a thing would be impossible, and the series was still largely dis-

---

25 *Buffy* had a vaguely *X-Files*-ian split between its "monster of the week" and "mythology" episodes, but elements of both were incorporated into every episode, so even in completely disconnected MOTW entries, the main villains were plotting to bring about doomsday somewhere, before bringing all of those elements together in its season finale. *The Sopranos* was structured like a collection of short stories that built atop each other, so you understood the characters better and better with every episode, all culminating in a finale that pulled those many disparate threads together.

cussed in the press as the one with the complicated story about aliens colonizing Earth. While Season Eight doesn't mark an abrupt shift in the style of *The X-Files'* serialization—there are still stand-alone episodes that have nothing to do with anything else—the hunt for Mulder gives it more of a throughline than any previous season (save maybe the Scully cancer arc in Season Four). Season Eight is, in some ways, the first *modern X-Files* season.[26]

The increased level of serialization inherent in this story means that the season feels like no *X-Files* season prior, and even when it makes missteps, they're more easily swept aside by the next big development in the overarching story line—a major hallmark of modern serialized dramas. Even more surprisingly, the plot never feels forced, like it might have on other shows. Mulder's disappearance and Scully's pregnancy are such seismic events within the world of the show that they can't just be ignored. Every episode has to check in on what's going on with the search, and short of that, it needs to let us know how Scully is dealing with this seemingly miraculous pregnancy. There are other minor threads here—like Doggett's quest to know what happened to his son—but for the most part, the aftermath of Season Seven gives Season Eight a propulsion that carries it through even the weakest hours.

"Per Manum" wasn't actually intended to air immediately before "This Is Not Happening." It was produced eighth in the season, between "Via Negativa" (S8E7) and "Surekill" (S8E8), and it's not hard to imagine airing it there, in its proper order. Yet it works much better falling where it does. The string of episodes before this entry admirably outlined Scully's attempts to force herself to become a believer, the better to honor Mulder's memory and to potentially find her missing partner. They also firmly situated Doggett as the man suited to carry on in Mulder's stead, even if he's much more of a skeptic than our missing hero ever could be. The dynamic between the two isn't as emotionally[27] charged as the one between Mulder and Scully, but it doesn't need to be, because the memory of Mulder is ever-present.

After that string of episodes, it makes sense to circle back to Scully's pregnancy, which is just fourteen weeks along.[28] The aliens have been quiet since they took Mulder off to parts unknown, so it's time to check in with them as well. "Per Manum" is appropriately scary when it comes to the extraterrestrials' intentions, setting the tone with a horrifying opening sequence in which a woman gives birth to a strange shrieking creature that appears to be some sort of human-alien hybrid. Add to that the scene in which Scully gets a look at her healthy, developing fetus, only to realize that she was actually being shown a videotape of some other woman's sonogram, and you have a beautifully executed misdirect, as Scully inadvertently

---

26 It's certainly the one that lends itself most to binge-watching, which I wouldn't have expected!
27 Or romantically.
28 To be honest, that time-line seems incredibly rushed, but let's just go with it.

leads the people looking for a woman pregnant with one of the hybrids right to her because she never guessed they could be looking for *her*.

All that said, the real reason to watch "Per Manum" is for the return of Fox Mulder, albeit in flashback. Unlike "The Gift" (S8E11), which perhaps tries too hard to insert Mulder into the story line by suggesting that he had been suffering from a debilitating disease for at least a season and didn't bother telling anyone, "Per Manum" fills in some happier blanks, implying that Mulder might be the father of Scully's unborn child (if the aliens aren't). It's not hard to guess that Mulder might be the father, but the inevitability doesn't change how lovely the flashback scene is; Scully asking him to help her conceive plays out as a touching moment between friends who are about to take a very big step together. David Duchovny steps right back into Mulder's innate tenderness in the scenes in which he and Scully chat about her desire to have a child and channels the character's empathy when Scully tells him that her first round of in vitro treatments didn't take.

In addition to even further strengthening the bond between our two favorite agents, these scenes help clarify Scully's motivation and emotional state at this point in the season. We now know that Scully isn't *just* looking for Mulder as her friend and partner; she's looking for the man who might be the father of her child, and one of the few people who can help her figure out exactly what's going on. She's also looking to build a better world for the life she carries inside of her—a place in which the government will not cooperate with advanced alien beings to plot an invasion of the Earth, a universe in which said aliens will not abduct defenseless women and impregnate them with interstellar horrors. *The X-Files* has done plenty of riffs on the terror inherent in the very idea of pregnancy, but once these terrors are affecting Scully, they suddenly feel much more immediate and visceral.

That's not to say that "Per Manum" doesn't have its issues. The actual alien conspiracy is so convoluted at this point that it's never clear why anything is happening, and the half of the episode that deals with Doggett feels weak in contrast to the emotional upheaval that Scully is going through. There's a sneaking sense that the show has done all of this before,[29] even if Anderson's performance knits it all together without any piece feeling too forced. Wedding the pregnancy and Mulder story lines into the same set of dramatic stakes was necessary, but the episode feels flabby and predictable around the edges.

"Per Manum," while solid, also suffers when compared to "This is Not Happening," which is one of the strongest episodes of the season. The series has portrayed alien abductions throughout its run as such an inevitable fact of life that it's rare to see the show really dig into how much abduction could rip a life in two, taking something that once felt normal and safe and turning everything into a reminder

---

29 Scary pregnancies, alien-human hybrids, and Scully in distress are all wells the show has pretty much run dry by this point.

of the most unexpected type of trauma. "Happening" drops returned abductees onto the ground in a horrible state, suffering from terrible injuries, on the verge of death. It builds and builds and builds, its central tragedy becoming more and more awful, climaxing in the horrific shock of Mulder's lifeless body appearing on the forest floor and the only man who can save him being sucked into a UFO returning to the depths of space.[30]

"This Is Not Happening" also folds in a piece of the mythology that the show seemed to have mostly forgotten about. Jeremiah Smith—that shamanistic alien who was healing humans all the way back in "Talitha Cumi" (S3E24)—returns to the show's forefront in this episode, turning up among a UFO cult in Montana headed by a doomsday prophet named Absalom (Judson Scott). Absalom and Jeremiah try to heal the abductees who are returned, but the task is thankless, as the aliens leave behind battered, mutilated bodies barely clinging to life. Once the FBI gets involved by raiding the cult's compound and interrupting their work, it sets into motion events that will leave Mulder lying dead on the ground, with no one at all who can save him.

The ending is truly spectacular, with Mark Snow's music and Anderson's performance and Kim Manners's direction working in tandem to create a sequence of images that shows Scully's absolute anguish at her inability to save Mulder at the moment when he was counting on her most. The whole episode feels *exhausted* (as a character who'd been dragged through year after year of this ridiculous conspiracy surely would be), and when Scully howls the episode's title in a moment that should feel a little dumb, it instead sounds like the cry of a woman at the end of her rope. What hope she had for the future is now left behind. The invasion is coming soon, and her only salvation is gone.

"Happening" is, for the most part, a terrific episode of *The X-Files*—one that would stand alongside the very best of the earlier seasons—*but* for the fact that it introduces Monica Reyes (Annabeth Gish), who feels entirely out of place here. When she pops up, sounding strangely chipper about Satanic cults that mutilate people, it throws the otherwise mournful episode into a tonal imbalance that seems wholly unintentional. Reyes, played by a well-known actress as she is, sure seems like she's meant to be the new Scully, who happens to possess Mulder's natural belief in the paranormal. But if we compare her perversely cheerful attitude here with Scully's utter torment at the episode's end, there's simply no question of who is going to be more compelling to the audience.

"Per Manum" and "This Is Not Happening" are the center of Season Eight. Both written by Chris Carter and Frank Spotnitz and directed by Manners, these episodes absolutely have to work if this season's approach to serialization is going

S8 E13–14

---

30 Mulder's return might have had a little more power if David Duchovny's name hadn't popped up in the opening credits. Oh well.

to carry the day. That they do is a testament to the show's inherent ability, even at this late date, to sweep everything aside and tell a simple but gut-wrenching story about the cost of living in a world in which unthinkable evil is wrought upon innocents. —TVDW

| "DEADALIVE" | SEASON 8 / EPISODE 15 |

| "THREE WORDS" | SEASON 8 / EPISODE 16
WRITTEN BY CHRIS CARTER AND FRANK SPOTNITZ
DIRECTED BY TONY WHARMBY |

NOT QUITE GONE
In which Mulder isn't dead!

"Deadalive" devotes a full hour to getting our second-favorite alien abductee back on his feet. It manages to make that transition suspenseful by putting Mulder through a series of increasingly unsettling crises. He starts the hour off by being buried alive and then things get even worse, so that by the time the happy ending rolls around, it feels truly earned.

"Deadalive" is the conclusion of the cliff-hanger from "This Is Not Happening" (S8E14), whereas "Three Words" gives us Mulder trying to reintegrate into his former life (without much success). The two hours are strongly connected as a result of the show's increasing focus on serialization, and there's a considerable amount of energy built over the course of these four entries, thanks to Mulder's return (first in flashback and then in actual fact) and reunion with his partner. In addition, for the first time, Mulder and Scully have an ally committed to their cause, an ally beyond the Lone Gunmen and Skinner. Doggett's presence alters the dynamic of the series, and while that dynamic has served Chris Carter and his writing staff well for a long time, it's exciting to see such a fundamental change.

Before Mulder can rejoin the living, though, he has to come back from the dead, and it's not a pleasant journey. Everything happens fast, and it's utterly nightmarish: Mulder is still alive, but his tissue is dead, so he's still in critical condition. Which leaves Scully, Skinner, and Doggett the daunting task of trying to find a cure for the impossible. It's a measure of the effectiveness of "Deadalive" that this struggle has real weight behind it. Given Mulder's long absence from the show, his presence is no longer as critical as it once was; and while it's unlikely that the show would bring him back just to kill him, it's not *impossible*. More importantly, Scully and the others are at the brink of despair throughout. Mulder's return feels powerful in a way that the mythology episodes didn't always , and the scene near the end of the episode, in which Mulder wakes up,[31] is a fitting denouement to what both the characters and the audience most dearly hoped for.

Apart from Mulder's return, the main focus of "Deadalive" is Billy Miles's[32] remarkable "recovery" and the reappearance of Alex Krycek. Billy's story is the creepier of the two. His reemergence into the plot serves as both an inspiration and a warning to our heroes; his return from apparent death convinces Scully to exhume Mulder's corpse to find her partner is still alive, yet Billy is literally a changed man, his death and transformation into something altogether new providing the clues that help Scully to cure Mulder's alien virus. Billy's fate lends weight to the hook of "Deadalive," ensuring that nothing feels certain until Mulder finally opens his eyes. As for Krycek, it's always fun to see him and his slimy smugness pop up to add dimension to the show as a more tangible threat to our agents.

"Three Words" finds Mulder back on his feet and Duchovny ready for action. The actor brings a new energy to his signature role, a semi-irritated vibe that's especially funny when it butts up against all these characters who have worked so hard to save him. Mulder doesn't even seem all that grateful! There's a sense that he's reached his wits' end, and his normal obsessions have overtaken what little sense and patience he had left. It's fitting that he would have been changed by his recent (horrifying) experiences, and Duchovny's approach helps to make sure his absence and return have as much weight for the character as they do for the audience.

That irritation is most evident in his confrontations with his "replacement." What becomes clear fairly quickly is that Mulder does not much care for Doggett. In the first meeting between the two men, Mulder shoves our new leading man, and relations improve only slightly from there. It makes sense that the two wouldn't get along upon first introduction, but the macho aggression comes off as too intense for the characters we know. Mulder's distaste works fine in theory but doesn't translate onto the screen. Infighting between heroes only works if everyone has a clear, understandable reason for disliking each other. Here, though, it just makes Mulder look like a territorial jerk; it's a dynamic which seems unnecessarily heightened, although the conflict does lend a semi-meta, additional friction to Mulder's reappearance—are we watching two actors squabbling over who gets to be the lead?

Perhaps the worst aspect of these two episodes is the way in which the story line sidelines Scully in the second half. After expending so much physical and emotional energy to bring Mulder back from the dead, it's perhaps fitting that she'd want to take a break, especially given her pregnancy. Yet it's disappointing to see the men take over in "Three Words," given how much Scully has accomplished. Furthermore,

S8 E15–16

---

31 And, of course, immediately plays a joke on his distraught partner.
32 As with his reappearance in "Requiem" (S7E22), Billy's presence here is a smart way to try to tie the show back to its origins—a callback which, even if it doesn't entirely make narrative sense, works to build a feeling of connection and an emotional throughline for a show nearing the end of its original run.

Mulder's later comment about how her priorities will change once she gives birth is disconcerting, as it suggests further downsizing of her role on the show. Much of the excitement of the two-parter comes from the chance to see *The X-Files* gesture to the way it used to be, with Mulder and Scully working together again to fight the forces of evil—which makes it especially galling to have Scully here pushed aside.

While "Three Words" lacks the emotional depth of "Deadalive," the later episode has a much stronger plot that builds to its inevitable conclusion in classic *X-Files* form. There's mystery, then hope, and then a betrayal that extinguishes almost all that hope except for the shred necessary for our heroes to survive. Mulder is back, the government is up to no good, the aliens are up to no good, and Scully is going to give birth any day now. Despite Mulder's mistrust in him, Doggett is still on the case. We now have more heroes than ever before. Can they can accomplish any good before it all goes to hell? —ZH

| "EMPEDOCLES" | SEASON 8 / EPISODE 17
WRITTEN BY GREG WALKER
DIRECTED BY BARRY K. THOMAS |

MULDER & SCULLY & DOGGETT & REYES

In which evil is a disease, and only Mulder
has the cure (but not really).

The central conceit of "Empedocles" is too nonsensical for the episode to work as a whole. Some genuinely unsettling things[33] occur in this episode, but it's just unbelievable to propose that evil is a virus that can be passed between people in moments of weakness. Perhaps genuine demonic possession would've fit the tone of the episode better and helped it all cohere. As it is, the notion of people being taken by *evil itself* feels slightly too much like a late-night argument in an undergrad dorm about why bad things happen to good people.

"Empedocles" is notable because it is one of the few episodes to feature all four FBI agents—past and future—in the same space, letting them bounce off one another. This crowdedness gives the episode a busier feel than most earlier episodes of the show, which could often feel as if they had a downright leisurely pace back when *The X-Files* was a true two-hander. Yes, the mythology episodes often had more "regulars,"[34] but in most episodes, it was all about Mulder and Scully, alongside B-story guest appearances by the people whose cases they were investigating. Now,

---

33 Look at that shot where poor Jeb (Jay Underwood) tears off his skin to reveal the fiery demon-self living beneath!

34 And consequently moved at a much brisker pace.

the show can play Reyes off Mulder, or Doggett off Scully, or return to the classic pairing of Mulder and Scully, and all of these relationships feel new and worth following.

Reyes doesn't exactly work as a character, but the show pulls off a clever trick by making her genre of supernatural "belief" very different from Mulder's, which produces some conflict between the two. It's also smart to tie her to Doggett in the form of a working relationship that extends back to the death of his son. Some of this dynamic was hinted at when Reyes first appeared in "This Is Not Happening" (S8E14), but giving it more weight here allows the two characters to share a bond without Mulder and Scully—an impulse that permits slightly more investment in Reyes.

Having all four agents around also allows the show to have a variety of story lines happening at once. Scully has to go to the hospital, and rather than sit by her bedside and wait for her to wake up, Mulder finds himself dragged into a case Reyes needs a consult on. This gives him a chance to spend serious screen time with someone other than his former partner for the first time in a while, which is doubly true once he gets to share scenes with Doggett. Because the producers almost certainly knew at this point that they wouldn't have David Duchovny for a prospective ninth season, it was imperative that the writing staff find some small ways to pass the torch from the older characters to the newer ones. To that end, Doggett talking with Scully about why she was able to finally believe, or Mulder and Reyes debating what's worth believing *in* makes these new characters feel like they fit into the show in valuable and fresh ways.

It's the Mulder and Scully scenes in "Empedocles," curiously, that fall flat. Granted, Scully is in a hospital bed for much of the episode, but the banter between the two in the scene in which they talk about whether she's sleeping with her pizza guy feels like it goes on forever. The final scene, in which the two of them talk over pizza and the gift Mulder has given her, is almost embarrassingly gooey for the show. The writers had made their peace with the idea that Mulder and Scully had become lovers (although they, of course, didn't want to just come out and say it), but the cheesiness of, say, Scully telling Mulder that he gave her the wonderful gift of being able to believe is a bit too much. The prickliness and joking sarcasm that has always animated their attraction is missing here. What we get instead feels like a version of the characters we've never really seen before.

The case is, then, the least interesting thing in this hour, and it turns out to be rock-bottom stupid, particularly once it's resolved. By the time Mulder is talking about how he thinks that people can be taken over by evil in moments of weakness, the wheels have come off the truck. This conceit might have worked if it were played solely on the level of metaphor, if the flaming man was just meant to be an unexplained monster or nebulous demon. A metaphor also would have avoided the icky philosophical implications of the "virus of evil" notion, which (if you think about it a bit more) ends up suggesting that people aren't really responsible for their own actions.

The episode also seems like it's setting up the plot as Doggett and Reyes's own form of the mythology, one they can investigate throughout their run on the show. Just as Mulder had his sister's disappearance, Doggett has his son's death to explore. The impetus makes sense, but the execution doesn't. Instead of aliens—who were obviously central to the mystery of Samantha's abduction—Reyes and Doggett are going to investigate . . . what, evil itself? If that's the case, then "Empedocles" doesn't exactly augur greatness. The episode is fascinating for how it allows all four agents to develop differing, sometimes squabbling, personalities in one another's company, but the actual plot deflates the excitement of that novelty. —TVDW

| "VIENEN" | SEASON 8 / EPISODE 18
WRITTEN BY STEVEN MAEDA
DIRECTED BY ROD HARDY |

BACK IN BLACK

In which the black oil resurfaces!

It's hard to know precisely when the mythology of *The X-Files* went belly up. You can make a convincing case for somewhere in Season Four, somewhere in Season Five, or even somewhere in Season Six. Regardless, the mythology episodes are usually absolute messes by the time Season Eight rolls around. And yet "Vienen" is a terrific roller-coaster ride that brings back one of the show's best inventions. It might be the best mythology episode since Season Three,[35] and it bolsters the argument that Season Eight somehow brought the mythology back to life, thanks to the decision to wed the conspiracy to the other ongoing stories of Mulder's disappearance (and return) and Scully's pregnancy. With its crackerjack plotting and terrific last act, "Vienen" is a season highlight, and certainly one of the hours that helps cement Season Eight as *The X-Files'* most underrated outing.

Most remarkable is how "Vienen" goes out of its way to mostly ignore everything that happened in the mythology arc *after* Season Three; it has no interest in the global conspiracy or the aliens' colonization plot. For the most part, the black oil that turns up here is the same black oil as it appeared all the way back in "Piper Maru" (S3E15) and "Apocrypha" (S3E16). Here, it isn't the first stage of some insidious alien colonization plot, a virus that eventually turns human hosts into incubators for the gray aliens. It is, instead, just a strange organism that can override the

---

35 Specifically since that season's finale, "Talitha Cumi" (S3E24).

body's functions and take control, and its total lack of explanation makes it all the more alarming. It's more *Invasion of the Body Snatchers* than *Alien*, and "Vienen" is all the better for it.

The episode is indicative of Season Three's mythology in other ways as well. The aliens might be around, but they're mostly offscreen here, and all they seem to be doing is listening and transmitting messages to the guys on the oil rig where the black oil appears. In practice, this lack of alien involvement causes the episode to resemble something like a zombie story, albeit one in which the zombies can disguise themselves as normal human beings.[36] Mulder and Doggett discover they're smack-dab in the middle of an infestation, then have to figure out what they're going to do about it. "Vienen" bears a lot in common with "Roadrunners" (S8E4) and other survivalist episodes, except this one somehow manages to rope in much of the series' master plot. It's not hard to see why this episode is the way it is, and why it's so surprisingly effective: It has an exemplary filming location.

In past seasons, the series had written to locations, and then the location managers had gone out to find the spot that would match the script. But before Season Eight, the location manager was encouraged to go to find places where episodes might be filmed, places that would stand out and make a unique episode of *The X-Files*. An offshore oil rig, what with its isolation and man-made island status, is definitely the sort of place that would look and feel different from every other episode of the show. Are there similarities to, say, "Ice" (S1E8)? Of course there are. But this episode has a budget Season One of the show never could have imagined, the benefit of which is proven by the exterior shots of Mulder and Doggett racing around the oil rig.

What do you do when you've got a story set on an oil rig? Well, bring back the black oil! The black oil's powers have always been so undefined that the writers constantly come up with new ones, when, in reality, the fact that a strange alien virus kept people alive at the bottom of the ocean for decades was compelling enough. "Vienen" unnecessarily brings back some powers you might have forgotten were even in the black oil playbook (like those radiation flashes), but it mostly scales it back to the mind-control virus we all remember. Its potential to crawl inside of you of its own volition remains as deeply disturbing as ever.[37] The isolation, the location, the stripped-down aesthetics, and the presence of the black oil conspire to create an episode that plays as a claustrophobic thriller. Our two male heroes suddenly find themselves in a place they can't easily escape with a bunch of people they know are their enemies—though those enemies are not yet aware that Mulder and Doggett know the truth about them. It's marvelously tense, particularly in the last fifteen minutes or so, when all hell is breaking loose; the two agents' only recourse

---

36 Again, just like in *Invasion of the Body Snatchers*!

37 Are you creeped out by shots of oil moving beneath people's skin? Then you're in luck!

is to find their way to the edge of the burning oil rig and leap into the water in slim hopes that the helicopter Scully sent will be able to rescue them. If nothing else, "Vienen" is a great example of a television episode that knows how to keep upping the ante.

The episode is also trying to do a couple of things the show will need to accomplish for the series to continue, and it performs one quite successfully and the other a little less so. The first is the need for David Duchovny and Fox Mulder to pass the torch to Robert Patrick and John Doggett. For *The X-Files* to work for years to come, somebody else needs to lead the charge of Mulder's quest.[38] The experience at the oil rig is meant to be a kind of turning point for Doggett, a point at which he will figure out exactly what's up, and the high stakes of the situation effectively convince him (and us) that he can't help but be at least curious about whatever is going on one hundred fifty miles offshore.

The episode is less skilled at reinstating that old *X-Files* dynamic of the skeptic and the believer, working together. "Empedocles" (S8E17), in which all of the characters are skeptics about some things and believers about others, was more believably flexible in this regard than this return to the show's rigid old format. "Vienen" presents Doggett's encounter with the black oil as something that he will have to struggle to eventually believe in, a journey from the way he's always thought of the world to a new way of looking at it. But this feels a little ridiculous at this late date in the series, as though the show was so intent on making a throwback to the early mythology that it also imported Scully's blunt skepticism in the face of all she had seen[39] and gave the lines she would have had in those earlier episodes to Doggett. It's as if the episode were *too good* at nodding to the show's past.

While the show has worked hard to differentiate Doggett's position from Scully's arc for the first seven seasons, this episode essentially reverts Doggett back to the same place where Scully began way back when. The scenes in this episode in which Mulder and Doggett argue about what is real and what isn't stop the story dead in its tracks. We've come far enough that it would be more sensible for someone like Doggett to take leaps of faith, particularly when everybody around him—even Skinner—is a believer by now.

In spite of this character shortcoming, "Vienen" packs a punch. It's a suspenseful, tension-wracked episode, and when it reaches its conclusion, in which Fox Mulder is fired from the FBI, there's a finality to this decision. The moment is filled with an overwhelming sense that we've reached the end of an era. Season Eight is a surprisingly orderly transition from one version of the show to another,

38 Which is, by the way, a quest that he won't have as many resources with which to pursue now that he's been fired from the FBI.
39 *Extreme Mulder voice.*

S8 E18

and with almost all of the pieces in place, "Vienen" clicks a few more together so that the puzzle starts to make just a bit more sense. —TVDW

I WOULDN'T BE HERE WITHOUT YOU

In which there is a changing of the guard.

Between Mulder, Scully, Doggett, and Skinner, the back half of the eighth season has a refreshing ensemble feel to it.[40] The show has pitted its two protagonists alone against the forces of evil for so long that it's thrilling to see a change in the configuration of the series. But these new dynamics can't last forever. Mulder may be back, but the actor clearly isn't invested in the long haul,[41] and the imminence of Scully's baby will force her to play a secondary role too.[42] As the season draws to a close, it's time to start setting up for the future. That means finding a way to say a strange (but strangely moving) sort of good-bye.

That is exactly what "Alone" feels like: a way to have closure without actually concluding the plot. The closest we get to an explicit ending comes in the first scene between Doggett and Scully in Mulder's office. It's a melancholy exchange as Scully suggests that this is, for all intents and purposes, the end of her time in the department. Intentionally or not, the scene is more a comment on the audience's response to Scully's absence than anything else, as Patrick conveys a sense of loss that feels excessive considering the amount of time the two of them have worked together.

That impression of self-awareness—of the show reflecting on its own internal changes—is heightened by the presence of Agent Leyla Harrison (Jolie Jenkins), Scully's ostensible replacement. Harrison, the most obvious audience surrogate the show has yet produced,[43] spends her screen time relating the episode's proceedings to previous Mulder and Scully cases. Her main purpose is to provide Doggett with someone who isn't quite capable of supporting him—someone to comment on the legacy of the past while providing a stopgap until the future arrives.

---

40 See also: "Empedocles" (S8E17).

41 The season has spent so much time getting us used to Doggett as leading man that Mulder seems almost superfluous at this point; it doesn't help that Duchovny's performance has a definite "last-day-of-school-before-summer-vacation" vibe.

42 It's possible to imagine a show that featured the two of them trying their luck as first-time parents, and it's a measure of how likable the actors are together that I think I would watch that show. But I won't fool myself into thinking that show would be *The X-Files*.

43 Harrison was named for a real life *X-Files* fan who died of cancer, which imbues her character with a bit more poignancy in an already melancholy episode.

Harrison is the most explicitly meta element to the episode, but even without her character, "Alone" plays like a statement. Seeing Mulder go through the old motions is wonderfully nostalgic, but we know things have changed. So much of the season has been spent on positioning Doggett as the new male lead that having our old hero return to the usual routine comes off as oddly artificial. Duchovny's desire to leave manifests in the text of the episode as Mulder reaching something of a crossroads. He still wants his truth, but there are things at stake now, not the least which is the existence of his son. Questing for truth and tilting at windmills is a single man's (or woman's) game, and the possibility of a family, however unconventional, would change anyone's priorities. There's a real sense that he's ready to move on.

None of these concerns would matter much if the episode didn't work well on its own terms. Spotnitz's direction makes elegant use of unusual angles and does a good job of conveying a constant impression of menace. The script wisely leaves most of the backstory of the creature to implication and suggestion, and the climax ranks as one of the show's better monster kills: Unarmed, Mulder has to tell a half-blind Doggett to shoot at the exact moment the monster jumps for him.

It's certainly a good time, but it feels a little strained too. The final scene involves Harrison asking how Mulder and Scully got back from the Antarctic after the climax of *The X-Files: Fight the Future*. It's a funny joke, and Scully and Mulder's immediate debate is a lovely callback to the old personas we know and love. But it's infused with a sense that it's time for them to go. The question, then, is whether the show can survive without them. —ZH

"ESSENCE"	SEASON 8 / EPISODE 20
"EXISTENCE"	SEASON 8 / EPISODE 21 WRITTEN BY CHRIS CARTER DIRECTED BY KIM MANNERS

WHAT ABOUT THE BOY

In which Scully finally has her baby.

How much does the mythology have to make sense in order for *The X-Files* to qualify as "good TV"? "Essence" builds to a fever pitch that makes questions of who-wants-what mostly irrelevant. "Existence" can't really maintain that level of intensity and tries to go for something more ambitious instead, to mixed results. However, the sense of ambition and the scope—and the visceral fact of Scully giving birth and screaming about how it's *her* baby and she's going to keep it—make it feel important.

As we've discussed, even the weaker episodes of Season Eight have a sense of purpose to them, and the mythology arc—beginning with the hunt for Mulder and ending with the alien-human hybrid, Christlike baby—maintains a strong sense of urgency throughout. Yet while there was a clear sense of emotional import and high-stakes danger from start to finish, that clarity unfortunately doesn't extend to the actual details of the plot. There are factions fighting against other factions, red herrings, God metaphors, and Krycek. You might have the creeping suspicion that none of it, in the end, makes a damn bit of sense. But hell, the season was a blast to watch.

That sense of fun doesn't make it less frustrating to see what this season has done to Scully's characterization, though. She's been reduced to a maternal symbol, with few scripts digging beyond that one-dimensional allegory. One of the plot points of "Essence" has Scully taking on a helper named Lizzy (Frances Fisher)—a woman who, it turns out, is working behind Scully's back for one of the various groups interested in the baby. This revelation is clearly a huge violation of trust, and yet we never get a sense of how Scully feels about being turned into a prop in this woman's game, how she feels about being betrayed and manipulated for reasons that passeth all understanding. It's infuriating to see the feelings, thoughts, and desires of such a forceful character—a character who has defined this show from the start—shoved into the background, even as the plot revolves around her. She gets more to do in "Existence," but even then, too much of what happens to her is related to us through the perspective of other characters. Scully herself is relegated to a secondary character on her own show.

Instead of dealing with Scully's sense of self, "Essence" utilizes the figure of Billy Miles, now a seemingly unstoppable killing machine fixated on Scully's baby. The climax of the episode has our heroes desperately maneuvering to get Scully somewhere safe so that she can deliver her child before Billy can catch up. One of the highlights of the season has been watching Mulder's absence bring everyone together, and the final scenes of "Essence" use the show's newfound ensemble to great effect, with Skinner, Doggett, Mulder, and Reyes all teaming up to orchestrate the final escape. The sense of near-miss triumph that concludes the episode sends viewers into "Existence" on something of a high.

Unfortunately, that high is then dampened by an hour that spends too much time with characters who find themselves sitting in various rooms and cars, waiting for something to happen. The intensity of "Essence" is gone, leaving us in a dull aftermath to try and parse out exactly what's happening and why. It's frankly exhausting. Too many twists build on top of one another, making the plot less a coherent story than a series of fake-outs designed to distract you from an empty core.

To an extent, incoherency has always been a key part of *The X-Files*. Grand conspiracy theories should have some circling madness in them, and part of the show's genius has always been in using that sort of nonsensical insanity to its advantage. In the mythology's best years, there was always a horrible, lurking possibility that Mulder and Scully might get to the bottom of everything and find out there was no bottom, just an endless series of digressions and reversals. But that sort of approach can't work forever, and the more "Existence" tries to build to some grand, awe-inspiring conclusion, the closer it comes to tipping over into total absurdity.

It all comes to a head with the birth of Scully's baby, and the diverse perspectives the show offers of that baby. We're told that he is the "perfect" child, "more human than human." We're told that it's a miracle, because Scully was medically barren. We're told that seemingly every major alien conspiracy now revolves around him, because he will save us from/help begin the alien invasion. We're told, by Mulder no less, that the baby is proof of the existence of God.

That's a lot of weight for a newborn to carry, to say the least. After watching Scully be constantly pursued and receive so many bizarre and unknowable threats, "Existence" has the entire situation resolved without any real sense of what happened. It feels downright lazy. The episode relies on mysticism and Scully's labor to carry the day, neither of which make for a satisfying conclusion to an otherwise good year. Yet "Existence" ends with Mulder and Scully embracing over little William[44] and sharing a definitely—and very much earned—romantic kiss. Thankfully, the humans at the core of *The X-Files* are as vibrant as ever. A pity that the aliens don't have the same spark. —ZH

---

[44] William is both Fox's middle name and the name of his father. Strangely enough, it's also the name of Scully's father and brother.

"NOTHING IMPORTANT HAPPENED TODAY" | SEASON 9 / EPISODE 1
WRITTEN BY CHRIS CARTER AND FRANK SPOTNITZ
DIRECTED BY KIM MANNERS

"NOTHING IMPORTANT HAPPENED TODAY II" | SEASON 9 / EPISODE 2
WRITTEN BY CHRIS CARTER AND FRANK SPOTNITZ
DIRECTED BY TONY WHARMBY

THE X-FILES (SUPER) SOLDIERS ON

In which the show reconfigures itself. Again.

The second episode of "Nothing Important Happened Today" is dedicated to the memory of Chad Keller. His birthdate won't strike many as notable, but the date of his death—September 11, 2001—is instantly recognizable. Keller was on board American Airlines Flight 77 on that tragic day; his life ended when terrorists flew the plane into the Pentagon. He left behind a wife, his family, and many friends, who included among their number fellow surf enthusiast Chris Carter. The marking of Keller's death is both a gesture of grief on the part of a man who was mourning a friend cut down far too soon and a tacit acknowledgement that these episodes were the first to air in the wake of attacks that would affect every aspect of American life—right down to which TV shows we preferred.

There were many good reasons to end *The X-Files* after its ninth season. It had run out of ideas, and its plan to shift the story from Mulder and Scully to Doggett and Reyes never worked. It had long since ceased to be the buzziest show on television, and it would soon find itself competing for the title of best drama on its own network when a new show named *24* aired—a series that would come to define the zeitgeist of the 2000s as thoroughly as *The X-Files* had defined the '90s. The biggest reason for the show's cancelation, though, was simple: Its ratings took a nosedive from the first episode of Season Nine on and kept dropping. At the time, Chris Carter said that the audience had simply gone away and he didn't know how to find them again. He admitted much later, when promoting the show's second movie adaptation,[1] that he thought the audience had actually lost interest because of September 11.

This is a telling theory—even if the biggest story to come out of a national tragedy should obviously never be the fate of a TV show. For shows to become as successful as *The X-Files* was in its heyday, they have to capture some element of public fascination. *The X-Files* was always a show about not trusting institutions, be they public or private, and more particularly about not trusting the government. In the wake of something like 9/11—at a time when the country relied more heavily on national unity and patriotism than it had for years—the last thing anyone wanted to

---

1 Which: more on that later.

do was suspect those institutions of trying to do evil things. You can see where this would be a problem for our little show about government cover-ups.

Which brings us to the mythology, and the alien conspiracy at its core. Sure, there are people out there who legitimately believe that the government or corporations or some other vast shadow network are collaborating with aliens to bring about an invasion that will end life as we know it, but most of us soldier on each day pretty certain that we're the only intelligent life in the universe. *The X-Files* had been savvy enough in the mid-'90s to pull the Oklahoma City bombing into its DNA and make it an implicit part of the show (and especially a part of *The X-Files: Fight the Future*). Timothy McVeigh was someone *The X-Files* might have done an episode about; Osama bin Laden fit less easily into its world. *The X-Files* always dealt best in gray areas. But in November 2001, when Season Nine debuted, the War on Terror was still an issue painted in black and white, and, with more pressing concerns overtaking the country, the idea of alien colonists sounded more ridiculous than ever. The show was simply too old to nimbly solve this problem.

On top of the real-world political upheaval that haunted the show, David Duchovny finally decided to leave it entirely in the summer of 2001.[2] *The X-Files* had always been centered on Mulder's quest. It had been somewhat successful last season at turning that into Scully's quest, and then Doggett's quest, but it still needed the promise of Mulder coming back to enliven the action. Duchovny had the ability to cut through the clutter of the alien conspiracy and bring everything back to the very human cost this lonely quest had had on the soul of Fox Mulder. Without Mulder around (and without the other characters searching for him), it becomes that much more difficult to believe anyone would carry the torch of his alien investigations forward. Mulder had the deepest and most personal connections to these investigations. Everybody else, even Scully, continues with them because of a vague sense of it being what Mulder would have wanted.

These problems, ultimately, were out of Carter and the other producers' hands. They couldn't control global geopolitics, nor could they control Duchovny. What *was* under their control was how the story would move forward under both of these ungovernable conditions, and the answer to that question was "haltingly."

"Nothing Important Happened Today" is a limp piece of storytelling that has *maybe* enough good ideas for three-quarters of an episode but is stretched across two for no particular reason. It has the good sense to pick up on the strongest thing about Season Eight—having an immediate goal that unites the season's stories around a central story line—and come up with a new riff on that concept.[3] But it's

---

2 Accordingly, the opening credits are given a complete revamp. It was well past time for the show to do this, but the redone credits look like an early 2000s screensaver.

3 This time it has something to do with William, Scully's child, displaying latent superpowers.

also scrambling to put together a brand-new mythology on the fly, one that will have more resonance to its new characters, who have no connection to, say, our old nemesis the Cigarette Smoking Man. Yet every time it introduces some new figure meant to carry the same weight as one of the old—like Doggett's old military buddy Knowle Rohrer (played by Adam Baldwin)—it struggles to get the audience invested.

Carter's belief that the series' premise was strong enough to carry it through many more seasons and cast changes could have proved accurate, were Season Nine more skillful. The slow integration of Doggett into the series in Season Eight was handled surprisingly well, and though the series had more trouble integrating Reyes, there were still some good ideas involved in the concept of her character,[4] and in the series' attempts to turn its "skeptic/believer" dynamic on its ear. You can't really say if Doggett or Reyes is "the new Mulder," because they both believe in different things. That ambiguity is a sign of the character complexity the show had earned over many seasons, now creeping into new characters.

The premise, too, is elastic enough that maybe the show could have run forever. The idea of two FBI agents traveling all over the country to hunt down monsters is about as simple and elegant as *Law & Order*'s central premise, and that show replaced its cast many times over on its way to running twenty seasons. Where *The X-Files* went wrong was in trying to extend Mulder's quest into a show that now existed without him. By ending the Mulder-versus-the-aliens story at the conclusion of Season Eight, then making Season Nine a season that carried none of the burden of the series' previous mythology and focused solely on Monster of the Week stories, the series could have slowly built Doggett and Reyes into a team that viewers were invested in, before introducing some new sort of ongoing story focused on more obviously supernatural evils and centered on the mystery of what happened to Doggett's son.

But that's easy to say with hindsight. In 2001, *The X-Files* was still known for its mythology and probably terrified of turning off some portion of its fan base by dropping that element of the show entirely. Enter the super-soldiers.[5]

The super-soldiers are out-and-out dumb. They're a rehash and regurgitation of ideas the show had executed better many times before. What are they but slightly altered versions of the alien bounty hunters or the alien-human hybrids? How is it that all of this ultimately boils down to more fears about women's fertility and Scully's fertility in particular?[6] *The X-Files* had the right *impulse* in ridding itself of most of its mythology and trying to instead tell a story about internal FBI cor-

---

4 Read more about those ideas in the review of "Empedocles" (S8E17).

5 *HEAVY SIGH*

6 The show has had some wonderful stories that pivoted around the inherent horror in being pregnant, in having another life-form inside of you. It's also had some very good episodes that also prominently featured sexual violence against women. But it's also gone to that well so many times that it's run out of water and now tends to simply feel sensationalist at best.

ruption, but it held on to a few too many elements of its old self and got lost along the way. Piling so much of the weight of this story on the shoulders of Cary Elwes as Assistant Director Brad Follmer—who doesn't make a particularly convincing good *or* bad guy in this setting—was another crucial miscalculation.

The idea of centering the season on William is a good one, and casting Lucy Lawless as Shannon, the first super-soldier we meet, is brilliant stunt casting.[7] The forthright approach to providing answers about the super-soldiers—with Shannon simply telling Doggett what happened to her and Scully's discovery onboard the mystery ship that the experiments there are being carried out on human ova (thus tying everything back to William)—is also a welcome and distinct shift from the mythology of yore. Though it's a retread of Season Eight, it's not a bad idea to have the question of what Mulder's up to hanging over the proceedings. That tactic at least allows the producers to play their wild card if Duchovny ever decides he wants to show up again.

These good ideas, however, are washed aside by the endless feeling of repetition. Even the race away from the ship that's about to blow up plays like everybody involved knows they have all the time in the world because of how many exploding government labs they've fled in the past. The episodes give Anderson far too little to do, and the fact that the show hasn't figured out what to do with Reyes yet is all too obvious when it immediately throws her into a lip lock with Follmer. These episodes also too often write Doggett—a compelling character with goals and interests of his own—as Fox Mulder because that's what the show knows how to do. Doggett even hangs out with the Lone Gunmen here!

The series just takes place in a different world in Season Nine. As this season wheezes to life, you can look at *The X-Files* and suddenly see its age, see how it's a product of the decade that birthed it and realize that it's not going to be able to adapt to the changing times it finds itself in. *The X-Files* was born in an age of peace and prosperity, and it spat in the face of those qualities with a kind of earnest cynicism. When the original run of the show came to an end, the United States was involved in a war that would go on to last longer than any other war in American history, and fewer people were worried about whether they were protected from the government than about whether the government could protect them. —TVDW

S9 E1–2

---

7 If the perpetually underrated Lawless was in every episode, maybe the show could have turned the super-soldier arc into something worth watching. If *only!*

DEMON DREAMS

In which "triumphs" is used ironically in a Scrabble game.

A great many things happen in "Dæmonicus," but none of them matter. The story is either a plot by a serial-killer mental patient or a tale of demon possession, but it's unclear. Either way, it's difficult to work up much enthusiasm. The meandering structure, overemphasized grimness, and deadening pace of the hour render any potential promise inert. After the tedium of the season's two-part opener, it's disheartening to get back to Monster of the Week episodes and find inspiration still lacking throughout.

"Dæmonicus" leans heavily on mood, but apart from a few isolated, eerie moments, this approach only manages to underline how hollow the story really is. There are shots in this episode that call more attention to themselves than any shot on the series before, like the fast-moving cloud cover or the bizarre overhead view of the tile floor at the mental institution that transitions into a grid of white-and-clear squares that block the screen. Bold directorial choices can work, but these feel absurd, and not in a good way.

Each increasingly desperate flourish has all the earmarks of Spotniz—a capable and creative person—trying to force intensity into a story that simply can't support its weight. As for Reyes and Doggett, the former can "sense" demons, while the latter is determined to prove that there isn't anything supernatural about any of this. A clash of philosophies between two well-intentioned people is one of the show's core concepts, but the conflict here is too poorly defined. It doesn't help that Reyes's position is simultaneously wishy-washy and preposterous. The over-the-top atmosphere of the episode requires either a dark sense of humor or an intriguing plot in order to deserve this heightened level of theatrics. "Dæmonicus" has neither. —ZH

SCHRODINGER'S AGENT

In which Doggett does and does not die.

"4-D" could have been a good episode. With some sharper editing, a stronger structure, more urgency, and a better understanding of how to translate this particular idea from the page to the screen, this could have been great. That it isn't quashes whatever little hope remained for the rest of the season.[8] The episode shows what happens when the creative team of the ninth season comes up a legitimately cool concept: It wastes the opportunity.

The episode revolves around a killer who is able to pass between two similar but distinct dimensions, which allows him to murder with impunity in one while living a normal life in the other. Interdimensional travel is not an easy concept to portray on-screen, because as helpful as spoken exposition may be, you still need a *visual* way to convey information about each parallel world so that your audience doesn't spend the time it should be using to care about the story trying to figure out what the hell is going on. There's a difference between an intriguing mystery and a muddle, and "4-D" gets muddled early, and then spends the rest of the hour trying to work its way out.

Moreover, a high concept needs rules in order to work. Not a ton of rules (too many rules and the concept feels overly designed), but the concept should at least communicate a sense that it doesn't simply exist at the whim of narrative contrivance. The dimension-hopping premise of "4-D" is such an unusual one that it needs clear storytelling to be effective. There has to be a sense that the writer knows why things are happening even if we don't, but the episode never builds to that level of trust. The most effective scenes show Reyes and the paralyzed Doggett trying to figure out what's happening; Reyes accepting his wishes and turning off his life support is powerful, because even if he isn't *our* world's Doggett, he's still a good man dying in a world that isn't his own. Yet given the bizarre reset that is the ending, even that sequence fails to have any lasting meaning. —ZH

---

8   Never a good sign, but especially depressing four episodes into a twenty-episode season.

"LORD OF THE FLIES"	SEASON 9 / EPISODE 5 WRITTEN BY THOMAS SCHNAUZ DIRECTED BY KIM MANNERS

THE BUGS ARE BACK IN TOWN!

In which what to our wondering eyes should appear but a young Aaron Paul.

"Lord of the Flies" is mostly notable for being the episode that brought Aaron Paul into the loose orbit of Vince Gilligan. Paul would go on to play one of the most important roles in Gilligan's critically acclaimed future series *Breaking Bad*, though there's never been any indication that Gilligan realized what a powerful actor Paul could be during his appearance on *The X-Files*. In this episode, he plays "Sky Commander Winky," a Johnny Knoxville wannabe who showcases dumb exploits that feature his friends for an obvious *Jackass* rip-off called *Dumb Ass*. An *X-Files* take on found-footage horror—in the form of teenagers filming their stupid pranks and stumbling upon something horrible in the process—could have made for a great episode. This is sadly not that.

The conceit behind "Lord of the Flies" seems to stem from the fact that *The X-Files* has showcased lots of creepy bugs in the past, but it's never had an episode in which flies eat people from the inside[9] . . . so maybe it's time for that to happen? The entry is meant to occupy a somewhat goofier portion of the *X-Files* spectrum, but it is largely devoid of real humor. The show has already covered a lot of this ground; the debt this episode has to other, funnier episodes like "War of the Coprophages" (S3E12) and "Syzygy" (S3E13), is enormous, to say nothing of all of the other non-comedic bug-centric hours.

The most notable reason to watch "Lord of the Flies," then, is that it features a guest cast full of people who are on the cusp of becoming famous. In addition to Paul (who's not really in it that much and mostly registers as a goofy and peripheral presence), Jane Lynch turns up as the mother of the bug-boy, who's given nothing to do but be stern to her son. Samaire Armstrong of *The O.C.* appears as the bug-boy's crush, Natalie. Only perpetual guest star Michael Wiseman as Dr. Rocky Bronzino really seems to get the arch sensibility the episode calls for. As Dylan Lokensgard, the bug-boy himself, Hank Harris isn't bad, but this also seems like the thousandth time the show has returned to the "isolated teenager is actually a monster" and "puberty is kind of a metaphor for transforming into something strange" tropes throughout its run. All of the deadening familiarity kills the comedy.

The humor also suffers thanks to a structural problem unique to Season Nine. Keeping Scully on the show while Doggett and Reyes do most of the investigating means that she needs to get stories of her own in order to justify her presence.

---

9 Though the tobacco beetles in "Brand X" (S7E18) are nearly the same conceit.

This move splits what had always been a show with two stories—following the FBI investigation in one plot and the guest stars of the week in another—into a show with three stories. Thus, the guest cast here doesn't get the time it needs to flesh out its third of the story, which might have made for better gags—and a better episode.

Even if that weren't the case, though, there's another problem with "Lord of the Flies": We don't really know Doggett and Reyes well enough to make jokes about or with them, nor are Robert Patrick and Annabeth Gish natural comedic actors like David Duchovny and Gillian Anderson are. When, for instance, Doggett is saying that the kids in *Dumb Ass* have "crap for brains," which must be what attracted the flies, it plays less like the kind of deadpan, offhand quip Mulder would deliver and more like Doggett is a boring suburban dad lecturing his kids about why their favorite television program is stupid. Doggett has been a solid addition to the show, but it turns out comedy is his Achilles' heel.

That means much of the humor to be found in the hour falls to Dr. Rocky and to the teenagers, which doesn't really work because it's never made clear how we should feel about the characters. Dr. Rocky is mostly a buffoon, but the relationship between Dylan and Natalie is supposed to make us feel genuine emotions, and it never really gets there. Even for a *Jackass* parody, this episode is weak, feeling overall like it was written by someone who read one newspaper article about *Jackass* and decided to fold it into *The X-Files*.

To the episode's credit, the sequences in which people are being eaten alive by flies from the inside out are genuinely creepy, as are the swarms of flies themselves. Those images and the fantastic guest cast almost carry this one, until Schnauz's[10] script largely loses track of exactly what Dylan and his mom are even supposed to *be*. *The X-Files* has been reheating its leftovers for several seasons now; "Lord of the Flies" extends that basic principle to the comedy episodes as well, to sour results. —TVDW

SEASON 9 / EPISODE 6
WRITTEN BY CHRIS CARTER AND FRANK SPOTNITZ
DIRECTED BY TONY WHARMBY

| "TRUST NO 1"

FOX.MULDER@GMAIL.COM
In which Mulder has an email address!

The X-Files accidentally made the very first TV episode about Edward Snowden, eleven years before Snowden revealed the depths of the National Security Agency's ability to spy on any American it wants at any given time. "Trust No 1" is an amazingly prescient piece of work, enlivened by PATRIOT

---

10 Schnauz, who joined the show after a stint writing on the Lone Gunmen spinoff, would also join Gilligan on *Breaking Bad* (and, later, *Better Call Saul*).

Act[11] paranoia, while also managing to be a really strong tribute to the connection between Mulder and Scully.

Yet one can't help but wonder: Why is the show still about Mulder and Scully when Doggett and Reyes are right there? Yes, obviously, the audience has more of a connection to the former partners than to the new ones, but that's why the series should be redoubling its efforts to get us to care about Doggett and Reyes even half as much. Instead, it feels like the show is unwilling to let anyone get too attached to the new partners when there's even a glimmer of a chance that Mulder might pop up somewhere. This instinct worked in Season Eight because the partners at the core of the show were Scully and Doggett. Of course Scully was obsessed with trying to find Mulder. But Season Nine should have a new normal. It makes sense that Scully is still seeking Mulder. But Doggett and Reyes caring this much—particularly once it's revealed to them that the NSA is spying on everybody all the time, which also might have something to do with the super-soldiers—seems less plausible.

Even though we've now had Adam Baldwin, Terry O'Quinn, and Lucy Lawless all playing super-soldiers, it's hard to care about this new piece of the puzzle. The connection the soldiers have to everything else in the mythology is tenuous at best, and the idea of an unstoppable force being stopped by a rock in the ground is silly.[12] The super-soldiers are awfully un-scary, and it's difficult to get past the inherent ridiculousness of the project's name. Even this early on, this thread already feels like a dead end.

"Trust No 1" makes a smart choice, however, by centering Mulder and Scully's connection without overplaying their relationship. *The X-Files* isn't always so seamless in attempting to convey romantic yearning, but the moments when Scully sadly emails Mulder to tell him that it's not safe for him to come home to be with her and William are surprisingly moving.

It's a shame, then, that this yearning gets in the way of the X-Files team stumbling upon an NSA espionage campaign that must have seemed far-fetched in 2001 but now seems only a little bit beyond what the agency is actually capable of. The scenes in which an NSA employee and his wife—possessed, as Scully is, of a superpowered baby—tell Scully, Doggett, and Reyes about how thoroughly they've been watched make for damned creepy television. Most impressively, these scenes don't require anything like aliens or monsters to unsettle you; instead, they merely hint at a government that wants to know everything and will do whatever it can to learn that information.

---

11 A bill passed in the immediate wake of the September 11, 2001 terrorist attacks, meant to bolster national security—which actually ended up providing ample fodder for those across the political spectrum who were already skeptical of government power to become even more skeptical.

12 Made even more so by the sight of O'Quinn gyrating around on the ground like he's dancing for a strobe light only he can see.

The X-Files was always at its best when it built its paranoid conspiracy theories in the shadow of reality, and simply setting this story on the fringes of a real government agency lends it some degree of power. This episode illustrates that the only way to make the super-soldiers arc hum is to separate it from the alien conspiracy. By shifting focus from the old (and clearly fictional) Syndicate to real-life agencies like the NSA, the show grabs for something that could end up being of interest, but it bungles the handoff by getting mired in an increasingly nonsensical story line with too much baggage. Perhaps this is the wisdom of the 2010s speaking in retrospect, but had The X-Files pivoted to making the NSA its true villain in 2001, it would have seemed prescient indeed. Instead, it opts for half measures that come just close enough to reality to frustrate all the more.

"Trust No 1" has a reputation as a terrible episode, which seems a little unfair in hindsight, given that it was accidentally right about something that would happen in the ten years after the show went off the air. The episode undoubtedly shortchanges Doggett and Reyes, and the super-soldiers thread is still too all over the place to register as thrilling. Yet when that shadowy figure races away from the climactic gunfight and you think, just for a moment, that it might be Mulder? Well, maybe there's still some kick left in that particular engine after all. —TVDW

SEASON 9 / EPISODE 7
WRITTEN BY VINCE GILLIGAN
DIRECTED BY MICHELLE MACLAREN | "JOHN DOE" |

WHO ARE YOU?

In which Doggett loses something twice.

What if you woke up in the middle of nowhere with no memory? How would you survive, and what would you do to get your memory back? That's the great hook that kicks off "John Doe," a stylish, pulpy thriller. Finally, the first good episode of Season Nine! There are a few clunky bits to be found here, but not many. This is an hour tied together by strong direction, a script that never makes the mistake of trying to explain too much, and a fitting, moving, conclusion—the presence of which are unsurprising, once you read the credits and see who is behind this hour.

"John Doe" marks the return of Vince Gilligan to The X-Files, after his wonderfully terrifying "Roadrunners" (S8E4).[13] One of the smartest touches of his script here is that even though Doggett doesn't remember his identity, his personality remains fundamentally the same. He's still the resourceful badass we know and

---

13 He spent his time away on the Lone Gunmen spin-off.

love, and he refuses to do anything illegal, regardless of how limited his options are. The best amnesia episodes are about stripping away all the noise and trappings from a character in order to get to the core of who they are. Finding out Doggett is a straight shooter right down to the bone isn't a revelation, but it does help solidify his value as a character. And it's equally important for us to see the one memory he keeps coming back to when all the others are gone.

In addition to being Gilligan's triumphant homecoming, this episode is Michelle MacLaren's directorial debut. She'd later go on to be one of the signature, Emmy-nominated directors (and producers) of Gilligan's *Breaking Bad*, and she brings considerable style to her first outing here. The washed-out look of daytime Sangradura conveys the heat and glare of Doggett's trap, and the action sequences are well composed. The confrontation with the bribed cops is a particular standout, with Doggett backing a bus out through a garage door and flipping the vehicle a hundred yards or so down the road. The sequence has a strong sense of rhythm, and the visual of Doggett and Reyes staring out through the smeared windshield at the shapes coming to kill them is quite striking. There's also a clever subversion of one the show's definitive visuals—the "a monster is about to do something horrible, so let's pull outside and view it from a distance" shot—only here, instead of a monster, it's Doggett jumping on top of a man who has been trying to kill him. It underscores how Doggett has become a monster himself in "John Doe"—a decent one trying to find his way out of a nightmarish situation, but nonetheless a creature driven to take violent action for reasons he doesn't yet understand.

In addition to the direction, a big part of why this episode works (and why so many other Season Nine episodes seem to struggle) is that Gilligan's script is driven by a character with a clear goal from start to finish. The escalation of Doggett's problems—from a man stealing Doggett's shoes to a confrontation with nearly the entire town—is well-handled, and the story's paranormal element—a memory vampire who works for the cartel—is kept largely in the background. The supernatural here acts as more of a justification for events than the focus of the events themselves, allowing Gilligan to play around with a crime noir staple like amnesia in an *X-Files* context. The strong sense of purpose combines well with the action, making for an episode that's always gripping to watch even before we know exactly what's going on.

There are, admittedly, a few stumbles throughout. Some of the otherwise excellent visuals are overly stylized, stressing events in a way that draws unnatural attention to them, and there are problems with the way that Doggett's one remaining memory is portrayed. The script makes smart use of Doggett's son's death by having it serve as the agent's connection to himself and his own history, but the actual images we see are overprocessed—the past is all soft, hazy white light and pastels. Yet Robert Patrick's commitment to Doggett's grief in the present makes the emotional connection work. If it's not possible for us to miss Luke because we don't really know him, it's at least easy to understand that Doggett does, and to empathize with his sorrow.

The greatest impression "John Doe" leaves is one of hellish desperation, a desperation mirrored in Doggett's increasingly haggard face. It's a fitting look for a character who ultimately has to embrace despair in order to find his way back to himself. In the end, Doggett remembers who he is because of the one thing that he is unwilling to forget: his son. But he can't remember his son without also remembering what happened to him. The horrible irony is, without that memory waiting to show him the way—without the tragic, life-shattering death—he never could have come back at all. It's tragic, and yet the episode suggests there are far worse fates. You either choose to accept your life for all its triumphs and its miseries, or you end up losing yourself entirely, waking up in a no-name town while someone is trying to steal your shoes. —ZH

NEW PARTNERS

As Season Nine progressed, a new partnership emerged, one that was also predicated on a skeptic/believer dynamic, but was still quite different from that of Mulder and Scully. Chris Carter offers insight on the conception of the Doggett/Reyes partnership: "You didn't want to just exit Mulder and bring in Mulder's mirror reflection—the same with the addition of Monica Reyes. We wanted her to be as different from Scully as possible. I imagined her as being more akin to Mulder, and him as being a little bit more akin to Scully, but in a more rigid and unscientific way. I think we cast just the right people for the parts. It really helped to push the series in a whole new direction, which is maybe what it needed right at the time, so that it didn't rest on its laurels, and it didn't just do the same, you know, the same expected thing time and again."

Inevitably there was pushback from audiences who missed the long-beloved, familiar chemistry of Mulder and Scully. Says Carter, "I think everyone hates change, and they don't want the things they love taken away from them. There's always going to be resistance to something new until they learn to love it. I think that's what happened with Robert Patrick and Annabeth Gish; they had the very difficult jobs of coming into a show that was moving like a freight train and figuring out how to climb aboard. They both did an amazing job."

Vince Gilligan agrees that Doggett and Reyes never quite got a fair shake from the show's audience. Says Gilligan, "[Patrick] is a wonderful actor. I want to give a quick shout-out to him. I think he got a raw deal. This guy is a brilliant actor; he did a wonderful job, as did Annabeth Gish. Both of them got such hate from the fans, and undeservedly so, for the 'affront' they exhibited in just showing up . . . and doing the job. It was a situation where David had briefly left and we needed the show to continue. We needed some new characters, and they kind of drew the shit end of the stick on that, which was a real shame, because I felt they were both wonderful."

Robert Patrick had high hopes himself for the Doggett/Reyes partnership: "I was so looking forward to exploring that, and seeing where that would go, and I thought Annabeth and I had our own chemistry. I was excited about the potential where that could go. I thought we could both have taken that into another whole direction and still honored the legacy of the original *X-Files*."

"HELLBOUND"

SEASON 9 / EPISODE 8
WRITTEN BY DAVID AMANN
DIRECTED BY KIM MANNERS

MORE THAN ONE WAY TO SKIN A MURDERER

In which Hell is a place where no one ever changes.

Late in this episode, Reyes tries to explain that this case been going on for centuries, and that she has some sort of connection to everything that's been happening. It's supposed to be a striking speech, a demonstration of forces working behind the scenes beyond either character's understanding. As it plays, it's just kind of silly. Annabeth Gish is nothing less than incredibly serious throughout, and yet the effect is negligible—laughable, even.

Every time "Hellbound" tries to use Reyes as a reason to care about what's happening, it falls flat. The character can only be described as "Not-Scully," a person whose primary characteristics—her supposed belief in the occult world and her affection for Doggett—fail to cohere into a memorable or compelling whole. Her "belief" is an attempt to invert the skeptic/believer relationship of Mulder and Scully, but neither she nor Doggett adhere to a strict philosophy. While that certainly makes for more dynamic conversations about cases between the two of them than Mulder and Scully were often allowed, Reyes (unlike Doggett) has no other personality to fall back on. Part of this is Annabeth Gish's performance, which lacks the intensity of that of her co-star; but it's hard to blame the actress when the character is so poorly conceived. The show's other leads have strong cores of conviction that drove them forward—Mulder's truth, Scully's science, Doggett's practicality. In making Reyes "spiritual," the writers fail to find an equivalent cornerstone to build off of, leaving the character adrift in a nebulous cloud of vague theories and affections.

Reyes's failure as a character greatly hinders "Hellbound," as the episode hinges on her obsession with a murder-by-skinning that turns out to have a long, long history. Reyes can't carry a story on her own. Without a major objective to motivate her, she's just a ghost, an empty space where a person ought to be; her obsession *should* be enough, especially considering her connection with the case, but it lacks the intensity to drive the action. Moreover, there's not much in the way of monsters that could make this episode more compelling. While the flayings are an arresting visual, the shock of seeing an excoriated body wears off. By the time the third guy winds up dead, it's as close to monotonous as "men being skinned to death" can be.

"Hellbound" also takes such a long time getting to the point that when the answers do finally come out, their effect is half lost in the mire of questions surrounding them. There are potentially fascinating issues here. The idea of a man getting vengeance on his killers not just once but over and over again through reincarnation raises some interesting questions about justice and karma, especially since the avenging spirit is always reincarnated as an officer of the law. The possibility that Reyes had been reincarnated herself, struggling and failing to stop the killer many times before, should make you wonder just what her role is and why she keeps getting pulled in. But in lieu of exploring any of these threads, we get a mediocre hour that serves mostly to evince how badly this show has done by its new female lead. —ZH

SEASON 9 / EPISODE 9
WRITTEN BY CHRIS CARTER AND FRANK SPOTNITZ
DIRECTED BY KIM MANNERS

"PROVENANCE"

SEASON 9 / EPISODE 10
WRITTEN BY CHRIS CARTER AND FRANK SPOTNITZ
DIRECTED BY CHRIS CARTER

"PROVIDENCE"

SAVE THE BABY, SAVE THE WORLD
In which Scully's baby . . . blah, blah, blah.

There are two major problems with the mythology in Season Nine. The first is that it has precisely zero new cards to play. After some of the Doggett and Reyes-centric episodes from early in this season made it seem as if the show might settle into a story about mysticism, the series heads right back where it started, with the aliens as the key to everything—including the origins of human religion, a thread that had been dropped after "The Sixth Extinction" (S7E1). The second problem is that the mythology remains relentlessly focused on Fox Mulder and his and Scully's son, William. Because Mulder isn't present, hanging so much of the story on him is a dead end, and William mostly serves to motivate Scully to make plot-contrived and out-of-character decisions.

These issues result in a season-long arc that has nothing of the urgency that once drove the best conspiracy episodes forward. Remember when Mulder had to get on that train way back in "Nisei" (S3E9), and then he jumped atop it from a bridge? Those thrilling, high-stakes days are long gone. Now, the characters do things largely because forces beyond their control (and/or the plot) require them to. The immediate goals—find Scully's baby!—are simple and logical enough, but long-term goals and character-based actions are nowhere to be found.

At the center of this two-parter is the notion that discovering more about the aliens' history on Earth will explain everything from the roots of modern religion to William's superpowers to whatever is going on with the super-soldiers. In Seasons Four and Five, the mythology struggled to take a more international focus but never quite stuck the landing. You can imagine how ill-equipped this team is to deal with expanding the focus of the mythology to include the entire history of life on Earth. Instead, it decides to cross its fingers, boil everything down to a story about malevolent forces with dark designs on William, and hope for the best.

There's a germ of an idea present in making the mythology all about the baby. With Gillian Anderson still on the show, the series needs to give Scully something to invest in, while continuing the process of weaning longtime viewers off Mulder and Scully and switching them to full-time Doggett and Reyes. But the William story line is too stocked with Chosen One symbolism the show purchased at a dollar store. Add to it all of the times we find out that both the UFO-worshipping cult *and* the new Syndicate want William and his father dead, and it's a recipe for dramatic stakes that have no real meaning because none of these threats directly affect anyone who is on-screen and capable of delivering dialogue.

Sure, it's nice to know explicitly that William will be humanity's salvation (but with the caveat that his father must remain alive). Yet the William story only really could have worked if the writers dug deep and came up with a story line that was all about a mother terrified of what her baby might have growing inside of him. Instead, the show bombards Scully constantly with external threats. Gillian Anderson was completely up to playing a ferociously protective maternal warrior, like Sigourney Weaver in *Aliens*. Instead, the season keeps asking her to play Meryl Streep in *A Cry in the Dark*. We don't want to see Scully being reduced to wailing about her baby and not being able to do anything about saving him. We want to see her walk into that cult compound, guns blazing, and take her son back.[14]

---

14 In its later seasons, *The X-Files* too often saw Scully as a paragon of suffering, not action. Without her trademark skepticism, it was like the show lost sight of everything else compelling about her too.

The idea of a cult that worships the aliens as gods was one that the show turned to a few times throughout its run, but the series never developed it as well as it might have. Yes, if this were a world in which aliens were literally interfering with human evolution, there would almost certainly be people who worshipped extraterrestrials. However, the show has always presented these cults as vague, hinted-at menaces that never present a real threat to anybody. "Roadrunners" (S8E4) isn't everybody's favorite episode, but there was a naturalistic presence to the slug cult in that episode; these UFO cults just feel a dime a dozen.

That sense is particularly strong with the cult in these episodes, an organization run by a guy named Josepho (played by Denis Forest with an air of pragmatic evil), who is the sort of guy who would kill a baby just because he thought that would further God's plan on Earth. Beyond Forest's performance, there's not a lot to this sect. We find out most of the information about this cult secondhand via the character of Comer (Neal McDonough), who infiltrated the cult and then eventually broke out of it to race back across the Canadian border to inform his FBI superiors of what he had learned. That story is filled with beats the show could hit in its sleep (and here seems to): somebody has infiltrated the FBI; information is being kept from the team who are working on the X-Files; I could go on.

The characters who get the short end of the stick in these two hours are Reyes and Doggett, who are by and large sidelined in favor of Scully, the FBI crew, the Lone Gunmen, and Josepho. In "Providence," Doggett spends a substantial amount of time confined to a hospital bed after getting run over, and nobody seems to care much. This twist is probably meant to inspire Reyes to become just as motivated by Mulder's quest as everyone else, but without Mulder on-screen, her investment is much harder to believe. Reyes and Doggett have become supporting characters on a show they're supposed to be taking over. That's rarely a good sign.

The mythology episodes have always given off an impression that the writers are just moving pieces around on a game board without ever really changing the landscape of the game. Pieces are occasionally removed, but they're just as quickly put back on once certain conditions are met, and the goals of the characters shift so rapidly that it doesn't matter anyway. This constant bait-and-switch was fun in the early days of the show, when the audience knew as little as Mulder did, and we got to watch him try to figure out just what that landscape looked like. But now that his piece is no longer on the board, and we've seen every possible configuration of all of the other pieces, we know that it doesn't matter what the show does. The game won't change. *The X-Files* is frantically trying to find a new reason to justify its own existence as it circles the drain. —TVDW

"AUDREY PAULEY"	SEASON 9 / EPISODE 11
	WRITTEN BY STEVEN MAEDA
	DIRECTED BY KIM MANNERS

SO MUCH I'D DO DIFFERENTLY

In which Reyes slips into a coma.

It took years for Mulder and Scully's relationship to turn romantic.[15] Eleven episodes into Season Nine, and Doggett and Reyes seem a few weeks shy of moving in together. "Audrey Pauley" starts with Reyes driving Doggett home from something like a date, and the two of them banter for while in a decidedly "more-than-friends" kind of way. After a car accident, Reyes spends the rest of the episode in a coma, and her connection with Doggett is the emotional underpinning of the story. One character even flat-out says to Doggett, "You love her, though."

However, the relationship this episode is predicated on feels rushed and unearned at this point in the season. "Audrey Pauley" is, in part, about how Doggett's feelings for Reyes drive him to investigate suspicious circumstances he might not otherwise have noticed. It's easy to imagine Mulder or Scully doing a similar thing for each other, but in their case, the history between them would justify the dynamic. Doggett and Reyes don't have much history to draw on besides what has been implied offscreen, and while the actors work well together, the ambiguity about what's going on between them in addition to their still-new relationship with the audience makes what should be a moving commitment appear artificial and forced.

Once the contours of the episode's premise become clear, there isn't much else for anyone to do until the final scenes. Reyes has fallen into a strange, other-world version of the hospital, the creation of an illiterate patient aide named Audrey Pauley (Tracey Ellis[16]) to house the souls of the living before they pass over to the other side. Doggett is stuck trailing behind in the real world, and no matter how determined Reyes is, her efforts in this parallel world can only uncover so much. It's all very spiritualist and hazy—and more than a little lazy—as the show once again introduces a magic disabled person to help facilitate a narrative. This is mitigated somewhat by Ellis, who does convincing work as Audrey, and the episode works best as a sad story about a lonely woman who finds the meaning in her life precisely when she's about to leave it.

Unfortunately, there are no deeper character revelations to come, and little suspense to be had, apart from the evil doctor's (Jack Blessing) hilariously

---

15 Maybe too long—even if you weren't hugely invested in the two characters becoming a couple, their chemistry was so evident from the start of the series that it's honestly strange that it took so long to become explicitly romantic.

16 This is Ellis's second appearance on the show; in her first appearance, "Oubliette" (S3E8), she played a woman with a psychic connection to a kidnap victim.

mustache-twirling attempts to keep his secret safe. It's not a disastrous episode, but there doesn't seem to be a lot of point to it. A few good ideas lean heavily on emotion to glue them together, but when that emotion isn't built on anything solid, it's easy to get lost in the mist. —ZH

SEASON 9 / EPISODE 12
WRITTEN AND DIRECTED BY JOHN SHIBAN | "UNDERNEATH"

DULL DARK SIDE

In which nobody was watching.

As a half-assed Jekyll and Hyde story, the only thing the episode really has going for it is the central mystery of the killer's identity. "Underneath" isn't the worst the show has ever been, and first-time-director-longtime-writer John Shiban manages to depict some shocking moments of grim violence. Overall, though, the episode feels overly familiar and rote.

W. Earl Brown, a talented character actor, guest stars as Robert Fassl, but he's forced to spend his screen time glowering in a kind of psychological deadlock. His character is a killer so intent on denying he's capable of sin that his sins take on a separate identity and start murdering on his behalf. Because Fassl is by design stuck in a perpetual state of denial, the emotional palate the actor can display is inherently limited. It's frustrating to watch someone as normally likable and down-to-earth as Brown stuck in such a thankless grimace of a role. The explanation for Fassl's psychological arrested development is given to us as a shallow gloss on religious faith and self-loathing. The lack of any further characterization or understanding of exactly what made Fassl into a monster makes him a poor villain.

Doggett's obsession with catching Fassl makes sense for our cop-turned-FBI agent, and his motivation at least gives a strong reason for him to be involved with the case. It's also perfectly in character that Doggett would need to have the case ultimately solved. Doggett's refusal to back down once again shows he shares some of Mulder's obsessive tendencies, even as his Scully-esque skepticism balks at the true nature of the crimes he's investigating. There's a potentially complicated moment when he finds out that his old partner planted evidence to try to ensure Fassl's conviction, but the partner disappears after his confession, and the planted evidence doesn't effect the story whatsoever, so the moment is drained of its power.

In the end, this is just a werewolf story with a slight twist, and that twist isn't enough to make "Underneath" worth watching. Fassl's internal conflict is unsettling, and the confrontation in the sewers is well done, but nothing more resonates here. The best Monster of the Week episodes in the series never felt pre-programmed or written solely to fill an airing slot; the strong story ideas always came first. Underneath it all, though, this episode is just going through the motions. —ZH

"IMPROBABLE"	SEASON 9 / EPISODE 13 WRITTEN AND DIRECTED BY CHRIS CARTER

SOLTANTO DIO SA

In which—seriously—God is Burt Reynolds.

If you need to find an actor to play God, there are worse choices than Burt Reynolds.[17] The God of "Improbable" is the God (or Godlike figure) that turns up in a lot of American folk tales and popular stories. He's a bit of a rapscallion, and he doesn't mind a naughty or winking aside that acknowledges his basic humanity. He's also a really good guy at heart, someone who just wants to make sure that people do their best to be good and kind to each other. If you're going to cast someone to play that version of God—that good guy with the big swingin' dick—why not Burt Reynolds?

There's not much else to "Improbable." It feels like a full third of the episode consists of Reynolds swaggering around with jazzy, Italian music burbling on the soundtrack. If you were going to sit down and describe what this episode was about to someone, you'd almost certainly get waylaid by the presence of the big guest star (as I am getting here). Indeed, the X-File here isn't actually our Lord and Savior Burt Reynolds, but rather a numerology-obsessed serial killer named Wayne (Ray McKinnon).

Chris Carter, who wrote and directed, chooses to make this episode one of the season's goofier ones, while also conveying how horrifying Wayne would be if he existed in our reality. Carter's attempt to get around this possible tonal issue by keeping Wayne's killings offscreen doesn't work as well as he might hope, but his script always manages to imply that this guy is a warped and twisted individual who needs to be stopped. What's fascinating about the proceedings here is that "Burt" (as the character was apparently referred to in the script) can't keep Wayne from doing what he does. All he can do is point to the patterns that are laid out in front of everyone and hope that somebody figures it all out.[18] There's a weary exasperation to Burt's attitude—and this episode overall—that fits well with the season as a whole. Maybe there's a grand design. Maybe there's not. What it really comes down

---

17 Particularly if you don't include any actors trained by the Royal Shakespeare Company in the mix.

18 This dynamic is reminiscent of both the killer and title character in "Clyde Bruckman's Final Repose" (S3E4)—another episode interested in the battle between free will and fate, though that episode interrogates the concept in a much more rigorous fashion than this episode does, in which the notion feels tossed off (mostly in a good way, however, I would argue).

to is: If you spent so much time trying to explain that to people, you'd be sick of it too.

"Improbable" is yet another episode that attempts to get the audience on board with Monica Reyes. The character is more approachable in a comedic story line than when she's trying to get us invested in her mystical spiritualism. Tossing her into a story with Scully—as "Improbable" does—is a strong move because the two already have a solid dynamic. The episode also more convincingly positions Reyes as the new Mulder than the rest of the season has done, as evidenced by the sequence in which she launches into a bunch of numerology crap when asked by others at the FBI what they should be looking for when hunting down the madman. She's Mulder with a difference, though; when Mulder pulled this kind of stunt, his speech always had the pitched frenzy of the conspiracy thriller. When Reyes does it, it's much gentler and funnier, and that's the right card to play for her character.[19] To run for a long while without its original two agents, *The X-Files* would have to find a tone that would have worked with and been unique to its new agents. "Improbable" comes close to finding that tone, and it's the best Monica Reyes gets in Season Nine.

The guest cast also bolsters the episode substantially. As Vicki, the numerology expert whose path unfortunately crosses with Wayne, Ellen Greene has a small part, but she makes it count. She lends Vicki the feel of a woman who has been at this a long time but still hasn't graduated from her tiny office. She's a fun character, and when her time comes, the show is able to draw a surprising amount of poignancy from it. Meanwhile, Ray McKinnon takes a rather thankless role—the serial killer attempting to complete his "pattern"—and imbues it with a startling amount of life, especially when he's paired with Reynolds.

But, of course, the real reason to watch this episode is to see Burt Reynolds play God. There's also an incredible amount of pleasure in seeing what the show does with the idea of God walking among his creations, begging them at length not to do anything stupid but knowing they always will. The scene that sells "Improbable" as a whole is the one in which Reyes, Scully, and God play checkers in a parking garage. It's never quite explained why God is there. Ostensibly, he wants to play checkers with a friend. In actuality, it's the one time he's able to intervene in the proceedings of us pitiful humans because here are two women who are capable of listening to him.[20] It would be nice, after all, to believe there's some sort of underlying pattern to everything, a system of figures and numbers that would allow the world to make sense, and that there would be something beautiful in how these sequences could transmute all of fate and free will into a symbiosis instead of an eternal struggle.

S9 E13

---

19 Or maybe Carter is interrogating how differently men and women have to present ideas in workplace settings? Yeah, probably not . . .

20 That God is able to commune with two women who have faith—even if those faiths are very different—feels pointed on Carter's part.

If we have the free will to realize where fate is taking us, then maybe we can figure out how to change it.[21]

If "Improbable" does something beautifully, it is because it's engaged with this point of its own philosophy. Early in the episode, God tells Wayne that the secret to three-card monte is to "make better choices," and it's easy to see that his intention is also to help Scully and Reyes understand the case by giving them little shoves until they too can look more fully at what lies before them. The opening credits replace "The Truth Is Out There" with "Dio Ti Ama," or "God Loves You" in Italian. What better way to describe love in the world of *The X-Files* than to poke and prod someone until they stop lying to themselves about what's really going on and see the truth for what it is? —TVDW

"SCARY MONSTERS" | SEASON 9 / EPISODE 14
WRITTEN BY THOMAS SCHNAUZ
DIRECTED BY DWIGHT LITTLE

SUPER CREEPS
In which "I made this!"

The fan surrogate character is tricky to make work on a television show. It's easy to see why a long-running show would enjoy writing a character who can allow it to poke fun at the fan base's obsession with the program. But it's also easy to have this mockery tip over into downright hostility toward the people who keep the series on the air in the first place. Consider Leyla Harrison, who first appeared in "Alone" (S8E19) and is Mulder and Scully's biggest fan. Whereas she was a "good" fan in "Alone," revering our two original heroes, in "Scary Monsters" she's a "bad" fan who spends much of her screen time complaining about being stuck with Reyes and Doggett, instead of her beloved pairing.

This attitude toward fandom takes on a particular cast when you also know that "Scary Monsters" was the episode during which the cast and crew of *The X-Files* found out they had been canceled. To be sure, they likely would have been able to read the writing on the wall for most of the ratings-challenged ninth season, but *The X-Files* was such a television institution at that point that it wouldn't have seemed inconceivable for the show to run for another couple of years (even if it was running on fumes). Instead, Fox gave Chris Carter and company a chance to craft a wrap-up story by announcing the end early in the season.[22]

---

21 Again, shades of "Clyde Bruckman" here.

22 At the time, all involved thought perhaps a few more movies would be made in the future, but nobody likely could have predicted the return of the show over a decade later for two additional seasons.

Suggesting that the cancellation led directly to the way Leyla acts in this episode would be inaccurate. After all, the script for this episode was written well before the production of the episode. But the writers surely knew what was coming, thanks to the ratings slide and fan backlash, so it's easy to imagine that some of the general sentiment of the room at the time crept into what was happening within it. Enter Leyla, a stand-in for those suddenly uninterested former fans.

Ironically, the show itself is still obsessed with Mulder and Scully, to the degree that whenever it pays more attention to Doggett and Reyes, it often feels like it has to make a meta-comment about just how much these new leads lack. If "Improbable" was an attempt to improve the Reyes character by softening her just a tad with some humor, then "Scary Monsters" is an attempt to make Doggett seem like just as much of a hero as Mulder was by having his skepticism be the only thing that can save the team stranded up in a mountain home. This is an episode in which it becomes glaringly obvious that this tactic is what the show has been doing with Doggett for two seasons now. It constantly reminds the audience that he's just as cool as Mulder ever was, all the while refusing to let him simply be his own man.

Another indication that this is the end: "Scary Monsters" has its Monster of the Week be the very *concept* of monsters of the week. Anything little Tommy Conlon (Gavin Fink) can imagine can be hallucinated by others. Hell, when the kid shows Reyes his pictures, he even says, "I made this," exactly like the kid in the Ten Thirteen Productions title card that appears at the close of every episode. Plus, the oldest scary story in the book is the monster under the bed, which this episode makes quite literal. There are fun *X-Files* Easter eggs here, if you're willing to dig around for them a bit, but Easter eggs do not a good episode make.

What makes "Scary Monsters" a lackluster entry isn't that it's too mean to fans or even that it's too self-involved about the concept of the show. Instead, this scenario just isn't interesting enough. Sure, the characters are stranded in the middle of nowhere, with a creature (or creatures) that could kill them at any time.[23] The true culprit is someone you won't expect right away. The details of the deaths—people killing themselves to get at something they believe is inside of them, say—are gruesome. But the whole formula feels tired and wheezy at this point, and, if you've seen every episode of *The X-Files* that comes before this one, it's incredibly easy to guess all the twists and turns within five minutes of this episode's start. Fans didn't connect with Doggett and Reyes not because they were too attached to Mulder and Scully. No, fans didn't connect with Doggett and Reyes because they were longing for a time when the show didn't seem like it was repeating its greatest hits over and over again, only to have the needle continually miss the groove. —TVDW

---

23 It's taken this long for the show to finally exhaust this durable format, first introduced in "Ice" (S1E8).

| SEASON 9 / EPISODE 15
WRITTEN BY VINCE GILLIGAN, JOHN SHIBAN, AND FRANK SPOTNITZ
DIRECTED BY CLIFF BOLE

THE ONES WHO NEVER GAVE UP

In which the Lone Gunmen can't hold their breath forever.

The X-Files has never been kind to its secondary characters; over the course of nine seasons, Mulder lost his entire family, Scully lost a sister and a father, and countless informants, friends, and background figures have died in a variety of horrible ways. Given that track record, it's almost shocking to realize that the Lone Gunmen lasted as long as they did. This world is a bleak, terrifying place even before you factor in the alien conspiracies and government cover-ups. Monsters are real here, and the fight against darkness is nearly always fatal. People like Byers, Langly, and Frohike were bound to get chewed up sooner or later.

But did they have to go out so half-heartedly? "Jump the Shark" serves as a conclusion to the short-lived *Lone Gunmen* spin-off series, introducing important players from that show with little fanfare here: Jimmy the Intern (Stephen Snedden) and Yves Adele Harlow (Zuleikha Robinson) both pop up, and both clearly have a history with the Gunmen, with the returning Morris Fletcher[24] filling in details from a one-season wonder that hardly anyone watched. Having Michael McKean do expository duty helps, as he manages to make most of it funny, but as with "Millennium" (S7E4), there's considerable clunkiness in this hour as the result of merging together two distinct shows.

There's sadness that pervades the hour as well, and a bitterness that doesn't always make sense in the context of this episode. The Gunmen are as willing to help as ever, but now there's a defeated air about them. Fletcher and Frohike get in a conversation in which Frohike seems to all but admit that he and his friends are basically screwed in the grand scheme of things. These guys' fundamental decency was one of the few reliably shining lights of *The X-Files*. If you put aside the fact that this sentiment reads like a bunch of writers complaining that their show got canceled, the characters' melancholy is fitting enough. All they have to show for their efforts over the years is their friendship and an underground newspaper most people treat as a punchline. Acknowledging the frustration of their unsung status, before giving them a hard-earned triumph, is classic drama.

The problem is, there is no triumph at the close of the hour. Frohike, Langly, and Byers sacrifice themselves to stop the spread of a human virus bomb. The show

---

24 Morris previously appeared in "Dreamland" (S6E4) and "Dreamland II" (S6E5), where he briefly swapped bodies with Mulder; he also showed up in "Three of a Kind" (S6E20), and did a single-episode guest spot on the *The Lone Gunmen*.

lets them go out heroically, but it's a waste; the sacrifice is semi-arbitrary, the sort of dangerous climax Mulder and Scully have wiggled their way out of countless times before. The plot has nothing to do with the season's ongoing story line, and while Byers, Frohike, and Langly get a send-off that leaves their dignity intact, it plays like a cheat on the part of the writers to get rid of suddenly inconvenient characters and to punish the audience[25] for not watching their spin-off show when it was on.

This feeling is compounded by the final scene, a funeral for the three men at Arlington National Cemetery that passes the point of honest grief and lapses into self-parody. Scully's characterization is the worst in this respect. Gillian Anderson (who appears in the episode only during the final scene) acts heavily medicated and goes off about how brave and wonderful and amazing her fallen friends were. It comes across as less like an appropriate acknowledgement of the loss of important characters, and more like salt intentionally thrown on an open wound. The Lone Gunmen were so incredible, but the audience didn't love them enough, and now they're gone. It's possible to accept a world in which these characters had to die, but not one in which their execution comes as a form of revenge. —ZH

SEASON 9 / EPISODE 16

WRITTEN BY CHRIS CARTER, BASED ON A STORY BY DAVID DUCHOVNY, FRANK SPOTNITZ, AND CHRIS CARTER

DIRECTED BY DAVID DUCHOVNY

"WILLIAM"

BYE-BYE, BABY

In which Scully gives away her son.

Throughout the first half of "William," Scully is, by turns, annoyed, curious, worried, bemused, and angry. Anderson conveys her wonder and horror at the possibility that the disfigured man sitting in front of her might actually be Mulder in "disguise" as layered and complex. But the instant the mystery man gets involved with William, all of Scully's complexity and personality vanishes in a rush of "My baby! My baby! Stay away from my baby!" An invisible switch gets flipped. Here's Scully the individual; now here's Scully the machine who worries about a plot device that is nominally a human being.

It makes sense that Scully would be on edge about William's safety. He's a helpless infant at the center of a vast conspiracy, which means he's in danger more or less constantly. That would, of course, make any mother nervous. The problem

---

25 Especially coming right on the heels of "Scary Monsters" (S9E14), with its "bad" fan surrogate; while it's possibly to sympathize with a creative team faced with unreasonable demands from their audience, having their frustration leak into the scriptwriting makes for some tonally awkward and mean-spirited entries.

is that the concern for William's safety overrides every other aspect of Scully's character—her humor, her faith, her iron will. It reduces the person we've gotten to know and admire over the past nine years into a one-dimensional caricature, which is immensely frustrating to watch. Mulder's obsession with the truth defined him as a character yet still allowed him to be a complete person. Scully's motherhood has, for the most part, been an excuse to remove her from the main action, something to hold her back while Doggett and Reyes get the job done.

So it should feel like a relief when, at the end of the episode, Scully gives up William for adoption. It should solve one of the season's biggest problems of characterization, and maybe it will. But it mostly feels like a bizarre, implausible, and frustrating conclusion to a supposedly life-or-death story arc. It's laughably naive to think that the forces searching for William will stop searching now just because it will take a little more digging to find him.[26] Even if you're willing to accept that this is a reasonable solution, the thin writing betrays itself. It's not impossible to imagine that Scully's devotion would eventually bring her to the conclusion that her son would be safer and happier without her. Given everything else that's happened, it might even be the most logical conclusion. But considering how badly the episode bungles her character, it's impossible to see the decision as anything other than the choice of the writers to close off a plot they're no longer interested in pursuing. To have Scully suddenly decide that the answer is to send William away is a sloppy way to back out of a fumbling story arc.

Mulder's disappearance this season has never made much sense, especially considering how unlikely it is that he would leave Scully (and their son) behind; the idea that it's somehow plausible that he could've been so disfigured by government tests that he would hide his identity from even the people he trusted the most doesn't improve upon this major issue. It turns out that the disfigured man is *not* him,[27] but the fact that Scully, Doggett, and Reyes are all willing to entertain the possibility that it could be underlines how much the writers have fallen into the laziness of the "characters just won't goddamn talk to each other" trap. *The X-Files* has always been a show about secrets and the way those secrets can corrupt just about everyone. But as much as "William" tries to sell the concept here, it just doesn't work.

What "William" accomplishes more than anything else is to remind the audience that the Mulder and Scully we grew to love are more or less completely gone. Duchovny directed the episode, and there are moments here and there in which the actor's personality shines through. The ambiguity of Spender's identity means we get a few exchanges that echo—in a sad and broken way—the old Mulder-and-Scully banter of the past, and a ghostly memory of how much that relationship grounded the show and brought it to life. Doggett is a great character, and Reyes isn't always

---

26 The baby even keeps his name, in case the Dark Forces need more help turning him up.
27 Weirdly, it's Spender, last seen in "One Son" (S6E12).

utterly bland; maybe with time, the two of them could've had their moment in the sun. But things are drawing to a close now, so those characters will always be shadows. What we're left with in their stead are just shadows of former greatness. —ZH

SEASON 9 / EPISODE 17
WRITTEN BY DAVID AMANN, BASED ON A STORY BY JOHN SHIBAN AND DAVID AMANN
DIRECTED BY KIM MANNERS

"RELEASE"

SOLVING THE MYSTERY

In which the mystery you had forgotten about gets wrapped up.

"Release" is a particularly frustrating episode of *The X-Files*. It contains some extremely moving and beautiful moments, as the show wraps up one of the major ongoing mysteries it has left. But those scenes just make it all the more exasperating to have so much of that episode taken up by Rudolph Hayes, a completely new character who spends much of his time staring at things and feels for all the world like he's about to be spun off into a totally pointless new show. "Release" reaches for profundity, falls short, but somehow still manages to get close enough to be worth watching—or at least worth watching when it's not trying to convince us that Doggett and Reyes should be falling in love because that's what all good FBI agent pairings do.

At the center of "Release" is a mystery you may have forgotten about: What happened to Doggett's son when he was murdered?[28] "Release" answers that question, but it does so in such a way that you feel like you don't know for sure what happened. Even when a character sits down and explains exactly how Luke Doggett died, it feels like, at best, ninety percent of the whole story. So much time has passed, and the details have gotten foggy. The answers Doggett gets are unsatisfying by design. No matter what he learns, it's never going to be enough to resurrect his son. Answers are one thing; emotional closure is another.

The question of closure is a note *The X-Files* played in the two-parter "Sein und Zeit" (S7E10) and "Closure" (S7E11), which served to wrap up the Samantha Mulder mystery. Purely judged on a story level, "Release" is more successful than those episodes, but we simply are not as invested in what happened to Doggett's son as we were in what happened to Samantha. Samantha's disappearance was Mulder's raison d'être, the drive behind his entire character. It took seven years for us to find out what happened to her. We've barely known Doggett for two seasons.

---

28 The two foremost episodes that revolve around this story arc are both Season Eight hours: "Invocation" (S8E5) and "Empedocles" (S8E17), but this story comes up in other episodes as well. It's notably important in "John Doe" (S9E7).

Still, finding *some* sort of answer is enough for Doggett and his ex-wife[29] to be able to finally scatter their son's ashes in the ocean, and is enough for us to have a bit of emotional catharsis as well. That final scene of the episode, the Doggetts standing in waves covering their feet, letting go of some of their grief, captures the heartbreakingly private moment in a way the series has rarely managed to do with such grace.[30]

The episode's greatest weakness, however, is tied inextricably to the solving of the murder of Doggett's son. Too much of the plot revolves around a super-crime solver named Rudolph Hayes (Jared Poe), as well as the character of Assistant Director Brad Follmer. As Follmer, Cary Elwes never really settled into his part this season or became someone who seemed like he belonged in this world. In the scenes in which he's being threatened with exposure by the mobster who has been bribing him for years, he goes comically over the top. Follmer has been a weird fit for the series since he first came on the scene. Unfortunately, that sense permeates his last appearance on the show too.

It's Hayes (revealed to actually be a former mental patient named Stuart Mimms) who really drags this episode down. Introduced as one of the trainees to whom Scully[31] is showing the finer points of forensic science, he seems to mostly solve cases by staring intently at the camera until something occurs to him. He has one Holmesian moment at the top of the hour in which he explains why a Jane Doe corpse was an unemployed single woman. But it all goes downhill from there. The character becomes far too much of a focus for the episode, when it *should* be properly focusing on unraveling the mystery of Doggett's son's death. The guest star hijacks the story here to a degree that the guest stars rarely do on *The X-Files*.[32] The emotional weight is with John Doggett, but what the episode is really interested in is Hayes.

"Release" could have worked better if it had revolved more around scenes like ones in which John and Barbara Doggett, still reeling from the untimely death of their child, try to come together to find closure. Yes, if the series had continued to run, the secret of Doggett's son's murder would have unspooled alongside it. The suddenness of the solution here *could* have made "Release" satisfying, instead of somewhat infuriating. When John and Barbara realize they simply have to let go of their son if they ever hope to move on, the episode actually touches some of the heartfelt emotion it aims for. But elsewhere . . . well, we just see a guy, staring at the camera, pretending to think really hard. —TVDW

---

29 Played by Robert Patrick's real-life wife, Barbara Patrick!

30 Credit here is due to director Kim Manners and probably *not* to the choice to have Reyes standing to the side, creepily watching the whole thing unfold.

31 With whom the show officially has no idea what to do at this point.

32 And, honestly, this is saying something on a show that had the tendency to be hijacked by its guest stars too often.

HERE'S THE STORY

In which everybody's smiling and everybody's happy.

"Sunshine Days" has its problems, but it is probably the best episode of Season Nine. Like its weird, pseudo-prequel "Je Souhaite" (S7E21), it's also an episode that maybe should have been the series finale. Whereas "Je Souhaite" put a perfect capper on both the character of Mulder and the relationship between him and Scully, "Sunshine Days" offers a great ending for the character of Dana Scully—and for the X-Files themselves. The quest for proof comes to an end, but it is subsumed by other, more important things. Yet there's another, deeper reason "Sunshine Days" makes the perfect ending: It understands that, at its heart, *The X-Files* is all about both loneliness and connection.

The characters on this series have always been defined by a central absence in their lives, beginning with Mulder's early loss of his sister and continuing on through Scully losing first her father and then everybody else she cared about over the course of the series, culminating in her long search for Mulder. The monsters that the agents track are almost always misfits, cast out of society and introduced to us as beings that inspire either pity or terror because of their isolation and alienation. The show's most famous episodes revolve in one way or another around the quest for a perfect other half,[33] and it's no accident that the series' most famous pairing was between two people who completed each other so neatly they may as well have been yin and yang.

Vince Gilligan, writer and director of both "Je Souhaite" and "Sunshine Days," understands this central theme above all else.[34] The end of "Sunshine" is more than a little hokey—with its insistence that there are things more important than proof of the paranormal, things like *human connection*—but the idea is tremendously moving in spite of itself. Here's Gilligan, wrapping up the series' central emotional conflict, while everybody else is more worried about drawing the show's plottier elements to a close. Gilligan's gentle humanism played well off the show's often-dark palette,

---

33 Especially true in classic comedy episodes, like "Jose Chung's *From Outer Space*" (S3E20) and "The Post-Modern Prometheus" (S5E5), but more of the horror episodes than can be counted were also about monsters seeking their perfect other half, especially "The Host" (S2E2), "Home" (S4E2), and every single episode about someone returning from the dead to right wrongs or protect an old love.

34 All of the show's best writers inevitably circled this idea several times, but Gilligan and Darin Morgan were the two to end up building their resumes atop it.

and that's deeply evident in the climax of this episode, in which one man realizes just how terribly he wronged another, then goes back to ask for forgiveness.

Moreover, Gilligan gives Scully the ending she deserves. The main plot of the hour is about Scully finally coming across incontrovertible "proof" of paranormal activity in the form of Oliver Martin (the great Michael Emerson, best known for his work on *Lost*), a telekinetic who's able to project his fantasies into reality, and thus has remade the interior of his home into that of the home from *The Brady Bunch*. Making the final Monster of the Week a bunch of sitcom characters works surprisingly well, particularly when grounded amid the great work we see from the regular cast members and Emerson, and particularly when viewed in light of this being the final "comedic" episode of the original run.[35]

Here, finally, is the proof Scully, Doggett, and Reyes have been seeking, and it's far, far weirder than they ever could have imagined. To exploit that proof ultimately means causing a man's death. Is sacrificing the soul worth the short-term gain? Within the confines of the episode, maybe not, but within the confines of the *series*, it's so hard to watch Scully get the one thing she's always wanted most and still know that she must do the "right thing" instead. TV characters on shows that run this long invariably turn into Sisyphus, but "Sunshine Days" is nice enough to push the rock alongside Scully, to let her know it understands how hard this is for her, and how long and impossible her struggle has been.

This isn't just Gilligan's farewell to *The X-Files* and the character of Dana Scully; it's also his love letter to the medium that made the show possible. Everything from the totally accurate re-creation of the *Brady Bunch* set to casting David Faustino (*Married with Children*'s Bud Bundy himself) as one of the luckless doofuses who finds himself killed after he breaks into Oliver's house, speaks to Gilligan's deep affection for television. But there's also a rich level of meta-commentary in all of the proceedings, as the characters talk about how the X-Files program could run for years thanks to the the proof they have found in Oliver, or as they reflect on how much a television series can mark somebody's life. *The X-Files* has always been a show in which a door could open and reveal just about anything, so why not reveal a whole other TV show?

Yes, "Sunshine Days" has some serious problems. Like "Je Souhaite," it doesn't have much of a plot. The ending, in which Oliver's problem is cured by having the doctor (John Aylward) who abandoned him as a boy vow to be his friend now and do a better job of looking out for him, is far too easy.[36] The doctor doesn't have any real obligation to Oliver beyond his own guilt. Do we really think he'll stick around

---

35 There's something hilarious on a meta-textual level about definitive proof of paranormal phenomena hanging out in the show's less-visited comedy corner, and it has a weird resonance with one of the earliest (and best) comedy episodes, "Jose Chung's *From Outer Space*" (S3E20).

36 Unless that's the point. This is an episode riffing on both *The Brady Bunch* and television's perpetually sunny belief that complex problems can be solved in thirty minutes or less, after all.

long enough for this man to finish healing? And yet, when the episode comes to this scene, it pushes not for answers or explanations . . . but for human connection.

There are plenty of people who will deride a show that chooses to leave its characters in a more or less happy place, instead of providing all of the answers it can think to contrive,[37] but wouldn't you settle for the bittersweet reverie that is "Sunshine Days"? Wouldn't you rather leave Scully realizing that all of the years she's spent pursuing the paranormal weren't for naught because of the people she worked alongside, than leave her anywhere else? Wouldn't you rather leave Doggett and Reyes quietly holding hands in a hospital hallway, imagining that they might have gotten the hang of this? The answer, to me, is simple. Always go for the ending that ties up the characters in a big, fat bow. Always go for the ending that understands what the show really is and where these characters deserve to end up. —TVDW

---

37 See also *Lost,* another Emerson project.

AN ELEGY

Robert Patrick remembers exactly where he was when he got the news that *The X-Files* was headed for cancellation: "Mr. Carter came to visit me on the soundstage. We went and had a chat in my trailer, and I found out the show wasn't going to be going past the two-year mark for me. I was . . . I don't want to use the word devastated, but I was so disappointed that it wasn't going to continue, because I thought we were doing a good job . . . . It hurt. I was so bummed out. The main reason was because of my enthusiasm for the job. I just couldn't believe it. It took me a while to get over it. . . . I loved John Doggett. It's probably one of my favorite characters I've ever played in my life. He was the personification of so many male role models that I'd had in my life, and I think he had great integrity, and it was so much fun for me to try to fill out the emotional life of the guy."

In the aftermath of September 11, and with the shifts in casting, *The X-Files* ratings struggled to return to their former heights. Chris Carter remembers: "Moving into Season Nine, there was something world-changing, and it would end up having an impact on the show that also no one could have predicted, which was the idea of government conspiracies and a government that was betraying us became anathema to everyone in America. . . .

[Post-9/11] we wanted to absolutely believe our government was doing everything in its power to protect us rather than to defy us."

In retrospect, Carter still stands by everything the show accomplished in the nine seasons of its original run. He recalls, "Vince Gilligan came up to me right about when we were ready to wrap the series in Season Nine and he said he didn't think there was one bad episode. I'm going to take that from one of the masters of television to heart and say that I think they all succeeded in their own ways."

Gilligan's own good-bye to the original run of the series came in the form of writing its penultimate episode, "Sunshine Days" (S9E19). "I did, in fact, write it, in my mind at least, as a bit of an elegy, as a bit of a good-bye. In fact, the very last scene, the very last lines of the episode, I think—it's been a while since I've seen it, but I very much wanted to have at least one of the two characters say good-bye to the audience—I gave it to Scully. . . . In that final scene Scully's talking to Doggett in the hospital, looking in on Michael Emerson's character, and that was my way of giving a good-bye to the audience and giving the thanks to the audience for keeping us on the air for nine years.

"It was kind of emotional for me. When the whole show came to an end, it was the end of a real era for me, it was the end of something very special and important to me and my career, and it meant a lot to me. So I wanted to slip in a subtle good-bye to everybody."

"THE TRUTH"	SEASON 9 / EPISODES 19 AND 20
	WRITTEN BY CHRIS CARTER
	DIRECTED BY KIM MANNERS

WE BELIEVE THE SAME THING

In which it sure was out there!

ZACK: I missed "The Truth" when it originally aired, which tells you how much my appreciation for the show had dwindled by that point; the first five seasons were some of my favorite television ever made, but at some point, my real life got in the way, and I lost track of things.

The first five minutes of "The Truth" aren't so bad. David Duchovny still looks half-stoned the way he so often looks in the final seasons, but there's not a lot of dialogue, and all the frantic running around serves to put more emphasis on action and visuals. Those visuals, at least initially, are pretty damn good: There's a cinematic quality to Mulder's brief trip into the heart of darkness, including the reveal of the giant chamber full of government (alien) scientists doing god knows what. The image of the office with the magic floating computer screen that reveals the end game[38] of the aliens' efforts is also indelible, classic *X-Files* mythology craziness.

Mulder's initial capture and the brutality of his treatment while held hostage are smart ways to set up the stakes for everything to follow. Then Skinner and Scully show up, the ghost of Krycek comes back, and things start to go downhill. The decline stems in part from how much Duchovny's evident boredom pales in comparison to Gillian Anderson's insistence on giving it everything she's got. It also doesn't help that the proceedings remind us that Mulder's disappearance was never very well explained or justified. Mostly, though, this episode suffers because of the seemingly endless trial that makes up most of its plot, in which half a dozen characters try to lay out the entire mythology over a series of monologues and "Previously On" montages.

The trial is a terrible, terrible device that stops any momentum or suspense dead in its tracks as we march inch by inch toward a verdict that will surprise absolutely no one. Even if I had been more into the mythology during the series' original run, I'm almost certain I still would have been frustrated with these scenes. Having all these characters—Scully, Skinner, Doggett, Reyes, Marita Covarrubias, Gibson Price and Jeffrey Spender—attempt to drag the murky, half-improvised backstory of the entire mytharc out into the open is both dramatically airless and enormously irritating.

For years, the contrast of Mulder's obsession against the skepticism and common sense of everyone around him (represented, of course, by Scully) was one of the series' main engines. The formula went like this: Mulder's explanations sounded unhinged, other people mocked him or lectured him in exasperation, and then Mulder, in the end, was proved right. *That* was the horror at the heart of the show. It wasn't just that there were real monsters and government conspiracies and aliens. It was the terrifying notion that what we typically dismiss as the ramblings of a lunatic could be true, that real life could be much stranger than fiction. To make characters like Skinner go along with tales of alien viruses and all the other ludicrousness—to make the only "skeptics" left be the villains—means that the tension and the fear at the core of the series is gone.

That's the problem with trying to unload answers onto us all at once, especially in such a pedantic, repetitive way: We need the mystery, the shadows, to bring the nonsense to life. The mythology should be a means to an end, a way to contextualize events within ongoing events, build the show's world, and deepen our engagement with the show's characters, not the end in and of itself. Structuring so much of the finale by demystifying something that was never designed to be explained assumes that handing the audience answers is what said audience wants most—a fundamental misunderstanding of why the show was so appealing in the first place.

S9 E19–20

---

38 Helpfully labeled "End Game," in case you weren't certain already.

TODD: I didn't watch much of Season Nine when it first aired either. I know I caught "Sunshine Days" (S9E18) on airing because I wanted to see how Vince Gilligan would close up shop on his corner of the show, and I also know I watched "The Truth." I remember the trial, and I remember the Cigarette Smoking Man burning to death. I remember that Doggett and Reyes were reduced to chauffeurs for other characters. But that's really all I retained upon first watch.

It's easy to see why I forgot so much of "The Truth": It's really, really boring television. "The Truth" lays all of the cards on the table and reveals just how much planning went into the show's mythology (which, somewhat surprisingly, turns out to be a lot). It gives viewers answer after answer after answer, until it feels like we're reading somebody's Geocities fan page for wild theories about the show. And sure, having all of this explained so explicitly appeals, in some way, to my inner nerd, who was really into this stuff around the series' midpoint. But it's also drastically, death-defyingly boring. The advantage to turning your finale into a dry lecture that's missing only a PowerPoint presentation is that it's difficult to get people really angry about it (as many nerds have gotten at other sci-fi TV show finales).[39] Instead, the viewers are too busy falling asleep.

There are some workable scenes throughout. It's neat to see all of the ghosts of characters who died along the way, and the very final scene in the motel is moving until Mulder starts randomly talking about the afterlife. The action is compelling, and William Devane makes a credible final boss (even if he only shows up once). The ultimate suggestion that Mulder can never truly win, that he must always hide in the shadows, is certainly in keeping with the show's ethos. Perhaps most admirably, the show's all-too-prescient government paranoia continued to the very last moment, as Mulder's sadistic treatment after his capture is all too similar to the many illegal detentions that were being carried out without the public's knowledge at the very moment this episode aired in 2002.

For the most part, though, "The Truth" is an onslaught of not particularly interesting information. It strangely feels like too little, too late. In attempting to squeeze everything into these two episodes, "The Truth" turns into an overlong version of someone showing you their vacation slides that you didn't ask to see. *The X-Files* gets a lot of guff for its mythology not making any sense. But this episode proves that *does* make a kind of sense. It's just that the more light you shine on the pieces, the goofier they all seem when put together.

The episode is also all too excited to get rid of Doggett[40] and Reyes in favor of Mulder and Scully. Mulder and Scully are obviously much better characters than

---

39 Notably *Battlestar Galactica* and *Lost*, both of which studiously avoided ever explaining their mysteries through long exposition dumps.

40 Who lets Mulder down in the clutch by believing in superpowered soldiers but *not* UFOs, which . . . OK?

the two later agents, but Doggett, in particular, is a hugely underrated figure both in the world of the show and in its lasting legacy.[41]

But at least the CSM gets killed by a helicopter. That feels like a fitting way for the character to go out.[42]

ZACK: It should have bothered me how much Doggett and Reyes (and even our poor, long-suffering Skinner, here reduced to a nice man who asks questions) were pushed to the side, but I'm not sure it did. I think I was more concerned with how patched together the finale was, how much the writers leaned on the thread of Mulder's quest when it hadn't really been all that relevant to the show for at least two seasons. We were given exposition-dumping instead of character resolution and closure. There isn't any closure whatsoever in this hour.[43] Apart from the CSM going out in a literal blaze of glory,[44] nothing gets resolved, no enemies are beaten, and there's no clear sense of where these characters are going to really end up. While I prefer endings that don't tie up everything too neatly, "The Truth" still feels like a couple of hours that had been sitting on a back shelf in the writers' room for a few years, only to now get dusted off, punched up with a few super-soldiers, and thrown to the wolves.

"The Truth" often plays like an abstract rendering of what an *X-Files'* finale should be, rather than an episode of television that originally builds off what came before it. The endless court testimony—so out of place on a show that did its best work by showing how the inexplicable lurked just under the currents of normal life—is quite possibly the least imaginative way to indicate that things are coming to an end. Yet there's laughably little here that's recognizable as an actual conclusion. Oh no, the X-files offices have been tampered with! Oh no, the CSM is dead[45]! Oh no, aliens are coming! Remove the live-action FAQ segment that is the trial, and "The Truth" plays much like any other finale of an *X-Files* season, cliff-hanger and all.

Mulder's concluding speech is also a grotesque self-parody, depicting the character at his most blindly insufferable. Worse, it's clearly intended to be a big hurrah moment, as though we had been waiting years to see Mulder finally get to tell a bunch of bureaucrats (and an alien!) just what he thought of them. The show had managed over the years to mitigate Mulder's all-consuming obsessions and self-righteous streak by giving him a healthy sense of humor and being more than willing to take him down a few pegs. At its best, *The X-Files* wasn't just the "Mul-

S9 E19-20

---

41 Reyes, on the other hand, is all right, I guess.

42 If you've gotten this deep into the series and this book, and you see how many pages you still have left to read, and you think the CSM is now actually dead, I'm actually impressed. I'd love to meet you.

43 Remember that this episode aired long before the series was guaranteed another movie, much less a short revival. The latter, especially, would have been essentially unprecedented in 2002.

44 Which, in this episode's defense, was pretty awesome.

45 Probably!

der Conspiracy Hour." Yet the finale often pivots in this direction, reducing every character to passive participants in his narcissistic drama. It's unpleasant to watch a show hero-worship its own lead at the expense of everyone else we've gotten to know and care about.

The worst is the way in which Scully is thrust into the background throughout. Given how much the character was sidelined during her pregnancy arc, the finale could have been a great opportunity to give her one last chance to shine. At the very least, it might have paid some attention to her own journey through the run of the show, a journey in which she suffered at least as much (if not more) than Mulder. Instead, she's right back to where she started: following her partner's lead. It speaks to what might be my biggest single disappointment in *The X-Files* as a whole, overarching narrative: the way the show so often seemed to forget that it had *two* leads, not just one, and that Scully (and Anderson) is just as critical to its success as Mulder (and Duchovny) was. By doubling down on Mulder, the finale essentially ignores half of its own soul, with inevitably poor results.

TODD: I'll admit, though, that when it comes to character moments, I do like that last scene, which leaves Mulder and Scully in a good place (even if it's tinted with a certain strange religiosity). I also do love the final encounter with the CSM, whose voice Chris Carter precisely captures as soon as he starts writing him again. I want my finales to leave the characters I love in a place that feels appropriate. In most dramas, that means saying good-bye to the characters in a place that feels commensurate with their actions throughout the show. *The X-Files* fails this test because, while it leaves Mulder and Scully at a surprisingly appropriate moment in their lives (they're on the run but still together and assured of their righteousness), it mostly just abandons everyone else in the midst of a cliff-hanger that will never be resolved.[46]

What kept *The X-Files* from running forever was how the final two seasons were driven by the twin impulses to make this a *new* television program while it was still openly pining for the days of Mulder and Scully. That approach worked in Season Eight, when the text was very much about returning to those days and coping with the grief that change could bring. In that season, the show managed to incorporate Doggett into those (sometimes painful) adventures as Scully's partner, but in Season Nine, it became a problem. This season is the worst of the show's run because the series quite obviously didn't care enough about making the Doggett-Reyes partnership anywhere near vital enough to carry a show that was always, at its heart, a two-hander.

---

46 Not even in future versions of the show. When some of these characters turn up again, we have no sense of how—or why—they might have survived.

Where "The Truth" ultimately fails is in drawing to a close not the show we had been watching—which had changed and evolved and adjusted over time—but the show *The X-Files* had been three or four seasons ago. It feels like an ending to a show that no longer exists, a show that never had the joyful, hilarious, or experimental hours that *The X-Files* had over its near-decade-long run. This was a finale less about taking an appropriate and final leave from characters to whom we were connected and more about trying to build something new for a future that might never come.[47]

---

47 Until it did! Turn the page.

THE X-FILES

I WANT
TO
BELIEVE

STILL OUT THERE

In which a franchise returns from the dead.

TODD: My primary memory of the second *X-Files* movie is one of disappointment. I wasn't disappointed in the movie itself so much as in the fact that it so quickly sank without a trace. Nobody was into *The X-Files* anymore when this thing hit theaters. I remember the excited reports from various conventions of new footage being shown and the moment the trailer came out. But as the release date got closer and closer in the summer of 2008,[1] it was hard to escape the feeling that whatever fan base the show once had was now scattered to the winds. The movie came out and disappointed at the box office. I ponied up for a morning matinee ticket; my wife and I were the only two people at the screening. I remember walking home feeling glum.

It is not, by any stretch of the imagination, a great movie. It's not even that good of an episode of *The X-Files*, though it is an overextended one. But it feels like something that could have been at home as one of the less successful episodes of Season Five or Six. It's nothing amazing, but it's occasionally thought-provoking and capable of providing a few jolts. Plus, it's got that incredible Mulder and Scully chemistry, that undeniably appealing dynamic that the original series so sorely lacked in its last few years on air. What's even more interesting to me is how little time the movie spends trying to dredge up fan-favorite things from the series. There's *some* fan service to be found here, but *I Want to Believe* mostly focuses on putting its best foot forward as a "Monster of the Movie" franchise, in which all you need to know about the series are the names "Mulder" and "Scully."

Of course, to have that sort of franchise be successful, the movie would have had to have a compelling Monster of the Week plot, and it's in this crucial element that *I Want to Believe* missteps. There's a former priest named Father Joseph Crissman (Billy Connolly), who is both a psychic and a pedophile. He's using his powers to help the FBI track down a missing agent because a couple of backwoods mad scientists

---

1 A year in which the man who would win the U.S. presidency built his candidacy around ideas of hope, change, and the phrase, "Yes, we can,"—none of which suggests an environment particularly welcoming to a paranoid horror movie with roots in a mythos concerning a grand government conspiracy. Then again, the other big factor in *I Want to Believe*'s collapse at the box office was that it was released shortly after *The Dark Knight* came and took over the American imagination, and that Batman saga certainly wasn't full of sunshine and roses. Whether you want to blame optimism or cynicism, there's something to pin the failure of *Believe* onto.

are conducting experiments with head transplants and the like.[2] The movie attempts to have more to it than that, but it's by and large a mad scientist tale with a sheen of religious connection threaded throughout.

Indeed, it's on the subject of religion that the film is most persuasive, particularly as it pertains to Scully. After the end of the original series, she has become a doctor at a Catholic hospital—which is exactly the sort of place where her strong scientific background and her foundational faith can keep rubbing elbows, jostling for her attention. Thanks to this career shift,[3] Scully becomes the protagonist of the story in a way she hadn't been throughout much of Seasons Eight and Nine. The film's title is *I Want to Believe* (of Mulder's poster fame) but aliens are nowhere to be seen. In this case, it's Scully who wants to believe, not in the supernatural, but in a God who hasn't abandoned his creations, despite all evidence to the contrary.

The strongest evidence *for* God emerges in the horror story. The idea of a pedophile who's also a psychic is the sort of thing the show could have turned into a terrific episode when it was firing on all cylinders,[4] but it would have required a defter touch than Chris Carter and Frank Spotnitz display here. The questions about whether God might use such a flawed vessel to deliver His message and about whether Crissman's physic ability stems, in some way, from the pain he caused his victims are explicitly made text here in a way that doesn't do them any favors. Moreover, on a structural level, there just isn't enough *here* to justify the 105-minute running time. It feels like there are five million chase scenes in this thing, and they're all oddly flat.

The final issue is how thoroughly out of whack the movie's sexual politics are, though in a very different manner from those of the original series.[5] Here, the villains are a gay couple who are killing women so that one of them (presumably a trans woman but never identified as such) can use female body parts for her gender confirmation surgery.[6] I would be interested in dissecting the film's portrayal of a gay couple shifting into a straight one due to one partner's transition, and how that notion might drive some of their murderous desperation, if I thought the movie had thought about this concept at all beyond Carter pointing to Spotnitz and saying,

---

2   The best scare in the movie is when a disembodied head opens its eyes and looks at Mulder.

3   And to a slightly clunky subplot about a young boy who's dying, clearly meant to remind Scully about giving William up for adoption and thus to resonate with her.

4   Though it's hard to imagine even the Fox network of the '90s—which was more permissive than other broadcast networks but not, ultimately, *that* permissive—letting a concept this dark get to air.

5   Which never met a threat of heavily sexualized violence against women it couldn't insert into a story.

6   Carter himself says the idea for this bit of mad science came from a news story he had read: "There was a guy who had done a head transplant on a monkey. Sure enough, I was able to go meet this guy in Cleveland and talk to him about how it was done, and what the difficulties are, and if it's possible on a human being. I found out, in fact, it is possible. It's not as far-fetched as it may seem."

"Dog Day Afternoon?[7]" before Spotnitz enthusiastically returned his nod. The use of queer themes here is so bad that it passes right by offensive and just becomes incredibly dumb.[8]

If there's a reason to watch *I Want to Believe*, then, it's to see Mulder and Scully together again, back in action. In particular, I like that the movie doesn't strain to put Mulder back in service, even if it feels absolutely ludicrous that *this* is the case the FBI would agree to work on with him again. If I'm being honest with you, it's just nice to see Mulder and Scully as, effectively, an old married couple. The level of trust and respect they have has over time nicely settled into a comfortable groove, and it makes for soothing viewing.[9] We as viewers have earned the right to see our original pairing interacting in such an unambiguously romantic way.

ZACK: I missed this in theaters,[10] but I'd seen it at least once before watching it again for review. Like Todd, I've always associated it with disappointment, although for me, that disappointment was always pinned to the movie itself. After *The X-Files* petered out in its final season, and after its first cinematic outing was only OK, I had hopes that a new movie based off the MOTW format might change things. It didn't. In retrospect, I know my expectations were impossibly high, but I still think we could've gotten something better than *I Want to Believe*.

I also don't think it's terrible. The plot pretty much holds together, and the story is a gratifyingly closed unit. And yes, it's absolutely fun to see Mulder and Scully together again; the easy chemistry between the two actors is as warm to watch as it is on the show. It doesn't resolve anything "The Truth" (S9E19/20) introduced, but on the whole, that's probably for the best.[11] A movie that's trying to get back in touch with a world that had been out of the public consciousness for over half a decade should try to keep things brisk and unencumbered, which this film does.

Perhaps that's exactly what frustrates me so much about watching the movie now. Beyond the (often bizarre) details of the plot, this is the exact approach I would've wanted the writers to take. Yet apart from the delightful interactions between Mulder and Scully, it just doesn't work all that well. I love Billy Connolly, but casting him as the pedophiliac priest only creates a black hole from which the

---

7   In which Sonny Wortzik (played by Al Pacino) robs a bank in order to help his wife obtain gender confirmation surgery.

8   It's here that I should cut Carter and Spotnitz some slack and point out that the movie's script couldn't be changed on set, because the movie was filmed during the 2007–08 Writers Guild of America strike, which meant that any writing Carter or Spotnitz did—right down to suggesting alternate lines—would be in violation of the strike. Could *I Want to Believe* have been saved with another script draft or two? We'll never know, but it certainly wouldn't have hurt.

9   Also: There's a moment in which Scully looks at a photo of George W. Bush hanging in FBI headquarters, and the famous theme song plays on the soundtrack, and it's weird and hilarious.

10 I was working as a projectionist at the time, so I remember watching the credit cookie of Mulder and Scully in swimwear and wondering what the hell was going on.

11 Flip back to that review if you want to remind yourself why that's the case.

rest of the movie can't extract itself. While his character's past ultimately connects into the main plot later on in the film, it's a device that works better in the abstract than in practice, as it becomes nearly impossible to settle into a good, diverting monster movie while the pall of child rape hangs over everything.

The worst sin of *I Want to Believe* is that this is a story that would've been uninteresting no matter how it had been told. It shies away from the paranormal almost entirely, relying instead on Father Joe's psychic visions and an admittedly exceptional form of organ transplant to hold our interest. The attack scenes are well shot but not particularly memorable, and the villains are never truly developed. We call it a MOTW-type format, but there's no real monster here, and apart from talking about psychics and their mysterious ways, Mulder doesn't even get to do any crackpot theorizing.

It all feels so perfunctory. This movie isn't a train wreck, but it also doesn't ever come up with more than a halfhearted defense of its own existence. Scully's story line reads like a contractual obligation inserted into the screenplay to make sure Gillian Anderson would sign on. The actress does her usual excellent work, but a sick little boy[12] who needs stem cell treatment does not make for gripping cinema.

I really just wanted more, which is always a frustrating thing to ask from a creator: a richer story, better characters, an actual monster. Watching the end credits, I think I enjoyed seeing the behind-the-scenes photos of the cast and crew more than anything in the movie itself. It reminded me of the reason I fall for shows like *The X-Files* in the first place—it feels like a reassuring, if often terrifying, existence of a home away from home. I wanted a great story, which I didn't get, but I also wanted to reconnect with some old (fictional) friends, which mostly worked out. That's certainly better than nothing.

It feels weird to go this far without mentioning Amanda Peet as Dakota Whitney. Could she have been more of an afterthought for this film? I guess it could've been worse; she could've been Agent Drummy (played by Alvin Joiner, AKA Xzibit).

TODD: Yes, introducing Agents Dakota Whitney[13] and Drummy only served to underline even more just how much this story has always been about Mulder and Scully, despite how much the writers might have wanted to make it about the X-Files Department in general. *The X-Files* was so tied to the chemistry between those two actors that it could never really break free of them, which must have frustrated the franchise ambitions of 20th Century Fox. This is the show that popularized the term "shipper" for a reason! Mulder and Scully are why we're watching, and that means any other characters—even one played by an actress

---

12 His name is Christian Fearon, which I found hilarious.
13 Which: What kind of name *is* that?

as generally solid as Peet—are just there to provide exposition and have shocking death scenes.[14]

The movie was shot in Vancouver—the first bit of *The X-Files* shot there since "The End" (S5E20)—and Chris Carter gets a lot of visual mileage out of characters tromping through the barren snowfields, poking at the white and hoping for a grim answer. Whatever faults the movie has aren't due to the performances or the film's technical aspects. It's just that the script is so very weak.

If this were the last bit of *X-Files*–related material we would ever get,[15] I think I'd be happier with this being the end rather than the "The Truth" (S9E19/20). This story tries to honor Mulder *and* Scully, whereas the series finale only really tried to do well by Mulder. The place that *I Want to Believe* leaves the two of them at the end of the film—assuming we excuse that hilariously unnecessary (but obviously welcome) credits cookie in which the two of them wave to the camera from a rowboat—is one that allows us to imagine them off having other adventures, together but without us watching. That's what I want to believe these two are still doing: fighting the good fight and never letting the darkness swallow them whole.

---

14 For as useless as she is to the film, I thought Dakota's death helped juice things up at a time when everything felt very bland.

15 Which it wasn't! Turn the page (again).

SEASON

TEN

REOPENED

In which we question how much one adjusts for nostalgia.

And then, suddenly, it was 2016, and *The X-Files* was back.

In the fourteen years *The X-Files* had been off the air (eight, if you count the 2008 movie), television had changed considerably. Serialization, once an anomaly for mainstream TV, had become the norm, with popular shows like *Lost* and *24* embracing its storytelling extremes to great popular and critical support. The advent of *The Sopranos* while *The X-Files* was still airing had ushered in an age of antihero television dramas that brought the medium greater critical attention than ever before, but the explosion of reality television and the rapid fracturing of the home audience resulted in a TV landscape that was filled with options but lacked certifiable crossover hits. That viewer splintering led to executives looking to leverage past phenomena into new content, and, in the context of network business and ratings grabs, bringing back *The X-Files* made sense. Time had been kind to the show in the years since it ended, with fans remembering the good times without lingering on the bad.[1] While it was easy to be skeptical at the prospect of a big, "event series" revival, the appeal of a new, revitalized *X-Files*—one which might not be bogged down by the original run's ballooning mythology—was too appealing for fans to ignore.

"My Struggle" is not a great hour of television. It's forced, unevenly paced, and exploits real-life tragedy to a degree that borders on tasteless. There's a certain queasiness to it as well, a sense that something isn't exactly what it ought to be. The world of the show is askew, and the new angle doesn't feel entirely intentional.

Still, how can you not feel a shiver up your spine when the first notes of that theme music kick in?

Of everything that happens in "My Struggle," Mulder and Scully's friendly estrangement makes the most sense, and there's a pleasantly meta charm to their reunion. Duchovny and Anderson's chemistry, thankfully, remains intact. While it's a shame to see Carter's script once again falling back on the same patterns these characters long ago outgrew (Mulder is fixated, Scully is the concerned outsider who sighs a lot before finally accepting the truth), it's still an absolute pleasure to see these actors working together again. And Mulder and Scully are not the only characters we're delighted to see again; it appears that

---

1   That nostalgia, which prompted online outlets to do legacy writing on classic shows, is a major part of why this book exists.

Skinner is still doing the same job he was doing when the show originally ended, and the Cigarette Smoking Man (surprise surprise) is not dead after all.[2] They're a little older, and a little tired of the material, but the spark between them is still there.

To be fair, it's not just Mulder and Scully that have a welcome familiarity about them. Carter's ability to spin labyrinthian theory into something *almost* rational gives Mulder and Tad O'Malley's (Joel McHale) rants a surprising amount of power—and while the mention of 9/11 as a "false flag" operation is in poor taste,[3] it's not entirely out of bounds for the show, which has previously draped tragedy in the guise of lunacy for its own storytelling ends.[4] If nothing else, there's still something to be said for hearing total madness expressed in such eloquent, formal language.

The big hook of "My Struggle" is Carter's attempt to spin the show's convoluted mythology off in a new direction. Some of this feels familiar; Mulder has decided "everything is a lie!" a dozen times or more by now in the history of *The X-Files*. The idea that the government weaved an increasingly convoluted lie about an alien civil war and invasion to cover for their own efforts to use alien tech to take over the world is a stretch, to put it kindly. One's willingness to accept this plot depends on one's ability to ignore both the troubling real-world implications and the fact that this latest version of "the truth" contradicts every *other* version of "the truth" that the show has thrown at us. Really, this premiere's greatest value is its ability to lay the groundwork for other writers to build on.

There are touches that work; Scully's date with Tad gives her something more to do than look worried all the time, and the fact that Skinner remains the assistant director of the FBI is at once hilarious and utterly reassuring. Of course, there are touches that don't work too. The transition from "Oh hey, I found proof!" to "Everything is being hushed up and nearly all of the relevant parties have been killed" is far too abrupt, and Sveta (Annet Mahendru) is too much of a prop to be a character in whom we can get invested.

If it's a mess, then at least it has the courtesy to cauterize its loose ends as it goes. Yes, there's absolutely some nostalgia at play here, even in the quality of the

S10 E1

---

2 We did warn you.

3 The world has changed considerably since Chris Carter first created the show, and one of the most unfortunate aspects of that change is the way conspiracy theory had gone from being a weird sideshow for the Internet's social maladroits and paranoid losers to a weird sideshow that also has some terrifying real-world consequences. The fact that this season doesn't even try to account for that social shift is a major creative failing, and yet another reason the mythology episodes are that much harder to stomach.

4 The third season episode, "Paper Clip" (S3E4), is literally named for the operation that brought Nazi scientists over to the U.S. to work for the government after the second World War. "Musings of a Cigarette Smoking Man" (S4E7) even had the CSM responsible for both John F. Kennedy and Martin Luther King Jr.'s assassinations.

mess itself—this is, after all, the sort of nonsense Carter got up to all the time during the show's original run, abridged by time constraints and of questionable necessity to the world of the show. "My Struggle" is not great. It might not even be good. But it's the start of a new era. Maybe for fans, that's enough. —ZH

A NEW CHAPTER

How exactly did a cult show that became a massive phenomenon suddenly return to television after fifteen years off the air? Chris Carter says that the door was still open after *The X-Files: I Want to Believe*, but the interest in a revival series nevertheless surprised him. According to Carter, he "got a call completely out of the blue, from 20th Century Fox, telling me that the actors were interested in bringing back *The X-Files*. Would I be interested as well? Knowing that the actors—or being assured that the actors were interested—I was interested." As for convincing some of the show's most beloved writers to get the band back together and return to write a few more scripts, Carter says "it took no coaxing at all. They were all available, luckily. [James Wong] has a regular job on *American Horror Story*, so he had to be sprung from that. That was the trickiest part. But, both Glen and Darin signed on enthusiastically."

Carter says that the truncated nature of Season Ten was a challenge, though, for all involved. When constructing a six-episode season for a show that ran for an average of twenty-two episodes a season in its heyday, Carter acknowledges that he and the writing staff had to take "a different approach to the show. Clearly, it's a much more focused approach to a series of episodes. But, we really took the same approach in the end, with the mixture of stand-alones to mythology episodes. It just happened in a much steeper arc."

The approach worked, as the debut episode of Season Ten was watched by 16.19 million people—the highest-rated premiere of *The X-Files* since "The Sixth Extinction" (S7E1) aired in 1999, as well as the most-watched episode of *The X-Files* since "This Is Not Happening" (S8E14) aired in 2001. *The X-Files*, without a doubt, had been reopened.

X-FILES-MEN

In which monsters still turn up on a weekly basis.

"Founder's Mutation" feels a bit like *The X-Files* got lost on its way back to television and swung through a few *X-Men* sets on the 20th Century Fox back lot. It was the fifth episode produced of this six-episode mini season, but it was chosen to air second, presumably to better set up some of this season's references to William. Mulder and Scully's imagined flashbacks to their son's childhood that they never got to see are clunky and unnecessary, but they're better integrated into the overarching story than these sorts of plot devices usually are. David Duchovny and Gillian Anderson bring real depth of feeling to the hour. You take your pleasures where you can find them.

That evaluation makes it sound like "Founder's Mutation" is a bad episode, and it's not. It features some superbly eerie moments, including one great gross-out jolt when a man, tormented by a high-pitched keening noise, plunges a sharp object into his own ear.[5] It has just the right set of twists and turns, it gives Mulder and Scully a case to actively solve, and its final reveal of the "monsters"—actually a set of twins who've been subjected to horrible experimentation—gets the proper amount of pomp and circumstance.

It's just that this episode suffers when compared with all of the shows that have aired since *The X-Files* left the air. Indeed, its biggest flaw has essentially nothing to do with the text of "Founder's Mutation" at all, but instead is due to how much it feels like *Fringe*, a Fox series that aired in its entirety between the release of *The X-Files: I Want to Believe* and the premiere of Season Ten and was probably the copycat show that was the most successful at capturing what made the original *X-Files* so very good. Whereas *The X-Files* started as a show about paranormal phenomena that dabbled in mad science, *Fringe* began as a show about mad scientists that occasionally suggested mad science might look very much like paranormal phenomena. It too was anchored by a core cast who gave great, minimalist performances (especially from Anna Torv and John Noble). It too was built around sins committed in the past that resonated in the present. And it too was eventually devoured by its own mythology.

It's not hard to imagine that the sorts of fans who anxiously anticipated the return of *The X-Files* were exactly the sorts of people who kept *Fringe* on the air against all odds for five seasons. Thus, when Mulder and Scully step into a secretive

---

5   Complete with an *incredibly satisfying* "Splorp!" sound effect.

lab where children with special powers are being enhanced and experimented on, one immediately feels a creeping sense of déjà vu—not just for *The X-Files* of old, but for one of its highest achieving progeny.

More personally, though, I feel that, as an adopted person, the story Season Ten tells about William is uncomfortable at best. I've tried not to bring my personal life into these reviews too much, but it's impossible to separate the content of the episode from my reaction to the way that Mulder and Scully act as though giving him up for adoption caused William to feel intense loneliness and sorrow, even though he presumably had adopted parents who loved him very much. To be sure, the show couches this argument in concern that William's powers would have marked him for interest from very powerful and unscrupulous men, and it's clearly rooted from the perspective of Mulder and Scully as William's birth parents, who feel some echoes of guilt, loneliness, or sorrow when confronted with one of William's possible fates. Yet the pair's certainty that William must have felt so very alone, much as it's rooted in their own grief, is inextricably tied to the way the series treats adoption as, at best, a necessary evil.

You can't just write all of this postponed sadness off as a clunky attempt at emotion in an episode that might be better off without it. "Founder's Mutation" is explicitly *about* what happened in the world of *The X-Files* when the Syndicate was thwarted. Despite Mulder and Scully's attempts to reveal the truth, experiments on human beings using alien DNA continued in the shadows. It is, like much of this season, about the horrors that seep from the foundations when empires crumble. Yes, the Syndicate was evil and filled with evil men. But its structure was also keeping some of the chaos at bay. Now, it's a free-for-all for all kinds of evil men,[6] and children are frequently the target of their dark designs.

That's the idea, at least, though I don't know if "Founder's Mutation" completely sells it. This episode probably would have worked better had it simply told its story in straightforward fashion, with Mulder and Scully slowly realizing that these are the kinds of atrocities that could very well have befallen the son they gave up. As is, the flashbacks never truly connect to the main story, and there's a definite sense of the script trying too hard to tie everything together. But this season is about two people trying to put back together a world now in shambles, and in its most powerful moments, "Founder's Mutation" steps into the rubble and starts gathering the pieces. It is not *The X-Files* at its best, but it *is* recognizably *The X-Files*. After "My Struggle" (S10E1), it's welcome just to see that the show hasn't forgotten how to do that work. —TVDW

6 Welcome to 2016, *The X-Files!!!*

IGNORANT IDIOTS

In which maybe this season wasn't such a bad idea after all.

It's no great truth that life loses some of its magic as you leave childhood behind, but what really stings is that the magic doesn't just leave you: It twists in on itself, making you bitter for all those years you wasted waiting for Santa Claus, Bigfoot, the bogeyman. Growing up doesn't ever end, and with every year that passes, we become a little more tired, a little more realistic, and a little less able to look at a monster and not try to see the zipper.

"Mulder and Scully Meet the Were-Monster" is the first legitimate defense of Season Ten's existence. That's somewhat ironic, considering this script comes from Darin Morgan, the man whose episodes for the original run aggressively questioned *The X-Files'* search for truth, and in doing so, helped transform it. Self-awareness is a risky turn for any narrative, but by acknowledging the fundamental stupidity of the alien abduction and government conspiracy theories that were key to the show's understanding of itself at the time, Morgan opened the series up to a whole new type of storytelling.

His script and direction in "Were-Monster" are exactly as ambitious and funny as one might hope. The episode is consistently goofy throughout,[7] right down to the murders of multiple generic white men.[8] The episode is, at its heart, a tribute to the pleasures of monster-hunting, body-slicing, and truth-hunting this show has always offered us.

Mulder starts the hour more conscious of his failings, and the failings of his lifelong search, than we've ever seen him. After hours spent combing through the X-Files backlogs, he's disgusted with the world and himself, no longer able to believe as willingly as he once did. Yet he and Scully go on a case anyway, after a pair

---

7 A full list of Easter Eggs and callbacks Morgan has scattered throughout the hour would require a whole separate review, but here are a few: Mulder throws pencils into the ceiling as he first did in "Chinga" (S5E10); Mulder is seen wearing the infamous red speedo from "Duane Barry" (S2E5); Scully reminds us that she's immortal, which was first suggested in "Clyde Bruckman's Final Repose" (S3E4), another Darin Morgan episode; Mulder's cell phone ringtone is the show's theme music; and Guy Mann runs around dressed in a seersucker suit and straw hat modeled after the outfit worn by Darren McGavin in the 1970s series *Kolchak: The Night Stalker*, a one-season wonder that was influential to the development of *The X-Files*.

8 Most genre shows aren't interested in the corpses they leave in their wake; one-offs and Dumpster prizes get a token nod at best. Morgan doesn't even bother with the nod.

of paint-huffing idiots[9] see a lizard monster attack Animal Control Officer Pasha (*X-Files* superfan Kumail Nanjiani). Scully starts to enjoy herself, even commenting on how much fun she's having, and her casual confession of pleasure serves as a sort of thesis statement for the hour.

The joyous tone that infuses the episode is why the identity of the corpses doesn't matter. They're made-up objects whose sole reason for existence is to allow the rest of the story to spring up around them. Pasha turns out to be another nebbish serial killer, and, as delightful as Nanjiani's performance is, he doesn't really matter either. Pasha is just another reminder of man's capacity for violence and the tediously familiar justifications that come with it. The search for truth, for monsters, is really about needing different answers for the same old questions.

There is another kind of monster in "Were-Monster," although he's innocent of any killing. Guy Mann (Rhys Darby) is a lizard creature bitten by a man and thus cursed to transform into a human during the day, complete with all of the horrible trappings human consciousness brings. It's a great joke to build an episode around, and one made even greater by Darby's infuriated bafflement at having all of the very human concerns about jobs and retirement funds and lying about his sex life. The premise that conscious thought has doomed us to unhappiness is not a new theme for Morgan,[10] and the surface-level silliness of Guy's struggles to cope with his newfound humanity don't distract from the melancholy running through the setup.

Mulder and Guy are ultimately suffering from variations on the same basic problem. Being human—being grown-up—means knowing the limitations of the world. More than anything, it means knowing that you are going to die, and the finality that comes from that realization. It means knowing that there are a finite number of possibilities for any given scenario, and that Occam's razor is the doom of all dreaming. Everything ends, and most of it ends in absolute, pointless nonsense, tantalizing us with a resolution we can't even grasp. You don't bring back a TV show more than a decade after it concluded and expect it to have any reason for existing. Mulder and Scully are gone forever, and they had some pretty shitty adventures in those last couple of years, so maybe you should just get over the whole thing.

The pleasure of "Mulder and Scully Meet the Were-Monster" is what holds it back from the edge of despair. It revels in the possibility that, well, maybe you don't have to let Mulder and Scully go quite yet. It's a surprising sentiment to come from a writer who so excels at embracing life's existential and essential cruelties. The brightest moments in the episode come from casual nods to beloved earlier outings, and from watching our heroes embrace the foolishness that held them together for so long. It's impossible to shed the maturity that masquerades as cynicism; we've

---

9 Played by Tyler Labine and Nicole Parker-Smith, who played the same druggie characters in "War of the Coprophages" (S3E12) and "Quagmire" (S3E22)—both episodes that Morgan was involved in writing.

10 See also: "Clyde Bruckman's Final Repose" (S3E4) and "Jose Chung's *From Outer Space*" (S3E20).

found the truth, and the truth is a box in the ground and a stone with your name on it.[11] But that doesn't mean we can't keep our eyes open, and if the monster we find isn't exactly what we thought it was, it might still let us shake its hand.

To put it another way: We still want to believe. —ZH

---

11 Speaking of, one of the better homages in the episode has Mulder hanging out in a cemetery, slumped down by a tombstone with Kim Manners's name on it. Manners was a key behind-the-scenes figure on *The X-Files*, serving as a producer on the show from Season Two on and a director who helmed more episodes of the show than any other director. He directed more than fifty episodes, beginning with "Die Hand Die Verletzt" (S2E14) and ending with the original series finale "The Truth" (S9E19). He died of lung cancer in 2009.

KOLCHAK: THE NIGHT MONSTER

Darin Morgan's contribution to Season Ten was unquestionably the most critically-acclaimed episode of the season, and was hailed as a return to form for one of the show's most iconic voices. But the script for the episode had origins in a different show, as Morgan had initially written it as an unproduced script for *Night Stalker*, the remake of *Kolchak: The Night Stalker* that ran for one season on ABC in 2005 and was co-created by Frank Spotnitz. The show, in paying tribute to the series that inspired *The X-Files*, featured contributions from many *X-Files* alums, including Vince Gilligan and directors Rob Bowman and Daniel Sackheim, in addition to Spotnitz himself. It makes sense, then, that the human form of the monster—Guy Mann—would be dressed as the original Kolchak throughout the hour.

When asked how Morgan managed to repurpose the script for *The X-Files*, he says, "It was both easy and really difficult." What was interesting to him, though, was how many critics, after the airing of the episode, pointed out its origins. He says critics often remarked, "'This is based on an old script for another show.' But I have several complaints about it. One is that most of the people that made that kind of complaint obviously had never seen the *Night Stalker* remake. Because the *Night Stalker* remake wasn't [really] a remake of *The Night Stalker*; it was a remake of *The X-Files*. They gave Kolchak a young skeptical lady partner, you know? The show was too much like *The X-Files*, and so to take an idea from that show wasn't really that much of a stretch. It was basically the same show except rather than being FBI agents, they were reporters."

Regardless of where the episode came from, many fans say this episode was their favorite of Season Ten. Even Mitch Pileggi claims it as one of his favorite hours, despite the fact that he doesn't appear in it. Pileggi says he loves Morgan's work, and resorted to teasing the writer to get him to include Skinner in one of his scripts. Pileggi remembers that, when shooting was going on for "Mulder and Scully Meet the Were-Monster," the actor wasn't "quite so nice. We were up in Vancouver and I was doing a couple episodes, and Darin was up there doing his episode that I wasn't in. I happened to run into him in the elevator and I didn't say anything to him. I just kind of looked at him and looked away. I hadn't seen him in a long time and he goes, 'I'm Darin,' and I said, 'Darin? Darin who?' And he goes, 'Darin Morgan,' and I go, 'Morgan? I'm sorry.' I was acting like I had no idea who he was, and I said, 'Until you put me into your episode, dude, I have nothing to say to you.'" Pileggi says that the joke was, of course, all in good fun, but that, "the look on his face when I was acting like I didn't know who he was was priceless."

| "HOME AGAIN" | SEASON 10 / EPISODE 4
WRITTEN AND DIRECTED BY GLEN MORGAN |

ALL THINGS MUST PASS

In which the Trashman testifies.

"Home Again" is the best Monster of the Week episode of the truncated tenth season. This is perhaps not as high of praise as it would seem since there are only two straight MOTW entries to be found in this season,[12] but it hits many notes that haven't been hit so skillfully so far in the revival, and it's comforting to see that *The X-Files* still has those notes in its repertoire. It's the first script for the series by Glen Morgan since "Never Again" (S4E13),[13] and it's the sort of creepy, darkly funny, and gross episode Morgan and James Wong used to specialize in. This one also pulls off something *The X-Files* usually struggles with: It has solid yet not overbearing political overtones.

The Morgan-and-Wong trademark is especially evident in the monster, who is a strong creation with an utterly gruesome method of killing (which seems to involve ripping people in half, with the requisite spatter of blood to mark the motion). Every time the story starts to flag—starts to get too caught up in the drama around Mother Scully's bedside, for example—one of these horrible kills arrives to send

---

12 The premiere and finale are straight-up mythology, while "Were-Monster" (S10E3) and "Babylon" (S10E5) are both experimental hours, which leaves only this hour and "Founder's Mutation" (S10E2).

13 Just as "Founder's Mutation" was the first script by Morgan's former writing partner, James Wong, since the two cowrote that Season Four episode.

the story back into overdrive. It's the precise blend of personal story and horror tale that Morgan and Wong were always best at,[14] and it's beautifully paced throughout.

In many ways, "Home Again" feels like an attempt to redo the misfire that was "The Jersey Devil" (S1E5). Once again, the monster highlights the class divide between the rich and the destitute, and once again, that monster is more effective in half-seen glimpses and moments of sheer impossibility. But where "The Jersey Devil" only halfheartedly engaged with these ideas, "Home Again" plunges into them headfirst. This episode is explicitly *about* how we've forgotten those who need our help the most, and how forgetting is too often the easiest thing for us to do.

Even better, Morgan doesn't make the theme too explicit until he's absolutely earned the right to do so. Whereas prior *X-Files* episodes with a political bent would often underline their points early and too often, Morgan holds back until the final few moments of the hour, when he finally nods toward the idea that this monstrous trash golem is the American class war given horrifying form and set loose on those who intend to destroy the homeless community of Philadelphia.

Really, "Home Again" is a delectable buffet of ideas from prior *X-Files* episodes that weren't realized as well as they could have been. The idea of a monster made from trash and human detritus, brought to life by the power of thought, is basically another iteration of the *tulpa* monster from "Arcadia" (S6E15), for which everything in the episode worked *except* the monster.[15] The scenes in which Scully stands vigil by her mother's bedside are quieter variations on a theme the show hit many, many times before with other family members of our two heroes. The nod toward William, mentioned here first by Scully's mother, is better handled than similar nods Wong attempted in "Founder's Mutation" (S10E2).

In particular, "Home Again" better acknowledges the immense weight of grief Mulder and Scully still feel at what they had to do to protect their son, and just how much they miss him, even if he's still out there, alive and perhaps unaware of their existence.[16] As with the other elements of "Home Again" that play better than their former incarnations, this theme works gracefully because of how delicately Morgan writes these scenes. Mulder and Scully miss William, and they can finally admit that to each other. But they've also lived with this pain for fifteen years now. Their son has grown up without them. They've had to learn to live inside of that space, at least a little bit.

This assessment is overpraising the episode, just a bit. If it were airing in one of the show's first five seasons, this entry would be strictly middle of the

14 See "Beyond the Sea" (S1E13), "Never Again" (S4E13), and "Home" (S4E2), among many other classics.
15 To say nothing of "Kaddish" (S4E15), another episode centered on a golem, though that entry used a much more classical version of the trope.
16 It makes you wonder if the whole William arc would have played more skillfully if "Home Again" had aired second and "Founder's Mutation" fifth as originally planned.

S10 E4

pack, and it's obvious here that "Home Again" stands out mostly because of the various failures of many of the hours surrounding it. But it's important not to undersell the episode either. By the hour's end—when Morgan has pulled all of the story's many strands together, and the Trashman is rolling out, his creation's work done—"Home Again," just for a moment, almost feels like the show's glory days have returned. It is a good, not great, episode of *The X-Files*. But a good, not great, episode of *The X-Files* is still a thing of wonder, so many years past the golden ones of yore. —TVDW

"BABYLON" | SEASON 10 / EPISODE 5
WRITTEN AND DIRECTED BY CHRIS CARTER

IT'S A BIT OF A MIND TRIP
In which mothers are the answer to everything.

"Babylon" is a messy, conflicted episode, one full of ambition and inspired strangeness, with jarring and unsettling pieces. The threat of a terrorist cell politically complicates things in a way Chris Carter's script never earns, and you can never really shake the fact that the script never digs much deeper into a one-dimensional conflict than "some artist made an offensive painting, *kaboom!*" The real-world relevance of these issues makes them feel especially opportunistic and distracting in a way the episode can't manage. Carter wants the power of the politically charged imagery without respecting its human cost, and it's a nearly fatal misstep.

Thankfully things get more interesting once the bomber (a young man named Shiraz, played by Artin John) fades into the background. He's more or less the Mac-Guffin for this story; as the only survivor of the bombing, he's left in a vegetative state, and it's up to Mulder, Scully, and two new FBI pals to make contact and find out the location of the cell that enabled him. This is a ridiculous premise, and while that's not entirely unusual for the show, the context (domestic terrorism) makes it harder to accept, especially given that it's never explained why Mulder and Scully would be working on this case. But to its credit, "Babylon" never really pretends this premise is anything other than ridiculous. One of Carter's strengths as a writer—the strength that arguably made this entire show possible—is his ability to write absolute bullshit with a straight face. And he keeps on writing it, with such conviction that you might start doubting yourself for doubting him.

Throwing a wrench into the usual Mulder-Scully dynamic are the new FBI agents who serve as younger versions of our heroes (right down to their hair color, in case you didn't catch the analogy). This isn't the first time the show has tried trotting out some doppelgängers,[17] but if these two are supposed to be potential spin-off material, I'm just not seeing it. Agent Miller (Robbie Amell) is a hunk of amiable nothing, and Agent Einstein (Lauren Ambrose) is aggressively annoyed by everything. Their chemistry and charisma pale in comparison to that of our two original protagonists. There's no clear justification in the script for their presence in the hour either. They are there to suggest that the questions of faith and skepticism are cyclical, or perhaps they just exist because Carter felt like being whimsical.

That suggestion of whimsy isn't as far-fetched as it sounds, because "Babylon" gets wildly whimsical as it goes along, and the episode is all the better for it. What starts as a seemingly serious look at serious things takes a hard left turn into Whacky Land when Mulder does mushrooms (or does he?) and trips like hell. Nothing else in the hour could ever prepare you for the sight of Duchovny line dancing or the Lone Gunmen in cowboy hats.[18] Then Mulder finds himself on a boat full of hooded oarsmen being whipped by the Cigarette Smoking Man, and sees Shiraz lying in his mother's arms, in an overt pietà in the back of the boat. To say it's bizarre would be a tremendous understatement.

There's something to be said for the way Duchovny commits to this incredibly wild material, and the way Carter has little shame in suggesting just about anything he can think of throughout the hour. The problem with the episode arises when you consider the lunacy in the original context of the opener: the very real and complicated threat of terrorism and religious extremism. The episode's take on religion—heavily symbolic and somehow ultimately all about motherhood—is at once saccharinely sincere and annoyingly vapid; "Babylon" can be charming in its absurdity, but that charm sits uneasily against any effort to parse out the episode's religious themes or draw any sort of real point from what you're watching. The use of Muslim characters as stock terrorists without any real acknowledgment for how that representation might register—as though a Muslim terrorist is such an immediately acceptable idea that it doesn't require any interrogation at all—is at once provocative and painfully naïve, mitigated only slightly by the fact that the script does its best to embrace everyone inside the umbrella of some vague, humanist version of God.

In the end, despite its religious themes, the closest reference point for insane shenanigans like these in Carter's work is "The Post-Modern Prometheus" (S5E5), as that earlier hour is one of the rare times Carter embraced absurdity with a passion that no other writer on his staff could really match. "Babylon" is quirkiness without restraint or common sense, surreality that lacks the necessary grounding

---

17 Carter has an affection for the concept, having used them before in "Syzygy" (S3E13) and "Fight Club" (S7E20); the latter even featured a pair of Mulder and Scully stand-ins in addition to the identical twins at the center of the story.
18 The supposedly dead (beyond the canon of *The X-Files* comic series) trio's only appearance in the season.

of nightmare to keep it from slipping into camp. It's not great, or even good, but at the very least, it's unique. —ZH

"MY STRUGGLE II"

SEASON 10 / EPISODE 6
WRITTEN BY CHRIS CARTER, BASED ON A STORY BY DR. ANNE SIMON, DR. MARGARET FEARON, AND CHRIS CARTER
DIRECTED BY CHRIS CARTER

THE END IS NIGH (AGAIN)

In which . . . wait, what?!

Despite all the anticipation, despite all the hype, despite all the hope, despite the monster ratings for the season premiere,[19] the six-episode revival of *The X-Files* ultimately came to be seen as a disappointment. This feeling persisted despite the presence of the roundly acclaimed "Mulder and Scully Meet the Were-Monster" (S10E3), and despite the generally liked hours of "Home Again" (S10E4) and "Founder's Mutation" (S10E2). All three of these episodes ranged from "solid" to "exceptional," and if at least one of the other three had joined them as a standout, the story surrounding the season would have been very different.

It's easy to imagine a world in which that happened. "Babylon" (S10E5) misses the mark, but it's so weird that you can see a reality in which it could have been something more worth watching. It's the kind of bad episode that is really going for something big and profound. Yet trying to imagine the season premiere or finale—this season's "My Struggle" (S10E1) diptych—taking a big leap in quality is very difficult to do. Their attempts to reconstruct the mythology feel wheezy and low on new ideas at best. Whereas an episode like "Founder's Mutation" turned a new conspiracy growing out of the ruins of the old one into something dark and sinuous, the "My Struggle" episodes mostly flail in the general direction of the status quo of seasons past.

The best example of this failure is made manifest in Tad O'Malley (Joel McHale), an overwrought figure who never coalesces into anything like the show's best informants or villains. He fulfills a similar function within the narrative of this season as earlier characters like Deep Throat or poor Max Fenig did. These were people whose presence reminded you at all turns of the human cost of the Syndicate's chokehold on society. But whereas Deep Throat and Max existed within the show's shadowy aesthetic, Tad is now the mainstream. He records his show on

---

19 16.19 million viewers watched "My Struggle" live when it premiered. Granted, it did so after a major football game, and that number isn't at the level of the show's most-watched episodes from the peak of the original run (the ratings for which regularly sailed over the twenty million viewer mark), but in 2016—in an age of deteriorating ratings for live TV whatsoever—it was massive.

a brightly lit set. He's a TV host, and when he pops up in the Mulder-and-Scully portions of the story, he carries with him the whiff of an alt-right charlatan.

There's a stab at commentary here, proposing as it does that the paranoia that drove so much of the original run of the series has now become popular and made Tad its surprisingly profitable face—a face which has become all too familiar in our age of YouTube conspiracy theorists.[20] Couple that with the way he seems like he just might be part of some deeper conspiracy (rather than just a better-looking Alex Jones), and you might have a germ of an idea that would ultimately bring the many pieces of the show together. Just because paranoia has gone mainstream doesn't mean that it shouldn't still exist in some form. The mythology of the season could have been an examination of the thin line between necessary skepticism and huckster-driven paranoid commerce, something Chris Carter had actually hinted at before in the show's middle seasons (and especially in the first movie, *The X-Files: Fight the Future*). Just because you're paranoid doesn't mean they're not watching you, goes the old saying, and *The X-Files* wrestling with its legacy of government mistrust in an age in which paranoia is seemingly everywhere (and getting stronger every day) could have been powerful.

But (heavy sigh) this is just *not that*.

"My Struggle II" feels like a weird and ineffective pit stop on the way to somewhere else, rather than a vital or concluding part of a bigger story. It's not the cliffhanger that ends the hour that irritates—at this point, it would be ridiculous to expect anything less than a lack of closure from *The X-Files*. No, what frustrates most is that everything leading up to that cliff-hanger feels like a half-assed redo of things the series had already done, with an apocalypse that seems localized to one TV set and one crowded bridge. "My Struggle II" wants you to believe that everything is hitting the fan, that the world is exploding, that the Syndicate's plan has finally been set in motion, even after the Syndicate has been torn apart. Instead, it all feels painfully anticlimactic. Most of the scenes in this hour can be greeted with a hearty, "Wait, what?"

Take, for instance, the return of Monica Reyes, who has apparently been secretly working with the Cigarette Smoking Man after he somehow survived being blown to pieces by a Tomahawk missile.[21] In and of themselves, none of these ideas are completely implausible. We already know that this is the sort of show in which a man could survive an all-consuming fire, and that it's the sort of show in which a formerly faithful agent would turn heel to save her own skin. But both developments are so quickly glided past—in a *flashback*, no less—that it's hard to truly invest in

---

20 Season Eleven (given the political climate in which it aired) deals with this idea in much more satisfying terms, so we'll talk more about it there.

21 That's got to be something like his third cheat of death itself, right?

either revelation. There's no emotional core to the episode. The entire enterprise is composed of awkward, halting momentum.

This plot-glossing approach could work with the right action movie pacing, but "My Struggle II" never manages that either. The big, final sequence takes place in standstill traffic, which is an apt visual metaphor for the whole hour. The mythology has reached a dangerous and feverish pitch in that it's really, really complicated (Good luck understanding a lot of plot points in this episode without remembering all the ins and outs of alien-human hybrids!) but also deeply simplistic. As a result, all we know is that aliens want to invade the planet, which is no surprise for anyone even remotely acquainted with any story about alien-human interaction. You're left with a too-predictable story that's both too easy to understand and simultaneously utterly impenetrable. This is, in no way, the legacy that a once-great show like *The X-Files* should leave behind.

Fortunately, then, this hour would not prove to be the last for *The X-Files*. Season Ten's high ratings meant a Season Eleven would eventually arrive. There's just enough in Season Ten to hint at what *The X-Files* can be in this dark, new decade that it's natural to hope Season Eleven will pull everything together. But maybe it won't.[22] Maybe it will just leave us in the middle of standstill traffic, waiting for answers that won't quite arrive and that we've probably already guessed. The mythology of *The X-Files* is a story about a world constantly on the precipice of ending that, nonetheless, never manages to end. Sounds familiar, if you think about it. —TVDW

---

22 Would you believe the answer is "A little from column A, a little from column B"?

THE STRUGGLE CONTINUES

In which everyone is mad about the boy.

After the disastrous finale of last season ("My Struggle II" [S10E6]), I was surprised to find myself somehow still excited at the prospect of more *X-Files*. Given how many of the show's problems were baked into the very core of the mythology itself, you'd think I'd be ready to give up. "My Struggle III" doesn't entirely allay those fears. Once again Mulder and Scully are doing . . . something while shadowy forces[1] work against them. Once again the fate of civilization is at stake. Once again there are aliens. And once again far too much emotional information is conveyed via clunky voice-over monologues that try to lend a certain amount of gravitas to the absurdity.

Yet the Season Eleven premiere is, at the very least, a bit better than it might have been. This episode evinces a degree of course correction for the show; the shift to focus more directly on our heroes simultaneously acknowledges the show's budgetary restrictions while still aiming for a world-ending threat and makes for an hour of television that doesn't send your friendly reviewer into fits of rage.

It turns out that the craziness that ended Season Ten was all a dream, a psychic whammy powerful enough to throw Scully into a coma. It's the sort of clunky feint that created so many problems during the late stages of the show's original mythology run (*You thought you knew the truth, huh? Well that was all a lie*; this *is the truth*). But given how baffling "My Struggle II" was, it's actually a relief to see all of its events reversed.

"My Struggle III" is well directed. Scully's great prophetic gulps are delivered in rapid edits and shaky camerawork that convey a sense of weight and danger even when the narrative details don't quite hold together. I especially like the final, quick reveal at the end, of a young man in terrible pain—William himself, we assume, who Scully says is responsible for her recent head trips. As far as scripting goes, though, there are the usual problems with character motivation for our protagonists. Gillian Anderson is set out to drift for large chunks of time, but David Duchovny is surprisingly game, which is always a welcome sight to behold.

Overall, the episode makes an effort to streamline the main arc of what's to come for Season Eleven. Where "My Struggle" (S10E1) struggled under the weight

---

1   The Cigarette Smoking Man is back again; Barbara Hershey also shows up as Erika Price, a new member of the Syndicate.

of an inchoate amalgamation of various Internet conspiracy theories, "My Struggle III" boils the plot down to the same type of threats that have always been a part of *The X-Files*. This time, it's the Cigarette Smoking Man intending to destroy most of the world's population with a virus he created using alien DNA and start humanity anew. That recentering on old foes gives this crisis clear stakes and lends the episode a certain amount of nostalgia—although, of course, it remains to be seen if Season Eleven can find a new angle on such familiar ideas.

The smartest structural choice this arc makes is bringing William back as the center of the mythology. At this point in the show's run, the character is still an abstract concept, a symbol of Mulder and Scully's bond and legacy more than anything tangible. The writers here suture our heroes' personal concerns to a larger narrative framework by making Scully's determination to find her son a story-driven need as much as an emotional one; she needs to reconnect with the child she left behind not only for her own sake, but also because the fate of the world might very well depend on it. It's something *The X-Files* has been doing ever since it revealed, way back in "Pilot" (S1E1), that Mulder's sister had been abducted by aliens. In making sure that even the most global, far-reaching conspiracy has intimate stakes, *The X-Files* has consistently attempted to keep its more outlandish ideas from launching completely into space.

Unfortunately, as smart as this decision may prove to be, it comes with a substantial drawback: the late-episode reveal that the Cigarette Smoking Man—not Mulder—is William's biological father. Given that we learn this directly from the CSM himself, it certainly *could* be a lie, but nothing we see in this hour suggests that it is. If it is the truth, it comes as a legitimate shock, but one that's so disturbing and ugly that it is difficult to appreciate it, even as a fictional narrative device. "My Struggle III" has several flashbacks to earlier episodes, including to "En Ami" (S7E15), which featured Scully and the CSM on a road trip. In that episode the CSM ostensibly drugs Scully, changes her clothes, and puts her to bed, which was bad enough when it first aired. To now retcon this scene to imply that the CSM actually impregnated her against her will is considerably worse. It's a sour, dark twist that will be hard for the rest of the season to surmount.[2]

Even putting the awful twist aside, the episode as it stands isn't very good, held back as it is by Carter's efforts to perform yet another massive reworking of the ongoing plot. Still, while that process of redirection is certainly frustrating to watch, the new status quo with which it leaves us with has some narrative potential (if you can, again, get past that stomach-churning twist). One can only hope that the remainder of the season presents things in a different light, once the show's other

---

2 Forced or duplicitous impregnation is a trope the show has used before, although, weirdly, it seems to come up most often in comedic episodes like "Small Potatoes" (S4E20) and "The Post-Modern Prometheus" (S5E5). See those essays for further discussion of this problematic device.

writers get on board. "My Struggle III" isn't a total deflation of expectations; to be brutally honest, at this point, there aren't many expectations left to deflate. There's potential here. But finding that potential means ignoring some significant warning signs from a revival that's yet to earn our faith. —ZH

NOT MY CONSPIRACY

Season Eleven of *The X-Files* premiered in a very different world than that in which Season Ten debuted. With the 2016 election, a new and controversial presidency, and the rising political traction of Internet conspiracies and alt-right racism, the show that had made its name by trusting no one now found itself keeping company with some unlikely—and sometimes unwanted—bedfellows.

Chris Carter explains that the notion of not trusting the government was, for him, dated to a specific time and place. "I grew up with conspiracies," he says. "I'm a child of Watergate. I believe that there are people acting in their best interests and not in ours. I question authority. It's kind of my natural character. That's where this conspiracy thinking really comes out of. It's like the idea that you can't be too paranoid, or just because you're paranoid doesn't mean they're *not* out to get you. Those things come out of my experience, and I think that they serve the kind of show that *The X-Files* is."

However, Carter is careful to explain that that kind of thinking "can go too far. . . . We see it right now with Infowars. There are certain things that are just beyond the pale, and that are so outrageous as to be ridiculous. Everything on *The X-Files* takes place—and this is by design—within the realm of extreme possible. While we suggest a conspiracy, we don't suggest something that is utterly ridiculous, unless it's in a comedy episode."

In fact, Carter explains that part of the reason that Season Eleven pivoted away from the story lines set up at the end of the previous season was because of the political climate of 2018. He says that, since the run of the original series, "So much time had passed, and [I felt] that people may have had a hard time picking up on the old conspiracy. And, in fact, so much had changed since the time of the previous conspiracy [in Season Ten], that it felt to me that the exploration of the other part of the previous conspiracy had been lacking, and was also more fitting with the world that we were living in. Which is a world where conspiracies dominate the news, and the truth is marginalized. We were at the beginning of that, because Trump had just

S11 E1

announced his run for the presidency in the previous series, Season Ten. But, I intuited what was going on, and so I thought, 'Let's explore the human side of that conspiracy.' As Mulder says, 'the conspiracy of men.' It felt to me that was the more logical and appropriate part of the conspiracy to investigate."

Carter admits, too, to doing some on-the-ground research into what popular fringe theories were being discussed at the time of writing Seasons Ten and Eleven; "I've been attending conventions. I attended a convention on the secret space program, which covered so many of the conspiracies that I ended up referring to in 'My Struggle' (S10E1) and beyond. . . . I have friends who are drunk on a lot of these conspiracy sites and conspiracy theories. I get earloads from them."

Still, the impulse of the conspiracy-minded to take Carter's work at face value was strong, and the ramifications unavoidable. Carter says that Infowars host Alex Jones himself contacted him after watching the premiere of Season Ten.

So, did Carter take Jones up on that offer? Carter says, flatly, "No."

SEASON 11 / EPISODE 2
WRITTEN AND DIRECTED BY GLEN MORGAN | **"THIS"**

HEAVEN IS A PLACE ON EARTH

In which the end isn't nigh—it passed us by several years ago.

Season Eleven is a much stronger season of *The X-Files*, on the whole, than either Season Nine or Season Ten. Where the show seemed tired in Season Nine and unsure of itself in Season Ten, this new batch of episodes feels confident and alive in a way that *almost* harkens back to the golden days of *The X-Files*. Indeed, the last season of the "classic" *X-Files*[3] to feel this attuned to what works and what doesn't was Season Six, which aired all the way back in 1998 and 1999.

The reasons for this season's shift in spirit are many, but a surprising number of them are thematic. It's clear that somewhere early in the writing process for Season Eleven, Chris Carter and Glen Morgan (the season's two core executive producers) sat down and thought on exactly what was worth embracing about *The X-Files* in

---

3 Season Eight is slightly better than Season Eleven, but it's also dominated by the serialization experiments around the missing Mulder story line, which makes it less like the show's traditional, Monster of the Week-versus-Mythology format.

2018 and what was less vital to the show. The terrific "This," the season's first stand-alone episode,[4] offers a compelling glimpse into their answers to that question.

In fact, it's worth breaking the episode down into its three major thematic thrusts, as these ideas can be understood to serve as theses for the season.

First: *The world of the 2010s is very different from the world of the 1990s.* To wit: Skinner seems like he's working with Russians. The very rich are almost worse antagonists than the aliens. Technology has run amok. The ghost of one Langly, of our lost Lone Gunmen, appears—only it's not precisely his ghost. And, oh, right, there are *Russians,* and they want Mulder and Scully dead.

By far the hardest thing *The X-Files* had to deal with in its modern-era revival was how dramatically the world had changed since the close of Season Nine, and how our ideas about conspiracy theories and paranoia had changed too. Yes, Season Ten took a stab at referencing these themes with an Alex Jones–style figure in the character of Tad O'Malley, but the paranoia of "This"—and, indeed, Season Eleven on the whole—is of a much richer type. The paranoia of Season Ten was a late Obama-era paranoia, more generic "the government is out to get you" business; the paranoia of Season Eleven is Trump-era madness. It not only *knows* the government is out to get you, but can provide citations if you ask. "This" borrows equally from the conspiracy thrillers (notice that race through Arlington National Cemetery) of the 1970s and the deep-dive Internet rabbit holes of our modern age (I mean, have you ever checked out #Russiagate on Twitter?). Ideas that sound sensible at first start to decay, and you can never be sure of what is true and what is "true."

Most of all, "This" suggests that it is Mulder and Scully themselves who helped the world spin-off its axis during their absence. After the X-Files were placed in a central database that allowed anyone (including Russian intelligence) to access them, in hopes that global cooperation could help solve spooky phenomena,[5] the sensitive information in those files became a vital part of the world's slow decay.[6]

Second: *The world is doomed.* In "My Struggle III" (S11E1) we learn that the aliens have lost interest in humanity thanks to how we've broken our planet and destroyed ourselves, which is by far the most compelling idea in the mythology in several seasons. Aliens once wanted to colonize us, but now, they're content to find some other planet. The Syndicate, meanwhile, has moved on to other schemes,

---

4   Though calling this episode a stand-alone is a touch misleading, since the new character of Erika Price, who is working with what remains of the Syndicate, turns up here for a scene or two.

5   That's my assumption, at least. Skinner isn't really clear on this point, beyond the idea that the X-Files belong to "everyone." It has echoes of, say, Edward Snowden exposing the NSA's spying powers and other leaking of government secrets, but the strokes here are broad enough that the reference doesn't seem to be to any one thing in particular.

6   *The X-Files* stops just short of suggesting that if Mulder had been around, he might have kept Donald Trump from becoming president, but boy, you can almost feel Morgan just off-camera, holding up a sign that says exactly that.

which presumably include the central invention in "This": a massive computer simulation to which one's consciousness can be uploaded after death. It's a kind of virtual heaven that becomes a hell once you realize what it is (as Langly eventually does, which leads him to attempt to contact Mulder). Sure, that world is a paradise on some level, but only if you never realize its limitations: it can never be escaped. It is not "real," at least not in the typical definition of the world. Which means this version of Langly isn't either.

Though undoubtedly nihilistic, the heart of this idea is compelling. No matter what Mulder and Scully do—no matter what the Cigarette Smoking Man does, no matter what *any* of them do—Earth is doomed. The best anyone can hope for is to find some way to survive the downfall and build a new life among the smoking wreckage. In theory, a computer paradise would be just the thing, except that Langly paints it as too much of a good thing, the kind of place so good you must know, on some level, that it can't be real.

Yet even if the world is doomed, Mulder and Scully—our eternal heroes—keep going, keep unraveling these mysteries. It's all they know how to do at this point, even if Russian gunmen who love The Ramones' "California Sun" keep coming to kill them.

Which brings us to our third thrust: *The world might be doomed, but it's not beyond salvation.* This is one of the most potent ideas of the show, sure, but especially of this episode.[7] Things might be dire, but things always seem dire right before you find your way out of the dark. In some ways, "This" functions as a meditation on the place of *The X-Files* in this different, doomed world.[8] What good is shining a flashlight into dark corners when all that's left are more dark corners? But what the episode concludes, over and over, is that so long as Mulder and Scully are together, walking into the dark, we might have hope.

The episode's melancholy undergirds this notion, a concept that reaches all the way back to the very earliest days of the series to brush up against some of its very first conspiracies, as if the show is reminding itself—now that it's racing at a clip—of when it barely knew how to walk. Mulder and Scully happen upon the grave of Deep Throat,[9] and for a moment, they're almost as young as they were at the series' start. By remembering where they have been, and where *the show* has been, *The X-Files* can find its way back to firm ground.

And then the gunfire rains down on them. Hope might still be possible, but it's no guarantee. —TVDW

---

7 And of future episodes of Season Eleven, so keep an eye out!

8 Skinner and Mulder, at one point, sigh and reminisce about how much less complicated all this conspiracy nonsense was in the '90s.

9 Whose name is revealed to be "Ronald Pakula," presumably a nod to Alan Pakula, the director of the 1970s political paranoia films *Klute*, *The Parallax View*, and *All the President's Men*—all notable influences on the series.

| "PLUS ONE" | SEASON 11 / EPISODE 3
WRITTEN BY CHRIS CARTER
DIRECTED BY KEVIN HOOKS |

DOUBLED TROUBLE

In which it's twins. Again.

"Plus One" is the first true Monster of the Week entry of Season Eleven, involving as it does murder, an investigation, a self-contained threat, and a conclusion that ends the story without offering much in the way of answers. Chris Carter's MOTW scripts are the definition of hit or miss,[10] but when he's on, he can produce unexpected and memorably quirky episodes that few other writers on the show can match.

And this episode is definitely quirky. The only problem is that there really isn't much else to it. There's no cohesive plot here, no coherent concept to be explored, exhausted, and put aside. There's just a collection of ideas that occasionally manage to connect, sometimes intentionally, sometimes by sheer accident. It's the sort of script that will be familiar to anyone who made it through Season Nine, a collection of theoretically interesting ideas that lack the necessary solid center to hold them all together.

Things start well enough, with a striking cold open that teases the idea of murderous doubles without belaboring the point. It's a good hook, and the episode keeps us interested by cutting to Scully and Mulder back in the old X-Files office. There's undeniable charm and stirring nostalgia to be found in seeing them in such familiar surroundings—just as, in the cold open, it's fun to see an idiot get chased by a supernatural force. But seeing our protagonists act as if this is the start of every other MOTW entry also undercuts the effectiveness of the previous two episodes; given everything that they've endured at the top of the season, it's disarming and disorienting that Mulder and Scully are back at work seemingly none the worse for wear.

It's not a plot hole, exactly. The end of "This" (S11E2) had Mulder and Scully turning to the FBI again, and the presumption is that they never really stopped working for the bureau after the close of Season Ten. In some respects, this is just *The X-Files* returning to the way it has always approached serialization: it makes routine nods toward continuity while still presuming that we understand that this is a TV show, and TV shows have their own internal logic and reset tactics, and that we should just all roll with it. Times have changed, though,[11] and the fits-and-starts

---

10 When he's good, he brings us Flukeman with "The Host" (S2E2), the meta-shenanigans of "The Post-Modern Prometheus" (S5E5), and the clever time travel romance of "Triangle" (S6E3). When he's bad, he brings us "Fight Club" (S7E20).

11 See the essay on "This Is Not Happening" (S8E14) for more on how *The X-Files* dealt with serialization when it became the storytelling norm in modern television.

method to fitting the serialized mythology into the larger framework of the show is more noticeably awkward than ever before.

This awkwardness alone wouldn't be a problem if the writing were more coherent, but "Plus One" is as much of a mess as it can be while still sticking to the established MOTW structure. Things seem somewhat promising when we're introduced to a mentally disturbed woman, Judy, and her jerk-ass twin brother, Chucky (both played by Karin Konoval),[12] but there's no real effort to bring any of this into focus. Sister and brother are responsible for the killings, but Mulder never comes up with a coherent crazy theory to explain where they got their power or even what their power is, exactly. The script commits the cardinal sin of introducing a premise without being able to make said premise pay off outside of exploiting it in the most obvious ways: a potential victim is introduced, they see their creepy double, and then they die. There's no development of the threat, and the only subversions of our expectations come from the episode simply refusing to provide concrete answers.

Your ability to enjoy "Plus One" depends entirely on how much pleasure you derive from Konoval's loopy double performance, and from scenes of Mulder and Scully flirting and discussing philosophy. The latter scenes are almost good enough to support a whole episode on their own, but unfortunately the "case" keeps pulling them back in. Even our two heroes seem barely interested in the proceedings, mocking corpses whenever they appear and failing to even try to protect the two men who die over the course of the episode. Scully and Mulder's total lack of response to either of the deaths of these men (beyond barely concealed amusement) enhances the general tossed-off quality of the whole enterprise.

Even the episode's best moments aren't entirely thought through. The actors have such easy, convincing chemistry together that Scully's question about what might happen when they get older[13] and lose track of one another is at once poignant and oddly misplaced. It suggests a reality for these characters outside *The X-Files*, and while that world is definitely one worth reflecting on, it feels so unrelated to everything else in the hour that it functions solely as a meta-textual moment. I found myself wondering not about the thoughts and feelings of Scully and Mulder but about those of the actors who portray them. That sort of self-commentary isn't inherently wrong or off-putting, but making such a device work requires a much stronger, more consistent authorial vision. Here it just comes across as one of the episode's more charming moments of flailing to find meaning.

Ultimately, the biggest failure of "Plus One" is its story's laziness. Judy and Chucky are funny enough, but forty minutes of watching Mulder and Scully chase their own tails while a pair of cartoonish buffoons snipe at one another makes one

---

12 An *X-Files* cameo veteran, who played both the fortune-teller killed in the cold open of "Clyde Bruckman's Final Repose" (S3E4) and the matriarch of the Peacock family in "Home" (S4E2).
13 Cue Mulder: "'When'?"

flash back to all the show's worst excesses.[14] By the time Mulder is wrestling with his double[15] and Scully is chewing on bread pills, you might be ready for the end credits. —ZH

FAKE NEWS

In which we're not alone in the universe, but nobody likes us.

We live in a world created in no small part by *The X-Files*, by late-night AM radio programs about government secrets, by barely legible GeoCities websites alleging horrific things based on dubious sources. We live in a world where anything can be true if enough people want to believe something enough, and where my version of reality might look nothing like yours. We live in the world of "nobody knows for sure."

Most of Season Eleven of *The X-Files* is fascinated by the idea that the world has passed it by. Other episodes play with this notion as it relates to the conspiracy, which has closed up shop for the most part, or the impending end of the world, which will have nothing to do with alien invasion. But "The Lost Art of Forehead Sweat," written and directed by the great Darin Morgan, is interested in all the ways that *The X-Files'* brand of skepticism seems downright quaint in the year 2018. If everyone's a skeptic, then finding the "real truth" is impossible, because truth lies in perception. If just one person disagrees, then the truth is no longer universal, and that tiny smidgen of doubt is enough to cause utter disaster.

"Forehead Sweat" is most similar to Morgan's "Jose Chung's *From Outer Space*" (S3E21), an elaborate story about how what we know is both open to interpretation and contingent upon any of us actually being able to know what we know. "Forehead Sweat" takes that idea even further, positing that the advent of the Internet has essentially rewired reality. Get enough people to watch your YouTube video about the September 11 terrorist attacks being an inside job, or about the rich and powerful being lizard people, and you introduce a little schism into reality for all of us. And in the reality of "Forehead Sweat," maybe that means what *seems* like reality isn't so real after all. Chrissy Giorgio in "Jose Chung" worried her memories were being stolen; Reggie Murgatroyd (Brian Huskey), the ostensible "hero" of "Forehead

---

14 More than anything the "twins" interaction here is reminiscent of Carter's "Fight Club," which is a bad, bad sign.

15 It doesn't help that Duchovny looks especially bored here.

Sweat," worries history is being rewritten in real time by the mysterious Dr. They (Stuart Margolin).

What's really devilish about "Forehead Sweat" is the way it obeys its own principles. Every time you think you're on solid ground, the episode introduces just enough doubt to leave you unsure of what you've watched—right up until its final moments, in which Reggie is taken back to the mental hospital where he's been living since a nervous breakdown, only for Skinner to burst through the door and ask where he's going. If Reggie is "real" to Skinner, should he also be real to us? The question isn't "Does it matter?" but "How much does it matter?"

Season Eleven is struck throughout with Trump anxiety, right down to the show's seeming unwillingness to show the forty-fifth president's mug up there on the wall outside Skinner's office.[16] If "Forehead Sweat" has a weakness, it is in the way it dives, headfirst, into roundabout portrayals of Trump—from an alien who tells Mulder, Scully, and Reggie that his kind will be building a wall around the solar system to keep humanity from exploring the cosmos to the invocation of Trump by Dr. They. It's not that The X-Files can't engage in political commentary. To the contrary; it's frequently very good at tackling these issues. Instead, the problem is that Trump's ongoing experiments with real-time reality alteration feel like they fit dangerously well within The X-Files' cosmos.

Look closer, and you'll see that what Morgan is really doing is taking a tour of the last twenty years of American policy: the two decades after the country won the Cold War and the two decades when it slowly started to lose its status as a moral superpower. Reggie casually waterboards a detainee in his CIA cubicle, then blows up a wedding via drone, before deciding to get lunch.[17] He listens in on a 2016 election argument between a Never Trumper and a Trump fan before switching over to listen to Mulder and Scully talk about Sasquatch (the conversation that opens the hour). None of this is normal, and none of it is good, but it's all stuff we've decided to live with, because it's the price of our American comfort. Trump isn't an anomaly; he's the product of a country obsessed with rewriting reality in order to forget its worst behaviors as quickly as possible.

But as Scully frequently points out throughout this hour, the Mandela Effect is self-evidently preposterous. We can check the historical record to see when Nelson Mandela died, or we can look up Sinbad's IMDb page to realize he never starred in a genie movie called Shazaam, or we can look at the spelling of the names

---

16 An honor accorded to Bill Clinton, George W. Bush, and Barack Obama, though Bush's portrait was featured in the infamous moment in The X-Files: I Want to Believe in which a close-up of it was accompanied by the whistling tones of the show's theme song. Spooooky!

17 Both of these are great, sick gags that only Darin Morgan could get away with. His split-second timing keeps the drone joke, especially, from becoming so dark that it turns the stomach, while still making your stomach do the tiniest of flip-flops. Your country is an X-File.

"Stan and Jan Berenstain" to find it was always the Berenstain Bears, not the Berenstein Bears.[18]

But that's the thing, right? We want so badly to be right—to believe that our recollection of events is infallible—that we will twist ourselves around to insist that it is. We'll misremember some odd bit of trivia, or lose track of the location of an important event in our lives, or just plain forget some fact we learned in high school but misplaced along the way. Our reaction, so often in the face of our own wrongness, is to be certain in our uncertainty, to believe that we could not possibly be wrong, so much so that reality itself starts to crumble.

This is an idea that was at the heart of the show's conception, and one Chris Carter manipulated beautifully when *The X-Files* launched in 1993. But twenty-five years later, it's an idea we're increasingly tiring of: a reality that will never resolve back into a clear picture of itself. As Donald Trump and Dr. They would remind us: Nobody knows for sure. And therein lies the power.

Like all Darin Morgan episodes, "Forehead Sweat" is terrifically fun, and the central trio of actors are having the time of their lives.[19] The script is filled with great jokes, Mulder mockery,[20] and Scully greatness.[21] It even has an ingenious *Twilight Zone* parody to act as a bookend to the episode's action, and the final scene is wistful and wise, as Mulder and Scully resolve to "remember how it was"—both a meta-commentary on the reboot of the show and on the less paranoid past it emerged from to (accidentally) help invent our increasingly nonsensical present.

And yet that final scene feels like a too-easy Band-Aid on a wound deep and festering. After all, "Forehead Sweat" also bears a dark, sad core that worries everything might be too far gone, that we might be handed a book entitled *All the Answers* and realize that the greatest truth in the universe is that nobody else likes us.[22]

But maybe they're right not to. Maybe humans are a virus, carrying our reality manipulation and our lies with us out into the cosmos. The alien insists that in all of the universe, only humanity has the capacity for lying. And while that seems unlikely to me, perhaps that's because the only life I've ever known—maybe the only life any human being has known—has been full of deception, and the destruction waged by that deception. Skepticism is healthy, but when you refuse to accept that the facts are the facts, a whole country can lose its mind.

S11 E4

---

18 The idea that "Berenstain" has been spelled with three *E*s and an *I*, instead of two *E*s, an *A*, and an *I*, is a popular false memory and gateway to the Mandela Effect, satirized here by Reggie having forgotten that the name of beloved children's book author Dr. Wuzzle was spelled with two *Z*s instead of two *S*s.

19 Check out Gillian Anderson's overplay of the quick turn in the car as the group goes to meet with the alien overlords.

20 In classic Morgan fashion; note the two FBI agents who write our handsome hero off as old and fat.

21 When the alien comments that Earth might have some good people, he looks pointedly at Scully.

22 Quoth the closing words of "Jose Chung's *From Outer Space*": "For although we may not be alone in the universe, in our own separate ways, on this planet, we are all alone."

And it's only going to get worse. Video software and image manipulation programs are getting so good that it will soon be incredibly difficult to ascertain when footage that seems too good (or too bad) to be true has been faked. We won't always know who's dead and who's alive, and all it will take for those in power to introduce suspicion around a particular set of facts is to stand up in front of all of us and shrug and say, "Nobody knows for sure." Laughing about the Mandela Effect is all well and good, because it's so ridiculous, but we live, every day, in the middle of a gigantic Mandela Effect, a world full of people who refuse to get on the same page because they're reading different books.

And no one will ever, ever know for sure. —TVDW

HOW IT ALL IS

Perhaps the most overtly politically engaged episode of Season Eleven—or *The X-Files* on the whole—"The Lost Art of Forehead Sweat" allowed Darin Morgan to spin disheartening current events into comedy gold. Much like Chris Carter, Morgan is quick to point out that the political climate of the last season of *The X-Files* had an undeniable influence on a show that was infamous for its love of conspiracies.

On the subject of the state of the world in 2018 and how *The X-Files* fits into the new post-Trump culture, Morgan says, "It's something that needs to be addressed if you're going to redo the show. And, whether or not it was that, or some other aspect of life that's changed. [James Wong was asked during a publicity circuit] if we felt guilty for, you know, having a character be this kind of conspiracy-thinking [person] now that it's so prevalent. [But the] difference to me, it seemed like, is that the old school conspiracies which we were addressing back in the original run had to do more with, 'Somebody is keeping knowledge from everybody else.' That kind of thing. Where now the conspiracies—as they're called—are just kookball bullshit, like, 'So-and-so has a child porn ring.' It's like, there's no basis, or there's no idea of something that needs to be uncovered, or something is actually being covered up. It's just crazy crackpot shit. It doesn't have evidence or anything. It's just, 'You just need to put it out there' and then people are crazy enough . . . to take that and run with it."

Morgan was particularly interested in how our favorite FBI conspiracy theorist would be affected by the new proliferation of wild notions, which he decided to make the center of "Forehead Sweat." To him, the episode is partly about "Mulder realizing that [this] is now the way the world is going. . . . It's like when you have a favorite band that no one's ever heard of, they're your favorite band. And then all a sudden they release an album and it becomes a huge hit. And now everyone loves that band and you just kind of don't like them as much anymore. It's like, you're the only guy that thinks the truth is out there, and someone is covering it up. Then all of a sudden [everyone], including the president now, believes in these crazy crackpot theories, [and] there's no more joy in it. You see that's where it went. Now it's just become foolish, or it's been sidetracked in a way that's made it pointless."

Despite the depressing real-world implications of the hour, "Forehead Sweat" had a happy ending in one sense: Mitch Pileggi finally got to make an appearance in a Darin Morgan episode, after years of hounding the writer. According to Pileggi, "I get the call and [Darin] goes, 'Okay, you're in my episode.' . . . And I go, 'That's cool,' and he goes, 'You've only got one line,' and I go, 'Oh, okay.' And he goes, 'But what a line!'"

| **"GHOULI"** | SEASON 11 / EPISODE 5
 WRITTEN AND DIRECTED BY JAMES WONG |

I WAS A TEENAGE MOTW

In which Scully meets her son.

Early in "Ghouli," Mulder complains about the state of modern monsters while Scully looks up creepypasta[23] on the Internet. "Where's the pathos?" he wonders. What happened to the creatures that were terrifying and yet strangely empathetic? It's a cute gag, and fits in well with the season's willingness to steer into the skid of its age; it also raised my expectations that we were going to get the *X-Files* equivalent of Slender Man. Unfortunately, that's not how this one goes, and I was a bit disappointed in the episode's midpoint course correction. Yet I found myself returning to that line. Because it turns out that the episode is, in fact, all about a monster with pathos: Scully's son, William.

Like "This" (S11E2) before it, "Ghouli" starts out as an apparent Monster of the Week entry before tying into the season's larger mythology. It's an awkward shift. There's an explanation for the attack that opens the episode, but no real justification for its horrible violence; the closest we get to understanding why this happened is because William was dating two girls simultaneously (for reasons that are never explained) and thought it would be funny to prank them. Given that they both end

---

23 For more on this idea, see the essay on "Familiar" (S11E8).

up in the hospital, and his adoptive parents end up dead, it's hard to have much sympathy for his short-sightedness. Yet the episode clearly wants us to have sympathy for him, blaming the whole "ghouli" incident (the origins of whom trace back to an in-world creepypasta) on a misguided sense of humor, and William's struggles to control his supernatural powers.

William's story line requires us to invest an awful lot of emotion into a completely new character (albeit one we met briefly as a baby), and "surly teen" is a hard sell for longtime viewers. I am admittedly biased, because when I watch *The X-Files*, I want to see Mulder and Scully going on adventures, not see them get bogged down by regret over past behavior. Acknowledging their history is one thing; being buried in it is another. Given how loopy and confusing the show's history has become, the temptation to just let it all go is nearly overpowering.

More frustratingly, the first part of "Ghouli" bears all the signs of a solid MOTW entry. The cold open is creepy and odd, and Scully's waking nightmare vision makes for an interesting connection with the case, connoting as it does some link between the phenomenon of sleep paralysis and an unknown monster. Regardless of whether or not this hour was always planned as a mythology episode,[24] the shift in focus from "What cool weird monster is causing all this chaos?" to "Is William dead?" quite suddenly supplants a question we wanted answered with one we aren't sure we care about. What seemed like a promising scary story turned into something more personal for our agents—for better and for worse.

To be fair, though, the deeper we get into Season Eleven, the more I realize that my grass-is-greener view of MOTW potential is a fantasy. There was plenty of bad in the last few seasons of the show (even the generally undervalued Season Eight), and a lot more that was mediocre; a fair chunk of the bad and mediocre content came from undercooked one-offs. The appeal of the MOTW concept is its endless possibility of a fresh slate, which means every hour can bring some unexpected classic, some magical and bizarre story to worm its way into your head. But the reality is that great ideas are rare, and there's no such thing as a fresh slate. Every new creature Mulder and Scully encounter has the weight of every other creature they've ever fought behind it. There's a reason Darin Morgan's entries have been the best part of Seasons Ten and Eleven: he's a talented writer who understands that the show's deconstruction and affectionate self-mockery is really the only novelty left.[25]

But much as I'd prefer it, not every week can be a Darin Morgan week. The refreshed *X-Files* is still trying to tell serious stories, and in that light, it makes sense to connect some of these outings back to the main arc. As weird and as clumsy as

S11 E5

---

24 In the revival seasons, the classic MOTW/mythology distinction isn't as useful as it used to be. Good thing this is the last season we cover in this book, or we'd have to find a new title!

25 Not that this episode doesn't have a sense of humor in its own right. The running gag of Mulder using a different name when ordering coffee is great: "It's an alternate reality. Fox doesn't exist in coffee shops."

that story line might be, it at least plays on our emotional investment in Scully and Mulder in ways that a more typical MOTW entry can't. Pulling William into the center of things means there are emotional consequences for our protagonists beyond the body count of this week's guest stars.

All in all, "Ghouli" works better than one might have expected. A large part of its success can be attributed to Gillian Anderson's commitment to portraying Scully's grief convincingly and realistically. Her monologue to William's "corpse" in the morgue has an impact regardless of what you think of William as a character (at that point, he isn't one), because Anderson (as always) just goes for it, throwing all her considerable gravitas into the moment. Even if you don't care about William, you can't help caring about Scully—the woman we've known and loved all these years, facing a surprising and unforeseen loss. Anderson's performance helps to give everything else that happens in the episode that much more weight, and while the season (and show) hasn't always done right by Anderson, her work remains exemplary.

"Ghouli" is bolstered, too, by the fact that William's powers are fun to watch in action, even if the kid himself doesn't make much sense as a character. The way he takes out the bad government guys chasing him in the climax is smart and resourceful, and his final scene with Scully is unexpectedly touching. The fact that he's pretending to be the author[26] of a pick-up artist book that Mulder and Scully found in his room suggests some unflattering angles to his character, but what's a monster without a little bit of asshole in him? —ZH

---

26 Played by *Lost* alum, François Chau.

THE LOST SON

The story of William hovered at the edges of Season Ten, but "Ghouli" marks the return of William to a place of centrality in the show's mythology—and in Mulder and Scully's lives. According to Chris Carter, addressing what happened to William in the final seasons of the show was important not only to the writers, but also to the fans: "The people who were passionate about the show really demanded that we return to it. They wanted to know what happened to that child. It was a command performance [by Miles Robbins], and something that, when you see "My Struggle IV" (S11E10), you'll see that it's William's struggle, and all about him."

Carter says that even when the show was off the air, he had ideas about what was happening in William's life, and what kind of kid he would grow up to be. "I think that there was this belief among the passionate fans that William was a golden child, and that he was safe somewhere growing up, like all children do," says Carter. "But, I always imagined that he—and this was all referenced and alluded to early on—had special powers. I think we saw him in his crib moving a mobile telekinetically [in "Nothing Important Happened Today" (S9E1)]. So, a kid growing up with those kinds of powers is going to grow up tortured, and maybe even marginalized, and certainly wondering about his situation as an adopted child."

James Wong, who wrote and directed "Ghouli," says his experiences as a father made him curious about William's story line: "I have kids, and I was just imagining what it would be like to not know who your kid was. In Season Ten [in "Founder's Mutation" (S10E2)], I really wanted to just touch on it, in a sense that, in a fantasy way, one would need to think about the loss of your child, and how that would affect you, and how that manifests itself in . . . a wish fulfillment way. What would Mulder and Scully do with a child?

"So I touched on that, and then by the time that Season Eleven came, it was just . . . we needed to [write more about it], it wasn't enough to [only reference it]. I felt like we needed to, everybody felt like we needed to see William. I was trying to figure out a way that it could be cool to see him, and not really see him, at least for Mulder and Scully to not really connect with him. Since William had these powers, I thought it would be cool that he could interact with them without really showing himself. Because he's worried about who they are. They weren't a part of his life. . . . William was the most interesting character for me to deal with, because he was more of a blank slate than all the other characters who have already done a bunch of stuff. I felt like I could sort of do what I wanted with William."

SEASON 11, EPISODE 6
WRITTEN BY GABE ROTTER
DIRECTED BY CAROL BANKER

THE AMERICAN WAR

In which even Skinner has an origin story.

"Kitten" does something incredibly risky, something that shouldn't work in the slightest: It takes what was already a serviceable character backstory (specifically, that of Walter Skinner) and attempts a direct dramatization of it. As mentioned throughout this book, the power of suggestion in horror often carries more weight than anything literal, anything we can see. That goes double for *The X-Files*, which became so beloved on the backs of episodes in which the monsters were often half-seen or hidden in shadow.

Yet "Kitten" works, more or less. There are things about it that are clunky, and it's never precisely clear *why* Skinner's Vietnam background—so hauntingly discussed in "One Breath" (S2E8) and eerily vague in "Avatar" (S3E21)—needs a full-on flashback, complete with Mitch Pileggi's nephew[27] playing the young Skinner. But the moments that need to sing strike their target, and the messier moments become easier to forgive in the light of the episode's overall successes. After all these years, maybe we don't *need* to know everything about Skinner, but it's nice to have the guy open up all the same.

There are two big reasons "Kitten" overcomes its weak points. The first is Pileggi, who has always been dialed in to his character but here comes to play with vigor that suggests he could have easily anchored some (likely misbegotten) Skinner spin-off, had Chris Carter and pals come calling. His closing monologue, in which he explains how haunted he is, every day, by what happened to his good friend John "Kitten" James in Vietnam, is the work of an actor who knows *exactly* where the breaking points are in his character. Pileggi knows, inside and out, the little fault lines in Skinner's soul that shake him and make him tremble.

It would be easy to complain about how frequently "Kitten" sidelines Skinner in an episode purportedly about him,[28] but "Kitten" is way ahead of you on that count. It knows you want more Skinner, and, in the end, it gives you the *most* Skinner: Skinner in every scene! Skinner displaying every possible emotion! So! Much! Skinner![29]

The second reason "Kitten" succeeds is because of how it ultimately justifies its decision to literalize a part of Skinner's backstory that probably could have been left as that monologue about Vietnam from "One Breath." See, this is a story about

---

27 Remarkably, despite Cory Rempel's strong resemblance to Mitch Pileggi, he is actually Pileggi's nephew through Pileggi's wife. The two are not biologically related.

28 He spends a remarkable amount of time being trapped in a hole in the ground.

29 Mulder and Scully figures sold separately; succubus not included.

how and why Skinner jettisoned a promising career to help Mulder and Scully, an idea underlined by our old nemesis Alvin Kersh,[30] who lets our heroes know that Skinner just might have run the whole damn FBI had he not kept sticking his neck out for two agents[31] who believed in things impossible.

Skinner has had a long and fruitful career, but one that got stuck in place, always at the level of assistant director. Skinner's career standing is the sort of thing you don't question on a TV show most of the time, because stasis is the norm on TV, but Gabe Rotter's script smartly incorporates Skinner's experiences in Vietnam into the answer. Skinner tanked his career to support Mulder and Scully, because he believes that Mulder and Scully's mission to expose the truth of what the country was doing to some of its most vulnerable citizens was more important than his personal advancement. Skinner himself suggested this way back in "One Breath" as well, but "Kitten" dramatizes it so effectively that it makes sense of the man's entire arc. That cold open—with Skinner watching what happens when Kitten is dosed with what amounts to fear gas, with a horned monster barely emerging from the smoke inside a hut, with Kitten killing Vietnamese civilians—is horrifying enough to make you see precisely why Skinner adopted Mulder and Scully's quest as partially his own.

The script is less successful at tying this into whatever has been going on with Skinner up until this point in the season, because . . . well, whatever has been going on with Skinner up until this point in the season has been kind of a mess. The show has played the "is he or isn't he on Mulder and Scully's side" card so many times that it's lost all potency, because we know he's *always* on Mulder and Scully's side.[32] The storytelling also struggles when it comes time to set Mulder and Scully on the path of Kitten's descendants and must fall back on having local law enforcement come right out and say, "Oh, hey, people say there's a monster in the woods, how about that?"[33]

But the central element of Skinner here works, which means that "Kitten" works. Kitten himself might have been a slightly better-developed character, but he's played by Haley Joel Osment, which at least makes him memorable. When Osment is playing Kitten's son, Davey, he conveys a sorrow similar to that portrayed by Pileggi. These are two men, of markedly different generations, who are both scarred by a government that should provide answers but never will. They are always out to get you. Skinner and Davey both know that, but only one chose to fight that "they" by becoming a part of it. —TVDW

S11 E6

---

30 Played, as ever, by James Pickens Jr., who presumably got one or two days off from his regular gig on *Grey's Anatomy* to pop up in what amounts to a cameo here, though an effective one.

31 OK, really just one agent.

32 See, again, his closing monologue here.

33 That said, Rotter gives Mulder a great one-liner when he says that monsters don't dig *pits*, and you can almost hear the *"Geez, Scully!"* he's holding back.

THE SPAM IS COMING FROM INSIDE THE HOUSE

In which you want to unsubscribe.

We're living in the future now, when things are supposed to be easier. And, for the most part, they are. Most of us carry small computers everywhere we go—machines that can play music, order a pizza, check weather, and even make phone calls. And it's only getting better. Right? Right. But websites still insist on emailing us customer service surveys as if the act of purchasing something online enters us into some weird, mandatory mentorship program. The tomorrow we were promised was a pristine utopia of a convenience-enhanced world, and we got some of that. But we forgot that systems don't always work the way we expect or want them to. We forgot the clutter of it all, the rush of electronic ephemera that blocks the rhythms of everyday life. We forgot that you can't ever entirely evolve away from junk mail.

That's bad. But what if it was worse? What if all that junk was its own kind of conspiracy, one guided not by selfish men in dark rooms but by a developing electronic consciousness learning what it means to be alive by watching us? That's the premise behind the clumsily named "Rm9sbG93ZXJJz,"[34] a stand-alone *X-Files* that has Mulder and Scully facing the irritating inadequacies of modern life—inadequacies that grow in pitch and number until they take a sharp turn toward the sinister. It's a terrific, funny, and eerie hour, a sharp blend of physical comedy and menace that serves as an excellent reminder of the show's infinite flexibility.

The format alone is enough to impress. After a cold open, narrated by an almost human computer voice, explains the fate of an AI Twitter account that learned a bit too well from its followers[35] (thus establishing the theme that will tie the whole episode together), we pick up with Mulder and Scully sitting together in a Washington, D.C., sushi bar. The place is upscale, sleek, gorgeous, futuristic, and, apart from our heroes, completely empty.[36] That emptiness sets the tone that will run through the hour to come; Scully and Mulder are the only major characters in the episode, and,

---

34 The name decodes to "Followers" in Base64—a nice riff on both the robots dogging Mulder and Scully throughout and online social media followers.

35 Based in part on the saga of Microsoft's failed AI Twitter bot named Tay, who learned racism and inflammatory content from other Twitter users resulting in Microsoft shutting it down less than twenty-four hours after its launch.

36 This scene is also almost completely devoid of dialogue, as Mulder and Scully communicate through gestures and pay more attention to their devices than each other.

until the final few minutes, the only people we actually see. But they aren't alone, not even when they're separated. At least, not exactly.

There's no real plot here, just a series of escalating incidents that plays out a bit like a silent film comedy. No one meets Mulder in a shadowy basement to explain how an evil government project has spun out of control. Instead, the episode foregrounds an idea that's been lurking at the margins for the duration of the season: Whatever is wrong with the world today has gone far beyond governments and conspiracies. We've already had a story line about evil cabals using technology to advance their aims in "This" (S11E2), but "Rm9sbG93ZXJz" focuses on something more universal, and harder to dispute. Things happen so fast now, and so much of what happens goes on in places we can't see or touch or even begin to understand. The constant rush of information makes it nearly impossible to grasp what really matters, and so we are reduced to reacting on the strength of our nerve endings. We snap, we get righteous, we rant, we rave. But what's watching us? And what sort of lessons is it learning?

That's a fair bit to unpack, but the genius of the episode is in how baldly it presents its thesis at the outset, and then doesn't strive to belabor it. There is no exposition in this hour, save that cold open, and there's no real breathing room. It's just a rhythmic build toward inevitable chaos. What makes it such a joy to watch is in how well that build is managed, how unforcedly it moves from one point to the next, each escalation at once absurd and immediately recognizable. Mulder orders sushi; he gets an inedible-looking blobfish; when he goes to complain, he finds a backroom full of robots just anthropomorphic enough to be threatening. He refuses to leave a tip, and the machines won't accept his decision. Hilarity, and fear by turns, ensues.

This plot setup works because it's silly and over the top and yet also strangely plausible. The constant phone notifications demanding you rate this or that; the automated operators who patiently refuse to understand what you're saying; the friendly symbols and language that double as barely disguised threats. The stakes eventually become absurdly high, but the route taken to get there is built of steps most of us can recognize. It captures the queasy, anonymous intimacy of all these apps and downloads and unseen minds—that feeling that something is tailoring itself to fit your needs (whether you like it or not) without ever revealing its own intentions. At one point, Scully runs out of Rock It Like a Redhead styling cream, and the instant she throws the empty tube into the wastebasket, a message on her phone pops up telling her she should buy more. It's funny, sure, but also unsettlingly reminiscent of when you do a search for underwear online and all of a sudden every site you visit is plagued with ads for briefs and bras. Yes, it's all just algorithms, but to what end? Is capitalism the goal or simply the means, with some larger, infinitely weirder purpose lurking behind the code?

Mulder and Scully are largely hapless throughout this entry, an everyman and everywoman struggling against a cybernetic tide. "Rm9sbG93ZXJz" is a perfect example of how *The X-Files'* approach to stand-alones (with its limited recurring characters, self-contained plots, and versatility when it comes to style and tone) allows it an anthology-style range, while at the same time ensuring our emotional investment thanks to the continuity and comforting presence of its leads. There's a zing of affection inherent in watching Duchovny and Anderson get put through their paces. Scully is the straight woman here just struggling to keep her head above water,[37] but Mulder's "kids-get-off-my-lawn" vibe is both a smart fit for the show's current direction and a believable development for his character. He was a man apart even when he was firmly in his own time; now that he seems to have lived past his obvious usefulness, his frustration and humor go a long way toward smoothing over the rougher patches of the show's return.

One of my biggest hopes for *The X-Files* revival was that the writers room would bring in some new voices. Kristen Cloke is a familiar name for any die-hard fan,[38] but this is the first time she and cowriter Shannon Hamblin[39] have written for the show, and the result is unexpected and rather wonderful. Seasons Ten and Eleven have good—even great—episodes, but this is the first in the lineup that feels legitimately fresh, and not just a rehash or a (delightful) deconstruction of what we've seen in the past. With Season Eleven now well past the halfway mark, we're bound to return to the not-terrible-but-also-not-great mythology soon enough (as we always do). But it sure feels nice to have something this old still be capable of finding such new devices. —ZH

---

37 Though there is a cute joke about her "personal massager"—I think, the first time a vibrator has been referenced on the show. Also, her password for her home security system is "Queequeg"!

38 She appeared as Melissa in "The Field Where I Died" (S4E5) and starred in *Space: Above and Beyond*. She is also married to Glen Morgan, who directed this episode.

39 Morgan's former writing assistant.

WHICH NO MORTAL COULD INVENT
In which Mr. Chuckleteeth is coming to get you.

"Familiar" is most reminiscent of two Season Two episodes: "Die Hand Die Verletzt" (S2E14), for obvious reasons,[40] and "Red Museum" (S2E10), for the sense that the episode is throwing everything it can think of into the stew and having a grand time doing so.[41] If asked to summarize the plot, you might just throw up your hands after a couple of minutes, but because the experience of watching the episode is so much fun, you would probably recommend it anyway.

Most importantly, "Familiar" finds a genuinely new form of horror tale for *The X-Files* to dabble in: the creepypasta.[42]

Creepypastas, for the unfamiliar, are scary stories posted in online forums[43] under dubious attribution, with the veneer of being true stories. Now, if you've read a creepypasta, you'll know that they are obviously *not* true stories, since most of them feature explicitly supernatural elements. But the idea is to *trick* yourself into believing them, so when a staircase turns up in the woods, or a group of campers is stalked by strange, unearthly beings they never see, everything feels *just true enough* to scare you. Many of these stories are presented in "installments"—much like a serialized TV drama—and even if they dabble in classic horror tropes (ghosts, Satan, etc.), they're often told in a genuinely new way.

The similarity of "Familiar" to a creepypasta story stems from how its story is ultimately rooted in the mundane details of everyday life. It's remarkable that an unsettling kids show has never featured in an *X-Files* episode before, but they're everywhere in creepypasta,[44] perhaps because most creepypastas are written by people in their twenties and thirties who are only now starting to realize how messed up some of the shows they watched as children were. The episode's villain,

---

40 That earlier episode, too, was about a small town infected with Satanic worship that made dark dreams come true.

41 Though "Red Museum," too, is about a small town infected with some dark, cult-like weirdness.

42 First introduced to the world of the show earlier this season in "Ghouli" (S11E5) but given significantly more attention as a theme here.

43 The name is a twist on "copypasta," itself a permutation of "copy-paste," used to refer to any block of text copied and pasted around the Internet. The most popular online forum for these stories is the subreddit NoSleep, which, true to its name, is not recommended for those of us who like to sleep.

44 Particularly in perhaps the most famous creepypasta, "Candle Cove," to which "Familiar" bears a vague resemblance. "Candle Cove" was adapted as the first season of the very good creepypasta horror TV series *Channel Zero*.

Mr. Chuckleteeth (who looks like a ventriloquist's dummy crossed with a game show host crossed with those occasional insert shots of the demon Pazuzu from *The Exorcist*) is another creepypasta standby: the obviously malevolent element of childhood that adults, nevertheless, don't recognize as evil.

The chief problem with "Familiar" is that it just suddenly *ends* in a way that's a little unsatisfying and barely answers any questions. Indeed, this failing would actually be a strength were this an actual creepypasta instead of an episode of *The X-Files*. In a creepypasta, the author[45] is just lucky to escape with their lives. "Familiar" tries to replicate that effect with Mulder and Scully skipping town while they still can, but their triumph is more muted because, well, they're Mulder and Scully. They live to fight another day all the time.

What's impressive, however, is how writer Benjamin Van Allen and director Holly Dale funnel the form of the creepypasta into something that's recognizably an *X-Files* episode. The arguments between Mulder and Scully about what's "really" going on are on point,[46] the "suffocating small town haunted by an unusual monster" vibe is exactly as you'd expect, and the idea that the monster is really rooted in personal problems[47] is straight out of a Season One Howard Gordon and Alex Gansa script.[48]

"Familiar" falters a bit when it tries to explain what's behind all these events, especially when it leans on the eye-rolling storytelling crutch of "Sure, most people killed at the Salem witch trials weren't actually witches, but *what if some of them were?*" To be sure, the episode draws a throughline from those witch trials to the Satanic Panic of the '80s to fears over violence in kids' TV shows to our modern era of justice meted out over social media—all of which are connected by a kind of mass delusion that truth can be found if we all yell together loudly enough. But all of those suggestions are better left in subtext than made text. When Mulder makes these themes explicit, it feels forced.[49] The need for an *X-Files*-esque explanation, or even the *hint* of any kind of explanation, ultimately works against the creepypasta atmosphere the episode otherwise nails.

But before the hour's perfunctory resolution, it builds up an impressive head of steam, with Mr. Chuckleteeth all but lunging out of the television to make the locals his plaything and an ever-escalating sense of chaos raining down all around

---

45 For almost every creepypasta is written in first-person.

46 Save for a somewhat strange argument in which Mulder seems to say that it's unconstitutional to investigate a sex offender who lives a couple of blocks from a local park to see if he's been involved in a series of child murders committed near that park.

47 In this case a woman summons a shape-shifting demon (or something like a hellhound) because she's upset that her husband was cheating on her, only for her to promptly lose control of said shape-shifting demon (like you do), which goes on to murder children, including her own daughter.

48 Think "Lazarus" (S1E15) and "Born Again" (S1E22).

49 Though I am fond of Mulder's closing line, in which he notes that "there's no escaping this town." We Americans will forever be defined by our inability to escape our own rushes to judgment.

the characters. The presence of literal hellhounds might be one element too many, but they also add to the terrifying sense of hell literally come to Earth with which each character is grappling.

For all its nods to *X-Files* past and online horror story present, the slyest trick of "Familiar" is the way it loops back to become a vital part of Season Eleven, which could itself easily be subtitled "Hell literally come to Earth." Mulder and Scully escape from Eastwood, Connecticut, with their lives—but only just. Mr. Chuckleteeth will come for them, as he comes for us all. —TVDW

SEASON 11 / EPISODE 9
WRITTEN BY KAREN NIELSEN
DIRECTED BY JAMES WONG | **"NOTHING LASTS FOREVER"** |

HOLDING ON THROUGH THE NIGHT

In which nothing tastes as good as youth feels.

It would be going too far to say that "Nothing Lasts Forever" is the goriest episode of *The X-Files*. For one thing, the show has roughly half a gazillion entries to its credit, so it would be difficult to make such a grand pronouncement; for another, "Sanguinarium" (S4E6) exists. But the lengths to which a former sitcom star and a mad doctor go to in this hour in order to hold on to their youth for just a few more days still manages to shock. The idea itself isn't particularly outrageous, as this is just another variation on vampires eating the young to stay fresh, but the details? I shuddered more than once, and there were a few scenes where I found myself actually unwilling to keep looking at the screen. The show may be far past its prime, but when it comes time to deliver the gore, it doesn't hold back.[50]

"Nothing Lasts Forever" is one of the season's stronger entries—not as great as "The Lost Art of Forehead Sweat" (S11E4) or "Rm9sbG93ZXJz" (S11E7), but certainly entertaining throughout, with a good hook, interesting guest stars, and, oh yes, copious amounts of the red stuff. There's also some fairly weighty thematic work going on, as the script brings in Scully's faith and Mulder's guilt over her time working on the X-Files. Like nearly every other episode in the season, this one includes some talk about how our heroes are getting older and what that means for both their work and their lives.

It's heavy stuff, made more immediately entertaining by the horror elements and the work of Fiona Vroom (who manages to make her character both grounded

---

50 Despite the existence of recent series like *Hannibal* (a show that treated serial murder, gore, and cannibalism as a form of artistic expression) and an uptick in graphic violence on television overall, *The X-Files* here proves it can still go for the jugular.

and over-the-top) as Barbara Beaumont, the former sitcom actress obsessed with maintaining the beauty that made her a (sort of) star. As we've seen with other Season Eleven episodes, not everything lands as solidly as it should. The longer the revival goes on, the more obvious it is that there will never be some sudden spark of inspiration that revitalizes the entire enterprise; that—as much as some of us might wish to pretend otherwise—there was no great creative justification for bringing back Scully and Mulder. The best we can hope for are some fun footnotes that make the most of the limitations inherent in this sort of "reboot." There's always an undercurrent of strain to just about every episode in these final two seasons, and the only way to reconcile that feeling is to incorporate the strain into the text itself—which limits just how effective any of these episodes can be as *X-Files* entries.

But "Nothing Lasts Forever" is a good one, even if not every connection lands. At worst, it's a collection of intriguing concepts that never quite gel into a fascinating whole, but that lack of cohesion doesn't make those concepts any less intriguing. Maybe the biggest problem here is that there is just a little too much going on; in addition to Barbara and Dr. Luvenis (played by the perpetually surprised Jere Burns—he's fine, but the role doesn't have much personality to it, which is a shame), we've got Juliet (Carlena Britch), an avenging angel determined to track down our villains for bringing her sister into their cult of bloodsucking (and bloodletting) youth. Which means we also have a cult, a group of lost young people clinging to Barbara and the good doctor for purpose and beauty in their lives while the doctor harvests their internal organs for his and Barbara's own perverse ends.

Any of these individual threads might have been enough to support an entire hour, and while they line up reasonably well, most story lines end up feeling underserved by the narrative, a collection of memorable moments and images that never sink beyond the surface. There's potential tragedy here, and some strong performances, but the guest stars struggle to rise beyond the archetypes they've been handed. Vroom is effective in that she embraces the cliché inherent in her role—the shallow actress willing to do anything to hold on to her looks—but it remains a cliché.

Still, some of those moments stick in your brain, like the organ donation gone wrong in the cold open, or the sight of Dr. Luvenis being stitched to the back of Juliet's sister, Olivia (Micaela Aguilera).[51] Mulder's confession to Scully—that he feels guilt over everything that has happened to her and believes she would have been better off if she had left the basement office after that first day on the job so many years ago—is unexpectedly moving, as are both characters' ongoing struggles with their own mortality. It's a more definitive version of a conversation the two have been having off and on for the whole season, one which acknowledges their past and tries to make some peace with it. Season Eleven is a stronger than the largely misbegot-

---

51 I'm particularly fond of Barbara singing "The Morning After," as one of her devotees guts himself for her pleasure.

ten tenth season, and exchanges like these are a large part of the reason why. The monsters are still fun and occasionally even scary, but ultimately, we keep coming back because we care about Scully and Mulder. Giving them a chance to behave like real people and to try to reckon with the immensity of their shared history is a way to honor that emotional investment. Mulder and Scully scenes like these go a long way toward making episodes like this worth watching—even when they don't entirely deliver on the goods. —ZH

BEGIN AGAIN

In which they all lived ever after.

Somewhat remarkably, "My Struggle IV" is probably the best of the four would-be endings of *The X-Files*.[52] It plays like something of a mixtape of *X-Files* mythology moments from years gone by, right down to an ending that involves Scully revealing a miracle pregnancy for the second time in the series' run. Once again she believes Mulder to be the father, and goodness, let's hope Chris Carter lets this one stick.

The element that distinguishes this episode over those other would-be endings is that it simply *goes for it* in terms of action and suspense. It's never immediately clear why most things in the hour are happening (beyond each party's vague need to get to William to hasten and/or prevent the end of the world), but the various car chases and gun battles on the way to the closing scene are well-staged. Moreover, Carter isn't afraid to let the body count run high. In some cases, this seems to reveal the show's general disinterest in bringing various characters back (Monica Reyes, in particular, given how unceremoniously she's gunned down). Other deaths, though, are sure to be reversed, were the show ever to return again (there is no way Walter Skinner dies like this).

But the most significant thing the episode seems to do is bring the story of Fox Mulder, Dana Scully, and their Syndicate torturers to a stopping point. "Seems" is the operative word here, since there's always a chance *The X-Files* will ride again, but it's possible to find some finality here, thanks to Gillian Anderson's avowal that she will take no part in future revivals.

To be sure, Carter and David Duchovny could trundle on alone, perhaps bringing in some new skeptical agent to roll her eyes at Mulder's theories, but given this

---

52 "The Truth" (S9E19/20), *The X-Files: I Want to Believe* (the second movie), and "My Struggle II" (S10E6) are the other three.

season's low ratings,[53] that seems unlikely too. *The X-Files* is valuable as a brand name, so it's hard to imagine it won't return in some form at some point. But that form will almost certainly have to be a semi-reboot, if not a complete one. With the Cigarette Smoking Man dead[54] and William swimming off into the night, this marks as solid an endpoint for this particular saga as any.

That raises the question, then: What does "My Struggle IV" suggest *The X-Files*, in the end, is about? Carter suggests that this show is about the tenacity of Fox Mulder, to the degree that the Cigarette Smoking Man chuckles and says, "You never give up!" like the two are characters in a 1980s video game. It's about the idea that the government is forever trying to keep something from you and that the only conduits to finding out what's really going on are decidedly unofficial ones.[55] It's about turning Dana Scully into the universe's punching bag.[56] And, finally, it's about the connection between Mulder and Scully, and how their partnership buoys both of them up—a realization that saves the episode in its last moments and helps it become a vaguely fitting capstone for the series. For if this show was about exploring our uniquely American darkness, then it was a show always at its best when these two were the ones inviting the viewers to follow them into the shadows. Leaving the series, at long last, with these two finally finding a small moment of peace? Well, it's almost hopeful.

Much of the credit for selling the power of Mulder and Scully's dynamic is due to Duchovny and Anderson, who play two people finally closing in on the answers they seek, only the "answers" in this case are to a very personal mystery: the location and safety of their long-lost son. This is a compelling inversion of the show's old format, in which the two were always chasing an elusive and grandiose truth. Season Eleven has done a surprisingly solid job of turning William into a character, rather than a plot mechanic. When Duchovny steps into the role of William[57] and

53 With "Nothing Lasts Forever" (S11E9) barely topping three million viewers, by far the lowest in the show's history.

54 PLEASE, FOR GOOD, THIS TIME.

55 I could never figure out just what the show was trying to do with Tad O'Malley, who sometimes seemed like a dupe and sometimes seemed like a vital conduit to get *the truth* out there. Considering how similar he is to Alex Jones, this is . . . disquieting. I think the show wanted to portray his journey from a Jones-style yahoo who inadvertently did the government a great service to someone using his considerable audience for good in this finale. But Tad probably appeared too few times to really read this way. (For a better treatment of similar material, see the sixth and seventh seasons of Showtime's *Homeland*, created by *X-Files* alums Alex Gansa and Howard Gordon.)

56 Anderson tweeted seemingly critical things about this episode in the immediate wake of its airing, and it's not hard to see why. Of the great many things "My Struggle IV" accomplishes, one of the most concerning is how it relegates Scully to worrying about the various men in her life, shifting her just off-center in a story theoretically about her. This device works to ensure the dramatic irony inherent in Mulder pursuing a son who isn't his biological child, but then you remember how casually the show introduced the idea of the Cigarette Smoking Man raping Scully by medically inducing a pregnancy. So it's a mess.

57 Who can, remember, make people see what he wants them to when talking to them.

has one last conversation with his mother, it's a lovely moment for both him and Anderson, who brings her A-game.

But these scenes are just one leg of an incredibly busy episode, one that keeps setting new goals for itself every few minutes and then obliterating them. The show's disinterest in William's adoptive parents clashes with the way Scully insists, at episode's end, that she's not his real mother. What's worse is that the rapidly diminishing pool of characters is meant to add dramatic stakes to an episode in which the threat of a global pandemic never quite manages to feel real.

It's ultimately hard to say "My Struggle IV" completely works, but it also doesn't utterly fail. *The X-Files*—218 episodes, eleven seasons, and two movies into its run—is still the story of a man chasing shadows and a woman pointing out the very real, very logical things casting those shadows. There are worse places to leave them than embracing, by the sea, their connection made manifest as a miracle between them. Maybe someday *The X-Files* will return and chase some other ending. For now, though, the world has yet to end, and Mulder and Scully are together at last. That's good enough for me. —TVDW

CLOSING *THE X-FILES*

After dominating the pop culture landscape for twenty-five years, the legacy of *The X-Files* can perhaps best be articulated by those who helped create it. When posed with the question of whether he thinks about how groundbreaking even small decisions on the show were, Chris Carter says humbly that, "*The X-Files* was built on what came before it, and people have just built on *The X-Files*. I think that what we showed mostly was that you could take a cinematic approach to television and it would work if they would give you the time and the money to do it—that TV could really rival movies in its storytelling. I think that's something that came out of *The X-Files*. I think the idea that you could do a running mythology helped inform and inspire shows like *Lost*, where it's completely serialized. *The X-Files* had that serial quality that we kept coming back to time and again. . . . I think the show will always be remembered mostly for the imaginative approach to time-worn genres."

The rest of the cast and crew are eager to talk about the show's influence closer to home, and how their time with the series forever changed their lives. When asked what he learned on *The X-Files*, Howard Gordon says, "That was really where I became a producer. I really learned about performance too. It was [about] how to tell a story really efficiently. It really was something that was based from a cinematic perspective—that action and suspense really are empty without prior point of view. [I learned to really understand] that unless you walk someone through, unless you know who you're with when something is happening to them, unless you're really squarely in their shoes, you're not going to feel what you want to feel. Whether you want to feel scared, whether you want to feel tense, whether you want to feel the fight-or-flight thing, it has to happen from that point of view. The show was really cinematic at the time. I do remember, as the budget just got bigger, the sheer cinematic quality of what television could be really became apparent. This really was, I think, a groundbreaker, in terms of the depth and the scope of what a TV show could be.

"At least for me it's where I learned that things were possible then. [The aim] really was to shoot high and shoot for a kind of excellence [which has always] stayed with me. There was a benchmark. . . . At the time, television was the second-rate stepchild of the movies. It just felt like we were doing some stuff that was actually better than a lot of the movies that were out there. It confirmed my own love for television."

James Wong, too, acknowledges the impact the show had on his life, saying, "I have an enormous amount of affection for The X-Files. X-Files changed my career, changed the course of my career. X-Files is the first episode of anything I've ever directed, and because I was nominated for an Emmy, it allowed me to direct movies. I felt like I found a show that I could apply my voice to, in a way that was natural, and fun, and exactly what I wanted to do. It wasn't another procedural; it wasn't just a cop show; it had everything for me. It had the extraordinary elements, a genre that I like to play with. But, it also had these great characters in Mulder and Scully. It was the one show that was the most important to me, I think."

Vince Gilligan also credits his wildly successful career to working on The X-Files. "I'd love to just put it into words just how important this show was to me, this job was for me," says Gilligan. "I wouldn't be where I am now if it weren't for The X-Files. I wouldn't have been equipped to run my own TV show. I wouldn't have been equipped to create Breaking Bad if it wasn't for the seven years I was on The X-Files. The job meant the world to me, the people meant the world to me, in front of and behind the camera. Chris Carter was a great boss, and I have such fond memories of this show. It was a great experience."

Robert Patrick shares Gilligan's enthusiasm for both his co-workers and Carter. "They were super kind," Patrick says. "Everybody involved with The X-Files—from Chris Carter, all the writers, all the executive producers, everybody involved with that show—are the best people. And I'm not talking about the best people in TV. I'm talking about they're genuinely very, very good people. There's a family feel that the show has, and I think you have to attribute that to Chris, and it trickles on down. Everybody involved was just super, super cool. They're wonderful people."

Gordon also has words of praise for Carter, saying, "As far as [what I learned from] Chris, he really trusted us. Which is to say, when someone could do the work, he let them do the work and let them have their voice. One of the traditional mistakes of showrunners—and Chris I think was a fairly green showrunner himself—is holding on very tightly to the reins. But Chris really let everybody do their own thing. That meant producing the episode, cutting the episode, and spending endless hours in the editing room. I really learned how to cut there, in a way I didn't on anything I'd done before that. [I learned] I was really someone capable of taking an episode from the beginning to the end. That's where I really felt the beginning of some, if not mastery, then at least an understanding of what it took, at a deeper level."

Gordon isn't the only one to express admiration for Carter as a show-runner and colleague. Frank Spotnitz says, "Since Vince is still a good friend of mine, he and I have both talked about how much we learned from Chris, and what a hugely formative and profound experience doing The X-Files was for both of us. Chris is incredibly smart, incredibly well-read, very driven, very competitive, and he demanded—he didn't ask—he demanded that you do your best work. And if you weren't willing to work that hard, then he didn't want you to stay. And if you look—especially the first four years of that show—there are a lot of writers there with one credit; there was a lot of turnover on that staff, because there are a lot of people in television, they make very good livings, and they just don't want to be pushed that hard. That was completely unacceptable to Chris, and I think Vince and I both hugely admired his ambition and intelligence. Chris was all about the work; if it was going to make the show better, he was for it, and if it wasn't going to make the show better, he was against it. And he was usually the first one there and the last one to leave. I think the success of The X-Files lies squarely on Chris's shoulders. There were a huge number of really talented people who worked on that show, but they did their best work because of him."

But Carter, true to form, isn't one to take sole credit for the massive success of the show. He says writers and co-workers are owed their due too: "These people all worked together, or individually, and so many people passed through our offices on the way to giant careers. I think that, while I can take credit, I can't take complete credit, and that needs to be said. . . . So many people came and directed; Vince made his directorial debut on the show; Jim Wong made his directorial debut on the show and then went off to do great things. So many people came, and it gave them an opportunity to show their stuff, and the show and I benefited from that hugely."

And as for the future of *The X-Files*, and whether or not the series will rise again? Carter says he has "lots of ideas" for possible future episodes. "I've got things, I write down ideas all the time. So many things never got made. So many things that I think would make a terrific Season Twelve. Whether that happens is anyone's guess. There is a musical *X-Files* to be made; whether it ever gets made I can't say."

Which begs the question: Is "My Struggle IV" (S11E10) well and truly the final episode of the television series that changed the medium forever? "I think I'm happy with it as a close of a chapter," Carter says. "I think *The X-Files* has a lot of life still left in it, so I don't want to start giving eulogies."

ACKNOWLEDGMENTS

Like most books, it took a lot of people to bring *Monsters of the Week* to print. Both of us would like to thank the kind folks at Abrams for all their efforts; in particular, this volume would not exist without the guiding hand and inspiration of Emma Jacobs, who reached out to us with the crazy idea of a complete collection of our reviews, and whose editorial vision made that idea into a reality. Ashley Albert's commentary and suggestions played a huge part in shaping this book into something worth reading, and Patrick Leger's fantastic illustrations helped bring it to life.

We'd also like to thank *A.V. Club* editors past and present for allowing us to pursue the quixotic dream of covering every season of *The X-Files*, including Season Nine. In particular, we'd like to single out Keith Phipps, Noel Murray, Tasha Robinson, and Erik Adams for their devotion to this project and TV coverage at the site as a whole. A big thanks, as well, to the countless great TV critics who wrote or write for *The A.V. Club* and who always inspired us to be better. Listing them all would take far too long. (Seriously, there are dozens of them.) Without the freedom to write and the encouragement to post reviews week in and week out, it's doubtful either of us would have seen this project to the end. The site's approach to pop culture coverage—thorough, accessible, and driven by the desire to mix enthusiasm with clear-eyed common sense—is one of the guiding lights for this collection.

As mentioned in the introduction, an earlier version of many of these essays originally appeared online, and we'd also like to take a moment to thank each and every person who read those earlier reviews, and especially those who took the time to add their own comments. The comment sections for these pieces were sometimes contentious, but they were always engaged, passionate, and more than willing to get down into the weeds. Our readers inspired us to dig deeper and think harder which ultimately made us write better. Writing on the Internet is a strange and noisy business, and knowing we had an audience as invested (if not more so) in the show as we were helped us get through the rougher patches.

Thank you, also, to Chris Carter, Vince Gilligan, Howard Gordon, Darin Morgan, Robert Patrick, Mitch Pileggi, Frank Spotnitz, and James Wong for spending so much time talking to us for the interviews spread throughout this book. Their openness and honesty about working on the show enriched the book considerably.

TODD: I can't talk about *The X-Files* without talking about the time my mom watched it, then sniffed, "I can see why Todd likes this," before turning it off entirely. (The episode was "Quagmire." She didn't understand why Mulder and Scully spent so much time stranded on a rock.) To my parents, Gail and Mary VanDerWerff, and to my sister, Jill Johnson, who was much more amenable to nerding out over *X-Files* with me—I wouldn't be here without you.

Thanks, also, to my wife, Libby Hill. We bonded over our love of this show, but she also watched so many hours of it with me in the process of writing these reviews and then of writing this book. I couldn't ask for a better partner in watching television or in life.

Thanks to Bonnie Nadell, Austen Rachlis, and everybody else at Hill Nadell. Thanks, too, to the crew at *Vox* who was completely understanding when I got a little scattered around big book deadlines. (That goes double for my genius editors, Jen Trolio and Genevieve Koski.) And a big thank you to Erin Moody, Todd Adair, Courtney Sylvia, Lauren Townsend, Jose Cabrera, Susan Patricola, and Katherine Pongracz who helped set up the interviews that pepper this book, as well as Benjamin Van Allen for graciously helping me carve out so much time with Chris Carter.

An enormous thank-you to all the TV critics whose work has inspired me since I was a young boy obsessively reading reviews; critics who have helped me think about this show (and all other shows) in so many new ways. The list includes (but is not limited to) Ken Tucker, Mike Hughes, Alan Sepinwall, Dan Fienberg, Matt Zoller Seitz, Maureen Ryan, Emily Nussbaum, James Poniewozik, Sonia Saraiya, David Sims, Pilot Viruet, Caroline Framke, Melanie McFarland, Genevieve Valentine, Inkoo Kang, and the entire crew of Shake Slack (especially Marisa Roffman, who fielded so many last-minute "Oh dear god, I've forgotten this piece of trivia" questions from me). I have learned so much from all of you over my career and over my life.

Finally, my portions of this book would not exist if Katy Schmidt had not said to me, in the eighth grade, that *The X-Files* was the best show on television, and it wasn't even close. Katy, thank you. You accidentally gave me a career and a book.

ZACK: I can still remember sitting in to watch *The X-Files'* first episode with my father and my sister, and how quickly the show became a Friday night ritual growing up; it may not have been the first TV show I fell in love with, but it's arguably the one that's had the longest and most important impact on my life. Thank you to William

Handlen and Jillian Lovejoy for watching through the show's first couple seasons with me, screaming and laughing and everything else; and thank you to my mother, Victoria Handlen, for putting up with what, to her, must've seem like an awful lot of fuss about little gray men.

I wouldn't have gotten into writing about *The X-Files* if I hadn't been a free-lancer for *The A.V. Club* in the first place, so all the thanks in the world to Tasha Robinson for offering all those years ago. Thank you to everyone I've worked with at the site since then, a vast roster of talent too numerous to get into here; but a special shout-out to Erik Adams and Danette Chavez for putting up with my nonsense. Of course, I wouldn't have gotten the *A.V. Club* job if I didn't already have some experience writing my own reviews, so thanks to the crew of the B-Movie Message Board and the B-Masters Cabal for giving me the inspiration to pursue this madness in the first place. A special shout-out to Freeman Williams who, I think, published my first review online. Don't blame him that it wasn't my last.

I'd like to offer my continuing gratitude to my agent, Jennie Goloboy, for her tireless efforts in supporting my writing and making sure I don't muck up the opportunities available to me.

Editing a book is a long, tedious, and often frustrating process. All my thanks and love to Caroline Glennon for somehow putting up with me through all of it; offering encouraging words as needed; and managing to convince me from time to time that I wasn't actually the worst writer in the world. Both Caroline and our cat, Ginny, kept me going when this all seemed like a terrible idea, and if there's anything in my part of this book that's worth reading, they deserve credit for keeping me from burning it all.